historical readings

Canadian Political Parties

NeW
CANADIAN
READINGS

SERIES EDITOR
J. L. GRANATSTEIN

Titles currently available

Dan Azoulay, ed., *Canadian Political Parties: Historical Readings*

Michael D. Behiels, ed., *Quebec Since 1945: Selected Readings*

David J. Bercuson, ed., *Canadian Labour History: Selected Readings*

Carl Berger, ed., *Contemporary Approaches to Canadian History*

Hartwell Bowsfield, ed., *Louis Riel: Selected Readings*

Bettina Bradbury, ed., *Canadian Family History: Selected Readings*

Kenneth S. Coates and William R. Morrison, eds., *Interpreting Canada's North: Selected Readings*

Terry Crowley, ed., *Clio's Craft: A Primer of Historical Methods*

Robin Fisher and Kenneth Coates, eds., *Out of the Background: Readings on Canadian Native History*, Second Edition

J.L. Granatstein, ed., *Canadian Foreign Policy: Historical Readings*, Revised Edition

J.L. Granatstein, ed., *Towards a New World: Readings in the History of Canadian Foreign Policy*

Norman Hillmer, ed., *Partners Nevertheless: Canadian-American Relations in the Twentieth Century*

Michiel Horn, ed., *The Depression in Canada: Responses to Economic Crisis*

B.D. Hunt and R.G. Haycock, eds., *Canadian Defence: Perspectives on Policy in the Twentieth Century*

Douglas McCalla, ed., *The Development of Canadian Capitalism: Essays in Business History*

Douglas McCalla, ed., *Perspectives on Canadian Economic History*

R.C. Macleod, ed., *Lawful Authority: Readings on the History of Criminal Justice in Canada*

Marc Milner, ed., *Canadian Military History: Selected Readings*

Morris Mott, ed., *Sports in Canada: Historical Readings*

Fernand Ouellet, *Economy, Class, and Nation in Quebec: Interpretive Essays*, ed. and trans., Jacques A. Barbier

Joy Parr and Marc Rosenfeld, eds., *Gender and History*

Michael J. Piva, ed., *A History of Ontario: Selected Readings*

John Saywell and George Vegh, eds., *Making the Law: The Courts and the Constitution*

Gilbert A. Stelter, ed., *Cities and Urbanization: Canadian Historical Perspectives*

Gerald Tulchinsky, ed., *Immigration in Canada: Historical Perspectives*

Joseph Wearing, ed., *The Ballot and Its Message: Voting in Canada*

Graeme Wynn, ed., *People, Places, Patterns, Processes: Geographical Perspectives on the Canadian Past*

historical readings

Canadian Political Parties

EDITED BY

DAN AZOULAY

YORK UNIVERSITY, TORONTO, CANADA

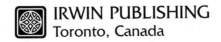 IRWIN PUBLISHING
Toronto, Canada

ISBN: 0-7725-2703-2

editor: Norma Pettit
design: Liz Harasymczuk
cover design: Liz Harasymczuk
typesetting: Liz Harasymczuk
cover photo: Adobe Systems Incorporated

Canadian Cataloguing in Publication Data

Main entry under title:

Canadian political parties: historical readings

(New Canadian readings)
Includes bibliographical references.
ISBN 0-7725-2703-2

1. Political parties – Canada. 2. Canada – Politics and government.
I. Azoulay, Dan André, 1960–   . II. Series.

JL195.C283 1998   324.271′009   C98-932149-5

Published by:
Irwin Publishing
325 Humber College Blvd.
Toronto, ON
M9W 7C3

Printed and bound in Canada

1 2 3 4 5   99 00 01 02 03

To Larry Beaton, Gillian Bartlett,
and Tony Young, early mentors

CONTENTS

O

FOREWORD _____ ix

INTRODUCTION _____ 1

section 1 OVERVIEWS _____ 3

　　　　　Introduction _____ 4

　　　　　JOSEPH WEARING ○ Ideological and
　　　　　Historical Perspectives_____ 5

　　　　　DAN AZOULAY ○ The Evolution of
　　　　　Party Organization in Canada, 1900-1984 _____ 27

section 2 THE RISE OF NATIONAL PARTIES,
　　　　　1867-1917 _____ 51

　　　　　Introduction _____ 52

　　　　　FRANK UNDERHILL ○ The Development
　　　　　of National Political Parties in Canada_____ 65

　　　　　H. BLAIR NEATBY AND JOHN SAYWELL
　　　　　○ Chapleau and the Conservative Party in Quebec _____ 83

　　　　　PAUL STEVENS ○ Laurier, Aylesworth, and
　　　　　the Decline of the Liberal Party in Ontario _____ 103

　　　　　JOHN ENGLISH ○ A Party in Opposition:
　　　　　The Conservatives, 1901-1911 _____ 121

　　　　　DAVID SMITH ○ The Well-oiled Machine:
　　　　　Liberal Politics in Saskatchewan, 1905-1917_____ 141

section 3 THE EMERGENCE OF PROTEST PARTIES,
　　　　　1918-1945 _____ 159

　　　　　Introduction _____ 160

　　　　　W.L. MORTON ○ The Western Progressive
　　　　　Movement, 1919-1921 _____ 174

WALTER YOUNG o The CCF: 1932-1945 _____ 189

JOHN IRVING o Social Credit in Alberta:
Interpretations of the Movement _____ 202

NORMAN PENNER o The United Front from
Above and Below: Canadian Communism in the 1930s _____ 213

HERBERT QUINN o The Formation and Rise
to Power of the Union Nationale _____ 238

JOHN SAYWELL o "I Swing to the Left":
Mitch Hepburn and the Ontario Liberal Party _____ 259

section 4 CONTINUITY AND CHANGE: 1946-1998 ___ 283

Introduction _____ 284

REGINALD WHITAKER o Party and State
in the Liberal Era _____ 299

GEORGE PERLIN o The Tory Syndrome:
Conflicts over Diefenbaker's Leadership _____ 317

DAN AZOULAY o "A Desperate Holding Action":
The Survival of the Ontario CCF/NDP, 1948-1964 _____ 342

ALVIN FINKEL o Social Credit in Alberta:
The Road to Disintegration _____ 366

GRAHAM FRASER o René Lévesque and the
Rise of the Parti Québécois _____ 391

SYDNEY SHARPE AND DON BRAID o Storming
Babylon: Preston Manning and the Reform Party of Canada __ 414

JUDY STEED o Shattered Dreams: The NDP's
1988 Election Campaign _____ 423

CHRISTINA MCCALL-NEWMAN o James Coutts and
the Politics of Manipulation: The Liberal Party, 1972-1977 ___ 445

JEFFREY SIMPSON o Mulroney 1988:
Power Despoiled _____ 462

FURTHER READINGS _____ 483

FOREWORD

o

Political history in Canada has not been a popular subject—with academic historians if not with the general public—for the last fifteen or twenty years. Party histories, election studies, and political biographies all have been seen as old-fashioned, boring, or the preserve of white, male practitioners—and all those terms are intended to be derisive. That this view is short-sighted seems obvious; that it is also wrong this book of readings should make clear. Yes, most of the writers, though not all, are male, but few are boring, whether young scholars or older well-established historians.

Indeed, this volume by Dan Azoulay, a young political historian, presents Canadian political history in its full variety. There are sweeping interpretations, national and provincial; there are detailed studies that illuminate the particular and make it general; and there are biographical interpretations of political leaders that demonstrate the impact of personality on politics and peoples. There is, in other words, the story of the supreme sport of politics in all its many varieties. Politics, after all, has been and is practised by more Canadians than even ice hockey. And frequently it is practised with more passion and always with much more at stake.

Political history remains important so long as Canadians practise democracy. That historians, political scientists, and journalists believe it important to study—despite prevailing trends in professional historical circles—is merely a reflection of reality, and it is absolutely certain that the pendulum of historiographical fashion will swing back towards a more reasonable position in which political history will be found at the centre. When it does, volumes of essays like this one by Dan Azoulay in the *New Canadian Readings* series will have mapped out the controversies, blazed a trail, and presented that firm base from which new interpretations can be discovered.

J.L. Granatstein
General Editor

INTRODUCTION

○

Until the 1960s, politics in all its dimensions, especially national politics, was the focus of most historical literature on Canada. By providing readers with an understanding of past political leaders, institutions, parties, and government policies, historians assumed that their work would create the highly elusive sense of national identity Canadians were thought to lack. In the New Left, anti-authoritarian atmosphere of the late sixties and early seventies, however, such a perspective was deemed elitist and was largely superseded by studies of how Canada's "limited identities" of class, region, gender, and ethnicity shaped the country's historical evolution. Since then, political history has experienced a revival of sorts. Realizing that Canada's development cannot be understood in the absence of key political events and individuals—that history is made from above as well as from below, in other words—academics have restored a measure of visibility and respectability to the study of political history. The last two decades have seen a steady increase in the number of studies, a good many of them by political scientists, that focus on one or another aspect of Canada's political heritage. Among these works are numerous biographies of civil servants and politicians, histories of Canada's foreign, defence and social policies, and neo-Marxist studies of the state's role in the economy. This renaissance is further reflected in the formation of the Organization for the History of Canada in 1994, a body devoted to studying and propagating, through its own journal and annual conferences, "the Canadian national experience in its broadest sense."

Not surprisingly, the study of Canadian political parties has ebbed and flowed in similar fashion. Numerous books and articles appeared on the subject in the 1950s and early 1960s, particularly on third parties like the CCF and Social Credit, but the number trailed off significantly thereafter. Since the mid-seventies, however, parties—and not just protest parties—have once again become legitimate objects of scholarly concern. And again, political scientists have led the way, followed closely by journalists. Of course this authorship has meant that much of the newer work on political parties lacks much in the way of historical perspective, for social scientists and journalists are naturally more present-minded than historians. There are, for example, a good number of textbooks about Canadian party politics, but none that takes a distinctly historical approach or that attempts to deal with the total party experience, as opposed to specific aspects thereof.

This, then, is one of the main rationales for this book: to provide students of politics and history with a reasonably comprehensive collection of readings on Canadian parties since Confederation, the first such collection of its kind. Another is to underline the importance of political parties to

Canadian history, for as most academics readily admit, parties have performed a number of functions vital to the proper functioning of a democratic polity, including recruiting leaders, serving as conduits for, and informers of public opinion, shaping public policy, bridging ethnic, class and regional divisions, and, of course, forming governments. Notwithstanding some recent claims that parties have largely outlived their usefulness, and despite the widespread cynicism toward politicians of late, few can deny that parties have had and will continue to have a significant impact on our society. Nowhere is this more apparent than in the emergence in recent years of powerful regional protest parties, whose weighty and conflicting concerns promise to dominate the public agenda for the foreseeable future.

Canadian Political Parties is divided into five sections. The first presents two readings that survey key aspects of Canadian party politics since Confederation. The next three sections mark what I believe to be the three main phases in the evolution of the Canadian party system. The fairly detailed introductions for Sections 2 to 4—necessitated by the absence of survey texts on Canadian party history—provide a contextual overview of the period, with an emphasis on the defining themes. Every attempt has been made in these introductions to avoid repetition with the individual readings in the sections. The final section provides a list of useful historical monographs specifically on Canadian political parties since 1867.

As for content, I have tried to be as inclusive as space permits. Of course the broad scope of the topic has demanded a measure of selectivity and, as such, readings have been included that to my mind best convey both the central themes of each era and the diversity of "major" and "minor" parties that have emerged federally and provincially since 1867. Consequently, only some of the more successful and enduring political organizations receive attention, while the smaller "fringe" parties that participate regularly in the electoral process—the Natural Law Party, the Christian Heritage Party, the Green Party, the Libertarian Party, to name a few—do not. Some information on such groups may be found in the Wearing article in Section 1.

I would like to thank the publishers and authors of the readings that follow for allowing me to reprint their work, especially those authors who generously agreed to waive their portion of copyright fees. I am also grateful to the editors and proofreaders at Irwin Publishing for their efforts at making this a more presentable text. Any mistakes or omissions in the final product are mine alone.

– D. Azoulay
August 1998

section

1

OVERVIEWS

INTRODUCTION

T he two articles in this section are meant to provide a broad introduction to Canadian political parties since Confederation. The first, by Joseph Wearing, is taken from the author's 1988 study *Strained Relations: Canadian Parties and Voters*. It deftly traces the ideological origins and evolution of Canada's major and minor parties, while at the same time providing a brief historical account of each. It concludes with an analysis of where voter support has traditionally resided for the major parties and how this "political geography" has changed over time. Admittedly, the piece is somewhat dated, given the dramatic changes in Canadian party politics since the late 1980s, but this minor drawback in what is otherwise a rich, and also rare, rendering of our political heritage is easily remedied with reference to the introduction and articles in Section 4.

The second reading is more focused than the first, but complements it well. Essentially an historiographic piece, it examines the literature on a neglected aspect of the Canadian party experience: organization. In the process, it provides an overview of the structure of Canada's federal parties since 1900, and more important, of how these parties have gone about mobilizing support. This piece is somewhat less anachronistic than that of Wearing, if only because few studies of party organization have emerged since its initial publication. Recent studies of the Reform party and Bloc Québécois, moreover, have had little to say on the subject of organization.[1] In any case, readers seeking more current information should consult Section 5, "Further Reading."

NOTES

1. Some information on the Bloc Québécois' organization can be found in Manon Cornellier, *The Bloc* (Toronto: James Lorimer, 1995), mostly in Ch. 5, which discusses the BQ's 1993 federal election campaign. The literature on the Reform party is more extensive. Although personality and policy are the focus in these mostly journalistic accounts, some information on organization can be gleaned from the following: Murray Dobbin, *Preston Manning and the Reform Party* (Toronto: James Lorimer, 1991), especially Chs. 5 and 6; Tom Flanagan, *Waiting for the Wave: The Reform Party and Preston Manning* (Toronto: Stoddart, 1995), Chs. 5 and 8; and Trevor Harrison, *Of Passionate Intensity: Right-Wing Populism and the Reform Party of Canada* (Toronto: University of Toronto Press, 1995), which easily contains the best account of the party's organization, in Ch. 5.

IDEOLOGICAL AND
HISTORICAL PERSPECTIVES

BY JOSEPH WEARING

o

Anyone looking at Canadian parties today [1988] is struck by how similar they are. Parties in other countries are supposedly more differentiated. This is ascribed to a richer political tradition and clearer class divisions. In a recent study of Western political parties Klaus von Beyme finds it inappropriate to analyze Canadian and U.S. parties by European standards,[1] and a Canadian writer attacks "the notion, as taught to every first-year poli-sci student, that Canada's three main parties represent three separate ideologies—conservatism, liberalism, and socialism...in truth they represent changing varieties of liberalism appropriate to an essentially liberal polity."[2] Canadian parties are not the only ones to have become similar. Otto Kirchheimer coined the term "catch-all" party in his 1966 analysis of how the major western European parties had broadened their ideological appeal.[3] If the Canadian Conservatives, Liberals, and New Democrats defy simple pigeonholing, so, too, do the German Christian Democrats, Social Democrats, and Free Democrats.

No individual political philosopher is entirely consistent with his own philosophy over a lifetime of writing and it would be surprising if a political party were not a good deal less consistent. For one thing, conditions change. An ideology is not fixed in stone. Preservation of the monarchy is a common feature of conservatism, but there is little point in a party pledging itself to restore the monarchy in a country such as France, for example, where the republican tradition is now deeply ingrained. The conservatives in France— the Gaullists—are in fact fully committed to maintaining the republic of

De Gaulle, not to resurrecting the Bourbons. On the other hand, even in the heyday of British "Butskellism"[4] there was no denying that Labour and Conservative parties had arrived at their consensus from very different origins and that those origins still mattered, especially after the consensus began to break down in the late 1970s....

It helps in understanding a political party to look to its ideological roots and origins. Two recent works dealing with political parties in a comparative framework find that most Western political parties fall into ten different types or ideological groupings as set out in Table 1[5]. By focusing on the origins of the various Canadian political parties, we can see that almost all the ideological traditions shown in the table are represented in the Canadian party system.

TABLE 1. *IDEOLOGICAL GROUPING OF WESTERN POLITICAL PARTIES*

IDEOLOGICAL TYPE	CANADIAN EQUIVALENT
1. Liberals	Reform/Liberal
2. Conservatives	Family Compact/PC
3. Workers'/Socialist	Labour/CCF/NDP
4. Agrarian/Rural	Progressives/United Farmers
5. Regional/Ethnic	Bloc populaire/Parti Québécois
6. Christian/Religious	None (or perhaps Union nationale)
7. Communist	Communist/Labour Progressive
8. Fascist/Ultra-rightist	National Unity party
9. Protest/Discontent	Social Credit/Créditistes
10. Ecological	Green

LIBERALS

The name, which originated with the Spanish *liberales* or constitutionalists elected to the Spanish parliament in 1812, was applied in Canada to the radical Reformers, Clear Grits, and Rouges beginning in the late 1850s.[6] The Reformers originated in the late 1820s to express popular grievances against the colonial government and to press for the adoption of responsible government as the answer to political unrest. Their belief in parliamentary, majority government and their success in using power to achieve it in the province of Canada and in Nova Scotia put them in the same camp as other liberal parliamentary groups in Britain, Belgium, France, and Italy. Like the European liberals, they also included a radical strand who wanted to carry democratic principles further by turning appointed government positions into elected ones, by extending the franchise, and by reforming the constituencies on the basis of equal population: Rep by Pop. There were even a few republicans.

Their allies, the Rouges, of Canada East had reservations about Rep by Pop, since it would reduce French-Canadian representation in parliament. Some Rouges wanted even more radical change—annexation to the United

States. Both the Rouges and the Grits, however, shared with their European counterparts the goal of maintaining a strict division between church and state, with the Rouges indulging in the more extreme anticlericalism of continental liberals.[7] When Wilfrid Laurier, in his younger days an outspoken Rouge, became leader of the Liberal party, the bonds of blood proved thicker than the water of religious dogma. French Canadians responded to a party led by one of their own and, after much perseverance, Laurier made peace with the Catholic bishops. By an ironic historical accident, the Catholic Church began to look upon the formerly dreaded Liberal party as its protector, much as the Conservative party had been under Macdonald.

Although the anticlericalism of the Rouges was derived from continental European liberalism, the various strains of British liberalism were the dominant influence for Canadian Liberals at least until the 1950s. Edward Blake's abhorrence of spendthrift Conservative policies was of a piece with Gladstone's public frugality. Laurier's belief in liberty, individual rights, and representative democracy clearly owes a debt to John Stuart Mill.

Liberalism also presented contradictions that were becoming painfully obvious. Canadian Liberals began to realize that the social problems created by industrialization could only be dealt with by government. On the other hand, like European liberals, they felt cross-pressured by their aversion to a paternalistic state and, apart from old-age pensions in 1926, Mackenzie King's Liberal government introduced little social welfare legislation before the Second World War. The crisis of capitalism in the 1930s further called into question the liberal belief in a free market economy and, for a time, only the socialists appeared to have a solution with their planned economy.

The ideas of two British Liberals, John Maynard Keynes and William Beveridge, provided a new set of liberal answers on which Canadian Liberals drew heavily.[8] Keynesian fiscal management of the economy was a heaven-sent answer to the liberal dilemma of how to retain a free market system even while government took responsibility for ensuring full employment, as the Liberal government did in its 1945 White Paper on Employment and Income. The Gladstonean belief in balanced budgets was conveniently discarded in favour of Keynesian deficits and surpluses. As Robert Campbell has shown, Keynesian doctrine was more honoured in the breach than the observance.[9] Nevertheless, Liberal governments in Canada after the Second World War had the good fortune to preside over a booming economy. Their policies were a shrewd combination of national development (from the gas pipeline of the 1950s to the National Energy Policy of the early 1980s), continentalism (from the American-financed resource boom of the 1950s to the Auto Pact of 1964), and the propagation of national symbols (from the flag in 1965 to the patriated constitution in 1982).

Earlier hesitations about social welfare policies were forgotten and, taking a cue from the wartime Beveridge Report—which laid the foundations of the British welfare state—Liberal governments launched family allowances (1944), hospital insurance (1957), the Canada Pension Plan (1964), and medicare (1968). Finally, traditional liberal values were reasserted under Trudeau by the promotion and entrenchment of language rights and other individual rights in the Official Languages Act (1969) and the Charter of Rights and Freedoms (1982).

In passing, we might note another common feature of Canadian and European liberalism that, according to von Beyme, has caused considerable difficulty over the years: nationalism.[10] For some Liberals, such as Gladstone, the logical extension of liberal principles lay in championing the rights of subjected peoples to be independent of the autocratic empires that ruled them. Others feared the divisive or the destructive force of nationalism. Consequently, nationalism produced acrimonious divisions within the Liberal parties of Bismarckian Germany and Victorian Britain. In Canada, apart from finding common ground in their dislike of Macdonald's plan for a centralized federation, Liberals encountered similar threats to party unity in the questions posed by nationalist forces. For many English Canadians, nationalism meant British imperialism. So they demanded Canadian participation on the side of the British in the Boer War, while many French Canadians, if anything, sympathized with the Boers. Although Laurier was able to find a compromise that smoothed over divisions within his party, the controversy foreshadowed much more serious threats to party unity when a world war broke out a decade later. For many Quebeckers, Canada's participation was yet another manifestation of British imperialism and so the issue of conscription split the party as Irish Home Rule had split Gladstone's Liberals thirty years before.

In the 1960s, nationalism again divided the party, though not as sharply. This time the issues were economic nationalism and the call for government measures to decrease the foreign (i.e., American) ownership of the economy. Walter Gordon, at one time Minister of Finance, was the protagonist; his continentalist opponents were led by another minister, Mitchell Sharp. By the 1970s, the Liberal party was firmly united in the cause of national unity under the leadership of Pierre Trudeau—which was not without its irony, since Pierre Trudeau, in the 1950s and early 1960s, had railed against the centralizing policies of Liberal federal governments and the emotional force of nationalism![11]

In one important respect, Canadian liberalism has differed from European liberalism insofar as the competition between right and left and the appropriation of liberal ideas by other parties have not yet marginalized it— at least not in central and Atlantic Canada, although this *has* happened in western Canada. Horowitz ascribes the triumph of the Canadian Liberal party to its position as "a *centre* party, with *influential* enemies on both right and left" and the need to meet the challenge of innovative socialism.[12] This is not a completely satisfactory answer, since even stronger challenges from the left and right debilitated European Liberal parties. Besides, a true centre position has usually proved treacherously difficult to maintain. As John Hancock maintained, "the middle ground is death."[13] A better explanation is that the Liberal party of Canada, in drawing much of its policy ideas from the rich and often conflicting statements of two centuries of liberalism, has been much more adept than its European cousins in fashioning an appealing electoral platform from those sources and especially in pre-empting the left.

CONSERVATIVES

According to von Beyme, generalizations about Conservative "programmatic principles" are among the most difficult to make because "Conservative programmes have undergone much more far-reaching change than the doctrines of other political groups."[14] However, four themes recur: (1) support for an established religion; (2) adherence to patriotism and nationalism combined, illogically, with a suspicion of the centralist state and support for regional rights; (3) "populist undertones" bordering on "plebiscitary collectivism"; (4) an acknowledgement that the state may sometimes have to act to compensate for the failings of society and human nature.[15]

All four themes are present in Canadian conservatism, although the first only to a vestigial degree. Before Confederation, Macdonald's Conservatives supported the four mainline churches—the Anglicans, the Presbyterians, the Roman Catholics, and the Wesleyan Methodists—in their claims to special privileges from the state. Now, with the country both more secularized and constitutionally opposed to religious discrimination, such religious favouritism would be an anachronism; however, in 1981, the party did campaign successfully to add to the Charter of Rights and Freedoms a phrase recognizing the "supremacy of God."

In common with its British counterpart, Canadian conservatism has frequently appealed to patriotism and nationalism. André Siegfried wrote that, by 1891, "patriotism had become one of the most effective planks in the Conservative platform"[16] and it was also a notable aspect of the Conservative appeal when Borden and Diefenbaker led the party. There were occasions in the past, however, when the Conservative party was torn between a broad, nation-building and region-bridging role—especially connecting French and English Canada—and a more narrowly conceived calling as the party of British imperialism and Protestant English Canada.

One of the ironies of Canadian ideological polarization is the Conservative and Liberal reversal on the provincial rights question, though clearly both sides of the issue are related to inconsistencies in the political philosophies inherited by each party. In the nineteenth century the Conservatives were the nation-building, centralizing party facing Liberal premiers, such as Mowat of Ontario and Mercier of Quebec, who staunchly defended provincial rights. In the twentieth century, the positions were reversed, with the federal Liberal party defending national unity and the need for a strong central government, while Conservative premiers such as Lougheed of Alberta and Peckford of Newfoundland safeguarded provincial jurisdiction and the federal leader, Joe Clark, described Canada as a "community of communities."

While the "plebiscitary collectivism" of the French right, most recently seen in De Gaulle and his love of the referendum, is not a feature of either British or Canadian conservatism, the populist overtones are certainly there, beginning with Macdonald. To quote Siegfried once again: "the main strength of the Conservatives consisted in their having a real leader who knew how to take up popular causes and make them his own."[17] Over half a century later, party leader John Diefenbaker was described by George Grant as representing a confusing combination of "populism, free enterprise, and nationalism."[18]

In the 1980s, a Conservative government was sufficiently captivated by Thatcherite and Reaganite "conservatism" (which is really eighteenth-century liberalism) to promise privatization, deregulation, and free trade. However, former PC leader Robert Stanfield is scornful of exaggerated claims for free enterprise and the free market, saying it is not part of the Conservative tradition.[19] Indeed, Canadian conservatism has historically recognized the need for compensatory action by the state. Conservative federal governments gave financial support to the Canadian Pacific Railway, created Macdonald's National Policy, and nationalized several companies to create the Canadian National Railway. R.B. Bennett laid the foundation for the Canadian Broadcasting Corporation and set up the Bank of Canada; Diefenbaker instituted a Winter Works program. Conservative governments in Ontario established the Workmen's Compensation Board and Ontario Hydro early in the century and, in 1981, acquired a 25 per cent interest in a major oil company, Suncor. This Canadian manifestation of what Horowitz calls "red Toryism" or "the corporate-organic-collectivist ideas of toryism" is questioned by Johnston, who finds that Red Tories at a leadership convention look not so much like socialists as "Liberals in disguise."[20] Thus, along with authentically Conservative ideas, Canadian conservatism has also been marked by liberalism, whether it is "business liberalism," in the words of Christian and Campbell,[21] or the "welfare liberalism" found by Johnston.

Finally, in common with Conservative parties elsewhere,[22] the PC party prefers a more comprehensive-sounding name than just Conservative. Macdonald's party was officially Liberal-Conservative and became the Progressive Conservative party in 1942 when it took on John Bracken, a former Progressive premier of Manitoba, as leader. (It was also, briefly, the National Liberal and Conservative party in 1920-22 and the National Government party in 1940.)

S O C I A L I S T S   A N D   S O C I A L   D E M O C R A T S

European observers tend to dismiss socialism in Canada as relatively unimportant,[23] and von Beyme asserts that "Canadian Socialism has little in common with European Socialism."[24] Socialism certainly developed more slowly in Canada than in Europe, yet even its troublesome factionalism before the Second World War came directly from its European models. When finally established, Canada's socialists (the CCF from 1932 to 1961 and the NDP from 1961) may not have got into the same electoral league as the British Labour party or the Social Democrats in Scandinavia and West Germany; they nevertheless compare favourably with socialist parties in France and Italy, as Table 2 shows. (Of course, the *total* leftist vote in the latter two countries has always been higher than in Canada because of a large Communist vote.)

TABLE 2. *PERCENTAGE OF VOTES FOR SOCIALIST PARTIES SINCE 1945*

	CANADA	FRANCE	ITALY	BRITAIN
1945	15.6	23.8		48.3
		21.1 (1)	20.7	
		17.9 (2)	30.1/7.1	
	13.4			
1950				46.1
		14.5		48.8
	11.3		12.7/4.5	
1955				46.4
		15.2		
	10.7			
	9.5	15.4	14.2/4.5	
				43.8
1960				
	13.5	12.6/2.0		
	13.1		13.8/6.1	
				44.1
1965	17.9			
				47.9
		18.7		
	17.0	16.5	14.5	
1970				43.0
	17.7		9.6/5.1	
		20.0		
	15.4			37.1 (1)
				39.3 (2)
1975				
			9.6/3.4	
		22.5		
	17.9		9.8/3.7	36.9
1980	19.8			
		37.5		
			11.4/4.1	27.6
	18.8			
1985				
		31.4		
			14.3/3.0	30.8

Source: K. von Beyme, *Political Parties in Western Democracies*; J.M. Beck, *Pendulum of Power*; Returns of the Chief Electoral Officer; *European Journal of Political Research*.

In all Western democracies, the sort of relationship a socialist party had with the country's trade unions was fundamental to the way it developed. There were three different models. In the case of the British Labour party, for example, the unions themselves took the initiative to have their own party represent them in Parliament. They created a party more pragmatic than doctrinaire. The second case is that of most continental northern European countries, where the trade unions concentrated on the industrial sphere and left the socialists to provide leadership in the political arena. Marxist ideas predominated in these parties at least in the early phases. Finally, in France and Italy, factionalism in both the unions and the parties of the left allowed integration to take place only gradually. The unions, as well as the parties, were much affected by Marxist and syndicalist ideas and took an active role in politics. Furthermore, divisions on the left were exacerbated by competition from a strong Communist party, which also made the socialists more radical.

Ironically, though Canadian socialists were inspired by British models, the historical development of Canadian socialism actually resembled that of France and Italy, especially in the early years. First, the low percentage of unionized workers and the very slow progress in creating a national federation of trade unions were similar to the situation in France and Italy rather than that in Britain and Germany. Membership in the Trades and Labour Congress (TLC), founded in 1886, did expand sharply after the turn of the century from 8,000 in 1900 to 100,000 in 1914.[25] However, it faced competition in Quebec from Catholic unions and in western Canada from radicals, who resented American domination exercised through so-called "international" unions. The climax of this western sentiment came with the short-lived One Big Union (OBU) and the Winnipeg General Strike of 1919. While the strike discredited militant strike action, it radicalized the working class in western cities and accentuated the sectionalism that always plagued socialist and labour unity in Canada.[26]

Finally, even though the Communist party of Canada (CPC) was never anything like as large as the Communist parties of France and Italy, its strategic position until the 1950s was similar. It had important positions of power within certain unions (though it also encountered much union hostility) and electorally it was not overwhelmed by a much larger and more successful social democratic party, as was the case in Britain.

A socialist party was not permanently established in Canada until 1932; before then, the array of socialist and labour parties was bewilderingly complex. In a country with so many different regional traditions and tenuous national links, it is not surprising that organizational initiatives were local and an effective national body was difficult to establish. There were also disagreements about whether to follow British or Russian models or to reject both and create a distinctive Canadian model based on a farmer-labour alliance.[27]

Before 1920, the principal manifestation of working-class politics consisted of locally based Independent Labour parties whose ideology was closer to the British Radical tradition than to socialism.[28] Domestic fallout from the First World War—in the form of inflation and profiteering—created the greatest class tension Canada has ever experienced, and, in its aftermath, Labour candidates won provincial seats in New Brunswick, Quebec, Ontario, Manitoba, Saskatchewan, and B.C.; two Labour MPs were elected in Manitoba and Alberta. Labour candidates had their biggest success in Ontario, where they won eleven seats and agreed to form a government with the United Farmers of Ontario. But success had come too easily. The group had neither leadership nor ideological cohesion; nor did the coalition government's failure to pass social legislation or the eight-hour day please rank-and-file party members. At the next election in 1923, all but four of its MPPs were defeated.[29]

In British Columbia, miners with a history of militancy were ready to engage in left-wing politics, even though this meant supporting the Socialist party of Canada, a party that attacked trade unions for being part of the capitalist system.[30] It had more electoral success at an earlier date than any other socialist/labour party in the country—holding the balance of power in 1903 and getting 13.9 per cent of the vote in 1912 to form the official opposition. But B.C. was rife with factions. The SPC split over whether to affiliate with the Communist International and was overtaken electorally by the Federated Labor party, a creation of the British Columbia Federation of Labor.

Throughout most of its history the Trades and Labour Congress was lukewarm to the notion of either establishing a labour party or formally endorsing a socialist party. This was due partly to the influence of Liberals and Conservatives who were active in the Congress and partly to the influence of Samuel Gompers of the American Federation of Labor (AFL), who believed strongly in political independence so that unions could play off the two older parties against each other. However, the TLC was less hostile to socialism than the AFL, and in 1906 it was persuaded to support the creation of a Canadian Labor party. In 1917, it went further and called for the cooperation of socialists, unionists, farmers, and others on the model of the British Labour party.[31] But the CLP never really got off the ground because the Independent Labor parties in the provinces were reluctant to give up organizational control to labour bureaucrats and the TLC found the CLP too socialistic for its taste.

The real impetus for the creation of a socialist party came from two Labour MPs elected in 1921—J.S. Woodsworth from Winnipeg and William Irvine from Calgary—who were the first Labour MPs not to slip into the Liberal caucus. A few years later they were joined by a number of radical Progressive MPs to form the Ginger Group and in 1932 they were finally able to unite the various labour and farm groups, socialists, Christian socialists, and Fabian intellectuals into the Cooperative Commonwealth Federation. The party had more electoral success than its predecessors. Its high point in federal elections came in 1945, when it won 28 seats with a popular vote of 15.6 per cent. In 1944 it took power in Saskatchewan and in the same period formed the official opposition in Ontario and B.C.

The CCF advance was hampered by uncertain union support, while party members themselves were unsure about the value of union affiliation. They feared domination of the sort exercised by unions through their block votes at British Labour party conferences and they were afraid of losing control over constituency nominations. However, serious electoral setbacks in the late 1940s and early 1950s convinced even the most apprehensive that they needed the unions as allies.[32]

In one sense, the splits in Canadian unionism eventually worked to the CCF's advantage. The 1940 merger of more radical, more nationalistic unions into the Canadian Congress of Labour (CCL) created a union federation to equal the conservative TLC and provided a union foothold for CCFers who took leadership positions in the CCL. Though falling short of direct affiliation, the political efforts of the CCL and the CCF gradually became more integrated. As well, throughout the early 1950s, a growing number of the TLC rank and file supported the CCF, and in 1954 they elected a discreet CCF sympathizer, Claude Jodoin, to the TLC presidency. This paved the way for the great breakthrough in 1956, when the TLC and the CCL united in a broad union federation, the Canadian Labour Congress (CLC). In response, the CCF attempted to reassure less socialistic union leaders by adopting a more moderate statement of principles—accepting a mixed economy and dropping an earlier commitment to eradicate capitalism. The shock of shattering electoral defeat in the 1958 election was the final push to get party and union leaders to accept marriage. A new, more broadly based party had to be formed.[33] This was the NDP.

Ideologically, the NDP is solidly in the social democratic camp. The 1956 Winnipeg declaration followed the trend of European social democratic parties, which one by one have also abandoned promises of wide-scale nationalization. In the postwar period, acceptance of membership in NATO has been one of the most controversial issues for democratic socialist parties. Eventually all the European parties accepted it as inevitable, though not without considerable debate.[34] (Even the Italian Communist party does not want Italy to leave NATO!)[35] The issue is no less controversial in the NDP. In 1969, the party's convention adopted a policy of withdrawal in what constituted the major victory of the Waffle, the party's radical wing. Against the urging of the party leadership, conventions reconfirmed the policy in 1983 and 1985....

COMMUNISTS

Although it has always been small, Canada has a Communist party with ties to the Soviet Union. Indeed, for the first thirty years, it was a complicating factor of some significance among the multitude of equally small groups making up the fractured left. Like many European Communist parties, it was born in the aftermath of the Russian Revolution and accepted the Third International's conditions for membership, which included unquestioning loyalty to the Communist party of the Soviet Union. Consequently, the Communist party of Canada had to follow the various turns and twists of Soviet foreign policy in determining who its friends and enemies were, including the shift from a popular front against fascism in the late thirties to outright opposition to the "imperialist" war in 1939, to wholehearted support for the war effort after the Nazi attack on the Soviet Union in 1941.[37] Beginning in 1929, this also meant attacking social democrats (as did Communist parties elsewhere) for being "the most dangerous elements in the ranks of the working class."[38] Some of the twists severely tested the party's credibility and undoubtedly hurt its public following, but it nevertheless had some propaganda successes during the thirties. The CPC organized a public campaign for the release of eight Communist leaders arrested in 1931. When he was freed, party leader Tim Buck addressed a rally of 17,000 at Maple Leaf Gardens and became a national celebrity. The party also led the On-To-Ottawa trek of unemployed men in 1935 to protest the policies of the Bennett government and recruited Canadians for the Mackenzie-Papineau battalion to fight in the Spanish Civil War.[39]

Although the party was banned at the beginning of the Second World War, it soon reappeared as the Labor-Progressive party. Its public esteem increased considerably when the Soviet Union became an ally and the Labor-Progressive party publicly supported the war effort of the Mackenzie King government. In 1943, it won a federal by-election in Montreal and elected two MPPs to the Ontario legislature. (The party already had a member in the Manitoba provincial legislature and won several municipal offices in Winnipeg and Toronto.) As with many western European Communist parties, the CPC reached the height of its electoral popularity in the immediate postwar period, getting 2.1 per cent of the vote in the 1945 federal election. It even entered into a short-lived electoral alliance with the Liberal party, which shared with the CPC an interest in preventing the CCF from emerging as a major political force, something that seemed very likely at the end of the war.[40]

The Gouzenko spy affair of 1946 brought discredit to the party, especially when its single MP, Fred Rose, was convicted of espionage. It was further weakened by later events that shattered Communist parties throughout the Western world. Khrushchev's denunciation of Stalin, the Hungarian uprising of 1956, and the 1968 invasion of Czechoslovakia each caused an exodus from the Canadian party of those who protested its blind obedience to the Soviet line.[41]

CHRISTIAN/RELIGIOUS PARTIES

There is a Christian Democratic party in most of the western European democracies: in Austria, Belgium, Germany, Italy, the Netherlands, it is either the largest or second largest party. This poses an obvious question. Why is there no Christian Democratic party in Canada?

Today's Christian Democratic parties arose at the end of the Second World War out of earlier Catholic parties that were created to defend Catholic rights from attack. Bismarck's *Kulturkampf* against German Catholics in the 1870s was one example; in Italy, the *risorgimento*'s goal of bringing the Papal States into a united Italy put the Church under siege quite literally. These earlier Catholic parties were also inspired by liberal popes, most notably Leo XIII, who sought a middle ground between dehumanizing capitalism and godless socialism. After 1945, Christian democracy was seen as providing the best indigenous protection against a resurgence of fascism on the one hand or a Communist takeover on the other. So the earlier Catholic parties were made less narrowly sectarian and broadened to include

Protestants where their numbers were significant (West Germany and, later, the Netherlands).[42]

Christian Democratic parties became important only in countries with a significant Catholic population, and since Catholics have never constituted less than about 40 per cent of the Canadian population since 1867, one would expect Canada to have produced a Christian Democratic party. However, Catholics in Canada never felt as threatened as they did in Bismarck's Germany, nor did liberalism ever become as extremely anti-clerical as it did in France and Italy at the turn of the century. This is not to deny the importance of Catholic issues in Canadian politics. Ultramontanism fired Catholic militancy in the late nineteenth century and the Church mobilized its adherents in the cause of separate school rights. The Church always found that at least one of the two major federal parties was sensitive to its political demands. First it was the Conservatives under Macdonald's leadership, until the tug-of-war between Quebec Ultramontanists (Castors), Catholic moderates, and Protestant McCarthyites severely tested even Macdonald's political agility and proved too much for his successors. Later the Church began to look to the Liberal party as its protector. As previously mentioned, Laurier had started his political career as an anti-clerical *Rouge*, but he calmed Church fears after his accession to the Liberal leadership in 1887 and absorbed former Conservative Catholic moderates into his party.[43]

With Laurier's assertion of provincial rights in the Manitoba Schools Question, the battle for Catholic separate school funding was relegated to the provincial arena, where the Catholic Church was not without friends, especially in the key province of Ontario. In an extremely long campaign (of over a century's duration), the struggle for full funding of separate schools up to the end of high school got successive help from all three of the province's major parties: the Conservatives under Premier Sir James Whitney in the early years of this century, the Liberals under Premier Mitch Hepburn in the 1930s, the Conservatives under Premier John Robarts in the 1960s. Final victory came when all three parties endorsed the final move to full funding under a Conservative government in 1984.

The closest Canada came to having a Christian Democratic party was the Quebec Union nationale, especially in its early days. The ideals of Catholic humanism, as defined in the papal encyclicals *Rerum Novarum* (1891) and *Quadragesimo Anno* (1931), had had considerable impact in the province, where they provided the philosophical basis of the Action libérale nationale, a dissident Liberal group that joined with Quebec Conservatives in 1935 to form the Union nationale. To begin with, the new party's policies owed a considerable debt to the Catholic Church's École sociale populaire, whose program of reform was inspired by *Quadragesimo Anno*. In 1936, the Union nationale took power in Quebec and governed the province for twenty-three of the next thirty-four years. Once in power, however, the party largely ignored the goal of reforming capitalism and became a right-wing anti-union, nationalist party.[44] European Christian Democratic parties have shown a similar tendency to rightist shifts, especially when in power, but none so dramatically as the Union nationale.

AGRARIANS

The Canadian experience with agrarian party politics provides a clear parallel with a number of other Western democracies. The Progressive party (or the United Farmers in some of the provinces) had a spectacular if short-lived success in the decade immediately after the First World War, when other agrarian parties also flourished in Scandinavia and eastern Europe. Von Beyme notes that farmers' parties emerged only in countries where the rural population was independent enough to stand up to the major landowners and where the "peripheral areas were still in revolt against the dominance of the urban population and its market orientation."[45] Certainly all of this was true of the Progressive revolt in Canada. In the words of the leading historian of the Progressive party, they had formed a concept of Canadian economic policy in which "a metropolitan economy designed, by the control of tariffs, railways and credit, to draw wealth from the hinterlands and the countryside into the commercial and industrial centres of central Canada."[46] The Progressives' program included free trade, government-owned grain elevators, cooperative buying and selling to give farmers market strength, and some of the political reforms of American populism, such as abolishing party discipline and instituting primaries. Unlike the American Populist revolt, which drew its main support from small entrepreneurs rather than farmers,[47] the Canadian movement was led by farmers and endorsed by farm organizations (although it also sought the cooperation of labour and in Ontario formed a government with labour). Even the Social Gospel Christianity from which the Progressives drew much of their inspiration (including their enthusiasm for prohibition) was not unique to the Canadian agrarian movement, since similar movements elsewhere "flourished best on the soil of a religious approach with sectarian traits" and especially in Protestant areas.[48]

In the first federal election after the First World War, the Progressive party was suddenly the second largest in Parliament and formed governments in Ontario, Alberta, and Manitoba. However, the party's biggest problem was its weak internal cohesion, particularly in Ottawa. Some MPs were former Liberals, who simply wanted to exert more leverage on the Liberal government on specific issues such as lower tariffs; others were idealists, who wanted to institute non-partisan government; others were radicals, who wanted to transform the capitalist system. Consequently, as the party disintegrated in the mid-1920s, some Progressives drifted back to the Liberal party, some joined Woodsworth's Ginger Group, which eventually gave birth to the CCF, and some got out of politics and poured their energies into the movement for Church Union, which produced the United Church of Canada.[49] One lasting effect of the Progressive revolt was that federal politics never again returned to the two-party system, which had held sway since Confederation.

REGIONAL AND ETHNIC PARTIES

It is important to distinguish between regional or ethnic parties as such and the situation where a region or ethnic group gives disproportionate support to a party with support from other regions or ethnic groups. Using the more restricted definition, regional and ethnic parties have not been as prevalent in Canada as in some other countries. The Austrian Reichsrat at the turn of the century had thirty-two ethnic parties out of a total of thirty-six parties. In present-day Belgium, the three major parties—Christian, Liberal, and Socialist—each split into French and Flemish sections as the result of linguistic parties getting elected to parliament.[50] There are regional parties also in the United Kingdom, Spain, Italy, and Finland. Support for ethnic parties is not correlated with an ability to speak the region's language. Welsh is much more widely spoken in Wales than is Gaelic in Scotland, but support for nationalist parties has been much higher in the latter region. Economic deprivation is not always a satisfactory explanation. In Spain a high level of interest in regional parties occurs in two of the country's most economically advanced regions, Catalonia and the Basque region.[51]

In Canada, the Parti québécois (PQ) is very clearly an ethnic or linguistic party, as was the Bloc populaire canadien, a short-lived Quebec party formed in 1942 to protest overseas conscription. The nationalism of such parties often leads them to be right-wing. However, at its foundation the PQ was not only committed to independence for Quebec but was clearly also in the social democratic tradition, since it rejected Quebec's place in North American capitalism and proposed to democratize economic structures through the device of "cogestion" or joint management-workers administration of the work place.[52] The PQ looked as if it might fill the void on the left of Quebec's political spectrum, a void the CCF/NDP had never been able to fill.

Once in power the party, in its efforts to cope with worsening economic problems, had a head-on collision with the unions, particularly those representing public-sector employees. After suffering defeat in a referendum asking for a mandate to negotiate "sovereignty-association" with the federal government, the PQ also gave a lower priority to its *indépendantiste* stance, following a bitter internal debate.[53] Without the support of public-sector employees, who had provided the core of PQ militants, the party was badly defeated in the 1985 provincial election, although it remained the second largest party. A further blow was the resignation and death of René Lévesque, the party's founder, who was apparently the only one who could bridge the gulf separating the leftist *indépendantistes* and the moderate technocrats in the party.

In the 1984 federal election, the Parti nationaliste de Québec attempted to carry the PQ's message into the federal arena—without actually getting the blessing of the PQ. It got only 2 per cent of the votes in Quebec, compared to 9 per cent for the NDP, whose subsequent support there, according to the polls,... soared.

PROTEST OR DISCONTENT

Social Credit is the most difficult Canadian party to categorize. As a sort of primitive Keynesianism that traced all economic problems to insufficient money in circulation, Social Credit was taken up by William Aberhart, who had already established a province-wide organization of fundamentalist Christian Bible study groups in Alberta. Under his leadership, it swept to power in 1935 and soon evolved from a radical protest movement into a conservative, almost reactionary defender of Alberta's interests. It continued to rule the province as a rural, conservative party until 1971, when it was replaced with the more urban Progressive Conservative party.[54]

In 1952, an election victory in British Columbia by a separate wing of Social Credit caused even more surprise than the success in Alberta seventeen years earlier. In B.C., it was partly a fluke of the electoral system. The Liberals and Conservatives, who had been together in a coalition and faced the CCF in opposition, devised an alternative vote to replace the standard simple ballot. They hoped their supporters would give first and second choices to the two former coalition partners and thus prevent the Liberal-Conservative split from benefiting the CCF. Antagonism between the two parties was so sharp, however, that many voters gave their second choice to a new party led by a former Conservative, W.A.C. Bennett. This was Social Credit. The party...continued to govern B.C....except for a three-and-a-half-year interlude by the NDP in the 1970s. Although Aberhart in Alberta attempted to implement Social Credit monetary theory when he first became premier, it has been ignored completely by the party leadership in B.C. In David Elkins's description, Social Credit in B.C. is now a party of populist individualism and a provincial-level coalition of Conservatives and right-wing Liberals.[55]

For a time, Social Credit looked as if it might become an important national party. Between 1935 and 1957 it captured most of Alberta's federal seats; it got two Saskatchewan seats in 1935; and it gained a few in B.C. between 1953 and 1965. In 1962, the Quebec Ralliement des créditistes came out of nowhere to take one-third of the province's seats and so Social Credit held the balance of power in Ottawa and in three of the next six parliaments. However, the western Socred wing faded quickly while Diefenbaker was prime minister and the Quebec wing operated more or less as a separate party under its fiery and erratic leader, Réal Caouette. In some respects, Caouette resembled Pierre Poujade, who led a movement of right-wing protest during the last years of the French Fourth Republic.[56] They both appealed to the forgotten "little guy," who was overwhelmed by modernization and wanted to protest its attendant problems of technology, urbanization, big government, and big unions.

Although it was the intention of Social Credit to become a national party that would force a realignment, it was unable to transform the national party system.[57] In 1987, Ernest Manning, who was a Social Credit premier of Alberta for twenty-five years, still saw the need for a moderate, western-based party appealing to those estranged from the three major parties. Social Credit remains a legally registered federal party, but it got only 0.13 per cent of the votes in the 1984 federal election and its right-wing extremism came to the fore when it chose as interim leader James Keegstra, who was convicted of promoting hatred of Jews. Manning described that as "the stupidest thing they could do" and looked to the newly formed Reform Association of Canada to represent disillusioned westerners.[58]

In Canada as elsewhere, petty bourgeois parties of protest have been more successful than right-wing extremist parties, which are discussed in the next section. In 1973 a Danish anti-tax party led by Mogens Glistrup got 15.9 per cent of the vote and remains an important factor in Danish politics. The Libertarian Party of Canada capitalizes on a similar frustration with government bureaucracy and spending, but got only 0.19 per cent of the vote in 1984. A satirical party, the Parti Rhinocéros, has waged brilliantly satirical election campaigns and, at 0.79 per cent of the vote in 1984, it was the fourth-largest party, though it got no seats.

RIGHT-WING EXTREMISTS

In the 1930s, fascist parties existed in most Western democracies. In Canada, no self-described fascist party won any legislative seats, but fascist ideas struck sympathetic chords. Anti-Semitism, though not as virulent as Hitler's, was nevertheless socially respectable. In Ontario, the Leadership League, founded by George McCullagh, publisher of *The Globe and Mail*, wanted to abolish provincial legislatures and establish a National Government in Ottawa to make government more efficient and to deal with labour unrest. There was even a Swastika Club in Toronto that instigated an anti-Jewish riot in the Christie Pits. In Saskatchewan, the Ku Klux Klan played a key role in stirring up anti-Catholic and anti-immigrant feeling (there being few blacks in that province), and in Quebec both the Catholic Church and the population at large supported the Francoist cause in the Spanish Civil War. In 1938, a fascist party, the National Unity party/ Parti unité nationale, was founded. It generated some serious press attention but soon disappeared.[59]

ECOLOGISTS

Ecology parties are the most recent party phenomenon, dating only from the 1970s. They are concerned about environmental damage and reflect a change to post-materialist values in the post-industrial age. Unlike other parties, they are difficult to place on a left-right spectrum, though their internal divisions are often acrimonious, as between the fundamentalists and the realists in the German Greens. The other parties, especially the NDP, have raised the same concerns, and in 1984 the Green party of Canada got only 0.21 per cent of the vote....

SAFE SEATS

. . ..The regional party strengths described in the preceding sections can be further illustrated by outlining the pattern of safe seats for each party. They may persist for long periods and then suddenly change. Some are in rural areas that have shown few social or economic changes from one generation to the next, while others are in urban areas. One of the most enduring is the band of Ontario Conservative constituencies that spread from Lake Huron through Lake Simcoe down to the eastern north shore of Lake Ontario and over to the Upper St. Lawrence south of Ottawa.... Many were Conservative even before Confederation—a phenomenon that may very well have originated with John A. Macdonald's success in organizing Irish support—both Orange and Green—for the Conservative party....[60]

Until very recently, the sharp linguistic cleavage in New Brunswick was displayed in a similar pattern of safe seats going back to the turn of the century. The North and East Shore Acadian counties (with singularly English names—Gloucester, Kent, and Westmorland) were all Liberal strongholds; the English-speaking counties of the southwest, especially those along the St. John River Valley, were staunchly Conservative. The two counties bordering Quebec in the northwest, which have a high percentage of French Canadians, tended to favour the Liberals, though not as strongly as the Acadian counties.[61] Only very recently have these patterns been broken. In 1984, Conservatives won all but one of New Brunswick's seats, apparently reaping the benefit of progressive policies on bilingualism adopted by the provincial Conservative government of Richard Hatfield. When Gloucester, on the Bay of Chaleur, went Conservative, it was the first time since 1896.

The most dramatic change in political geography occurred with the Diefenbaker sweep in 1957-58. This reflected not only western disillusionment with the Liberals, but also confidence in a Conservative government where western voices were stronger than ever before. Formerly, the Conservative party had just three safe seats in Calgary and southwestern Manitoba and two recent acquisitions in B.C. The Liberals had fourteen loyal ridings in a band running from the southeastern corner of Manitoba to the northeastern section of Alberta—the Parklands belt—and another four or five in B.C. In the eight elections up to 1957, the Liberal party won an average of twenty-three seats out of fifty-three in the Prairie provinces, while the Conservatives won seven.

The 1958 shift is shown in Table 3. From then until 1965, the Liberals had no safe seats in all of western Canada, while the Conservatives suddenly had forty-three. The Liberals did slightly better during the early Trudeau years, but beginning in 1979 they held only one safe seat (Winnipeg-Fort Garry) to the Conservatives' forty-seven. The other parties were also affected. Beginning in 1935, Social Credit had regularly carried all rural Alberta seats (except for a couple in the northeastern section of the province), but it lost them all for good in 1958. The CCF lost all its safe seats in Saskatchewan and Manitoba, though it won back the two Winnipeg seats in the next election.

The NDP continued to regain previous strongholds, and by 1979-84 it had as many safe seats as before the Diefenbaker realignment.

TABLE 3. *SAFE SEATS BY PART AND REGION, 1958-1984*

REGION	PC			LIBERAL			NDP		
	'58-'65	'68-'74	'79-'84	'58-'65	'68-'74	'79-'84	'58-'65	'68-'74	'79-'84
Atlantic	12	17	13	8	7	4	0	0	0
Quebec	4	2	1	13	53	17	0	0	0
Ontario	20	15	37	14	36	14	2	5	3
Prairies	39	24	33	0	3	1	0	4	7
BC	4	0	14	0	2	0	4	1	6
Yukon, N.W.T.	1	1	2	0	0	0	0	0	0
Totals	80	59	100	35	101	36	6	10	16

NOTE: Social Credit had ten safe seats in Quebec in the 1968-1974 period. A "safe seat" is defined as one held continuously by the party through the indicated period.

B.C. has become more volatile. Trudeaumania eliminated the Conservatives in 1968 and the polarization between Trudeau and Stanfield in 1974 hurt the NDP. Even with the volatility, the pattern of consistently held seats illustrates how B.C. politics is based on class divisions more than any other province[62]. Conservative strength lies in the agricultural areas—Prince George, the Peace River, the Okanagan, the Lower Fraser Valley—and in the prosperous Vancouver suburbs of Richmond, Delta, and North Vancouver. The NDP has a secure hold in ridings with a high concentration of unionized labour in forestry, mining, and smelting on the northern coast and in the working-class ridings of the east end of Vancouver.

In the Atlantic provinces, the shift in the party balance has been less striking than in western Canada. The biggest change was in Nova Scotia, where most of the seats were safely Liberal from 1935 to 1953 (with the notable exception of Cape Breton South, which was heavily unionized and CCF). However, in 1957 the Conservatives took all but two of the province's twelve seats and half a dozen have been safely Conservative ever since.

While the Conservative party has branched out from its Ontario rump of the 1940s and 1950s, the Liberal party has shifted in the opposite direction. It has lost almost all its safe seats in western and Atlantic Canada, retained its core of safe seats in Quebec, and added a much less dependable but potentially large number of ridings in Ontario. The striking shift has been in Toronto, where changes in the ethnic character of the city have had a dramatic impact, partly in response to the large number of immigrants coming in under Liberal governments and to the Liberal party's support for multiculturalism. Until 1930, there was no place in all of Ontario as staunchly Tory as Toronto. Beginning in 1878, Toronto elected only one Liberal (1896) over the next fifty years. Toronto's population was overwhelmingly of British origin—80 per cent. The largest non-British group at that time was Jewish, in the Spadina area of the central-western section of the city (then Toronto West

Centre), which elected Toronto's first Liberal in 1930. A second Liberal was elected in neighbouring Trinity five years later. In 1949, there were eight. As the population of British origin dropped to 52 per cent in 1961, so, too, did the number of safe Conservative seats. Only the four most Anglo-Saxon ridings in the north and east (Eglinton, Broadview, Greenwood, and Danforth) remained loyally Conservative, and then only to the early 1960s. (Eglinton briefly went Liberal in 1940.)[63]....

Three other large Canadian cities also exhibit striking patterns. The Francophone ridings of Montreal were the mirror image of Tory Toronto and remained loyally Liberal well after the Toronto bastion had fallen. In the 1960s, The Conservatives took only one seat in Montreal and none in the next decade. In the Conservative sweep of 1984, the thirteen central-core ridings that remained Liberal occupy more or less the same area as the eleven ridings that withstood the Diefenbaker sweep of 1958.

The NDP has two safe seats in working-class north Winnipeg, which have been faithful to the left (with only an occasional apostasy) since Labour candidates were first elected in 1925. Two ridings in the east end of Vancouver trace their ancestry back to a single riding that has gone CCF-NDP in almost every election since 1935.

CONCLUSION

The pattern of safe seats is intriguing and instructive, but nothing persists forever. Tory Toronto fell to the Liberals and the NDP, the Liberal Parklands seats were lost in the Diefenbaker sweep. Much of rural Quebec went Conservative in 1958 and then Créditiste. The Liberals gradually regained those seats in succeeding elections only to lose them again in 1984. Although the Conservatives' sweep through Quebec in 1984 now seems unlikely to be repeated, the province's support for the NDP (as the polls indicated in 1987)[64] suggests that it could become a volatile three-party battleground as Ontario has become. For Quebec to be no longer a Liberal stronghold could have a profound impact on national party politics. Will the Prairies and the Atlantic provinces stay as solidly Conservative? There are indications that western disillusionment with Conservative patronage practices may end the Conservative dominance that began with Diefenbaker. Finally, provincial Liberal victories in P.E.I., Quebec, Ontario, and New Brunswick could be the harbinger of a new shift in which the Liberal party again becomes the party of provincial concerns as it was in the nineteenth century. Predicting long-term trends is extremely hazardous, particularly when the electorate is as volatile as it is now. We noted earlier, however, that past cycles of party politics have lasted about thirty to thirty-five years. While historical patterns do not necessarily repeat themselves, it is worth observing that the present cycle began in 1958. A new cycle could well be imminent.

NOTES

1. Klaus von Beyme, *Political Parties in Western Democracies* (Aldershot, Hants,1985), 2.

2. Ron Graham, *One-Eyed Kings* (Toronto, 1986), 17.

3. Otto Kirchheimer, "The Transformation of the Western European Party Systems" in Joseph LaPalombara and Myron Weiner, eds., *Political Parties and Political Development* (Princeton, 1966), 177-200.

4. "Butskellism" was coined by combining the surnames of the moderate Conservative, R.A. Butler, and the moderate Labourite, Hugh Gaitskell, who had been most influential in refashioning their respective parties' policies in the late 1950s and early 1960s in such a way as to represent a broad, left-of-centre consensus that characterized British politics until the mid-1970s. See S.H. Beer, *British Politics in the Collectivist Age* (New York, 1965); *Britain Against Itself* (New York, 1982); and Dennis A. Kavanagh, *Thatcherism and British Politics* (Oxford, 1987).

5. von Beyme, *Political Parties*, 23-141; Jan-Erik Lane and Swante O. Ersson, *Politics and Society in Western Europe* (London, 1987), 97-105. Lane and Ersson add an eleventh category, left-socialist parties.

6. P.G. Cornell, *The Alignment of Political Groups in the Province of Canada* (Toronto, 1962), 90, n.2. The short-lived Brown-Dorion ministry of 1858 was in reality the first "Liberal" government. W.L. Morton, *The Critical Years* (Toronto, 1964), 19.

7. In Canada several denominations received special privileges from the government—the Church of England, the Church of Scotland, the Roman Catholic Church, and, to a lesser extent, the Wesleyan Methodists. This took the form of land grants (the Clergy Reserves), aid to religious universities and separate school rights.

8. J.L. Granatstein, *Canada's War; The Politics of the Mackenzie King Government, 1939-1945* (Toronto, 1975), 249-88.

9. Robert M. Campbell, *Grand Illusions: The Politics of the Keynesian Experience in Canada, 1945-1975* (Peterborough, 1987).

10. von Beyme, *Political Parties*, 42-3.

11. See Pierre Elliott Trudeau, *Federalism and the French Canadians* (Toronto, 1968), especially "Federal Grants to Universities," "The New Treason of the Intellectuals," and "Federalism, Nationalism and Reason."

12. Gad Horowitz, "Conservatism, Liberalism and Socialism in Canada: An Interpretation," *Canadian Journal of Economics and Political Science* (1966), 143-71.

13. John Hancock, "The script is set for two-party play in the Commons," *Globe and Mail*, 1 October 1987.

14. von Beyme, *Political Parties*, 48.

15. Ibid., 49.

16. André Siegfried in *The Race Question in Canada*, F.H. Underhill, ed. (Toronto, 1966), 160.

17. Ibid., 158.

18. George Grant, *Lament for a Nation* (Toronto, 1965), 17.

19. William Christian and Colin Campbell, *Political Parties and Ideologies in Canada*, 2nd ed. (Toronto, 1983), 87.

20. Richard Johnson, "The Ideological Structure of Opinion on Policy," in George Perlin, ed., *Party Democracy in Canada* (Scarborough, Ontario, 1988), 65. The now-classic definition of red Toryism is contained in Horowitz, "Conservatism, Liberalism and Socialism in Canada," 143-71.

21. Christian and Campbell, *Political Parties and Ideologies,* 85.

22. von Beyme, *Political Parties,* 48.

23. See, for example, Maurice Duverger, *Political Parties: Their Organization and Activity in the Modern State,* 2nd ed. (London, 1959), 223. Duverger links "Labour" with Social Credit as "local parties." von Beyme, *Political Parties,* 65, groups Canada with "those Anglo-Saxon countries in which no Socialist party of any significance emerged."

24. von Beyme, *Political Parties,* 66.

25. Martin Robin, *Radical Politics and Canadian Labour* (Kingston, 1968), 117.

26. Ibid.,182-99. Gregory S. Kealey argues that the working-class unrest in 1919 was widespread and that "regional particularism" has been exaggerated. "1919: The Canadian Labour Revolt," *Labour/Le Travail* (1984), 15. On the other hand, Craig Heron finds that capital and labour in general were willing to cooperate in southern Ontario, whereas the most bitter confrontations occurred in the mining, forest, and transportation industries west of the Lakehead. "Labourism and the Working Class," *Labour/Le Travail* (1984), 69-70.

27. Norman Penner, *Canadian Communism: The Stalin Years and Beyond* (Agincourt, Ontario, 1988), 112.

28. Heron, "Labourism and the Working Class." 45-75.

29. Robin, *Radical Politics and Canadian Labour,* 219-51.

30. Ibid., 92-3.

31. Ibid., 81-2, 132-3.

32. Gad Horowitz, *Canadian Labour in Politics* (Toronto, 1968), 73-4, 136-7, 151.

33. Ibid., 63-7, 151-6, 162-7, 174, 194.

34. The exceptions are the socialist parties in Sweden and Switzerland, where a traditional policy of neutrality enjoys a broad political consensus, and in Austria, where neutrality was imposed in the Four-Power peace treaty.

35. Frederic Spotts and Theodor Wieser, *Italy, A Difficult Democracy* (Cambridge, 1986), 272.

36. Desmond Morton, *The New Democrats 1961-1986: The Politics of Change* (Toronto, 1986), 95, 227.

37. Penner, *Canadian Communism,* 128-90.

38. Quoted ibid., 93.

39. Ibid.,110-11, 118-22, 136-8.

40. Ibid., 204-7; Horowitz, *Canadian Labour,* 102-6.

41. Penner, *Canadian Communism,* 23-66.

42. See Ronald E.M. Irving, *The Christian Democratic Parties of Western Europe.*

43. H. Blair Neatby, *Laurier and a Liberal Quebec* (Toronto, 1973).

44. Herbert F. Quinn, *The Union Nationale: A Study in Quebec Nationalism,* 3rd ed. (Toronto, 1979); Kenneth McRoberts, *Quebec: Social Change and Political Crisis,* 3rd ed. (Toronto, 1988); R. Jones, *Community in Crisis: French-Canadian Nationalism in Perspective* (Toronto, 1967).

45. von Beyme, *Political Parties,*112-13.

46. W.L. Morton, "The Progressive Tradition in Canadian Politics," in Hugh G. Thorburn, *Party Politics in Canada,* 5th ed. (Scarborough, Ontario, 1985), 186.

47. von Beyme, *Political Parties,* 112.

48. Ibid., 113-14.

49. W.L. Morton, *The Progressive Party in Canada* (Toronto, 1950). For the interplay of religion and politics see W.E. Mann, *Sect, Cult and Church in Alberta* (Toronto, 1965); Richard Allen, *The Social Passion: Religion and Social Reform in Canada* (Toronto, 1973).

50. A. Mughan, "Accommodation or Defusion in the Management of Linguistic Conflict in Belgium?" *Political Studies* (1983). 434-51.

51. von Beyme, *Political Parties*, 120. See also Lane and Ersson, *Politics and Society in Western Europe*, 65-81.

52. See Vera Murray, *Le Parti québécois de la fondation à la prise de pouvoir* (Montreal, 1976).

53. Raymond Hudon, "The Parti Québécois in Power: Institutionalization, Crisis Management and Decline," and J.-P. Beaud, "The Parti Québécois from René Lévesque to René Lévesque," in Thorburn, ed., *Party Politics in Canada*, 5th ed. 220-33, 234-41.

54. For Social Credit in Alberta, see J.A. Irving, *The Social Credit Movement in Alberta* (Toronto, 1959); C.B. Macpherson, *Democracy in Alberta: The Theory and Practice of a Quasi-Party System* (Toronto, 1954); J.R. Mallory, *Social Credit and the Federal Power in Canada* (Toronto, 1954).

55. David Elkins, "British Columbia as a State of Mind," in Donald E. Blake, *Two Political Worlds: Parties and Voting in British Columbia* (Vancouver, 1985), 49-73; G.L. Kristianson, "The Non-Partisan Approach to B.C. Politics: The Search for a Unity Party, 1972-1975," *B.C. Studies* (Spring, 1977), 13-29.

56. Michael B. Stein, *The Dynamics of Right-Wing Protest: A Political Analysis of Social Credit in Quebec* (Toronto, 1973), 238.

57. Denis Smith, "Prairie Revolt, Federalism and the Party System," in Hugh G. Thorburn, ed., *Party Politics in Canada*, 1st ed. (Toronto, 1963), 126-7.

58. Quoted in Matthew Fisher, "Flame of western party still burns in former Socred premier," *Globe and Mail*, 14 August 1987.

59. Neil McKenty, *Hepburn* (Toronto, 1967), 193; C.H. Levitt and W. Shaffir, *The Riot at Christie Pits* (Toronto, 1987); David E. Smith, *Prairie Liberalism: The Liberal Party in Saskatchewan 1905-71* (Toronto, 1975), 143-8, 189-93; John H. Thompson with Allen Seager, *Canada 1922-1939* (Toronto, 1985), 323-4.

60. Joseph Wearing, "Elections and Politics in Canada West under Responsible Government, 1847-1863" (D. Phil. thesis, Oxford University, 1965), 297-8.

61. Hugh G. Thorburn, *Politics in New Brunswick* (Toronto, 1961), 45-82.

62. Martin Robin, "British Columbia: the Politics of Class Conflict," in Robin, *Canadian Provincial Politics*, 1st ed. (Scarborough, Ontario, 1972), 27-68. For a discussion of how class divisions have moderated in recent years, see Blake, *Two Political Worlds*.

63. Toronto, City Planning Board, "A Report on the Ethnic Origins of the Population of Toronto, 1960" (Toronto, 1960); A.H. Richmond, "Immigrants and Ethnic Groups in Metropolitan Toronto" (Toronto, 1967).

65. *Globe and Mail*, 16 July 1987.

THE EVOLUTION OF PARTY
ORGANIZATION IN CANADA, 1900-1984

BY DAN AZOULAY

○

INTRODUCTION

Writing at the turn of the century, British political theorist James Bryce observed that "although political parties are as old as popular government itself, their nature, their forces, and the modes in which they have been organized have received comparatively little [scholarly] attention."[1] Unfortunately, this is still largely the case almost a century later, at least with respect to Canadian parties and, specifically, their organization. Until very recently, historical studies of Canadian political parties have dealt almost exclusively with such things as their electoral performance, ideology, composition, legislative activities and leading public figures. How parties have gone about mobilizing public support, through membership recruitment, fundraising, publicity, patronage distribution, and so on—that is, how they have been "organized"—has not been an issue of pressing concern to most academics.[2] This is true despite the importance which interested observers have attributed to the leading Canadian parties historically, particularly their role in bridging sectional, class and racial animosities and thus adding a significant measure of stability to Canadian politics.[3] Even in the numerous studies of the Cooperative Commonwealth Federation/New Democratic Party (CCF/NDP), where one would expect to find a treasure trove of detail on something as basic to its existence as organization, the focus has been on elections, ideology, leadership and party structure; some of these subjects are related to the question of organization,[4]

Dan Azoulay, "The Evolution of Party Organization in Canada since 1900" in *The Journal of Comparative and Commonwealth Politics,* Vol. 33, No. 2 (July 1995), pp. 185-208. Published by Frank Cass & Co. Ltd., London, England. Used with permission.

to be sure, but CCF/NDP organization per se has not been given the detailed attention it deserves. Most of what little work has been done on party organization in Canada, historically, focuses on *other* third parties and to a lesser extent on the main parties, the Liberals and the Conservatives.

The main objective of this paper, therefore, is to review that which has been written on the question of party organization in Canada for the period 1900 to 1984, and in so doing, to suggest new avenues of research. A secondary objective is to foster a clearer understanding of the concept of party organization, one which will in turn allow for a more precise classification of parties on the basis of their organizational structures and activities. A major problem with much of the existing literature on political parties, including the pioneering works of such notables as Bryce, Michels and Ostrogorski, is that there is no consensus on what is meant by "party organization." Many, for example, have tended to equate organization primarily with party structure, that is, with the constituent parts or anatomy of a party, and to a lesser extent with party composition, namely the nature and size of social groups associated with the party.[5] What Michels refers to as the inevitable tendency towards oligarchy in party organization is a reference to structure, and specifically, how power within that structure becomes centralized over time.[6] Duverger offers a somewhat broader definition, although the typology he offers to differentiate among party organizations, in particular the distinction between "mass-extra-parliamentary" (mass) parties and "elite-parliamentary" (cadre) parties, refers almost entirely to the structure and composition of parties. The emphasis is still on party components, the degree to which these units and the individuals within them are organized or "articulated," the social bases of the party, and how power and responsibilities are distributed therein.[7] More common perhaps has been the equation of party organization with electoral "machine." In such cases organization is defined primarily as the "organizational apparatus" put in place to mobilize public support during election campaigns, with patronage distribution a key tool employed by a machine to achieve its goals.[8] Others have referred to party organization as consisting either exclusively or largely of *extra-parliamentary* units within the party, such as national, regional, or local councils and associations.[9] Perhaps the main problem with defining party organization in such structural and compositional terms, however, is that, as Duverger himself noted, "constitutions and rules never give more than a partial idea of what happens [in a party], if indeed they describe reality at all."[10]

Even on those rare occasions when the concept of organization has been disentangled from that of party structure and an emphasis placed on party *activities*, there has been no consensus on what constitutes organizational activity. In his lucid and trenchant *Political Parties in Western Democracies*, for example, Leon Epstein defines organization as patronage distribution and door-to-door canvassing, especially the latter, whereas activities like publicity and policy-revision are labelled "counter-organizational."[11] Students of the CCF, in particular, see organization as membership-recruitment and simple vote-getting, and draw a sharp distinction between such supposedly crass activities and those more appropriate to a political "movement," such as membership discussion and proselytization (i.e., "political education").[12] On the other hand, many writers consider such educational activities as publicity, policy conferences and speech-making integral aspects of party organization, especially in the modem age of mass communication.[13] Some also portray organizational activities as separate from fundraising activities, while others make no such distinction.[14] In short, although little effort has been made to define the concept of party organization explicitly (another problem with the existing scholarship), it is clear that it has come to mean different things to different writers, or at least each has chosen to emphasize certain aspects of the concept over others.

It is my view that the concept of party organization must include many of the elements identified in the existing literature. To emphasize one element over another or, worse still, to ignore some elements altogether, risks obscuring important aspects of party experience and this, in turn, makes the comparison and classification of parties on the basis of organizational criteria that much more difficult. In this paper, therefore, organization is defined broadly to mean both the structures and the methods by which supporters of a party have mobilized public support, during and between election campaigns, with the ultimate goal of sustaining or enhancing their party's political power or influence. Organizational structures may include such things as riding associations, study groups, campaign committees, influential notables or "clients" coopted by a party, workplace "cells," advertising agencies and affiliated organizations such as trade unions. Among the wide array of organizational methods or tools available to such structures in the party's quest to achieve or maintain power—to the extent that these methods further this quest, even indirectly—one might include patronage or the promise thereof, publicity, membership education, program revision, fundraising, canvassing, and getting one's supporters to the polls on election day. This definition is similar to that adopted, at least implicitly, in several existing studies,[15] and when applied to the main political parties in Canada this century—Liberal, Conservative, Social Credit, Progressive, CCF/NDP and Communist—it provides a useful way of understanding and classifying them.

MAJOR PARTIES

Only a few good monographs have been written on the post-1900 organization of Canada's two oldest parties, the Liberals and Conservatives. Reginald Whitaker's lengthy account of the "organizing" and "financing" of the federal Liberal Party between 1930 and 1958, appropriately entitled *The Government Party*, has been supplemented recently by Joseph Wearing's *The L-Shaped Party*, an examination of the party since 1958, and Christina McCall-Newman's *Grits*.[16] What Whitaker describes is essentially a cadre party *par excellence*, organized by the top parliamentary leadership, financed by a small number of well-connected party supporters in central Canada and characterized by minimal input from a relatively small membership. But it was a *dual* Liberal Party organization, one in which the responsibility for organizing funds and electoral support shifted back and forth between the parliamentary and extra-parliamentary bodies depending upon whether the Liberals were in power or not. When the party was in power, which was most of the time, ministers were responsible for making speeches, raising money, arranging federal nominating conventions, formulating party policy, supervising federal elections in their regions and, most important of all, distributing government patronage in exchange for support, financial or otherwise.[17] Whitaker labels this type of organization "ministerialism" and emphasizes the "crucial" importance of patronage, or the promise thereof, in securing funds and motivating party activists. When the party was in opposition between 1930 and 1935, many of the organizational duties were handled by the extra-parliamentary party, the National Liberal Federation (NLF). But for most of the period in question, the NLF's functions were limited to a bit of publicity, political education and research for caucus, and it focused largely on fundraising and directing patronage seekers to the appropriate minister or government official. Although the NLF president would occasionally assume the role of national organizer, organizational matters remained largely the responsibility of the prime minister, through his "informal network of personal contacts," and his ministers.[18] By the 1950s, when prosperity and political apathy undermined the NLF's purpose further, and powerful cabinet ministers took care of almost "all partisan activity," the extra-parliamentary organization virtually withered away. With most of the partisan functions now under the control of the state, its bureaucracy, and its professional advertising agencies, the Liberal party did indeed become the "government party."

Whitaker's study is more than a description of the Liberal party's approach to political organization. It is also a subtle indictment of the dominant element of that approach, ministerialism. While he attributes the Liberal party's return to power in 1935 to the efforts of the extra-parliamentary party, and grudgingly concedes that ministerialism helped maintain the party's hegemony for the next two decades, he openly attributes the decline of the party in the late fifties to the rise of the "government party" form of organization.[19] Unfortunately, Whitaker does not explain in any detail why this was so, except to say that with the rise of the welfare state bureaucracy in the 1950s, ministers had less time to devote to purely partisan activities and key party organizers were lost to the party when they were rewarded with positions in the civil service. David Smith has also pointed out, in his study of the Liberal party in the West, that regions without strong or influential representatives in cabinet did not "benefit" from the ministerial form of organization and so rejected the party.[20] It is perhaps more precise to say, however, that ministerialism per se was not to blame, but should have been supplemented by a more highly developed extra-parliamentary organization, especially after the Second World War.

Not surprisingly, efforts to revive the Liberal party after 1958, as Wearing's account tells us, focused on strengthening the NLF and using the latter to revitalize provincial constituency associations.[21] This policy of centralized extra-parliamentarianism was based on the assumption that stronger provincial parties, once they came to power, would assist the federal party to do the same; it was a strategy employed by the federal Conservatives in the 1950s with much success. After some debate as to which section of the party would take prime responsibility for reviving the provincial parties, the provincial Liberal associations themselves or the NLF, the forces of centralization prevailed. Under the influence of the NLF's aggressive National Director, Keith Davey, a new federal organizing structure was established to supersede the NLF. Resembling a sort of merger between ministerialism and extra-parliamentarianism, with Davey and several key cabinet ministers in charge, the revamped NLF attempted to introduce the so-called "new politics" into the provincial parties. It tried, for example, to infuse new blood into local constituency executives, give a greater voice to members in policy decisions and candidate selection, broaden the party's financial base, train members in the techniques of poll organization and remove patronage as an incentive for party workers. The goal, in short, was to convert the Liberal party from a cadre party to a mass party, all the while promising not to interfere with the traditional autonomy of the provincial sections in the area of organization.

The success of the "new politics" was mixed. The stronger extra-parliamentary organization continued to depend on patronage and large business donations, but the revitalization of some constituency associations, primarily in Ontario, contributed to the Liberals' return to power in 1963. The success of the new organizational approach could have been greater had the strengthening of extra-parliamentarianism not coincided with a decline in ministerialism (Prime Minister Pearson ordered his ministers to focus their energies on Parliament instead of organization). Consequently, in those ridings where the extra-parliamentary party was weak and the Liberals could have used the assistance of key ministers in finding quality candidates, making speeches and raising money, support for the party was low. Once again the Liberals failed to realize that the dual nature of their organizing activities had to be maintained for political success to follow. Furthermore, the centralizing aspects of the new politics created a backlash within some of the stronger Liberal provincial parties, particularly in the West. The latter resented the imposition of democratic, progressive reforms in their organizational jurisdiction and refused to assist the federal party during elections; cooperation was also hindered by basic philosophical differences between the federal party and western provincial parties.[22]

A more useful account of Liberal party organization in the Pearson and post-Pearson years is Christina McCall-Newman's *Grits*. Colourfully written and displaying a keen appreciation for the personality factor in politics, it fills in some of the nitty-gritty details obscured in Wearing's often convoluted text and, for that matter, in most analyses of party organization. What emerges is a fascinating picture of the "modern," highly centralized political machine, directed by the Prime Minister's closest political advisers and replete with slick television advertising, sophisticated polling techniques, and an array of professional imagemakers hired to fabricate just the right image of the party leader at a time when the cult of leadership was, and still is, pronounced.[23]

Not that the more traditional instrument of organization (i.e., patronage) was discarded. Although it was disparaged by the small clique of professional organizers, the proverbial "backroom boys," people like Senator Davey and Prime Minister Trudeau's Principal Secretary, Jim Coutts, whose activities almost supplanted ministerialism, appointments to the bloated federal bureaucracy continued to be used to reward and motivate party workers or relocate "dead wood" from within party ranks. In any case, responsibility for organizing the party remained concentrated at the upper levels of the party, with the "democratized" extra-parliamentary section, the NLF, playing a mostly symbolic role.[24]

As for the national Conservative party, too little has been written on the subject of organization to allow for firm generalizations. Nevertheless, several studies suggest some of the main components of the Tory approach. John English's study of the party in the first two decades of the century, *The Decline of Politics,* draws an organizational picture not unlike that drawn of the Liberal party, though in far less detail. Out of power between 1896 and 1911 and under the guidance of their new leader, Robert Borden, the Conservatives used party policy as their main organizational tool (Borden's famous Halifax Platform of 1907). The program was meant to appeal to the ascendant "progressive" interest groups of the day, including businessmen, Quebec *nationalistes,* and English-Canadian imperialists, as well as Conservative provincial administrations. Against the background of the naval and reciprocity issues, which alienated key segments of the electorate from the Liberals, it was the alliance of these extra-parliamentary interest groups and Tory premiers which helped return the Borden Conservatives to power in 1911. Not unlike the Liberal party, moreover, the Tories relied heavily on prominent central Canadian business interests to lubricate what English properly describes as an innovative reform of party organization, though one which fell far short of the "root-and-branch restructuring of the party" Borden had originally set out to effect. Unfortunately, information on the exact nature of the supposedly powerful patronage-dispensing Tory machines at the provincial level is, as the author admits, "almost as scarce as items on the most intimate details of politicians' lives." Details of the party's organizational approach after 1911 are equally sketchy, although English assures us that the "politics of patronage" which Borden so lamented in the previous Liberal administration, coupled with the government's emphasis on certain key policies, was not substantially altered under the Tories. Meanwhile, the extra-parliamentary organization of interest groups which Borden had worked so assiduously to construct, and which had returned the Tories to power was allowed to atrophy.[25]

The state of the Tory party's organization in the inter-war period has only recently been brought to light. Larry Glassford's survey of the party under R.B. Bennett, *Reaction and Reform,* discusses briefly the efforts to establish a national extra-parliamentary organization in the late twenties and the rapid dismantling of this organization after the 1930 election.[26] Under Bennett's predecessor, Arthur Meighen, the party had no national organization to speak of and at election time relied exclusively on the party machinery of provincial Tory administrations to mobilize campaign workers, funds and votes, especially in Ontario. This was to change somewhat under Bennett. A Dominion Liberal-Conservative Association (DLCA) was established, with a national organizer and small staff responsible for publicity and research. Financed largely by the personal resources of the party leader and several wealthy Tory MPs, the DLCA created a prolific and innovative publicity machine which Glassford credits with returning the Conservatives to power in 1930.

But the DLCA was short-lived. With the Depression raging, Prime Minister Bennett had little time (or additional money) for organization, which he felt should be handled, instead, by his ministers. Why the latter chose not to assume such duties for the most part is not clear, although Bennett's indifference to their doing so was certainly one reason. What *is* clear is that when opportunities arose for soliciting political contributions and distributing patronage they were mishandled. The last-minute attempt to revive the DLCA was too little, too late to exploit the Prime Minister's New Deal broadcasts and the party hobbled through the 1935 campaign in a much-weakened state. The Tory party's neglect of organization, concludes Glassford, was a key factor in the defeat which followed and continued for the duration of Bennett's tenure as leader.

The only full-length study of the national Conservative party's organization is J.L. Granatstein's *The Politics of Survival*.[27] Although it focuses largely on the party's organizational aberration during the Second World War, it is a solid account of how a party internally divided, lacking funds and generally unpopular, devises new organizational methods to "survive" as a political entity. Initially, the party responded to its weakened state in an orthodox way, by changing the leaders and appealing to the business community for funds. Like the national Liberal party, the Conservatives were a cadre party organizationally. When the party was out of power, prime responsibility for organizing and financing the party lay with the leader, whose tools consisted of a large network of influential contacts and control over party policy. After the disappointing election of 1940, however, the Conservative party decided to revive its long-defunct extra-parliamentary organization, the Dominion Conservative Association (DCA). With a central office, a national organizer, and a national chairman, the DCA would try to revive the provincial parties with funds raised among the business community by finance committees in Toronto and Montreal.[28]

But the Association never got off the ground, and instead, organizational renewal took a different turn. Led by a group of progressive rank-and-file party members in Ontario who believed that the only way to stop the CCF from becoming the second most popular party in Canada was to move the party in a more progressive direction, the Conservatives liberalized their program, chose the progressive ex-premier of Manitoba, John Bracken, as their leader, and changed the party's name to Progressive Conservative. Under Bracken another attempt at organizational renewal was made through the DPCA (now the Dominion Progressive Conservative Association), whereby the latter assumed significant responsibilities in the area of publicity, public relations, organization, and fundraising. By June 1945 the extra-parliamentary party had raised sufficient funds (almost exclusively from the business community) to allow for a substantial publicity barrage during the federal election of that month. But despite what Granatstein calls "a campaign organization...as efficient as any in Canadian history to that time," the gains in seats were offset by the less than progressive issues the party chose to emphasize during the campaign.[29]

In the final analysis, therefore, the Conservative party's new organizational approach was based largely on image-making. A new policy, a new leader, and a new name were adopted to give the party a more progressive image. Certainly the Tories displayed some of the shift from ministerial organization to extra-parliamentary organization experienced by the Liberals when they were out of power, but like the NLF, the main function of the DPCA was raising money—in this case to finance speakers and advertisements reflecting the new image.

After the war, the Conservative party largely returned to its prewar organizing approach, in which the leader and the organization were almost one and the same. What little information exists for this period indicates that it continued to rely heavily on the personal qualities of successive party leaders to broaden its base of support and very little on grassroots organization. Unfortunately, the majority of these leaders lacked the talents and vision of their predecessors and were, partly as a consequence, less adept at presenting innovative policies which might have revived party support. Perhaps a more significant feature of the Conservative party's postwar organization, however, was its growing reliance on the assistance of several strong and virtually autonomous provincial organizations, especially in Ontario and the Atlantic provinces. It was the coming together of both of these elements of the party's organizational approach, in fact, that allowed the Conservatives to regain power in the late fifties, albeit temporarily. Diefenbaker's ability to capture the imagination of Canadians with his "northern vision" and to move audiences with his tremendous oratorical skills—Goodman calls him "the greatest [campaigner] of this century" — made him the party's strongest asset. The Tories also had the good fortune, in spite of Diefenbaker's egomaniacal and abrasive tendencies, to be assisted by strong provincial organizations, particularly in Ontario, where popular premiers not only endorsed Diefenbaker in each federal election campaign, but also mobilized their powerful provincial machines on behalf of the federal party. One might even argue that since the mid-sixties the Ontario party's organization *was* the federal party's organization, even more so of late, with the former virtually abandoning the provincial field in the mid-eighties to serve the federal party exclusively.[30]

Additional insights into the Conservative party's organization can therefore be extracted from several published accounts of the Ontario party: principally, Jonathan Manthorpe's *The Power and the Tories,* a lively account of the party's domination of Ontario politics since the war, Rosemary Speirs' *Out of the Blue,* describing the decline of the Tory dynasty, and, to a lesser extent, two recent publications of the Ontario Historical Studies Series.[31] As with the federal Conservative party, organization in Ontario depended almost exclusively on the efforts of the caucus, particularly the leader. But apart from the use of patronage distribution and policy formulation as standard organizational tools for governing parties, successive Tory leaders in Ontario also had at their disposal the indispensable services of a principal organizer.[32] The latter was a party pollster first and foremost, and judging from the ability of the Ontario Conservative party to respond successfully to shifts in public opinion, a very efficient one at that. The principal organizer secured his information from a large network of personal contacts (i.e., ward "heelers") in almost every constituency poll; these contacts, who tended to be well-known business persons and professionals in the community and who depended on government largesse to some degree, also gave the party a constant presence in the ridings. Consequently, Tory leaders relied heavily on the information which their organizers passed on regarding concerns at the local level to help them in formulating party policy. In addition, the principal organizer would usually oversee campaign activities, including the nomination of candidates and the hiring of poll workers, and recommend loyal supporters for government jobs or contracts.[33] In the Ontario case, therefore, the party leader still played a key role in organization, but was assisted by his own personal organizational apparatus.

But by the late 1960s, the same winds of change blowing through the federal Liberal party's organization swept through the Ontario Conservative party as well, giving rise to what the media quickly dubbed the "Big Blue Machine." Largely superseding the traditional hierarchy of "patrons and clients," which S.J.R. Noel argues was the dominant feature of machine politics in Ontario to that point,[34] the Big Blue Machine consisted of a small coterie of professional political managers, advertising executives, fundraisers and pollsters, whose collective talents were invoked by party leader William Davis in 1971 to rescue an organizationally moribund party from possible defeat at the hands of an ascendant NDP. In the provincial election of that year, and in subsequent contests, the Machine drew heavily upon a variety of new electoral techniques, imported primarily from the United States, including slick radio and television advertising, sophisticated polling and well-planned photo opportunities for the party leader, who was made the focus of the campaign. As a result, Davis's image was completely transformed. Rather than the boyish, awkward-looking and bland individual Ontario voters were accustomed to seeing and hearing, they were suddenly presented with a mature, well-groomed, sharply dressed and dynamic Premier, ready to lead Ontario into a progressive and prosperous future. The electoral results were impressive and the enduring efficiency of the Machine extended the Tory dynasty into the mid-eighties; so successful was the party's new "organization," in fact, that it was often conscripted to serve the electoral needs of other provincial Tory parties as well as the federal party. But it was not to last, for over time the Big Blue Machine drew the enmity of grassroots party members, who more than ever felt cut off and ignored by party leaders, in matters of policy especially. The resulting divisions and the continued "lack of proper grassroots organization" were too much for the professional political gurus to overcome, and by 1984, as Speirs puts it, the Machine had "run down."[35]

MINOR PARTIES

The organization of Canada's minor or "third" parties has been much better documented. The Social Credit party has been particularly well-served.[36] In Alberta, where it enjoyed its greatest success, the party was organized largely through the efforts and inspiration of one man—its leader, the teacher and fundamentalist preacher, William Aberhart. Blessed with tremendous organizational abilities and a charismatic personality which instilled deep loyalty among his followers, Aberhart began laying the structural foundations for the party in the early 1930s through his Prophetic Bible Institute in Calgary. Here he presented lectures, produced and distributed religious pamphlets, and delivered a very effective weekly radio sermon that was heard throughout the province. These activities allowed him to accumulate a large following, which he then organized into Bible study groups. When Aberhart decided to take up the cause of social credit, therefore, he already had at his disposal an impressive organization, consisting of hundreds of study groups across Alberta, through which he disseminated his social credit theories. In 1935, when he decided to form a political party to advance his cause further, this organization formed the basis of a formidable political machine, with the Institute as the party headquarters and the study groups as the constituency associations.[37]

Provincial organizers, trained by Aberhart at the Institute, toured the rural areas, speaking to farmers about the virtues of social credit, distributing literature, and assisting in the formation of additional study groups. This secondary leadership was complemented by an even larger corps of local study group/riding association leaders and candidates who, driven by their intense personal devotion to Aberhart, worked tirelessly to spread the word and establish more groups; so aggressive were these local leaders that they succeeded in infiltrating and converting many United Farmers of Alberta (UFA) locals to the movement, much to the dismay of the ruling UFA government. Party headquarters supplemented regular radio broadcasts, speaking tours and literature distribution with colourful parades, large picnics and well-attended open air meetings to foster the impression that Social Credit was a force on the move. These image-making techniques, which demonstrate the meticulous nature of the Social Credit organization, worked to perfection as more and more citizens jumped on the party bandwagon.

In short, what began as a religious and then social movement directed by one man was, by 1935, a highly organized political party consisting of many enthusiastic followers who carried the social credit message and organization to the far reaches of the province. Certainly the party organization was highly centralized in some respects. Aberhart produced most of the propaganda himself, trained and instructed the secondary leadership, and retained final authority over the selection of candidates. But his authority was exercised primarily in Calgary and surrounding regions, and the farther afield one travelled, the more autonomous the local organization tended to be. This looser structure on the fringes of the organization worked to the party's advantage, for it allowed enthusiastic local leaders free rein on the further and more rapid organization of study groups in remote areas of the province. At the same time, the "closely knit and highly centralized organization" allowed the movement to mobilize quickly for political action.[38] In the end, the Social Credit phenomenon was a monument to political organization, an ideal example of how a political party could adapt a well-developed, non-partisan organizational base to political purposes and under certain necessary conditions, in this case severe economic hardship, mobilize a large section of the electorate and win power. The precipitous organizational contraction which the party endured shortly after taking power, however, remains a fruitful avenue of inquiry.[39]

Although little research has been done on the subject, Social Credit organization in Quebec just prior to the 1962 federal election,[40] in which the party won a surprising 26 seats, seems to have displayed many of the same characteristics as its western counterpart.[41] Much of the party's support, for example, stemmed from its leader's effective use of a relatively new election-eering medium: television. In a context of worsening economic conditions, the charismatic Réal Caouette was able to win over many converts to the Social Credit philosophy through his weekly Sunday evening political "sermons," and party organizers were able to raise a lot of money to finance this costly publicity by promising to extend his broadcasts into local areas. Another crucial factor, as in Alberta, was the enthusiasm of party organizers in establishing riding associations and spreading the good word. Focusing their proselytizing efforts largely in "primary groups" of workers, friends and neighbours, many were strategically located in workplaces containing a high concentration of low-income manual labourers and, as a result, met with great success. Finally, the Social Credit organization within the ridings themselves was highly developed well in advance of the actual campaign. Ridings were divided into a hierarchy of organizing units, consisting of sections and polls, each with a chief organizer. This structure gave Social Credit a strong visual presence in the ridings and facilitated the transmission of instructions from the party's central office to the local leadership. Not surprisingly, students of the Social Credit phenomenon in Quebec agree that the relative strength of the party's organization was as important as the "economic climate" in the party's success.

The organizational dimension of three other third parties, the Progressive party, the CCF/NDP, and the Communist party, has also received some attention. The Progressive movement's organizational approach was very different from that of either the Social Credit party or the two "old parties."[42] The Progressive party and the various provincial farmers' parties had virtually no central direction. The former, for example, had no central office, and hence no national organizer, no central revenue fund, no national publicity, no political education services, and no general election strategy. Nor was there really a national leader, for Thomas Crerar was, strictly speaking, simply the party's House leader. Instead, organizational matters were entirely the responsibility of the local constituency associations; the latter nominated candidates, raised their own funds, and basically ran their own campaigns without "outside" assistance or interference. In effect, concludes one observer, the Progressive party had no "distinct political organization."[43]

The reasons for this are clear. First, the farmers' political movement was the result of a spontaneous, grassroots uprising of farmers across Canada in response to long-felt injustices aggravated by the First World War. Unlike the Social Credit party (or the old parties), therefore, the impetus to organize came not from the top, but from the bottom. Only when the pressure from the rank-and-file become so strong that it could no longer be ignored did leaders of the numerous farm organizations agree to take independent political action. Thus from the very beginning the initiative for political organization was strongly entrenched at the local level. More important, many farmers viewed the traditional political parties, with their powerful, middle- and upper-class caucuses, as essentially undemocratic; strong caucus discipline and heavy reliance on corporate business donations, they complained, reduced the freedom of elected representatives to act freely on behalf of their constituents. Consequently, the aversion to partisanship and any sort of central direction in organizational matters was reflected in the highly decentralized organization of political Progressivism.

In terms of the political consequences, it is likely that this highly localized organizational structure contributed to the decline of the progressive movement in the long run.[44] In the short run, however, the policy of "constituency autonomy" was probably beneficial. The organizational autonomy enjoyed by riding associations no doubt facilitated the rapid mobilization of supporters, as enthusiastic local party activists faced no structural-bureaucratic obstacles in their efforts to get their candidate elected; this resembled the success enjoyed by the autonomous Social Credit clubs in rural Alberta in 1935. But once the initial zeal waned, tempered by time and changing economic circumstances, and the impetus for organization therefore faded, no central body remained to fill the void and sustain party organization. The lack of centralization may have also precluded any attempt by a more politically astute central organization to broaden the appeal and base of the party to non-farmers.[45] It might be noted, as well, that the localized party organization did little to foster the necessary public image of the party as a serious contender for provincial or national power, or as a united legislative force.

The literature pertaining to the CCF/NDP, as mentioned at the outset, is lacking in its detailed attention to matters of organization.[46] The one notable exception is Seymour M. Lipset's landmark study of the Saskatchewan CCF, first published in 1950. Ironically, Lipset's main interest was in using the Saskatchewan CCF to test Michel's iron law of oligarchy[47]—which is essentially a matter of structure—but in the process he provides some useful insights into party organization. It is clear, for example, that the CCFs organizational structure was quite decentralized, though not to the same extent as the Progressive movement. Responsibility for organizing lay to a large extent at the local level, with the leaders of the main farm organizations in the province; they created the CCF, and using their influence in the large network of community organizations with which they were associated were able to attract support to the party. Nevertheless, the CCF in Saskatchewan and across Canada boasted a fairly complex and hierarchical organization in its own right, one consisting of National and Provincial Offices, constituency associations, CCF clubs and poll committees; run primarily by volunteers, and guided by the advice of the upper levels of the party, this machine was responsible for educational work, fundraising and signing up new members.[48] Some sections of the CCF, particularly the Ontario party, also adopted the strategy of infiltrating other organizations in order to find recruits; an excellent description of the sometimes bitter fight to capture the support of the country's main labour unions, for instance, can be found in Irving Abella's *Nationalism, Communism and Canadian Labour*.[49] In later years, following the party's transformation into the NDP in 1961, the grassroots organizing approach of the party was refined in the direction of more intensive canvassing methods and supplemented by more modern organizing techniques, especially television advertising.[50]

It is clear, therefore, that the CCF/NDP's organization was based on the individual efforts of an array of private citizens working at different levels of the movement and using methods that were roughly uniform across the country. Although many party supporters were driven by a strong commitment to democratic socialism, and worked tirelessly to promote the cause, a good many more had only a mild or ephemeral commitment. This is clear from the wild fluctuations in membership levels which the CCF experienced in its 28-year history. When political and economic conditions turned against the party after 1945, many rank-and-file members simply left, leaving the more ideologically-motivated leaders to carry on.[51] This organizational instability makes the question of how successful CCF organization was difficult to answer. Certainly the well-tuned Saskatchewan machine which was in place when public opinion swung towards the CCF during the Second World War helped bring the party to power there, but the relationship between organization and popularity is more dialectical in other parts of the country, where organizational expansion was as much a *consequence* of the CCF's growing popularity in these years as it was a *cause*.[52]

As for the Communist party of Canada (CPC, later renamed the Labour Progressive party or LPP), its basic organizational approach for many years can best be described as organization by infiltration and co-optation.[53] Armed with specific instructions from the party's small, but omnipotent politbureau of the central executive committee based in Toronto, party organizers went about establishing "cells" or "units" of members in factories, mines, lumber camps and communities across Canada (primarily in Ontario and the West).[54] Although the party contested few elections before the Second World War, these local clubs nevertheless formed the basis for the party's electoral organization. More important, however, were the efforts to

infiltrate and control existing "mass organizations," mostly trade unions, and
to establish front organizations, such as the Workers' Unity League, in order
to find new party recruits and win the membership over to the goals of the
international Communist movement. Occasionally, when the ruling body of
the international movement, the Comintern, decreed it, the CPC would
actively seek the alliance of other left-wing or liberal parties in a "common
front" against right-wing enemies at home and abroad, again, to win
converts to the CPC's perspective. Organizers were known for their loyalty,
dedication and willingness to make sacrifices, and for their strong organizing
abilities. Other methods used to attract support and keep party members
busy and motivated included parades, marches, petitions and delegations.

By the late 1940s, with the intensification of the Cold War, the CPC
underwent organizational contraction. Faced with growing hostility in
various quarters, its strategy of infiltrating or cooperating with non-
communist organizations was superseded to a large extent by efforts to
strengthen the electoral apparatus of the party, by creating more active and
autonomous local units, similar in nature to the average CCF constituency
association, for example, but with fewer powers. In the early fifties the CPC
also moderated its program, adopting a more anti-American posture and
abandoning its revolutionary methods in favour of the parliamentary road to
socialism. Because organizers and activists were forced to keep a low profile,
however, membership recruitment, fundraising and electoral activities were
kept to a bare minimum. By 1956, with the exodus of members, organizers
and leaders following Khrushchev's anti-Stalin diatribe and the USSR's
invasion of Hungary, the CPC went into a severe organizational decline from
which it never fully recovered.[55]

The success of the CPC's organizational approach prior to the Cold War
is unquestionable. During the 1930s Communist organizers mobilized large
numbers of unemployed and pressured local governments for relief. They
also established a number of industrial unions under the CIO label, gained
positions of influence in the CCL and TLC, attracted large numbers of non-
Communists to the party's front organizations (apart from the unemployed),
and in the 1940s elected a number of party members to municipal office.
These advances helped swell the ranks of the Communist party proper in the
interwar period and were significant accomplishments for a party which was
forever short on organizers and which laboured under official repression for
much of its history. That the party did not enjoy greater success, therefore,
was due less to its organizational strategy than to a hostile political climate,
one which hindered its public organizing activities and forced it to operate
covertly.[56]

This, then, is a brief review of the significant literature on party organization in Canada for the years 1900 to 1984 as well as some of its
short-comings. Clearly some important strides have been made on the
subject. But a lot remains to be done, for much of the information is
fragmentary, with few studies attacking the subject of organization directly.
There is, in particular, a dearth of research on the Conservative party and
CCF/NDP. Nevertheless, what information does exist can be used to

differentiate the parties on the basis of their organizational approach. The most common approach used by the Liberal and Conservative parties to attract support, broadly defined, can be described as simple, authoritarian and patronage-driven. It was simple and authoritarian in that the organizational structure has consisted almost entirely of a relatively small number of elected representatives, usually focused in the cabinet, who attracted and maintained support through the manipulation of policy and, in particular, the distribution of patronage in all of its forms. The extra-parliamentary structure of such parties has never been very highly developed or enduring. In short, the old parties have been primarily "parliamentary" parties.[57]

By contrast, the organizational approach adopted by parties lying on opposite ends of the political spectrum, the Communist and Social Credit parties, has been complex, authoritarian and messianic. The structures erected to mobilize support have been multi-faceted, reflecting a highly developed hierarchical network of individuals and groups whose success has often depended on the infiltration or conversion of existing structures and whose methods have leaned heavily on proselytization. Moreover, organization in these parties has been strictly controlled from the top, by a select group of individuals who commanded almost fanatical loyalty from the secondary leadership and rank-and-file. The primary fuel driving these sophisticated, and often meteoric political machines has been rigid adherence to ideology, which in turn accounts for their crusading spirit and aggressive organizing methods.

Parties in the final category, under which we can group the moderate left-wing parties such as the Progressives and the CCF/NDP, display an organizational approach which is fairly complex, quite democratic, and driven by mild to strong ideological commitment. These parties have erected structures which, although lacking in the infiltration and conversion aspects of the extremist parties, were nevertheless fairly well developed into a system of central bodies, committees, constituency associations, clubs and affiliated groups. Unlike any of the other party types, furthermore, sovereignty lay at the grassroots of the party. Finally, while most party members were driven by ideological commitment and made great sacrifices for the cause, their degree of loyalty was not as intense or as enduring, perhaps, as that of the more extreme parties.

CONCLUSION

This paper has sought to make clear the different organizational approaches adopted by Canada's political parties this century.[58] But such a cursory review cannot, of course, do justice to the complexity of each party and the variations in organizational form and strategy over time, across regions, and between federal and provincial sections of the same party. Nor do the variations discussed here necessarily help us to distinguish among parties far into the future, for recent research indicates that, since the 1960s, differences in organizational structure and methods among the major parties have lessened considerably. In the last two decades or so, as a result of new data-gathering and data-dissemination technologies, there has been a significant convergence in the structures and methods used by the three major parties to organize support. Each has come to rely less on extra-parliamentary or rank-and-file organization to gauge public opinion, formulate and publicize policy positions, raise money and structure the vote, and to rely more on what some have termed "elite clientelism" or "supra-party organization," in which a select group of well-paid professional pollsters, political consultants, "ad men" and "media communicators" use the new media technologies to market parties, particularly their leaders, to the electorate, as they would any other product. Paltiel writes that:

> ...the face-to-face style of electioneering on the hustings, at rallies of the faithful, and in the columns of the party-owned or subsidized press of an earlier age has been replaced by image-building campaigns via television and radio whose currency are announcements, spots, skillfully contrived "events," and photo opportunities prepared by advertising agencies and "advance" men.[59]

Even the NDP has adopted these Madison Avenue techniques, to the point where their campaigns, as Wearing concludes, "are now virtually indistinguishable from Liberal and PC campaigns."[60]

As well, many questions remain unanswered. What, for instance, is the precise relationship between organization and electoral success? Existing studies seem to suggest, albeit quite unobtrusively, that organization has been an important factor, especially for the party in power, but how much difference does organization really make in relation to such powerful "structural" determinants as socio-economic developments, electoral laws, and political culture? We also need to know more about the connection between organization and ideology, if one exists. Is the organization of extremist groups inevitably more "complex," while that of the more pragmatic, brokerage groups necessarily more "simple"? Or are organiza-tional forms and strategies, even for the more ideologically based parties, determined primarily by the party's proximity to power? The experience of Social Credit in Alberta and Quebec's Parti Québécois, for example, suggests that the nature of a party's organizational apparatus may undergo significant changes once that party reaches office.[61] It would also be useful to know more about how tensions between federal and provincial parties have affected organization. While several researchers have described the nature and origins of such tensions, the organizational repercussions have not been clearly identified.[62] From these analyses one can only assume that such in-fighting weakened party organization, by alienating party supporters, dividing resources, duplicating organizational structures, and expending party energies in a wasteful fashion. Nor have the effects of the electoral system and electoral reforms on party organization been examined in sufficient detail. Certainly the single-member plurality system has forced parties to target the more winnable ridings in their organizational strategies, while such important reforms as the 1974 Elections Expenses Act have clearly changed the ways in which parties go about raising and allocating funds. But the most pressing task remains that of delineating the day-to-day organizational activities of political parties, that is, how they went about building and sustaining what were and, to a lesser degree, still are, important components of the political system and key instruments of the regional, class and ethnic identities that together constitute the national fabric. If the foregoing review-analysis leads to further study along these lines, it will have achieved its purpose.

N O T E S

I am grateful to the *Journal of Commonwealth and Comparative Politics* editors/reviewers for their suggested revisions to an earlier draft of this paper.

1. Bryce, "Introduction," in M. Ostrogorski, ed., *Democracy and the Organization of Political Parties Vol. 1*, and abridged by S.M. Lipset (London: Macmillian, 1902; New York: Anchor Books, 1964), lxvii.

2. In the McGraw-Hill Ryerson Series in Canadian Politics, the only volume devoted to political parties contains no articles on organization per se. C. Winn and J. McMenemy, eds., *Political Parties in Canada* (Toronto: McGraw-Hill Ryerson Ltd., 1976). A more recent compendium, *Canadian Parties in Transition: Discourse, Organization, Representation* (Scarborough: Nelson, 1989), edited by Alain Gagnon and A. Brian Tanguay, contains three articles dealing with "Political Marketing and Party Financing," but these focus on contemporary parties, as does the bulk of the political science literature. Two good reviews of the literature on Canadian political history are Reg Whitaker, "Writing About Politics," in John Schultz, ed., *Writing About Canada: A Handbook for Modern Canadian History* (Scarborough: Prentice Hall, Inc., 1990), 1-26, and John English, "The Second Time Around: Political Scientists Writing History," *Canadian Historical Review* 67:1 (March 1986), 1-16.

3. See, for example, Frank Underhill, *In Search of Canadian Liberalism* (Toronto: Macmillan of Canada, Ltd., 1960), Chs. 1, 6; see also articles by H. Thorburn and E. Reid in Thorburn, ed., *Party Politics in Canada* 4th Ed. (Scarborough: Prentice-Hall of Canada, 1979).

4. Although elections certainly involve organization, they are usually the culmination of months and years of preparation and are in no way representative of the day-to-day activities.

5. In Canadian political historiography, for instance, see Leo Zakuta, *A Protest Movement Becalmed: A Study of Change in the* CCF (Toronto: University of Toronto Press, 1964), and Dean McHenry, *The Third Force in Canada: The Cooperative Commonwealth Federation, 1932-48* (Berkeley: University of California Press, 1950). Both define organization strictly in terms of structure and membership. When Zakuta speaks of the CCF's "organizational decline" or "stability" he is referring to fluctuations in formal party membership and changes in party structure.

6. Robert Michels, *Political Parties: A Sociological Study of the Oligarchical Tendencies of Modern Democracy*, translated by Eden and Cedar Paul (Hearst's International Library, 1915; reprint, New York: Dover Publications, 1959).

7. Maurice Duverger, *Political Parties: Their Organization and Activity in the Modern State* 3rd Ed. (New York: John Wiley and Sons, 1966). See also F. Engelmann and M. Schwartz, *Canadian Political Parties: Origin, Character Impact* (Toronto: Prentice-Hall of Canada, Ltd., 1975), Ch. 1.

8. Leon Epstein, *Political Parties in Western Democracies* (New York: Frederick Praeger, 1967; reprint, New Brunswick, NJ: Transaction, 180), Ch. 5. Epstein uses the term "organizational apparatus." See also Engelmann, *Canadian Political Parties*, Ch. 9, and Escott Reid, "The Saskatchewan Liberal Machine Before 1929," *Canadian Journal of Economics and Political Science, 2* (1936), 27-40.

9. See, for example, S.J.R. Noel, "Dividing the Spoils: The Old and the New Rules of Patronage in Canadian Politics," and Whitaker, "Between Patronage and Bureaucracy: Democratic Politics in Transition," *Journal of Canadian Studies* (Oct. 1987): 72-95; Whitaker, *The Government Party: Organizing and Financing the Liberal Party of Canada 1930-58* (Toronto: University of Toronto Press, 1967).

10. Duverger, *Political Parties*, xvi.

11. Epstein, *Political Parties*, 115-16. Many Canadian studies of political parties also exclude educational activities from their definition of organization. See, for example, Zakuta, *A Protest Movement Becalmed*, and Engelmann, *Canadian Political Parties*, Ch. 8.

12. Zakuta, *A Protest Movement Becalmed*; Walter Young, *The Anatomy of a Party: The National CCF 1932-1961* (Toronto: University of Toronto Press, 1969).

13. See, for example, S.M. Lipset, *Agrarian Socialism: The Coopera- tive Commonwealth Federation in Saskatchewan, A Study in Political Sociology* Rev. Ed. (Berkeley: University of California Press, 1971), Ch. 3; Joseph Wearing, *Strained Relations: Canadian Parties and Voters* (Toronto: McClelland and Stewart, 1988), 12-15; and Whitaker, *The Government Party*.

14. Using the Canadian example, once again, see Whitaker, *The Govern- ment Party*, and Granatstein, *The Politics of Survival*, both of whom see party organization and party finances as separate. For an oppos- ing view see Khayyam Zev Paltiel, "Political Marketing, Party Finance, and the Decline of Canadian Parties," in Gagnon and Tanguay, *Canadian Parties in Transition*, 332- 53.

15. With respect to organizational methods, for example, Paltiel defines these aptly as "raising funds, mobilizing the electorate, building coalitions, and communi- cating their messages." Ibid., 352. Similar though less explicit defini- tions may be found in Whitaker, *The Government Party*, and Wearing, *Strained Relations*, Ch. 3. Note: in this paper the terms "organiza- tion," "organizational approach," "organizational dimension" are used synonymously.

16. Whitaker, *The Government Party*; Joseph Wearing, *The L-Shaped Party: The Liberal Party of Canada, 1958-80* (Scarborough: McGraw-Hill Ryerson, 1981); Christine McCall-Newman, *Grits: An Intimate Portrait of the Liberal Party*, (Toronto: Macmillan of Canada, 1982). It should be noted that while Whitaker prefers to dis- tinguish between organizing and fundraising, I prefer to see the latter as simply another way of building the party machine or organization, similar to educating existing mem- bers or recruiting new members. Moreover, Whitaker tends to focus more on the relationship between the extra-parliamentary party and the parliamentary party rather than on the functions and efficacy of each.

17. Practically all of the federal party's funds came from contractors, who were asked by ministers or party "bagmen" with important business contacts to contribute to the party

in exchange for government contracts. This was known as the "contract levy system." Whitaker, *The Government Party*, 198-9.

18. Wearing, *The L-Shaped Party*, 13.

19. Whitaker, *The Government Party*, 185, 211-12, 408-9.

20. David E. Smith, *The Regional Decline of a National Party: Liberals on the Prairies* (Toronto: University of Toronto Press, 1981), 52-7. Several excellent chapters on the political organization of the Saskatchewan Liberal Party up to 1971 may be found in Smith's *Prairie Liberalism: The Liberal Party in Saskatchewan, 1905-71* (Toronto: University of Toronto Press, 1975); Reid's "The Saskatchewan Liberal Machine Before 1929," remains useful as well.

21. Up to that point the Liberal party was a federation of highly autonomous federal and provincial wings. Each level had its own riding associations and sources of funding, and leaders from both sides rarely interfered with the organizational efforts of the other, even though they both competed for the same funds and personnel. Whitaker, 77 and Ch. 8 *passim*; Wearing, Ch. 2 *passim*.

22. Wearing, *The L-Shaped Party*, 18-85; Smith, *The Regional Decline of a National Party*, 75-7.

23. It has been argued that the substantial resources channelled by parties and governments into advertising, polling, consulting services and other aspects of contemporary electioneering, since the 1960s, represent a *new*, more elitist form of patronage. See, for instance, Noel, "Dividing the Spoils," and Whitaker, "Between Patronage and Bureaucracy: Democratic Politics in Transition," *Journal of Canadian Studies* (Oct. 1987), 55-71. For more on modern electioneering techniques, see David Walker, "Pollsters, Consultants, and Party Politics in Canada," and Khayyam Paltiel, "Political Marketing, Party

Finance and the Decline of Canadian Parties," in Gagnon and Tanguay, eds., *Canadian Parties in Transition*, 384-403, 332-53.

24. Unfortunately, McCall-Newman provides little information on organizing activities *between* elections; one suspects they were minimal given the high-powered organizations erected just prior to election campaigns. Because the study focuses primarily on the key personalities involved in this period, information on organization is widely scattered throughout the study.

25. J. English, *The Decline of Politics: The Conservatives and the Party System, 1901-20* (Toronto: University of Toronto Press, 1977), especially 44-54, 62-77.

26. L. Glassford, *Reaction and Reform: The Politics of the Conservative Party under R.B. Bennett, 1927-1938* (Toronto: University of Toronto Press, 1992).

27. Granatstein, *The Politics of Survival*.

28. Ibid., 69-83. Unfortunately, Granatstein provides no further details on the precise activities of the Dominion Conservative Association, except to say that it was basically moribund by 1942. Nor does he describe the impact of the new organization, if any, on the return of the Tories to power in Ontario in 1943.

29. The DPCA established study groups across Canada to discuss the party's new policy direction, appointed provincial organizers, and held a nationwide fundraising campaign (unsuccessful at that) to broaden the base of the party's finances. Granatstein, *The Politics of Survival*, 156-75.

30. Bits and pieces of information on the federal Conservative party's organization since 1945 may be found in the memoirs of long-time party adviser and organizer, Eddie Goodman. See *Life of the Party: The Memoirs of Eddie*

Goodman (Toronto: Key Porter Books, 1988); see also George Perlin, *The Tory Syndrome* (Montreal: McGill-Queen's University Press, 1980), and "The Progressive Conservative Party," in H. Thorburn, ed., *Party Politics in Canada* 4th Ed. (Toronto: Prentice-Hall Inc. 1985), 161-8; and Rand Dyck, "Relations Between Federal and Provincial Parties," in Gagnon and Tanguay, *Canadian Parties*, 186-219.

31. Jonathan Manthorpe, *The Power and the Tories: Ontario Politics—1943 to the Present* (Toronto: Macmillan of Canada, 1974). Rosemary Speirs, *Out of the Blue* (Toronto: Macmillan of Canada, 1986). See also A.K. McDougall, *John P. Robarts: His Life and Government* (Toronto: University of Toronto Press, 1986), and Roger Graham, *Old Man Ontario: Leslie M. Frost* (Toronto: University of Toronto Press, 1990), for brief references to the Ontario Conservative party's provincial organization.

32. The principal organizer in Ontario between 1938 and 1960 was A.D. McKenzie. Manthorpe attributes the succession of Tory victories in Ontario largely to the efforts of this individual.

33. Manthorpe, *The Power and the Tories,* Chs. 2-4; McDougall, *John P. Robarts,* 20-22; Graham, *Old Man Ontario,* 68-70. Much like the federal Conservative party's strategy during the war, a good deal of the Ontario party's success was based on the deliberate strategy of trying to revitalize its image by changing its leaders and repackaging its program every ten years or so.

34. Noel, "Dividing the Spoils."

35. Manthorpe, *The Power and the Tories,* Chs. 4, 5; Speirs, *Out of the Blue,* 1-31.

36. See John Irving, *The Social Credit Movement in Alberta* (Toronto: University of Toronto Press, 1959), especially Chs. 2-5, 7, in which the author delves deeply into the "strategy and tactics" of the party's promoters in that province. See

also, Harold Schultz, "Aberhart, the Organization Man," *Alberta Historical Review* 7 (Spring 1959), 19-26.

37. By August of that year there were over 1,600 study groups in the province. Schultz, "Aberhart, the Organization Man," 20.

38. Ibid., 23.

39. Unfortunately, Alvin Finkel's recent study of the Social Credit party between 1935 and 1971, *The Social Credit Phenomenon* (Toronto: University of Toronto, 1989), sheds little light on the question of organization.

40. The most comprehensive accounts of Social Credit in Quebec, Maurice Pinard, *The Rise of a Third Party: A Study in Crisis Politics* (New Jersey: Prentice-Hall, 1971), and Michael B. Stein, *The Dynamics of Right Wing Protest: A Political Analysis of Social Credit in Quebec* (Toronto: University of Toronto Press, 1973), are also the least informative with respect to the organizational side of the party between 1957, when the Ralliement des Créditistes was formed, and 1962, its year of greatest success. Pinard agrees that a strong organization was instrumental in the party's success, but he focuses exclusively on the impact of structural and socio-economic factors. Stein provides a good organizational analysis of the party's predecessor, La Ligue du Crédit Social, but little on the organization of the Ralliement itself. For a brief, but useful account of the Ralliement's organization in one Quebec riding, see Vincent Lemieux *et al.*, "Election in the Constituency of Levis," in John Meisel ed. *Papers on the 1962 Election* (Toronto: University of Toronto Press, 1964), 33-52.

41. A word of caution is necessary here. The original Social Credit party in Quebec, La Ligue du Crédit Social, which existed between 1936 and 1957, was very similar in its organizational characteristics to the Alberta case. Education and the conversion of a highly developed

structure of study groups into political units were the main thrust of the movement. Its more politically-oriented successor, however, differed from the Alberta party in several respects. First, it appears to have been subject to far less central direction in organizational matters. Second, the top leaders and provincial organizers were not as strongly motivated by ideological concerns, although the rank-and-file, many of whom had absorbed the Social Credit message through years of propaganda by La Ligue, certainly were. See Stein, *The Dynamics of Right-Wing Protest*, 39-79.

42. The best study of the national farmers movement is still W.L. Morton, *The Progressive Party in Canada* (Toronto: University of Toronto Press, 1950), especially 89-136, 213-15.

43. Morton, *The Progressive Party*, 89.

44. Ibid., Ch. 9.

45. Ibid., 213-14.

46. A few examples will suffice to illustrate. In his celebrated study of the national CCF, *The Anatomy of a Party*, the closest Walter Young comes to talking about organization is his brief analysis, in chapter seven, of the type of person who joined the CCF and the nature of CCF propaganda; Gerald Caplan's *The Dilemma of Canadian Socialism* (Toronto: McClelland and Stewart, 1973) occasionally refers to the *lack* of organizing efforts on the part of "sectarian" party members in Ontario, but says little about how the existing organization came to be or was maintained; Terence Morley, *Secular Socialists: The CCF/NDP in Ontario* (Kingston: McGill-Queen's University Press, 1984), refers only briefly to the CCF's renewed "organizational capacity," in the early 1950s, and almost exclusively in terms of the key "organizers" involved and the electoral consequences; and McHenry, *The Third Force in Canada*, provides an excellent, albeit brief introduction

to the CCF's organizational capacity, but his remarks are of a general nature and say nothing about different organizing techniques and strategies.

47. In his influential study of European socialist parties at the turn of the century, Robert Michels argues that such parties, and indeed all modern political parties, have centralizing tendencies. "The democratic external form which characterizes the life of political parties," he asserts, "may readily veil from superficial observers the tendency towards aristocracy, or rather towards oligarchy, which is inherent in all party organization." This process is driven by party leaders, who try to consolidate their power within their organizations, often by hiring paid (and hence obedient) party bureaucrats and otherwise wooing party members. *Political Parties: A Sociological Study of the Oligarchical Tendencies of Modern Democracy* (Hearst's International Library, 1915; reprinted, New York: Dover Publications Inc., 1959), 11.

48. Lipset, *Agrarian Socialism*, 66-7, 75-87, 250-3.

49. 1. Abella, *The CIO, the Communist Party, and the Canadian Congress of Labour 1935-1956* (Toronto: University of Toronto Press, 1973).

50. Little has been written on NDP organization, although some insights may be gleaned from Desmond Morton's lively, but short survey, *The New Democrats, 1961-1986: The Politics of Change* (Toronto: Copp, Clark, Pitman Ltd., 1986), as well as his two shorter pieces, *The Riverdale Story: a by-election campaign* (Ontario NDP, 1964), and "The Effectiveness of Political Campaigning: the NDP in the 1967 Ontario Election," *Journal of Canadian Studies* 4 (1969). See also selected chapters in Alan Whitehorn's more recent study, *Canadian Socialism: Essays on the CCF-NDP* (Toronto: Oxford University Press, 1992).

51. For more on the organization of the Ontario CCF/NDP in the 1950s and early 1960s. see D. Azoulay, "Keeping the Dream Alive: the CCF/NDP in Ontario 1951-1963," (PhD diss., York University, 1991).

52. See Caplan, *The Dilemma of Canadian Socialism*, Chs. 7, 9; and Young, *The Anatomy of a Party*, Ch. 5.

53. The most comprehensive discussion of CPC organization is found in Ivan Avakumovic, *The Communist Party in Canada: A History* (Toronto: McClelland & Stewart, 1975), especially Chs. 2, 4 and 7. Ian Angus, *Canadian Bolsheviks: The Early Years of the Communist Party of Canada* (Montreal: Vanguard Publications, 1981), is largely an indictment of the party's slavish adherence to the Soviet line, but provides some insight into the negative organizational implications of this phenomenon. Norman Penner's more recent study, *Canadian Communism: The Stalin Years and Beyond* (Toronto: Methuen, 1988), is a disappointment as far as party organization is concerned, but has the merit of extending the history of the party to the near present. For a general account of the party's activities in Montreal at mid-century, particularly the organizational efforts of key local leaders, see Merrily Weisbord, *The Strangest Dream: Canadian Communists, The Spy Trials, and the Cold War* (Toronto: Lester and Orpen Dennys, 1983).

54. Initially, the majority of the party's rank-and-file consisted of Finnish and Ukrainian immigrants organized in fairly autonomous language federations. The central leadership abolished this semi-federal structure in the late twenties, thereby consolidating its authority over party activities. Angus, *Canadian Bolsheviks*, Ch. 4.

55. Avakumovic, *The Communist Party*, Ch. 9; Penner, *Canadian Communism*, Chs. 8-10; and Weisbord, *Strangest Dream*, Chs. 17-19.

56. The CPC's organizational approach did have some weaknesses, however. Avakumovic, 87-7, 116-17, notes that Party leaders who had gained positions of influence in the trade unions, for example, often became so involved in their day-to-day union work that they forgot to promote the CPC among the rank-and-file. As well, any unitary organization which depends as heavily on its central leadership for direction as did the CPC is bound to be immobilized without those leaders, which is why the authorities made a habit of arresting the top leaders. Angus, *Canadian Bolsheviks*, Ch. 5, argues that the "undergroundism" was more a matter of preference among some party members, who enjoyed working covertly, and this hindered the party's growth. To the extent that this was true, particularly in the early years, this can be seen as an additional weakness in the organization, rather than an obstacle imposed from without.

57. The major parties have not needed a complex party organization for two reasons: if they were in power or close to it, the lure of patronage was enough to attract funds and support from individuals, groups and regions; second, when they were the main alternative to the ruling party, they could count on being the most likely recipients of any anti-government vote (unless they were too closely equated ideologically with the ruling party during times of great social dislocation, as during the 1930s), and, therefore, needed only to maintain the *appearance* of being a viable alternative, which in turn required only a minimal organizational presence at the local level, at least in the short run.

58. The only study I have come across which attempts, albeit briefly and only for Ontario, to compare the various party organizations in Canada, from a historical perspective, is Joseph Wearing, "Political Parties: Fish or Fowl," in Donald C.

MacDonald ed., *The Government and Politics of Ontario*, 2d Ed. (Toronto: Van Nostrand Reinhold, 1980): 291-313.

59. Paltiel, 335; Noel, "Dividing the Spoils." For a good overview of the new electioneering and fundraising techniques, see Wearing, *Strained Relations*, Chs. 3, 6.

60. *Strained Relations*, 90-1; see also Morton, *Politics of Change*, Ch. 4.

61. Finkel, *The Social Credit Phenomenon;* H.M. Angell, "Duverger, Epstein and the Problem of the Mass Party: The Case of the Parti Québécois," *Canadian Journal of Political Science,* 20 (1987), 363-78.

62. See Edwin Black, "Federal Strains within a Canadian Party," in Thorburn, ed., *Party Politics in Canada*, 4th Ed. (Toronto: Prentice-Hall, 1979), 89-99; and Whitaker, *The Government Party*, Ch. 2.

THE RISE OF NATIONAL PARTIES, 1867-1917

○

INTRODUCTION

C anadian party politics in the period 1867 to 1917 are distinguished by several main themes, among them the emergence of national parties, the remarkable stability of the party system, and the convergence of the major parties in their approach to organization and to the leading issues of the day.

The national parties that emerged after 1867, the Liberals and the Conservatives, had their roots in the old province of Canada. In both Upper and Lower Canada (later Canada West and Canada East), political loyalties prior to the coming of responsible government tended to divide between supporters of the Crown and established Churches, generally referred to as Tories, and those who opposed the ruling clique, generally known as Reformers. Tories and Reformers were further distinguished by their opposing views toward democracy, the separation of Church and state, affection for the US (as opposed to Britain), unfettered economic activity, and dedication to rural life and values, with the Reformers generally displaying or favouring such things to a greater degree than the Tories. In the 1830s and 1840s, however, the leading point of division, politically, was the issue of responsible government: should the government be the instrument of the voters, acting through their elected representatives, the position favoured by the Reformers, or of the Crown, acting through the governor and his appointed councils, favoured by the Tories? The issue was settled in the later 1840s when an opportunistic alliance of Reform MPs from both sections of the province succeeded in bringing about a system of responsible party government, one in which power was thereafter wielded by the party able to hold the support of a majority of MPs in the legislature.

The coming of responsible government also produced a fundamental realignment of political groupings in the province. With little left to hold the original Reform alliance together, the more conservative Reformers in Canada East, known as the Bleus, joined hands with moderate Reformers and a handful of remaining Tories in Canada West to form the Liberal-Conservative party. The new party was led principally by the Kingston lawyer and businessperson John A. Macdonald and his highly popular Quebec lieutenant George-Étienne Cartier, leader of the French Canadians in the elected assembly. Both individuals were instrumental in bringing this bicultural alliance together and in purging it of its Tory vestiges, transforming it into the moderate party that controlled the government of the Canadas for much of the 1850s and early 1860s.

At the same time, the more radical Reformers in both sections of the province went on to form their own parties. In Canada West they were known as the Grits. With their largely rural, moralistic, and anti-strong central government orientation, the Grits were the successors of the Mackenzie radicals of the 1830s, with one exception. No longer tied to the moderate Reformers in Canada East and upset with what they considered the undue influence of French Catholics in the governing of the province, the

Grits adopted an increasingly anti-Canada East stance. Their counterparts in Canada East, with whom political cooperation was at best sporadic, were known as the Rouges. The Rouges were a relatively small faction that came to be defined largely by their republican and anti-clerical views. Needless to say, these views did not endear the Rouges either to the powerful Catholic Church or to most French Canadians. Together, the Grits and Rouges were the forerunners of the future Liberal party.

An equally dramatic realignment in the party system occurred as a result of Confederation. The rising popularity of the Grits in Canada West by the early 1860s created a situation of great political instability, as neither they nor their Liberal-Conservative opponents could win and maintain enough legislative support to form enduring administrations. A federal union of all the British North American colonies was seen as the main solution to this problem and in 1864 the Grits agreed to join with the Liberal-Conservatives in a coalition government aimed at bringing this union about. The effects on the party system were far-reaching. In the Maritime colonies, where traditional political differences ran along Tory-Reform lines, much as in the Canadas, the issue of Confederation produced groups that either favoured or opposed the proposed union. Using a potent combination of nationalism and patronage, the ever-shrewd John A. Macdonald seized the opportunity presented by the Confederation debate to permanently attach to his party the "pro" politicians and their supporters in both the Maritimes and the Canadas, including a good many Grits. Macdonald's appeal to patriotism and individual self-interest not only gave birth to what soon became known as simply the Conservative party, but was also an appeal that would serve the Conservatives well in the post-Confederation period.

Several key changes in the electoral laws after Confederation solidified support for the two main parties and facilitated their expansion beyond Ontario and Quebec. Until 1874, voting was neither secret nor held simultaneously in all constituencies. Not having a secret vote hindered genuine partisanship, for voters were reluctant to be seen voting for a party that might lose the election. In such instances voters could expect retribution from the winning party in terms of lost government "favours," such as civil service jobs, government contracts, and public works projects. Many voters, therefore, preferred to support "independent" or "loose fish" candidates who could (and did) shift their support according to the party that was in power, thereby maximizing the returns to their constituents. Non-simultaneous elections across the various constituents had a similar effect on partisan attachments, as both candidates and voters would refrain from declaring their partisanship until it was clear which party was leading in the constituency elections that had already taken place. Thus Western constituencies, for example, would wait until results from the East were known before casting their ballots and candidates could then declare their party allegiance with more certainty. Even if candidates declared for the eventual loser in the election, they could usually be counted on to support the government. Such loose party loyalties were more appropriately called "ministerialist," rather than Liberal or Conservative, for they changed with each government or ministry.

Under such circumstances, parties were clearly "parties" in name only, for they could not count on consistent support in either the ridings or the legislature. The introduction in the 1870s of secret balloting and, in Ontario, Quebec, and the Maritimes, simultaneous elections did much to solidify support for both of the major parties across central and eastern Canada and thus make party lines more clear. The West followed shortly. Voters in the new province of Manitoba, comprised increasingly of partisan Ontario settlers, adopted firm party allegiances by the 1880s—being ministerialist prior to this. Once the CPR was completed to their province later that decade, and simultaneous elections held, British Columbians did the same. The result was that by 1896, in the words of Escott Reid, "the Conservative and the Liberal parties had at last become national and...a national two-party system was established in Canada for the first time."[1] Thereafter, and until the wartime election of 1917, party loyalties wavered little and neither party received less than 36 percent of the popular vote in any province.[2]

Closely related to the rise of national parties in the post-Confederation period was the tremendous stability of the party system. Truly national parties foster stability by successfully accommodating under one roof a myriad of regional, class, and ethnic interests. That the Liberal and Conservative parties were able to do this more or less consistently, notwithstanding the wide expanse of the country, its ethnic heterogeneity, lingering resentment with Confederation, and the religious and cultural tensions of the time, explains why the two parties dominated Canadian politics in the half-century following Confederation and why they each did so for such long stretches.

The Conservative party was the leading political force in the period 1867 to 1917, winning seven of twelve federal elections, six of them before 1900. After winning the 1867 election on the issue of Confederation, the party returned to power by a narrow margin in 1872, only to be defeated two years later on the heels of the Pacific Scandal that followed the revelation that Macdonald and the Conservatives had asked for and received large sums of money during the election from a consortium hoping to secure a contract to build a railway to the Pacific. But the Liberal interregnum was brief. In 1878 Macdonald's party returned to the helm under the banner of the National Policy—a policy designed to revive prosperity through high tariffs, western settlement, and immigration. Largely on the strength of this policy's promise, the Conservatives enjoyed eighteen more years of uninterrupted rule. It was also the dominant party provincially in five of the seven provinces before 1900. Indeed, the late nineteenth century very much belonged to the Conservatives.

The broad appeal of the Conservative party's nation-building agenda, particularly among those regions and classes benefitting materially from it, was an important factor behind its success. With the construction and completion of the Canadian Pacific Railway, in particular, André Siegfried noted at the time, "the Conservatives earned for themselves a reputation as a party of vast enterprises, with the great interests of the nation profoundly at heart."[3] But there were other reasons, not least of which was the shrewdness of the party leader. John A. Macdonald was a master at securing the support of key and, in some instances, antagonistic segments of the electorate. As subsequent events would demonstrate, no other leader could reconcile as well the Protestant, anglophone, imperialist wing of the Conservative party, residing largely in Ontario, with the Roman Catholic, francophone, anti-imperialist wing in Quebec. He achieved this reconciliation of interests by generally avoiding the divisive cultural issues of language and religion and by focusing, instead, on issues of territorial and economic expansion. It did not hurt, either, that the Roman Catholic hierarchy in Quebec was bitterly opposed to the Liberal party and made sure that its flock felt the same. Even with the death of Cartier in 1873, therefore, Macdonald could count on the support of that crucial province come election time.

Just as important to the party's success, perhaps more so, was Macdonald's adept use of patronage. While the spoils of office were not nearly as extensive as they would be later in the next century, incumbency in the Macdonald and Laurier eras did provide parties with enough to elicit, reward, and maintain support and keep the party solvent. In exchange for their efforts at election time, party activists would be given or promised any one of a number of local government jobs. In return for campaign contributions business people would receive lucrative government contracts and privileged access to the leader himself. For their support at the polls, voters would be promised a new government building, wharf, or road for their riding, which meant jobs and additional services. These rewards were all powerful inducements, especially in the years of slow economic growth before 1900, and Macdonald and his ministers used them to great effect. Patronage was perhaps the key ingredient in keeping the fragile bicultural conservative alliance intact for close to thirty years. Moreover, because Macdonald managed party patronage himself and was careful to distribute these favours and plums only to the most dedicated of party workers, the Conservatives received more in return for their patronage than they would have otherwise, for party activists saw that one day they would likely be rewarded for their years of service. Macdonald also had a knack for silencing influential critics, whether in a particular region or within a particular organization, by offering them public employment, including cabinet positions. Thus was he able, for example, to diffuse much of the lingering anti-Confederation sentiment among Maritime MPs in the 1870s and 1880s.

Of course some credit for the success of the Conservative party lies with their main opponents, the Liberals, who for much of the period were not an attractive alternative. Weakened by the co-optive tactics of the Conservatives and lacking any unifying vision, the Liberal party that assumed office in 1874 was not really a party at all, but a weak coalition of disparate groups, including a good many anti-Confederates, disaffected Conservatives, and assorted ministerialists. Nor could the party count on their leader, Alexander Mackenzie, to create the necessary cohesion or consolidate the party's support, for although Mackenzie was a man of deep integrity, he was also overly cautious and dreadfully uninspiring. When combined with a caucus united only in their aversion to bold or expensive government initiatives, Mackenzie's leadership convinced voters that his party was incapable of resolving the many problems that beset the young nation in the 1870s, or any that might follow. Liberal fortunes remained pretty much unchanged in the 1880s under the leadership of Edward Blake, who, while brilliant, was as lacklustre as his predecessor and just as loathe to play the political game. Nor did he move the party in new policy directions. The Liberals continued to oppose the basic components of the National Policy without offering much in its place. Thus, while the Liberal party's popular vote rose marginally in the elections of 1882 and 1887, it continued to face huge Conservative majorities in Parliament.

In the late 1880s, however, the Conservative party's hold on national power began to weaken. The signs of this loosening grip became evident first at the provincial level, where by 1887 Liberal governments ruled in the four most populous provinces, including the long-time Conservative bastion of Quebec. Since the death of Cartier, the Quebec wing of the Conservative party had struggled to maintain unity between its moderate Bleu supporters and a faction of militant Catholics known as the Castors. Through the use of patronage and reasonably effective secondary leaders in his cabinet, Macdonald managed to maintain this uneasy alliance. However, the execution of Louis Riel in 1885 and the rise of militant Protestant sentiment within the Ontario wing of the Tory party thereafter, finally fractured the Quebec Conservatives. Responding to an appeal for racial solidarity, many Castors defected to Honoré Mercier's revamped provincial Liberal party, the Parti National, which rode to power in 1886. In view of the traditional animosity shown by the Catholic Church toward the Liberals, the shift toward the provincial Liberals—who had, it should be noted, purged their Rouges element some years before—was indeed an ominous sign for the national Conservative party, whose success had always rested heavily on Quebec. The party's loss of eighteen Quebec seats in the federal election the following year, and the Liberals' gain of nineteen, further confirmed the political realignment that was taking place in the province. The stridently anti-French position of a handful of Conservative Ontario MPs regarding the linguistic and educational rights of French Catholics outside Quebec would continue to erode Conservative support in Quebec into the 1890s.

The turning tide of Canadian party politics was accelerated by the emergence of Wilfrid Laurier as national Liberal leader in the late 1880s. Laurier, the party's first francophone leader and a repentant ex-Rouge who had worked hard to disassociate his party from its radical past, gave French Canadians one more reason to abandon their traditional Conservative loyalties. The fact that Ontario Liberals had largely shed their anti-French "Grit" image was another. Premier Oliver Mowat's Liberal administrations had adopted policies beneficial to the province's Catholic and French-speaking minorities and this rebounded to the benefit of the federal Liberals in Quebec. Moreover, at a time when many Canadians were becoming disillusioned with the limited benefits of the National Policy, the Liberal party increased its support in English Canada, particularly among farmers, by proclaiming its support for "unrestricted reciprocity" with the US. The Liberals might even have won the 1891 federal election had the Conservatives not launched an emotional attack on reciprocity, calling it a veiled scheme to make Canada the fifty-first American state.

The "Old Flag, the Old Man, and the Old Policy" may have rescued the Conservative party in 1891, but the die had already been cast. The Liberals had narrowed the Conservative's majority of seats in Ontario to four and for the first time since Confederation had captured a majority of the seats in Quebec, both clear signs that the process of political realignment was continuing. This process was advanced by the death of Macdonald shortly after the election and by the party's failure to find a leader with the old chieftain's ability to offer grand visions or keep the increasingly fractious Conservative alliance intact; the departure from cabinet of the party's popular Quebec minister, Adolphe Chapleau, was almost as devastating. These leadership problems, when added to the party's stale image, the frequent charges of corruption it faced as a government, vocal Protestant extremism among Ontario Conservatives, and vacillation over the issue of passing remedial legislation reinstating separate schools in Manitoba, foretold the demise of Canada's first "government party."

The Liberals, meanwhile, increased in strength. Laurier wisely decided to drop unrestricted reciprocity as a key Liberal plank, calling instead for "freer trade." As well, by promising a more conciliatory approach to the Manitoba schools question, one that respected provincial rights in the area of education (a key concern in Quebec) by eschewing remedial legislation in favour of friendly persuasion, he managed to win the support of most English and French Canadians. In the all-important province of Quebec, Laurier was now seen as the person best able to defend French-Canada's interests, and young Liberals, directed by former Conservative organizer Israel Tarte, came together in droves to assist the Liberal campaign. The growing support for the Liberals across the country was made manifest in the 1896 election. On the strength of their strong showing in Quebec, where they boosted their seat total by twelve, the Liberals returned to power after almost two decades in Opposition.

The Liberal party totally dominated federal politics between 1896 and 1911, winning large parliamentary majorities in 1900, 1904, and 1908. It had consistently strong support in the Maritimes in this period, and in most western provinces as well, but its overwhelming majorities in Quebec, where it won over three-quarters of the seats between 1896 and 1908, lay at the root of the party's success. This record was all the more remarkable given the rising tensions over language and schooling and since the late 1890s, over Canada's relationship to the mother country. These were years of growing labour organization and militancy as well. That the Liberal party was able to maintain such high levels of support across the country's growing regional, class, and ethnic divides was due to several factors. Primary among them was Laurier's ability to bridge such divisions. His pan-Canadian nationalist vision, eloquently and charismatically articulated on numerous occasions, his effusive optimism about the country's future, which seemed to be borne out by events, and his ability to find the middle ground in highly divisive issues—he was a master of compromise—ensured the solid support of the electorate. Laurier's success in getting the papacy to restrain the anti-Liberal political intrusions of the Catholic Church in Quebec did not hurt the Liberal cause either. Nor did his government's use of patronage, which in its scope and efficacy came to rival that of the late Sir John.

Certainly another key to the Liberal party's great success prior to 1911 was the tremendous growth and optimism of the period. Immigrants by the thousands moved to the West, many of whom expressed their gratitude by voting Liberal. Two new provinces, Saskatchewan and Alberta, were created in 1905. Wheat production boomed in response to rising world prices, exports rose, new mineral discoveries helped fuel the recovery of the resource sector, secondary industries finally began to bloom under the protection of the tariff, a new round of railroad construction began, including a second transcontinental line, and many new jobs opened up in the quickly expanding service sector. It was, on the whole, a time of unprecedented growth, and for much of it the Liberals gladly assumed, and were generally awarded, credit.

The Conservative party, by contrast, was during the Laurier years a mere shadow of its former self. When Robert Borden assumed the leadership of the party in 1901, replacing the eminent but aging Sir Charles Tupper, he found himself in control of a party that was badly divided, poorly organized, outdated in its policies, and, thanks to intemperate racist remarks by Ontario Conservatives, still lacking firm support outside Anglo-Protestant Ontario. Borden himself was hardly a breath of fresh air. The former Halifax lawyer, though blessed with great intelligence and resolve, was rather dull in public, and not a particularly inspiring orator. Nevertheless he was determined to restore the party to its former glory by modernizing its policies and organization. His Halifax Program of 1907 committed the party to a more "progressive" approach to politics and the economy, calling as it did for such things as greater state intervention in the economy and a more efficient, less partisan civil service. Contentious cultural and foreign policy issues, on the other hand, were studiously avoided. His efforts to reform the party's organization, while less successful than expected, were equally innovative. An effort was made to establish a more systematic party organization, with a strong base of local Conservative organizations. These reforms, along with the gradual emergence of supportive Conservative administrations in New Brunswick, Ontario, Manitoba, and British Columbia, resulted in some minor gains for the party in the 1908 election.

More important to the resurgence of the Conservatives after 1908 were two issues that the Liberals proved unable to handle: naval policy and reciprocity. After almost a decade, the issue of Canada's military relationship to Britain returned to centre stage. The Conservatives and their imperialist supporters favoured a closer relationship, beginning for the moment with financial contributions to the Royal Navy. Laurier, ever aware of the strong anti-imperialist sentiment in Quebec, devised yet another compromise, proposing instead the creation of a Canadian navy, one that could be loaned to Britain in time of war. Unfortunately for the Liberals, this compromise failed to please. English Canadians deemed it a sell-out of the mother country while many French Canadians worried that it was but a prelude to Canadian involvement in imperial wars. The harshest attacks in Quebec came from Henri Bourassa, an influential politician and editor whose Nationalist movement was no longer as enamoured of Laurier as it had once been. The Nationalists, on whom the Liberals had depended heavily for marshalling electoral support in the province, began to turn against Laurier in 1905, after his government backtracked on the issue of minority education rights in the new provinces of Saskatchewan and Alberta. The so-called Autonomy Bills that created the two provinces had initially guaranteed public funding for separate schools as well as French-language instruction, where desired. But after pressure from his English-speaking ministers, Laurier allowed the Bills to be amended, with the result that religious and French-language instruction in Saskatchewan and Alberta were severely restricted. The naval policy of 1909, asserted the Nationalists, was simply the latest assault on French-speaking minority rights. Evidently the Nationalists' compatriots were convinced, and in 1911 the Liberal party suffered the first real blow to its power base in the province.

The issue that fatally wounded the Liberals, however, was reciprocity, the same issue that had buried them in 1891. The Conservatives, initially demoralized by Laurier's announcement in 1911 that a free trade agreement had been signed with the US, seized the opportunity to once again paint their opponents with the brush of disloyalty. Borden's decision to pursue this line of attack was aided immeasurably by the disaffection of many prominent Liberal business leaders in Ontario, who viewed free trade a threat to their economic interests. In the election campaign that a confident Laurier called to decide the issue, the Conservatives eagerly allied themselves with the dissident Liberals and together they launched a blistering (and well-financed) attack on the government. Reciprocity and the proposed navy, English Canadians were warned, would sever the British connection and lead to annexation with the US. French Canadians were told almost the exact opposite. An "unholy alliance" forged by Borden between leading Quebec Conservatives and Bourassa's Nationalists contended that the naval policy would drag Canada into every imperial war. Laurier was doomed and he knew it. The electoral cooperation among his enemies in central Canada, including the running of jointly selected "anti-government" candidates in several Quebec ridings, cost his party sixteen seats in Quebec and twenty-four in Ontario, where an added factor was the weakened state of the Liberals' electoral machinery and the resurgence of the Conservative organization under Premier James Whitney's Conservative administration. Perhaps, too, after fifteen years in office, the Liberals had come to take their power for granted and had been punished for their arrogance. Lingering hints of scandal and inefficiency in the expenditure of public monies did not help either. In any case, the Liberals' long reign of power was over.

The election of 1911 was an important turning point in Canadian party politics. On the surface it appeared as though the torch was being passed back to the "other" national party. However, this apparent continuity masked the beginning of another political realignment, one that would culminate in the permanent dissolution of the two-party system in 1917. For although the Conservatives had returned to power in a convincing way, with a forty-seven seat majority, their true strength continued to be concentrated largely in Protestant-imperialist Ontario. As such, they could not hope to maintain their support in Catholic, anti-imperialist Quebec at a time when matters of minority ethnic rights or foreign affairs continued to draw national attention. And, indeed, the Conservative-Nationalist alliance quickly fell apart when in 1912 Borden's government, pressured by its predominantly English-speaking caucus and several staunchly imperialist Tory premiers, decided to extend financial assistance to the British navy. Frederick Monk, the most prominent French-Canadian in the government, resigned, leaving Quebec without a strong voice in cabinet for the first time since Confederation. The Liberal party's status as a national party was equally precarious. With forty-four percent of its seats now located in Quebec, it had become even more a regional party. That it managed to hold on to its representation out West in 1911 was due primarily to strong rural support in the region for free trade. When the issue of Canada's precise relationship with Britain came to loom even larger, however, the ethnic divisions that had been largely masked by the free trade issue in 1911 would fundamentally transform the major parties and the party system itself.

The coming of the First World War brought the question of Canada's relationship with the Empire to centre stage. In the early stages of the conflict, both parties rallied to the cause and consensus reigned. But the unanimity was short-lived. Government scandals and the insensitive handling of recruitment in Quebec, combined with further restrictions on French-language education in neighbouring Ontario, about which Borden's government seemed uninterested, further alienated Quebec from the Conservatives. The introduction of conscription in 1917, however, sealed the Tory party's fate, as French-Canadian politicians and their supporters moved *en masse* to the Liberals, who under an aging Laurier, refused to endorse the policy. The effect of conscription on the Liberal party was equally dramatic, as most English-Canadian Liberal MPs, favouring both conscription and progressive reform, left the party to support Borden's coalition government and ran under the Unionist banner in the December 1917 election.

Clearly the war had a major impact on the party system. Traditional party loyalties were shed and for the first time Canada's two major parties were divided almost purely along ethnic lines, with most French Canadians and other cultural minorities supporting the Liberals and most English Canadians backing the Unionists. Under such circumstances, neither party could claim to be genuinely national in scope. The election of 1917, which the Unionists won handily, finally made evident the deep ethno-cultural tensions that the previous election had to a large degree obscured. Even the Liberal bastion of Saskatchewan succumbed to the Unionists' strident racial appeals during that most intense of Canadian elections. Thus the political stability that was so distinguishing a feature of the Canadian party system since 1867, a stability characterized above all by the long incumbency of inclusive national parties, disappeared during the war, never completely to return.

The final theme worth noting for this period might best be called the decline of traditional "partyism." That is, the parties themselves changed, both ideologically and, to a lesser extent, organizationally. For much of the late nineteenth century the Conservatives were distinguished by their greater paternalism, as demonstrated by their willingness to use the powers of the state to foster economic development, promote closer state-Church ties, and protect minority cultural rights, and by their stronger attachment to Britain and British institutions. The Liberals, on the other hand, were more voluntarist, self-righteous, and continentalist, favouring smaller government, the moral purification of politics and society, respect for individual and provincial rights, and looser ties to the mother country. Of course such ideological differences should not be overstated, for within each party there existed varying shades of opinion on these issues. But as general tendencies the distinctions hold.

By the early 1900s, however, these ideological differences narrowed substantially. Under Laurier the Liberals discarded much of their continentalist and laissez-faire approach, beginning with the adoption, virtually unaltered, of the former Conservative government's National Policy. The maintenance of a protective tariff, the fostering of western settlement through immigration, and the construction of major railways were as much hallmarks of the Laurier years as of the Macdonald era. So was the Liberal party's increasing sympathy for the mother country, expressed in its preferential imperial tariff, which admitted imperial products at a lower rate, and in its limited participation in the Boer War.

The Conservative party shifted course as well, though perhaps less perceptibly. While it still had a strong imperialist, anti-Quebec strain, one that became more prominent in the absence of influential francophone representatives in party councils, Borden tried hard to present a more moderate and progressive front for his party. Under Borden the Tories became less overtly anti-French, favoured freer trade within the Empire, and supported progressive reforms aimed at regulating business, making government more efficient, and cleaning up politics—not unlike the Grits of old in many ways.

Generally speaking, therefore, the major parties converged ideologically. Of course some sort of convergence toward the pragmatic centre of the ideological spectrum was arguably part and parcel of the rise of national parties: the more "national" a party became, the less likely it was to endanger this growth by taking controversial stands. More important, this ideological convergence was necessary because the electorate *itself* was changing by the early 1900s, becoming larger and more differentiated, and, as economic and community associations spread, less firmly attached to one party or the other. Under such circumstances, party leaders realized that only moderate, middle-of-the-road "brokerage" parties able to accommodate a variety of groups and regions under one roof could hope to form a government. When Laurier told voters in Strathroy, Ontario, during the 1908 campaign that "the

Liberal party is broad enough, [and] Liberal principles are large enough to give an equal share of Justice and Liberty to all men," he was practising the new art of consensus politics.[4] Party leaders did their best, therefore, to squelch extremist views within their party, so as to preserve the broad coalition of support necessary for political success. The dilution of party principle also gave rise to a growing emphasis on the character of party leaders, so that by the 1900s (and excluding 1911), elections became contests not so much between different visions of the country or philosophies of government, but between different personalities and political machines.

The ways in which the Liberals and Conservatives approached the matter of party organization also converged over the period. As mentioned, both parties relied heavily on patronage as a method of building and maintaining support. Federal Liberals might not have been as enthusiastic, initially, about building their political machine in this way, but they were eventually converted. Oliver Mowat's long-ruling Liberal government in Ontario formed the basis for a powerful patronage-driven machine, the elements of which were later used to good effect by their brethren in Ottawa. Both parties also relied heavily on the media to trumpet their cause and keep spirits high among the party faithful. In return for regular editorial support, governing parties would, through lucrative printing and advertising contracts, finance the operations of a variety of newspapers.

But as the size and composition of the electorate changed, these methods were not as reliable as they had once been in attracting and keeping supporters. Patronage positions could not possibly keep stride with either population growth or the growing number of eligible voters, and in an era of rapid economic growth, ambitious, well-educated individuals found the private sector a more promising avenue for their talents. Voters were in any case becoming less tolerant of the practice, calling instead for a more efficient—this being perhaps the key word of the progressive era—system of assigning civil service positions, one based more on individual merit than on party affiliation. The party press was losing its usefulness, too, as voters increasingly turned to the many independent papers that appeared after 1900, papers whose political content was in many instances negligible.

Of the two major parties, only the Conservative party attempted to adjust to the new realities. Led by Borden, it took steps to supplement older methods of mobilizing support and establish the foundations for a more permanent party organization, one that relied less on members of the Tory caucus and their patronage-oriented activities in the ridings, and more on alliances with groups outside the caucus, including an extra-parliamentary structure of councils and committees staffed with volunteers and paid officials. In contrast, the Liberal party, apparently satisfied with the efficacy of patronage as on organizing tool, made few attempts to remake itself organizationally. This lack of change proved especially fatal to the party in 1911, both in those provinces with recently installed Conservative governments and in Quebec, where the only political organization of any significance—Bourassa's Nationalists—placed their machine at the service of the Conservative party.

In any case, the limited organizational changes that did take place were not enough to stem the growing cynicism among voters with the party system, particularly as the programs of the major parties became more ambiguous and less distinctive. Rightly or wrongly, more and more Canadians came to see the party system as severely flawed: as remote, outdated, parochial, corrupt, inefficient, lacking creativity, and presided over by individuals whose main concern was not with advancing the "national" interest, but with advancing the interests of their party, their friends, and worst of all, themselves. It is in this growing disaffection for the two-party system, based largely on the convergence in policies and methods of its main players prior to 1917, that the roots of the postwar third-party backlash lie.

There are, of course, other themes that run through the party history of this period: the symbiotic and, at times, corruptive ties between the major parties and their corporate benefactors; the often debased level of political discourse and crass vote-getting methods engaged in by both parties at election time; and the sporadic appearance of third-party candidates, mostly farm, socialist or labour candidates in Ontario and the West. But these themes were minor compared to those outlined above. Nor were they necessarily unique to the period 1867-1917. By contrast, the emergence of national parties, the prevalence of political stability, and the growing similarity of the major parties were stronger and more characteristic of this period than any other.

The articles that follow illustrate well these major themes, or aspects thereof. In the first, Frank Underhill examines the emergence of Canada's national parties. Underhill's main argument is that by the early 1900s the Liberal and Conservative parties had become indistinguishable servants of the big business community, in turn laying the groundwork for the rise of alternative parties in the interwar years. More significant, perhaps, are his insights into the ways in which the parties used patronage, economic programs, and government favours to keep the conflicting sectional, racial, and religious interests in their coalitions united. Underhill's article is followed by H. Blair Neatby and John T. Saywell's piece on the decline of the Conservative party in Quebec, in which the authors emphasize the unsuccessful efforts of the party's chief Quebec lieutenant, J.A. Chapleau, to heal the divisions in the party between the Castors and moderates or to stem the growing disaffection among Quebec Conservatives, Chapleau included, with the federal government's failure to pass remedial legislation for Manitoba. A similar failure of regional leadership contributed to the decline of the Laurier Liberals in Ontario prior to the 1911 election. This failure is the focus of the article by Paul Stevens, who contends that the Liberals' Ontario "political boss," Allan Aylesworth, undermined Liberal support in that province by alienating puritanical rural voters, neglecting practical organizational matters, and failing to act as a strong voice in cabinet or on the hustings for party supporters concerned about reciprocity and "French domination." By contrast, the early 1900s were years of successful rebuilding for the Conservatives. John English describes this process in an excerpt from his book *The Decline of Politics,* a process dominated by Robert Borden's attempt to forge alliances with groups outside his poor-quality, unrepresentative caucus. The final piece in this section, taken from David Smith's study of the Saskatchewan Liberal party, describes the intricacies of the party's "political machine" between 1905 and 1917. The use of patronage to reward Liberal party supporters in that province and the key role of government ministers in managing party organization were typical of the organizational methods employed by the major parties at the time. They were also, as Smith suggests, highly effective.

NOTES

1. Escott Reid, "The Rise of National Parties in Canada," in *Papers and Proceedings of the Canadian Political Science Association,* IV, 1932, 199.

2. J.M. Beck, *Pendulum of Power: Canada's Federal Elections* (Toronto: Prentice-Hall Canada, Inc., 1968), 72-136 *passim.*

3. André Siegfried, in F. Underhill, ed., *The Race Question in Canada* (Toronto: McClelland & Stewart 1966), 158.

4. Cited in Beck, *Pendulum of Power,* 107.

THE DEVELOPMENT OF NATIONAL
POLITICAL PARTIES IN CANADA

BY FRANK UNDERHILL

○

"The most common and durable source of factions," declared James Madison in 1787,[1] "has been the various and unequal distribution of property. Those who hold and those who are without property have ever formed distinct interests in society. Those who are creditors, and those who are debtors, fall under a like discrimination. A landed interest, a manufacturing interest, a mercantile interest, a moneyed interest, with many lesser interests, grow up of necessity in civilized nations, and divide them into different classes, actuated by different sentiments and views. The regulation of these various and interfering interests forms the principal task of modern legislation, and involves the spirit of party and faction in the necessary and ordinary operations of the government."

"In the course of political evolution," declared Mr. W. L. Mackenzie King, addressing the National Federation of Liberal Women in 1928,[2] "we witness a constant struggle of two contending principles, the principle of the future and the principle of the past.... To the ever-present conflict of these principles we owe the birth and growth of political parties.... By whatever names those parties may be designated, they tend more and more to owe their existence to this conflict of principles between the future and the past, a conflict which, when the history of the future is unfolded, will be found to have been continuous from the dawn of civilization to the eve of the millennium."

F. Underhill, "The Development of National Political Parties in Canada," *Canadian Historical Review* (December 1935), pp. 367-87. Toronto: University of Toronto Press Incorporated. Reprinted by permission of University of Toronto Press Incorporated.

This paper is an attempt to apply to the history of Canadian political parties the materialist analysis of Madison, and to show by implication the irrelevance of commonly offered idealistic explanations, such as that provided by Mr. King. I shall, therefore, not spend time inquiring what Canadian Conservatives have been trying to conserve since the achievement of responsible government or what Canadian Liberals have been trying to liberate. I shall devote myself to studying that struggle of different interests to which Madison drew attention; and I shall discuss how out of "the regulation of these various and interfering interests," involving as it did "the spirit of party and faction in the necessary and ordinary operations of the government," the Canadian party-system was evolved.

Madison and the founders of the American constitution apparently expected a multiplicity of parties in the new republic corresponding to the different forms of propertied interests. Instead, there developed a peculiar North American two-party system, centring mainly about the conflict between the industrial and financial interests on the one side and the agricultural interests on the other. But in the course of the struggle for the control of the presidency each party had to make some appeal to all the sectional groups within the nation; so that the two national parties tended to become loose opportunistic collections of politicians, containing in their membership representatives from competing sectional and class groups all across the continent, maintaining an uneasy unity by appeals to traditional symbols and by an intricate and unprincipled system of bargaining and compromise.

In Canada a similar two-party system grew up and developed with the geographical expansion of the Dominion. The fact that the British names for the parties were preserved and that the parties operated within a British constitutional framework made little difference to their essentially North American quality. The stage properties were imported from Britain, but the plot of the play and the characters on the stage were all native products.

2

The present-day Canadian party system goes back to a starting-point in the old province of Canada, in 1854, in the period immediately following the achievement of responsible government. The so-called Reform party of LaFontaine and Baldwin, which was never quite a party but rather a coalition of groups, was in process of disintegration into its original elements. Out of the confusion there was formed a new coalition, which at the start seemed to contemporaries only one of several possible coalitions. But it gave itself the inspired name of the Liberal-Conservative party, and, under the long leadership of John A. Macdonald, it slowly consolidated itself from a coalition into a party which dominated Canadian politics for forty years. Over against the Liberal-Conservatives, the various groups and individuals who found themselves wandering in the wilderness of opposition gradually in their turn coalesced into a new Reform or Liberal party, claiming to base themselves upon the traditions of Baldwin and LaFontaine, but achieving party cohesion more slowly than the Liberal-Conservatives because, until the day of Laurier, they seldom enjoyed the sweets of national office.

The differences between the two parties were never, before or after Confederation, as clear-cut as the differences between their two outstanding leaders, Macdonald and Brown. In fact, in the early days they never quite became parties at all in the modern sense. There were too many individuals whose allegiance was uncertain—"loose fish," "shaky fellows," "waiters on Providence." There were too many constituencies whose practice it was to elect "independents" of one stripe or another—i.e., representatives who were expected, by a realistic bartering of their votes, to get the utmost possible concessions for their locality or their economic group from the party leaders who sought their support. Members of the legislature, both frontbenchers and backbenchers, passed with remarkable ease from one political camp to another. The reader of Canadian newspapers in the 1850s and 1860s is struck at once by the fact that the papers never agree with one another in reporting the results of general elections. Each claims for its side all the doubtful members, and the controversy is not cleared up until there have been two or three divisions in the newly elected house. Nor is it entirely cleared up then. For, as Macdonald was wont to complain, the trouble with so many of these independents was that, after being bought, they often refused to stay bought. Hence the extreme instability of Canadian governments in the 1850s and 1860s, and the bewildering rapidity with which new experimental combinations of politicians succeeded one another in office. Hence the general low level of political morality. Hence also the ferocity with which the fight was carried on.

Still it was out of this confused turmoil that the lines of party division were gradually laid down. And, since it was this party system of the original province of Canada which established itself over the whole dominion after 1867, it is necessary to begin by inquiring what these lines of division were.

Who, then, were the Liberal-Conservatives? Popular tradition has it that Macdonald brought together all the moderate elements in Canadian politics into his new party, leaving the extremists in the cold of opposition. Yet one reads the books in vain to discover in what sense these moderates were moderate, or what were the two extremes between which they formed the golden Canadian mean. To be sure there were the Clear Grits and the Rouges at what may be called the one extreme; but the representatives of the other extreme, the old Family Compact Tories, were, as a matter of fact, part of Macdonald's "moderate" party. And why, after all, should the railway promoters and manufacturers who supported the Liberal-Conservatives because that party looked after their interests be called moderate, while the frontier farmers who fought for their interests in the Clear Grit party are designated as extreme? Historians who apply such adjectives to competing party groups demonstrate merely that they have prejudged all the issues by accepting in advance the standards and the scale of values of one side in the discussion.

The Liberal-Conservative coalition of 1854 was composed of four main groups. A short examination of each of them in turn will reveal what was their chief bond of union.

The group which was numerically strongest was that of the French-Canadian Roman Catholics of whom George-Étienne Cartier was by 1854 rapidly becoming the recognized leader. We have been told that Macdonald sensed the natural conservatism of the French and set out from the start of his career to woo them. This is no doubt true as far as it goes, but it does not take us very far. There still remains a blank period in the political evolution of the French Canadians which has never been properly explored. In the 1820s and 1830s there was going on in Lower Canada a bitter struggle between the Montreal mercantile interests, who were dreaming of a commercial state which should extend across the continent and pour its traffic (and profits) into the St. Lawrence, and the French-Canadian peasants who had no taste to be taxed for such far-reaching purposes but wished only to be left to enjoy their accustomed static agricultural civilization. Lord Durham reported in alarmist language in 1839 that relations between the two races were so embittered that neither would ever again accept the government of the other. Yet fifteen years later they are living together in beautiful amity. In the fifteen years after Durham there somehow or other developed that alliance which has been the permanent dominating factor in Canadian politics ever since— the alliance between the Montreal commercial and industrial interests intent upon consolidating an economic empire and the great mass of the French-Canadian voters who accepted the leadership of the church.

In support of this alliance of French and English interests in Quebec, Macdonald brought from Upper Canada a sufficiently large body of Orange Loyalists to give his party a fairly continuous majority from the 1850s to the 1890s. To regard this Anglo-French *entente* of Macdonald and Cartier as merely a case of mutual racial and religious tolerance, and to neglect the dynamic economic purposes which lay behind it, is to take a very superficial view of Canadian politics.

We have very little light on the processes, between the 1830s and 1850s, by which this new alignment of forces in Lower Canada was brought about, but at any rate it is clear that in the career of Cartier we find its personification. Cartier was the avowed and recognized spokesman of the French-Catholic hierarchy. He was also the solicitor of the Grand Trunk Railway Company and the recognized spokesman for Grand Trunk interests during the fifties and sixties when the affairs of the Grand Trunk were the most important subject of political controversy. Cartier represents in his own person the break with the long previous French-Canadian tradition of opposition to the commercial ambitions and policy of the English elements in Montreal. On the eve of Confederation, looking back over his own career, he took occasion to explain that he had never accepted all of Papineau's policy,—"Mr. Papineau not being a commercial man, and not understanding the importance of these measures. He considered Mr. Papineau was right in the struggle he maintained against the oligarchy of that time in power; but he had never approved of the course which he took with reference to commercial matters and in opposition to measures for the improvement of the country."[3]

In the thick volume of 817 pages in which Joseph Tassé collected the speeches of Sir George Cartier, the first speech printed is one in the election campaign of 1844 on responsible government; but the second is on the Montreal and Portland Railway. It was delivered on August 10, 1846, at a great open-air meeting, presided over by LaFontaine, and held for the purpose of working up popular enthusiasm in behalf of this project of equipping Montreal with a winter port. "The prosperity of Montreal," Cartier told his hearers, "depends upon its position as the entrepôt of the commerce of the West.... We can only maintain that position if we assure ourselves of the best means of transport from the West to the Atlantic by means of our canals and of this railway."[4] Here in 1846 is the whole gospel of the Montreal mercantile class upon the lips of a French Canadian; and, at the close of the meeting, so M. Tassé informs us, many shares were subscribed in the projected railway, "Messrs. LaFontaine and Cartier giving the example."

When he became a member of the legislature Cartier continued his active interest in railway development. He served as legal adviser to the Grand Trunk promoters, and the first resolution of the board of directors of the Grand Trunk Company in 1853 appointed him as its solicitor for Canada East. In the later 1850s and through the 1860s the Grand Trunk had to come repeatedly to the legislature for financial help of one kind or another, and it was Cartier who took the leading part in seeing that the help was forthcoming. "The Grand Trunk," he boasted, "and the Victoria Bridge have flooded Montreal with an abundance of prosperity. What would Montreal be without the Grand Trunk? It has assured for us the commerce of the West."[5] His biographer, Mr. John Boyd, quotes the admiring comment of William Wainwright, one of the leading Grand Trunk officials: "It was undoubtedly through the Arrangements Act, the passage of which by the Canadian parliament was secured by George-Étienne Cartier, that the company was saved at that time [1862].... Cartier in this connection rendered a service that should never be forgotten by Canadians, for through his influence the collapse of a railway enterprise that meant so much for the country was undoubtedly prevented. George-Étienne Cartier was the biggest French Canadian I have ever known."[6] Exactly. On Montreal standards, the test of bigness in a French Canadian was the degree of his assistance in advancing the cause of the commercial empire of Montreal.

"For fourteen years, from 1852 to 1867, Cartier was chairman of the Railway Committee of the Legislature of United Canada"; and finally, to quote Mr. Boyd's delightful euphemism, "he crowned his career by having passed by parliament the first charter for the construction of the Canadian Pacific Railway."[7] The charter to which Mr. Boyd refers was that which was granted in 1872 to Sir Hugh Allan of Montreal and his associates and which gave rise to the incident famous in Canadian history as the Pacific Scandal.

So much for the French-Canadian place in the Liberal-Conservative party. It should be added, of course, that during the same time that it provided this support to business enterprise, the Catholic vote obtained many things which were of interest to the church—the incorporation of religious communities with the locking up of large landed estates in mortmain, the clerical control of education in Lower Canada, the extension of separate schools in Upper Canada, and so forth.

The second group in the Liberal-Conservative party consisted of Montreal big business and such voting support from the Eastern Townships as it could command. Numerically the Lower-Canadian English did not count for much, but they had an importance out of all proportion to their numbers because of their connection with the commercial and industrial enterprises of Montreal. On the whole, the Eastern Townships tended to follow this Montreal leadership in politics; and it is interesting to observe the arguments by which the majority of their votes were attracted into the Liberal-Conservative camp. If race and religion had been the dominating factors in Canadian politics of the fifties and sixties, as the traditional accounts of the pre-Confederation period would have it, the Lower-Canadian English would surely have been attracted into an alliance with the Upper-Canadian Grits; and it was a frequent complaint of the Toronto *Globe* that they did not vote with their western fellow citizens who shared their language and religion.

Alexander Galt[8] was the outstanding representative in politics of the Lower-Canada English section. Note the arguments which Galt addresses to his constituents in his great speech at Sherbrooke on November 23, 1864, when he is presenting the project of Confederation to them and when he has to allay their fears of handing themselves over to a permanent French majority in the Province of Quebec:

> The interests of the British population of Lower Canada were identical with those of the French Canadians; these peculiar interests being that the trade and commerce of the Western country should continue to flow through Lower Canada.... He felt that in taking his position in the [Quebec] Conference he was charged, not altogether with the simple duty of a representative of the British portion of the population of Lower Canada, but he felt that he equally represented his French-Canadian friends; and his conviction was that, instead of there being any clashing and division of interests, they would be found in the future more closely bound together than ever before. It would be found that the effect of the combination of all the Provinces would be to benefit Lower Canada—not French Lower Canada or British Lower Canada—but the whole of Lower Canada—by giving it the position of being the commercial heart of the country.... He thought our material interests would have to govern us in this respect.... He thought it was plain that Lower Canada was going to be the great commercial centre for the whole of the Provinces, and even when we extended the boundaries of our Empire to the countries bordering on the Saskatchewan and the Rocky Mountains, the whole wealth of that great country must pour down the St. Lawrence and stimulate the industry of the cities of Lower Canada.[9]

Confederation, in other words, meant the final realization of the dream of a commercial empire with the lower St. Lawrence for its focus; and, in face of such an opportunity, it behooved the two races on the St. Lawrence to rise above their mutual suspicions. Let me repeat that, of course, the Liberal-Conservative party stood for a policy of appeasement between French and English; but the dynamic purpose for which appeasement was sought was the establishment of Montreal's "commercial state."

In the field of journalism the chief exponent of the ideas and ambitions of the Montreal business group was, then as now, the Montreal *Gazette*. Copious quotations could be extracted from the *Gazette* illustrating this same thesis which Galt expounded at Sherbrooke, and it is worth noting that in all these quotations from the *Gazette*, from Galt and from Cartier, there is practically no talk about those vague abstractions which are called political principles. The emphasis is entirely upon interests. "Their politics," said the Toronto *Globe* of the two Montreal papers, the *Gazette* and the *Pilot*, "have been conducted on a mercantile basis.... The five loaves and two fishes are their seven cardinal principles."[10]

On the other two groups, both from Upper Canada, who made up the Liberal-Conservative coalition, there is no need to dwell so long. It is clear that the Hincksite Reformers, the third group in the coalition, the so-called "moderates" amongst the Upper-Canadian followers of Robert Baldwin, were primarily urban. Francis Hincks himself was notoriously on very intimate terms with the Grand Trunk promoters—too intimate, so his critics charged. When he retired from active politics in 1854, he bequeathed to Macdonald the Hincksite group and its leader, John Ross. Ross had gone to England to complete the Grand Trunk deal, and he was one of the five cabinet ministers sitting upon the directorate of the railway company to denote the close connection between the Canadian government and the transportation enterprise. In due course he became president of the Grand Trunk Railway Company.

Macdonald's own Upper-Canadian Tory following, the fourth element in the Liberal-Conservative coalition, is important for the voting power which it contributed and for the intensification of anti-American feeling which it gave to the party, but for little else. We need only note here that it was the old high and dry Family Compact Tory hero, Sir Allan MacNab, who contributed the slogan of the new coalition when he declared in a famous phrase that "railways are my politics."

The main element in the coalition which gradually formed itself in opposition to the Liberal-Conservatives was, of course, composed of the Clear Grits of Upper Canada. Grittism had the centre of its strength in the pioneer farming area of the Ontario peninsula, and was a characteristic expression of frontier agrarian democracy. The vigorous and growing young city of Toronto, from which railways were beginning to radiate westward and northward, formed the intellectual as well as the economic capital of these pioneer wheat farmers; and its relation to them was like that of Winnipeg in our own day to the radical pioneer wheat farmers of the prairie. In Toronto the Grit movement found an incomparable leader with an incomparable organ through which the gospel of Grittism might be preached—George Brown and his *Globe*. East of Toronto the strength of the Grits gradually declined; and along the eastern end of Lake Ontario, down the St. Lawrence and up the Ottawa, while there were men calling themselves Reformers, pure Grittism made little appeal. These districts were connected economically with Montreal rather than with Toronto. When the Montreal *Gazette* appealed for the interests of the St. Lawrence route against the "Peninsular interest" of western Grittism, it met with sympathetic response in the eastern parts of Upper Canada.

The appeal of the *Globe* was essentially to the West. The commercial and financial interests of Toronto often joined hands with the *Globe's* "intelligent yeomanry" of the peninsula in fighting against the schemes of Montreal for tariffs that gave differential advantages to imports *via* the St. Lawrence, and against Montreal's monopolistic control of transportation, credit, and wholesale distribution. The *Globe* criticized the protectionist tendencies of Galt's tariffs in 1858 and 1859, but Brown could not get the Reformers nearer Montreal to agree with him in his free-trade views. It was the *Globe* which initiated and led the campaign for the extension of Canada westward to the Red River and the prairies; and on this question the Grit attitude was very much like that of the radical Republicans to the south with their free-homestead policy and their election cry of "Vote yourself a farm." The main purpose of this campaign and of the "Rep by Pop" agitation, as Montreal interests very clearly perceived, was to increase the influence of the western agricultural districts in the provincial legislature so that they could more effectively checkmate policies which had their origin in Montreal head offices.

The *bête noire* of the *Globe* and the Clear Grits was the Grand Trunk Railway. In spite of popular tradition to the contrary, it is the Grand Trunk Railway rather than the French Catholic Church which occupies the major portion of the *Globe's* space during the decade before Confederation. To the *Globe* the Grand Trunk stood as a symbol for the whole corrupt system, as it believed it to be, of the domination of the country's government and politics by eastern business interests.

> With the Grand Trunk and the Bank of Montreal at his back, there is no saying how far the reckless financier of the present government may carry his schemes. These institutions are the enemies of the people and of popular rights. They have special interests to advance in Parliament.... It is time that Upper Canadians were united together in resisting these monopolies, and the Government which has created and supported them. It is time that we had a Government above being the servant of railway or banking institutions. It is time that we had a Government which would consider the interest of the whole people and not of a few wily moneymakers who can bring influence to bear upon Parliament. It is above all a necessity that the people of the West...should elect men who will be able to prevent the mischief which Mr. Galt is still anxious to do to the interests of the Western country.

This is from an editorial in the *Globe* of 10 August 1867, an editorial written in the midst of the first general election of the new Dominion of Canada which had just come into existence on 1 July. Nothing could show more forcibly the *Globe's* clear understanding (in those days) of the economic basis of politics, and nothing could show more clearly the class and sectional lines dividing the Liberal-Conservatives of the 1860s from the Grits.

The Rouge group from Lower Canada, who worked in cooperation with the Grits in the legislature, were never able to attain the numerical strength in their French-Canadian community which the Grits attained in Upper Canada. Their anti-clerical tendencies made the church a bitter enemy, and by 1867 they were steadily declining in strength under clerical attack. The democratic and republican ideas which they derived from the revolutionary Paris of 1848 made them unpopular both with the church and with Montreal business, though they did form a short alliance with the Montreal mercantile interests in 1849 for the purpose of advocating annexation to the United States. (This is the only occasion on which Montreal ever lost faith in its mission.) But their voting strength was mostly in the pioneer agricultural districts south of the St. Lawrence. Dorion, their leader, opposed Confederation partly because he thought it was a Grand Trunk "job," which it partly was. They shared with the Grits a general sympathy for the democratic ideas which came from the United States. Some of the more advanced of them had imbibed from France an economic radicalism which went far beyond any native North American doctrines, and were beginning to talk about bourgeoisie and proletariat. But these were a small minority of what was only a minority party. The focus of Rouge interest was mainly local; the party had its hands full in fighting the declining power of French-Canadian feudalism and the growing power of the French-Canadian church.

–
3
–

Such were the main lines of party division in the pre-Confederation province of Canada. After 1867 these party divisions of Liberal-Conservatives and Reformers were gradually extended from the central area to the outlying sections of the dominion. Inevitably the politics of Canada dominated the politics of the Maritime Provinces and of the little far-western communities of Manitoba and British Columbia. In 1871 the population of Ontario and Quebec together was 2,812,367 (Ontario, 1,620,851; Quebec, 1,191,516) out of the dominion's total population of 3,689,257; while Nova Scotia had only 387,800; New Brunswick, 285,594; Prince Edward Island, 94,021; Manitoba, 25,228; and British Columbia, 36,247. Confederation had been due primarily to the continental ambitions of the Canadians; it was they who had brought the other partners into the union. And it was Canadian ambitions, reaching their highest intensity in Montreal and Toronto, which continued to supply the driving force for both the economic and the political life of the new dominion.

In the politics of the new federal state after 1867, accordingly, there is to be discerned a double process. Most important and fundamental is the continuing drive of great business interests for the conquest and consolidation of this expanded economic empire which lay open to their exploitation; and it was the primary function of Macdonald's Liberal-Conservative party to make the state a partner in this enterprise, a function which was taken over by Laurier's Liberal party after 1896. But to achieve this end of a united centralized economic empire a great variety of particularist sectional, racial, and religious interests had to be conciliated, manipulated, and kept moving together in some kind of practical concord. It was the second function of the party system to perform this task of conciliation and management of the diverse sectional interests in the new loosely knit nation.

The first generation after Confederation is dominated by Macdonald's Liberal-Conservative party. Clearly it was a constructive nation-building party and it earned its support, as against its Reform rival, by the wider sweep of its national ideas and ambitions and by the greater vigour of its administrative policies. But the nationalism of the Liberal-Conservatives was of a particular quality. The nation which they were helping to build up was a nation under the strong centralized control and leadership of the great capitalist *entrepreneurs* of Montreal and Toronto.

In short, the Liberal-Conservative party under Macdonald was a Hamiltonian federalist party. Macdonald would never have subscribed to Alexander Hamilton's whole-hearted contempt for the common people, but he and Cartier and their lieutenants were agreed in opposing the manifestations of American democracy which expressed themselves in Canada through the Grit and the Rouge parties. "The rights of the minority must be protected," said Macdonald to his fellow delegates at Quebec when they were discussing the proper constitution of the Senate, "and the rich are always fewer in number than the poor."[11] In all essential points Macdonald's fundamental policy was Hamiltonian. A strong central government was needed to carry through the drive for westward economic expansion, to win the confidence and attract the capital of the investing classes whose support was necessary for this expansionist policy. The great interests of finance and industry and transportation must be tied to the national government by putting the national government solidly behind their ambitions for power and profit. So the "National Policy" lays the basis for the development of a many-sided economic life, and at the same time fosters a class of industrialists who depend for special privileges upon the national government. Similarly the Canadian Pacific Railway makes an economic unity out of the half-continent where hitherto there has been only the framework of a political unity, but again the result is achieved by the creation of a specially privileged group who depend vitally upon the incitement and patronage of government. Most important of all, the development of these interlocking groups of railwaymen, manufacturers, and financiers serves to bring about not merely a closer national unity within the northern half of the continent, but a unity which is set off against the United States, which is based predominantly upon the St. Lawrence and its tributary routes, which is constructed for the purpose of consolidating this area against American penetration, of making it a closed preserve to be triumphantly exploited by Canadian business enterprise.

While, however, the economic process of expansion, consolidation, integration, and concentration went on steadily, the accompanying political process by which the diverse sections of public opinion were managed and manipulated towards the one supreme end was carried on only with great difficulty. It was Macdonald's genius in the arts of bargaining and conciliation that gave him his unquestioned position of leadership. Ontario and Quebec were constantly at odds over racial and religious issues. The outlying sections of the dominion were only slowly incorporated into any real union. "Seven years have elapsed since Confederation was accomplished," said the young idealists of the Canada First movement in 1874, "and to this day neither one nor the other of our old parties has established itself, as a party, in Nova Scotia, New Brunswick, Manitoba or British Columbia. Patronage and vituperation were equally inefficacious to give a lasting foothold to either party."[12] "Their politics were and perhaps still are 'better terms'."[13] A decade later when Goldwin Smith visited British Columbia *via* the new Canadian Pacific Railway, he reported with grim enjoyment that a citizen of the Pacific province, on being asked what his politics were, had replied "Government appropriations."[14] In fact "government appropriations" formed the basic element in the technique by which Macdonald kept the different sections of the dominion marching together in some semblance of order and by which he slowly constructed a united party out of diverse sectional groups.

Let me select but one incident in the long history of the Macdonald system, an incident which throws a vivid light on the inherent sectionalism of Canadian politics, on the kind of difficulties Macdonald had to meet, on his methods, and also on the dominant purpose which his whole system subserved.[15]

In 1884 the Macdonald system had reached its zenith. The old chieftain had lived down the disgrace of the Pacific Scandal, and the crisis of the Regina scaffold was not yet upon him. The National Policy had been established and the C.P.R. was being pushed rapidly across the continent. The country seemed at last about to reap the economic harvest which had been promised by Confederation. But the C.P.R. was in financial difficulties. In the winter of 1883-4, Stephen, Angus, McIntyre, Van Horne, and Abbott came up to Ottawa to interview Macdonald. They could raise no more money in the open market in London or New York, and if the government did not come to their help the company would have to go out of business. They proposed a temporary loan from the government of twenty-two and a half million dollars.

Macdonald saw them at his home, at Earnscliffe, late one evening, and rejected their proposal. He told them that they might as well look for the planet Jupiter. He wouldn't give them the money; if he did agree, the cabinet wouldn't follow him; and if the cabinet did agree it would smash the party.

They returned disconsolate to their lodgings where they met J. H. Pope, acting minister of railways during Tupper's absence as high commissioner in England. Pope went back to Earnscliffe, woke Macdonald up out of bed, and persuaded him to reverse his decision. "The day the Canadian Pacific busts," said John Henry Pope, who was famous for his homely language, "the Conservative party busts the day after." Next morning the C.P.R. delegation saw the cabinet, and Pope's arguments were again successful. But there still remained the party majority in the House. Tupper was brought back from England and he rammed the loan through caucus. In due course the resolutions and then the bill for the loan were introduced into Parliament.

Here difficulties arose. Macdonald was vitally dependent upon the large bloc of Bleu votes from Quebec and the French members saw their opportunity. The province of Quebec, like the C.P.R., was in financial difficulties. It had undertaken the construction of a north-shore line from Ottawa to Montreal to Quebec. At this critical moment the premier of Quebec arrived in Ottawa, and together with the French members of the dominion house he proceeded to hold the government up. They demanded that three million dollars be paid to Quebec by the dominion as a subsidy in assistance of the north-shore line on the ground that it was a work of national importance, and they announced that they would not vote for the C.P.R. loan until Macdonald came to terms. The C.P.R. debate began in the House and the seats of the Quebec members were ominously vacant. Macdonald sat with anxious face as the debate progressed from day to day, while agents negotiated for him with the recalcitrant Quebeckers in a committee room down the corridor. The debate went on, finally the last speech was delivered, Mr. Speaker called for a division, and still there were no Quebec members in the House. At the last moment, on the second division bell, they trooped in; the C.P.R. loan was carried, the C.P.R. was saved, the government was saved, and the unity of the Conservative party was saved—but the Quebeckers got their blackmail.[16] The members from the other provinces, who had been interested spectators at these manoeuvres, then demanded compensation also. Finally it was agreed that there should be a general levelling up all round of provincial subsidies.

On the whole incident and on its implications as to the nature of Canadian politics the comment of Goldwin Smith in the *Week* is very illuminating:

> Though the Government majority voted solid at last, a rift was distinctly seen in it, and through the rift a glimpse was caught into a troubled and chaotic future. Sir John Macdonald may be the Prince of Darkness; with some of its imps he is certainly far too familiar. But an angel of light would perhaps have not been so successful in holding together the motley and discordant elements, local, ethnological, religious, social and personal, on a combination of which the Dominion government has been based; or if he had, it would not have been without detriment to his seraphic purity. Not Cavour or Bismarck was more singularly fitted for his special task

than Sir John.... When this man is gone, who will there be to take his place? What shepherd is there who knows the sheep or whose voice the sheep know? Who else could make Orangemen vote for Papists, or induce half the members for Ontario to help in levying on their own Province the necessary blackmail for Quebec? Yet this is the work which will have to be done if a general break-up is to be averted. Things will not hold together of themselves.[17]

This is the excuse, if not the justification, of Sir John Macdonald. The task of his political life has been to hold together a set of elements, national, religious, sectional and personal, as motley as the component patches of any "crazy quilt," and actuated, each of them, by paramount regard for its own interest. This task he has so far accomplished by his consummate address, by his assiduous study of the weaker points of character, and where corruption was indispensable, by corruption. It is more than doubtful whether anybody could have done better than he has done.... By giving the public the full benefit of his tact, knowledge and strategy, he has probably done the work for us as cheaply as it was possible to do it. Let it be written on his tomb, that he held out for the country against the blackmailers till the second bell had rung.[18]

4

A study of the Alexander Mackenzie régime, 1873-8, the only period during which the Reformers were in office before Laurier, throws into relief the same characteristics which we have observed in the Macdonald system.

When Macdonald retired from office over the Pacific Scandal and the new Mackenzie government sought public support in a general election, the *Globe* proclaimed: "The poll tomorrow is the Thermopylae of Canadian political virtue" (28 January 1874), and it announced that the Macdonald system was at an end. "By sectional legislation, by tampering with individual members, by holding out threats and inducements in turn, they [the Conservatives] had utterly destroyed the *morale* of the first Parliament of the Dominion" (6 January 1874). "The Pacific Scandal shattered at one blow the fabric which Sir John Macdonald kept together by his skill in manipulation of individual interests, and the cohesive power of public plunder" (22 January 1874). "Appeal will henceforth be made not to warring interests but to a community of hopes, not to rival claims of battling representatives but to a national sentiment co-extensive with our wide domain" (10 January 1874).

Mackenzie, however, quickly discovered that the Thermopylae of Canadian virtue had not altered any of the essential conditions under which Canadian politics was carried on. The cabinet which he formed was as much a coalition of sectional groups as had been that of Macdonald in 1867. With the outlying sections of the dominion Mackenzie had constant trouble. His government was at odds with British Columbia continuously because he was unwilling to pay enough in railway concessions to win the support of the

Pacific coast politicians. With the Maritime Provinces he had similar difficulties. The Alexander Mackenzie letter-books in the Public Archives at Ottawa are full of letters from the prime minister in which he is trying to appease the appetite of his Maritime followers for spoils and to make them see that the new Intercolonial Railway must be run as a railway by technical experts and not as an employment agency for deserving Maritime Reformers. "It seems," he wrote on 27 July 1874, to Lord Dufferin, the governor-general, "that the smaller the province the more trouble it will be. Columbia, Manitoba, and Prince Edward Island give me more trouble than Ontario and Quebec." And about the same time, 18 November 1874, he bursts out to his Nova Scotia lieutenant, A. G. Jones of Halifax: "I am in receipt of your extraordinary letter about railway and other appointments, and I confess nothing has been written to me for months that has astonished me more. It is really too bad. Half my time is taken up with this question of patronage in Nova Scotia and Prince Edward Island. My life has become a torment to me about it."

Mackenzie, in fact, was too scrupulous and stiff-necked in his puritanism to make effective use of the technique by which alone a strong united party could be constructed in a country such as Canada. More important, he was not in sympathy with the intellectual atmosphere of the dominion capital. He was never at his ease with railway-contractors or concession-hunters or with any of that swarming tribe of adventurers who were eager to do their share in building up the new nation by being given a slice of its natural resources to exploit for their own profit. He remained hostile to the whole Hamiltonian tradition of an alliance between government and big business which Macdonald had established at Ottawa. He boggled over the expense of the Pacific railway. He failed to seize the opportunity of winning the manufacturers to the support of his party by giving them the protection which they were demanding with more and more insistence through the 1870s. As Goldwin Smith remarked, if his strong point as prime minister consisted in his having been a stone-mason, his weak point consisted in his being one still. No party equipped with such leadership and inspired by such ideals could compete successfully with the Hamiltonian forces gathered together by John A. Macdonald. Mackenzie's failure provides as clear a demonstration of the fundamental basis of Canadian party politics as does Macdonald's success.

5

It was left to Laurier to take up the work where Macdonald had laid it down. Many observers have remarked on the similarity between the two men and their methods, and it is true that under Laurier Canadian politics continued to consist of an intricate process of sectional bargaining and log-rolling just as under Macdonald, the necessary work of adjustment now being carried out under the auspices of the Liberal rather than of the Conservative party. But what is equally important to observe, and what has not so often been pointed out, is that it was a condition of Laurier's success that he should make of his party an instrument for the same Hamiltonian purposes which had been pursued by the Conservative party under Macdonald. So Laurier had a more difficult and subtle rôle to play, because he led a party in which the radical agrarian Grit tradition in Ontario and the radical anti-clerical Rouge tradition in Quebec were still strong. Under Laurier the old party of Brown and Mackenzie and Dorion had to combine Jeffersonian professions with Hamiltonian practices.

After his struggle with the hierarchy in 1896 Laurier quietly smothered what was left of Rougeism in his party, took over the old Bleu faction, and made his peace with the church. The appointment of Fielding rather than Cartwright to the ministry of finance was a sign that he was about to make his peace with the manufacturers also and accept the National Policy. He succeeded in doing this while at the same time keeping hold of his low-tariff agrarian followers by the most brilliant political coup in Canadian history, the invention of the British preference. This served also to help to wean his agricultural constituents from their dangerous habit—dangerous, that is, to Canadian capitalist interests—of looking southward for markets. Having made these preliminary adjustments, Laurier then proceeded to put his party in charge of the one really first-class boom which the country had enjoyed since 1867. In the rush of prosperity of the early 1900s sectional difficulties for the moment disappeared. At last Canada was a nation, for there was so much prosperity to distribute that every section could be satisfied and every individual could become a capitalist.

Incidentally Laurier built up for his party a railway and banking connection to offset the old alliance of the C.P.R. and the Bank of Montreal with the Conservatives. In his working partnership with the Grand Trunk-Mackenzie and Mann-Canadian Bank of Commerce interests he completed the Hamiltonian alignment of his party. The Laurier of the railway boom had come a long way from the Laurier of the 1877 speech on political liberalism— but he had brought his party all the way with him and had established its place in the essential Canadian tradition. "Consult the annals of Canada for the past fifty years at random," said a twentieth-century observer, "and whatever party may be in power, what do you find? The government is building a railway, buying a railway, selling a railway, or blocking a railway."[19]

At this point we reach the golden age in the evolution of the Canadian two-party system. Both parties were now completely national in the North American sense; that is, both appealed for support to all sections and classes of the nation and both preached the same policy—the continuous fostering of material prosperity through the incitement and patronage of government. The class differences which had been discernible between the original Liberal-Conservatives and the original Reformers in the 1850s had disappeared; class conflicts and sectional conflicts were now reconciled and settled within each party rather than as between the two parties. All that remained to distinguish the parties were the two old English names. Not even in the United States had the functioning of the North American two-party system achieved a greater degree of perfection than this.

And then suddenly in 1911 there broke out a storm which showed that all was not quite so harmonious as appeared on the surface. The reciprocity election of 1911 bears the same significance in Canadian political history as the election of 1896 in that of the United States. It marks the emergence of a movement of protest against the tightening grip of industrial plutocracy upon the national economy; and from that time on the murmurs of discontent have grown steadily louder. The old agrarian radicalism of the Upper Canada Grits was coming to life again in a fresh incarnation among the wheat farmers of the new West.

For the moment, however, the incipient revolt was ruthlessly and triumphantly crushed. When Laurier made the one serious mistake of his career and listened to the cry of the western farmers for American markets he was quickly repudiated by the governing classes of the country and of his own party. Merely to call the roll of the famous eighteen Toronto Liberals who deserted Laurier over reciprocity and brought about his defeat is to provide eloquent testimony of where the real issue of the election lay. The list begins with the head of the Canadian Bank of Commerce, includes two other financiers prominent in the Commerce group, three men high in the directorates of other banks, the legal adviser of Mackenzie and Mann, two managers of great insurance companies, several ex-presidents of the Toronto board of trade, and it concludes with the head of the largest department store in Canada.[20]

In 1911 Canadian capitalism celebrated its coming of age. The dream of the Montreal merchants of one hundred years before had at last come true. The northern commercial state was a reality. Slowly, in spite of many discouragements and setbacks, it had been built up, and now its trade flowed in and out by the St. Lawrence, "the River of Canada." Its three and a half million square miles [5.6 km^2] were well organized under the direction and control of Montreal. Toronto capitalists, who at times had shown some inclination to challenge the position of the senior metropolis, were now working hand in hand with it. And on 21 September 1911, the Canadian people put behind them the temptation to break the economic bonds by which they had been welded into a nation, affirming their determination to remain loyal subjects of St. James and King streets.

Yet perhaps the discerning observer might have felt some reason for uneasiness at the very moment of this triumph. Perhaps the agrarian revolt of 1911 was the first sign that there was developing within the Canadian economy, as in that of the United States, a deeper cleavage of interests, another irrepressible conflict which could not be avoided or adjourned indefinitely by the happy process of geographical expansion. Perhaps the unrest which has shown itself in the Progressive movement of the 1920s, and in the C.C.F. and other movements of political protest in the 1930s has pointed in the same direction. Perhaps the more intense strains and stresses which seem likely to test the social structure in the second generation of the twentieth century will make the old Macdonald-Laurier two-party system no longer adequate. It grew up as a free-and-easy opportunistic adaptation to the sectional divisions of a continental area. It worked well enough in an expanding capitalist economy. But the age of the frontier is passing away, and the sectional divisions of North America tend to be transformed into the European class divisions of the "haves" and the "have-nots." Will the party system also be transformed? Or will Canadians still cling to the orthodox faith, in which idealist academic students and cynical practical politicians find a curious bond of union, and maintain that the North American two-party system has still a long life ahead of it, that age cannot wither it nor custom stale its infinite variety?

NOTES

1. The *Federalist*, no. X.

2. W. L. Mackenzie King, *Liberalism, the Principle of the Future: An Address* (published as a pamphlet, n.d.).

3. *Parliamentary Debates on the Subject of the Confederation of the British North American Provinces* (Quebec, 1865), 61.

4. Joseph Tassé, *Discours de Sir Georges Cartier, Baronnet, accompagnés de notices* (Montréal, 1893), 7.

5. John Boyd, *Sir George Étienne Cartier, Bart.: His Life and Times* (Toronto, 1914), 161.

6. Ibid., 165.

7. Ibid., 167.

8. Galt had gone into politics in 1849 in order to advance the interests of the British American Land Company of which he was the Canadian manager. Explaining his action to the directors in London, he wrote: "I consider the interests of the Company and of the country to be identical.... I ought perhaps to add that I am not the least likely to become a political partisan; my views are all for objects of material advantage" (see O. D. Skelton, *The Life and Times of Sir Alexander Tilloch Galt*, Toronto, 1920, 143). Here speaks the perfect "moderate."

9. A. T. Galt, *Speech on the Proposed Union of the British North American Provinces, Delivered at Sherbrooke, C.E., 23 November 1864* (Montreal, 1864).

10. 2 Nov. 1859.

11. Sir J. Pope, ed., *Confederation, Being a Series of Hitherto Unpublished Documents Bearing on the British North America Act* (Toronto, 1895), 58.

12. *Canada First: A Memorial of the Late William A. Foster, Q.C.* (Toronto, 1890), 55.

13. Ibid., 59.

14. Goldwin Smith, *Canada and the Canadian Question* (London, 1891), 220.

15. This account of the proceedings concerning the C.P.R. loan of 1884 is based upon O. D. Skelton, *Life and Letters of Sir Wilfrid Laurier* (Toronto, 1921), Ch. vi, and the columns of the *Week* for the early part of 1884.

16. It was not only fastidious persons like Goldwin Smith who referred to this process as blackmail. Next year the C.P.R. came back for a further loan of five million dollars.

    Macdonald writes to Tupper on this occasion (17 March 1885): "The C.P.R. will make its appeal for relief this week. I don't know how Council or Parliament will take it.... Our difficulties are immense. The Quebec M.P.s have the line to Quebec up again. The Maritimes are clamorous for the short line, and we have blackmailing all round. How it will end God knows, but I wish I were well out of it" (see E. M. Saunders, *The Life and Letters of the Rt. Hon. Sir Charles Tupper*, London, 1916, II, 47).

17. The *Week*, 28 Feb. 1884.

18. Ibid., 10 April 1884.

19. Quoted in O. D. Skelton, *Life and Letters of Sir Wilfrid Laurier,* I, 244.

20. The names of the eighteen Liberals and the text of their manifesto against reciprocity may be found in the *Canadian Annual Review,* 1911, 49.

CHAPLEAU AND THE CONSERVATIVE PARTY IN QUEBEC

BY H. BLAIR NEATBY AND JOHN T. SAYWELL

o

Until the 1890s Quebec was considered a Conservative province; since the 1890s it has been a Liberal stronghold. This transfer of political allegiance has long been recognized as one of the most significant developments in Canadian political history. And yet historians have never satisfactorily explained why the change occurred. Possibly Canadians have been too concerned with national parties and national leaders, and so have concentrated on Laurier's assumption of national leadership and his policy as a national figure. It is apparently assumed that French-Canadian voters deserted the Conservatives in 1896 because Laurier was a French Canadian, although he had become leader of the national party in 1887; or because Louis Riel was hanged, although the execution took place in 1885. In concentrating on Laurier's victory, the role of regional and provincial leaders and the interaction of provincial and national politics has been overlooked or drastically simplified.

In 1896 the Conservatives lost Quebec. They lost Quebec because the party was divided and leaderless as it had seldom been before, at a time when both unity and leadership were essential. Chapleau might have provided the leadership and saved Quebec for the party in 1896 as he had done in the past, but he made no effort to do so. A study of Chapleau's career gives some insight into the complexities of Canadian politics, and also provides a partial explanation for the transition from the Macdonald era to the Laurier era in Canada.

H. Blair Neatby and J. Saywell, "Chapleau and the Conservative Party in Quebec," *Canadian Historical Review* (March 1956), pp. 1-22. Toronto: University of Toronto Press Incorporated. Reprinted by permission of University of Toronto Press Incorporated.

The *débâcle* of the Conservative party in 1896 might be said to have its origins in 1871 with the publication of the *Programme catholique*. This political manifesto signified the formation of an ultra-Catholic lay party corresponding to the ultramontane faction within the church. Weak in numbers but influential because of its leadership and its rigid principles, this group maintained that politics must have a firm religious and moral basis and that "la separation de l'Église et de l'État est une doctrine absurde et impie." The group—soon to be labelled the Castors—became the right wing of the Conservative party, but as the *Programme* stated, it was not concerned with party loyalty in the political sense:

> C'est assez dire que par *le parti conservateur* nous n'entendons pas toute réunion d'hommes n'ayant d'autre lien que celui de l'intérêt et de l'ambition personelle, mais un group d'hommes professant sincèrement les mêmes principes de religion et de nationalité, conservant dans leur integrité les traditions du vieux parti conservateur, qui se résument dans une attachement inviolable aux doctrines catholiques et dans un dévouement absolu aux intérêts nationaux du Bas-Canada.[1]

This was hardly a definition of the Cartier-Macdonald Conservatives, and it is significant that the *Programmistes* were an important factor in Cartier's defeat in 1872.

Cartier's Conservatism was more comprehensive. He was certainly willing to accept clerical assistance but not to submit to clerical domination, and while willing to uphold the legitimate interests of the church he tended to emphasize material progress. Although staunchly nationalistic and concerned with French-Canadian interests, as all Quebec leaders must be, he sought a compromise between English and French, Protestant and Catholic. Perhaps Cartier could in time have averted the danger of an ultra-Catholic faction in the party, but his death in 1873 left no one who could. The *Programmistes* became a virtually autonomous faction within the party, seeking its own ends and following its own leaders. His death also intensified the regional and personal rivalries that had long existed but which had never got out of hand. After 1873 too there was no Quebec Conservative who alone spoke for his province in Ottawa. Would a new leader arise? If so, would he be of *l'école de Cartier* or would he be a Castor? On the answers to these questions hung the political future of Quebec.

Although only thirty-three when Cartier died, Joseph Adolphe Chapleau was one of the many to seek the succession to Cartier as the political "boss" of Quebec and the leader of a united party in the federal field. The son of a stone mason, Chapleau was a liberal Conservative, even feeling free on one occasion to inform Laurier that "tu es moins démocrate que moi."[2] His close association with the family of L. F. R. Masson, *le grand seigneur de Terrebonne,* whose protégé he was, served to offset his humble origins and democratic leanings. Although Chapleau derived political support from the labouring population throughout his career, he was still at home with big business and finance capital which, like Cartier, he was willing to have associated with him in the work of government. Like Cartier, he was a firm believer in the value to Quebec of material progress, and his interest in the development of Montreal made him acutely aware of the need to develop the Canadian economy. Thus in 1867, at the outset of his career, he had become "an active and loyal advocate of Confederation" and later boasted that he "was almost alone, amongst those of my generation, who escaped the contagion of the 'mouvement national' which then broke out, (as it does periodically in our too sensitive Province)."[3] But, again like Cartier, Chapleau was also conscious of sectional interests. Concerned with the role of French Canada in national politics, he believed that the interests of the minority could only be protected in a predominantly Anglo-Saxon and Protestant federation by uniting the French Canadians in one political party under one regional leader. Because of his political philosophy Chapleau had become a loyal lieutenant of Cartier; on Cartier's death he was a prominent contender for the succession.

His natural endowments made his political success even more probable. Indeed, a political opponent admitted as early as 1874 that "comme talent naturel, Chapleau est, peut-être, l'orateur le mieux donné que le Bas-Canada a produit."[4] His facility for the right metaphor, his brilliant and often sarcastic wit, his emotional intensity, and a powerful but pleasing voice, made each of his public appearances a momentous occasion. Few men dared to face him in the *assemblées contradictoires* then so loved in Quebec. His oratorical style was more suited to the hustings than to a legislative assembly, it is true, for he persuaded by passion rather than by logic, but this was no handicap to a man who sought political power. For twenty years, until his death in 1898, Chapleau was the most popular and perhaps the most powerful Conservative in Quebec. His political career in many ways is simply a struggle to have this primitive power recognized and rewarded by due influence in party councils.

Chapleau first entered the provincial Cabinet in 1873, but when the Government was reorganized by the *Programmiste* Charles Boucher de Boucherville in the following year he was not included. Too strong and able a man to be excluded from any Conservative administration for long, he was asked to enter a little more than a year later. It was an uneasy coalition between the ultramontanes and Chapleau, made possible by the agreement upon the necessity of building the North Shore Railway, and made necessary because Chapleau's assistance was needed to pass the measure. But it soon became apparent that the agreement on policy was superficial. While Chapleau regarded the railway as a means of economic development, the de Boucherville faction saw it as an agency of colonization which would further the interests of the French-Canadian race and religion.[5] If ever economic and religious interests conflicted, the coalition would be shattered.

Meanwhile, Chapleau was consolidating his position. He was already regarded as the leader, in the Cartier tradition, of the moderate Conservatives who were restless under the leadership of the extreme *bleus*. Stimulated perhaps by his growing popularity and sense of personal power, Chapleau even contemplated a new coalition which would eliminate the ultramontanes. In 1879 he held out the olive branch to the moderate Liberals.

Such a coalition would have meant a truly Liberal-Conservative party, isolating both the extreme *rouges* and the ultramontanes. This first hesitant overture came to nothing, although it meant that Chapleau "a profondément scandalisé un groupe important du parti conservateur" since to the ultramontanes all Liberals were anti-clerical *rouges*.[6] But henceforth talk of coalition was always in the air. Unable to bring it about under his leadership, yet unwilling to tolerate the Castors, Chapleau was paving the way for the assimilation by the Liberals of *l'école de Cartier*, or *l'école de Chapleau* as it was often known, under the leadership of Wilfrid Laurier.

The political confusion in Quebec in the next few years brought Chapleau to power. Party leaders took advantage of Lieutenant-Governor Letellier's *coup d'état* of 1878 to send de Boucherville to the Senate. Chapleau accepted the post of party leader following Macdonald's promise to remove Letellier and to support Chapleau in his provincial railway policy.[7] Letellier was dismissed in 1879 and with the assistance of his successor Robitaille, the Conservatives returned to power. Chapleau seemed to have Quebec under control; all that remained was to move into federal politics and assume the mantle of Cartier. Within a year, Macdonald asked him to enter the federal Cabinet.

But before Chapleau could leave Quebec he had to consolidate his position, for his strength in Ottawa would be directly proportional to his strength in Quebec. Two closely related problems remained to be solved: the first was to rid the province of its white elephant, the North Shore railway; the second was to crush the *Programmistes*. Through Macdonald's influence the Canadian Pacific purchased the Ottawa-Montreal section of the railway and made it part of the transcontinental, while the Montreal-Quebec section was purchased by a syndicate headed by L. A. Sénécal, to whom Chapleau had confided the administration of the road before its sale. As Sénécal was a close friend and political associate of Chapleau, and presumably his financial adviser and supporter, the sale was widely believed to have been more in the interests of Sénécal than of the province. Moreover, this sad materialistic fate of the railway was particularly obnoxious to the ultramontanes, who had regarded it as a colonization road which would consolidate the French-Canadian race and the Roman Catholic religion in the province. Thus the sale of the railway divided the two Conservative factions on the issues of political morality and religion. The rupture in the party was complete.

Chapleau had long realized that the uneasy truce with the ultramontanes would sooner or later end in open conflict and he knew that only if his opponents were impotent would his position be secure. He wrote to Macdonald:

> Since the day I received your letter asking me to arrange affairs in Quebec so as to be ready to be sworn in without delay, I have been at work to prepare my departure from here. I have not yet succeeded in putting things into shape, and I am sorry to say that I cannot go at the present moment....

There are two classes of men here into the hands of whom I cannot allow the power to fall: the ignorant set which, with a few exceptions, composed the majority of the preceding government, and the contemptible *clique* of enviers, who are hiding their venality under the cloak of religion and conservatism. The latter have of late been defiant, calculating upon my early disappearance. They are decided to impose themselves into the reorganization of the government or they will force a dissolution. I want time to reduce them to complete submission or to break this parliament upon their heads and crush them for a long time.[8]

Apparently unable to reduce the ultramontanes to "complete submission," Chapleau called an election. His platform discussed only commerce and finance, railways and bridges.[9] This emphasis could not help but disturb those members of the party who sought a State subordinate to the Church, on the grounds that "L'État dépendant de l'Église sera soumis à Dieu."[10] But Chapleau's personal dominance seemed established by an overwhelming victory in the election. From this new position of strength he again took up the plan of a provincial coalition which would drive the Castors from the party or neutralize them if they wished to remain. It is not clear whether Chapleau initiated the *pourparlers*, but his friend Arthur Dansereau was an active participant in them. To Dansereau he wrote on 16 October 1881: "Maintenant, tu me dis que XZ et quelques autres veulent absolument de la coalition, qu'ils m'accepteraient comme chef, avec le programme que j'ai posé. Cela ne me surprend pas; nous ne différons, les chefs libéraux et moi, que sur une couple de points...nous sommes tous protectionnistes, et le pays est avec nous. Nous nous entendons sur l'opportunité de vendre le chemin de fer un bon prix."[11] The discussions ended when it became clear that neither Chapleau nor Mercier could persuade the bulk of his followers that a coalition was essential or desirable at that moment.

By the summer of 1882 Chapleau felt sufficiently secure to leave Quebec for Ottawa. From the federal Cabinet came J. A. Mousseau, a man of mediocre ability, who was to be Chapleau's puppet in Quebec City. "Few men have had such an opportunity of taking the leadership of a party, with such a majority and such a well disciplined House," boasted Chapleau to Macdonald.[12] In fact Chapleau had underestimated the tenacity and determination of the ultramontanes. His departure occasioned a venomous personal attack upon him and gave new life to his opponents, to whom Mousseau could offer only a fitful resistance.

The open war began in August, 1882, with the publication of a pamphlet, *Le Parti, le Pays et le Grand Homme,* by "Castor."[13] Reference was first made to Chapleau's repeated promises to remain in Quebec until the province had achieved material prosperity. "Suivant *la Minerve,* le gouvernement fédéral faisait regulièrement, tous les trois mois, un siège en règle autour de M. Chapleau pour le prendre d'assaut et l'emporter de force à Outaouais. Mais M. Chapleau, plus fort qu'Ulysse, résistait héroïquement à cette sirène enchanteresse que l'on appelle 'Sir John'."[14] Seventeen times Chapleau had refused the call, each time basing his decision on "raison d'État" and the interests of his province, yet his patriotism always seemed to coincide with his personal ambition. And so "on affirmait déjà le nouveau principe: le grand homme d'abord; le parti ensuite, et le pays...quand les intérêts du grand homme le permettraient."[15] Castor's dislike of Chapleau is evident on every page:

> Non pas que l'hostilité de M. Chapleau pour les ultramontains procède des principes raisonnés, adverses à cette école: il les hait d'abord par instinct, ensuite à cause de son ignorance absolue de toutes les questions religieuses et sociales, enfin et surtout, *parce qu'il n'en est pas*. Ses goûts bohèmes et ses tendances boulevardières l'ont éloigné des ultramontains qui, de leur côté, n'ont pas songé à lui faire une douce violence et à lui ouvrir leurs portes à la façon dont on reçoit les heros.[16]

Chapleau was thus an unprincipled renegade whose sole ambition Castor correctly surmised, was to unite Quebec under his leadership. But in the province were two opposed principles, "le principe conservateur catholique et le principe libéral plus ou moins anti-catholique. Pas d'union donc sans la destruction de l'un de ces deux principes."[17] Since Chapleau was not a true Catholic Conservative, that is, an ultramontane, he must be a liberal; and so "Guerre implacable! guerre à mort! guerre sans trève! guerre sans merci! *Delenda est Carthago*."[18]

War to the death it was to be, both in Ottawa and in Quebec City. In Ottawa Chapleau found the same elements opposing him, principally in the person of Sir Hector Langevin, the doyen of the French-Canadian Conservatives. Langevin was not truly an ultramontane, yet through his association with the hierarchy he had come to be recognized as the Castor spokesman in the Cabinet. Moreover, the two men personified the age-old rivalry between Montreal and Quebec. And since Chapleau openly sought Langevin's position of primacy, the older man naturally resented the audacious intruder and envied his immense popularity. Sir Adolphe Caron too, who was closely associated with the Castors, lacked sympathy for the *parvenu* and, with Langevin, had been working against Chapleau in Quebec for some time.[19] Laurier, who had begun to despair of Liberal prospects, saw a glimmer of hope and acutely analyzed the situation for Edward Blake:

> ...there is just another thing which is possible: it is a split amongst the Conservatives. Already there is an intense hatred between some of the members of the party. The party is at present divided into two sections: the Chapleau section & the Langevin section. Langevin rather hates Chapleau: at all events is both jealous & afraid of him. Chapleau hates or loves nothing. He is a clever, able & designing fellow. He & Langevin would not sit in the same cabinet but for the presence of Sir John A. Macdonald. Let Sir John disappear, & immediately there is a split, & either the one or the other, if not both

will go to you. Sir John living it is probable that these conflicting elements will remain united though a mere trifle might bring a rupture, for some of Langevin's followers, such as Tarte, have sworn eternal war to Chapleau. It is more likely still, that Chapleau will remain quiet, courting Langevin, biding his time, & will endeavour gradually to work his way to the leadership. His policy will be to be able at some time to give himself as the head of the Quebec deputation, & to make himself indispensable to the other provinces, I mean the Conservatives of the other provinces.[20]

Chapleau could maintain his position at Ottawa, but within a year the Castors had forced Mousseau to the wall and Chapleau was forced to go to his assistance. He first attempted to reorganize the provincial Cabinet by bringing in two moderate ultramontanes, J. J. Ross and L. O. Taillon, and so split the Castor wing.[21] But Mousseau completely bungled the negotiations.[22] The Premier's position was further weakened when he was convicted of election irregularities and was forced to re-contest his seat in the Assembly. Opposing him was a Castor who could boast of Liberal support! To Chapleau this opposition, supported, it would seem, by Langevin and Caron,[23] was an "insurrection," and at an *assemblée contradictoire* at St. Laurent he launched an attack against the Castors:

> Leur parti comprend toutes les médiocrités ambitieuses qui ne peuvent arriver par les voies ordinaires, tous les désappointées, et un bon nombre d'hypocrites qui se prétendent religieux et conservateurs, pour mieux détruire chez le peuple le vrai sentiment religieux, dont la base fondamentale est le respect à l'autorité et l'amour du prochain. Ils n'ont du reste qu'un trait de resemblance avec le vrai Castor. Ils font leur ouvrage avec de la boue, ils détruisent les chaussées des bons moulins pour construire leurs tanières et ne sont vraiment utiles que lorsqu'on vend leur peau.[24]

With Chapleau's support Mousseau won his election, but even Chapleau's guidance could not make the Premier a successful party leader. Once again there were rumours of a coalition to drive out the Castors; as usual nothing came of them, and Mousseau was soon forced to resign.

By 1885 Chapleau's ambitions had been checked. The dream of succeeding Cartier, of being master of Quebec and leader of a solid Quebec bloc at Ottawa, seemed to have vanished. Then came a crisis, and with it an opportunity which if seized might have altered the course of Canadian history. Quebec was united as never before in opposition to the proposed hanging of Louis Riel. The Macdonald Cabinet, Langevin and Caron included, had agreed on execution. The man who refused could be the leader of Quebec. Honoré Mercier saw the possibilities and realized Chapleau's opportunity; he himself could never gain the support of the bulk of the Conservatives on any issue, but Chapleau could take both parties with him. In what he regarded as the interests of the French-Canadian minority, Mercier even offered to insure success by accepting Chapleau as leader of a *parti-national*.[25]

Tempted, disillusioned and disappointed perhaps, Chapleau wavered. The fateful decision was made on the night of 11 November 1885, when, accompanied by Tarte, Dansereau, and Lacoste, he was on his way to a crucial meeting of the Cabinet in Ottawa. Fortunately the documents speak for themselves. According to Tarte:

> Nous passâmes la nuit à discuter, à feuilleter l'histoire, à peser les pour et les contre. Les opinions étaient divisées. Nous laissâmes M. Chapleau juge.... Nous nous mîmes au lit à quatre heures du matin. Au déjeuner de huit heures, M. Chapleau, qui n'avait pas dormi, nous annonça qu'il en était venu à la résolution de ne pas démissioner: il nous donna ses raisons avec une grande force et une grande clarté. "Nous sommes dans la fosse aux lions," ajoute-t-il.[26]

Shortly after having finished his breakfast, Chapleau wrote to a very close friend:

> I have just thrown the lot in Riel's affair. In spite of all and many temptations, I have decided to uphold the law and the Crown. I may be sent home for my courage at the next electoral contest. I prefer staying at home with sense than to become a *mob-being* with sensation. I don't care about having the many with me, if I have the good testimony of my intelligence and conscience.
>
> Tomorrow the storm will rage; I rely upon sunshine at another date.
>
> I had thought of yielding to the temptation. There was more than one reason for it. I had so many personal spites to satisfy. I have pocketed all that and I have done what I thought was my duty. And if I succumb I shall retire without grumbling, taking my retreat with dignity. "Peace with honor."[27]

He then informed Macdonald of his decision:

> I have spent the greater part of the night in preparing my memorandum in support of my disagreement in the Riel case. Just as I was sending it in this morning I hesitated in the face of the terrible responsibility of an agitation on such a question where national animosities would surely meet to fight their battle. And after long meditation I have decided not to incur that great responsibility.[28]

Ten days later—after the execution of Riel—came the most dramatized version of all:

> The world is full of unexplainable wonders. Present *chaos* in our Province is a terrible evidence of the proposition. The savants have not yet found what electric(ity) is; they know it is a force & they use it, but where does it come from, where does it go? Mystery.
>
> An electric current is running through Quebec, the force of which is not known even to those using it. (It may burn some who are

abusing of it). It was generated in the sli(p) of a rope on the scaffold at Regina & it will end...where? If I was told: "on another scaffold at this end of the Dominion land" I would not feel incredulous.

On the night of the 11th instant (the first night I spent sleepless since the 29th of October/79)[29] I felt the rising of the magnetic wave which has since carried everything before it in Quebec. At the dawn of the day on the 12th I had decided to give up the seat I had in the Cabinet and follow the current, but suddenly I glanced in front of me, in the distance such a sight, tumult, fighting, bloodshed, misery and prostration; and a madman looking from the window of a prison and laughing, rubbing his hands and shouting incoherent words of malediction. I was horrified. I then read over my report & the conclusions, which amount to a resignation with the assumption of the popular movement, and before I could sign it, my resolve was changed & I wrote to Sir John asking him to inform His Excellency that I was giving my assent to the decision of my colleagues on the question of the execution of Riel.[30]

And so Chapleau showed himself to be more than a self-seeking politician. It must have been difficult for a man of his ambition to reject the opportunity to unite Quebec, and also for a man of his temperament to reject the role of tribune. But he realized that a racial struggle in Canada would be disastrous for French Canadians, and his personal desires were suppressed by a sense of responsibility for his compatriots.

The common front thus presented against the nationalistic movement in Quebec proved to be temporary, and the old bickering continued. Fully aware of the real meaning of the role he had played, Chapleau openly attacked Langevin's position as *primus inter pares* in the Quebec delegation by demanding full control of the large and important political region of Montreal. After the provincial election of October, 1886, when Mercier and the Nationalist Conservatives (some Castors under a new name) defeated the Ross Government, Chapleau became more insistent: "the absolute ruling must be centered in one hand, in my hand, for the political region of Montreal."[31] Threatened with Chapleau's resignation just before the critical election of February, 1887, Macdonald was forced to give way and consent to the division of political authority in Quebec.[32] Another stage had been reached.

Chapleau was in many ways the only defence the Conservatives had against Mercier. Proof of that could be found in the results of the 1887 federal election in which, although the Conservatives lost fifteen seats in Quebec, only three of them were in the district of Montreal, where Chapleau had conducted the campaign. Convinced that he had saved the party in Quebec by his efforts and his great ability, Chapleau sought his reward and recognition:

Il me fallait une affirmation hardie du pouvoir que je revendiquais dans la region que je devais et que je voulais conduire. Je l'ai choisie aussi éclatante que possible, dans deux spheres élèvées et distinctes au Senat et sur le Banc. On a compris et on a suivi. Jamais dictature n'a été plus généralement accueillie que la mienne, durant la campagne électorale. J'ai dû, il est vrai, me faire tout à tous pour soutenir la position que j'avais prise. Je l'ai fait, j'ai réussi.[33]

In a gesture calculated to humiliate his rivals, Chapleau recommended for the senatorship none other than the infamous Sénécal, the *bête noire* of the Castors.

Finding the two-horse team difficult to handle—the hands on the reins were not as supple as they once had been—Macdonald sought to end the rivalry by sending Langevin to an honourable exile in Spencer Wood, the luxurious residence of the lieutenant-governors of Quebec.[34] If Chapleau had not won, it was at least evident that his rival was losing. Langevin's prestige had been declining ever since 1885, and only the final blow was needed. Tarte, who later delivered the blow, informed Caron that "Sir Hector a fait son temps: il est d'une incroyable impopularité; je le regrette, mais il a si mal manoeuvré sur l'affaire Riel qu'il est devenu absolument impossible."[35] But Langevin refused the offer and Macdonald, anxious to see peace in his time, turned to Chapleau. "Voyant qu'il n'y a pas moyen que Langevin & lui restent plus longtemps dans le Cabinet sans en venir à une rupture éclatante." Chapleau wavered again.[36] Could he ever achieve his end or had the time come for a fresh start? He decided to resign and his decision was only changed as the result of pressure from his supporters and from the followers of Caron, who now regarded him as the strongest figure in Quebec. Tarte predicted "le désastre au lendemain de la retraite de Chapleau,"[37] while T. C. Casgrain was even more explicit in a letter to Caron:

> Si Chapleau était nommé Gouverneur, Sir Hector aurait le champ libre & votre position serait bien précaire. Voici une excellente occasion de donner à Sir Hector la récompense qu'il mérite. Vous êtes jeune, Chapleau aussi; à vois deux, avec vos amis, vous pouvez certainement mener la barque. Il y a longtemps que je vous conseille de faire alliance avec Chapleau & si vous l'avez faite je vous en félicité. Si Sir John se retire après la session, comme tout le monde le croit, Sir Charles pourra être appelé à former un ministère. Mais si Sir Hector reste, il insistera, je suppose, à être appelé. Bien je vous le demande, pourra-t-il former un Cabinet assez fort dans les circon-stances pour gouverner? Gardera-t-il l'appui des nationaux? Je suis certain que non. Sir Charles entrera-t-il sous lui? Chapleau servira-t-il sous lui? Enfin Sir Hector est-il capable de gouverner la Province de Quebec? Jamais de la vie.[38]

Chapleau's Montreal friends insisted that he remain in Ottawa and consolidate "the good work of the last electoral campaign." "If I tell you that my departure might cause some disorder in our political world," he wrote to Macdonald, "I do not wish to allude to my personal merits or preferences, but to the unfortunate crisis which the Province of Quebec is just after traversing and which is not quite yet annihilated although it has been overpowered." Nonetheless if the Prime Minister's offer was to be taken as an order, Chapleau was willing to go to Spencer Wood, but only on condition that he was relieved "from all the political consequences which may result therefrom."[39] Macdonald was in no position to push either of his Quebec colleagues from the Cabinet; both men stayed and the rivalry continued.

As restless and independent in Macdonald's Cabinet as he had been a decade before in de Boucherville's, Chapleau alone seems to have realized that the situation in Quebec made sweeping changes imperative. Mercier's overwhelming victory in the provincial election of 1890 was proof enough of that. Although he regarded the position of the party as "hopeless" because the party organization was "radically vicious" and there was no "political authority in our province in Federal matters," he undertook once again to strengthen the party. But he did so only on the understanding that he was to be given "entire liberty of action":

> ...not an apparent and only "for courtesy" liberty, but a thorough and practical freedom in the choice of the means which I think best to secure success. I know my fellow countrymen well enough to allow nobody's judgment to supersede mine in the direction to be given for an electoral battle. Machiavelism [*sic*] if needed, should be allowed to fight men who publicly profess to surrender our birthrights to a foreign power and *lettres de marque* should be obtained against the pirates who have seized the ship of State in our Province.[40]

Four months later, on the eve of the federal election, believing his work had been "more or less neutralized" by "intriguers, leeches and parasites," Chapleau had almost given up hope for the Conservative party:

> I may remain to see it crumble down, or I may step aside leaving the responsibility of its fall to others. I speak of course of Quebec only, but remember this: Quebec has been made the pivot of the representation of the other Provinces in Parliament, it may also prove to be the pivot of the party forces in the next Parliament. If I were Prime Minister, I would hesitate before risking the battle if Quebec is dismantled.[41]

Sir John Thompson and Mackenzie Bowell should have marked well those words.

The new Machiavellianism probably included Tarte's revelations of the Langevin-McGreevy scandals. The time had come perhaps for the headsman to wield his axe. Even Macdonald, who remained faithful to Langevin to the end, was forced to admit that his colleague was "inert and useless except in office, but he doesn't move much in Quebec politics."[42] Long before 1890 Tarte had deserted his former employer, taking all his accumulated secrets with him, and with that awareness of political realities which was soon to lead him into the Liberal party, had become intimate with Chapleau and Dansereau. His determined attack on Langevin and his boast that he would "chase him from public life" should be regarded as another episode in the Chapleau-Langevin feud, for it is impossible to believe that Chapleau was not a party to it.[43] Sir Charles Tupper, back from London to assist his colleagues in the election of 1891, realized that Tarte held a bombshell which, if allowed to explode, might destroy the Government. Would Tarte be satisfied if Langevin was sent to Spencer Wood? Tarte said he would.[44] Macdonald wrote to Angers, then Lieutenant-Governor of Quebec, and asked him to enter the federal Cabinet. There was no need for Angers to be told that Langevin was to be exiled:

> On reading your letter, I have naturally conjectured who was to retire. I look upon Mr. Chapleau and Sir Adolphe Caron as indispensable, for reasons which you yourself can better appreciate. True, Caron has been, for the last year, a little frivolous, but I am sure a friendly warning would bring him back in vias rectas, and if he had his coudées franches & was not hampered by the nefarious influence of McGreevy acting through Sir Hector you could not have a more active and popular colleague in this district....
>
> Starting from there, I conclude that Sir Hector is likely to withdraw, of course assumably for reasons of health....
>
> Now I must go further, as if we were conversing together although such things put in writing appear harsh: I well know the influence that carries the long career of Sir Hector by your side, and the sympathy which you naturally feel for him in his critical position. But sentiment cannot be your only guide in the saving of your policy and in the continuation of the prosperity of the Dominion. Millions of dollars have been invested on the faith of your protective tariff.
>
> If Sir Hector, although often warned, has wittingly lessened his usefulness, he has to blame himself alone. And he can expect an acknowledgement for his rendered services only in proper time, and without compromising the Ministry. His state of health must be the reason of his withdrawal and care must be taken that the public have no pretext to say that he goes as a fugitive from justice, by his accepting immediately another office elsewhere.[45]

Angers refused to enter the Cabinet although he willingly placed his office at Macdonald's disposal. But the planned deception, futile as it unquestionably would have been, of the exchange of a young and healthy for an old and tired politician was no longer possible. Nor did Langevin like the idea. The federal election and the death of Macdonald postponed Langevin's fall, but the irrepressible Tarte forced his resignation in August, 1891.

It seemed that Chapleau had won, and yet within a year it was Chapleau who resided in Spencer Wood. Owing to the nature of the evidence it is impossible to state precisely why this eclipse occurred, although the general picture is clear. After Langevin's retirement Chapleau alone could be regarded as the leader of Quebec. The provincial Premier, once again de Boucherville, was an unsympathetic partner, it is true, and would never be Chapleau's puppet as Mousseau had been, but his tenure need not be permanent. Anticipating Langevin's resignation, Chapleau had strongly pushed Thompson as Macdonald's successor in June, 1891,[46] not, as is commonly supposed, because Thompson was a Roman Catholic, but because the position he desired in the hierarchy could not be achieved—because of the complicated provincial and regional balances within the federal Cabinet—with Abbott as Prime Minister. Confronted with Thompson's adamant refusal, Chapleau "caved in and accepted the shilling."[47] Like most Canadians, however, Chapleau and his followers regarded the Abbott Administration as a temporary measure. A new and lasting structure was to rest on three firm pillars: Thompson as Prime Minister, Chapleau as leader of Quebec, and "X" an Ontario Protestant.[48]

Meanwhile, to assert himself and to establish his position, Chapleau claimed the Department of Railways and Canals, left vacant by Macdonald's death. Reconstruction was delayed until after the session of 1891 when Abbott, again foiling Chapleau, gave the department to J. G. Haggart. For a time Chapleau's resignation appeared certain. Dissatisfaction in Quebec was increased by the rumour that W. R. Meredith, the Ontario Conservative leader who had frequently spoken disparagingly of the Roman Catholics and was known to be opposed to separate schools, would enter the Cabinet. Abbott had ventured on very dangerous ground as Meredith himself realized:

> I fancy that Abbott's stand in the Chapleau matter will strengthen him and his government in Ontario though if Chapleau goes out and I should go in a big race and religion cry will be raised. If Chapleau means mischief he is playing his cards well by seeking to turn the issue into a fight between the French Conservatives and the Ontario "Orangistes." He could only make a fiasco if the break were made because he did not get the Railway Department while on the other issue he could pose as a champion of French-Canadian rights and probably carry his people with him.[49]

Chapleau was not "posing" as a champion of French Canadian rights—he was sincere. Since he was the representative of French Canadians in the Cabinet, the Railway portfolio would be a recognition of French-Canadian influence at Ottawa as well as a recognition of Chapleau's personal prestige. To Chapleau there could be no distinction between the two. In any case Chapleau accepted a lesser place, the Department of Customs, but with ill-concealed annoyance. From this moment dates his gradual defection from the Conservative party; and from this moment, until the victory of Laurier, Quebec was without an effective leader in Ottawa.[50]

In time Chapleau's grievance might have been overcome, particularly as Thompson's accession came closer. A problem that Macdonald, the great conciliator, had left unsolved made the rupture complete. For a number of reasons Macdonald had refused to take any action on the Manitoba legislation of 1890 abolishing separate schools. Lieutenant-Governor Schultz wanted to reserve the bill but permission was denied; Roman Catholics throughout Canada petitioned for disallowance but their request was refused. With Macdonald's consent—likely at his urging—Chapleau had given pledges to "certain parties"[51] that if the courts upheld the Act the federal government would protect the rights of the minority by remedial legislation.[52] When in July, 1892, the Judicial Committee of the Privy Council declared the statute valid the time had come to fulfil that pledge. The Conservatives were to find it difficult to fulfil, not only because of the many political pitfalls in the way, but also because the constitutional authority of the federal government to redress grievances was no guarantee that it could enforce its will in Manitoba.

Chapleau differed sharply from his colleagues as to the responsibility to be assumed by the central government. The Sub-Committee which considered the appeal for redress intended to evade political responsibility by treating the question as a judicial problem. As its report stated, the application of the petitioners "was not to be dealt with as a matter of political character or involving political action or policy."[53] The decision was thus to be the responsibility of the "Law," an impersonal abstraction, in order that human politicians could pose as instruments who could not be held responsible for the political results of the decision. To Chapleau the decision was political as well as judicial. He refused to sign the report unless it was amended to read "not to be dealt with *at this moment* as a matter of political character," explaining that he "would not consent to shelter the final responsibility of the Council behind a mere judicial interpretation of the statute. The different Acts that have built Confederation are in the nature of Treaties the execution of which rests with those that made them." In other words, Chapleau would not accept the judicial interpretation if it sacrificed the rights of the minority in Manitoba. The pledges that he had made, he continued, "were too much in accordance with my deep-rooted convictions, and an equally deep sense of justice and tolerance, to allow them to be branded today as political devices, or election promises. I felt that I would be missing in my duty if I were to sign any document which would in any way affect my freedom of action in that great and delicate question."[54] On the school question, then, Chapleau was immovable, and Thompson, who objected to Chapleau's suggested amendment on the grounds that it precluded "the non political role of conduct of the Council in disposing of the appeal," did not include Chapleau in his Cabinet, but instead sent him to Quebec as Lieutenant-Governor. Laurier only spoke half the truth, however, when he later declared that Thompson had forced Chapleau's retirement,[55] for Chapleau, believing that he had "neither the influence nor position in the ministry his service and ability entitle him to," preferred "recuperating his powers in the repose of the Lieutenant-Governorship" to remaining in a cabinet where on questions vitally affecting his province he was not recognized as the man who spoke for Quebec.[56] He had stepped aside as he had once warned he might, and the Conservatives were to risk the battle with Quebec "dismantled."

As a general rule only those whose political importance has passed have been appointed to the office of Lieutenant-Governor. It was not so with Chapleau. After his appointment, as before, he was the leading Quebec Conservative; in fact his political power and personal reputation increased during his residence at Spencer Wood. As the Conservative party disintegrated in the face of internal dissensions and external pressures, and as the failure of his ex-colleagues to solve the Manitoba school question became more and more apparent, Quebec Conservatives—indeed all

Conservatives—looked to Chapleau. His relations with both the federal and provincial administrations were close, for no one dared to offend him. He did not subscribe to the doctrine that the Lieutenant-Governor should have no political opinions, but frequently spoke his mind on matters of state, either personally or through Dansereau in *La Presse*. Each of his pronouncements had a great effect in Quebec—particularly when they related to minority rights in Manitoba, a subject on which he continued to claim complete freedom of action. Since the fate of the Conservative Government hinged on Quebec, it is no exaggeration to say that Chapleau was the most important political figure during the last two years of the Conservative decline.

That Chapleau's political significance was recognized by his contemporaries is shown by the attempts to bring him back into active politics. These attempts began with Thompson's death in December, 1894. After consultation with Sir Frank Smith, a Roman Catholic who assured him that Sir Mackenzie Bowell would be acceptable to his co-religionists, Lord Aberdeen asked Bowell to form a government. Before this selection had been decided upon and made public, letters written by both Dansereau and Laurier indicate Chapleau's importance. As usual, Dansereau was over-dramatic:

> Les morts vont vite, surtout les Sir John. En dehors du sentiment chrétien qui ne manque pas de nous émouvoir sur le sort de notre prochain, je n'éprouve aucune regret politique du malheureux événement. Je me demande si le parti conservateur n'est pas l'ancien peuple de Dieu, que la Providence dirige selon les fins qu'elle a décidées. Cet homme tuait surement son parti, plus encore peut-être qu'Abbott. Bang! Tout s'en va.... Inutile de te dire que dans la rue aujourd'hui il n'y a à peu près, comme commentaires de la mort de Sir John, que ton nom de prononcée. S'il voit tout cela de la haute, il a compris qu'il a fait quelques erreurs dans sa vie, "Will Chapleau come and save us?"[57]

Laurier believed that Chapleau might come out of retirement and try to save the party. The death of Thompson was an "irreparable" blow to the party, he declared, but recuperation might be attempted by a Tupper-Chapleau combination. "Nothing can prevent it, if the offer is made to the Quebec man. It is an open secret that Thompson was the man who forced him to withdraw, now he may see his opportunity to come back to active life, & and if the offer is made to him from Ottawa, he will jump on it.... Remember that he is by no means a coward. He is on the contrary, a most daring fellow."[58] But it was Bowell and not Tupper who succeeded and no offer was made to the Quebec man.

A year later Bowell may have made such an offer. Angers resigned in July, 1895, when it became apparent that Bowell had no intention of introducing a remedial bill during the session, and had it not been for a canny subterfuge by the Prime Minister his resignation might well have resulted in the defeat of the Government.[59] By this time Angers was the strongest member from Quebec and a successor of eminence was essential. In October, when Chapleau stopped off in Ottawa on his return from Manitoba where he had been in close communication with Mgr Langevin, the journalists were convinced that Bowell had asked him to enter the Cabinet. M. Rumilly says that the offer was made but that "Chapleau ne sauverait pas une dernière fois son Parti."[60] Two months later, after a consultation with a prominent Conservative who had seen Bowell, Dansereau told Chapleau that "si tu voulais donner le moindre encouragement à B——il mettre immédiatement les deux autres à la porte."[61] There is no reason to question Dansereau's report, for Bowell was desperate by this time. No successor to Angers was in sight and, using this as a pretext, the "nest of traitors" was preparing for his overthrow.

Bowell was a failure as Prime Minister. Only his temporary position as acting Prime Minister could justify his selection, and Aberdeen was even reluctant to admit that this was an adequate qualification.[62] Bowell's colleagues had never really accepted him as their leader; "Here we are, twelve of us, & every one of us as bad, or as good as the other—Jack as good as his master," Foster once commented.[63] The Prime Minister seemed unable to agree upon any course with regard to the school question, deciding in turn upon dissolution, a remedial bill, and another session, until his colleagues were never sure what might happen tomorrow. Resolute leadership was needed as never before, but it was quite apparent that Bowell could not provide it. It was equally obvious that he was never going to find a successor to Angers.

Sir Charles Tupper, many of the Conservatives believed, could supply the leadership and decision and could restore the confidence of Quebec. Tupper had a reputation as a fighter and, better still, as a winner. His position as the elder statesman assured the proper subordination of his colleagues, and as a newcomer he could adopt a fresh approach to the educational problem in the West. But above all, he could win back Quebec. As A. R. Dickey, one of the *"group of seven,"* wrote: "If you wd come out as first minister you could get Chapleau, Lacoste (Chief Justice) & Pelletier from Quebec, Hugh J. Macdonald from Manitoba & I believe Chief Justice Meredith from Ontario, while Blair of N.B. who has so recently shown his power is very anxious to come in. This wd form a powerful govt that wd sweep the country."[64] Everybody seemed to agree—Chapleau could save Quebec for the party and Tupper could bring him back. J. A. Macdonell assured Tupper before the crisis of January, 1896, that "with you at the head of the Government, Chapleau to put heart into his friends in Quebec...we may be saved from destruction.[65] Even such an extreme ultramontane as Archbishop Langevin grudgingly conceded that Chapleau was needed if the Conservatives were to remain in office: "Chapleau le fortifiera politiquement, mais ce n'est pas lui qui le consolidera au point de vue doctrinal."[66] When news of the revolt became public on 6 January 1896, Chapleau was given as much publicity in the press as Tupper. On the same day Tupper himself informed a close political friend that "if sent for by the GG I propose to ask Chapleau to be the French leader and if he can get Lacoste I will give him the office of Minister of Justice."[67]

Tupper did offer Chapleau the leadership of Quebec and was even prepared to let him select his own colleagues. Until the eve of the June election he repeated the offer and there were constant rumours that it had been accepted. But by that time it had become an elaborate political farce, for Chapleau had no intention of returning to Ottawa and again compromising his freedom of action. M. Rumilly, who has had access to private correspondence of the period, writes that "Tupper lui envoya Nantel et Bergeron, et Mgr. Laflèche lui écrivait, l'engageant à entrer dans le ministère, pour y mener à bien l'acte réparateur. Mais le lieutenant-gouverneur persista dans son refus."[68]

The acceptance of Tupper's offer would have given Chapleau the position to which he had long aspired. Why then did he refuse? Unfortunately there is no simple or single explanation. Chapleau himself offered one reason in a letter to Bowell:

> You must not have been so surprised as others pretend to have been at my refusing to enter the new administration. You knew as those others did, that the passing of a Remedial Bill, was a *sine qua non* condition of my reentering the federal cabinet....
>
> Sir Charles in the heat of temper aroused by this disappointment accused me of having deceived him, after having promised in a letter to him, that I would join his cabinet. I readily excused his bad humor, and I truly forgave him for that unjust accusation. I told and wrote Sir Charles that, at the request of Sir John A. Macdonald in 1891, I have given assurances to Archbishop Taché which were sanctioned by my solemn, though private, written pledge, in the face of which I could not, in honor, re-enter the Cabinet before the Remedial Bill was put through Parliament.[69]

Chapleau's reason was in part an excuse, for honour might just as easily and perhaps more logically have compelled him to help pass remedial legislation. His associate Dansereau offered another explanation:

> Pourquoi ne vint-il pas? Parce que ce grand Canadien avait bien mesuré certains de ses compagnons d'armes et la situation. Il avait compris que le chef d'une maison divisée était condamné à l'impuissance et que les influences auxquelles il devait l'arrêt subit, la neutralisation, dès son arrivée à Ottawa, de cette carrière si brillamment commencée à Québec, était encore en pleine activité.[70]

In other words, the Castors still made impossible the unity of the Conservative party in Quebec. The time had passed for crushing his enemies; that had been the task of the 1880s when be was young and ambitious. And unless he could lead a united Quebec he preferred not to lead at all. Moreover, the problem was no longer as pressing as it had once been. A new leader of a new party had arisen in Quebec. Was it not possible that the coalition of moderates could be formed under his wing? One word from Chapleau on behalf of the Conservatives in May or June of 1896 would have been extremely important. But Chapleau was silent and, in Dansereau's words, "le peuple à qui il faut une idole se tourna vers Laurier en 1896."[71]

Chapleau fully realized the consequences of his silence. Tarte had moved into the Liberal fold long before and Tarte in 1896 was still Chapleau's confidant. In many ways Tarte symbolized the union of the Chapleau Conservatives and the Laurier Liberals. The two leaders were not very far apart politically. Like Cartier and perhaps even more so, Chapleau was a liberal Conservative, who had always preferred a Liberal to a Castor. And Laurier was a moderate Liberal who had shed his *rouge* associates, who had long been anxious to win over *l'école de Cartier*, and who was to prove his conversion by having about him such men as Tarte and Fitzpatrick. Complete fusion of the two parties was to be a long process but it was accomplished. A decade later Laurier could agree with a correspondent who wrote that "vous avez réussi à obtenir le concours absolu, sincère, sans restrictions de ceux qui, dans notre province, appartiennent à l'école de Cartier."[72] If the end was the greater unity and strength of Quebec, nothing would have pleased Chapleau more. Of this there is no better evidence than a letter he wrote to Laurier after the Liberal victory in Quebec province in 1897 had assured Laurier's hegemony in both spheres—the position Chapleau himself had sought:

> Maintenant qu'allez-vous faire dans et de la province de Québec? La majorité triomphante va-t-elle enterrer ou se faire fonctionner la hache de guerre? Va-t-elle relever les ruines ou raser jusqu'au sol et labourer dans les débris encore fumants? Le problème est entre tes mains. Je n'abandonne pas mon rêve d'une Province unie et forte. Mais je ne vois guère plus le moyen de la réaliser. Les éléments restent, mais la transformation est difficile avec l'atmosphère politique dans laquelle on vit à Québec en ce moment.... Si vous avez quelque chose à me suggérer, dans les *circonstances*, je suis à vos ordres, pour tout ce qui pourra profiter au bien de la Province, et à l'appaisement de la fièvre de combat qui doit sévir encore dans le corps électoral et dans l'âme des élus.[73]

Chapleau died a few months after his departure from Spencer Wood in 1898, at the age of fifty-eight. In spite of his talent and ambition he had failed to dominate Quebec as Cartier had done. Yet his career is significant in the history of his province and his country. He had consistently fought against the ultra-clerical faction and had probably saved the Quebec Conservative party from becoming a narrow Roman Catholic party. His failure to unite his party might be attributed to his temperament, to his instinctive preference for destroying the Castor faction rather than compromise, but he was not entirely to blame. The Castors were no less determined to destroy him. Nor would it be just to describe him as no more than an ambitious or self-seeking politician. He was an ambitious man, it is true, but in two national crises, the execution of Riel and the Manitoba school question, he refused to seek personal power at the expense of the interests of his compatriots and the nation. His career illustrates the dilemma of a national politician representing a minority group. It helps to explain why Quebec became a Liberal province. And it should be a warning to historians that to speak exclusively of national parties and national leaders is to superimpose on a pattern of great variety and intricate design another of the utmost simplicity which, while simplifying Canadian political history, may at times tend to distort it.

NOTES

1. *Mandements, lettres pastorales, circulaires et autres documents publiés dans le diocèse de Montréal,* vol. 8 (Montreal, 1887), 397.

2. Chapleau to Laurier, 31 May 1897, Laurier Papers, 31 May, 1897. (Unless otherwise stated all manuscripts are from the Public Archives of Canada, Ottawa.)

3. Chapleau to Thompson, 5 March 1888, Thompson Papers, P.A.C.

4. L.O. David, *Mes Contemporains* (Montreal, 1894), 29.

5. See E. Auclair, *Le Curé Labelle* (Montreal, 1930), 131, for an illustration of the ultramontane point of view.

6. Charles Langelier, *Souvenirs politiques,* vol. I (Montreal, 1909 and 1912), 121.

7. Chapleau to Macdonald, 19 September 1878, Macdonald Papers, 39, P.A.C.

8. Chapleau to Macdonald, 31 October 1880, Ibid., 204.

9. *L'Administration Chapleau* (Montreal, 1881), pamphlets in P.A.C., second series, no. 352.

10. Robert Rumilly, *Monseigneur Laflèche et son temps* (Montreal, 1938), 70.

11. *Mémoires sur la coalition* (St. Hyacinthe, 1886), 19, Pamphlets in P.A.C., second series, no. 1021.

12. Chapleau to Macdonald, 25 July 1882. Macdonald Papers, 204.

13. *Le Parti, le Pays, et le Grand Homme* (Montreal, 1882), Pamphlets in P.A.C., second series, no. 459.

14. Ibid., 1.

15. Ibid., 20.

16. Ibid., 11.

17. Ibid., 82.

18. Ibid., 108.

19. For example, see Chapleau to Macdonald, 25 March 1882, Macdonald Papers, 204, where Chapleau complains that "it is strange to see just the bodyguard of Langevin and Caron leading the battle against me" and refers to the opposing faction as "that disgusting clique of religious pickpockets, the pest of all government."

20. Laurier to Blake, 31 July 1882, Blake Papers, 12, Ontario Department of Public Records and Archives (P.A.O.).

21. Chapleau to Macdonald, 6 May 1883, Macdonald Papers, 204.

22. Mousseau to Macdonald, 22 August 1883, Macdonald Papers, 253.

23. P. Landry to Caron, 16 October 1884, Caron Papers, 4752, P.A. C.

24. A. de Bonneterre, ad., *L'Honorable J. A. Chapleau, sa biographie, suivie de ses principaux discours, manifestes, etc.* (Montreal, 1887), 297.

25. R. Rumilly, *Histoire de la Province de Québec,* 26 vols. (Montreal, 1940-52), vol. 5, 105.

26. J. 1. Tarte, *1892 Procès Mercier* (Montreal, 1892), 21, Pamphlets in P.A.C., second series, no. 1767.

27. Chapleau to W. Lynch, 12 November 1885, Chapleau Papers.

28. Chapleau to Macdonald, 12 November 1885, Macdonald Papers, 204.

29. The day when Joly was refused a dissolution and Chapleau, always at the Lieutenant-Governor's elbow, assumed the responsibility for forming a Conservative administration.

30. Chapleau to W.V. Lynch, 21 November 1885, Chapleau Papers.

31. Chapleau to Macdonald, 31 October 1886, Macdonald Papers, 205.

32. Chapleau to Macdonald, 15 January 1887, ibid.; Macdonald to Chapleau, 21 January 1887.

33. Chapleau to Tarte, 4 March 1887, Tarte Papers, 13.

34. Macdonald to Chapleau, 21 May 1887, Macdonald Papers, 527.

35. Tarte to Caron, 30 May 1887, Caron Papers, 10883.

36. T. C. Casgrain to Caron, 30 May 1887, ibid.

37. Tarte to Caron, 30 May 1887, ibid.

38. T. C. Casgrain to Caron, 30 May 1887, ibid.

39. Chapleau to Macdonald, 20 June 1887, Macdonald Papers, 205.

40. 11 August 1890, ibid.

41. Chapleau to Thompson, 22 December 1890, Thompson Papers.

42. Macdonald to Tupper, 5 June 1890, Tupper Papers.

43. See J. S. Willison, *Reminiscences Political and Personal* (Toronto, 1919), 192; Langevin too, drew Macdonald's attention to the *rapprochement* between Tarte and Chapleau. Langevin to Macdonald, 11 January 1891, Macdonald Papers, 227.

44. Rumilly, *Histoire,* vol. 6, 221.

45. Angers to Macdonald, 22 January 1891, Macdonald Papers, 186.

46. Thompson to Mrs. Thompson, 10 June 1891, Thompson Papers.

47. Edgar to Mrs. Edgar, 16 June 1891, Edgar Papers, P.A.O.

48. M. F. J. Quinn to Chapleau, 4 October 1891, Tarte Papers, 13.

49. Meredith to Whitney, 31 October 1891, Whitney Papers, P.A.O.

50. M. Rumilly (*Histoire,* vol. 6, 273) states that Abbott promised Chapleau the Lieutenant-Governorship when Angers retired.

51. Chapleau to Thompson, 29 December 1892, Thompson Papers.

52. *L'Electeur,* 2 June 1893.

53. Chapleau to Thompson, 22 December 1892, Thompson Papers.

54. 29 December 1892, ibid.

55. Laurier to Edgar, 14 December 1894, Edgar Papers, P.A.O.

56. R. S. White to Thompson, 19 September 1892, Thompson Papers.

57. Dansereau to Chapleau, 12 December 1894, Lemieux Papers.

58. Laurier to Edgar, 14 December 1894, Edgar Papers.

59. See Lady Aberdeen's Journal, 15 July 1895.

60. *Histoire,* vol. 7, 233; *La Presse,* 1-2 October 1895.

61. Dansereau to Chapleau, 21 December 1895, Lemieux Papers.

62. Lady Aberdeen's Journal, 12 December 1894.

63. Ibid.

64. Dickey to Tupper, 1 November 1895, Tupper Papers.

65. E. M. Saunders, ed., *The Life and Letters of the Rt. Hon. Sir Charles Tupper, Bart, K.C.M.G.,* 2 vols (Toronto, 1916), vol. 2, 192-3.

66. L. G. (Roulx), ed., "Correspondance Langevin-Audet," *Revue d'Histoire de l'Amérique française,* vol. 1, no. 2 (1947), 276. Letter dated 14 February 1896.

67. Tupper to Van Horne, 6 January 1896.

68. Rumilly, *Histoire,* vol. 8, 43.

69. Chapleau to Bowell, 9 May 1896, Bowell Papers.

70. *La Presse,* 30 November 1901.

71. Ibid.

72. T. Coté to Laurier, 19 November 1907, Laurier Papers, 488, 131977.

73. Chapleau to Laurier, 15 May 1897, Laurier Papers, 45, 14686. For the actual mechanics of the fusion, see H. Blair Neatby, "Laurier and a Liberal Quebec: A Study in Political Management" (unpublished doctoral dissertation, University of Toronto, 1956), Ch. 8.

LAURIER, AYLESWORTH, AND THE DECLINE OF THE LIBERAL PARTY IN ONTARIO

BY PAUL STEVENS

o

The Liberal party collapsed in Ontario in 1911. This was one of the most significant developments in Canadian political history for it resulted in the defeat of the Laurier government. Yet historians have failed to provide an adequate explanation. They have generally attributed the débâcle to reciprocity, although the proposal should have been popular in rural Ontario; or to charges of disloyalty to the British Empire, although Laurier and the Liberal party had survived a more blatant Anglophile and Francophobe campaign in 1900. For the most part they have overlooked the role which regional and provincial leaders play in the Canadian political system. Reciprocity might or might not have brought economic prosperity to Ontario and the Dominion. It might or might not have been destructive of a Canadian nationality. But in the face of growing skepticism about the nature of Laurier Liberalism and the social and political values of its chief spokesman in the province, the people of Ontario put the American temptation behind them. At a time when leadership was essential, the Liberal party in Ontario was found lacking.

Ontario had been a predominantly Conservative province in national politics since Confederation. By the beginning of the 1890s, however, it was turning toward the Liberal banner. Laurier played a leading role in this transfer of political allegiance. In 1887 he had hesitated to accept the party leadership because be believed that a French-Canadian Roman Catholic leader would be a handicap in the English-speaking provinces, particularly

Excerpt from *Historical Papers 1968* (The Canadian Historical Association, 1968). Reprinted with permission of Paul Stevens and The Canadian Historical Association.

in Ontario. But after assuming the leadership, he persistently pursued an Ontario policy to minimize the disabilities of his racial and religious background. He adopted a platform of unrestricted reciprocity to gain political support in the province. During the Manitoba school controversy, he maintained a position consistent with the principles of provincial rights and non-denominational schools, the twin pillars of Ontario Liberalism for over two generations. And in response to imperialist pressures from the province, his government introduced the preferential tariff and agreed to assist Great Britain against the Boers in South Africa. By the end of the decade Ontario had become a Liberal province.[1]

But federal politics in Canada involves more than national policies and national leaders. The task of leadership in a national political party is particularly onerous because of the deeply rooted regionalism which permeates Canadian life. The centrifugal forces of race and creed have been reinforced by geographical divisions, economic differentiation, and the beckoning smile of a wealthier neighbour. National parties have therefore been to a large extent merely the momentary reflections and temporary alliances of heterogeneous provincial organizations. The Liberal party remained essentially in this condition until 1896, anti-Catholic, anti-French Ontario Grits in an uneasy alliance with anti-clerical Quebec Liberals. Although Edward Blake and Laurier had begun to rid the party of its separate provincial outlooks and to formulate policies which would attract support from Ontario and Quebec, the ideology and traditions of the Grits and Rouges had not been obliterated, and it was of the utmost importance that the Liberals have effective leaders from both provinces to hold their followers in line. For Ontario the fact that Laurier was a French-Canadian Roman Catholic made this essential. John Willison reflected the views of many when he noted during the Autonomy Bill's debate: "I do not think it just, but it is nevertheless the fact, that a Protestant leader could do what Sir Wilfrid Laurier is doing much more safely, and that many Liberals will remember what they regard as the treason to their principles of a Roman Catholic, when they would not so remember if their leader were a Protestant."[2]

One of the reasons for the success of the Liberal party in Ontario during the latter part of the 1890s was Sir Oliver Mowat's decision to become federal leader in the province. Liberal strategists portrayed Mowat as an English co-premier during the election campaign of 1896, while Laurier spoke rapturously of the days of Baldwin and Lafontaine. After Mowat's resignation in 1897, one of Laurier's weaknesses in Ontario was his inability to find a leader who could inspire a similar confidence. The stalwart old warhorses of Ontario Liberalism, Sir Richard Cartwright, David Mills, John Charlton, Richard Scott and William Paterson were all in the twilight of their political careers; and William Mulock, though an effective administrator, lacked the oratorical force and eloquence necessary to a man who sought political power. The loss of 16 constituencies in Ontario in the election of 1900 was in part a reflection of the belief that the Liberal party was dominated by Quebec and under the influence of individuals whose Liberalism was incompatible with the province's social and political values.[3] "Our province is hopelessly overborne in the councils of the Liberal party by the strong delegations from Quebec and the East," observed one member of the Ontario caucus, "and the resultant effect upon Ontario is that of apathy and indifference throughout our ranks."[4]

The man whom Laurier selected as "political boss" in Ontario was Allan Aylesworth. The son of an eastern Ontario farmer of United Empire Loyalist stock, Aylesworth was imbued with the contempt and scorn of the Upper Canadian reformer for the despotism of the Family Compact and the aggressive tendencies of a centralized authority. He was a brilliant student at the University of Toronto and rose quickly to a prominent position at the Ontario Bar. In 1903 he was one of Canada's nominees on the Alaska Boundary Tribunal, and his refusal to sign the tribunal award won him popular acclaim. Since 1900 Laurier and his Ontario strategists had been attempting to induce Aylesworth to enter federal politics.[5] Optimism was widespread that Aylesworth could provide "the vitalizing influence necessary to raise the party in public esteem and restore its former prestige."[6] Aylesworth, however, was reluctant to relinquish his briefs until he had provided for the future of his sons;[7] and, when in the general election of 1904, he agreed to take the plunge, he was defeated in the eastern Ontario constituency of Durham. In October 1905 be finally entered the House when Mulock resigned after a by-election in York North. He immediately became Postmaster General and eight months later succeeded Charles Fitzpatrick as Minister of Justice.

Aylesworth was well suited for the position of chief lieutenant in Ontario in many ways. Laurier and Aylesworth were intellectually and temperamentally congenial; and in Aylesworth, Laurier had discovered a colleague to whom he could give his complete trust. On most of the important issues of the day, and particularly on the subject of imperialism, the two had common principles and common opinions.[8] Like Mowat, Aylesworth's Reform credentials were impressive. He was a staunch defender of provincial rights and economy and efficiency in government. Although his political support came primarily from the farming population, he had roots in the business and financial community through his legal practice. He was a strong orator on the political platform, accurate, lucid and disarmingly frank, and his speeches were continuously dignified and convincing. "I have never listened to any Ontario minister who enthused Liberals as he did" applauded one Ontario Liberal. "He simply electrified the electors here, both Grits and Tories."[9]

Aylesworth's task was not enviable. The Liberal party in Ontario was demoralized and dispirited when he entered the federal cabinet. For a generation of Liberals, schooled in the tradition that their party was the custodian of political purity and public morality, the charges of electoral corruption against the provincial administration of George Ross following the election of 1902, and Ross' reluctance to introduce effective legislation to control the sale of liquor, were a rude awakening. "Ontario has lost something of her ascendancy in the Canadian Confederation," declared one prominent political observer. "She has lost in political leadership, in political vigour, in public spirit, and in moral purpose."[10] The defeat of the Liberals in 1905 was overwhelming. As the Governor-General, Lord Grey, noted, "it was not a party vote, it was the uprising of an honest and indignant people who have given warning in the most emphatic manner that they will not tolerate dishonest government."[11]

In the federal field as well, Liberals found themselves under heavy attack for abandoning the traditions of their Clear Grit heritage. Many Liberals maintained that the educational clauses in the Autonomy Bills of 1905, securing separate schools in Saskatchewan and Alberta, violated the principle of provincial rights.[12] What heightened the disillusionment of many Liberals in Ontario was the widespread belief that Laurier's Manitoba school policy had been based on provincial rights and opposed to denominational schools. Willison later explained that his early esteem for the Liberal leader had been based "on his devotion to the federal principle and his resolute resistance to clerical interference in education.... With the Western Autonomy Acts he turned squarely in the other direction."[13] Laurier, in fact, was not opposed to denominational schools, and on several occasions during the 1890s he had pointed out that provincial rights were abbreviated in the field of education.[14] Nonetheless, disconcerted Laurier supporters deplored that "the hierarchy, the modern Rouges (who have changed their colour somewhat) and the Irish agitators, have a better key to his heart than native British sentiment in Canada."[15] Willison, for one, severed his allegiance with Laurier and the federal Liberal party in protest.[16]

Aylesworth stepped into the political arena to stem the tide. Almost immediately he was confronted with a further deterioration of public confidence in Laurier Liberalism. Between 1905 and 1908, the Laurier government's administration of the country's business was the subject of a succession of opposition charges and allegations. In the sessions of 1906, 1907, and 1908, Conservative leaders waged war on Clifford Sifton's stewardship of the Interior Department prior to his resignation in 1905. Charges that the Department had sold 250,000 acres [101,175 hectares] of choice land to members of the House and their friends at unduly low rates; that the Department had entered into a contract with the North Atlantic Trading Company, a group of European Shipping Agents, to bring immigrants to Canada at the rate of five dollars per head; and that the Department had granted to a syndicate of Sifton's friends a timber limit belonging to the Indian Department at Algoma were all laid at the government's doorstep. In 1908 a commission headed by Mr. Justice W.G.P. Cassells turned up evidence of petty graft in the Department of Marine and Fisheries involving a number of high-ranking civil servants. More serious politically were charges against the personal conduct of the Minister of Militia and Defence, Sir Frederick Borden, and the Minister of Railways, H.R. Emmerson, and of electoral corruption against the Minister of Public Works, Charles Hyman. For many Ontario Liberals, the allegations against Hyman, and the evidence of bribery and corruption which came to light in his London constituency, were particularly distressing. "Liberals in the past have been proud of their traditions," declared one Liberal journal, "proud of their accomplishments, jealous of their honour. They cannot afford to be less proud or less jealous today.... If it is necessary to teach any of the leaders or workers in the Liberal party that the party at heart is honest and earnest and jealous of its honour, the sooner the lesson is taught the better. Even if the lesson is a bitter one, eventually it will be a wholesome one."[17]

Aylesworth delivered a series of speeches throughout the province to answer these charges. He retorted that the Conservatives, fresh from their success with the cry of scandal in the provincial campaign, had embarked upon a similar course at Ottawa. "I do not pretend," he admitted, "that when millions of dollars are spent yearly every dollar is spent where full value is given in contracts of various kinds."[18] But Aylesworth declared that there was no foundation for the opposition's charges. "Show me one instance in which there has been corrupt practices by any member of the Government, and I will admit the justice of the attacks."[19] The Minister of Justice saved his strongest words for the Conservative leader, Robert Borden, reproaching him for his continued association with George Foster in light of the report of the Royal Commission on Life Insurance which had criticized Foster's handling of the funds of the International Order of Foresters and the Union Trust Company.[20] With what the Toronto *Globe* described as "the true ring of militant democracy,"[21] he attacked the hollowness and pretense of Borden's recently unveiled reform platform.[22] The Opposition leader's promise of "honest appropriation and expenditure of public moneys in the public interest" was the height of political platitudes, while his electoral purity plank was already covered by the present election law. Aylesworth charged that Borden, his high-sounding phrases notwithstanding, was not above playing the political game himself, and that in view of a contribution of $30,000 by the Montreal newspaper publisher Hugh Graham to the Conservative campaign fund in Quebec, it was hardly surprising that the Conservative leader now wished to restrict such contributions to other than corporations, contractors, and promoters of companies. "No member of the Government," he proclaimed, "is conscious of political corruption to any greater extent, if as great as Mr. R. L. Borden himself."[23] The campaign was an unqualified success, and in the election of 1908, the Liberals turned back the Conservative challenge.[24]

The extent of this success, however, was in some ways illusory. For the first time since 1874, the Liberals had failed to gain a majority of the popular vote outside of Toronto, and many constituencies in rural Ontario were clearly in jeopardy. Nor had the leadership question been satisfactorily settled. Although Laurier had strengthened the Ontario wing of the party by bringing George Graham and Charles Murphy into the cabinet on the eve of the election, the President of the Toronto Reform Association pointed out that "the old Liberals are becoming discouraged and disinterested and the leaders of the party in the province are not putting their claim before the people in such a way as to hold their own with the young men."[25] Particularly disturbing to many Liberals in rural Ontario was the feeling that a new and less responsible element was dominating the party and that the virtues of the old liberalism had been lost right of. Apart from Aylesworth, none of the

Ontario leaders had gained their confidence. As one member warned, "Ontario Liberalism is on the expectant for something to happen. We are not going to be dominated by the new element in the Liberal party, as has been the case."[26]

Of concern as well was the position of the Minister of Justice. It was becoming apparent that Aylesworth's leadership in the province was far from secure. In the midst of the campaign, he had begun to grow deaf, and he told his constituents that he would be forced to retire from politics unless his hearing improved. At the beginning of 1910, his troubles continued when he became embroiled in bitter controversy with the leaders of moral reform in Canada, undermining his authority with a wide section of the Liberal party in the province. In December 1909, H.H. Miller, the Liberal member for South Grey, proposed an amendment to the criminal code which would have prevented professional gambling on Canadian race tracks.[27] The measure was supported by the Moral and Social Reform Council of Canada which represented all the major Protestant denominations, the Canadian Purity Educational Association, the Trades and Labour Congress, the Dominion Grange, and the Farmers' Association.[28] Laurier voted for the proposal himself, but he refused to adopt it as a government measure, and in committee the chief clause was defeated by one vote.[29] For the promoters of the bill, the villain of the piece was the Minister of Justice. Aylesworth had little use for the puritan conscience of Protestant Ontario, and he possessed neither the inclination nor the political dexterity to conceal his impatience. He maintained that the legislation would make a crime of something "which the ordinary sense of the average man does not consider a crime." Rubbing salt into the wound, Aylesworth derided those who supported the bill. "Very possibly before the end of this parliament, we shall have a proposition to make it a crime to play cards, or to dance, or to indulge in any of the other amusements which there are some in the community think constitute, very nearly, if not quite a sin."[30]

Aylesworth's attitude angered many Liberals in the rural and Protestant sections of the province. N.W. Rowell, a young Toronto lawyer and a leading spokesman for Canadian Methodism, informed Graham that he now regarded him rather than Aylesworth "as the real leader of the Ontario Liberals in Dominion politics."

> There appears to be on all sides the deepest regret, and on many sides the deepest resentment at the spirit and character of the speech of the Minister of Justice in opposing the bill; not that he should not agree with the principle of the bill, but that in voicing his opposition he should have treated with contempt the conscientious convictions and the sentiments of the church-going people at least of the province, and, I believe, largely of all the provinces. As a man said to me last evening in the car, whatever Conservatives may do, Liberals will not follow that leadership. They may not say much about it, but they will not vote or work for its support.... There is the belief that had one of the influential members of the Government who are

believed to be in sympathy with the bill spoken at all as strong in favour as Mr. Aylesworth did against it, the bill would have been carried, and however correct the theory may be that the government is in no way responsible for the bill, it will be difficult to remove from the minds of many that had the members of the Government who are nominally in favour of the bill, really desired that it should pass, the vote would have been different. The strength of the Liberal party throughout this country will be found in those classes who believe in the church and in religious institutions and who have strong views on moral issues, and who do not believe in legalized professional gambling, and while up to the present time the agitation has not been strong in my judgment it is because the issue has not been raised, and unless during this session something is done to retrieve what appears to me to be the serious blunder which has already been made, you will inevitably find an agitation during this coming year which necessarily will, by reason of the speech delivered by the Minister of Justice, more or less reflect on the Government however little those concerned in it may desire to do so.[31]

The editor of the Toronto *Globe*, Rev. J.A. Macdonald, also rebuked the Minister of Justice. "It would be to Canada's discredit if, with a new start in a new country, free from the incubus of age-long social custom, we were not able to lead the way into a cleaner democracy."[32] On 15 April the House reached a compromise that allowed legalized book-making but limited race meetings at any track to two weeks a year. Although the *Globe* and the Moral Reform Council were far from satisfied, they accepted the legislation as a step in the right direction.[33]

But the conflict between Aylesworth and the "church-going" section of Ontario Liberalism continued over another issue which lasted for several months. On 4 March Aylesworth announced the release of two men, King and Skill, who had been convicted of selling obscene literature, after they had served only two months of a one-year sentence. Aylesworth explained that in his opinion the two men were not guilty of the offence with which they had been charged. He admitted that certain passages in the books in question, as well as in "that best of books that we all revere," might properly be described as indecent. But he declared that the books themselves, which included the English translations of Balzac, Petronius, and Brantôme, were classics "which are to be found on the shelves of our own library."[34] New evidence later revealed that salacious advertising had been used to sell the books, but Aylesworth remained adamant. He admitted that though his judgment might have been at fault, his opinion had been a purely legal one, which he still thought to be right.[35]

The decision outraged the "Ontario puritans." The protests were led by Macdonald in the editorial columns of the *Globe*. For Macdonald, the affair was another example of a dangerous tendency in Canadian society "to regard lightly offences against purity in life and morals." "Canada," he explained, "can do without the 'science' of depraved perverts or the 'classics' of the modern French lust-sewer."[36] Politically, the question was charged with explosive potential. "There is more political gunpowder in this than in almost anything else that has come up of late," Macdonald warned Laurier. "Following hard upon Mr. Aylesworth's speech on the Gambling Bills, it makes thing well nigh intolerable."[37] The Minister of Justice, he contended, had lost his hold on the Ontario Liberals.

> Men who care nothing at all about the ethical interests involved, but who are interested only in the popularity of the Government, do not hesitate to say that Aylesworth can never be anything but a weight. If this is true, it is largely the result of his own persistent blundering in dealing with questions in which public opinion is involved. I say this with the utmost frankness.... I do not propose to say anything against him, but I shall never have the least enthusiasm for him so long as he follows the lines he has pursued in the past.... And more than that, the great body of the Liberal Party is with me and not with him.[38]

Macdonald was not the only Liberal to express alarm. As one leading Protestant clergyman explained, "the people of Canada are a moral people. They love purity in their homes. They will not tolerate a Minister of Justice whose sentiment and opinion would allow the circulation of literature so loathsome as to affront and shock the moral sense of all decent people."[39]

Throughout the dispute, Laurier stood firmly behind the Minister of Justice. He explained that Aylesworth had not condoned the sale of immoral literature but had merely expressed an opinion that the sale of books which were acknowledged as classics could not be held to be a violation of the criminal code. "I am quite familiar with Brantôme," he added. "It is one of the classics of the French language of the sixteenth century. It is coarse, as were the manners of that day but it is not lascivious. It deals with matters of rather risky character but he does not write with the view of exciting passion but rather of provoking mirth. I do not consider it half so dangerous for youth as some other books of almost daily circulation such for instance, as Shakespeare's sonnets or Shakespeare's Adonis."[40] He agreed that King and Skill were not respectable booksellers and admitted privately that Aylesworth's opinion had been "too drastic."[41] But he was content to point out that "this is one of the many questions as to which lawyers can disagree."[42]

In the midst of the controversy, the divisions within the ranks of Ontario Liberalism were publicly and dramatically exposed. For some time a young and ambitious group of Toronto Liberals had been disenchanted with the lack of active and aggressive leadership in Ontario.[43] At the end of April, Hartley H. Dewart, a prominent member of the Ontario Bar, and the son of a former editor of the *Christian Guardian*, charged in an open letter to the *Globe* that the Liberal party in Ontario was lamentably weak in its organization. For Dewart, the responsibility for the apathetic condition of the party's electoral machine lay with the Ontario ministers. "A commander-in-chief, even if he be as brilliant and skillful as Sir Wilfrid Laurier undoubtedly is, cannot be expected to achieve the success that he should without able tacticians between himself and the men in the ranks." But it was upon Aylesworth as leader of the Ontario Liberals and central Ontario's representative in the cabinet that Dewart fixed his sights.

> In the City of Toronto and the surrounding ridings we have suffered and are suffering as a party because the Minister who is supposed to represent this district is not a political force or even a factor in organization. A district or even a constituency may be lost if feather-weight advisors are the main sources from which knowledge of the political situation is derived. The local Minister should at least be the mouthpiece through which the political views or needs of the district are expressed.... The consideration locally that these matters have received and to which they are entitled is due in nearly every instance to the direct representations made by active Liberal workers to the Minister in charge of the department interested. Surely the public at large are justified in expecting the directing force of the Minister of Justice in these matters of local policy, just as much as Liberals are in matters of political organization. If our policy is sound and our views are right, as we believe them to be, the party leader who sees to it that organized effort and wise direction are brought to bear to achieve success performs a public as well as party service.

Dewart concluded that the country was entitled to the "best service of the best men" and that political prescience as well as sound executive ability was needed.[44]

The charges were not without secure foundation. Although one political observer had described the Liberal electoral machinery in Ontario during the 1908 federal election as "the most effective organization that had ever been known in a Dominion election,"[45] it had fallen into disrepair particularly in Toronto and central Ontario. "With the present organization," admitted one party stalwart, "it would be impossible to elect St. Peter to any one of our seats."[46] So exhausted was the provincial organization that party officials were forced to cancel a proposed policy convention for September 1910 because none of the local constituency associations had prepared policy measures for the organizing committee.[47] That Conservative strategists could predict with such accuracy the results of the election in Ontario in 1911 was indicative not so much of the strength of the Conservative organization, for the Tory machine had been unable to deliver significant results in 1908, but of the moribund state of the Liberal organization.[48]

Moreover, Aylesworth had done little to enhance his position with the political activists in the party. A master intellect, of high character, and with rare executive ability, the Minister of Justice had many deficiencies as a practical politician. It is one of the remarkable aspects of Laurier's career that, though an astute and calculating politician himself, he was more concerned with the administrative capacity of his political advisors than with their ability to master the details of political organization and to keep the party in line. Aylesworth had little interest in the intricacies of party organization, while frequent forays to Europe and the United States took him out of the political arena for months at a time. In cabinet, he seldom spoke on political matters, admitting to Laurier on one occasion that "in all such respects I am content to trust you blindly."[49] One of the reasons was his deafness which limited further his effectiveness as the spokesman for Ontario Liberalism. As he pointed out to Laurier some years later :

> My last four years in the House at Ottawa were purgatory to me. To sit there like a dummy when perhaps something I knew all about was being discussed—to know absolutely nothing of what was being said and then to read next day in Hansard speeches that I could have torn to tatters if I could have heard a word of them—kept me raging in impotent anger. And it was even more dreadful in council when there was something under consideration that I knew about or was perhaps specially interested in. I might talk a little while and then somebody across the table might say something—or even if you spoke, sitting by my side—I had no idea whether it was in agreement with me or in criticism....[50]

On the eve of his departure for the Hague Tribunal at the beginning of May, Aylesworth informed Laurier that his continued presence in the cabinet would be "a weakness and an injury" to the government and offered his resignation.[51]

Laurier, however, stood by his beleagured colleague and refused to agree to his leaving the cabinet. "I am only too well aware," he explained, "that there are in the ranks of the party, some, who, I regret to say, are your personal enemies, but they must learn that, outside their very limited number, the whole party is behind you."[52] There were a number of reasons for Laurier's loyalty. The Liberals could not afford to have Aylesworth resign under a political cloud and thereby give credence to his critics' charges. Another factor undoubtedly was the failure of the younger Liberals in the province to emerge as potential successors to the Minister of Justice.[53] Moreover, Laurier had personal motives as well. The aging Liberal leader had become increasingly withdrawn from his political colleagues in Ottawa. The retirement of most of his friends from public life had contributed to a growing sense of isolation. Aylesworth was one of the few men with whom Laurier still enjoyed intimate companionship, and he was determined that this not become the victim of the political wars. But in spite of Laurier's determination, it was clear that Aylesworth had little control over the Ontario Liberals. At a time when new issues demanded party cohesion and unity, the Liberal party in Ontario was divided and leaderless as it had seldom been in the past.

In time Laurier might have been able to put the pieces together, particularly as Graham and the new Minister of Labour, W.L.M. King, began to emerge as political forces in the province. But the debate over reciprocity threw the party into complete disarray. From the outset of the controversy, the political climate in Ontario was not favourable to a reciprocity treaty with the United States. Although unrepentant free traders recalled the Liberal success in the province in the election of 1891,[54] the passage of years and the glow of prosperity had somewhat beclouded the motives and circumstances of the unrestricted reciprocity campaign. The economic depression of the late 1880s had given way to a period of unexampled growth and development, calling for tariff permanency, financial stability, and a minimum of change. Between 1891 and 1911, the industrial development of Ontario had greatly accelerated, and a population which had been predominantly rural, had become predominantly urban.[55] These changes had been accompanied by a growing confidence in the Dominion's ability to stand alone, and an increasing desire to avoid intimate connection with a nation which had repeatedly rejected Canadian overtures toward lower tariffs, and which, as the intervention in Venezuela, and the founding of the American Empire in the Caribbean and the Pacific had demonstrated, was following the path of expansionist imperialism. As Willison warned, "we would be selling our birthright for a mess of theoretical pottage put up by Cobden and Company, Manchester."[56]

Members of the Ontario caucus were divided on the issue. Aylesworth and Paterson were in favour of an agreement which they believed would substantially benefit the farming community.[57] But the majority showed little enthusiasm. Graham was opposed to any "large measure of reciprocity,"[58] while King maintained that "the less done on these questions for the present, the better, both for the Government and the country."[59] Even rural members restrained their applause, contending that Canada should realize her own strength and not "grovel or feel in any way dependent upon the United States."[60] "We have developed markets of our own," one Ontario Liberal pointed out, "are enjoying good prices and have paid a tremendous sum to divert trade East and West, and should a tariff be arranged to alter these conditions it will be difficult indeed to foresee the result to Canada.[61]

There is no simple explanation for Laurier's determination to press for reciprocity in the light of this opposition. He always believed that a large measure of free trade with the United States would be advantageous to Canada and that once the question was placed in this perspective, the opposition would be overcome. Strident demands from western Canada for tariff relief and the desire for a new and dramatic policy after fourteen years in office made the proposition politically attractive. He was also concerned for the preservation of harmonious relations with the United States. The establishment of the International Joint Commission in 1909 and the agreement to refer the problem of the North Atlantic fisheries to the Hague Court in 1910, were the marks of a new spirit of accommodation between Ottawa and Washington which had gradually replaced the animosity and resentment engendered by the Alaskan dispute; and Laurier was anxious not to place this in jeopardy. Since the Americans had made the proposal, he was prepared to treat it with courtesy and respect. As Grey informed James Bryce, the British Ambassador in Washington, "the necessity of saving the face of the United States Government will have to be borne in mind."[62] Once the negotiations had begun, Liberal leaders discovered the breadth of the American proposals, and they ultimately accepted a much more comprehensive agreement than they had intended.[63]

The agreement brought forth a storm of criticism throughout Ontario. In the vanguard of the suddenly mounting wave of resistance to reciprocity was a group of prominent Liberal industrialists, manufacturers and financiers. On 20 February eighteen Toronto Liberals led by Zebulon Lash, a leading Toronto lawyer, and Sir Edmund Walker, President of the Canadian Bank of Commerce, issued a manifesto opposing ratification of the agreement.[64] Reciprocity was not the first issue upon which members of the Toronto Eighteen had found themselves in opposition to the Laurier administration. In 1909 Laurier's refusal to disallow Ontario hydro legislation involving the expropriation of private power companies led many to the conclusion that the federal government approved a measure which they believed would seriously affect Canada's interests in the British financial market.[65] But for the Liberal establishment in Toronto, reciprocity represented a more direct challenge to its position of economic ascendancy throughout the province and the nation. The fears of industrial and financial interests for the future of Canada as an autonomous nation within the framework of the British Empire were genuine and deeply felt. But their apprehension was undoubtedly based to a large extent on the assumption that their interests were intimately tied to the continuance of the policies of economic nationalism which both Macdonald and Laurier had pursued. The identification of the Liberal cabal with the fledgling Canadian Northern Railway was particularly impressive. Of the eighteen, five were directly connected with the Canadian Northern or with its principal financial backers.[66] And while Walker admitted that "the growth of Canada would in time do away with the loss of any carriage because of trade diverted to the United States," he was quick to point out that "we have been trying to build up a nation running east and west with a large and rapidly growing inter-provincial trade, and we need transportation of our commodities in order to make our three transcontinental railways pay."[67] Accordingly, on 1 March, Lash, Clifford Sifton, John Willison and the Liberal M.P. for Brantford, Lloyd Harris, met privately with Robert Borden in Ottawa and presented the Conservative leader with a series of conditions upon which they would cooperate with the Tories to oppose reciprocity and bring down the government; and when Borden agreed to "use every possible endeavour to give them effect," they pledged to proceed at once to organize for the coming battle.[68]

As the controversy continued, political factors played an increasingly important part. They were particularly crucial because they aroused and brought into play many of the issues that had confronted Laurier during the earlier years of his administration. Already the *nationaliste* campaign in Quebec had led many in Ontario to question French Canada's loyalty to the Empire.[69] The rapid growth of French-Canadian population in the province and the demand by the newly formed French-Canadian Educational Association of Ontario for "equal rights" for the French language strengthened charges that the *nationalistes* sought greater political power throughout the Dominion.[70] According to the Ontario organizer of the Liberal party in November 1910, "the whole tory campaign in Ontario today is an anti-French crusade because of our leader's French-Canadian origin."[71] Of concern as well were the activities of the Roman Catholic Church. The prominent part which members of the government played at the Eucharistic Congress in Montreal in September 1910 and the struggle in Quebec over the application of the Ne Temere decree aroused Protestant apprehension that the influence of the Roman Catholic hierarchy was in the ascendancy.[72] And it was not without significance that the first point to which the dissident Liberals insisted Borden agree was that a Conservative government "should not be subservient to Roman Catholic influences in public policy or in the administration of patronage."[73] Reciprocity added fuel to fire. Fear that reciprocity would lead to annexation and the resulting loyalty cry were the catalysts which brought anti-French-Canadianism and anti-Catholicism to the surface. As Graham later explained, "three things militated against us in Ontario, first this Province is Protectionist, second it dislikes the Yankees, and third it is ultra Protestant, and it yielded easily to the cry that Laurier and the French-Catholics wanted to give us to the United States."[74]

The Liberals fought back with little success. Laurier replied that closer commercial relations with the United States would not affect Canada's autonomy within the Empire or lead inevitably to absorption into the American Republic. "This Treaty," he pointed out to one ardent and confirmed Imperialist, "will lead to added prosperity and may I ask you to point to me a single country which when prosperous and happy, was ever led to change its allegiance. Prosperity everywhere confirms loyalty."[75] But the lack of a leader in whom Ontario had complete confidence effectively undermined Laurier's appeal. The revolt of the Toronto Eighteen and the widely held fear that the lowering of duties on farm products would be followed by similar reductions on manufactures were the expressions of a business and financial community which no longer felt it had adequate representation at Ottawa; while the strength and resilience of the loyalty cry was in part the result of long-standing doubts and suspicions about the nature of Laurier Liberalism. Aylesworth did his utmost to ease these apprehensions. "There is not a thought, nay, not a breath drawn by Sir Wilfrid Laurier that is not single to the good of Canada and her people. He is a loyal subject, a true believer in that form of Imperialism which he thinks and I think is the true form; that Imperialism which gives to every component part the fullest freedom and seeks equally the well-being and closer binding together of the whole."[76] But Aylesworth's influence in the province had been greatly weakened; and the Minister of Justice had already advised Laurier that he would not seek re-election in the next election.[77] Indeed effective leadership in Ontario had passed into the hands of the Young Turks of the party, Graham and King who had few ties with the old guard of Ontario Liberalism. King summed up the situation: "With the exception of one colleague, Mr. Graham, who is much over-worked, I have no other who is in shape to do much work through the province, in the way of speaking. There are six of us from Ontario, two are too old and infirm to get about, one is deaf, the other is there mostly because be is an Irish-Catholic—that leaves Graham and myself."[78]

The weakness of leadership in Ontario also hampered efforts to place the case for reciprocity before the province. Liberal leaders in Ontario were unable to provide the direction necessary to galvanize party spokesmen into action and launch a concerted and effective campaign in the constituencies. Plans for a public meeting in Toronto to answer the charges of the hastily formed Canadian National League did not get off the ground.[79] Graham complained that "the discouraging part of it is the apathy of the members in the House, whom we have been after for weeks, begging them to hold meetings, but they seem to be standing it off until the roads will be so bad that there will be little use in calling a meeting."[80] Early in March, the Ontario Reform Association set up a committee to provide speakers for political meetings throughout the province,[81] and constituency associations were urged to arrange meetings to pass pro-reciprocity resolutions.[82] Conservative obstructive tactics in the House, however, demanded that Liberal members be in Ottawa and the brunt of the campaign thus fell upon the lacklustre provincial leader, J.F. Mackay. In April, the death of Graham's son forced Laurier's chief strategist in Ontario to withdraw from the campaign for over three weeks, further decimating the Ontario contingent. Moreover, as the summer began and the pamphlet propaganda of the Canadian National League flooded into the province, the Liberal counter-attack had yet to begin. Graham was dismayed that "not a blow has been struck. It is discouraging here—not a single envelope.... There is literature waiting to be sent out, but it will take a long time to address the envelopes after they come."[83] The sluggishness of the Liberal machines in Ontario was serious. As one Liberal organizer warned, "Unless a very vigorous educative campaign is undertaken, taking township by township and polling subdivision by polling subdivision, I would not like to do any prophesying as to the result. Our fellows simply MUST realize that it is their business to dig in and earn their indemnity."[84]

But little time remained as the Ontario Liberals suddenly found themselves in the midst of an election campaign. Their task was immense. Liberal strategy was designed to enlighten a misinformed and befuddled electorate. "I must confess," wrote King, "I find everywhere the need of the people in different ridings being more fully informed as to just what the nature of the proposal is. The press and the speakers are taking it for granted that the people know the agreement and that it is only its effect that needs consideration. The truth is our strongest side of the case is the agreement itself."[85] Liberal strategists believed that once the province was fully aware of the true character and extent of the proposed pact, it would readily see that there was nothing disloyal in it.[86] But as the campaign began, the Liberals had clearly lost the initiative. The argument that the agreement would open a vast third market to the Canadian farmer was no longer useful, particularly in the cities and towns where the consumer was convinced that greater farm prosperity would result in an increased cost of living. One Liberal candidate advised Graham "to say very little about the farmer, which I find has the same effect on my constituents as a red flag is supposed to have on a bull."[87] Efforts to present candidates from the business and financial community to counter the impression that the agreement would imperil their interests were largely unsuccessful.[88] Charles Hyman turned down Aylesworth's overtures to return to public life: "I could not hope to carry the city of London at the present time, the party organization is gone, the party itself only a skeleton of its former self, and enthusiasm over reciprocity in a city constituency could hardly be expected."[89] In the end, Laurier and the Ontario Liberals were forced to concentrate on the British and Imperial question; and by focusing attention upon the dangers of a Borden-Bourassa alliance, they brought into play still further the racial and religious question upon which they were already so vulnerable.[90]

Laurier lost the election of 1911 because he lost Ontario. Of eighty-six seats in the province, the Liberals won only thirteen, a loss of twenty-three seats from dissolution. In spite of his efforts, Laurier failed to win in Ontario the support he felt his policies deserved. He had persistently tried to keep in personal contact with the province. His failure to find a lieutenant in whom the province had implicit confidence might be attributed to his instinctive preference for advisers with intellectual and executive talent over political astuteness, to his own withdrawal from his political colleagues, or to the vagaries of fate which took from him some of his brightest supporters. Perhaps no one man could effectively represent and speak for Ontario like Fielding in Nova Scotia, Blair in New Brunswick, or Sifton in the west. For its geographical extent, religious and racial diversity and economic disparities makes Ontario a province not like the others. But Laurier never lost sight of the importance of regional and provincial leaders in the Canadian political system. In the final analysis, they provide one of the keys to the collapse of the Liberal party in Ontario. Laurier's inability to secure a strong leader acceptable to his Ontario supporters left the party deeply divided and swung the electoral pendulum in the province toward Borden and the Conservative party.

NOTES

1. At the dissolution of Parliament in 1900 the Liberals held 52 seats in Ontario. Of the 52, six had been won by McCarthyites and Patrons [of industry] in 1896 but were regarded as Liberal by 1900. In addition, the Liberals had gained four seats from the Conservatives in by-elections since 1896.

2. Public Archives of Canada, J.S. Willison Papers, Willison to R.L. Borden, 22 April 1905.

3. For an analysis of this election campaign see Paul D. Stevens, "Laurier and the Liberal Party in Ontario, 1887-1911" (unpublished doctoral thesis, University of Toronto, 1966), Ch. IV.

4. P.A.C., Wilfrid Laurier Papers, George D. Grant to Laurier, 26 May 1904.

5. Ibid., Laurier to Charles Murphy, 10 November 1903; Charles Hyman to Laurier, 20 January 1904.

6. Ibid., Charles Murphy to Laurier, 9 November 1903.

7. Ibid., Laurier to W.S. Calvert, 19 February 1906.

8. *The Globe*, 15 October 1904.

9. Laurier Papers, C.M. Bowman to Laurier, 31 October 1906.

10. J.S. Willison, "The Party System of Government," *Proceedings of the Canadian Club*, 15 February 1904, 72.

11. Grey of Howick Papers, Grey to Alfred Lyttleton, 13 February 1905.

12. Laurier Papers, James McMullen to Laurier, 9 March 1905.

13. Willison Papers, Willison to George Beer, 29 November 1912.

14. Stevens, "Laurier and the Liberal Party in Ontario, 1887-1911" Ch. II; H. Blair Neatby, "Laurier and a Liberal Quebec; A Study in Political Management" (unpublished doctoral thesis, University of Toronto, 1956), 258.

15. James Cappon, "The Principle of Sectarianism in the Constitution of Canada," *Queen's Quarterly*, Vol. XII, No. 4, April, 1905, 436.

16. Stevens, "Laurier and the Liberal Party in Ontario, 1887-1911," 287-93.

17. *Sentinel-Review* (Woodstock), 17 October 1906.

18. *The Globe*, 15 June 1907.

19. Ibid., 17 June 1907.

20. Ibid., 27 February 1907.

21. Ibid., 12 September 1907.

22. *The Mail and Empire*, 21 August 1907.

23. *The Globe*, 11 September 1907.

24. Liberal representation in the House of Commons dropped from 39 to 37 as a result of the general election; and the party's popular vote was reduced by almost two percent. But in view of Conservative predictions of between 60 and 70 seats in the province, most Liberals were not unhappy with the result. Laurier Papers, J.A. Macdonald to Laurier, 28 October 1908; Laurier to Macdonald, 30 October 1908.

25. Laurier Papers, W.K. George to Laurier, 1 August 1908.

26. George Grant, *The Evening Journal* (Ottawa), 17 January 1906.

27. Canada, House of Commons, *Debates*, I, 1909-10, 96, 16 November 1909.

28. *Canadian Annual Review, 1910*, 239.

29. Canada, House of Commons, *Debates*, IV, 1909-10, 6587, 7 April 1910,

30. Ibid., 6543, 7 April 1910.

31. P.A.C., George Graham Papers, N.W. Rowell to Graham, 9 April 1910.

32. *The Globe*, 8 April 1910.

33. Ibid., 16 April 1910.

34. Canada, House of Commons, *Debates*, IV, 1909-10, 7185, 15 April 1910.

35. Ibid., 8350, 28 April 1910.

36. *The Globe*, 23 April 1910.

37. Laurier Papers, J.A. Macdonald to Laurier, 19 April 1910.

38. Ibid., Macdonald to Laurier, 5 July 1910.

39. Ibid., Laurier to Macdonald, 22 November 1910.

40. Ibid., Laurier to Macdonald, 21 April 1910.

41. Ibid., Laurier to Macdonald, 25 April 1910; Ibid., Laurier to Rev. C.W. Gordon, 16 November 1910.

42. Ibid., Laurier to Rev. C.W. Gordon, 16 November 1910.

43. Graham Papers, H.H. Dewart to Laurier, copy, 12 February 1909.

44. *The Globe*, 27 April 1910.

45. J.W. Dafoe, *Clifford Sifton in Relation to His Times* (Toronto, 1931), 341-2.

46. Laurier Papers, J.L. Richardson to Laurier, 7 November 1910.

47. The General Reform Association for Ontario, *Proceedings of the Sixth Annual Meeting* (Toronto, 1910), 24.

48. R. Cuff, "The Conservative Party Machine and the Election of 1911," *Ontario History*, LVII (September, 1965), 149-56; C.W. Humphries,

"The Political Career of Sir James P. Whitney" (unpublished doctoral thesis, University of Toronto, 1966). It is interesting to note as well that the so-called "Whitney Machine" was singularly unsuccessful in by-elections between 1908 and January 1910. Of the three by-elections in the province, the Liberals won two with increased majorities.

49. Laurier Papers, Aylesworth to Laurier, 31 August 1910.

50. Ibid., Aylesworth to Laurier, 19 October 1917.

51. Ibid., Aylesworth to Laurier, 5 May 1910.

52. Douglas Library, Queen's University, Allan Aylesworth Papers, Laurier to Aylesworth, 8 May 1910.

53. Three of the brightest lights in the Ontario caucus had failed to live up to Laurier's expectations. George Grant, the Ontario whip, had resigned at the beginning of 1906 after giving an interview to the Ottawa *Journal* criticizing the Ontario leadership. Leighton McCarthy had not sought re-election in 1908 for personal reasons, while Hugh Guthrie had been denied promotion apparently because of personal financial difficulties.

54. Laurier Papers, W.D. Gregory to Laurier, 14 January 1911.

55. Between 1891 and 1911, the rural population in Ontario decreased from 1,295,323 to 1,194,785, while urban population increased from 818,009 to 1,328,489.

56. *The News*, 6 September 1910.

57. Aylesworth Papers, Letterbook, Aylesworth to J.F. Edgar, 3 March 1911.

58. Graham Papers, Private Letterbook, Graham to A. Davis, 9 November 1910.

59. P.A.C., W.L.M. King Papers, King to E.W.B. Snider, 28 October 1910. Both Graham and King distributed questionnaires to the manufacturing and industrial interests in their constituencies during the summer of 1910 and discovered that they were overwhelmingly opposed to a reciprocity agreement.

60. *The Weekly Sun*, 10 August 1910.

61. Laurier Papers, D.A. Gordon to Laurier, 17 November 1910.

62. Grey Papers, Grey to George Bryce, 5 January 1911.

63. Laurier Papers, Laurier to Fielding, 18 January 1911; King Papers, King to Arthur Pequegnat, 30 January 1911.

64. R. Cuff, "The Toronto Eighteen and the Election of 1911," *Ontario History* LVII (December, 1965), 169-80.

65. Laurier Papers, B.E. Walker to Laurier, 4 June 1909; J.L. Blaikie to Laurier, 11 June 1909; E.R. Wood to Laurier, 17 June 1909; H. Blain to Laurier, 18 November 1909.

66. The Canadian Bank of Commerce and the National Trust Company.

67. University of Toronto Library, Sir Edmund Walker Papers, Walker to J. H. Fulton, 16 March 1911. Another former Liberal who joined in the anti-reciprocity campaign, John Willison, had written of Walker: "He has been the chief apologist for the Electrical Development Company, the Toronto Electric Light Company and the Canadian Northern Railway Company. He has absolutely no public spirit except in the field of banking and in his own particular pursuits while his arrogance on questions which he does not understand is intolerable. Of course I agree that he is a man of distinction, of great service in his own field, and even a worthy national figure. But so many corporations centre in the Bank of Commerce and he is so utterly their slave that he is dangerous." Willison Papers, Willison to C. F. Hamilton, 3 May 1907.

68. Willison Papers, J. S. Willison, Memorandum, undated. The Committee insisted that a new Conservative administration, should one

be elected, should not be subservient to Roman Catholics in policy or patronage matters; that it should resist American encroachments on Canada's economic integrity and strengthen Canadian nationality; that Borden, in forming his cabinet should consult with Lash, Walker and Willison, to ensure that it be "so constituted as to guarantee the effective adoption and application of this policy, and that there should be reasonable representation therein of the views of those Liberals who may unite with Conservatives against the policy of reciprocity"; that Borden should bring men from outside Parliament into cabinet; and that he should set up a Civil Service Commission, reorganize the Department of Trade and Commerce, and appoint a Tariff Commission.

69. Laurier Papers, James McMullen to Laurier, 26 August 1910. It is interesting to note as well the number of articles on the *nationalistes* which appear in the English-Canadian Press, particularly after the Drummond-Arthabaska by-election.

70. Ottawa *Citizen*, 17 October 1910; *The Weekly Sun*, 10 November 1909.

71. Laurier Papers, J.M. Mowat to Laurier, 5 November 1910.

72. *The Globe*, 2 September 1910; Laurier Papers, Rev. R.E. Langfeldt to Laurier, 19 October 1910; *The News*, 28 March 1911. It is difficult to assess the impact of these issues, but one Conservative organizer in Ontario informed Borden: "I also find a strong prejudice against Sir Wilfrid on the 'mixed marriage' question and this with the Liberals. If the feeling in my county is any omen as to Ontario as a whole I believe we will surprise them.

Borden Papers, 27 October 1910. J. D. Reid to Borden, 25 May 1911.

73. Willison Papers, J. S. Willison, Memorandum, undated.

74. Graham Papers, Private Letterbook, Graham to J. A. Carman, 27 September 1911.

75. Laurier Papers, Laurier to Hugh Graham, 6 February 1911.

76. *The Globe*, 13 August 1911.

77. Laurier Papers, Aylesworth to Laurier, 5 May 1910.

78. King Papers, King to Violet Markham, 1 January 1911.

79. Laurier Papers, Graham to Laurier, 8 March 1911.

80. Graham Papers, Private Letterbook, Graham to N.W. Rowell, 15 March 1911.

81. Ibid., Graham to N.W. Rowell, 15 March 1911.

82. Graham Papers, F.G. Inwood to H.H. Mowat, 29 March 1911.

83. Ibid., Private Letterbook, Graham F.F. Pardee, 5 July 1911.

84. Ibid., J. Macdonald Mowat to Graham, 29 May 1911.

85. Ibid., King to Graham, 26 June 1911.

86. Ibid., Private Letterbook, Graham to F.F. Pardee, 31 May 1911.

87. Ibid., J. Macdonald Mowat to Graham, 16 September 1911.

88. Laurier Papers, M. K. Cowan to Laurier, 1 August 1911; Laurier to William Harty, 12 August 1911; Graham Papers, Graham to W.J. O'Reilly, 2 August 1911.

89. Aylesworth Papers, Charles Hyman to Aylesworth, 19 August 1911.

90. Graham Papers, J. Macdonald Mowat to Graham, 16 September 1911.

A PARTY IN OPPOSITION: THE CONSERVATIVES 1901-11

BY JOHN ENGLISH

o

How does an opposition party leader organize his party for victory when he is denied all but a few drops of that lifeblood of political existence, patronage? This was the question facing Robert Borden, the new leader of the Conservative party in 1901. The answer was not clear, but Borden's attempts to discover it form an interesting chapter in Canadian political history. Between 1901 and 1911 the Conservatives under Borden became the focus of an uncertain but often creative experiment in transformation. The pressure for such change came from the leader, from a few Conservative members of Parliament sharing his views, and from increasingly powerful groups outside Parliament to whom Borden turned in lieu of organized Conservative support. The resistance to reform arose among the majority of party backbenchers, lower-level party officials, and financial and commercial interests traditionally influential within the Conservative party. The succession of Conservative defeats after 1896 reinforced both factions in their beliefs. To the resisters, Borden's tentative changes bore the responsibility for past failures; to Borden, the party reactionaries had caused the defeats. In 1910 and 1911 these antagonistic viewpoints met in an open clash. This collision, which improbably culminated in a Conservative victory in September 1911, reflected and even perhaps predetermined the political events, alliances, and divisions of the succeeding ten years, particularly the politically complex Union government formed in 1917. To examine the creative pressures exerted within the Conservative party is to study a mirror of the changes throughout Canadian political life.

Excerpt from John English, *The Decline of Politics: The Conservatives and the Party System, 1901-20* (Toronto: University of Toronto Press Incoporated, 1977), pp.31-53. Reprinted with permission of University of Toronto Press Incorporated.

LEADERSHIP AND POLICY

During the first three decades of Canada's existence the Conservative party was the party of Confederation, the political embodiment of the spirit of 1867. By 1901, however, the party was in opposition and without Macdonald, and lacked such a clear definition. Party differences seemed to be less meaningful and less fundamental. The issue of the survival of Confederation had all but vanished from the political arena; while annexation to the United States and its counterpart, imperial enthusiasm, which had greatly vexed Canadians until recently, now seemed condemned to political death by the mutual consent of both the Liberal and Conservative parties. More than anything else, the ease of the transition from Conservatism to Liberalism in 1896 had produced this widespread sense that party differences had disappeared. The Fielding budget, imperial preference, and Laurier's knighthood further confirmed this belief. While the struggle continued with flourish and fury in the constituencies, national political leaders and commentators hailed the new comity as they groped for an explanation of its emergence.

When the seventy-nine-year-old Sir Charles Tupper led the Tories to a second consecutive defeat in 1900, the "Cumberland warhorse" knew that he must give way. The Tuppers—Sir Charles and his talented but unpopular son, Sir Charles Hibbert—were reluctant to lose the leadership, but they knew they could prevent the choice of anyone abhorrent to them and, given the absence of a clearly recognized alternative leader, probably nominate the successor. Most of the members of Parliament and senators who gathered in a caucus room on 5 February 1901 to choose the new leader were aware of and accepted the Tuppers' view of the role they would play. After courteously considering some of the party's old warriors, including George E. Foster, J.G. Haggart, and Clarke Wallace, and two unlikely French Canadians—Thomas Chase Casgrain, the prosecutor of Quebec's most recent martyrs, Riel and Mercier, and Boer War supporter Frederick D. Monk—the younger Tupper proposed the name of Robert Borden for the party leadership. Although his principal qualification seems to have been his earlier law partnership with Tupper, the device was nevertheless successful: Borden, a member for only four years, was unanimously chosen leader.[1] The many Tupper enemies were either weary of the fray or, more likely, simply stayed away from a meeting which they could not control.

What does the choice of Borden tell us about the character of the Conservative party and of Canadian politics? First, it substantiates the impression of Canadian party politics as predominantly local in orientation. The method of choice of the new leader minimized rather than created public excitement. No thought was given to consultation with Conservatives throughout the Dominion. Indeed, the number of politicians at the leadership caucus suggests that there was not even much interest in the choice among Tory parliamentarians themselves: in fact only 70 of 112 eligible parliamentarians attended. Here surely is further evidence that national party leadership was less important than local party leadership, and that national consciousness in the modern sense of nationally focused politics was yet unformed. Another striking illustration of this is the prominence that Canada's largest English-language daily, the *Montreal Star*, gave to the leadership change—two columns on page six. The *Star* was certainly concerned: its owner, Hugh Graham, regarded himself as the *eminence grise* of the Tory party, but apparently the *Star's* readers were not thought to be much interested.

Secondly, the selection of Borden and the manner in which it was accomplished betrays the transitional and uncertain state of the party.[2] The great names of the Tory past, the Tuppers, Sir John Thompson, and, most of all, Macdonald, were all absent from the Parliament of 1901 and with them had disappeared the style of leadership and most of the political controversies which they embodied. Even George Foster, who for all his deficiencies was a powerful link with earlier Tory greatness, was not on the Tory front bench because of his election defeat. Borden was, it is true, the choice of the past, but he was scarcely representative of it. That Borden was given "an absolutely free hand [by the caucus] to do whatever he pleases" means that the Tories recognized that the past could not be recaptured and that the party must come to terms with the success of Sir Wilfrid Laurier and the new political milieu. Borden therefore possessed an opportunity which his predecessors—Tupper, Sir Mackenzie Bowell, Thompson, and Sir John Abbott—never really had: the opportunity to reconstruct the party in his own image.

Borden had more freedom than past leaders but, in his biographer's words, he sensed "...that his work would be slow, demanding, often discouraging. He recognized that it would call for patience and understanding far beyond what he had been called upon to exhibit in his legal career.... The security of the law, of its established precedents, of its traditional procedures, of its professional respect, had no real equivalent in politics.[3] And there certainly was much discouragement and even embarrassment in Borden's first few years as leader when he could use only what he inherited. During 1903 and 1904, for example, the inexperienced leader became involved in an extraordinary plot with Montreal Conservative interests, the Canadian Pacific Railway, and Hugh Graham, which included bribery of journalists, resignations of Quebec Liberal candidates late in the campaign, and large transfers of funds to the Conservative party in return for certain promises. The plot failed and so did Borden when Laurier triumphed in the 1904 election.[4] Not surprisingly, Borden's initial reaction to the defeat was a decision to return to Halifax where before he entered politics in 1896 he had earned $30,000 annually. His wife disliked politics, and the performance of his "extremely lazy" caucus frustrated him. The caucus, he told his wife, "continually neglected" what he considered to be "matters of moment."[5] But Borden did not return to Halifax, to the security of the law and his comfortable income. His impulse to flee was halted by a unanimous appeal to his sense of duty by the Conservative caucus, which overrode—not for the last time—the wishes of Borden's wife.[6]

Having decided to remain, Borden began to reorganize his party and to lure new interests and men to the Tory cause, and it was then that policy became important. An opposition party without much patronage had little chance in a party-to-party confrontation. If, however, the opposition could attract significant "interests"—we call them "pressure groups" today—their financial and other resources could dramatically alter the political balance. By 1905 there were several groups which had organized their committed followers and, indeed, were performing many of the functions which parties had previously undertaken. They defined national goals and in many cases repudiated local interests, and they existed as alternate forms of socialization to the political party. There were many such groups who shared Borden's dissatisfaction with Laurier Liberalism: "farm and labour leaders who believed that their followers had received less than a fair share of the new affluence, French-Canadian *nationalistes* fearful for the future of their society's distinctiveness, feminists demanding political equality, urban reformers concerned about slums and sanitation, prohibitionists zealous to 'Banish the Bar,' and advocates of 'Canadianization' uneasy about the foreign immigrant." The differences among these groups were great, and Borden knew that any dreams that all reformers might rally to the Tory standard were chimerical. Yet each group in its own way did assert, in the words of Craig Brown and Ramsay Cook, "the increasing irrelevance of Laurier's kind of liberalism" and thus represented "the search for a new public philosophy."[7]

It was to this search and to this mood that Borden's Halifax Platform of 1907 responded. Historians have devoted much attention to the intellectual origins and significance of these Halifax proposals; what concerns us here is their political utility. The platform, Borden wrote, would be "an effective and honest rallying cry which will appeal to the more progressive spirits and communities."[8] Like W.S. Gilbert, Borden knew:

> That every boy and every gal
> That's born into the world alive
> Is either a little Liberal,
> Or else a little Conservative.

But little boys grew up (until 1917 a politician did not need to worry about little girls). And although usually reluctant to cast off their political birthright, sometimes they did—in fact, Borden himself had.[9] Those who did so were likely to be the most thoughtful, intelligent, and concerned—in short, the "more progressive spirits and communities." Thus the planks of the Halifax Platform promising "civil service reform" and "clean elections" would appeal to the many Canadians who felt wronged by the strong political machines and who might be willing to become Conservatives. The "restoration" of public lands to Saskatchewan and Alberta, rural free mail delivery, and a public utilities commission to regulate railways and telephone and telegraph companies would surely win the approval of those western "farm leaders" who believed their followers had not received their "fair share." There were few independents in Canadian politics, but given the extraordinary stability of Liberal and Conservative party support (in the three elections, 1900, 1904, and 1908, the Tory popular vote varied only 5 per cent), the independent's choice was all important. Because a very small swing could mean success in the election, the independent or "floating vote" was most carefully tended.[10] This was the essence of political leadership, and Robert Borden eventually proved to be its master.

There were three major groupings which Borden eventually drew into alliances of varying degrees of formality with the federal Conservative party: the Quebec *nationalistes,* the imperialists and "progressives" of English Canada, and the Conservative provincial premiers, who, of course, would have voted Tory federally but who, without Borden's wooing, might not have worked very hard for them. Yet, while these groups may have provided the margin of victory, they did not provide its foundation. This was the part of the Conservative voters and their representatives, the Conservative members of Parliament, and for that reason they deserve our first attention.

RANK AND FILE

Borden regarded his party's rank and file as narrow men of limited talent. Thus he wrote to a friend who had objected to his strong support for a bill providing for an increase in the members' indemnity: "Those who are opposed to any increase of indemnity would have their views altered if they had undergone my own experience in endeavouring to get representative men to enter public life. This is rapidly becoming impossible under present conditions."[11] What type of men were entering public life? Laurier once described a member's typical career pattern: "...In the average rural riding, the large majority of all ridings, the member had served in township and county councils and possibly been warden. This has brought him close acquaintance with the electorate. He is an honest, faithful conscientious member, but with no outstanding ability."[12]

An examination of the characteristics of the Conservative members largely verifies Laurier's impressions. Unexciting, unambitious, and always alert to the whims and needs of their constituencies, the Conservative rank and file were an unimpressive lot. But however unimpressive, they *were* the Conservative party to most Canadians and therefore should be studied in some depth. Fortunately, the diligence of contemporary chroniclers, of the Public Archives of Canada, and of Norman Ward, whose 1950 study of representation has remained unsurpassed, has created a strong framework upon which to carry out an analysis.[13] For our purposes here the year 1909 has been selected to examine the Conservative members—Borden had been leader of the party for eight years and within two years was to come to power.

When Borden assumed the leadership, Conservative representation was geographically maldistributed although the Conservative popular vote was relatively high in all provinces. This pattern continued through the next two elections, as can be seen in Table 1. The stability and the pattern are striking,

TABLE 1. CONSERVATIVE SUPPORT IN CANADIAN GERNERAL ELECTIONS, 1900-1908

	1900			1904			1908		
	Conservative Seats	Total Seats	Percentage of vote	Conservative Seats	Total Seats	Percentage of vote	Conservative Seats	Total Seats	Percentage of vote
Prince Edward Island	2	5	48.2	3	4	50.9	1	4	49.6
Nova Scotia	5	20	48.3	0	18	44.5	6	18	49.0
New Brunswick	5	14	47.8	6	13	48.8	2	13	46.2
Quebec	8	65	43.5	11	65	43.4	11	65	40.8
Ontario	56	92	49.7	48	86	50.3	48	86	51.4
Manitoba	3	7	48.2	3	10	41.8	8	10	51.5
British Columbia	2	6	40.9	0	7	38.8	5	7	46.8
Northwest Territories	0	4	44.9	3	10	41.5			
Yukon				1	1	58.6	0	1	10.8
Alberta*							3	7	44.4
Saskatchewan*							1	10	36.8
Total	81	213	47.4	75	214	46.9	85	221	47.0

*The provinces of Alberta and Saskatchewan were formed in 1905 from the former Northwest Territories.

Source: M.C. Urquhart and K.H.Buckley, eds., Historical Statistics of Canada (Toronto, 1965), section W.

as are the inequities of the electoral system. Ontario was the core of the Conservative party, electing more than half of the Tory representation throughout this period. Borden could not capture his home territory, the Maritimes. In the west, the Conservative provincial governments of Manitoba and British Columbia used their prestige and patronage to advance the federal cause; but the Conservatives were distressingly weak in the most rapidly growing provinces, Saskatchewan and Alberta, which, it should be noted, were Liberal creations in 1905. Yet it was Quebec which kept the Conservatives on the opposition benches. Whether Louis Riel's execution, Tory indifference, or Laurier's French-Canadian background were responsible for the death of Conservative Quebec, each succeeding election confirmed that the province was now a Liberal bastion.

Given the predominance of Ontario representation, one would expect that the main racial and religious characteristic of Conservative members would be British Protestant. Still, the degree to which British Protestants did dominate the Tory caucus in 1909 is nevertheless quite astonishing (see Table 2). That Borden was bound by the prejudices and perceptions of middle-class English Canada is therefore quite understandable. The well-known witticism that the Church of England is the Tory party at prayer might properly be applied to the Conservative party of Canada in 1909 if one added to the Anglican total the Methodists and the Presbyterians. Canadian Conservatism bore the unmistakable marks of its origins, British and established; but for all its outward similarity, it possessed little of the excellence of its British counterpart—it was, at best, a pale reflection.

TABLE 2. *RELIGIOUS AND NATIONAL BACKGROUNDS OF CONSERVATIVE MEMBERS IN 1909*

	Number	Percentage of total caucus	Percentage of group in population
Anglican	33	37.9	14.47
Presbyterian	17	19.5	15.48
Methodist	18	20.6	14.98
Roman Catholic	12	13.7	39.31
Baptist	2	2	5.31
Other Protestant	5	5	10.45
British	79	90.8	54.08
French Canadian	6	6.9	28.51
German	2	2.3	5.46
Astro-Hungarian	0	0	1.79
Others	0	0	10.16

Where an individual is of mixed British and French parentage he is included as a French Canadian (for example, Monk). In all other cases the father's nationality has been used to determine the member's nationality.

Source: *The Canadian Parliamentary Guide, 1909,* and Morgan, *Canadian Men and Women of the Time.*

One reason for this weakness was, of course, the absence in Canada of any hereditary aristocracy trained from birth for state service and endowed with ample means. There was a very rapid turnover of members and political inexperience was all too common. Fully 45.9 per cent of the Conservative members in 1909 had been elected first in 1908, an election with an overall turnover of 38.4 per cent. The average parliamentary experience of Conservative members in 1908 was 5.8 years, the median only 4 years. Borden's difficulties stemmed from the fact that there were too many new members who were willing to innovate but lacked prestige and political skill and too many veterans who feared change yet possessed manifold political skills and prestige.[14] The inexperience and the high rate of turnover indicates that the Conservatives were having great difficulty in retaining their members. Limited interest in politics, faulty organization, and frustration with the party itself are all possible explanations for this failure. Even more serious in light of the number of new Tory members in 1908 is the information that the median age for Conservative members in 1909 was 51.5 compared to an overall parliamentary median of 50. The Liberals, thirteen years in power, were a younger party than the Conservatives. If little comfort could be derived from these statistics, greater unease undoubtedly arose from the knowledge that, despite Borden's recruitment efforts, nearly all the new members were largely cast in the mold of the old.

The Conservative members of Parliament were, on the whole, men who had entered politics after years of participation in the affairs of their constituency. Typical careers would be those of Richard Blain, MP for Peel in Ontario, G.H.Barnard of Victoria, and Pierre Blondin of Champlain in Quebec. Blain entered federal politics at the age of forty-three after serving on a town council for ten years and as reeve and as warden of the county. Barnard, a lawyer, had been elected for Victoria in 1908 at forty years of age after serving as an alderman and as mayor of Victoria. This pattern transcended cultural boundaries: Blondin, also a lawyer, had been the clerk of the circuit court for Champlain and an alderman in the town of Grand-Mère. Of the 87 Tories elected in 1908, 42 identified themselves as having local political experience (undoubtedly many more neglected to mention it); 23 noted that they were mayors of towns before their election to Parliament.[15]

The occupations of the Conservative members in 1909 reflect the local interest of the candidate:

Lawyers	26	Doctors	10	Journalists	3
Merchants	13	Farmers	10	Others	6
Manufacturers	10	Financiers	6	Unknown	3

Very few had advanced training of any type. If one excludes legal training from university education (but includes lawyers with degrees), twenty-two Conservatives had university degrees, only two of these degrees in science or engineering and ten in medicine. The manufacturers in Tory ranks scarcely fitted Borden's rather romantic conception of that group: they were such men as John Stanfield, the owner of a knitting mill and a notorious political manipulator, or George Taylor, the Conservative whip since the time of Macdonald and "an Orangeman and proud of it." The merchants and doctors were mostly from small towns as were the few journalists and publishers, professions which were often fertile sources for political talent but not for the Conservative party in 1909. The lawyers predominated, as they always have in Canadian politics where the propinquity of the courtroom and the political backroom has been marked.

What, then, can be said about the Conservative rank and file in 1909? Earl Grey, one of a long series of governors-general who had great contempt for Canadian politicians, thought he had found a perfect descriptive phrase for the Tories: "the stupid party." One suspects that Borden, in his more despondent moments, might have agreed. More fundamentally, however, the disappointment of Borden, Grey, and many others lay not with the men but with the representative system which produced them. The weak members were a symptom of a weak party and of an electorate blind to any political world beyond their own constituency. Borden favoured, to use Max Weber's term, but not in Weber's sense, a "plutocratic recruitment"[16] of those who would "live exclusively for politics and not off politics," men who were not merely the tool of "local notables" but the representatives of the best elements in the nation. Could the representative system of constituencies in a land so broad, spiritually and geographically, as Canada bring forth not delegates but trustees who would subordinate local to national ends? Between the Scylla of plebiscitarian democracy and the Charybdis of political feudalism, Borden sought a clear course.

His course was obscured by lack of information about who voted for the Conservatives; he simply did not possess the sensitive political antennae of Mackenzie King, Laurier, or Macdonald whose wide range of correspondents fed them political details which they quickly assimilated and used. Nor did he have the public opinion surveys which a later generation of politicians have both cherished and feared. While the historian also suffers from this absence, some conclusions about voting behaviour are possible. But before we examine how people voted, we should ask who voted in the elections of 1900, 1904, and 1908.

By 1900 "the notion that the franchise was a trust accompanying property, rather than a right normally accompanying citizenship"[17] had all but disappeared. With the adoption of provincial franchises in 1898 full manhood suffrage obtained in all provinces but Quebec and Nova Scotia. The effects upon the size of the electorate in the various provinces can be seen in Table 3. A large percentage of those who could vote did, an indication of partisan loyalty as well as of political interest. In 1900, 77.4 per cent of those on the voters' list voted; in 1904, 71.6 per cent; and in 1908, 70.3 per cent. In certain provinces the turnouts were astonishingly high (in 1900 in Ontario 85 per cent voted and in Nova Scotia 75 per cent); in other provinces rather low, undoubtedly a product of such factors as distance from polls, bad weather, recent immigration, and lack of interest in the campaign (in 1900 in British Columbia 59 per cent, in Manitoba 64, in Quebec 69, and in New Brunswick 76).[18]

TABLE 3. THE FRANCHISE IN 1900

	Constituencies in sample	Average electorate	Average population	Average electorate as percentage of average population
Ontario	12	5530	20,420	27.1
Quebec	10	4905	23,262	21.1
Nova Scotia	4	5802	23,382	24.8
New Brunswick	4	5328	19,730	27.3
Prince Edward Island*			20,652	
Manitoba	3	11,282	40,443	27.9
British Columbia	3	5443	24,903	21.9

*Under provincial law the Island had no voters' lists since open voting still applied there.

Source: Ward, Canadian House of Commons, 225.

Were these voters inspired to vote for the party or for the candidate? No conclusive answer is possible, but the presence of several double-member constituencies does give some indication that the party was paramount in the decision of most Canadians. The strongest evidence for this is the relatively small difference between the vote of the two candidates running for the same party. Only once between 1904 and 1911 did the margin between the candidates of the same party in the three double-member constituencies vary more than 6 per cent. Similarly, a close analysis of double constituencies in the last decades of the nineteenth century led one analyst to conclude, with André Siegfried, that for most Canadians the party was "almost a sacred institution, to be forsaken only at the cost of one's reputation and career."[19]

If stability and partisanship were the salient features of Conservative support, what were the foundations of these features? As can be seen in Table 1, the Conservatives did exceedingly well in 1908 and 1911 in three of the four provinces which had Conservative governments. In the provinces with Tory governments in 1908, the Tories won 67 per cent of the seats and 54 per cent of the total vote. It is not surprising that Borden considered control of provincial governments the stepping stones to federal victory.

In separate studies Douglas Baldwin and Kenneth M. McLaughlin have examined in considerable detail the basis of party support in the last years of the nineteenth century. Baldwin found that in Ontario Macdonald's Tories received support from all areas, but especially strong support in cities and from Anglicans and Irish Protestants. Interestingly, he discovered that Conservative support among Franco-Ontarians declined considerably between 1879 and 1891. In his analysis of the 1896 election, McLaughlin argues that there is "no statistical evidence to support the existence of a 'Catholic vote.'" He also claims that Protestants similarly refused to place "religion before the interests of their party." In Quebec, 1896 witnessed a change as French Canadians sought leadership and stability under a French-Canadian prime minister, but, McLaughlin strongly emphasizes, Conservatism did not collapse in Quebec.[20] The pattern of support described by Baldwin and McLaughlin was Borden's inheritance from Macdonald and Tupper.

The Conservatives continued to do very well in the cities. Of the 85 seats won by them in 1908 fully 46 per cent were urban at a time when only 30 per cent of all seats were urban.[21] The Anglican support seems to have remained as well: in the ten constituencies[22] where Anglicans made up more than 28 per cent of the population the Tories were victors in nine and took almost 55 per cent of the popular vote in the 1908 election (compared to 47 per cent of the overall vote). The Conservatives also garnered fairly strong support in Quebec in the constituencies where English Canadians made up over 40 per cent of the population, [23] taking 49.5 per cent of the vote and three of the seven constituencies. Nevertheless, Conservative weakness in French-Canadian areas continued. They lost all six constituencies outside of Quebec where French Canadians constituted more than 50 per cent of the population[24] and won only 39.5 per cent of the popular vote in those constituencies. Of the 48 Quebec constituencies where French Canadians totalled more than three-quarters of the population, the Tories won only five in 1908. Their popular vote in the 48, however, was a more respectable 42.75 per cent.[25] Finally, of the twelve constituencies where "others" outnumbered "British" and "French" combined,[26] the Tories won three (all in Manitoba) and 44 per cent of the popular vote.

In general, then, the Conservatives had a broader base than the character of their Commons membership suggests. While weaker in French Canada and non-British areas than elsewhere, the Tories were certainly far from vanquished, and Borden might conceivably expect a significant Conservative revival in Quebec once the Liberals turned to an English-Canadian leader. In fact, one of the most troubling aspects of the Conservative supporters in the Conservative caucus was their failure to represent Conservative support in the nation. In an age before the party convention, those unrepresented could seldom make their presence felt. The danger lay in the possibility that the leader would see the caucus as the microcosm of Conservatism in Canada and fail to notice how certain elements were absent. Borden, fortunately, managed to retain a perspective, and he did this most effectively by bringing others forward to represent and speak for those who remained without a voice in the caucus.

OUTSIDERS AS INSIDERS

Borden's major goal was to defeat the Laurier Liberals; secondary and complementary goals were surmounting the mediocrity of the parliamentary Conservatives and attracting allies for his battles with Laurier. Great politicians achieve the support and freedom Borden desired by appealing beyond Parliament to the electorate. "Gladstone," the Duke of Argyll observed, "exercises such a sway over the constituencies, that the members are afraid to call their souls their own."[27] The failure of the Halifax Platform campaign in the election of 1908, when the Tories suffered a second defeat under Borden's leadership, proved that such a direct route was closed to Borden. One alternative was to begin at the lowest level and build a well-structured national organization based upon widespread participation. Not surprisingly, newspaper clippings on Chamberlain's famed "caucus" are plentiful in the Borden Papers. The influence of such experiments is apparent in a 1903 letter from Borden to a North-West Territories convention chairman: "No cause however good can prevail unless its supporters are thoroughly organized and equipped for battle. Organization is all important. If the people remain inert the Government naturally falls into the hands of professional politicians, men whose chief interest in the country is their own political existence, men accustomed to rely upon the unscrupulous methods of the machine."[28]

But Borden was no populist content with vague images of "the people" liberating themselves, and modern political organizational methods were unknown. Political participation would be primarily educative, with a clear sense of direction, and inspired from above—not by "professional politicians" but by men with vision and detachment and, in Borden's words, a "moral earnestness."[29] If this is a contradiction, it is one shared by the most prominent social thinkers of the age who were so intoxicated by the possibilities of the state that they could not enunciate a coherent and cogent course for popular action.[30] Borden, however, was no philosopher, and action for him meant seeking out men who conformed to his idea of what public men should be. Many he found outside of politics, and we shall deal with these later, but others he found involved in political life, notably the Conservative provincial premiers. In his struggle to remake the party, Borden used the premiers to overcome the stagnation of the parliamentary party and to create a new organization which undermined the traditional sources of power in the party. It was, therefore, not simply fortuitous that federal Conservatives did very well wherever provincial Tories held sway.

With the exception of James Whitney, history has not treated the Conservative premiers of the early 1900s well. The scandals and inefficiency surrounding the last years in office of Rodmond Roblin and Richard McBride are as lamentable as they are comic. Yet in 1905 these new governments seemed to be popular, progressive administrations which "guaranteed stability and positive growth."[31] Borden accordingly decided to link his party's fate to that of these provincial parties. After the 1904 defeat which revealed the bankruptcy of the old party organization, Borden turned to Whitney, McBride, and Roblin for assistance in constructing a new organization.

In Ontario, Borden had worked quite closely with Whitney since 1901, and by 1907 this friendship had become an organizational alliance. During Borden's period of hesitation about political life, Whitney had encouraged him to stay on as leader—indeed, Whitney later claimed that Borden "was mainly influenced in his decision to remain in public life by a letter which I wrote him on the subject."[32] In May 1907, after consultations with the premier, Borden created an organization to serve both federal and provincial Conservatism in Ontario with A.E. Kemp, the manufacturer, as financial manager and J.S. Carstairs, an historian, as the organizer. Carstairs later pointed out how indistinguishable the federal and provincial parties became in this new organization:

> In the eighty-one federal ridings (without counting the five Torontos) which may be properly considered to be by bailiewick [sic] there are 115 Liberal Conservative Riding Associations, which may be classified as follows:
>
> A. Purely Federal Associations 14
> B. Mixed Federal Associations; that is, where two Provincial Organizations have been united to form a Federal Association 6
> C. Purely Provincial Associations 35
> D. Associations that perform all political functions both Federal and Provincial[33] 60

There remained two nominal organizations, but, as Carstairs' figures suggest, actual work was done in unison in most cases. A newspaper jointly owned was planned for Toronto, but for various reasons the enterprise failed.[34] Whitney advised Borden on federal party policy and thought that the Halifax Platform "hit the nail pretty fairly on the head."[35] Because he believed this and because he believed that Borden would introduce into the federal area the programs he advanced provincially, Whitney actively campaigned for Borden in the 1908 election.

In the other provinces ruled by the Tories—British Columbia, Manitoba, and, after 1908, New Brunswick—similar attempts at organizational unity were made. Premiers McBride, Roblin, and Douglas Hazen, then at the height of their popularity, joined Whitney on federal platforms in 1908, their presence itself becoming a campaign issue.[36] After 1908 Martin Burrell, McBride's former secretary, became the British Columbia premier's representative in the federal caucus.[37] For his part, Roblin lent his most powerful deputy, Robert Rogers, to the federal Conservatives to act, according to one report, as the Conservative chief organizer. Rogers' reputation was yet unsullied and Borden's confidant Charles Hamilton even told a story of three *Manitoba Free Press* detectives "who followed Rogers for months—were in his office as confidential clerks etc.—& got nothing." More probable was Hamilton's other claim that Rogers was "a greater campaigner and organizer than Sifton." These remarkable skills became the property of the federal party after 1908. Rogers' precise role in the organization is unclear, but evidence clearly suggests it was a major and effective one.[38] Borden's tactics were similar in provinces where the Conservatives were in opposition. Charles Tanner, the Conservative leader of the opposition in Nova Scotia, noticed the remarkable change in federal-provincial party relations: unlike Sir Charles Tupper who had "candidly acknowledged that he had preferred to see the locals in opposition," Borden took a genuine interest in the fortunes of the provincial party and expected the provincial party to do the same in return.[39]

The rewards of Borden's actions were soon apparent. On the one hand, the campaigns of Whitney, McBride, and Roblin gained decisive victories for the Conservatives in their respective provinces, the only provinces which the federal Tories won in 1908. Furthermore, a great number of youthful, ambitious, and able provincial Conservatives became involved in federal politics with some, such as Burrell, even being elected. Those who remained outside Parliament continued to take part in organizational work for both the provincial and federal parties. The "sleeping sickness" which had usually afflicted the Tories after earlier elections was thus warded off.[40] Most important, however, was the increased power which the federal-provincial alliance gave Borden within the parliamentary party itself. With the premiers' help, Borden might yet make the federal party his own.

Unfortunately for Borden, there was no Conservative premier of Quebec; indeed, there were few leading Quebec Conservatives. When Borden assumed the leadership of the party in 1901 he had only eight colleagues from Quebec. Obviously something had to be done about this situation, but Borden—a Protestant, unilingual, Halifax lawyer—knew no remedy. Acting upon tradition rather than considered judgment, he moved quickly to appoint a French-Canadian lieutenant.

Borden's choice for the post first held by the great Sir George-Étienne Cartier was Frederick Monk whose principal goal in political life was, by his own admission, an appointment to the judicial bench.[41] During the next three years Monk fought Borden's attempt to ally with Joseph Israel Tarte, who had resigned from Laurier's cabinet, assailed Borden with demands for special favours, and engaged in fierce internecine warfare with other Quebec Conservatives.[42] By mid-1903 Borden was complaining to his wife that "Monk spends the most of his time in brooding over imaginary conspiracies which he thinks are being hatched against him...my work would have been infinitely easier during the present session if he had never entered the Chamber."[43] Finally in an "act of treason" in January 1904, Monk abdicated with an election close at hand. Never again did Borden appoint a French-Canadian Conservative leader: the post would remain vacant until French-Canadian Conservatives showed sufficient "maturity" to warrant such special consideration.[44] With only eleven seats in Quebec in 1904 and again in 1908, Borden could afford to act boldly, and he did. He attempted to construct an alliance with one of the most virulent critics of corruption in Canadian and Quebec politics, Henri Bourassa.

Borden had met the most prominent *nationaliste* when they boarded together in their first years at Ottawa.[45] No doubt he was charmed and impressed by the vibrant Bourassa, but there is no evidence that close friendship developed. Certainly Borden would not have approved Bourassa's stand on the Boer War or on imperialism in general, but other features of La Ligue nationalist canadienne programme—provincial rights, opposition to foreign economic domination, and protection of natural resources—were quite similar to Borden's own views. Bourassa gathered about him a well-educated, articulate, and highly political group of young men who "became convinced that the root of much of the evil lay in politics. And that meant the Liberals: Gouin at Quebec, Laurier at Ottawa."[46] Contacts between Conservatives and *nationalistes* were therefore inevitable, and they first occurred informally and at the provincial level.

The provincial Conservatives began, after 1905, to detach themselves from their federal counterparts (who in 1905 were opposing the separate school clauses in the Autonomy Bills) and to seek the support of the *nationalistes*.[47] English-Canadian reformers in Montreal, who were often active Conservatives, began to make common cause with the *nationalistes* against various wrongs. Herbert Ames, a Conservative MP and perhaps Canada's best known urban reformer, was a leader in this regard. Hugh Graham's *Montreal Star* also became a supporter of many of the *nationalistes'* reform policies, and it was through Graham and his editor, Brenton Macnab, that Borden came into contact with Bourassa. In July 1907 Bourassa, through Macnab, indicated to Borden his willingness to work with the Conservatives "to raise the flag of absolutely honest government over the province." He was referring to provincial politics, but he did promise more: he praised Whitney's Ontario policies, similar to Borden's Halifax Platform, and asked for "an alliance—not open, but real—with Mr. Ames' and a meeting with Borden.[48]

This meeting apparently did not occur—too little time and too many differences prevented any alliance for the 1908 federal election—but the provincial Conservatives and *nationalistes* together fought the government of Sir Lomer Gouin in the 1908 Quebec election. Borden continued to think of Bourassa as an answer to the Conservatives' Quebec weakness and as an ally against corruption and the politics of the past represented by Laurier Liberalism. Bourassa could bring to Conservatism the most talented young men, proven political deftness, a vital organization which Quebec Conservatism lacked, and utter impatience with political corruption and frivolity. The time-servers and the place-seekers so abundant in Quebec Conservative ranks would lose their place to men committed to a different style and understanding of politics.

One hesitates to employ the term "progressives" to describe the third major grouping which Borden courted: the word has had too many meanings in American history and, in Canadian history, a too specific one, the name of an agrarian political party. Nevertheless, the contemporary use of the word justifies its application here. Borden, the reader will recall, believed his Halifax Platform would appeal to "progressive" spirits and communities. Similarly, Bourassa thought Whitney's bold political program was "progressive," and newspapers regularly characterized politicians or their politics as "progressive."

What Borden understood by "progressive" is indicated in several of his public statements. To be sure, he meant that the state should assume a more active role than it had in the past and than Laurier was willing to allow it in the future. More fundamentally, though, Borden—in common with Canadians as diverse as the Manitoba visionary E.A. Partridge and the Toronto imperialist George Denison—was rejecting the kind of politics that was marked by compromise and where decision only occurred at the level of the lowest common denominator. Borden sought a larger vision, one which would go beyond mere consensus and would spurn the "parish pump" politics of Canadian parliamentary democracy: "Looking to every man as a citizen to stand for that which makes for the interest of the whole country, and overlooking mere transient, temporary and local considerations, we cannot doubt that the interest of the East is the interest of the West, the interest of Nova Scotia is and always must be the interest of British Columbia."[49]

This Borden speech and many others like it clearly reflect "the sense of power" that so many Canadians exuded at that time. There was, on the one hand, self-confidence and, on the other, frustration with the limits imposed by geography, tradition, and human weakness. No matter what the primary focus of interest—imperialism, government ownership or regulation, or economic development—the progressives were united by a disposition to become politically involved and to see national politics as a means of attaining their individual goals. For an opposition leader they presented great opportunities, but how could one take best advantage of them?

In 1904 when Borden was advocating government construction and ownership of the new Grand Trunk Pacific, the Conservative whip received a letter from Watson Griffin, the publicist for the Canadian Manufacturers' Association, commending Borden's stand and proffering advice: "Let the Conservatives gain the support of the capitalists who are interested in manufacturing industries and they do not need to fear the railway capitalists in carrying out the Borden policy of public ownership of the national transcontinental railway."[50] Borden needed little coaxing. Even before Griffin's letter arrived, he had developed close ties with J.W. Flavelle and A.E. Kemp, major figures in Toronto financial and industrial circles. Kemp, Flavelle, B.E. Walker, and Herbert Ames, who was elected to the House of Commons in 1904, were in fact the kind of "progressives" Borden tried to draw into political life. They were mostly businessmen, but not, Borden believed, men whose vision was restricted to their private interests. They were willing to countenance and indeed to encourage a more active, responsible state; and, at least in Borden's eyes, they would "make their stand" for the "whole country."

Borden, Roger Graham observed, "admired successful businessmen and was inclined to be heavily influenced by their views...."[51] And why not, at a time when business attracted men of the greatest capacity and vision? Every age has an avenue of energy which the brightest young men seek out. Perhaps the Empire attracted the most creative young Englishmen in 1900; certainly the Church called the best to its fold in the Middle Ages. But in Canada in 1900, business with its excitement and opportunity was an irresistible siren to a young Max Aitken, R.B. Bennett, or Joseph Flavelle. Even the Marxist and the muckraker gave credit to the vitality and talent of their enemies.[52] Laurier traced the decline in the calibre of members of Parliament to the attraction of business—no longer were the chief openings for advancement for a young man law and politics: "Today...and this is particularly true of Ontario, there are such opportunities in business with large remuneration that politics with its uncertainties has little attraction for young men of ability."[53] Borden hoped to change this for two reasons. First, politics dealt with the most serious matters affecting national life and must therefore involve the most intelligent in the land. Second, Borden realized that mere pursuit of wealth was "a menace" to the political structure of

Canada. Political activity could serve as an educator for businessmen to make them aware of national problems and their own responsibilities as citizens. Moreover, their financial aid could free Borden from the dependence upon Montreal interests, notably the CPR, for party funds.[54] In the religious, philanthropic, and cultural activities of businessmen like Flavelle, B.E. Walker, and Thomas White, Borden saw the first stage of full-scale political participation. In the task of bringing order to the chaos of late nineteenth- and early twentieth-century economic change, he envisaged such men as his strongest and most valuable allies.

Borden, it has been seen, had significant personal and political reasons for developing these relationships with extra-parliamentary interests. Indeed, the nature of the prewar party system, with its patronage, its partisanship, its unrepresentative electoral system, and its stability, meant that the prudent opposition leader had to depend upon such groupings to carry out certain functions which were normally those of the party. Inevitably, Conservative parliamentarians became suspicious of Borden's aims. As Craig Brown has noted, Borden seemed to his caucus "distant, moody, imperious, sometimes almost scornful of their worth...he had made policy by memoranda with outsiders; businessmen, journalists, provincial potentates, men who understood little and cared less about the demands, the whims, and the welfare of the parliamentary party."[55] That this was often necessary few members appreciated. They correctly saw that Borden's larger aims could threaten them even as they brought ultimate victory to the party. Such was the paradox that underlay both the turmoil within Conservative ranks and the triumph of Borden's party in the election of 1911.

NOTES

1. This account is taken mainly from the *Montreal Star*, 7 Feb. 1901, and J.C. Hopkins, *The Canadian Annual Review, 1901* (Toronto, 1902), 436. The former account is obviously the product of a "leak" and differs substantially from the one in Borden's *Memoirs* which minimizes Tupper's role in the selection. See H. Borden, ed., *Robert Laird Borden: His Memoirs* (Toronto, 1938), I, 72-5; also *Toronto World*, 20 July 1905, and R.C. Brown, *Robert Laird Borden: A Biography, 1854-1914* (Toronto, 1975), I, 47-9. The younger Tupper had raised the issue of the leadership with Borden over two months before the meeting, although Borden appears to have forgotten this contact in his *Memoirs*. See Borden to Tupper, 5 Dec. 1900, C.H. Tupper Papers, 1914-16, PABC.

Borden's experience included party organization work for Tupper in Nova Scotia; Borden to C.H. Tupper, ibid.; and C. Tupper to C.H. Tupper, 15 Aug. 1897, Charles Tupper Papers, v.11, PAC.

2. It should be noted that there was an agreement never publicly stated that Borden would serve as temporary leader for a year. This was undoubtedly an "escape clause" in the event that Borden proved entirely unsuitable. Borden, *Memoirs*, I, 73. Laurier also began with a one-year probationary term.

3. Brown, *Borden*, 51.

4. For fuller details, see my "Sir Robert Borden, the Conservative Party and Political Change in Canada, 1901-1920" (unpublished

PhD thesis, Harvard University, 1973), 72n. Borden himself was possibly corruptly involved in the plot.

5. Brown, *Borden*, 83-6, and Borden to Laura Borden, 5 July 1904, cited in ibid., 87.

6. See Laura Borden to Borden, 11 Feb. 1906, Borden Papers (BP), v. 327, PAC, for evidence of Mrs Borden's dislike of politics, apparently a common trait among Canadian prime ministers' wives.

7. R.C. Brown and Ramsay Cook, *Canada, 1896-1921: A Nation Transformed* (Toronto, 1974), 186.

8. See Brown, *Borden*, 129-35. The quotation is from Borden to R.P. Roblin, 2 Aug. 1907, BP, v.351.

9. See his *Memoirs*, I, 42.

10. Interestingly, the stability of partisan choice remains in those areas of Canada where third parties have made relatively minor inroads, namely the Maritimes and Quebec. See Mildren Schwartz, *Politics and Territory: The Sociology of Regional Persistence in Canada* (Montreal and London, 1974), 148-53. On the importance and character of the floating vote, see V.O. Key, *The Responsible Electorate* (New York, 1966).

11. *Memoirs*, I. 150; see also Borden to Laura Borden, 5 July 1904, cited in Brown, *Borden*, 87.

12. Cited in Arthur Ford, *As the World Wags On* (Toronto, 1950), 126.

13. The sources consulted are Henry Morgan, *Canadian Men and Women of the Time* (Toronto, 1912); J.K.Johnston, *The Canadian Directory of Parliament* (Ottawa, 1968); E.J. Chambers, ed., *The Canadian Parliamentary Guide, 1909* (Ottawa, 1909); ibid., *1910; Fifth Census of Canada*, II (Ottawa, 1913); and Ward, *The Canadian House of Commons: Representation* (Toronto, 1950). On the subject of the reliability of statistics, Ward cites J.F.S. Ross: "Gaps there are and, it is to be feared, errors; but I am satisfied that they are not so extensive, nor of such a characheter, as to impair the general accuracy of the conclusions reached." This admirable warning should also be applied to the data given in this paper.

14. Length of service of Conservative members in 1909:

Years served	Number of members	Years served	Number of members
1	40	9 to 12	1
2 to 4	3	12 to 18	8
4 to 6	21	18 and over	6
6 to 9	8		

The Canadian Parliamentary Guide, 1909. All calculations are my own. The turnover of members in Canada has always been high. See Ward, ibid., 115-17. A high median age is quite common among opposition parties, but is not of course desirable.

15. For an evaluation over time of pre-parliamentary experience, see Ward, ibid., 121-4.

16. "Politics as a Vocation." in H.H. Gerth and C. Wright Mills, eds., *From Max Weber* (New York, 1958), 85-6. Weber uses the term "plutocratic recruitment" to refer to the recruitment of those who are [not] economically dependent on politics. Borden accepted this, but he also saw that economic freedom alone was not enough; politicians should be "detached" in a much wider sense.

17. Ward, *Canadian House of Commons*, 225.

18. H.A.Scarrow, "Patterns of Voter Turnout in Canada," in John Courtney, ed., *Voting in Canada* (Scarborough, 1967), 105, 200; and M.C. Urquhart and K.H. Buckley, eds., *Historical Statistics of Canada* (Toronto, 1965), 616.

19. Douglas Baldwin, "Political and Social Behaviour in Ontario, 1879-1891: A Quantitative Approach" (unpublished PhD thesis, York University, 1973), 274-5. On the basis of a study of polling districts in Ontario, Baldwin claims (277) that at least 68 per cent of the voters

in federal elections between 1882 and 1891 voted for the same party every time. See also Norman Ward, "Voting in Canadian Two-Member Constituencies," in Courtney, *Voting in Canada*, 127.

20. Baldwin, ibid., 116, 140, 262. Liberals obtained strong support from Scotch Presbyterians; McLaughlin, "Race, Religion and Politics: The Election of 1896 in Canada" (unpublished PhD thesis, University of Toronto, 1975), 426-9.

21. These calculations are my own. Sources are the *Canadian Parliamentary Guide, 1909*, and the *Census of Canada, 1911* (Ottawa, 1913).

22. Victoria City, Lanark South, London, Toronto East, Toronto North, Toronto South, Toronto West, York South, Nanaimo, and Brome (they lost the last).

23. Brome, Montreal Ste Anne, Montreal St Antoine, Argenteuil, Huntingdon, Pontiac, and Stanstead.

24. Russell, Prescott, Victoria-Madawaska, Restigouche, Kent, and Gloucester.

25. These are Bagot, Beauce, Beauharnois, Bellechasse, Berthier, Chambly and Vercheres, Champlain, Charlevoix, Chicoutimi and Saguenay, Deux-Montagnes, Dorchester, Drummond-Arthabaska, Gaspé, Joliette, Kamouraska, Labelle, Laprairie and Napierville, L'Assomption, Laval, Lévis, L'Islet, Lotbinière, Maskinonge, Mégantic, Montcalm, Montagny, Montmorency, Mont St Jacques, Mont Ste Marie, Nicolet, Portneuf, Quebec Centre, Quebec East, Quebec County, Richelieu, Richmond Wolfe, Rimouski, Rouville, St Hyacinthe, St Jean Iberville, Shefford, Soulanges, Temiscouta, Terrebonne, Trois-Rivières, Vaudreuil, Wright, and Yamaska.

26. Strathcona, Victoria, Comox-Atlin, Dauphin, Lisgar, Selkirk, Lunenburg, Waterloo North, Humboldt, Mackenzie, Saltcoats, and Saskatoon.

27. Quoted in John Vincent, *The Formation of the Liberal Party, 1857-1868* (London, 1966), 227.

28. Borden to Chairman, Conservative Convention, Moose Jaw, 17 March 1903, v. 350.

29. "An Ideal of a Continental Relationship," 23 March 1910, BP, v. 300.

30. See, for example, Christopher Lasch, *The New Radicalism in America* (New York, 1965), especially Ch. 5.

31. Martin Robin, "British Columbia," in Robin, ed., *Canadian Provincial Politics* (Scarborough, 1972), 46. See Brown, *Borden*, 132.

32. Whitney to H.H. Ross, 13 Sept. 1907, Whitney Papers, PAO.

33. "Memorandum Concerning the Organization in Ontario," 23 May 1912, A.E. Kemp Papers, PAC. Whitney's hesitations about a joint organization, which are understandable in light of the patronage demands of federal members, are detailed in Catherine Pick Warner, "Sir James P. Whitney and Sir Robert L. Borden: Relations between a Conservative Leader and His Federal Party Leader, 1905-1914" (unpublished MPhil thesis, University of Toronto, 1967).

34. See Floyd Chalmers, *A Gentleman of the Press* (Toronto, 1969), 166-9. The plan was to buy out the moribund *Mail and Empire*. Colonel J.B. Maclean acted as the Tory negotiator. Maclean to Kemp, 17 Dec. 1912, Kemp Papers, v. 9.

35. Whitney to Borden, 11 Sept. 1907, BP, v. 351. It should be added that Whitney expressed uncertainty that Borden had gone far enough in advocating public ownership. Earlier evidence of the close consultation between the two can be found in Borden to Whitney, 11 Jan., Whitney Papers, v. 10; Whitney to Borden, 4 Nov. 1907, and Whitney to R.H. Pope, ibid., v. 12.

36. The British Columbia federal and provincial organizations were completely merged by 1911. "British Columbia Conservative Association," McBride Papers, box 1911, PABC. Although Hazen's provincial government did aid the federal party, the organizations remained distinct. A.R. Slipp to O. Crocket, MP, University of New Brunswick, Crocket Papers, box 7. Rogers' extensive federal activity suggests a merger, but I was unable to find any evidence in the Manitoba Archives on this. J.C. Hopkins, *The Canadian Annual Review, 1908* (Toronto, 1909), 160.

37. Interview with Mrs Margaret Macintosh (McBride's daughter), Sidney, BC, Oct. 1970.

38. Hamilton to J.S. Willison, 24 May 1908, v. 37, Willison Papers, PAC. Unfortunately the Borden Papers for 1908 are missing, but evidence of Rogers' large role may be found in Borden to Rogers, 25 and 30 Jan., Rogers to Borden, 6 March 1911, BP, v. 133; see also Hugh Graham to Borden, 18 Feb. 1911, BP, v. 327, which tells of Rogers acting as a Borden emissary to Montreal.

39. Tanner to Borden, 3 Dec. 1909, BP, v. 352.

40. The phrase is from H.B. Ames in "The Organization of Political Parties in Canada," American Political Science Association, *Proceedings* (27-30 Dec. 1911), 184.

41. Borden, *Memoirs*, II, 401.

42. Monk to Borden, 18 Nov. 1903, T.C. Casgrain to Borden and Casgrain to Taylor, 20 Feb. 1904, Monk to Borden, 29 Jan. 1904, BP, v. 350; *La Patrie*, 1 March 1904; Michael Carroll, "Henri Bourassa and the 'Unholy Alliance'" (unpublished MA thesis, Carleton University, 1969).

43. Quoted in Brown, *Borden*, 57.

44. Casgrain to Borden, 20 Feb. 1904, BP, v. 350. Monk did become French-Canadian Conservative leader again

in 1909, but the position had clear restrictions and was not the same one he left in 1904. "Memo of Conversation between Messrs. Borden, Monk and Casgrain," 29 Jan. 1909, BP, v. 351.

45. Bourassa to Borden, 18 Oct. 1935, BP, v. 261.

46. Brown and Cook, *Canada, 1896-1921*, 139.

47. See J.A.A. Lovink, "The Politics of Quebec Provincial Parties, 1897-1936" (unpublished PhD thesis, Duke University, 1967), 98, 148, 321 ff; and H.B. Neatby, *Laurier and a Liberal Quebec* (Toronto, 1973), 177-81.

48. Macnab to Graham, 9 July, Macnab to Borden, 11 and 18 July 1907, BP, v. 327. See also Brown, *Borden*, 128-9.

49. Speech in BP, v. 79. See also Borden, *Memoirs*, I, 373.

50. Griffin to George Taylor, Conservative whip, 2 June 1904, BP, v. 350.

51. *Arthur Meighen: The Door of Opportunity* (Toronto, 1960), I, 152.

52. Two examples would be Gustavus Myers, *A History of Canadian Wealth* (London, 1914), and Edward Porritt, *Sixty Years of Protection in Canada, 1846-1907: Where Industry Leans on the Politician* (London, 1908). On business thought, see Michael Bliss, *A Living Profit* (Toronto, 1974).

53. Laurier's remarks are paraphrased in Ford, *As the World Wags On*, 126.

54. Graham and the CPR, for example, had probably contributed approximately $300,000 to party funds in 1904, that is, well over $1000 per constituency. Charles Hibbert Tupper told Graham that "Every penny of what we received outside [British Columbia] came from you." Tupper to Graham, 10 Dec. 1904; also Graham to Borden, 15 July 1904, and 17 May 1907, BP, v. 327. Graham and the CPR expected favours in return, something Borden knew and resented.

55. Brown, *Borden*, 166.

THE WELL-OILED MACHINE: LIBERAL
POLITICS IN SASKATCHEWAN, 1905-1917

BY DAVID SMITH

o

Some of the most prominent features of Saskatchewan politics first appeared in the long span of Liberal rule after 1905. An important contribution to the province's political heritage was the operation of the Liberal party itself. The Liberals developed a model for electoral success which other parties had to emulate if they hoped to enjoy similar long-run dominance. The victories resulted from the Liberals' concern for their party organization and their eclecticism in matters of policy. This acumen for organization thwarted Conservative bids for power, and after a time contributed to the opposition's internal division and electoral weakness.

During their record of unbroken success between 1905 and 1929 the Liberals had four leaders: Walter Scott, 1905-16, W.M. Martin, 1916-22, C.A. Dunning, 1922-6, and J.G. Gardiner, 1926-9.... The initial twenty-four years of Liberal dominance in Saskatchewan may be divided into two periods of twelve years each. Until 1917 and the upheaval in federal politics caused by the formation of the Union Government and the accompanying federal election, the Liberal party in Saskatchewan remained in absolute control of events in the province. It was in this period that the party organization, or Liberal machine as it was frequently called, became entrenched. No comparable era of Liberal dominance was to recur in Saskatchewan's history, for the turmoil of 1917 set in motion changes that profoundly affected the province's political structure in the next decade. Thus, it is to the first twelve-year period that attention will now be directed.

Excerpt from David Smith, *Prairie Liberalism: The Liberal Party in Saskatchewan 1905-71* (Toronto: University of Toronto Press Incorporated, 1975), pp. 25-45. Reprinted with permission of David Smith and University of Toronto Press Incorporated.

POLITICAL MACHINES AND SASKATCHEWAN

Analysis of Canadian political machines is rare.[1] Discussions of patronage can be found and examples of corruption have been documented, but together they do not constitute an adequate description of machine politics. Recourse has usually been to American example where "the word 'machine' conjures up certain pictures: a boss who sits in a central headquarters and issues orders down through a neat chain of command, sub-bosses who execute the orders through blocs of workers who in turn supervise blocs of voters, and the whole held together by some mechanistic power."[2] This type of machine is not only American, but urban American, and is identified most frequently with organizations like Tammany Hall in its heyday in New York City, or with the...Cook County Democratic organization led by the mayor of Chicago, Richard Daley. These machines, found mainly in the large eastern cities of the United States, flourished at the beginning of this century. They were characterized by strong leadership, frequently by a person not holding political office, a disciplined hierarchy, and the distribution of rewards, both material and non-material, to party workers and supporters.

Since the fundamental feature of the urban machine was tight organization, it did not lend itself to state-wide application, particularly in states that were basically rural. Few rural states possessed political machines: Louisiana under Huey Long and Virginia under Harry Byrd were the outstanding exceptions. But in each of these cases the personalities of these leaders and the use they made of established local elites in communities where racial questions bulked so large suggested that neither of these Southern states had much in common with the provinces of Canada.[3]

Thus the relevance of American experience would seem remote except for one significant similarity between the situation of the urban machines and that of Saskatchewan. In both, after 1900, there lived a growing number of foreign immigrants unfamiliar with Anglo-American civic values.

In the United States, these were the people who provided the basis for the American urban machine. A machine, it is said, cannot operate unless people "place a lower value on their votes than they do on the things which the machine can offer them in exchange for them."[4] What the urban machine offered the immigrant was, first, status or recognition for his ethnic group through rewards to individual members of these groups and, second, help, "none of your law or your justice, but help" to individuals who needed it, at a time before social services had become a branch of government.[5] In their response to the immigrant the American machines may have been humanizing structures in the political system, they may even have played an indispensable role as agencies of assimilation, but eventually they were charged with corrupting the newcomer. The machine's irresponsible structure and its practice of trading services for votes incurred the wrath of reformers, who appeared most noticeably in the Progressive movement before the First World War, and whose success led to the overthrow of almost all of the existing urban machines.

In Saskatchewan, too, large numbers of non-English immigrants, brought to Canada and settled upon the land by Liberal governments, became a principal pillar of the Liberal party. In exchange for status and help the Liberals expected and received votes. Opposition to this practice arose in much the same form as in the United States. The Liberals were charged with corrupting the immigrant through the operation of the machine. References in Saskatchewan to the venality of machine politics were borrowed from the Progressive vocabulary. In an address to the 1913 convention of the Saskatchewan Grain Growers' Association, W.J. Rutherford, the dean of Agriculture of the University of Saskatchewan, called for a new political party to make politics "a holy thing in Canada" and condemned "the jackals of politics—the healer, the briber, the grabber of franchises, the seeker of privilege, the plunderer of the poor."[6]

The comparison between urban America and rural Saskatchewan clearly cannot be pushed too far. The two localities could hardly have been more different. Saskatchewan's rural population was scattered over a huge area, with its European settlers living in scores of ethnic communities cut off from the predominant, anglo-saxon society by distance as well as by differences in language and culture. The most fundamental feature of Saskatchewan's political system, one which was clearly absent in the United States, was the parliamentary form of government. Unlike any machine directed by a boss in an American city, the Saskatchewan government faced an opposition in a legislative assembly and was subject to the restraints that that political reality imposed. The Liberal party used public funds and offices to reward its friends and relied on intensive party and electoral organization. But it did not have the American bosses' goal of maintaining itself in power at almost any price, and although considerations of partisan advantage informed its choice of policies, the party conceived, developed, and later defended its politics on the public platform against opposition. For many years the party was so successful at attracting support from significant segments of the electorate that it was able to withstand charges of patronage, machine politics, and even outright corruption, although the latter assertions were few and speedily dealt with by Liberal leaders. These charges damaged the party only when other divisions in Saskatchewan public life, its society, and its economy became apparent.

STRUCTURE AND PERSONNEL
OF THE PARTY ORGANIZATION

The lubricant of political machines is patronage. Every party—past or present, old or new—is under pressure to reward its friends when it comes to power. However, in contrast to the active governments of today, whose armies of bureaucrats administer welfare programs which help the poor without regard to political allegiance but whose lucrative contracts are often given to the partisan rich, governments at the beginning of this century generally distributed only a few contracts of modest amount but used low paying civil service jobs to reward their supporters.

Those in Saskatchewan, as elsewhere, who held political power were constantly plagued by job seekers. Because there was a scramble for preferment for every position, demand always exceeded supply and some supporters had to be turned away. Moreover, patronage had to stop somewhere. Not all positions within the gift of the government could be given to friends. Certain of them, like those on the Local Government Board, which was established in 1913 with power to approve or refuse applications by local authorities to raise money by loans and to supervise the expenditure of this money, were considered too sensitive and too important to the well-being of the province to be filled solely on the criterion of party loyalty. Even an old and trusted confidant like Peter Bredt had his request for appointment rejected by Scott because "this was one body the members of which should be selected absolutely without regard to any personal or political consider-ations which is a view after all impossible to combat successfully."[7] The Farm Loan Board, created prior to the 1917 election to meet the growing demands for government financial support to the farmers, also came within the category of non-partisan bodies. A former Liberal member of Parliament for Prince Albert, who had been defeated in the 1911 federal election and who had been appointed shortly afterwards by the provincial Liberal government as an issuer of marriage licences, was rebuffed in his search for a more exalted position on the board on the grounds that the board was completely separate from the government and must be kept free from political influence because "it is a business institution."[8]

But, aside from bodies like these, the field was open to manipulation. A multitude of jobs, including poundkeepers, game guardians, inspectors of boilers, and many others, were constantly sought after, although the pressure around election time was greatest. It was not unusual for an MLA to advise a minister to rush some appointment because it would mean "3 votes for me," or for the provincial organizer of the party to ask for the appointment of an official because "this fulfills an election promise."[9] The alacrity with which such appointments were made reflected both low esteem for the public service and strong conviction that party supporters deserved recognition. Such restraint as did exist with regard to appointments to the public service arose from the practical considerations that too much patronage might reduce what efficiency the public service possessed and that an "efficient public service is a mighty good thing for the Government's friends to be able to point to when appealing for public approval."[10] But the public servant fortunate enough to be judged efficient and therefore to be retained despite partisan considerations must nevertheless take no active part against the government in an election.

Between the two extremes of special, non-partisan appointments and ordinary partronage appointments, stood the justices of the peace. Their importance in the administration of justice encouraged frequent reiteration of the pledge that "nothing but a man's fitness for the position regardless of his political leanings" would enter into his selection, but the number of such appointments—in 1909 there were over seven hundred—suggests that the temptation to use the office for political reward was too great.[11] It was generally agreed that a justice of the peace could be removed only after cause was shown and there was an investigation. Consequently, at least twice, the commissions of all justices of the peace were cancelled "for the purposes of getting rid of some of these objectionable parties."[12]

The accepted manner of making minor appointments was to solicit suggestions from MLAS or defeated Liberal candidates who, in turn, usually had loyal supporters in each community of the constituency from whom information could be secured. In the early years of the Scott administration, before Scott's illness forced him to be absent from the province for long periods, letters seeking this information would emanate from the premier's office. In later years they were sent from Calder's office because he assumed the position of acting premier during Scott's absences. But it was Calder who from the very beginning was responsible for party organization and who watched over and authorized all appointments.

Memoranda from all ministers reached his desk asking if an appointment was "in the public interest"; in turn, Calder and his deputy ministers notified other departments of "friendly" people "whose services should be availed of by your outside travelling staff, when seeking advice, awarding patronage, etc."[13] Calder advised other provincial ministers on patronage matters even to the extent of warning one of them to place his correspondence regarding appointments in a personal file separate from departmental matters.[14] He also advised federal Liberal ministers which appointments within their jurisdiction were of advantage to the Saskatchewan Liberal government. There was no question but that, excluding the very few non-partisan boards, patronage appointment was the rule for filling government jobs, and it was equally obvious that in Saskatchewan Calder's influence was paramount. A single illustration of both of these features of the provincial political system in this period was Calder's memorandum to a political organizer and former deputy minister of Railways advising him that the government gardener should be watched because he "is not as solid as he should be. The matter should be inquired into quietly. He has from time to time a good many people working for him and therefore has some influence."[15]

Quite separate from dispensing government jobs, but as much a part of patronage, is the awarding of contracts and the handling of government business. In return for favours of this kind governments customarily expect a sympathetic response, generally in the form of some financial contribution. As with the two old federal parties, the financing of election campaigns by the Liberal party in Saskatchewan remains a matter of considerable secrecy. Comments on the subject by political leaders are extremely rare and thus Walter Scott's passing reference to the problem faced by the Liberal party on the eve of autonomy is valuable despite its brevity:

> I sometimes wonder where in the world the people imagine that the money comes from. We have friends all over the country who seem to think that there is an inexhaustible fund to draw upon but at the same time whenever anything is said to lead to the suspicion that the

Government has made a deal which might leave room for the parties of the other party to make a subscription to party funds these friends are the first to hold up their hands in horror at the idea.[16]

In this early period of limited government involvement in the economy, the Saskatchewan government was restricted in what it might do to make business beholden to it. Aside from the distribution of government insurance and legal work, there was relatively little that it could grant. Instead, correspondence, usually from Calder or at his instigation, would be directed to the head offices of larger business, such as the farm-implement companies or national banks, suggesting that they assure the political loyalty of their agents or managers. The unspecified implication of this correspondence was that the businesses might otherwise face a hostile government in future.[17] An exception to this general statement of the relationship between Saskatchewan Liberal governments and big business in this early period was the railways. Once the provincial government began to guarantee bonds for railway construction in the province after 1908, it was possible to bring direct pressure on the railways by threatening to withhold guarantees of further credit on railway ventures once under way. The problem associated with such action was that railway line extensions were as important to the government's political success as they were to the companies' financial success. As a result government pleas with the railways for the completion of construction were as frequent as government threats.

One aspect of government patronage which eventually brought the Saskatchewan Liberal government into direct financing of a business enterprise was government support given to friendly newspapers. As the sole medium of communication in a province with a large, widely scattered, rural population the press was in an unique position to influence political sympathies. Every political party sought a friendly newspaper in every major town. In the cities the Liberals could count on loyal support from the Regina *Leader* and the *Moose Jaw Times*, both papers controlled by Walter Scott, and the *Saskatoon Phoenix*. Only in Prince Albert, with its one Conservative daily, the *Herald*, did they initially not have a champion. In 1917, however, the *Herald* switched sides and supported the Liberals because the Borden government did not appoint a senator from Prince Albert to fill the vacancy caused by the death of Senator T.O. Davis, a prominent resident of the northern city.

In the rest of the province close to 150 weekly newspapers were published, of which approximately fifty were judged by the Liberals to be Conservative or Conservative-leaning in 1916.[18] Such newspapers could not expect to receive the small but important government patronage in the form of legal and court advertisements, liquor licence application notices, and departmental publicity that totalled, at the most, two or three hundred dollars a year. Weekly newspaper publishing appears to have been a contingent financial enterprise because ministerial files are full of pleas from distressed editors for government help. More often than not the ministers attempted to aid these friendly newspapers through additional advertising or by shifting the existing allocation of advertising to the benefit of the hard-pressed paper and away from those temporarily better off.

A distinct type of newspaper patronage involved the ethnic press. Here the problems of communication were compounded by the barrier of language. Early in the life of the first Saskatchewan Liberal government Scott wrote that it was "our duty to enter upon a line of policy to enable us to assist in some fairly substantial measure a number of the papers which circulate in the Province."[19] While some of the foreign-language papers were published in Saskatchewan a number emanated from Winnipeg and a few even from eastern Canada. However, each was distributed in the respective ethnic settlements of the province. On different occasions all of these papers—Icelandic, Norwegian, Swedish, Ruthernian, German, Hungarian, and Hebrew—received a sympathetic hearing by the Liberal governments of Saskatchewan usually accompanied by concrete aid. In addition to regular government advertising several of the more prominent ethnic papers also received orders for the publication of government statutes in their own language.

Of special interest to the Liberal leaders was the growing German population because next to persons of anglo-saxon origin the Germans were the second largest ethnic group in Saskatchewan: "There is not a Dominion or local Constituency in Saskatchewan in which there is not a very heavy German vote, and as the majority of them have been voting Liberal in the past it is very important indeed that they should be kept thoroughly posted regarding the political questions of the day.[20] To insure the continuation of Liberal influence among the Germans, the Scott government undertook to establish a German-language paper, the *Saskatchewan Courier*. Initial financing involved both provincial Liberal MLAS and federal Liberal members of Parliament who subscribed to shares in the publishing company and sold a portion of these in their own constituency. The federal representatives each received an equal number of shares, while the provincial members received shares in proportion to the German-speaking voters in their riding. This scheme of financing was not successful, and early in 1908 the first of a series of pleas for government assistance began from the paper which, in Calder's words, was "always 'up against it' to a greater or lesser extent for funds."[21]

The giving of jobs, the awarding of contracts, and the granting of favours to friends of the party was a distinctive part of political life in the province. It constituted Saskatchewan's version of the "spoils system," except that the defence of the spoils system as a method of democraticizing public life carried little weight where the same party controlled all offices for years—even decades.[22] Rather than alternating parties in Sasketchewan, one party was entrenched.

With its monopoly of power the Liberal party used public offices and funds not only as rewards to supporters but also as a basis to build its party organization. Any man or woman who benefitted from the government's largesse was expected to work for the party when requested, but there was another kind of public official whose party responsibility was far greater. His formal duties as a public servant might be extensive—this was certainly true of deputy ministers like D.C. McNabb and S.P. Porter in the Department of Railways, Telegraphs, and Telephones—but he was also a key party man. McNabb and Porter were sent by Calder to Alberta to help organize the provincial Liberal campaigns in 1909 and 1913. The "army of inspectors" was the way the Liberals' critics used to describe these party officials who held government jobs that allowed them to travel around the province inspecting roads or public institutions. While any one of a number of special inspectors might be singled out to illustrate the point, perhaps one of the most interesting and least known is the secret service of Saskatchewan.

The Royal North-West Mounted Police continued after autonomy as the basic law enforcement body in Saskatchewan and Alberta. A series of agreements, initially of five years' duration beginning in 1906, provided that each province would pay $75,000 per year toward the cost of this service. Generally the arrangement worked well from the Saskatchewan government's point of view until 1911 and the change of government in Ottawa. Although direct political involvement by the provincial government in the affairs of the RNWMP had been minimal before 1911, the Scott government was soon irritated by the new federal Conservative government's handling of police affairs and gave notice in 1913 that it would not renew the agreement at the expiration of the current five-year contract in 1916.[23] The outbreak of war modified its attitude, although the new agreement of 1916 was altered to allow termination after one year's notice. The following year the RNWMP was withdrawn from the province by the federal government as a war measure. For the next decade, except for purely federal tasks such as patrolling the international boundary, law enforcement in Saskatchewan was the responsibility of the Saskatchewan Provincial Police.

While the SPP was formally created in 1917, its origin may be traced to the influence of the temperance movement upon the Scott government in 1906 and 1907. The temperance advocates found a sympathetic audience in Scott and some of its supporters, particularly W.R. Motherwell, the minister of Agriculture.[24] Saskatchewan instituted prohibition early in 1917 after first "banning the bar" and establishing government control of the wholesale and retail liquor business in 1915 and then, by referendum, in late 1916, abolishing the stores. But some years before these achievements the government, under temperance pressure, had established a Board of Licence Commissioners and a corps of inspectors. This machinery was supplemented by the appointment of a number of "spotters" or detectives who would be less visible than the inspectors and who could secure information on the administration of the system from less public sources.[25] The chief inspector's position, after being offered to the Manitoba Liberal organizer, eventually went to C.A. Mahony, a Roman Catholic and a "strong Liberal" from Ontario with a background in police work.[26]

At its creation the secret service was that specific group of men who acted as detectives. It was the intention of the government that the individuals employed in the service should be few, anonymous, and mobile.

Over the years, the term "secret service" came to be used more broadly to describe all provincial inspection or police work and the number of both inspectors and detectives grew. The secret service became something of a regular part of the government establishment, with towns pressing the attorney general to locate a detachment of detectives.[27] Both the inspectors and detectives reported on general political conditions in their areas; sometimes they advised on local organizational matters and suggested the names of individuals who should receive special consideration from the Liberal government in Regina.[28]

ELECTIONS AND THE PARTY ORGANIZATION

If there was one fundamental principle of party organization that continually received lip service from Liberal party leaders in Saskatchewan it was that they would not interfere with local associations, especially in the selection of candidates.[29] In the period from 1905 through 1917 the only instance of open intervention by a provincial Liberal leader was prior to the 1917 campaign in the provincial constituency of South Qu'Appelle. A saw-off of MLAS in the ridings of South Qu'Appelle and Hanley had been arranged at the instigation of the Conservative leader, W.B. Willoughby. The premier, W.M. Martin, asked the constituency association to secure the resignation of the Liberal candidate already nominated in South Qu'Appelle, so that the Conservative candidate, a soldier, could run unopposed there while a Liberal candidate, who was also a soldier, ran unopposed in Hanley. Although the Liberal candidate agreed to the request, the local association objected, calling it undemocratic and "a form of machine politics."[30] An independent Liberal, who had been the official Liberal candidate in 1912, eventually ran in South Qu'Appelle and lost to the Conservative candidate.

From the very first, local associations were sensitive about their prerogative in the matter of selecting candidates and forthrightly rejected any candidate whose selection might be interpreted as a result of "boss or clique rule."[31] This particular accusation arose more frequently with regard to federal nominations than provincial, although as long as Liberal governments were in power both in Regina and Ottawa, and Scott was the acknowledged leader of all Liberals in Saskatchewan, the criticism tended to ignore jurisdictions.

The provincial and federal elections of 1908 provided a good example of the special difficulties a political party in power at both levels of government could expect to face. In one respect the difficulties were not undeserved; for despite their disclaimer that the August provincial election was called for purely local reasons—among others to seek a mandate to extend provincial credit to railway construction and to expand the Legislative Assembly from twenty-five to forty-one members, thus allowing broader representation in the next legislature to discuss new municipal legislation—the leaders of the Liberal party in Saskatchewan could not avoid the charge that this election, less than three years after that of 1905, was called at Ottawa's instigation to test party feeling in the West.[32] The Scott government's strong showing, a 2 per cent decline in popular vote but a 2 per cent increase in legislative representation in the expanded chamber, seems to have convinced the Laurier government to go ahead with the federal contest two months later. The course of the Liberal and Conservative parties between autonomy and the end of the period under review in this chapter is given in Table 1.

TABLE 1. POPULAR VOTE AND LEGISLATIVE SEATS WON BY PARTIES IN SASKATCHEWAN PROVINCIAL GENERAL ELECTIONS 1905-17

			LIBERAL		CONSERVATIVE*		OTHER	
Election	Total popular vote	Total no. of seats	% of vote	%of seats	% of vote	% of seats	% of vote	% of seats
1905	34,057	25	52	64	47	36	–	–
1908	58,302	41	50	66	49	34	–	–
1912	87,632	54	57	85	42	15	1	–
1917	187,635	59	57	86	36	12	7	2

*The Conservatives campaigned as the Provincial Rights party in the provincial elections of 1905 and 1908.

Source: Evelyn Lucille Eager, "The Government of Saskatchewan," unpublished Ph.D. dissertation, University of Toronto, 344.

Scott nonetheless foresaw trouble in this close federal-provincial relationship, especially with regard to federal nominations, and eventually prevailed upon Calder to resign from a committee which had been arranging federal nominating conventions in the West.[33] He reasoned that provincial officials should remain clear of the federal contest until this stage had been completed since the frictions that inevitably accompany such selection could hurt the provincial party. He may well have had in mind the comments of an old acquaintance who wrote to him that in the Regina federal constituency the Liberals "made a great mistake in calling the convention on very short notice in a semi-private sort of way, suppressing all newspaper advertisement and setting a date in direct conflict with the election of the local improvement councillors.[34] Such insensitiveness to local feeling was not typical of the provincial Liberals, although there were a number of minor problems that arose during this particular provincial campaign that might have been averted had Calder not been occupied with federal matters. As it was, matters were left in the hands of the provincial organizer and his activity tended to agitate local associations. The experience of 1908 suggests that federal-provincial party cooperation, even in this period of staunch loyalty to one party and enmity to the other, could lead to discord. Its benefits should not be devalued, however, for when Calder and Motherwell were defeated in their provincial constituencies seats were opened for them by the resignation of two sitting MLAS who then stood successfully for Parliament in October 1908.[35]

The defeat of the federal Liberals in 1911 simplified party strategy and organization for the 1912 provincial campaign. This time Calder took complete charge with impressive results—a 7 per cent increase in the popular vote and a 19 per cent increase in legislative seats, which in a chamber of fifty-four members meant that there were forty-six Liberals. Scott described the result of 1912 as a "great triumph for Calder" and claimed that he had "never [seen] a campaign organization approach the perfection of our organization."[36] Concentration upon organization was the first priority of the Liberal party for the 1912 campaign. In contrast to the disorganized, almost hurried, campaign of 1908, the province's third election was approached by the Liberals with methodical care. Without any doubt this was due to Calder's efforts to stimulate local associational activity throughout 1911. During the spring and summer of that year Scott was absent from Saskatchewan and Calder, as acting premier, reported on his organization work. These letters and his directions to local associations, which were being issued at approximately the same time, reveal an informative picture of what might almost be called democratic centralization.[37]

Extensive efforts were made to involve large numbers of local Liberals in the selection of their candidates. In the spring of 1911 letters were sent out over Calder's signature as president of the Saskatchewan Liberal Association informing local Liberals of the provincial central executive's decision that nominating conventions should be held. These conventions, the letters stated, should be arranged by the executive committee of the central association of each constituency; where such a committee did not exist, "authority could be issued by the provincial executive to a provisional committee to be named by it." The persons receiving these letters were to be asked to suggest the names of five active Liberals residing in different parts of their constituency who might be appointed to a provisional committee. Either the executive of the central association or the provisional executive was empowered to fix the basis of representation at nominating conventions. The suggested scheme of representation was two delegates for each rural poll, four for a combined village or town and rural poll, and three for a town or village poll. Further correspondence from Calder informed those in charge of poll subdivisions of their responsibility to see that delegates to the nominating conventions were chosen at a full turnout. Each of these individuals received directions regarding the location of his poll, the number of delegates to be selected, and standard publicity to advertise the "primary meeting." Calder was too good a party organizer to insist on undeviating adherence to these directions. He recognized that in some constituencies the electoral principle might stimulate division rather than promote unity and that it might better be replaced by the appointment principle. The important consideration was that a consensus on a candidate be achieved.

In contrast to these efforts at stimulating local participation was Calder's insistence that he "see each prospective candidate for the purpose of sizing him up."[38] Although he made no public attempt to remove candidates selected by local conventions, his influence could nevertheless be effective. In the Milestone constituency, where Calder's scheme for selecting a candidate was not followed, tensions between Liberal factions threatened the party's electoral success. Also, it was Calder's opinion that the candidate who had been selected lacked "those qualities which go to make up a successful political candidate." He suggested to a friend in the constituency that if the candidate could be convinced to step down he "has our best wishes" and the government would do anything "within reason" to give him a position or other favour. The candidate quickly stepped down.[39]

The success of the 1912 campaign guaranteed that the party organization in operation for that election would be utilized in subsequent contests. In 1917 the party machinery with Calder once again at its head duplicated its former success. The Liberals' share of the popular vote remained the same but they increased, though slightly, their proportion of seats in the Legislative Assembly. The Conservatives, however, suffered a setback in popular vote and legislative representation. The number of Independent candidates tripled, as farmer unrest was more widespread than in 1912 on account of the Non-Partisan League, which had entered Saskatchewan from North Dakota.[40] As a portent of later political turmoil this event was of great significance, but in terms of its immediate effect upon Liberal party organization, it was relatively unimportant. In the words of one observer of the 1917 Saskatchewan campaign: "The exodus from the States to Saskatchewan of the farmers league (I forget the name they call it) has caused complications, giving the Conservatives a chance to make trouble in their many weak districts but Calder appears to be responding to the trouble in a most capable manner."[41]

The management of party organization and the distribution of patronage were only preliminaries to the principal goal of winning elections. Excluding the federal campaign of 1917, there was no distinction drawn between federal and provincial Liberal party organizations in Saskatchewan. The same people were active in both. Patronage was clearly federal or provincial in origin, but either might be rewarded to individuals whose claim rested on service in the other realm. This was particularly evident after the federal Liberal defeat in 1911, as many federal office holders removed by the incoming Conservative government sought refuge in Saskatchewan. Provincial Liberals took to heart the counsel of Senator Ross, Scott's long-time friend and political confidant: "Don't be afraid, fill up your pay rolls and get the information and work you require," and recruited these people in anticipation of a Conservative attack from Manitoba and Ottawa during the 1912 provincial elections.[42]

Since few issues divided the parties, emphasis during campaigns tended to be placed on manipulating electoral machinery to attract voters. The fundamental, indeed crucial, part of that machinery was the voters' lists. In 1905 the old territorial law was still in effect and there were no lists. In that election the voter went to the poll, declared himself, and was given a blank ballot. He designated his party choice on the ballot by marking an x with one of several coloured pencils provided. The colours were assigned according to order of candidate nomination. Although territorial law allowed for up to six colours for six candidates, the emergence of only two parties restricted the colours used to two: blue and red. By agreement in the 1905 election the Provincial Rights candidates were nominated first and received the colour blue; Liberal candidates, nominated second, received the colour red. But while there were no formal voters' lists, the parties each drew up their own, and these were used by scrutineers who might challenge voters. A voter so challenged could make an oath which recited the franchise qualifications and cast his ballot, but this reserve ballot, as it was known, was subject to investigation. Whenever the results of an election were close in a constituency, these ballots became the centre of dispute and the cause of delay in determining the final decision.

In 1908 both printed ballots and official voters' lists were introduced as part of the province's first election law.[43] The voters' lists were to be compiled in two ways: in towns by personal registration and in rural areas by enumeration. Personal registration was carried out in public by a registrar or his deputy; representatives of the parties were present and could challenge the applicant's right to be placed on the list. If the registrar rejected the applicant, the individual could go to a court of revision and seek to have his name placed on the list at that time. The opposition's major complaint with the system was that, given the unexpected dissolution of the legislature in 1908 and the hurried election campaign, there was not sufficient time, as set down by the statute, for the courts of revision to meet. Moreover, they charged, registrars would frequently not be present when the voter turned up to register and enumerators appeared selective about which rural voters they canvassed.[44] The advantage of the system was that the eligible electorate was determined prior to the election and there was not the opportunity for endless debate over the legality of ballots already cast by challenged voters as in 1905.

In 1912 the system was changed again, principally at opposition demand, to provide for permanent voters' lists or what were called "closed lists." After the experience of 1908 the opposition feared another snap election and hurriedly compiled partisan lists. They extracted from the premier a statement in the Legislative Assembly that he could see no immediate or pressing reason to seek a dissolution. Scott made political capital out of this by commenting that it was highly unusual in a parliamentary system for the opposition to seek to keep the government in power.[45] The new system of voters' lists once in operation made the opposition less happy, if possible, than in 1908. Whereas in 1908 they had argued that the trouble was getting on the lists, now they complained that they were being taken off in favour of aliens who had not yet qualified for naturalization. This particular problem arose because the registrar acted alone, drawing up lists on the basis of "any and all sources of information."[46] While the law provided that persons improperly registered might be removed from the lists, the fact remained that great discretion now rested with the registrar. The selection of registrars, too, made them subject to suspicion, for it was as much a part of Liberal party organization as the selection of acceptable candidates, the only difference being that the prospective registrars were interviewed by the provincial Liberal organizer rather than by Calder. That large numbers of ineligible persons, particularly newly arrived foreign immigrants, were placed on the lists in 1912 seems indisputable. In light of these violations of the Act, the opinion of the attorney general, W.F.A. Turgeon, that 'both sides suffered" under the new system was of little consolation to the Conservatives.[47]

In the 1917 election, along with female franchise, a dual system was introduced once again. This time, closed lists were provided for the cities and towns of over two thousand population and enumeration lists for the country. Although the government was now led by W.M. Martin, the attitude of Liberals had changed little and the opposition faced a tough partisan fight on the subject of election lists. The president of one local Liberal association, who was also appointed an enumerator, wrote the new premier that he was trying to "augment our power" and that "when the Provincial Elections take place there shall not be a conservative vote polled in our locality."[48]

This easy, almost carefree, approach to the voters' list indicated the prevailing attitude to elections. Calder admitted that he looked forward to the 1912 contest and that its conduct would be "a game of cards."[49] The analogy of the election to a game was not inappropriate. The Liberals, and their opponents too, took delight in challenging voters when they privately admitted there was no reason to doubt their qualifications.[50] They thought it sport to bait the opposition into making blanket charges of Liberal electoral wrong-doing and then to single out some isolated instance of local constituency honesty, preferably substantiated by some local Conservative's evidence.[51] But if elections were a game they were a game to be won. Immense amounts of time and effort went into securing loyal workers— Calder, for instance, kept lists of correspondents' names and turned them over to the provincial organizer, while another MLA had a federal census taker in 1911 compile a separate list for him of potential workers in this constituency.[52]

Equal diligence was exerted to see that those who benefitted from patronage between elections got out and helped the party at the time of the contest. This applied not only to job holders, who literally were watched on election day, but to railroads who had enjoyed government help in financing their lines.[53] They were told to press on with their construction work or, if that was not possible, at least to have surveyors in the constituency as an indication to the electorate of some progress.[54] The government itself would act in a similar manner prior to election day by announcing guarantees for railway extensions or setting about road construction in a politically doubtful area.[55]

The preparations for election day were minute and thorough, the Liberals overlooking nothing in their resolve to carry the electorate. A directive to Conservative scrutineers in 1912 possibly reveals more about Liberal practices than it does about Conservative watchfulness: "See that there is no window, pipe hole, crack, or even knot hole, in ceiling, walls or floor, through which [a] Grit spy could look or voter himself show his ballot."[56]

NOTES

1. A recent and welcome exception to the dearth of comment on patronage in Canadian politics is J.E. Hodgetts, William McCloskey, Reginald Whitaker, and V. Seymour Wilson, *The Biography of an Institution: The Civil Service Commission of Canada, 1908-1967*, Montreal, 1972, 9-19.

2. T. Harry Williams, *Huey Long*, New York (Bantam edition), 1970, 271-2.

3. While the literature on political machines in the United Studies is plentiful, studies of rural state machines are scarce; for Louisiana, see Williams, *Huey Long*, and for Virginia see V.O. Key, Jr., *Southern Politics* (New York, 1949), 19-35. Some of the most useful general literature is: Lee S. Greene, ed., "City Bosses and Political Machines," *Annals of the American Academy of Political and Social Science*, 353, 1964; Edward C. Banfield and James Q. Wilson, *City Politics* (Cambridge, Mass., 1963), Ch. 9; Leonard D. White and T.V. Smith, *Politics and Public Service: A Discussion of the Civic Art in America* (New York, 1939), Ch. 3; James Q. Wilson, "Corruption: The Shame of the States," *The Public Interest*, 2, 1966, 28-38; Theodore J. Lowi, "Machine Politics—Old and New," *The Public Interest*, 9, 1967, 83-92; and James Q. Wilson, "The Economy of Patronage," *Journal of Political Economy*, 69, 1961, 369-80.

4. Banfield and Wilson, *City Politics*, 116-17.

5. This "pious declaration" of a Boston political boss was quoted by Lincoln Steffens, *The Autobiography of Lincoln Steffens* (New York, 1931), 618, and is critically reviewed by Raymond E. Wolfinger in "Why Political Machines Have Not Withered Away and Other Revisionist Thoughts," *Journal of Politics*, 34, 1972, 388-9.

6. SGGA, *Convention Report*, 1913, 24.

7. AS, Scott Papers, Scott to P.M. Bredt, 26 Dec. 1913, 11838.

8. AS, Martin Papers, W.M. Martin to W.W. Rutan, 25 Sept.1917, 13418.

9. AS, Turgeon Papers, General Correspondence, R.M. Mitchell to W.F.A. Turgeon, 10 June 1912, and General Correspondence, M.C. Wright to Turgeon, 20 Oct. 1911.

10. Scott Papers, Scott to D.H. McDonald, 16 Jan. 1905, 6142-3. Where public officials were blatantly partisan or corrupt, the government could argue the opposite case: "The very stupidity and brazenness of [conduct] is a good feature in this way that it goes to prove that nobody above...had a hand in it." Ibid., Scott to Ross, 14 Feb. 1906, 7394-9. W.R. Motherwell went so far as to suggest that when a man did not seek assistance or preferment once in a while "it is sometimes taken as an indication of [his] allegiance in other respects." Motherwell Papers, Appointments File 18, Motherwell to Dr R.E. Monteith, 27 May 1909.

11. Scott Papers, Scott to Malcolm Millar, 6 April 1906, 7292. For lists of appointments see fortnightly issues of the *Saskatchewan Gazette*.

12. Motherwell Papers, Appointments File 20, Motherwell to W.G. Robinson, 18 Feb.1909.

13. AS, Calder Papers, D.C. McNabb to E.J. Wright, deputy provincial secretary, 20 Sept. 1915, 6373. Earlier patronage lists may be found in correspondence in Motherwell Papers, Patronage File 88, between Motherwell and F.J. Robinson, deputy minister of Public Works, 25 March 1907, 4 Jan. 1908, and 14 Oct. 1908.

14. Turgeon Papers, General Correspondence, Calder to Turgeon, 19 April 1910.

15. Calder Papers, Calder to S.P. Porter, 7 May 1912, 6272.

16. Scott Papers, Scott to D.H. McDonald, 25 May 1905, 6149-50.

17. Calder Papers, Calder to Norman MacKenzie, 30 April 1912, 6253-4 and Calder to Alex Laird, general manager of the Bank of Commerce, 10 Oct. 1911, 6493-4. In reply to Calder, Laird thanked him "for making it possible to correct an infraction of the proprieties [of a bank manager] without unenviable publicity for the Bank." 25 Oct. 1911.

18. For lists of daily and weekly newspapers with party allegiance and patronage noted, see Martin Papers, 35059-69.

19. Scott Papers, Scott to Motherwell, 30 Nov. 1907, 7698-9.

20. Calder Papers, Calder to Ross, 22 Feb. 1908, 7399-400.

21. Ibid., Calder to W.B. Somerset, 5 March 1915, 7623. Provincial government patronage to newspapers was reckoned to run between $100 and $300, Scott Papers, Scott to Thomas Sanderson, 2 Nov. 1907, 50301, but in the case of the *Saskatchewan Courier* it usually ran about $500. Calder Papers, F.H. Auld to Calder, 15 April 1915, 7634.

22. In the classic defence of the spoils system Andrew Jackson stated that "in a country where offices are created solely for benefit of the people no one man has any more intrinsic right to official station than another. Offices were not established to give support to particular men at the public expense." James D. Richardson, *A Compilation of the Messages and Papers of the Presidents, 1789-1897*, 10 vols (Washington DC, 1896-9), 2, 448-9, quoted in Ari Hoogenboom, ed., *Spoilsmen and Reformers*, (Chicago 1964), 3.

23. Correspondence with the federal government on this subject may be found in PAC, Borden Papers, RLB283. It was the opinion of the comptroller of the RNWMP that the Scott government sought to create a local police force "whom they would be able to employ for political purposes." Ibid., L. Fortescue to Borden, 19 March 1914, 95956-7. For a review of Saskatchewan's position on the matter, see Dunning Papers, J.W. McLeod, clerk of the Executive Council, to C.A. Dunning, 7 Feb. 1924, 34887-8, and a copy of memorandum from Scott to Turgeon dated 8 June 1915, 35865.

24. For more on the influence of the temperance forces on the origins of the provincial police see Motherwell Papers, Liquor File 71.

25. Scott Papers, Scott to Rev. T. W. McAfee, 10 Feb. 1906, 7237-8.

26. Turgeon Papers, General Correspondence, H.E. Perry to Turgeon, 16 Sept. 1910. Mahony was favourably recommended to Scott by the Church hierarchy and by the commissioner of the Dominion Police. Turgeon Papers, Appointments File, 8 Dec. 1910 and 3 Jan. 1911, 35620.

27. Ibid., Humboldt Constituency File, Turgeon to J.H. Crerar, 5 May 1914; General Correspondence, secretary of Lloydminster Liberal Association to Turgeon, 6 May 1911; and Appointments File, Turgeon to S.S. Simpson, 20 April 1911. For a detailed breakdown of the cost of police administration in Saskatchewan for 1916, see Martin Papers, 35620.

28. Ibid., General Correspondence, C.J. Hogg to Turgeon, 28 March 1912. Probably the most interesting appointment to the secret service was that of D.S. Irwin who was hired at $1,000 per annum, although his expenses were another several hundred dollars, while still in the service of liquor licence authorities in Alberta. This dual appointment continued for nearly a year during which time Irwin advised on local appointments, the establishment of a local Saskatchewan Liberal organization in Lloydminster separate from the Alberta one, and helped in the 1912

campaign. He returned to Alberta to help the Liberals there in the 1913 election. Ibid., General Correspondence, 11 Dec. 1909 through 31 Dec. 1911, Scott Papers, Scott to Dr. W. W. W.Amos, 18 March 1911, 10245-7, and Calder Papers, Calder to Irwin, 31 Oct. 1912, 6293. While the secret service and liquor inspectors were partisan Liberals, they could nonetheless embarrass the party by "pulling" friends. One Liberal MP wrote Turgeon: "For Heaven's sake, Turgeon, you shouldn't let your men pull out friends until after the next election—if then." Turgeon Papers, General Correspondence, D.B.Neely to Turgeon, 15 Nov. 1911.

29. Scott Papers, Scott to J.G. Turriff, 9 Jan. 1906, 7510-11; Turgeon Papers, General Correspondence, Turgeon to G.D. Weaver, 26 March 1912; Martin Papers, Martin to Pelly Liberal Association, 3 May 1917, 24226.

30. Martin Papers, A.E. Nicholls, secretary, South Qu'Appelle Liberal Association, to Martin, 20 June 1917, 24254-5.

31. Turgeon Papers, Political Material File, 1908, J. Robinson to Scott, 29 June 1908.

32. Regina, *Daily Standard*, 23 July 1908 and 27 July 1908, editorials. See also John T. Saywell, *The Office of Lieutenant-Governor*, Toronto, 1957, 160-1.

33. Scott Papers, Scott to W.A. Lamont, 31 Aug. 1908, 37458-9.

34. Ibid., T.M. Bryce to Scott, 6 July 1908, 7951-3.

35. The two MLAS who eventually went to Ottawa were D.B. Neely and Thomas MacNutt. MacNutt, who was the first Speaker of the Legislative Assembly in Saskatchewan, did not want to go to Ottawa, but Scott said that he, Scott, "was compelled to give [his] consent" to the proposal. Ibid., Scott-MacNutt correspondence, 24 Sept. and 2 Oct. 1908, 39053-6 and 39058-60.

36. Ibid., Scott to Bulyea, 16 July 1912, 39427-8.

37. Compare the account of the party organization in 1911 in the next paragraph, drawn from the Calder Papers, 5814-6092, *passim*, and this view of party organization in 1908: "Our defeat [in Moose Mountain] in my opinion was again due to defective organization. I do not mean so much the organizing at the time of the election, but the "Rip Van Winkle" between elections. Nothing whatever is done to keep the party active in the interval. Since the fight in 05 I do not think the Executive has been called together once, or any conference between the central body at Grenfeld and its Octopus feelers with the straggling outside representatives…. What wins elections [is] not the rush and scurry for a few days before a poll. Every Local Improvement District and similar small official bodies should be made the stepping stones for Liberals to assert their influence and get a footing among their neighbours. There are more votes to be got by a man who knows his book in a quiet talk with his surrounding neighbours, than by a dozen public speeches from a platform. At a meeting, it is the speaker alone who does all the talking, the listener has no chance, but get one or two together and haggle it out, to use a slang expression, and you start them thinking and wondering whether you are not right after all and round they come, in time." Scott Papers, J.J. Bell to Scott, 14 Sept. 1908, 7932-6. Mr. Bell had organized the constituency in the 1908 election and he reported that "at halftime…I handed out of the Polling places, to my assistants, a list of all who had not voted and they started off to hunt the laggards up and get them to come." The thoroughness of organization which Mr. Bell described does not appear to have been so typical of the Liberals in the 1908 election as it was to become later. Compare the

similarity of this account of party organization with that given by Escott M. Reid. "The Saskatchewan Liberal Machine Before 1929." *Canadian Journal of Economics and Political Science*, 1936, 27-40.

38. Scott Papers, Calder to Scott, 23 April 1911, 10368-9.

39. Calder Papers, correspondence between Calder and Dr Hugh McLean, 13 Feb. 1912 and 6 March 1912, 6162-3 and 6197-8.

40. One successful candidate, D.J. Sykes of Swift Current, was nominated by the Non-Partisan League as well as by local Liberals and Conservatives. When the legislature met he took his seat with the Liberals.

41. Scott Papers, Norman MacKenzie to Scott, 17 May 1917, 14513-17. The agrarian unrest and its impact upon the Saskatchewan political system is discussed in detail in the next chapter.

42. Calder Papers, Ross to Calder, 19 Jan. 1912, 6120-2.

43. *Statutes of Saskatchewan*, 1908, Ch. 2.

44. Regina *Daily Standard*, 11 Aug. 1908, 1 and 2.

45. Scott Papers, Scott to W. F. Kerr, 20 March 1911, 10698.

46. *Statutes of Saskatchewan*, 1910-11, Ch. 5, s. 298. One former Liberal MLA, J.W. Horsman, 1948-64, recalled that while working on a railroad gang during this particular campaign, he witnessed many of his fellow workers, immigrants who had arrived in Canada a matter of weeks before, being placed on the voters' lists. Interview, Aug. 1970.

47. Turgeon Papers, Miscellaneous: Elections File, 1908-10, Turgeon to Laurier, 22 Nov. 1912.

48. Martin Papers, William Lee to Martin, 7 April 1917, 27076. For changes in the Election Act, see *Statutes of Saskatchewan*, 1917, Ch. 5.

49. Scott Papers, Calder to Scott, 22 April 1912, 11299-308.

50. Ibid., Scott to Ross, 24 Oct. 1907, 7786-7.

51. Turgeon Papers, General Correspondence, S.R. Moore, MLA, to A.P. McNab, minister of Public Works, to Turgeon, 19 Oct. 1912, and Turgeon to Daniel Dupuis, 30 Oct. 1912. The Conservatives, too, could indulge in election pranks, such as publicizing, through "agents," a cheap land scheme in Alberta, hiring a passenger coach to take Liberal electors from the Francis constituency free of charge to Alberta, but making the service available only on election day. Regina *Morning Leader*, 5 July 1912, I.

52. Calder Papers, Calder to M.C. Wright, 19 May 1911, 5832, and H.C. Pierce, MLA, to Calder, 29 May 1911, 5870-2.

53. Turgeon Papers, Humboldt Constituency Files, G.A. Palmer to Turgeon, 25 June 1912.

54. Calder Papers, Calder to M.H. McLeod, general manager of the Canadian Northern Railway, 25 May 1912, 8094; Calder to E.J. Chamberlain, general manager of the Grand Trunk Pacific Railway, 7 May 1912, 8396.

55. Turgeon Papers, General Correspondence, correspondence between Calder, Turgeon, and William MacKenzie, president of the CNR, 8-15 May 1912; Calder Papers, Calder to H.S. Carpenter, superintendent of Highways, 22 June 1912, 7739.

56. AS, Pamphlet Collection. *Special Instructions for Conservative Scrutineers, Provincial Elections,* 1912.

THE EMERGENCE OF PROTEST PARTIES, 1918-1945

○

INTRODUCTION

I n contrast to the extension, consolidation, and relative stability of the two-party system in the period before 1917, the interwar years and the Second World War witnessed the emergence of competitive third parties and, largely in response to the new parties, the gradual transformation of the two old parties. While no major political realignment occurred in these years, except in Alberta and Saskatchewan, where third parties were elected to office for more than one term, the two-party system was replaced by the multi-party system in most jurisdictions.

The demise of the two-party system was heralded, in the first instance, by the rapid rise of farmer and labour parties shortly after the First World War. The discontent of the rural sector, particularly in Ontario and the West, had been growing since the late nineteenth century. For years Canadian farmers had complained of high freight rates, inadequate transportation and storage facilities, unfair grading and weighing practices by private grain elevator owners, rural depopulation, urban immorality, political corruption, and, above all, the protective tariff, on which they blamed most of their problems. Initially farmers responded by forming self-help organizations, such as cooperatives and Grain Growers Associations, whose approach was largely educational and apolitical. Only the Ontario-based Patrons of Industry ventured into the political arena, in the early 1890s, and its foray was both brief and ineffectual. Politically, like other groups at the time, the farmers' needs found expression through the old parties, especially the Liberals, whose lip service to freer trade held much appeal in rural areas.

The farmers' faith in the two-party system was severely shaken, however, by two events. The first was the defeat of reciprocity in 1911, proof to farmers that their political influence was waning and that the Liberals and Conservatives were ultimately beholden to the big business interests in central Canada on whom the parties depended financially. As a result, farmers came to believe that they could expect little in the way of serious reform from the old-line parties, especially on the tariff. The second event was the First World War and its immediate aftermath. In the name of prosecuting the war effort to its fullest and keenly aware of Prime Minister Borden's promise to exempt their sons from conscription, Canadian farmers rallied behind the Union government in 1917. However, the cancellation of the exemptions the following year, combined with the postwar dismantling of government-controlled grain marketing, the failure of the Union government to lower the tariff, and the onset of recession left many farmers disillusioned once again with the old parties and, for the first time, eager to take independent political action. In part this change in attitude was also due to the influence and inspiration of the Non-Partisan League, an American-based radical farmers organization that spread to Alberta and Saskatchewan in 1917 and contested several elections, with some success.[1]

The farmers' political movement began at the provincial level with the decision of United Farmers organizations in central and western Canada to field candidates in provincial elections. Consequently, between 1919 and 1922, farmer or farmer-labour governments were formed in Ontario, Alberta, and Manitoba, and a half-dozen farmer candidates were elected in both Nova Scotia and New Brunswick. Equally dramatic changes took place at the national level. In 1919 the prominent farm leader and Minister of Agriculture in the Union government, Thomas Crerar, along with eight of his western colleagues, left the government benches to form the nucleus of the first national farmers party, the Progressive party. The central plank in the movement's platform was tariff reform, but other demands were heard as well—for direct democracy, an end to government patronage, more services to rural areas, government ownership of utilities, and prohibition. On the strength of this left-populist message the Progressive party won an astounding sixty-four seats in the 1921 federal election, and the right to form the Official Opposition. The two-party system, severely wounded by the war, had suffered a fatal blow.

Some mention should also be made of the growing number of labour parties that emerged in the immediate postwar years, especially as they allowed farmer parties to govern in several provinces and would later contribute to the formation of the CCF. Independent labour parties, formed by local and provincial labour councils, first appeared in the late nineteenth century, primarily in the larger urban centres of southern Ontario and the West. The labour parties were supplemented by a myriad of small socialist parties across Canada, many of which were either formed or endorsed by labour organizations and, at the very least, claimed to speak on their behalf. While this smorgasbord of parties reflected the vitality of a nascent Canadian left, it also meant political impotency. Had these organizations been able to overcome the ethnic and ideological differences within and among themselves as well as the working man's preference for *economic* action as a means to reform, their political impact would undoubtedly have been greater. As it was, only a handful of labour party representatives won office before 1917.

This situation was soon to change. With the growth of labour militancy during the latter stages of the First World War, spurred mainly by conscription, inflation, alleged profiteering, and the triumph of Russian Bolshevism, a record number of labour candidates (22) ran in the 1917 federal election under the aegis of the country's largest labour body the Trades and Labour Congress. This early foray into national politics was hurried and poorly organized, however, and results were accordingly dismal. After an equally unsuccessful experiment with syndicalism in the two years that followed—the 1919 Winnipeg General Strike being the most dramatic example of this—workers turned even more forcefully and systematically to partisan political action. In the immediate postwar years, the number and popularity of municipal and provincial labour parties grew quickly. Moreover, an unprecedented number of labourites were elected to local, provincial, and federal office across Canada. In Ontario and Alberta, independent labour parties shared the seat of power with their colleagues in the farmers' movement and in the 1921 federal election four labour candidates won seats, including J.S. Woodsworth, the future leader of the

CCF. "Class" thus competed almost equally with "region" as the basis for political protest in the turbulent postwar years.

Neither the labour nor the farmers' protest was enduring, however. By the early twenties, working-class political action was already in decline, weakened by poor results in office, Communist infiltration and distraction, a backlash against unions, and the gradual return of prosperity. Many independent labour parties as well as branches of the Canadian Labour party—formed by socialists, communists, and unionists in 1922, but wracked by debilitating internal divisions until its demise in 1926—would survive the decade, but barely. The farmers' political protest receded just as quickly. Serious divisions between the minority of farmers who demanded radical reform to the political and economic systems and those who, as disaffected Liberals, favoured more cosmetic reforms, such as tariff reduction, left the various farmers' parties fairly impotent, both as governments and as opposition critics. This impotence, in turn, bred disillusionment among the movement's supporters, concentrated in rural Ontario and the West. So, too, did the Progressive party's principled refusal to act as Official Opposition, thereby depriving itself of a valuable national platform from which to expound further its views.

The disintegration of the Progressive party was aided, as well, by the wily tactics of Prime Minister Mackenzie King, whose minority Liberal government's survival in the early twenties rested on the support of the Progressive caucus. In return for this support and to lure Progressives back into the Liberal fold, King made some minor concessions to farmers' demands, including tax and tariff reductions. He also managed eventually to convince Robert Forke, Crerar's replacement as leader of the Progressive party, to join his cabinet. The Progressives' internal divisions and the Prime Minister's ability to exploit them, combined with the return of rural prosperity in the late twenties, help explain the virtual disappearance of the Progressive movement, outside of Alberta, by 1926. The handful of radical Progressives MPs who remained formed an alliance with the two Labour representatives in the House and became known, collectively, as the "Ginger Group," the embryo of what was soon to become the CCF.

With the disintegration of the Progressive and labour and farmers' parties, the old two-party system again became dominant in the late twenties. The return of two-party dominance was short-lived, however. The onset of the Great Depression in late 1929 gave renewed impetus to regional political protest, especially in western Canada, where the cataclysmic events of the decade hit hardest and where governments possessed fewer financial resources to deal with the crisis. Initially voters continued to place their faith in the traditional parties, but with each passing year, as unemployment worsened and suffering increased, more and more Canadians lost faith in the capitalist system and, more important, in the ability of the old parties to patch it up using orthodox methods. For the first time, many began to demand positive government intervention in the social and economic life of the country. The growing discontent, in turn, spawned three new political parties, raised significantly the profile of a third, and effected changes to the old parties.

The most radical and popular of the new parties was the CCF, a national, though largely western-based, federation of provincial farm organizations and independent labour parties, including socialist intellectuals from central Canada, formed largely at the behest of the Ginger Group in 1932. Led by J.S. Woodsworth, a highly respected former Methodist minister, social worker, and western labour MP, who was largely responsible for uniting the disparate elements of the party, the CCF espoused a distinctly socialist philosophy. In its statement of principles, endorsed at its founding convention in Regina in 1933, the CCF supported the replacement of the capitalist free-enterprise system, with its recurring unemployment and its grossly uneven distribution of wealth, with a "cooperative commonwealth" in which governments would control or regulate key sectors of the economy and provide a wide array of social services to ensure a decent standard of living for all Canadians. It was a philosophy based largely on the ideas of British Fabian socialists and indigenous Christian-progressive reformers.

Despite its moderate, evolutionary brand of democratic socialism, the party's enemies nonetheless portrayed it as a revolutionary Bolshevik movement seeking to overthrow capitalism by violent means and expropriate all private property. This unfavourable image, validated by the occasional intemperate remark from more radical CCFers, limited the party's appeal. Most Canadians were simply not willing to take a chance on an avowedly socialist party, especially at a time when day-to-day survival preoccupied their thoughts. In Catholic, anti-socialist Quebec and across the perpetually poor Maritimes, in particular, the CCF had virtually no support. Added obstacles included the official non-partisanship of the country's main labour organizations and the competition of other protest parties. Nevertheless, within three years of its founding the CCF enjoyed Official Opposition status in BC and Saskatchewan, based on substantial popular support, and held seats in the legislatures of Ontario, Manitoba, and Alberta. It also won nine percent of the popular vote in the 1935 federal election, a reasonably impressive amount for a young, radical movement.

Not until the 1940s, however, did the CCF become a major party, and far and away the leading protest party of the era. Despite the return of prosperity that accompanied wartime economic mobilization, Canadians retained strong memories of the Depression and had no wish to return to such conditions at war's end. Centralized economic planning and comprehensive social security, both mainstays of the CCF's program, seemed to offer the answer, not least because of the government's success in eliminating unemployment during the war. The CCF's popularity was given an additional boost by the rapid wartime expansion of the labour movement, led by the newly formed Canadian Congress of Labour (CCL). Industrial unionists were not only more sympathetic to political action than their brethren in the craft-oriented unions but were also more sympathetic to the CCF, which the CCL quickly endorsed as its "political arm."

These factors account in large part for the CCF's meteoric rise during the war. In September 1943 polls ranked it the most popular party in the country. One month before, it had come within four seats of forming the government of Ontario. The following year it took power in Saskatchewan, becoming North America's first openly socialist government. And in the June 1945 federal election it tripled its existing representation, to twenty-eight, despite a vicious anti-CCF propaganda campaign financed by segments of the business community. Party membership, meanwhile, ballooned, as Canadians from all walks of life jumped on the CCF bandwagon. The Second World War marked the apex, however, of the party's popularity. Never again would the CCF reach such dizzying heights.

Almost as successful, although far less sweeping in its critique of the status quo, was the other western protest party formed in the thirties: Social Credit. Like the CCF, the Social Credit party was born in response to the severity of the Depression on the prairies and, in particular, to the failure of the existing parties to sufficiently alleviate the people's suffering. Like the CCF, the Social Credit party owed its existence and success primarily to the efforts of one individual, William "Bible Bill" Aberhart, a respected fundamentalist minister, teacher, and Sunday School broadcaster who found the answer to his province's woes in the monetary theories of a Scottish mining engineer. Insufficient purchasing power among consumers lay at the root of the Depression, claimed Aberhart, and an infusion of money in the form of monthly dividends from the government (or social credit), combined with greater government regulation of the banking system, would restore purchasing power and get the economy moving again. Social Credit's message was deceptively simple—or so Aberhart made it seem—and for a province whose rural inhabitants were heavily in debt, desperate for answers, and mesmerized by Aberhart's tremendous oratorical powers, Social Credit was widely embraced as God's word on the economy.

Determined to put his ideas into practice, Aberhart converted his extensive religious organization into an equally impressive political one, and in 1935 Social Credit scored major electoral triumphs. It won 56 of 63 seats in the provincial election that summer, displacing the aging, scandal-ridden United Farmers of Alberta party, whose CCF-related platform it was not above appropriating on the hustings, and captured 15 of Alberta's 17 seats in the subsequent federal contest. Once in power, the party's fairly conventional and at times reactionary approach to governing, accounted for, in part, by the unconstitutionality of its monetary policies, was in marked contrast to the left-leaning rhetoric that lay behind its rapid ascent. Most historians agree that Social Credit provided honest and efficient government, but not much else. Nevertheless, the party was an enduring force, dominating Alberta politics, provincially, to the late 1960s, and federally, to the late 1950s.

One hesitates to call the third party born in the 1930s, Reconstruction, a new party, as it was essentially an offshoot of the national Conservative party. It was, however, a separate and fairly distinct entity, programmatically speaking, and garnered almost as many votes as the CCF in the 1935 election. The Reconstruction party was founded a few months before the 1935 federal election by Harry Stevens, a disgruntled minister in R.B. Bennett's Conservative administration who felt that not enough was being done by Bennett's government to curb the exploitative wage and pricing practices of large, monopolistic manufacturers and retailers, practices unearthed by Steven's much-publicized Parliamentary Committee on Price Spreads and Mass Buying of 1934. Forced to resign from the cabinet for his continuing public denunciations of big business and convinced that the Conservative party could not be a vehicle for reform, Stevens formed his own party. Its candidates, numbering an impressive 174 of a possible 245, called for greater government regulation of big business to ensure a fair return to producers and small business, and a more equitable distribution of wealth, through fair wages, extensive public works, and higher taxes on the rich. The platform was in some ways a typical Depression-era refrain, with its David and Goliath overtones. In the end, only Stevens was elected. The three-month-old party had not had time to create an effective electoral machine and no Conservatives of stature had come to Stevens' side. The nine percent popular support earned by Reconstruction, a not insignificant amount under the circumstances, was largely a reflection of the sympathy and respect Canadians had for the party's leader, particularly in the urban areas of Ontario and the Maritimes. The party disappeared shortly after. It was succeeded, in some respects, by W.D. Herridge's New Democracy movement, another anti-big business party, though with a social credit bent, which ran a small number of candidates, unsuccessfully, in the 1940 federal election.

Another party that came to prominence in the thirties was the Communist party of Canada (CPC). The CPC was born shortly after the First World War from the remnants of several small socialist parties fractured by the war and inspired by Russia's successful Bolshevik revolution to unite into what became the largest left-wing party in Canada at the time. The CPC's popularity in its early years, however, was severely limited by its doctrinaire Marxism, which held little appeal to most Canadian workers, by its subservience to the USSR, which caused erratic shifts in party policy and provoked charges of disloyalty, and above all by the strict opposition and repression of employers and police (the CPC was officially banned until 1936). As such, Canadian Communism's following was restricted largely to east European immigrants in the resource sector of the West and northern Ontario whose radical background and horrendous working conditions made them receptive to the party's revolutionary message. There were, as well, bitter divisions within the movement over the party's structure and over how best to accomplish its goals. These struggles, too, limited the party's ability to hold and attract adherents.

By the early 1930s, however, the CPC's message about the inevitable dissolution of capitalism seemed vindicated by events. More important, its adherents took the lead in organizing the unemployed and demanding adequate relief. To many desperate workers, the CPC seemed to be the only voice speaking on their behalf, and at substantial risk to their own safety. Communist influence in the labour movement expanded as well, as party activists played a leading role in establishing industrial unions in the primary and mass production industries. More surprising was the fact that the CPC managed to attract a good many middle-class followers to the various "front" groups it set up to preserve civil liberties at home and resist the spread of fascism abroad. The adoption of more moderate reform proposals and rhetoric during the "Popular Front" period of the late 1930s, during which the party sought alliances with all "non-reactionary" groups, further expanded the party's base of support among native-born Canadians, particularly youth and intellectuals. However, this growing support did not translate into electoral victories, as only a handful of Communists were elected to office in the thirties, usually at the municipal level. But then, the CPC placed little emphasis on winning elections in these years, preferring, instead, mass demonstrations and direct action.

Not until the Second World War did the CPC—renamed the Labour Progressive party (LPP) in 1942—take a serious interest in electoral politics. In so doing, it managed to capitalize on the public's growing support for the left in general at this time, as Canadians became more amenable to collectivist ideas and, with the USSR a military ally after June 1941, more sympathetic to communists in particular. The communists' active involvement in the spread of industrial unions also began to pay off, in terms of elevating working-class support for the LPP in heavily unionized, mostly urban ridings, usually at the expense of the CCF. The LPP was able, in turn, to parlay this growing support into seats. During the war it won more seats than ever before at the municipal and provincial levels. In 1943 it won a Montreal by-election, and in 1945, on the strength of 100,000 votes in sixty-seven ridings, re-elected its MP. More important, perhaps, was the assistance it gave to Liberal (or Lib-Labour) candidates across Canada, a number of whom won office with LPP endorsement. Like the CCF, however, the Communist party would never again attain the level of success it enjoyed in this period. The Cold War that followed, as well as the tremendous prosperity of the postwar years, inflicted irreparable damage on its support and morale.

The other prominent theme in the party politics of this period, one closely linked to the rise of third parties, was the transformation of the old parties, particularly at the provincial level. Largely in response to the discontent fostered by recession and farmer and labour discontent immediately following the First World War, the Depression of the thirties, and the high expectations for continued prosperity and postwar security that emerged during the Second World War, both the Liberals and the Conservatives chose new, more progressive leaders and proclaimed new, more forward-looking policies. Indeed, in their attacks against the status quo and in their promises of reform, the old-line parties at times came to resemble the protest parties against which they competed. The new approach was especially true in the 1930s, when new-look Liberal and Conservative parties appeared, and won office, in BC, Ontario, and Quebec.

Perhaps the most genuine of the self-proclaimed reform parties was the BC Liberal party under T. Dufferin ("Duff") Pattullo, one of several somewhat eccentric personalities to occupy the political stage during the Dirty Thirties. Patterning himself on US President Franklin Roosevelt, Pattullo professed a strong belief that the state had an important role to play in creating a more equitable, humane capitalist system—that governments had a responsibility for the well-being of their citizens and toward this end should regulate the economy and provide social services, including health and unemployment insurance, even if this meant running a budgetary deficit. This rather novel perspective—novel for an old-line party at least—in conjunction with an intense fear among conservative British Columbians that the CCF's "socialist hordes" would come to power if the non-socialist vote was divided, allowed the BC Liberals to trounce the ruling Conservatives in the 1933 provincial election. Its massive victory also gave the new Pattullo administration a mandate to proceed with what came to be called the "little New Deal." And proceed it did. Among the Pattullo government's many initiatives were an expanded public works program, improved welfare services, a shorter work week, minimum wages, and subsidies to sustain employment levels in the mining and fishing industries. Largely on the strength of this record, the Liberals remained in power until 1941, sharing power thereafter in a Liberal-Conservative coalition.

If substance triumphed over style among BC Liberals, the same cannot be said of their Ontario counterparts. After nearly thirty years in Opposition, the Depression provided the backdrop for the Ontario Liberal party's return to power, if not necessarily respectability. Just as important in this resurrection was the party's new leader, Mitchell ("Mitch") Hepburn, an onion-farmer and former MP whose brashness, flamboyance, and verbal recklessness contrasted sharply with the colourless Conservative Premier, George Henry. Like so many other Depression-era populists, moreover, Hepburn promised to fight for the "common man" against the big interests and against corrupt, wasteful, cold-hearted governments. "I swing well to the left," he assured voters while campaigning, "where even some Liberals will not follow me."[2] He was typically vague on specifics, but the implication, at least, was that a Liberal government would regulate big business, make government more honest and efficient, and at the same time expand social services for average Ontarians. Given Hepburn's passion and charisma on the campaign trail, voters were inclined to believe him and gave his party a massive majority in the 1934 election.

Hepburn was a traditional, laissez-faire "Grit" at heart, however, and as such his response to the Depression was strictly orthodox: balancing budgets and reducing the cost of government. True, some progressive labour legislation was passed—though without Hepburn's endorsement— and higher relief payments were given to the unemployed, but on the whole the "new" Liberals did little for the "average man" (or woman) in those desperate years. Indeed, in his personal war against industrial unions and in the financial assistance he extended to his close friends in the mining industry, Premier Hepburn demonstrated where his true sympathies lay. As his first biographer stated succinctly, "his rhetoric was radical; his policies were not."[3] What he *did* do was give vent to the unfocused anger and frustration many average citizens felt in this period, and for this he remained popular throughout the decade, easily winning re-election in 1937.

An equally dramatic political resurgence occurred in the neighbouring province of Quebec, although in this case it was a refurbished Conservative party that replaced an aging Liberal regime. It did so with an appeal to the voters that was more nationalist than populist. In the early thirties, Quebeckers, like voters elsewhere in Canada, sought scapegoats for their economic woes. They found them primarily in the English-speaking capitalists who controlled Quebec's economy and supposedly exploited French-Canadian workers. Because the Liberal government of L.A. Tashereau had over the years given substantial support and encouragement to such "foreign" monopolistic elements, it, too, became the object of growing public indignation. This anger was expressed within the ruling Liberal party itself by a faction of young nationalist intellectuals, closely allied with and inspired by the views of Catholic social reformers in the province. The renegade Liberals, in turn, formed an organization known as L'Action Libérale Nationale (ALN) to pressure the Tashereau government into curbing the power of foreign investors and providing more social services to rural and urban areas.

The leader of the province's Conservative party, Maurice Duplessis, saw an opportunity here and seized it. He offered to form a political alliance with the ALN, one aimed at implementing the latter's left-wing nationalist economic and social program. The ALN agreed and the Union Nationale was born. Led by Duplessis, who lambasted the Liberals for their relationship with foreign monopolies and their allegedly corrupt ways in office, and who promised a better deal for the workers of the province, the Union Nationale won a convincing victory in the 1936 provincial election.

The election of the Union Nationale was the first in a string of victories that, except for two brief Liberal interregnums, stretched into the late 1960s. Less enduring was the reformist agenda on which the party was first elected. Most members of the ALN became quickly disillusioned with the essential conservatism of Duplessis and his former Conservative colleagues and returned to the Liberal fold. This allowed Duplessis an even freer hand with which to run Quebec according to his own rural-Catholic, laissez-faire views. This freedom, in turn, meant few restrictions on foreign capitalists, minimal social services, restrictions on the rights of organized labour (sometimes by force of arms) as well as on the rights of free speech and assembly, and substantial financial assistance to the Catholic Church and to the rural areas from which the Union Nationale derived most of its support. It is largely for these reasons that historians generally describe the Duplessis years as Quebec's "Dark Ages," an epitaph unmitigated by the strong-arm tactics, bribery, and manipulation that the Union Nationale employed at unprecedented levels to win re-election. Like many of the "protest" parties of the interwar period, therefore, the Union Nationale proved to be far less reformist once in office.

Federally, too, the look of the old parties changed, although here the changes were slower in coming. Of the two, the Conservative party proved the most resistant to change. Its decision in 1920 to replace the more progressive and pragmatic Robert Borden with the more conservative and notoriously uncompromising Arthur Meighen signalled a return to a more traditional approach, one emphasizing the benefits of a high tariff and closer imperial relations. The first held little appeal, however, to the aggrieved farmers of the West and Ontario, and the second was guaranteed to keep French Canada—still seething from conscription—firmly in the Liberal camp. These policies, plus Conservative Prime Minister Meighen's unwillingness to compromise one iota to secure Progressive support in Parliament and his constitutionally questionable "shadow cabinet" of 1925, consisting of "acting" ministers who had yet to be re-elected as bona fide cabinet ministers, kept the Tories in the opposition benches for all but three days between 1921 and 1930. The Conservative party was not forgiving. In spite of the fact that Meighen had through his eloquence and intelligence helped restore the party to national prominence, the party replaced him at its first leadership convention, in 1927, with millionaire lawyer and businessperson R. B. Bennett.

Bennett's optimism, vigour, and ample financial resources revived the Tory party once again and contributed greatly to its 1930 election victory. Luck was a factor too. Whereas Prime Minister Mackenzie King refused to "give a 5 cent piece" to any Conservative provincial government for "alleged unemployment"—an uncharacteristically imprudent remark—Bennett pledged to fight the Depression, using the tariff to "blast" Canadian exports into the markets of the world. But tinkering with the tariff, balancing the budget, providing emergency unemployment relief, rounding up suspected communists, and establishing work camps for the legions of unemployed marked the extent of the Conservative party's creativity and Canadians soon began to look to other parties for answers. Realizing this, and sensing the desire for change within a segment of his own party, Bennett experienced a sudden conversion. Virtually overnight he became a harsh critic of the economic system that had served him so well and which, as prime minister, he had staunchly defended. In his "New Deal" radio broadcasts of January 1935, Bennett declared that "the old order is gone . . . [and] will not return."[4] In its place he promised a system of "government regulation and control," including unemployment and health insurance, minimum wages, higher profits taxes, and strict federal regulation of business. Not since the Halifax platform of 1907 had the Tories demonstrated such progressive inclinations, a foreshadowing of the even greater progressive shift to come during the war. Nevertheless, and with good reason, voters found their arch-conservative prime minister's sudden conversion to reform principles, especially in an election year, somewhat incredible, while most long-time Conservatives were shocked. The paucity of reform legislation that followed as well as the RCMP's brutal dispersal of relief camp strikers in Regina in July did little to boost Bennett's credibility, and in the 1935 election the Tories were reduced to a mere 40 seats, their smallest parliamentary contingent since Confederation. Within three years Bennett would resign as party leader. His successor was R.J. "Fighting Bob" Manion, an Irish Catholic whose bad temper and often tactless invective, when combined with his party's vaguely right-wing, pro-Empire platform, kept the party's support concentrated in Ontario.

The federal Liberal party's record of innovation in the interwar years was only slightly better. The process of change began in 1919 when the party held its first-ever leadership convention to choose a replacement for the recently deceased Laurier, a function previously performed by the party's federal caucus. At the same time the party adopted a remarkably forward-looking program, one which included support for old-age pensions, health insurance, proportional representation in Parliament, and lower tariffs. What's more, the new Liberal leader, Mackenzie King, seemed well-suited to implement this progressive agenda. Young, well-educated, an expert in the emerging field of industrial relations, and a documented proponent of a more humane, government-regulated capitalism, King's reform credentials, if not impeccable, appeared sound.

In reality, King was an excessively cautious individual whose tenuous interest in reform was greatly overshadowed by his almost fanatical determination to keep his party united and to alienate as few voters as possible, particularly in the Liberal bastion of Quebec. In a phrase that aptly summarizes King's political credo, he once told his cabinet that "it is what we prevent, rather than what we do that counts most in Government."[5] To this end, King introduced reforms only to the extent needed to gain or to maintain power. These reforms included minor revisions to taxes and tariffs, to satisfy the Progressives, and an old-age pension plan, to secure the support of the Ginger Group in 1925. Foreign policy commitments were studiously eschewed, for they could only mean divisiveness, government expense, and possibly war. Not that the Liberal government's inaction proved to be a political liability. As the intense ideological battles of the progressive era faded and as prosperity returned in the late twenties, Canadians turned their attention to less weighty matters, being generally satisfied with a less obtrusive national government. Political apathy, in conjunction with King's adroitness in diffusing the Progressive challenge and in turning the "King-Byng affair" of 1926 to his party's advantage—King cited the Governor-General's refusal to dissolve Parliament and call an election in June of that year as evidence of imperial tyranny—account for the Liberal party's domination of federal politics in the 1920s.

Canadians were not nearly as apathetic in the 1930s. The emergence of third parties and of new-style "old parties" provincially, was proof enough of this. On the other hand, it remains a fact that most voters were unwilling to take a chance on the more radical and, to many Canadians, frightening alternatives, such as the CCF or the Communist party. Mackenzie King knew this and exploited it, telling voters in 1935 that the choice they faced was between "King" and "Chaos." Almost 45 percent opted for the former and returned the Liberals to power with the largest majority in Canadian history to that point. Having been elected without the mandate (or desire) to introduce reform, and despite sporadic references to aspects of their 1919 program while in opposition, the Liberals felt little need to change direction. Royal commissions were established to study the questions of unemployment relief and federal-provincial constitutional powers, and the

Bank of Canada was nationalized, but balanced budgets at home and "no commitments" abroad remained the touchstones of Liberal practice.

Not until the early 1940s did the old-line federal parties alter significantly their image. The immediate cause of this transformation was the political threat of the Canadian left. With the popularity of the CCF, and to a lesser degree the Communists, rising quickly during the war, both the Conservatives and Liberals felt compelled to present a more progressive front. The Conservatives became the "Progressive" Conservatives, selected a new leader—the former Liberal-Progressive premier of Manitoba, John Bracken—and adopted a more left-wing program that, among other things, promised universal old-age pensions, medicare, a large-scale housing program and advanced labour legislation, albeit with few details. The Liberal party went even further. As a government it had already introduced an unemployment insurance scheme and in 1944 it expanded the emerging welfare state with a program of family allowances. In addition, it promised full employment through extensive postwar "economic planning" and a national minimum standard of living through comprehensive social security. These changes to both parties did much to stem the surging CCF in the 1945 federal election. While the Liberals and Conservatives did, indeed, lose ground to the left in that contest, many—particularly the CCF—had expected the losses to be much greater.

While the emergence of third parties and the ideological liberalization of the old are the leading themes in this period, a related development worthy of note is the democratization of the parties themselves, in terms of their internal organization. This theme is covered in sufficient detail in Section 1 and need not be discussed here at any length. Suffice it to say that with the growing disrepute of "partyism" after 1900 and the rise of third parties after the First World War, the older methods of mobilizing popular support became less predominant than before. Generally speaking, the new parties were organized and financed much more democratically than the old. Not only did they have many more official members, who without hope of material compensation (i.e., patronage) gave their time and money to get their candidates elected. They also gave their members a greater voice in the running of the party and in the formulation of its programs. This was particularly true of the Progressive and CCF parties. In short, these years saw the emergence of so-called "mass" parties.

Even the older parties changed with the times. Although still essentially elitist and caucus-based in their organization and financing, the Liberal and Conservative parties in this period allowed their members a greater voice in choosing party leaders, candidates, and policies. They also tried to place themselves on a more secure and broadly based footing by creating extra-parliamentary organizations, such as the National Liberal Federation and Dominion Conservative Association. These bodies coordinated and enhanced the fundraising and electioneering efforts of regular party members and went some distance in democratizing the old parties, particularly when the latter were in opposition and thus bereft of patronage resources.

The readings that follow focus on the emergence of protest parties, clearly the leading development in the party politics of this period. The first three deal with the left-populist, largely western-based movements. Manitoba historian W.L. Morton outlines the origins of the Progressive political insurgency on the Prairies, emphasizing the deepseated sectionalism of the region as well as the catalytic effect of the First World War. Just as important are his observations about the fragile nature of the movement, divided as it was between two competing and ultimately irreconcilable visions of progressivism. The more radical wing of the Progressives went on to play a key role in the formation of another regional party, the CCF. This is the focus of Walter Young's concise, yet comprehensive overview of the party from his well-known book *Democracy and Discontent*. Young contends that the CCF was very different, ideologically and structurally, from previous protest and old-line parties—that it was a "movement" as well as a party, and, as such, was an enduring force with strong grassroots support. At the same time, he points out the serious obstacles, both internal and external, faced by the CCF in its bid to advance electorally prior to the Second World War. The third significant protest party to emerge from the West, Social Credit, is the subject of John Irving's piece. In it the author reviews the philosophy, leadership, and strategy/tactics of the Alberta Social Credit movement in an attempt to explain its broad and sudden appeal. Without denying the powerful influence of the Depression in the party's meteoric rise or of Aberhart's tremendous organizational and communicative skills, Irving nevertheless emphasizes the powerful "psychological functions" of the three main factors he reviews. To Irving, Social Credit was above all a phenomenon of "mass psychology."

From interwar regional protest the readings move to the more unequivocally class-based protest of the Communist party. In the excerpt from his book *Canadian Communism*, Norman Penner examines one phase in the strange history of the country's Communist party. In particular, he outlines the efforts of the party in the 1930s to forge an alliance—through a variety of front groups, a more moderate, "liberal-reformist" program, and a closer relationship with mainstream labour—of progressive forces to combat the growing threat of international fascism. Penner admits that this "united front" strategy failed to unite the left, as most democratic socialists eschewed cooperation with Communists, but argues that the Communists nevertheless tapped into the idealism and fear of many working- and middle-class Canadians, and that this ability brought the party unprecedented electoral gains.

Changes in the nature of the older parties in this period are examined in the last two readings. Herbert Quinn, in his detailed and highly readable piece on the origins and rise of the Union Nationale, documents the Quebec Conservative party's return to power in the mid-1930s under their new, politically savvy leader, Maurice Duplessis. Quinn shows how the Conservatives—now called the Union Nationale—adopted a left-nationalist platform to exploit the province's rising reform sentiment and discredited the ruling Liberals by exposing their widespread corruption in office. He also provides valuable insights into the often unsavoury methods of the Liberal machine. The last article, by John Saywell, describes what was in many ways a similar process in neighbouring Ontario. Here, however, it was the Liberal party that donned the mantle of populist reform (minus the nationalist component) and accused the incumbent Conservatives of widespread corruption and "extravagance." Particular attention is given to the demagogic bombast of Liberal leader Mitch Hepburn. Indeed, in Saywell's portrait of Hepburn's aggressive style and the tensions Hepburn's style caused within the Liberal party one can easily detect the seeds of the party's eventual fall from grace. From this excerpt we also gain an appreciation for Hepburn's tremendous energy and his organizing abilities on the hustings, qualities not often associated with the infamous onion farmer from St. Thomas.

NOTES

1. In the Alberta election of 1917, for example, two of the League's four candidates were elected. J.H. Thompson, *The Harvests of War: The Prairie West, 1914-1918* (Toronto: McClelland & Stewart, 1978), 128.

2. Cited in Neil McKenty, *Mitch Hepburn* (Toronto: McClelland & Stewart, 1967), 100.

3. Ibid.

4. Cited in H. Blair Neatby, *The Politics of Chaos: Canada in the Thirties* (Toronto: Macmillan Canada, 1972), 65.

5. Cited in J.C. Courtney, "Prime-Ministerial Character: An Examination of Mackenzie King's Political Leadership," in J. English and J. Stubbs, eds., *Mackenzie King: Widening the Debate* (Toronto: Macmillan Canada, 1978), 82.

THE WESTERN PROGRESSIVE MOVEMENT, 1919-1921

BY W. L. MORTON

o

The Progressive Movement in the West was dual in origin and nature. In one aspect it was an economic protest; in another it was a political revolt. A phase of agrarian resistance to the National Policy of 1878, it was also, and equally, an attempt to destroy the old national parties. The two aspects unite in the belief of all Progressives, both moderate and extreme, that the old parties were equally committed to maintaining the National Policy and indifferent to the ways in which the "big interests" of protection and monopoly used government for their own ends.

At the root of the sectional conflict, from which the Progressive Movement in part sprang, was the National Policy of 1878. Such conflict is partly the result of the hardships and imperfect adaptations of the frontier, but it also arises from the incidence of national policies.[1] The sectional corn develops where the national shoe pinches. The National Policy, that brilliant improvisation of Sir John A. Macdonald, had grown under the master politician's hand, under the stimulus of depression and under the promptings of political appetite, until it had become a veritable Canadian System Henry Clay might have envied. Explicit in it was the promise that everybody should have something from its operation; implicit in it—its inarticulate major premise indeed—was the promise that when the infant industries it fostered had reached maturity, protection would be needed no more.

This, however, was but a graceful tribute to the laissez-faire doctrine of the day. This same doctrine it was which prevented the western wheat grower from demanding that he, too, should benefit directly from the

Excerpt from *Historical Papers* 1946 (The Canadian Historical Association, 1946), pp. 41-54. Reprinted with permission of The Canadian Historical Association.

operation of the National Policy. That he did benefit from the system as a whole, a complex of land settlement, railway construction, and moderate tariff protection, is not be be denied. But the wheat grower, building the wheat economy from homestead to terminal elevator in a few swift years, was caught in a complex of production and marketing costs, land values, railway rates, elevator charges, and interest rates. He fought to lower all these costs by economic organization and by political pressure. He saw them all as parts of a system which exploited him. He was prevented, by his direct experience of it, and by the prevailing doctrine of laissez-faire, from perceiving that the system might confer reciprocal benefits on him. Accordingly, he hated and fought it as a whole. Of the National Policy, however, the tariff was politically the most conspicuous element. Hence the political battle was fought around the tariff; it became the symbol of the wheat growers' exploitation and frustration, alleged and actual. Like all symbols, it oversimplified the complexities it symbolized.

This clash of interest had, of course, to be taken into account by the national political parties. The Liberal-Conservatives, as creators of the National Policy, had little choice but to extol its merits even in regions where they seemed somewhat dim. They could stress its promise that a good time was coming for all, they could add that meanwhile the Yankees must be held at bay. When the Liberals quietly appropriated the National Policy after attaining national power in 1896, the task of the Conservatives became much easier. Not only could the Liberals be accused of having abandoned their principles; they could even be accused of unduly prolonging the adolescence of infant industries. A western Conservative, Mr. Arthur Meighen, could indict the Laurier administration on the charge of being maintained in power "behind ramparts of gold"[2] erected by the "interests." This echo of the "cross of gold" was not ineffective in the West, where the charge that there was no real difference between the parties on the tariff not only promoted the growth of third party sentiment, but also prolonged the life of western conservatism.

The Liberals, for their part, had not only abandoned "continentalism" in the Convention of 1893, but with the possession of power had developed that moderation without which a nation-wide majority may not be won or kept in a country of sectional interests.[3] Liberal speakers might proclaim that the party was the low tariff party; Fielding might make the master stroke of the British preferential tariff; certain items might be put on the free list here, the rates might be lowered on certain others there; but the Liberal party had become a national party, with all the powers and responsibilities of government, among them the maintenance and elaboration of the now historic National Policy. In consequence each national party began to appear more and more in the eyes of the wheat grower as an "organized hypocrisy dedicated to getting and holding office,"[4] and the conditions were created for a third party movement in the West.

The tariff, then, was a major predisposing cause of a third party movement in the West. Down to 1906 the British preference and other concessions of the Fielding tariff, together with reiterated promises of further reductions, kept the western Liberals within the fold. The completion in that year, however, of the three-decker tariff marked the beginning of more serious discontent. It grew with the offer of reciprocity in the Payne-Aldrich tariff of 1909. With the increase of agricultural indebtedness, concomitant with the settlement of the West, and the disappearance of the advantageous price differential between agricultural prices and those of manufactured goods, on which the wheat boom had taken its rise, the discontent deepened. It found expression through the grain growers' organizations, those "impressive foci of progressive ideas."[5] In 1909 came the organization of the Canadian Council of Agriculture, in 1910 Laurier's tour of the West, [6] and the Siege of Ottawa by the organized farmers. Plainly, the West was demanding its due at last. The Liberal party, which had lost support in Ontario in every election since 1896, which saw its hold in Quebec threatened by the Nationalists under Bourassa, could not afford to lose the support of a new and rapidly growing section. In 1911 the helm was put hard over for reciprocity, and Liberal prospects brightened in the West.[7] But this partial return to continentalism in economic policy was too severe a strain for a party which had become committed as deeply as its rival to the National Policy. The "Eighteen Liberals" of Toronto, among them Sir Clifford Sifton, broke with the party, and it went down to defeat under a Nationalist and a National Policy crossfire. At the same time the Conservative party in the West, particularly in Saskatchewan and Alberta, suffered strains and defections which were to show in a lowered vitality in succeeding elections. But the offer of reciprocity remained on the statute books of the United States for another decade, and year by year the grain growers in convention demanded that the offer be taken up.

The demand of the western agrarians for the lowering of the tariff, however, was by no means an only factor in the rise of the third party. Into the West after 1896 poured immigrants from the United States and Great Britain. Most of the Americans came from the Middle West and the trans-Mississippi region. Many brought with them the experience and the political philosophy of the farmers' organizations and the third parties of these regions. Perhaps the clearest manifestation of their influence on the political development of the West was the demand for direct legislation which found expression in those forums of agrarian opinions, the grain growers' conventions, and which also found its way to the statute books of the three Western Provinces. From the British Isles came labour and socialist influences, felt rather in labour and urban circles, but not without effect among the farmers. These populist and socialist influences were mild; their exponents were in a minority. Nonetheless, they did much to give western discontent a vocabulary of grievance. Above all, they combined to repudiate the politics of expediency practised by the national parties, to denounce those parties as indifferently the tools of the "big interests," and to demand that the farmer free himself from the toils of the old parties and set up a third party, democratic, doctrinaire and occupational.[8]

In the Canadian West this teaching fell on a soil made favourable not only by a growing disbelief in the likelihood of either of the national parties lowering the tariff, but also by a political temper different from that of

Eastern Canada. (One exception must be made to this statement, namely, the old Canadian West in peninsular Ontario, from which, indeed, the original settlement of the West had been largely drawn.) This difference may be broadly expressed by saying that the political temper of the eastern provinces, both French and English, is whiggish. Government there rests on compact, the vested and legal rights of provinces, of minorities, of corporations.[9] The political temper of the West, on the other hand, is democratic; government there rests on the will of the sovereign people, a will direct, simple, and no respector of rights except those demonstrably and momentarily popular. Of this Jacksonian, Clear Grit democracy, reinforced by American populism and English radicalism, the Progressive Movement was an authentic expression.

No better example of this difference of temper exists, of course, than the Manitoba school question. Manitoba was founded on a balance of French and English elements; this balance was expressed in the compact of the original Manitoba Act, the essential point in which was the guarantee of the educational privileges of the two language and religious groups. The balance was destroyed by the Ontario immigration of the eighteen-seventies and eighties; in 1890 Manitoba liberalism swept away the educational privileges of the French minority and introduced the "national" school, the chief agency of equalitarian democracy. This set in train a series of repercussions which, through the struggle over the Autonomy Bills in 1905, the introduction of compulsory education by the Liberal party in Manitoba in 1916, and the friction caused by Regulation 17 in Ontario, led up to the split in the Liberal party between the western and the Quebec Liberals on the Lapointe resolution in the federal Parliament in 1916. This split not only foreshadowed and prepared the way for that on conscription; it also contributed to the break-up of the old parties which opened the way to the rise of the Progressive party after 1919.[10] The western Liberals, that is to say, were turning against Laurier because they feared Nationalist domination of the party.

Thus it was that the ground was prepared for the West to throw its weight behind Union Government, first suggested as a war measure, then persisted in to prevent a Liberal victory under Laurier. Western Liberals and radicals did so with much reluctance and many misgivings. An independent movement was already taking root.[11] For the Liberal party, an electoral victory was in sight following a succession of provincial victories and the discontent with the Borden Government's conduct of the war.[12]

This probable Liberal victory, to be based on anti-conscription sentiment in Quebec and low tariff sentiment in the West, was averted by the formation of the Union Government. The issue in that political transformation was whether the three western Liberal governments could be detached from the federal party. But the attempt made at the Winnipeg convention in August, 1917, to prepare the way for this change was defeated by the official Liberals.[13] The insurgents refused to accept the verdict of the convention; and by negotiations, the course of which is by no means clear, the support of the three western administrations and of the farmers' organizations was won for

Union Government. Thus the leadership of the West was captured, and assurance was made doubly sure by the Wartime Elections Act. At the same time, the nascent third party movement was absorbed by the Union Government, and the Liberal party in the West was wrecked by the issue of conscription, as the Conservative party had been mortally wounded by reciprocity.

Though the Union Government was constituted as a "win the war" administration, which should still partisan and sectional strife, other hopes had gone to its making. It was thought that a non-partisan administration might also be an opportunity to carry certain reforms, such as that of civil service recruitment, that it would be difficult, if not impossible, for a partisan government to carry. There was also, and inevitably, the tariff. The Union Government was not publicly pledged to tariff reform, but there can be no doubt that western sentiment had forced Unionist candidates to declare themselves on the tariff; indeed many western Unionists were low tariff Liberals, or even outright independents. The eastern industrialists, on the other hand, were alert to see that the weighty western wing of the Cabinet should not induce the government to make concessions to the West. Thus there was an uneasy truce on the tariff question during the remainder of the war, the issue lying dormant but menacing the unity of the Government and its majority once the pressure of war should be removed. The test was to come with the first peace budget, that of 1919.

These, then, were the underlying causes of the rise of the western Progressive Movement. In 1919 they came to the surface, unchanged in themselves but now operating in a heated and surcharged atmosphere. That there would have been a Progressive Movement in any event is not to be doubted; the war and the events of the postwar years served to give it explosive force.

Certain elements in this surcharged atmosphere were general, others peculiar to the farmer, in effect. Chief of the general elements was the fact that the War of 1914-18 had been fought without economic controls of any significance. The result was inflation with all the stresses and strains inflation sets up in the body economic and social. The high cost of living, as it was called, was an invariable theme of speakers of the day, particularly of spokesmen of labour and the farmer. The farmer was quite prepared to believe that he, as usual, was especially the victim of these circumstances, and would point to the "pork profiteers," to clinch his contention. Inflation was at the root of the general unrest of the day, and the influence of the Russian Revolution, the radical tone of many organizations and individuals, the Winnipeg strike, and the growth of the labour movement are to be ascribed to inflation rather than to any native predisposition to radical courses.

Among the farmers' special grievances was the conscription of farmers' sons in 1918. The farming population of English Canada, on the whole had supported conscription, but with two qualifications. One was that there should also be "conscription of wealth," by which a progressive income tax was meant. The other was that the farms should not be stripped of their supply of labour, a not unreasonable condition in view of the urgent need of producing food. But the military situation in the spring of 1918 led to the revocation of the order-in-council exempting farmers' sons from military service. The result was a bitter outcry from the farmers, the great delegation to Ottawa in May, 1918, and an abiding resentment against the Union Government and all its works, especially in Ontario.

In the West itself, drought, especially in southern Alberta, had come to harass a farm population already sorely tried. Suffice it to indicate that in the Lethbridge area of southern Alberta, the average yield of wheat between 1908 and 1921 ranged from sixty-three bushels to the acre [1.6 ha] in 1915 to two in 1918, and eight in 1921.[14] This was the extreme, but the whole West in varying degrees suffered a similar fluctuation in yield. It was a rehearsal of the disaster of the nineteen-thirties.

To the hazards of nature were to be added the hazards of the market. In 1917 the government had fixed the price of wheat to keep it from going higher and had established a Wheat Board to market the crops of the war years. Now that peace had come, was wheat once more to be sold on the open market, or would the government fix the price and continue to market the crops through the Wheat Board, at least until the transition from war to peace was accomplished? Here was a chance to make the National Policy a matter of immediate benefit and concern to the western farmer, a chance not undiscerned by shrewd defenders of the National Policy.[15] Here also, under the stimulus of war, was the beginning of the transition from the old Jeffersonian and laissez-faire tradition of the frontier West, to the new West of wheat pools, floor prices, and the Cooperative Commonwealth Federation. The point of principle was clearly grasped by the farmers, but their response was confused. The Manitoba Grain Growers and the United Farmers of Alberta declined in annual convention to ask the government to continue the Wheat Board, but this decision was severely criticized, one might almost say, was repudiated, by the rank and file of the membership. The Saskatchewan Grain Growers, who met later, emphatically demanded that the Wheat Board be continued. In the upshot it was, but only for the crop yield of 1919 and in 1920 it was liquidated. From this action came much of the drive, indeed the final impetus, of the Progressive Movement.[16] Thereafter the western farmer was caught between fixed debt charges and high costs on one hand and falling prices on the other; his position seemed to him desperate. From his despair came first, the Progressive electoral sweep in the West, and then the economic action which created the wheat pools.

Finally, there was the question of tariff revision. It was, however, no longer the simple clash of sectional interests it had been. The customs tariff had been increased to help finance the war. Any revision now would affect governmental financing of the war debt, and also the financial resources of private individuals and corporations in the postwar period. In short, the question had now become, what place should tariff revision have in reconstruction?

It was to this question that the Union Government had to address itself, while preparing the budget of 1919 under the vigilant eyes of the farmers' organizations on the one side and of the Canadian Manufacturers'

Association on the other. The decision was, in effect, to postpone the issue, on the ground that 1919 was, to all intents and purposes, a war year and that only a very moderate revision should be attempted. The decision was not unreasonable, and was clearly intended to be a compromise between eastern and western views on the tariff.[17] But western supporters of the Union Government were in a very vulnerable position, as the McMaster amendment to the motion to go into Committee of Supply was to show.[18] The pressure from the West for a major lowering of the tariff was mounting and becoming intense. In the outcome, the Honourable Thomas A. Crerar, Minister of Agriculture, resigned on the ground that the revision undertaken in the budget was insufficient. In the vote on the budget he was joined by nine western Unionists. This was the beginning of the parliamentary Progressive party.

The position of the remaining western Unionists became increasingly difficult, though also their pressure contributed to the moderate revision of 1919.[19] The fate of R. C. Henders is very much in point. Henders had been, as President of the Manitoba Grain Growers, an ardent and outspoken agrarian. In 1916 he had been nominated as an independent candidate for Macdonald. In 1917 he accepted nomination as Unionist candidate and was elected. In 1919 he voted with the Government on the budget, on the ground that this was in effect a war budget, and the time premature for a revision of the tariff. In 1920 the United Farmers of Manitoba, following the action of their executive, "repudiated his stand, accepted his resignation, and reaffirmed [their] confidence in the principles of the Farmers' Platform."[20] In 1921 he vanished from political ken. An honest man had taken a politically mistaken line and was mercilessly held to account. Such was the fate of western Unionists who did not cross the floor and find refuge in the Senate. Western low tariff sentiment would admit of no equivocation.

The third party movement, stirring in the West before 1917 but absorbed and over-ridden by the Unionist Government, was now free to resume its course with a favourable wind fanned by inflation, short crops, and postwar discontent. The Canadian Council of Agriculture had in 1916 taken cognizance of the mounting demand that political action be taken by the farmers. Without committing the Council itself, it prepared the Farmers' Platform as a program which the farmers' organizations might endorse and which they might press upon the government. The events of 1917 diverted attention from it, but in 1918 it was revised and enlarged, and in 1919 was adopted by the farmers' organizations. In substance, the platform called for a League of Nations, dominion autonomy, free trade with Great Britain, reciprocity with the United States, a lowering of the general tariff, graduated income, inheritance, and corporation taxes, public ownership of a wide range of utilities, and certain reforms designed to bring about a greater measure of democracy, such as reform of the senate, abolition of titles, and the institution of direct legislation and proportional representation.[21] The platform gave the incoherent western discontent a rallying point and a program and was the occasion for the organized farmers entering federal politics. Its title, "The New National Policy," was a gage of battle thrown down before the defenders of the old National Policy, a challenge, direct and explicit, to make that policy national indeed.

This decision to enter federal politics was opportune beyond the dream of seasoned politicians. The prairie was afire in a rising wind, and soon the flames were flaring from one end of the country to the other. In October, 1919, the United Framers of Ontario carried forty-six seats in a house of 111, and formed an administration. Later in the same month O.R. Gould, farmers' candidate in the federal seat of Assiniboia, defeated W.R. Motherwell, Liberal stalwart and a founder of the Grain Growers' Association, by a majority of 5,224.[22] A few days later Alex Moore carried Cochrane in a provincial by-election for the United Farmers of Alberta. In 1920 the organized farmers carried nine seats in Manitoba, seven in Nova Scotia, and ten in New Brunswick.[23] By-election after by-election went against the Government, usually to farmer candidates, until the smashing climax of the Medicine Hat by-election of June, 1921, when Robert Gardiner of the U.F.A. defeated a popular Unionist candidate by a majority of 9,764.[24] Even the Liberals' tariff plank of 1919 did little to check the sweep of the flames. The political prophets were estimating that of the forty-three seats west of the lakes, the Progressives would carry from thirty-five to forty.[25]

All was propitious, then, for the entry of the Progressives into federal politics. There they might hope to hold the balance of power, or even emerge as the largest group. The work of organization was pushed steadily. In December, 1920, the Canadian Council of Agriculture recognized the third party in the House of Commons as the exponent of the new national policy and endorsed the members' choice of the Honourable T.A. Crerar as leader.[26] During 1920 and 1921 Progressive candidates were nominated by local conventions in all federal constituencies in the West.

Two major difficulties, however, were arising to embarrass the Progressives in their bid for national power. The first was the charge that they were a class party. The second was the demand that political action be taken in the provincial as well as the federal field.[27] These embarrassments were eventually to split the Movement, defeat its bid for national power, and reduce it to the status of a sectional party.

The origin of these divisions in the Movement may best be examined by turning to provincial politics in the West. That the entrance into federal politics could not be kept separate from a demand that political action be taken in the provinces, arose in part from the federal composition of national parties. Any federal political movement is driven to attempt the capture of provincial governments, in order to acquire the means, that is to say, the patronage, whereby to build an effective political organization. It is not to be supposed that this political maxim was unknown to the leaders of the Progressive Movement. They hoped, however, that national success would be followed by a voluntary adherence of the western governments, which would render capture by storm unnecessary.

The Progressive Movement, at the same time, was a genuine attempt to destroy machine politics, and there was in its leadership a sincere reluctance to accept the facts of political life. They hoped to lead a popular movement, to which the farmers' economic organizations would furnish whatever direction was necessary. It was the zeal of their followers, eager to destroy the old parties wherever they existed, that carried the Progressive Movement into provincial politics.

Province by province, the leaders were compelled to bow to the pressure of the rank and file, and allow the organized farmers to enter the provincial arenas. The methods and the results, however, were by no means identical, for they were conditioned by the different political histories of the three provinces.

In Manitoba the dominating fact was that from 1899 until 1915 the province had been governed by the Conservative Roblin administration. The sheer power and efficiency of the Roblin-Rogers organization, perhaps the classic example of the political machine in Canadian history, accounts in great part for the victory of the anti-reciprocity campaign in Manitoba in 1911. Its spectacular demise in the odour of scandal in 1915 left the provincial Conservative party badly shattered. Henceforth there were many loose Conservative votes in the most conservative of the Prairie Provinces, a province a whole generation older than the other two, and during that generation the very image and transcript of Ontario. But the succeeding Liberal Government, that of the Honourable T.C. Norris, was reformist and progressive. There was little the Grain Growers could ask of the provincial administration that it was not prepared to grant. Why then should the organized farmers oppose the Norris Government? The answer was that the Progressive Movement was, for many Progressives, a revolt against the old party system, and the provincial Liberal organization had been affiliated with the federal Liberals. It might, indeed, become a major buttress of liberalism as the breach between the Laurier and the Unionist Liberal closed. If the old parties were to be defeated at Ottawa, they must be rooted out at the source of their strength in the provinces. Out of this conflict, largely one between leaders and rank and file, came the decision of the new United Farmers of Manitoba in 1920 that the organization as such should not enter provincial politics, but that in the constituencies the locals might hold conventions, nominate candidates, and organize. If a majority of constituencies should prove to be in favour of political action, then the executive of the United Farmers would call a provincial convention to draft a platform.[28] As a result, political action was taken locally, and nine farmer representatives were elected to the Manitoba legislature in 1920.[29] As a result of this success, the U.F.M. placed the resources of the organization behind the farmers' political action,[30] and in the election of 1922 the farmers won a plurality of seats in the legislature. The suspected *rapprochement* of the Norris government with the federal Liberals may have contributed to its defeat.[31]

In Saskatchewan and Alberta the dominating factor was that at the creation of the two provinces in 1905 the federal Liberal government used its influence to establish Liberal administrations. In Canada the possession of power is all but decisive. Governments fall not so much by the assaults of their enemies as through their own internal decay. From 1905 until 1921 the Liberals ruled in Alberta; from 1905 until 1929 they were in power in

Saskatchewan. Moreover, in both, the Conservative party was cut off from the patronage and unnaturally compelled to be a party of provincial rights. Both provincial Conservative parties declined from 1911 on, and rapidly after the provincial elections of 1917. In these provinces too, the administrations were careful to govern in harmony with the wishes of the organized farmers. Why then should the farmers enter provincial politics against the Liberal government? Again the answer is that the provincial Liberal parties were affiliated with the federal party, and were examples of the machine politics which Progressives hoped to destroy, politics rendered noisome by the corruption arising from the scramble for the resources of the West, and the political ruthlessness of the professional politicians of the day.

Down to 1917 the political developments of the two provinces were alike, but a remarkable diversion occurs thereafter. In Saskatchewan the Liberal party enjoyed shrewd leadership, considerable administrative ability, and a fine political organization. Threatened by scandal in 1917, it made a remarkable recovery under Premier William Martin. In that almost wholly rural province, the Liberal government was a government of the grain growers. Leadership, as in the instance of the Honourable Charles A. Dunning, graduated from the Association to the government. The slightest wish of the Saskatchewan Grain Growers became law with as much dispatch as the conventions of government allow.[32] When the demand for provincial political action arose, Premier Martin met it, in the Preeceville speech of May, 1920, by dissociating the provincial from the federal party. At the same time the weight of the executive of the Grain Growers was thrown against intervention as a separate party in provincial politics. As in Manitoba, when the demand, partly under pressure from the Non-Partisan League, became irresistible, it was referred to the locals.[33] The locals gave little response during 1920-21, and an attempt of third party men in 1921 to commit the central organization to political action was foiled.[34] As a result, the provincial Progressive Movement in Saskatchewan became largely an attempt at organization by independents, under the leadership of Harris Turner of Saskatoon.[35] Before organization could be well begun, Premier Martin dissolved the legislature and headed off the movement by a snap election. This was decisive. Only thirteen independents were returned, to a great extent, it would seem, by Conservative votes, for the provincial Conservative party simply did not contest the election. Thus the Liberal administration in Saskatchewan survived the Progressive rising, but at the price of severing temporarily its ties with the federal party.

In Alberta the same story was to have a very different outcome. Not only was the Liberal party of that province less fortunate in its leadership, though no less realistic in its tactics, not only did it suffer division by the quarrel over the Alberta Great Waterways Railway scandal, which created a weakness in the party that the division into Laurier and Unionist Liberals did nothing to mend;[36] but the farmer organization of that province was separate in its leadership from the government, and that leadership was from 1915 the leadership of Henry Wise Wood. In Alberta, the forceful personalities were outside the government; in Saskatchewan, they were, on the whole, in the government or close to it. Alberta lost the brilliant A.L. Sifton to the Union Government in 1917, and Alberta alone possessed a Henry Wise Wood. Wood and the executive of the United Farmers of Alberta were no more anxious than other leaders of the farm organizations to go into provincial politics. He, indeed, was on principle opposed to going into politics at all. The drive for a third, independent, farmer party, however, developed much greater force in Alberta than elsewhere. This was partly because the decline of the Conservative party was even more pronounced in Alberta than in Saskatchewan. It was also because the Non-Partisan League became more powerful in that province than in Saskatchewan. American populism and British radicalism had freer play in frontier Alberta than in older Saskatchewan. The Non-Partisan League, for example, captured two provincial seats in Alberta in 1917, whereas it had captured only one in Saskatchewan in the same year, and that by a fluke. The League went on to threaten to capture the locals of the U.F.A. by conversion and infiltration. This was a threat that could not be ignored, because it was in and through the locals that the farmers' organizations lived. Wood and the U.F.A. leaderships were therefore caught on the horns of a dilemma. They knew that political action had invariably ruined farm organizations in the past, as the Farmers' Alliance in the United States had gone to wreck in the Populist party. They knew also that they might lose control of the U.F.A. if the Non-Partisan League obtained control of a majority of locals and assumed leadership of the drive for political action. Wood solved the dilemma by his concept of "group government," and in doing so crystallized the strong tendency of the Progressive Movement, a tendency which owed much to the Non-Partisan League, to become a class movement, deeply averse to lawyers, bankers, and politicians. The U.F.A. would take political action, but it would take it as an organization. It would admit only farmers to its ranks; it would nominate only farmers for election; its representation in the legislature would constitute a separate group, cooperating with other groups but not combining with any to constitute a political party. Guided by this concept, the U.F.A. in 1919 entered politics, both federal and provincial.[37] In 1921 it won a majority of the seats in the Alberta legislature.

These varying fortunes of the Progressive Movement in the three provinces were significant for the character of the federal Progressive party. Broadly speaking, two concepts of the character and future of the party prevailed among its members. One, which may be termed the Manitoba view, was that the Progressive Movement was one of insurgent liberalism, which might have the happy result of recapturing the federal Liberal party from the control of the conservative and protectionist Liberals of the East. This was the view, for example, of J.W. Dafoe, a mentor of Progressivism. It aimed at building up a national, popular movement by "broadening out," by "opening the door" to all sympathizers. The Saskatchewan federal Progressives also accepted this view, the more so as the provincial movement had been headed off for a decade. The other concept may be called the Alberta concept. It was that the Progressive Movement was an occupational or class movement, capable of extension by group organization to other economic classes, but not itself concerned with bringing about such extension. Farmer must represent farmer, the group must act as a group

It may be noted in passing that neither view of the Progressive Movement demands an explicit farmer-labour alliance. Why Progressivism did not develop this characteristic of the earlier Populist party and the later Cooperative Commonwealth Federation cannot be explained here, but it may be said that the leadership of both wings of the Movement was averse to an open alliance with labour.

Here again is the two-fold character of the Progressive Movement postulated in the opening paragraph. Progressivism which was an economic protest, seeking a natural remedy by political action little more unconventional than a revolt from caucus rule, is here termed Manitoban. Progressivism which was doctrinaire, class conscious, and heterodox, is here called Albertan. The former assumed that exploitation would cease in a society made competitive by the abolition of protection; the latter proposed to produce a harmony of interests by putting an end to competition by means of the cooperation of organized groups. Both tendencies, of course, existed all across the Movement. Each was personified and had as respective protagonists the Honourable T.A. Crerar and Henry Wise Wood.

The extremes, however, were fundamental and irreconcilable. Manitoban Progressivism sought economic ends through conventional political means and admitted of compromise with the old parties. Albertan Progressivism sought much the same economic ends, but also sought to transform the conditions of politics. In this it was closer to the essential nature of Progressivism, with its innate distrust of elected representatives and of party organization.[38] Its pledging of candidates, its frequent use of the signed recall, its levy on members for campaign funds, its predilection for direct legislation and for proportional representation, establish its fundamental character. That in so conducting itself, it was to give rise to forms of political organization which old-line politicians were to envy, is one of those little ironies which delight the sardonic observer.

An examination of the course of the general election of 1921 adds little to the exposition of the theme. As revealed in the campaign literature, it turned on the issues of protection and of the class doctrines of Henry Wise Wood. Prime Minister Meighen, first of those western men with eastern principles to be called to head the Conservative party, put on the full armour of protection, and fought the western revolt in defence of the National Policy. It was courageous, it was magnificent, but it was not successful. His party attacked the Progressives as free traders seeking to destroy the National Policy for selfish class advantage. Mr. W.L. Mackenzie King stood firmly on the Liberal platform of 1919, which, marvelously contrived, faced squarely all points of the political compass at once. Liberal strategy was to avoid a sharp stand, to pose as the farmers' friend—"There never was a Farmers' Party while the Liberals were in power"[39]—and to denounce the class character of Progressivism. Mr. Crerar was in the embarrassing position of a leader whose followers persist in treading on his heels, but he fought the good fight with dignity and moderation, protesting that his was not a class movement.

In the upshot, the Progressives carried sixty-five seats, and emerged as the second largest group in the House. Coalition with the Liberals was seriously considered and was rejected only at the last moment, presumably because Messrs. Crerar and Drury could not obtain from Mr. King those pledges which would have ensured the identity of the group and the curbing of the protectionist elements in the Liberal Cabinet. This decision marked the beginning of the disintegration of the Movement, for the Progressives neither imposed their policies on the Liberals nor definitely became a parliamentary party seeking office. With that fatal tendency of third parties to avoid responsibility, of which George Langley had warned a decade before,[40] they declined to become even the official opposition.

Thereafter Manitoban Progressivism lost its bright speed amid the sands and shallows of official Liberalism. Albertan Progressivism represented by the Ginger Group, the federal U.F.A. members and a few others, alone survived the decay of Progressive zeal, and remained for fourteen years to lend distinction to the national councils, and to bear in its organization the seeds at once of Social Credit and the Cooperative Commonwealth Federation.

NOTES

1. cf. Frederick Jackson Turner, *The Significance of Sections in American History* (New York, 1932), 314.

2. *Hansard*, 1910-11, I, 1918.

3. Wilfred E. Binkley, *American Political Parties* (New York, 1944)—"Madison's principle that a nation wide majority can agree only on a moderate program," 87; also 17-18.

4. Dafoe Library of the *Winnipeg Free Press*, Dafoe Papers, Dafoe to Sir Clifford Sifton, 21 July 1919; on the prospects of reorganizing the Liberal party.

5. *Manitoba Free Press*, 10 April 1917, 9.

6. *Grain Growers' Guide*, 14 September 1910, 13. Fred Kirkham, advocate of a third party, wrote to the editor from Saltcoats, Saskatchewan: "If the memorials presented to Sir Wilfrid Laurier have failed to imbue him with the determination to battle with the vested interests of the East to grant our just requests, we have no alternative but to become democratic insurgents, and form a new party and find a new general to fight under. We must be courageous in politics before Laurier will treat with us as a big community of votes to be reckoned with."

7. Laurier Papers, 3089, J.W. Dafoe to Laurier, 28 April 1911, Public Archives of Canada. "In my judgment reciprocity has changed the whole political situation in the West. Until it was announced the drift out West was undoubtedly against the government; but now it is just the other way about."

8. *United Farmers of Alberta, Annual Report*, 1910, 43. "Moved by the Vermilion Union: Resolved, that ten farmers, as members of Parliament with votes would have more weight in shaping the laws and influencing government than one thousand delegates as petitioners:

Therefore be it further resolved that the farmers, to secure this end, should vote for farmers only to represent them in Parliament and vote as a unit and cease dividing their voting power. Carried."

9. I am indebted to Professor J.R. Mallory of Brandon College, now of

McGill, for a discussion clarifying this point.

10. *Manitoba Free Press,* 13 May 1916. Editorial, "Consequences." "Whatever may be the political consequences of this blunder to Liberalism in Canada at large, Western Liberalism will not suffer if it adheres to the independence which its representatives have displayed at Ottawa this week. These developments at the capital must tend to strengthen the feeling which has been growing steadily for years that Western Liberals need not look to the East, at present, for effective and progressive leadership.... Canadian public life will thus be given, what it sorely needs,...a group of convinced radicals.... To your tents, O Israel!"

11. Ibid., 28 June 1917, 9. "The Saskatchewan Victory." "The Canadian West is in the mood to break away from past affiliations and traditions and inaugurate a new political era of sturdy support for an advanced and radical program. The break-up of parties has given the West its opportunity; and there is no doubt it will take advantage of it." At least four independent candidates had been nominated in the West before June, 1917, in provincial and federal seats. In December, 1916, the Canadian Council of Agriculture had issued the first Farmers' Platform.

12. Henry Borden, ed., *Robert Laird Borden: His Memoirs* (Toronto, 1938) II, 749-50, J.W. Dafoe to Borden, 29 September 1917.

13. Dafoe Papers, Dafoe to Augustus Bridle, 14 June 1921. "The Western Liberal Convention was a bomb which went off in the hands of its makers. It was decided upon at Ottawa by a group of conscription Liberals; the intention was to bring into existence a Western Liberal group free from Laurier's control who would be prepared to consider coalition with Borden on its merits, but the Liberal machine in the West went out and captured the dele-gates with the result that the convention was strongly pro-Laurier."

14. *Report of the Survey Board for Southern Alberta,* January, 1922.

15. *Hansard,* 1919, 1, 558. Colonel J.A. Currie (Simcoe). "I am quite in agreement with the hon. member for Maple Creek (J.A. Maharg) when he says we should fix a price for the wheat of the West. That is in line with the National Policy." See also the Right Honourable Arthur Meighen's proposal for a modified Wheat Board in his speech at Portage la Prairie during the campaign of 1921. *Canadian Annual Review,* 1921, 449-50.

16. *Cf.* Vernon C. Fowke, *Canadian Agricultural Policy* (Toronto, 1946), 268.

17. The changes were as follows: the 71/2 per cent increase for war purposes was removed from agricultural implements and certain necessities of life; the 5 per cent war duty was modified; an income tax was levied.

18. Fourteen western Unionists voted for the amendment. *Hansard,* 1919, IV, 3, 678.

19. *Hansard,* 1919, IV, 3475. W.D. Cowan, Unionist (Regina). "I believe that the changes which have been made in the tariff have been made entirely because of the agitation which has been carried on by the West. We have had, for the first time, I fancy, in the history of Parliament, a western caucus and in that we have been united. Old-time Liberals united with old-time Conservatives. On the one point that they should try to get substantial reductions in the tariffs...."

20. *Canadian Annual Review,* 1920, 741.

21. See ibid., 1919, for text, 365-68.

22. *Parliamentary Companion,* 1921, 196.

23. *Manitoba Free Press,* 25 February 1921; *Grain Growers' Guide,* 4 August 1920, 4 and 27 October 1920, 5.

24. *Parliamentary Companion,* 1922, 247.

25. Dafoe Papers, Dafoe to Sir Clifford Sifton, 20 January 1920.

26. *Grain Growers' Guide*, 15 December 1920, 3. Resolution of executive of the Canadian Council of Agriculture in meeting of 7-9 December 1920.

27. Dafoe Papers, Dafoe to Sir Clifford Sifton, 26 January 1921. "Crerar's only troubles out here arise from the ardor with which certain elements in his following insist upon organizing a purely class movement against the three local governments, thereby tending to antagonize the very elements which Crerar is trying, by broadening its basis, to add to his party."

28. *United Farmers of Manitoba Year Book*, 1920, 67.

29. *Grain Growers' Guide*, 7 July 1920, 6. Editorial, "The Manitoba Election." "The United Farmers of Manitoba, as an organization, took no part in the election, and each constituency where farmer candidates were nominated and elected acted entirely on its own initiative."

30. Ibid., 19 January, 1921, 3.

31. *Manitoba Free Press*, 28 April 1922. Dafoe Papers, Dafoe to Sir Clifford Sifton, 7 July 1922.

32. *Minutes of the Annual Convention of the Saskatchewan Grain Growers' Association*, 18-21 February 1919, 4. Report of Premier Wm. Martin's address. "There are questions now coming before you affecting the welfare of the whole community of the Province. It is the policy of the present government and will continue to be the policy of the present government to carry out these suggestions."

33. Ibid., 9-13 February 1920, 114-19.

34. Ibid., 31 January - 4 February 1921. The debate on provincial political action was involved; a motion to enter provincial politics as an organization was defeated (118) and a motion to support action by constituencies was, it would seem, shelved (93).

35. *Saskatoon Daily Star*, 1 June 1921. Report of the convention of independents at Saskatoon, 31 May 1921.

36. John Blue, *Alberta Past and Present* (Chicago, 1924), 125. "The session of 1910 witnessed a perturbation and upheaval that split the Liberal party into two factions, which more than a decade afterwards regarded each other with some jealousy and distrust."

37. *United Farmers of Alberta, Annual Report*, 1919, 52-3.

38. *Grain Growers' Guide*, 5 March 1919, 26. Article by Roderick McKenzie on "Political Action." "The purpose of the movement inaugurated by the farmers is that whenever the time comes to make a choice of representation to parliament, the electors get together to make their selection."

39. Pamphlet no. 5081, *Group Government Compared with Responsible Government*, P.A.C.

40. *Grain Growers' Guide*, 21 September 1910, 13-14. "It may be urged that a separate farmers' party might influence the government even if it did not become strong enough to take on itself the actual work of governing. The answer to that is this. The legitimate objective of a political party is to control the legislative and administrative functions. Without [that] objective it cannot exist for any length of time...."

THE CCF: 1932-1945

BY WALTER YOUNG

o

The depression not only affected the lives of people in the thirties, it affected the ideas and attitudes of a generation, instilling both caution and pessimism. Things would never be the same again. For those already convinced of the inequity—if not, indeed, the iniquity—of the capitalist system, the depression deepened their conviction and spurred their determination to take more direct action. The men and women in the several socialist and labour parties in the west had begun to move toward concerted action as early as 1929. The farmers, many of whom regretted the failure of the Progressive party and were anxious to try again, were joined by others as the fluctuations of the world market and crop conditions revealed once more their vulnerable position.

UNITING FOR THE COOPERATIVE COMMONWEALTH

There were many labour and socialist parties in western Canada at this time, each with a different name and most with their own preferred socialist doctrine. In British Columbia there was a Canadian Labour party and a Socialist party of Canada. In Alberta there were branches of the Canadian Labour party and the Dominion Labour party. There was an Independent Labour party in Saskatchewan and one in Manitoba—the one for which J.S. Woodsworth was M.P. In 1929 delegates from these parties and from several trade unions, some of which held radical political views, met in Regina to

Excerpt from Walter Young, *Democracy and Discontent* (Toronto: Ryerson Press, 1969), pp. 51-67.

"correlate the activities of the several labour political parties in western Canada."[1] The *Manitoba Free Press* saw the conference as the beginning of a Western Canadian Labour party, but it was not quite that. The groups did not amalgamate, they merely passed resolutions of a radical nature and agreed to meet again the following year in Medicine Hat.

The second meeting of what became known as the Conference of Western Labour Political Parties was more radical than the first, and with reason. The effects of the depression were being felt. It was not until the third gathering, in Winnipeg in July of 1931, that delegates undertook to form a national labour party. Several of the farmers' organizations were invited to that conference. It was recognized that the plight of farmers and workers was similar and that from concerted action results satisfactory to both could be achieved. There was no disagreement on policy; the farmers' groups had been moving further from the reformist doctrines of the Progressives toward a more distinctly socialist position. All the delegates at Winnipeg in 1931 agreed that, "capitalism must go and socialism be established."[2] Their aim was the establishment of a "cooperative commonwealth."

Formal steps were to be taken to build a new political movement at the fourth meeting of the Labour Conference. As the labour parties moved closer together, submerging philosophical differences in a common cause, so too the farmers' groups, as they moved leftward, moved together and came to accept more fully the need for direct political action. The decision of the labour parties to unite coincided with a similar decision on the part of the United Farmers of Alberta to invite all groups sharing a faith in the ideal of the cooperative commonwealth to attend a conference in Calgary in 1932.

The United Farmers of Alberta (UFA) had formed the government of Alberta in 1925 but had resisted the call of federal politics, largely because of the anti-party philosophy of their leader, Henry Wise Wood. Wood retired in 1931 and was succeeded by Robert Gardiner, a member of the Ginger Group in the federal House of Commons. Gardiner was determined to put together a national political party and consequently led the UFA to the point where their convention called for the formation of a party to fight for the rights of farmers and workers alike. The cooperative commonwealth they, and the other groups, were seeking was defined as:

A community freed from the domination of irresponsible financial and economic power, in which all social means of production and distribution, including land, are socially owned and controlled either by voluntarily organized groups of producers and consumers, or...by public corporations responsible to the peoples' elected representatives.[3]

In Saskatchewan the Independent Labour party, formed by M. J. Coldwell, a school principal and Regina alderman, had been working with the Farmers' Political Association led by George Williams. The two had collaborated as the Farmer-Labour party in provincial elections and both groups were active in organizing farmers and workers into local groups of one or other of these organizations. One such group was formed in Weyburn in 1932 by a young Baptist clergyman, T.C. Douglas. That same year the farmers and city workers agreed to present a single joint program and to undertake joint political action, creating in effect a Saskatchewan farmer-labour party, although both groups retained their identity. As the leader of the agrarian side of the new movement put it, the philosophy of the farmer-labour alliance was "fundamentally socialistic."[4]

The Manitoba ILP, with headquarters in Winnipeg and active branches in the smaller towns like Brandon and Souris, assumed responsibility for the development of the movement toward a new political party. The United Farmers of Manitoba were not hostile to the activities of the labour party but were not prepared to officially endorse their activities. Rural Manitoba was more in the Liberal-Progressive tradition and there was less agrarian support for the socialism of the ILP. In Winnipeg itself, however, with its large proportion of industrial workers, many of whom were immigrants, there was a lot of support.

In eastern Canada there was considerable activity among the labour and socialist parties, but it was disorganized and sporadic. There were more than a dozen labour and socialist parties of various colorations in Toronto alone. What organized political activity there was occurred largely through the efforts of the United Farmers of Ontario, a farmers' organization that was closer to the old Progressives in outlook than to the radical UFA or the Saskatchewan Farmers' Political Association. Nevertheless, the presence of these bodies did indicate that a national party of the left might find some support in Ontario.

There was some support in the intellectual community as well. In 1931 two university professors, one from McGill and the other from the University of Toronto, agreed that Canada needed a new political party, one which would not share the fate of the Progressives and be devoured by Mackenzie King's Liberals. The two, Frank Scott and Frank Underhill, established a society to provide such a party with a doctrine that would prove unpalatable to Mr. King. The society was known as the League for Social Reconstruction and soon had branches in Montreal, Toronto, Winnipeg and Vancouver. In many respects it was like the British Fabian Society, and, like it, hoped to become the intellectual wing of a Canadian socialist party.

The farm and labour MPs in the House of Commons were not unaware of the activities of the farm and labour groups across the country. Woodsworth had attended the conferences of the Western Labour Political Parties, had been in touch with Coldwell and Williams in Saskatchewan, and was honorary president of the League for Social Reconstruction. Robert Gardiner was president of the UFA. Miss Agnes Macphail was in the United Farmers of Ontario. On May 26, 1932, the members of the cooperating groups in the House of Commons met in the office of William Irvine and decided to bring all these strands together in a single political movement, which they tentatively called the "Commonwealth party." Each member was given specific organizational responsibilities and all were to take every opportunity to organize support for the new party. Each one had, so to speak, grown up in the tradition of radical protest. The fact that they were meeting together as representatives of the farm and labour groups was evidence of a fundamental unity that had always existed but which had required the stress of the depression to become manifest across the land. Each had learned the lessons taught by the failure of the Progressive party and all were determined to avoid these mistakes.

The new venture they were beginning had a considerable advantage over the Progressive movement in that there was one obvious leader in the figure of J.S. Woodsworth. A man of heroic determination and devotion to principle, Woodsworth was accepted by farmer and worker alike as the symbol of the emerging movement. He had been a Methodist minister earlier in his career but had resigned from his church because of its failure to apply the teaching of the gospels to all men, and because of its attitude toward free speech. He had worked as a longshoreman in British Columbia, had travelled through the prairies on behalf of the Non-Partisan League and had edited the *Western Labor News* during the Winnipeg general strike.

In his own actions as well as in his statements on the public platform and in parliament, Woodsworth symbolized the aspirations of the men and women who were working through the farm and labour movements to bring about a better society. He spoke for all these when he moved in the House of Commons the first of what became annual resolutions:

> That in the opinion of this House the government should immediately take measures looking to the setting up of a cooperative commonwealth in which all the natural resources and socially necessary machinery of production will be used in the interests of the people and not for the benefit of the few.[5]

The submerging of political division and animosity in creating a federation of the diverse groups in Calgary in 1932 was a tribute to the symbolic and actual leadership of J.S. Woodsworth. He was subsequently described by a Liberal journalist as "a saint in politics."[6]

Outside the circle of his own followers and those commentators of a fairly liberal outlook, Woodsworth was seen almost as the devil incarnate, corrupting young minds when he spoke to university students, and preaching revolution and totalitarianism in his speeches in the House of Commons. It would have been surprising had the reaction to Woodsworth and his colleagues been anything else, for what they proposed constituted, at that time, a major reallocation of the nation's economic resources—and that was gross interference with the rights of private property.

Those who believed that private property and free enterprise—the capitalist system—formed the basis of individual freedom could not accept the proposals of the socialists despite the evidence of the depression that the system was clearly not working well for all the people. A majority of Canadians believed that socialism was evil and that poverty and unemployment were the result of bad luck or poor management. They were unwilling to accept the arguments of Woodsworth that the economic system was stacked against the many in the interest of the few. Proposals for unemployment insurance were scoffed at as subsidizing laziness; public ownership was said to be a form of theft that led to dictatorship.

It was characteristic of Woodsworth that despite the criticism of his ideas, he persisted when lesser men would have withdrawn from the struggle. As many of his ideas and the policies of the party he helped create were adopted and enacted by the Liberal government, many of his critics recognized the essentially noble character of the man. Pacifist, humanitarian and socialist, he was a key factor in knitting together the various strands that emerged as the fabric of a new political party, the Cooperative Commonwealth Federation or, as it was usually called, the CCF.

The depression, acting as a catalyst, hastened the growth of the CCF but it did not, in the strict sense, cause it. By 1929 radicals in the cities and on the farms had already seen the need for a broader and more united base. The depression served to validate this belief, for it was proof of both the inadequacies of the capitalist economy and the insensitivity of the "old-line" parties. Furthermore, despite the prevalence of hardship in western Canada, the depression would not bring immediate victory to the new party in the 1935 election. This was largely because the CCF was very new and, paradoxically, because its "revolutionary" character, in comparison to the other parties, had no direct appeal to those who were down and out. Socialism was to receive its greatest support at a time when prosperity had returned and those enjoying it were prepared to adopt a radical stance in order to retain it. As Professor Lipset has pointed out, support for radical movements on a large scale comes on the flood of rising expectations, not on the ebb of desolation and depression.

Woodsworth, Irvine and the Ginger Group had a foothold in parliament. The formation of the CCF gave them the beginnings of a nation-wide organization based on an alliance of what were essentially movements—bodies of like-minded people, dedicated to reform and prepared to make remarkable sacrifices to achieve their goals of social and political reform. As politicians, the leaders of the CCF recognized the need to weld the groups together into a democratic party that would aim for power. As participants in a movement, they could, as well, draw satisfaction from the achievement of any of their goals, whether they were in power themselves or not. In this regard they were soon able to see the results of their efforts as Mackenzie King reacted to their presence and edged his party leftward.

The tragic consequences of the depression and the ineptitude of governments in dealing with it hardened the determination of men like Woodsworth to do their utmost to ensure that it never happened again.

The conference in Calgary in August of 1932 brought together for the first time delegates from most of the major farm and labour groups in the west. Their purpose was the founding of a new political party, but it was not to be a duplicate of the "old-line parties," nor was it to be like the Progressive party. The new organization was to be a federation of the existing labour and farm groups; it was also to have a clearly defined political philosophy— socialism. Its purpose was spelled out in the formal resolution passed unanimously by the delegates:

The establishment in Canada of a cooperative commonwealth in which the basic principle regulating production, distribution, and exchange, will be the supplying of human needs instead of the making of profits.[7]

The name of the new party was to be The Cooperative Commonwealth Federation (Farmer, Labour, Socialist).

The three words included parenthetically at the end of the name indicated that while all the delegates accepted the ideal of the cooperative commonwealth, not all would call themselves socialists; even among those who did, there was some disagreement about what socialism really was. Among the delegates from British Columbia, for example, were those who thought of socialism as the doctrine formulated by Karl Marx. Others had learned their socialism from the writings of the members of the British Fabian Society or from other English socialists. And for some socialism was just a general term that meant that they were against the government and the existing economic system because it had reduced them to poverty.

Because all shared the same misgivings about the capitalist system and the working of Canadian politics, they were able to forget their doctrinal differences and agree to work together to bring about changes that would improve their lot and that of Canadians in general. In their enthusiasm for change they could unite behind a program that was more radical than anything ever advocated by the Progressives, one which declared that "social ownership and cooperative production for use is the only sound economic system."[8]

GOALS AND A PROGRAM

The new organization was not simply a political party, it was a political movement as well. The purpose of the CCF as it emerged from the Calgary conference was not just to win the next election, it was to bring about radical changes in the nature of Canadian society. What the members wanted was to replace the profit motive with that of service to the community and to others. It was a noble ideal. As one observer of the Calgary meeting commented, the delegates "oozed idealism to the detriment of practical experience."[9] The purpose of the movement was to win converts to a new way of thinking. Activity in the House of Commons and on the hustings in election campaigns were two ways of doing this, but not the only ones.

During the winter of 1932-3 the members of the new party devoted themselves to the problems of organizing. The provisional executive invited the League for Social Reconstruction to prepare a statement of the party's principles, a Manifesto. This task was performed largely by Frank Underhill, who wrote the first draft of what became the Regina Manifesto at his summer home in June of 1933. It was discussed by other members of the League and then presented to the first convention of the CCF, which met during August, 1933, in Regina.

Some changes were made but the Manifesto that the convention adopted with enthusiastic cheers was essentially as it had been prepared by Underhill and his colleagues. It remained the most specific statement of Canadian socialism.

The aim of the CCF was made very clear in the opening paragraphs of the Manifesto:

> We aim to replace the present capitalist system, with its inherent injustice and inhumanity, by a social order from which the domination and exploitation of one class by another will be eliminated, in which economic planning will supersede unregulated private enterprise and competition, and in which genuine democratic self-government, based on economic equality will be possible.[10]

The Manifesto proposed the public ownership of all financial machinery—banks, insurance companies, trust companies and the like—as well as public ownership of public utilities and "all other industries and services essential to social planning." Emphasis was laid on the development of cooperatives, and particular attention was given to the problems of the farmers. There were, as well, proposals for medicare, hospital and dental insurance schemes to be run by the state. The Manifesto closed with a ringing declaration:

> No CCF Government will rest content until it has eradicated capitalism and put into operation the full program of socialized planning which will lead to the establishment in Canada of the Cooperative Commonwealth.

The program of the new party was most assuredly socialist. It was more socialistic than some of its founders had expected or, in a few instances, were prepared to accept. Farm and labour groups had proposed similar measures before but there had never been such a specific and deliberate program as the Regina Manifesto. The guardians of the sacred institutions of Canadian capitalism declared the program preposterous. The Press and opposition politicians saw it as naked communism.

At Regina, J.S. Woodsworth was elected National Chairman—in effect the party leader. But he was not a leader in the traditional sense. The CCF was a federation of smaller parties and movements and it was deliberately designed to ensure the fullest participation by all members in making policy and in directing the affairs of the party. One of the chief criticisms western radicals had of the old parties was that they were undemocratic, controlled by a small clique that was dominated by eastern businessmen. No such state of affairs would be allowed to prevail in the CCF. There would be annual conventions, annual elections of officers, and the party platform would be prepared by the delegates at the annual conventions.

REACTION TO THE NEW PARTY

Despite its democratic structure, critics and opponents of the CCF saw it as a totalitarian and alien force. Few of them understood socialism; most of them equated it with communism. Yet the CCF was clearly a direct descendent of the British Labour Party, at least as far as its ideology was concerned. The program of the CCF advocated radical changes in the Canadian economy and attacked the principle of competition and free enterprise. For many observers this was evidence enough that it was a serious threat to "the Canadian way of life." It was ironic that the CCF soon built up an enviable record in defence of individual liberties and parliamentary democracy.

The opponents of the CCF saw a revolutionary force when they looked at the new party. They feared for their property and their privileges. Some members of the CCF found the party philosophy too radical, while others complained that it was not radical enough. Short of having no political philosophy at all, such disagreement was inevitable. So, too, was the opposition of many people in Canada inevitable, for the kinds of change advocated by the CCF were sweeping and bound to arouse serious disagreement.

Because it stood for radical change, because it proposed to reshape sectors of the Canadian economy and reform aspects of Canadian society, the CCF attracted to its ranks people who were deeply concerned about the nature of the Canadian economic and political systems. Many were convinced that future depressions were certain and would remain incurable unless changes were made. The CCF also attracted people whose own situation drove them away from the old parties into the new movement in search of a satisfactory explanation of a poverty that was not of their making. The commitment of all these people to radical change meant that the CCF was able to succeed where an ordinary party could not. It had little money, only a sketchy organization and no political foothold in any legislature, but it had a growing membership of dedicated people prepared to sacrifice their time and what money they had in the cause of reform.

Typical of this kind of dedicated enthusiasm was that shown by M.J. Coldwell. A school principal in Regina when the party was founded, he seldom turned down an invitation to speak about the CCF. This often meant travelling in freezing weather by sleigh to a distant farm. Sympathetic farmers along the way would supply fresh horses, coffee and hot water bottles. In good weather he would hire a plane, leave after school, fly perhaps a hundred miles [160 km] to speak and then spend the night at a farm. The next morning he would return to start the school day at nine. Money was scarce but farmers would contribute what produce they could spare: a sack of grain here, a bushel of potatoes there.

The CCF stimulated dedication because it offered an explanation of what had gone wrong and proposed what seemed to be a sensible way of preventing the same thing from happening again. In addition, it was a party that clearly belonged to the members. It provided a social focal point, bringing together men and women with similar problems and similar points of view. On the prairie the party meetings were social activities, as were the fundraising efforts—box socials, picnics, and the like. In the cities the CCF groups provided a congenial social nucleus for the unemployed, helping many to overcome the feeling that they were Canada's forgotten people. It helped combat the loneliness of the underdog. The character of the CCF as a movement gave it strength and determination far beyond its numbers and financial resources.

THE STRUGGLE FOR POLITICAL SUCCESS

Despite its strengths, however, the CCF did not ride the crest of a wave to political success; it achieved office in only one province, and even there not until 1944. At the beginning there was public suspicion to overcome, as well as the internal divisions and inconsistencies of the movement. The CCF was not a united party; it was a federation of provincial movements and parties, each with a fairly high degree of autonomy of both action and viewpoint. In the three prairie provinces there was a good deal of consistency of philosophy. But British Columbia socialism was more militant and more highly spiced with Marxist or "scientific socialism." Some members in that province had little use for the farmers. The Ontario wing was troubled with discontent resulting from the willingness of some members and some CCF clubs to enter into an alliance with the Communist party. In 1934 Woodsworth had to reorganize the Ontario party to overcome these problems.

The lack of unity was not surprising. Ideology invites dispute, and there were members of the CCF whose main interest was argument rather than political organization. The movement also had a different character in different regions. For example, on the prairie it was growing as part of the rural community. The active leaders of the wheat pools and the cooperative movement were virtually all active in the CCF. On the other hand, in British Columbia, and to a slightly lesser extent in Ontario, the militants were more the "outsiders" of society, the determined non-conformists. Thus, although the CCF was growing, it was growing slowly and not without some internal discomfort.

The national party faced its first serious test in the 1935 federal election. It nominated 119 candidates but only seven were elected: two in Manitoba, two in Saskatchewan and three in British Columbia. This was not an auspicious beginning. The Ginger Group had been wiped out and there were no CCF members at all from Alberta. In that province an even newer political phenomenon, Social Credit, had swept all before it. In all, the CCF got only 9 per cent of the total popular vote and only 2 per cent of the seats in the House of Commons.

The election of 1935 was a confusing one for the voter. In many constituencies there were five and occasionally six candidates. A former Conservative cabinet minister, H.H. Stevens, had created a new party, the Reconstruction party. It ran 174 candidates but elected only one.

Nevertheless, it attracted close to 400,000 votes. Social Credit, in winning every seat in Alberta, cut heavily into support that might otherwise have gone to the CCF. It is likely that some of those who voted Reconstruction and Social Credit would have voted CCF, although it is impossible to say how many. However it was explained, though, the result of the election was a blow to the CCF.

The party fought a vigorous and direct campaign. Party literature pulled no punches; if anything, it was a bit too sharp in its criticism of capitalism. One CCF pamphlet read:

> Bank Robbers Get Millions, but the BIG SHOT BANKER IS A BIGGER CRIMINAL THAN THE GUNMAN because the banker's greed hurts all the people all of the time.[11]

Another urged voters to "Smash the Big Shots' Slave Camps and Sweat Shops."[12] From the CCF point of view capitalism had caused the depression; but this was not quite the same thing as accusing bankers of criminal greed. For the active members of the CCF the enemy was plain to see—the men who controlled the financial structure of Canada, those who suffered little during the depression. Rid the economy of their unwholesome influence, place the public in control, and the problem would be solved. There was some truth in their analysis, and their vehemence was understandable, but it did not attract many voters who were not already socialists. Indeed, it repelled many.

With only seven members in a House of Commons composed of 254, the CCF seemed to be of little consequence when the new parliament opened. But as session followed session it became clear that Woodsworth and his colleagues were the real opposition to Mackenzie King's Liberal administration. After the departure of R.B. Bennett, the Conservatives groped for leadership and policy; they were to stumble in the darkness of opposition for twenty-two years. The CCF, however, did have a leader of considerable ability and a clearly defined policy. The members of the small group were dedicated to their cause and managed to do the work of a caucus at least thrice their size. In the first session, for example, T.C. Douglas, spoke sixty times, more than most members and as much as most cabinet ministers.

The role the CCF played was that of the conscience of the House of Commons, speaking out on behalf of those whose interests seemed to be ignored by the government, and championing the cause of civil rights. In the latter cause the small band was able to bring about the repeal of section 98 of the Criminal Code, the infamous section that had first made its appearance during the Winnipeg general strike in 1919, permitting the arrest and deportation of "aliens." In 1937 the CCF led a concerted attack on the inroads being made into civil liberties by provincial governments, notably those of Premier Mitchell Hepburn of Ontario and Premier Duplessis of Quebec. In both cases the police power of the state was being used to interfere with the legitimate activities of trade unions in strikes and union organization. In particular, the CCF attack was directed against the Padlock Law in Quebec, a law that enabled the arbitrary arrest of individuals who, contrary to established procedure, were then required to prove their innocence. While the CCF could not change these laws, by bringing them to the attention of the nation through debate in the House of Commons they were able to arouse public opinion and, on occasion, force the government to act.

In 1939 Woodsworth had the satisfaction of seeing the government introduce legislation guaranteeing the right of employees to form and join trade unions. He had been advocating such a bill for three years. By standing firmly on principle, by raising issues again and again and by patient and carefully prepared argument, the CCF members were able to induce the government to introduce reforms that would otherwise have been much longer in coming. Their very presence in the House of Commons was a constant reminder to the Liberal government of the sizable body of the electorate that were in favour of broad and far-reaching reform. Political commentators may not have supported the CCF philosophy, but they were forced to admit time and again that the seven CCF MPs were an efficient and formidable opposition to the government.

During this early period the members of the CCF were active across the country, bringing in new members, organizing clubs and constituency associations and eagerly looking toward the day when a CCF government would be in power. In Saskatchewan in 1934 the Farmer-Labour party had become the official opposition in the provincial legislature winning five seats—the Liberal government held the other fifty. In 1938 the CCF increased this standing to ten seats. In British Columbia the CCF became the official opposition in 1941, winning more votes than any other party. Membership in the party grew, but not as quickly as party leaders had hoped. Despite its British ancestry, Canadian socialism remained a strange and, for many, a sinful doctrine. The fact that opponents of the CCF constantly referred to it as a communist "front" did not help. Nor did the repeated public invitations of the Communist party to join forces help the CCF image.

THE CCF DURING THE WAR

The outbreak of war in 1939 found the CCF stronger than it had been in 1933, but not as strong as its founders had expected. The war brought a more prosperous economy. The production of war materials took up the slack in industry, the prices of farm produce improved, and the army offered employment for many who had spent the previous three or four years on relief. The war also brought a crisis in the CCF.

As a man of deep religious faith and strict adherence to principle, Woodsworth had opposed war all his life. For him the organized slaughter of one's fellow men, regardless of the cause, was not an acceptable policy. He could not support Canada's entry into the war. A majority of his fellow party members, however, did not take this position. Most were opposed to war in principle, but at the same time they accepted the fact of Hitler's ambitions in Europe and the unfortunate necessity of resisting him with force. From the day of its foundation the CCF had officially opposed war. The crisis of 1939 brought about an agonizing reappraisal of that policy.

At a long and emotionally charged meeting of the party's National Council, it was decided that Woodsworth would stand alone, stating his opposition to the war while M.J. Coldwell would speak for the party and support Canada's entry at Britain's side. In his speech to parliament Woodsworth said:

> I have every respect for the man who, with a sincere conviction, goes out to give his life if necessary in a cause which he believes to be right; but I have just as much respect for the man who refuses to enlist to kill his fellow men and, as under modern conditions, to kill women and children as well....[13]

The point was, he insisted, that "brute force" was being allowed to overcome "moral force."

During the debate Prime Minister Mackenzie King said:

> There are few men in this parliament for whom, in some particulars, I have greater respect than the leader of the Cooperative Commonwealth Federation. I admire him in my heart because time and again he has had the courage to say what lay on his conscience regardless of what the world might think of him. A man of that calibre is an ornament to any Parliament....[14]

It was a fitting tribute to Woodsworth at a time when, his health failing and the party he had led opposing him, he stood firmly on those principles that his intellect and his conscience had told him were right and just.

The CCF entered the wartime parliament after the 1940 election with seven seats, only one more than before; but this time five were from Saskatchewan. They had lost one seat in Manitoba and two in British Columbia. There had been little change in the popular vote received. There was one ray of hope—the party had an MP from Nova Scotia, Clarence Gillis. His election was a direct result of the affiliation with the party, in 1938, of the Cape Breton local of the United Mine Workers Union. From 1936 on the party had made a determined effort to interest trade unions in providing support. The case they made was a good one: the CCF was the only party in the House of Commons that supported all the demands of organized labour. The election of Gillis was the first dividend from that policy.

The role of opposition in wartime is awkward and difficult. The government of the day tends to seek refuge in the cloak of patriotism or the spurious caves of secrecy. The CCF entered the war uneasily, with an ailing and alienated leader and little hope of improving its political position. As it turned out, during the period 1940-1945 the CCF was to reach the highwater mark in its fortunes.

NOTES

1. CCF Papers, Minutes, 1929 Conference, Western Labour Political Parties, P.A.C.

2. Ibid., 1931 Conference.

3. CCF Papers, *Declaration of Ultimate Objectives*, passed by UFA Convention, 1932, P.A.C.

4. W.L. Morton, *The Progressive Party in Canada* (Toronto: University of Toronto Press, 1950), 180.

5. Cited in K.W. McNaught, *A Prophet in Politics: A Biography of J.S. Woodsworth* (Toronto: University of Toronto Press, 1959).

6. The Liberal journalist was Bruce Hutchison, cited in G. MacInnis, *J.S. Woodsworth: A Man to Remember* (Toronto, Macmillan, 1953), 320.

7. W.L. Morton, *The Progressive Party in Canada* (Toronto: University of Toronto Press, 1950), 282.

8. *The Co-operative Commonwealth Federation, An Outline of Its Origins, Organization and Objectives* (Calgary, 1932).

9. Cited in B. Borsook, "The Workers Hold a Conference," from *Canadian Forum*, XXV, September, 1932.

10. The Regina Manifesto is appended to K.W. McNaught, *A Prophet in Politics: A Biography of J.S. Woodsworth* (Toronto: University of Toronto Press, 1959).

11. CCF Papers, CCF Pamphlet, 1940, P.A.C.

12. Ibid.

13. McNaught, *op. cit.*, 311.

14. Ibid., 309.

SOCIAL CREDIT IN ALBERTA: INTERPRETATIONS OF THE MOVEMENT

BY JOHN IRVING

o

The Social Credit upsurge in Alberta was essentially a people's movement which sought to reform, but not to revolutionize, the existing social order by changing the pattern of certain institutions...during the years it rose to political power, this movement passed through the stages of social unrest, popular excitement, formalization, and institutionalization...it exhibited, in the course of its evolution, the mechanisms of agitation, *esprit de corps,* morale, ideology, and operating tactics. Considered as a phenomenon of mass psychology, the Social Credit movement may best be interpreted in terms of a tripartite pattern which involves its philosophy, its leadership, and its strategy and tactics. There is no implication here that these three aspects are exhaustive, but they do offer a convenient framework in terms of which the important psychological factors may be grouped.

...the philosophy of Social Credit includes both a severe criticism of certain phases of the present capitalistic system and a number of constructive proposals for its reform. The psychological functions of this philosophy in the development of the Social Credit movement in Alberta will be discussed here in terms of four principal factors—the social context, the desire for meaning, the satisfaction of needs, and the conditions of suggestibility.

On its negative or critical side, Social Credit appealed to Albertans for two reasons: it exploited the preferred group tendencies connected with economics and politics that had been developing in the province for over a generation; and in "explaining" the causes of the depression it did not run counter to, but rather accentuated, the extremely hostile attitudes towards

Excerpt from John Irving, *The Social Credit Movement in Alberta* (Toronto: University of Toronto Press Incorporated, 1959), pp. 334-46. Reprinted by permission of University of Toronto Press Incorporated.

the existing economic system that had arisen in a period characterized by "poverty in the midst of plenty."

Of these preferred group tendencies, the most significant was the criticism of the capitalistic banking and financial system that had long been encouraged by the U.F.A....at its annual conventions, especially during the decade preceding 1935, there were bitter debates on resolutions attacking the system and calling loudly for its reform...there was scarcely a U.F.A. local that did not have a member or members dedicated to the task of keeping up an incessant criticism of the monetary system. When Major Douglas himself appeared before the Agricultural Committee of the Alberta legislature in the spring of 1934 the U.F.A. members applauded his devastating criticisms of the system, while at the same time they were highly dubious of his constructive proposals. On its critical side, the philosophy of Social Credit definitely fitted into old social norms; in this respect, Albertans were perhaps more suggestible to the appeal of Social Credit than the people of any other Canadian province.

During the depression, which, for a variety of reasons, was probably felt with greater severity in Alberta than in any other part of Canada, social unrest and widespread discontent developed on a hitherto unparalleled scale, but the provincial government, grown conservative through long years in office, offered no solution of the people's economic problems. Further...the representatives of the Eastern financial interests who visited Alberta to discuss the payment of loans and mortgages were insistent that the obligations of the hard-pressed farmers must be met in full: the lowering of interest rates was unthinkable; there could certainly be no adjustment whatever of principal indebtedness. Confronted with the depression on these terms, it is not surprising that thousands of people had developed embittered and hostile attitudes towards both the government and the monetary and financial system. Social Credit was a philosophy made to order for distribution among people with such political and economic attitudes.

In recent years social psychologists have emphasized the importance of the "desire for meaning" in the individual's organization of his experience. The desire for meaning arises when primary, or even derived, needs are frustrated of realization, that is, in critical situations. These situations arise when an individual finds himself involved in a chaotic social environment which he cannot interpret and which he wants to interpret. In such circumstances people who have become accustomed to the established order of society are susceptible to social change. Under the impact of an appropriate philosophy, old values may be overthrown and new social norms may arise.

The feature of the depression which puzzled Albertans most was the discrepancy between the abundance of goods produced and offered for sale on the one hand and the shortage of purchasing power in the hands of the consumer on the other. According to the Social Credit analysis, this discrepancy was simply due to the fact that under the monetary and financial system the rate of flow of purchasing power to the masses was always less than the rate of flow of prices, that is, the purchasing power of consumers was always less than the cost of production. It was also argued that in Alberta the depression, although an inevitable and recurrent feature of an unreformed monetary system, had been accentuated by the machinations of bankers and financiers (the "Fifty Big Shots") who controlled financial credit. To thousands of people this "explanation" of the depression seemed to make meaningful the grievous shortage of purchasing power from which they were suffering, the paradox of "poverty in the midst of plenty." Social Credit interpreted the chaotic external environment in a form simple enough to be "understood," and during the rise of the movement the A plus B Theorem became part of the everyday vocabulary of nearly all adult Albertans.

As the depression increased in severity, Alberta passed into a phase approaching social disorganization: psychologically considered, conditions could scarcely have been more ideal for the setting up of new social norms. Social Credit thus satisfied the desire for meaning and intelligibility amidst a chaotic social environment. On its positive or constructive side, Social Credit advocated new norms, and the upsurge of the movement represented an active attempt to realize a new social order through a specific program of monetary and financial reform. It was maintained that if the Social Credit proposals could only secure legislative approval, the horrors of the depression would automatically end and a new world would surely come into being. There are also indications that to many of Aberhart's personal religious following the philosophy took on the character of an eschatology, a prophetic vision of a divinely ordained future for the world.

The major factor in the psychological appeal of the philosophy of Social Credit was unquestionably the promise it held out for the satisfaction of the primary needs of food, clothing, and shelter. In a depressed and debt-ridden province where thousands of people were unemployed and living on relief, and where farmers were forced to sell their products at such incredibly low levels that they were often on the verge of starvation, the prospect of a basic dividend and a just price had an almost irresistible attraction.

In its offer of a basic dividend, generally understood to be $25 a month for each adult citizen, the Social Credit plan resembled to a certain extent the Townsend Plan which was attracting millions of adherents in the United States, especially in California, at the same time.[1] This "fountain-pen money" (as it was called in derision by the opponents of Social Credit) would provide every family with economic security and would banish forever the fear of poverty. Further, the basic dividend was to be presented without any eleemosynary taint, for was it not the people's right, their cultural heritage? Like many another panacea in the long procession of schemes for the salvation of society, the promise of a basic dividend gave the leader of the Social Credit movement the chance to take his followers along a Glory Road.

The social context, the desire for meaning, and the prospect of satisfying their needs combined to produce in Albertans a psychological condition in which they were extremely open to the appeal of Social Credit. At the same time, most of them lacked sufficient knowledge of philosophy and the social sciences to enable them to assess its claim to be *the* authentic interpretation of their world. Unable to deal with Social Credit in any critical way, thousands of people accepted it because it brought order into their confused world.

They were at once bewildered and had the will to believe. They were in a condition of readiness to respond, and the philosophy of Social Credit lent itself admirably to shortcut rationalizations in the form of slogans and symbols. For those who could not understand the philosophy as a whole, slogans like "Control of Credit," "Monetization of Natural Resources," "Basic Dividend," "Just Price," and "Cultural Heritage" became crowded with meaning. No small part of the appeal of Social Credit was simply due to the fact that it met so well the conditions of suggestibility which existed in Alberta at the time that Aberhart began his crusade in 1932.

An emphasis on the profound and multivalent appeal of the philosophy of Social Credit to the people of Alberta must not obscure the importance of the leadership of William Aberhart as a major factor in the rise of the Social Credit movement.... Aberhart brought to the movement his great prestige as an educationist and religious leader: it is doubtful if the movement would have won political power in Alberta without his leadership. This does not imply that we should think of him as a sort of genius with a mystic power of prestige that compelled assent and loyalty for Aberhart, like the leader in any field of social life, was both cause and effect. He was the product of the life of his people, and his power lay in his offer to lead in a direction in which those people wished to go, to resolve a difficulty for which no other man had so good a solution.

In his leadership of a mass movement, Aberhart combined the functions of the prophet with the executive capacities of the great planner and organizer. As a prophetic leader, Aberhart may be interpreted in terms of his unification of Christianity and the philosophy of Social Credit, his resolution of his followers' problems of ego involvement, and his charismatic appeal.

Aberhart's leadership gave the Social Credit movement a threefold religious context: he used the excellent facilities of the Calgary Prophetic Bible Institute as the headquarters of the movement; he attracted into the movement most of his large personal religious following which had been built up over a period of some twenty years; and he identified unmistakably the philosophy of Social Credit with the variety of Bible prophecy and Christian fundamentalism he had long been advocating. Aberhart had no hesitation in presenting Social Credit to Albertans as a Divine Plan for the salvation of society, the parallel in the economic sphere of the Divine Plan for the salvation of the individual. While such an approach infuriated many institutional religious and political leaders, it had a powerful attraction for thousands of people who were undoubtedly led in this way to join the movement.

Aberhart's presentation of Social Credit as a Divine Plan enabled him to insist that ultimate victory was inevitable: the cosmic forces were all on his side. In building up this feeling of inevitability in his following, he swept into the movement many persons who might otherwise have hesitated, but who wished to be on the winning side. He was shrewd enough, however, not to rely entirely upon the Divine Plan for the cosmos: he also used extensively the secular appeal. The names of noblemen, dignitaries of the church and state, and "experts," mostly in *England*, who accepted the proposals of Social

Credit were constantly invoked as an answer to the criticisms of orthodox economists in *Canada*. No name, apart from that of Major Douglas himself, was more useful in this connection than that of Dean Hewlett Johnson of Canterbury Cathedral, who at the time was an ardent advocate of Social Credit. To Aberhart's earlier prestige as an educational and religious leader there was now added the halo that came from his advocacy of a philosophy which not only mirrored the Divine Design, but which had the support of many great and powerful authorities on earth as well.

As a result of the depression, such economic chaos had developed in Alberta that the majority of the people were experiencing at least the threat of economic insecurity, if they had not already become unemployed, been forced to the verge of starvation, or gone on relief: as has been said above, there was a widespread disturbance of cultural norms and frames of reference, and thousands of people felt that they had lost their status in society. This impairment of status was naturally accompanied by problems of ego-involvement. In a society that had emphasized so strongly that individual effort was the key to success and respectability, many people now appeared as hopeless failures: they were obsessed with feelings of guilt for their inability to cope with the system. To these people, Aberhart's explanation of the "real" causes of the depression—and of their plight—brought a new outlook on life. In making clear to them that they were not personally responsible for their desperate situation, in naming the bankers and financiers as the "devils" who had ruined them, he lifted (as in the religious confessional or the psychiatric clinic) the heavy burden of the guilt of failure from their lives and started them on the road back from ego-displacement to ego-enhancement.

In a society in which the individual is also motivated by the desire to maintain or increase his own feelings of self-regard, Aberhart helped his followers to achieve ego-enhancement by insisting on their direct participation in the activities of the Social Credit movement. Through incessant *personal* effort, a new orientation was given to their lives and...many of them exhibited surprising qualities of local leadership. In addition, the movement appealed to their feelings of self-regard in that it promised a restored, a redefined, or a greatly improved status for all of them when victory should be achieved. Aberhart's success as a leader was partly due to his ability to persuade so many people to work so vigorously for the "cause": these people, on the other hand, were willing to work so hard because they experienced thereby so much psychological healing of their disorganized lives. They escaped from the horrors of the depression by developing new ego-involvements in the Social Credit movement.

Although Aberhart always paraded his Queen's University degree and his titles as Principal of Crescent Heights High School and Dean of the Prophetic Bible Institute, he was careful also to preserve membership character with his followers. To maintain a "folksy" appeal, he had an act...in which he would come on the platform in a tattered, patched up "coat of many colours" to illustrate the fallacious approaches of various well-known political leaders to the problems of the depression. His grammatical errors, although made unintentionally, served to increase this folksy appeal. He received rich and poor alike in his office at the Bible Institute, with the same unflagging interest in their problems. He appeared to his followers as a man who was absolutely devoted to their cause. It is not surprising that people identified themselves with a leader who possessed such characteristics. This identification included an acceptance of *his* objectives as *their* objectives, of *his* unusual mixture of religion and economics as *their* interpretation of the world. His followers were so convinced of his sincerity and conviction that they felt, in their turn, that he identified himself with them, and Aberhart naturally encouraged the development of this attitude.

Ego-involvement in the movement became so acute for many people that they refused to discuss the validity of the Social Credit proposals with opponents or, finally, even to listen to the speeches of leaders of other political parties, whose meetings they boycotted. By the summer of 1935 a large number of Social Crediters had developed such intolerance that they viewed any attempt to analyze Social Credit theories critically as a personal attack on William Aberhart...the incisive, scientific analyses of Social Credit presented by the vice president of the U.F.A., Norman F. Priestley, in a brilliant series of radio broadcasts, lashed them to fury: they retaliated, not by rational arguments but by writing abusive and even scurrilous letters to Priestley, questioning his right to criticize "that Man of God, William Aberhart." Nor would they listen to Professor Angus, spokesman for the Economic Safety League. Two weeks before the election, several of the U.F.A. leaders finally realized the nature of the social movement with which they were confronted. "A dead calm," one of the then Cabinet ministers has put it, "descended over our meetings. We moved like ghosts across Alberta, and everywhere the Social Crediters faced us in ice-cold silence. We carried out our assignments and kept up a bold front, but I knew we had hopelessly lost."

The social disintegration into which Alberta drifted as the depression wore on had produced a state of mind in which thousands of people were expressing a desire for a strong-willed, dauntless leader who would take them out of the wilderness: they realized, however dimly in many instances, that only collective action under a great leader could solve their problems. Aberhart's imposing physical presence, his performances as orator and organizer, his resolute and inflexible will, his infinite resourcefulness, his ability to hypnotize people by his voice, his contagious belief in himself—all these characteristics combined to produce in many people the attitude that "Here is the *Leader*." In the crises which occurred at various times it was always personal allegiance and absolute loyalty to William Aberhart that finally prevailed, and not any agreement on thought or action. Charismatic leadership gave singular unity and additional drive and momentum to a movement that already maintained, on the philosophical side, the inevitability of the realization of Social Credit in the world. To the assertion that Social Credit could not, under the B.N.A. Act, be applied in the province of Alberta, his followers had one simple, confident answer—"William Aberhart will find a way. If we all stand behind him we can build a new world under his leadership."

If Aberhart's character as the prophet of the Social Credit movement gave his leadership a Messianic quality, his ability as an organizer and planner was no less remarkable. Around his person the whole movement gravitated and, with the exception of the short period in the spring of 1934, he maintained undisputed control over its development. The strategy and tactics that gradually emerged in the course of this development may be considered in terms of six major factors: systematic instruction, a people's movement, the use of old norms, the media of propaganda, dramatization, and the groups.

Throughout our analysis of the rise of the Social Credit movement we have emphasized its continuity with a long-existing religious movement. But, as a movement in its own right, it was born in the basement of the Bible Institute the night its leader began systematic instruction in the literature of Social Credit. Those who received this instruction had an irresistible feeling that they had gone back to school to study the causes of the depression and its remedy under a master teacher. The experiment was so successful that its members enthusiastically invited others to take part. Systematic instruction was the dynamic underlying the organization of the groups. As the movement developed, hundreds of people had been so well trained in the philosophy of Social Credit that they could organize and conduct new study groups on their own initiative. Organization within organization gathered momentum and enabled Aberhart to extend the movement indefinitely.

The response of the people was, indeed, so enthusiastic that Aberhart was able, after a few months, to maintain truly that it was a "people's movement." He invariably said to his audiences, "It's *your* movement; *you* must carry it to others; I can't solve the problems of the depression but *you* can. Study! Study! Study! And then *you* carry the truths of Social Credit to others." Sometimes the appeal was grimmer, especially after the decision to take the movement into politics, as in the radio refrain, "If *you* have not suffered enough, it is *your* God-given right to suffer more; but if *you* wish to elect *your* own representatives to implement the Social remedy, this is *your* only way out." A person whose interest in Social Credit had been aroused was immediately put to work for the movement, in his family circle, among his relatives, in his neighbourhood district. These tactics account for both the tremendous drawing-power of Social Credit meetings and the remarkable coverage of Alberta that the movement achieved in a short time. People were attracted to a movement which gave so many signs of being aggressive and dynamic.

The structure of the Social Credit organization was given added strength because it paralleled so closely that of the U.F.A. which had been functioning in Alberta for nearly twenty-five years;.... Aberhart's study groups corresponded to the U.F.A. locals; his zones (usually containing ten or a dozen groups) were modelled on the U.F.A. districts; there was little difference in the constituency organizations of the two movements; and, finally, the Social Credit League was inspired by the U.F.A. provincial convention. For nearly two-and-a half years, Aberhart, as well as other Social Credit leaders and speakers, had the use of both organizations:...they engaged actively in functional penetration of the U.F.A. locals until the Social

Credit movement was finally transformed into a political party in April, 1935, only five months before the election. The similarity in the organizational structure of the two movements and Aberhart's tactics of functional penetration made it easier for members of the U.F.A. to transfer their allegiance to the Social Credit movement;...in some locals nearly the whole membership deserted their leaders and went over to Social Credit groups.

Apart from the remarkable personal activity of the people themselves, Social Credit ideas were promoted mainly through the use of the radio, the lengthy speaking tours of Aberhart and Manning [leading organizer and speaker for the party] in the summers of 1933 and 1934 (and later of numerous local and secondary leaders), the *Social Credit Chronicle*, and the large-scale distribution of literature. Paradoxically enough, newspapers hostile to the movement (and eventually there were scarcely any exceptions) helped to spread the philosophy. The very publicity they gave to the movement through the violence and bitterness of their personal attacks on Aberhart, and the ridicule they heaped on the Social Credit proposals boomeranged; they turned people to the movement who might otherwise merely have watched the great contest from the sidelines.

The most effective medium of propaganda was unquestionably Aberhart's use of the radio...he had already had nearly ten years of experience as a broadcaster; a representative of the British Broadcasting Corporation who visited Canada in the middle 1930s declared there was no device or technique of the radio speaker that Aberhart had not thoroughly mastered; a former Prime Minister of Canada concluded that "Aberhart had the greatest mass appeal of any leader in Canadian history." Whoever has observed in Alberta the far-flung loneliness of the countryside (as in the vista from the great hill east of Cochrane on the Banff road) can appreciate the psychological significance of the penetration of Aberhart's radio voice into thousands of isolated farm homes. He thundered his exposition of Social Credit in a voice which had many tones and ranged up and down the octaves, but perhaps his greatest attraction was his capacity to project his personality over the air. Through his radio addresses, Aberhart built up contacts in every region of Alberta except the Peace River and the far north, to which the Calgary radio station CFCN could scarcely penetrate at that time. Correspondence resulted from these contacts; radio instructions for the formation of groups were sent out and the movement was on its way even in the most isolated districts. It may be doubted if there could have been a Social Credit movement without Aberhart's use of the radio.

Aberhart brought to the promotion of Social Credit ideas all the techniques of dramatic appeal he had developed during twenty-five years as an expounder on Sunday afternoons of Bible prophecy and Christian fundamentalism: whether in religion or politics he could always be depended on to give the public a good show...the response of the people was aroused and sustained through the wide publicity he was able to secure for the movement at each critical stage in its development: by the use of numerous devices such as petitions, appeals to the U.F.A. government, the straw vote, the radio calls for "One Hundred Honest Men," mass meetings, and great picnics and teas. He thus kept the movement rolling so effectively that people listened to the radio or read their papers eagerly for news of it and tried to anticipate what he would be up to next. Even the split in the movement which occurred in the spring of 1934 merely heightened the tension among the people and dramatized anew the movement.

Dramatic effects were perhaps nowhere so successful as in his radio plays in which a cast of characters representing various vested interests (the Banking system, the mortgage companies, industry, etc.) argued with Aberhart and Manning (always the heroes of the piece) the merits of Social Credit.... The opponents of Social Credit were never able to put their case before the public with anything approaching Aberhart's effectiveness and his use of dramatization must be considered an important psychological factor in the appeal of the movement.

The study groups were the genuine organizational foundation of the movement. When public enthusiasm for Social Credit was approaching the stage of mass hysteria in the summer of 1935 there were sixty-three groups in Calgary alone, and some 1,800 in the whole province. Membership in the groups ranged from 10 to 800; many of them had between 100 and 200. The groups were privileged to send delegates directly to the Central Council or later to the Social Credit League in proportion to their numbers; they also functioned as the principal medium through which funds were raised for the movement. Groups usually held weekly or fortnightly meetings, and for years the main item on the agenda was the study of Social Credit literature.

Other social movements have used the group form of organization, but a close examination of the Social Credit groups suggests that they probably played a much more important role in Alberta than in movements elsewhere. Considered psychologically, the groups had three important functions: they sustained the microcosm; they developed a remarkable type of primitive comradeship; and, as the movement changed into a political party, they maintained in the minds of their members the hope of the ultimate realization of Social Credit in the world.

Why did Social Credit, rather than some other philosophy, for example socialism, become so widely accepted among the people of Alberta as the hope of salvation? Would Aberhart have been equally successful as the leader of a socialistic movement? Only speculative answers can be given to such questions, but various considerations may be adduced. Let us explore the possibilities in terms of philosophy, leadership, and methods.

...we have stressed repeatedly that Social Credit fitted in with the norms of a province where monetary reform as a solution of economic problems had long been advocated. As such, it exhibited a remarkable congruence with preferred group tendencies. Socialism, as contrasted with Social Credit, had no real roots in the Alberta community. The weakness of the appeal of socialism may be attested by the fact that its devotees among the U.F.A. Members of Parliament were themselves strongly attracted to monetary reform in general, and to Social Credit in particular, both as an explanation and as a solution of the problems created by the depression. The indecision that existed in the minds of leading Alberta founders of the C.C.F. concerning the competing claims of socialism and Social Credit confirms our view that the existing social norms were heavily weighted in favour of the latter.

Given more favourable circumstances than actually existed for its reception in the Alberta of the 1930s, it is conceivable that the philosophy of socialism could have been presented in such a way as to satisfy "the desire for meaning" of the better educated classes of the community. Socialism offers at least as plausible an explanation of the cause and cure of depressions as Social Credit. But the former represents a much more penetrating, as well as a much more comprehensive, critique of the capitalistic system than the latter. Then, too, the objectives of socialism seem to be much more remote and difficult of realization than those of Social Credit. As such, the latter offered the more immediate and, therefore, under depression conditions, the more attractive lure of the satisfaction of needs than the former. Social Credit was undoubtedly presented in such a grossly oversimplified form that even the most economically and politically illiterate person thought he understood it. It may be doubted whether even Aberhart could have presented socialism in such a way that it would have met the conditions of suggestibility that existed in Alberta during the 1930s. Nor should it be forgotten that Social Credit lends itself admirably to the kind of exposition of which Aberhart was capable, whereas socialism does not.

Socialism is not, in fact, the type of philosophy that would have appealed, in any significant sense, to a man of Aberhart's capacities and temperament. Whether considered in terms of nature or nurture, Aberhart was an arch-conservative in education, religion, and politics. The Social Credit movement has always been at great pains to appear as a *reform* rather than a revolutionary movement. As such, it has differentiated itself sharply from socialism (whether Fabian or Marxian) in several important respects. It seeks a limited objective, the transformation of the monetary and financial system of capitalism (it will make capitalism "work"), never the revolutionary reconstruction of society at large. It is strongly steeped in the current *mores* of capitalistic society. It attempts to establish a claim on existing institutions by emphasizing its respectability and its essentially Christian character. Finally, as a merging of social reformist and religious interests, Social Credit has constantly reaffirmed the ideal values of Christian capitalistic society. Aberhart would not, therefore, have been equally successful as the leader of a socialist movement for the reason that the philosophy of socialism was utterly foreign to his mind and personality. But it would probably be difficult to discover a leader whose intellectual and emotional capacities were more ideally suited for the acceptance and propagation of the philosophy of Social Credit.

In the light, then, of the conditions that existed in Alberta, as well as of Aberhart's actual capacities and personality, it was inevitable that a Social Credit rather than a socialist movement would prevail. This conclusion is confirmed by the historical fact that socialism was, in reality, an alternative to Social Credit in 1935. While it is true that socialism appeared as such an alternative only within the equivocal context of the U.F.A. movement, it was still an alternative. Surely the inability of socialist ideas to revitalize the decaying U.F.A. movement may be adduced in further support of our argument.

Indeed, for well over two decades following its disengagement from the U.F.A. in 1938, the C.C.F. was unable to make headway against the Social Credit movement. The perennial failure of the C.C.F. in the province of its birth to defeat the Social Credit party may be taken as a final justification of our view that not even Aberhart could have led a socialist movement to victory in 1935. But such a final justification requires a consideration of the bitter struggle between the Social Credit and socialist movements in Alberta in the years following the memorable election of 1935, a consideration that would take us far beyond the scope of the present book.

We have offered a pluralistic interpretation of the rise of the Social Credit movement. Given the social, economic, and political situation in Alberta, the principal psychological factors were the philosophy, the leader, and the strategy and tactics of that leader. Each of these major factors includes, as we have seen, a variety of subsidiary elements, so that as a phenomenon of mass psychology the movement appears as a complex pattern of events functioning in conjuncture within the wider social context. Finally, our functional and phenomenological analysis has never lost sight of the fact that the Social Credit movement was ultimately based on the experiences of people who had endured incredible frustration and suffering. Considered as a whole, the movement was *their* dynamic assessment of the possibilities of their world.

NOTES

1. Dr. Francis Everett Townsend, a physician, proposed a $200 monthly pension to American citizens 60 years of age and over who had not been convicted of a felony. Early in 1936 the Townsend movement claimed more than 3,500,000 paid members in the United States. This movement was responsible for the collapse of a rising Social Credit movement in California during the 1930s.

THE UNITED FRONT FROM ABOVE AND BELOW: CANADIAN COMMUNISM IN THE 1930S

BY NORMAN PENNER

o

The Seventh Congress of the Communist International, which took place in Moscow from 25 July until 20 August 1935, was the first Comintern congress to make the united front *tactic* its main theme rather than a minor point in an otherwise revolutionary program. Certainly there were enough references at the congress to the revolutionary aims of the world Communist movement, but these were relegated to a secondary position at least temporarily, because the defeat of fascism had become the immediate objective of the Communists, and a broad popular front tactic was the only way to realize this objective.

It had taken almost a year after the victory of Hitler in Germany and the subsequent smashing of the Communist, Social Democratic, and all other non-fascist parties, before the German Communists and Comintern recognized that their main foe was not the Social Democratic party, but the National Socialist German Workers' (Nazi) party and similar fascist-type parties in France, Austria, and Spain, which were growing rapidly, and in Italy, where the fascist party under Mussolini had been in power since 1922.

The Communists had come to the conclusion that fascism had replaced social democracy as the main threat some time before they decided that a communist-socialist alliance was the necessary means for stopping the further growth of fascism. The main theme of R. Palme Dutt's celebrated book *Fascism and Social Revolution,* which first appeared in late 1934 with Comintern approval, was that the central conflict had become fascism versus communism:

Excerpt from Norman Penner, *Canadian Communism: The Stalin Years and Beyond* (Toronto: Methuen, 1988), pp. 128-160. Reprinted with the permission of Norman Penner and Stoddart Publishing Co. Limited, North York, Ontario.

To many the alternative of Fascism or Communism is no welcome alternative.... [T]hey dream of a third alternative which shall be neither Fascism or Communism.... This dream of a third alternative is in fact illusory...if social revolution is delayed, then Fascism becomes inevitable.... [T]he only final guarantee against Fascism is the victory of the proletarian dictatorship.... Therein is the urgency of the fight, not only for the ultimately inevitable victory of Communism, but for the rapid victory of Communism.[1]

This analysis was developed relentlessly in page after page and ended with the rallying cry: "The workers' dictatorship is the *only guarantee* against the victory of Fascism.... The path of bourgeois democracy ends in Fascism.... The battle for the workers' dictatorship must be fought, not merely after Fascism, but *before Fascism*, as the sole means to prevent Fascism.[2] In the event, however, that the revolution did not happen before the fascists took power as in Germany, Dutt assured his readers that socialism was imminent:

Germany is nearer to the final victory of the proletarian revolution than any country in the capitalist world. The fact that the German workers are going through the extremist hell of Fascism is the reflection of the fact, not that their movement is more backward, but that it is relatively more advanced and close to the revolution.[3]

This was, of course, the Comintern's appraisal at that time, embellished by the "theoreticians" in each party such as Dutt. In his book *Socialism and the CCF*, which came out earlier in 1934, Stewart Smith writing for the Canadian Communists under the name G. Pierce made the astounding statement:

As a matter of fact, there is no fundamental difference between the capitalist democracy of Canada and the Fascist dictatorship of Germany. THEY ARE BOTH DICTATORSHIPS OF THE SAME RULING CLASS, THE CAPITALIST CLASS.[4]

It was not until after Georgi Dimitrov's speech at the Seventh Congress, and particularly his reply to the discussion, that the full extent of the change that the Communist International was ordering could be seen:

Now the toiling masses in a number of capitalist countries are faced with the necessity of making a definite choice and of making it today, not between proletarian dictatorship and bourgeois democracy, but between bourgeois democracy and fascism.

In this reply to the discussion, Dimitrov also made the first public criticism of the German party by the Comintern:

It was the mistake of the Communists in a number of countries, particularly in Germany, that they failed to take into account the changes which had taken place, but continued to repeat those slogans, maintain those tactical positions which had been correct a few years before.[5]

The proposition that the fight was now between fascism and bourgeois democracy, and therefore the Communists had to take up the struggle to defend bourgeois democracy, was the startlingly new direction charted by the Seventh Congress. The Communists, in spite of everything they had been told and preached, were now told that they must bend all their efforts to defend the liberal democratic state against the onslaught of fascism. Dimitrov had some stern words to say about the social democratic and liberal parties, but the main thrust of his remarks was directed not at them but at the Communists, to make them change their concepts and practices, if there was to be any hope of a genuine popular movement in any country to stop fascism.

The pervasive feeling among the delegates at the Seventh Congress was that they were repudiating the Sixth Congress of 1928, which had ushered in a whole period of extreme leftism that resulted in the isolation of most Communist parties in the Western world. Ironically, this happened everywhere except Germany, where the Communist party grew rapidly in votes and membership, and this encouraged the German Communist leadership to escalate its attack on the social democrats instead of joining with them against the Nazis. The *combined* vote of the Communists and socialists at every election before the last one in March 1933 was sufficient to defeat the Nazis. But they were *not* combined, and the Communists, for some time after Hitler took power, continued to agitate as though the social democrats and not the fascists were the main danger. Their post-Hitler manifesto declared that with the extinction of the social democratic party organization it was now clear to everybody in Germany that the fight was between communism and fascism.

There were, however, disagreements developing, especially within the French Communist party. It was beginning to feel the hot breath of fascism in France and simultaneously was coming under strong pressure from the French Socialist party (SFIO) for united action against the fascist gangs. After 6 February 1934, when the fascists had attempted a coup in the Chamber of Deputies, the movement towards a united front became irresistible, and at the end of July the Communists and Socialists concluded their first working agreement for joint action. Later this agreement embraced the ruling Radical party as well to form what became known as the "popular front."

The spontaneous development of pressure for the adoption of the popular front tactic coincided with new developments in Soviet foreign policy. When Hitler came to power, the Soviet government made discreet inquiries as to whether he would continue the treaty of friendship which had been in force between Germany and the Soviet Union since 1922. As late as 29 December 1933, Maxim Litvinov, the Soviet foreign minister, reported to the Supreme Soviet:

> Of course, we have our own opinion about the German regime and of course we sympathize with the sufferings of our German comrades, but we as Marxists are the last who can be reproached with allowing sentiment to prevail over policy. The entire world

knows that we can and do maintain relations with capitalist states whatever their regime, even if it is fascist. Our relations with Germany are determined not by its internal but its external policy.[6]

Less than a month later, on 26 January 1934, at the opening of the Seventeenth Congress of the Communist party of the Soviet Union, Stalin repeated, in slightly different words, Maxim Litvinov's statement:

> Of course, we are far from being enthusiastic about the fascist regime in Germany. But fascism is not the issue here, if only for the reason that fascism in Italy, for example, has not prevented the USSR from establishing the best relations with that country.[7]

When it became clear in April 1934 that Hitler was not interested in renewing the previous Soviet-German treaty, or in negotiating a new one, the Soviet government began to press vigorously for alternative policies. It joined the League of Nations, which it had denounced since the foundation of the League in 1919, and began to press for collective security. It started negotiations with the French government under Pierre Laval for a mutual assistance pact. Simultaneously, the Comintern began to show genuine enthusiasm for the idea of an all-inclusive united front, beginning with its approval of an agreement between the French Communist party and the Socialist party, which was cited as a shining example.

The coincidence of Soviet diplomatic interests and the needs of the French and other Western Communist parties made it possible and necessary to change the direction of the Comintern; however, there was still considerable resistance from many important figures as to how far the tactic could be stretched before it became a matter of principle, rather than a temporary diversion to achieve an immediate goal, as many viewed it.

The debate in Comintern circles delayed the convening of the congress several times before the Secretariat felt that it had sufficient agreement to go ahead. The congress opened 25 July 1935, but it was not until 2 August that Georgi Dimitrov made his keynote speech. As the discussion developed, it became clear that there were still wide variations in the way the tactic of a united front was perceived. Dimitrov's reply to the discussion underlined those differences, which concerned the question of whether he had proposed a major change or a cosmetic one, whether he meant that the Communists were going to be defending bourgeois democracy, or merely exerting themselves more energetically to enlist rank-and-file and middle-level social democrats in the *revolutionary* fight against fascism.

These differences continued in varying degrees to plague the Comintern for the duration of the popular front period, which came to an abrupt halt on 23 August 1939, with the signing of the Soviet-German Non-Aggression Pact. During the period of the "popular front" the Communists pursued the central aim laid down by the Seventh Congress, with varying success, depending on the strength of the party in each country, and according to the way each party understood the new connotation of the old united front slogan.

One of the major difficulties in implementing this stage of the united front was that Dimitrov's address was pitched at the level of the French Communist party, which was the only party in the West, after the demise of the German, that had any clout in the political arena, and therefore had something to offer socialists and liberals. He did not ignore the problem of the small Communist parties but his answer was not very helpful:

> [I]t must not be forgotten that the Communist Parties of Austria or Great Britain, with all their insignificance in numbers...are not only the tens of thousands of workers who are supporters of the party, but are parts of the world Communist movement, are sections of the Communist International, the leading party of which is the party of a proletariat which has already achieved victory and rules over one-sixth part of the globe.[8]

THE LEAGUE AGAINST WAR AND FASCISM

During the 1920s the Comintern had instructed the member parties to launch united front organizations, such as the Friends of the Soviet Union, branches of the International Red Aid (in Canada, the Canadian Labor Defence League), workers' sports associations, working women's leagues, and others. These were characterized later by the Comintern as unsatisfactory. They were made up largely of party members and never able to go much beyond the ranks of the Communist parties which had set them up.[9]

The Comintern's first experience with a new kind of united front was at the World Congress Against Imperialist War in Amsterdam between 27 and 29 August 1932. It was initiated by the Comintern but publicly called under a distinguished sponsorship of world celebrities including Henri Barbusse, Romain Rolland, Madame Sun Yat-sen, Albert Einstein, Upton Sinclair, and Theodore Dreiser. The united front did attract people outside the ranks of the Communist parties. According to the official report, there were 2,196 delegates from 27 countries, of whom 1,041 had no party affiliation, 830 were Communists, 291 were Social Democrats, 24 Left Socialists, and 10 of the Communist Opposition.[10]

The congress was closely supervised from the floor by Georgi Dimitrov[11] and Willy Munzenburg,[12] two of the Comintern's most experienced organizers, who were able, by directing the 830 Communist delegates, to ensure that the resolutions adopted were those that the Comintern wanted adopted. The discussion centred on one theme—namely, that the capitalist powers were preparing to launch a war on the Soviet Union, and that the League of Nations and pacifists were attempts by the capitalist powers and their social democratic allies to paralyze the anti-war struggles of the masses. A continuing committee was set up with headquarters in France, changing the name of the movement late in 1933 to "World League Against War and Fascism," which played a key role in implementing the Comintern's new and broader united front tactic. The Communists in many countries established national affiliates, taking care to ensure that the united front character of this movement was preserved.

The First Canadian Congress Against War and Fascism took place in Toronto from 6 to 8 October 1934, and was considered by its sponsors to be a success. It launched the Canadian Communists into the anti-fascist popular front period. The representation at the congress included well-known Communists, of whom the most important were Leslie Morris, Sam Carr, and Matthew Popovich; prominent left CCFers such as Fred Fish, Bert Robinson, E.A. Beder, and Arthur Mould; religious figures such as Rabbi Maurice Eisendrath and Reverend Salem Bland; and a few non-Communist trade union leaders such as A.R. Mosher, president of the All-Canadian Congress of Labour (ACCL), and John Bruce, of the AFL's Plumbers' Union and of the Toronto Trades and Labour Council.

The congress was presided over by A.A. MacLeod of Nova Scotia, who had spent the previous five years in the United States, first as secretary of the YMCA of Chicago, then as business manager of the radical liberal magazine *The World Tomorrow*, edited by the renowned theologian, Reinhold Niebuhr. MacLeod had participated in the founding of the US League Against War and Fascism and was asked by the Canadian Communists to return to Canada to take charge of their united front work, which he did with considerable success.

The "Manifesto" that summed up the outlook of the three-day congress reflected the changes in Communist thinking since the Amsterdam Congress of 1932. The main change was the elevation of fascism as a threat to the world equal to that of war, although fascism was not yet considered the only or even the main threat to world peace. The United States, Great Britain, and Japan, as embodiments of capitalist imperialism, were considered to be the driving forces toward world war because this was inevitable for big imperialist powers. The League of Nations was no longer regarded as a tool of the imperialist states, but the congress warned that "it is futile to rely solely upon the league of nations...to maintain world peace." The congress supported the "proposals for total disarmament such as those sincerely advanced by the Soviet Union" and emphasized that its main activities would be "mass meetings, demonstrations, lectures, parades."[13]

Such actions were indeed the main fare of the League, including frequent trips abroad to attend world congresses as well as national congresses in other countries. By example, or by careful planning, the League also brought into being the Canadian Youth Congress, which became independent of the League and which went on to become the most successful united front initiative in this whole period. The League was also instrumental in setting up committees among the ethnic groups, especially in the Jewish community, where committees against fascism and anti-Semitism were established in Winnipeg, Toronto, and Montreal and succeeded in drawing in many non-Communist organizations. It published a number of pamphlets on the subject of fascism, including one that exposed the home-grown fascist groups which had begun to sprout in Canada and were duplicating the Blackshirts or Brownshirts of Europe.[14] The League also took the initiative in establishing the Canadian Committee to Aid Spanish Democracy; later under its changed name, the Canadian League for Peace and Democracy, it established a similar committee to aid China.

AID TO THE LEGAL GOVERNMENT
OF THE SPANISH REPUBLIC

Although the idea of a popular front alliance in the electoral sense had been worked out with France in mind, the first government of a popular front character came to power in Spain in the parliamentary elections of 16 February 1936, almost three months before it happened in France. It was a coalition of the left republicans, socialists, Communists, and some anarchists, with a program which had been worked out with the active assistance of Jacques Duclos, a leading member of the French Communist party, who represented the Comintern in the negotiations.[15] In exactly six months, on 17 July, however, the military, headed by General Franco—and having support from the top bishops of the Catholic Church, the wealthy landowners, capitalists, and sections of the middle class—attacked the legally elected government, plunging the country into a bloody civil war that lasted for two and a half years.

It became immediately evident that Franco had the fascist regimes of Hitler and Mussolini behind him. They financed and supplied him with arms, aircraft, pilots, and military advisers, while the democratic countries and the Soviet Union agreed at the League of Nations not to supply similar equipment to "either side." Shortly after, the Soviet Union ended this hypocrisy and shipped equipment of the same type to the loyalist side but was unable to match the quantities coming from Germany and Italy.

The democratic countries' idea of "non-intervention" was motivated by their policy of appeasing Germany and Italy, out of fear or out of hostility to the Soviet Union, or both. Thus, as the insurrection stepped up, the war turned into a contest between a rebel army that was sustained by the main Fascist powers in Europe, and the legal government of Spain, which had become totally dependent on the Soviet Union for its needs.

The Soviet Union met its obligations in two ways: through direct shipment of arms, ammunition, tanks, artillery, and aircraft, together with advisers, and through the Communist International, which brought volunteers from all over the world to form what became known as the International Brigade. Before the war was over, the brigade had enlisted over forty thousand men from twenty countries. The Soviet Union sent in over two thousand military personnel, who were assigned to the regular Spanish Army and Air Force, completely separate from the International Brigade, although the reason for that separation was never made clear.[16]

The Communist party of Canada likewise met its obligations in two ways: it recruited and made all the arrangements for sending Canadians to the International Brigade, and it channeled all other aid through the League Against War and Fascism, which, in turn, set up the Committee to Aid

Spanish Democracy, which raised funds for the Canadian blood transfusion unit under Dr. Norman Bethune. Dr. Bethune became world renowned as a result of his later work with the Chinese Communist Eighth Route Army under Mao Tse-tung, but he was already a celebrity in Canada as a result of his pathfinding work in refrigerating blood for transfusions and administering them on the battlefields in Spain.[17]

The organization of the Canadian battalion, which took on the name Mackenzie-Papineau after the two leaders of the 1837 reform rebellions in Upper and Lower Canada, was a monumental effort. It involved recruitment, transportation through unknown routes, passports, financing, and coordination with the authorities in Spain. Without detracting from any other underground railroad in history, this was indeed a prodigious feat.[18] The problems encountered were likewise enormous, because they were political. In Canada's case, there was the prohibition by the Mackenzie King government on enlistment in foreign wars through an Act that was amended to cover the specifics of the Spanish war. Moreover, a clause was inserted in the Act that made even the blood transfusion institute of Dr. Bethune illegal on the grounds that he was not ministering to both sides![19]

The Communists made a commitment to the Comintern to screen recruits thoroughly so that, as far as possible, people accepted into the International Brigade would be politically reliable. They did not succeed in all cases,[20] but it was not for lack of trying:

> Meanwhile Hunter and Phillips continued to screen the volunteers searching for RCMP officers and for Trotskyites. As Hunter put it, "we didn't know which we hated the most."[21]

The activity that the Spanish Civil War generated in the Communist movement and around it brought significant benefits in terms of membership participation and recruiting of new members. This was particularly true in the Young Communist League, which ran highly successful campaigns to provide parcels and cigarettes for the Mac-Paps in Spain and to entertain them when they returned home. The national tour that Dr. Bethune made on his return in 1938 was a highlight in the history of the Communist party, even surpassing the enthusiasm, the crowds, the money raised, and the radio and press publicity of [party leader] Tim Buck's release from Kingston.

The war ended in January 1939 with the popular front government defeated and General Franco the head of state. The defeat was, of course, a heavy blow for the Spanish people and strengthened Hitler's and Mussolini's confidence that they could win a war in Europe. It was also a setback for the world Communist movement, which had made immense sacrifices, especially of its members who went to fight the fascists in Spain and did not return. In Canada close to half the twelve hundred Mac-Paps were killed. It was at least some consolation that, because of the wide support for the Spanish Republic among Canadians, the King government did not prosecute any of the veterans who had clearly defied the Foreign Enlistments Act of 1937.

The organizations that the Canadian Communists established as their direct contribution to the united front against fascism were moderately successful in the activity they generated and in the breadth of their appeal. They never succeeded, however, in reaching far beyond the representation at the founding congress of the League Against War and Fascism in October 1934. Some of the personnel changed from time to time, and the most important CCFer to join the League was Tommy Douglas, MP, who became one of its vice-presidents in 1938. But the main leadership of the CCF refused to associate with the League although they supported many of its demands in Parliament.

The Trotskyists, who were represented at the founding of the League by Maurice Spector and Jack MacDonald, former leader of the CPC, were barred from further gatherings of the League. The Communists were always in firm control, and even though the program had broadened, restrictions on admissions were mainly directed at the followers of Trotsky. In this respect the Communists adhered to the precept that Zinoviev had laid down at the Comintern as far back as 1921—namely, that "united front action could not be taken except on communist terms."[22]

THE CANADIAN YOUTH CONGRESS

The Canadian Youth Congress, which started as the youth wing of the League Against War and Fascism, had a different development. While it began slowly in August 1934, it was inspired by the founding convention of the American Youth Congress, which was held at the same time. It was an outstanding event, which came as a big surprise at the time to the American Communists. One thousand delegates, ranging in political opinion "from YMCA to Communist," established the congress and agreed to a program covering everything from youth unemployment to the threat of war and fascism.[23] There is no doubt that the success of the American Youth Congress from 1934 on was the result in no small measure of the unfolding of Roosevelt's New Deal, which the Communists had not yet fully appreciated.

The strong winds of reform sweeping through the US were just beginning to have an impact on Canada and the second meeting of the Canadian Youth Congress, held in Ottawa in 1936, looked very much like the 1934 meeting of the American movement. Kenneth Woodsworth, the main figure in the leadership of the Canadian Youth Congress, described this meeting as "the first really national youth congress in Canada...out of which came the Declaration of Rights of Canadian Youth, resolutions on Canadian youth and world peace and the proposed Canadian Youth Act."[24]

Every important youth organization in English Canada, including the youth divisions of the Conservative, Liberal, CCF, and Communist parties, was present at the Ottawa Congress and remained so at all further annual congresses and in the local and provincial councils, which met between the national gatherings.

In 1937, at the congress meeting in Montreal, a strong effort was made to convince the French-Canadian youth movements, most of which were under the control of the Catholic Church, to join. One of the strongest appeals to

Catholic youth was made by William Kashtan, national secretary of the Young Communist League, who accommodated his organization to every one of the conditions that the Catholic Action had laid down. He put forward his organization's agreement in these words:

> The Young Communist League accepts these conditions in the interests of the unity of Canadian youth. We support internal and world peace. We oppose those who cause warfare between the classes and between racial groups. We respect the religious beliefs of others; we favor the right of the individual to private property; we oppose those who destroy the sanctity of the home. We struggle to aid in a more complete development of the human personality.[25]

One question was not dealt with by Kashtan, or any other person at this juncture, and that was the attitude of most of the Quebec youth groups to fascism, because of the fact that the Catholic Church and all its organizations supported Franco and Mussolini. Thus the Communists were prepared to accept a form of unity with groups that did not oppose fascism. From this point of view, it cannot be said that the united front established in the Canadian Youth Congress was part of the worldwide unity against fascism which the Comintern had called for at its Seventh Congress.

It is true that, given all these concessions from the existing Canadian Youth Congress, including the stand of the Communist delegates, the French-Canadian delegates did not join; nevertheless, there was nothing to stop them from joining, given the unanimity of the delegates from English Canada in their desire to have unity among youth of both Canadian nations.

Canadian historians of both traditional and radical schools, and Communists themselves, talk and write about the Youth Congress as one of the front organizations that the CPC was able to lead or dominate. Although the chief executive officers at the national, provincial, and local levels were always Communists, the program was far broader than that of the League Against War and Fascism. It was based mainly on the economic needs of Canadian youth, which were supported by practically everyone. In that sense the Communist affiliation of most of the leaders was not a major problem, because they were working within congress policy. When that ceased to be the case in 1940, with the Communists opposing the war, the Canadian Youth Congress disintegrated.

A CHANGE ON THE LABOUR FRONT

> It must be clearly understood that the Workers' Unity League is the centre of all revolutionary trade-union and economic work of the Communist party and the left-wing.
>
> > -Tom Ewen, February 1931.[26]

And the old poppycock about the Workers' Unity League being a section of the Communist party of Canada is also failing to fool the workers, because everybody knows that our unions comprise a very representative cross-section of the Canadian workers—all sorts of nationalities, all kinds of political and religious opinions.

-*Tom Ewen, 9 November 1935.*[27]

These two statements illustrate not so much an effort to hide the truth, but the perceptions of two different strategies that the Comintern had imposed on all its sections within six years. The first was Stalin's policy of organizing revolutionary unions, openly led by Communists, and was based on the perspective that the proletarian revolution was just around the corner. Despite some success in organizing the unorganized and the unemployed, the Workers' Unity League was a failure; however, it left the Communists with small bases in mass production industries such as auto, mining, lumber, chemical, furniture, packinghouse, electrical, rubber, and the needle trades.

The second statement made by Ewen reflected the new united front tactic as laid down at the Seventh Congress of the Comintern. The Communists were in the process of disbanding their "ideal, revolutionary" unions to return to the mainstream of the labour movement, which meant the American Federation of Labor and its Canadian counterpart, the Trades and Labour Congress. Moreover, this turn was taking place at a time when a spontaneous upsurge among factory workers toward unionism had begun, especially in the United States, where the New Deal added impetus to the movement. The first piece of labour legislation, enacted in the United States in 1935, codified the right of workers to belong to unions of their own choice.

The Seventh Congress was clear in its new direction for Communists in the trade union movement. "The communists are decidedly for the re-establishment of trade union unity in each country...for one international of trade unions," and then specifically the resolution stated:

> In countries where small Red trade unions exist, efforts must be made to secure their admission into the big reformist trade unions, with demands put forward for the right to defend their views and the reinstatement of expelled members. In countries where big Red and reformist trade unions exist side by side, efforts must be made to secure their amalgamation on an equal footing, on the basis of a platform of struggle against the offensive of capital and a guarantee of trade union democracy.[28]

Tom Ewen, in his speech at what turned out to be the last convention of the Workers' Unity League, presented this resolution of the Comintern as the path ahead for the WUL:

> We want to make it clear that the WUL will not let any minor question or program, policy, or organization, act as a hindrance, even to the slightest degree in the fight for trade union unity.....[29] [W]e are prepared to agree that WUL unions shall merge with other unions...even if this means that they would sever their affiliation with us and affiliate to the AFL....[30] [W]e have managed to rectify that terrible mistake that some of our organizers and members used

to make of branding every leader or member of any AFL or ACCL union as a labor fakir, or of branding these unions as company unions.[31]

Ewen, a member of the party leadership, had access to information that was not generally available—that is, that John L. Lewis, director of the newly formed AFL Committee for Industrial Organization (CIO), was negotiating with the Communist party of the United States to hire some of its most talented and experienced trade union organizers in the projected drive to organize the unorganized in the mass production industries.[32] He brought on to his personal staff two prominent radicals, whom everyone knew were Communists, and he allowed, even encouraged, the industrial unions that were being built under his chairmanship to hire well-known Communists as part of their staff. At the same time he made it clear to the leaders of the CPUSA that they must not try to place Communists in leading positions in *his* union, the United Mine Workers of America, from which all known Communists had been expelled in the 1920s, in the United States and Canada.[33]

There were many reasons for this drastic reversal in John L. Lewis's attitude to the Communists, as he had been one of the most aggressive red-baiters in the AFL. But it was equally a reversal for the Communists, who were abandoning their go-it-alone policy of building revolutionary unions in order to rejoin what they had so contemptuously called "reformist" trade unions, and to work now with and for labour leaders whom they had universally described as labour "fakirs."

The policy to which the Communists were now committed was to carry out the organization of the unorganized through the established trade union body, mainly the AFL, without any connotation that this was, in fact, revolutionary work. This has remained the trade union policy of the Communist parties in Canada and the United States ever since, and nobody in the leadership of these parties has suggested a return to the go-it-alone policy.

The Communist party of Canada lost no time in abolishing the Workers' Unity League after the party's delegation had returned from the Seventh Congress of the Comintern. The Central Committee met at the beginning of November 1935 to formalize the steps to be taken. This was followed within a week by the third and last convention of the WUL, which merely ratified the decisions of the CPC and the Comintern.

At that time there were few WUL affiliates eligible to join the AFL or TLC, but those that were—such as the Industrial Needle Trades Union, the Lumber Workers Industrial Workers Union, and a few small local unions such as the Longshoremen in Vancouver and the Furniture Workers in Stratford—quickly merged into their AFL counterparts.

The specific problem that faced the Canadian party in carrying out the new united front policy was what to do with the small groups that had been organized under the WUL in some of the mass production industries but which had literally nowhere to go if the WUL were suddenly dissolved. They were not eligible to join the AFL, either because there were no AFL unions in that industry, or because AFL headquarters refused to accept industrial unions, or because they were not big enough to warrant serious attention by the AFL. At the Ninth Plenum of the Central Committee in November 1935, the person reporting on this topic proposed that the WUL continue in existence until a solution could be found for these groups.[34] What he really meant was that the party was counting on the CIOs coming into Canada quickly, at which time these minuscule groups would become very important as bases for the organizational drives in the respective industries. This is approximately what happened, although only after some agonizing delays.

The WUL was dissolved a few weeks after its convention. It was not, however, until the end of 1936 that the first big effort of the CIO in Canada was undertaken—namely, the formation of Local 222 of the United Auto Workers in Oshawa, followed by a spectacular strike at the General Motors plant. After the strike was won, in April 1937, the CIO became a magic watchword in Canada, around which successful organizing drives were undertaken in steel, electrical, rubber, textile, chemical, woodworking, hard-rock mining, and other plants in the automobile industry. Between 1938 and 1943 union growth was the greatest in Canadian labour history, from 385,000 to 664,000, most of it in industrial-type unions in the CIO, but also in the AFL and Catholic trade union federations, which jumped on the bandwagon generated by the CIO.[35]

The Communists made a major contribution to this growth, starting with their pioneering work in the WUL but mainly as a result of their unremitting energy in the massive drive under the CIO banner to organize industrial unions in Canada. The willingness of John L. Lewis to have Communists on his staff and in the major unions of the CIO (except for the United Mine Workers) was an undeniable factor in the sudden emergence of the Communist parties of the United States and Canada as a force to be reckoned with in the North American labour movement. This was indeed the culmination of the parties' efforts in this direction from 1921 until the late 1930s. The prominency of the parties was also the result of the profound change in trade union policy brought about, not by the party leaders in Canada and the US, but by the decisions of the Seventh Congress of the Comintern, and, in particular, the emphasis put on labour unity by Georgi Dimitrov. All these subjective factors, plus the favourable pro-labour climate created by the New Deal, ended, at least for a time, the isolation of the Communists from the mainstream of the trade union movement.

That it was a two-way process was cheerfully acknowledged by Earl Browder, leader of the American Communists, in his speech to the US party's convention in June 1936:

> This great mass movement needed our still small Communist party in order to achieve these results, just as we needed this great mass movement to find scope for our program and energies, to bring us once and for all out of our isolation into the broad streams of the mass life of America.[36]

The changes that took place in the Communist approach were far-reaching, even though they were defended in Canada as merely a temporary shift in tactics. The fact that Tim Buck, in his opening speech at the Eighth Convention of the CPC in October 1937, could publicly boast of the alliance between the Communist party and such prominent trade union figures as "P.M. Draper, president of the Trades and Labour Congress of Canada, Bob Tallon, secretary, John L. Lewis, leader of the CIO, and dozens of others"[37] indicated the extent of the changed relationship.

The Communist party, which from its foundation considered itself to be the only force in constant opposition to the trade union bureaucrats, or "labour fakirs," now regarded most of them as allies. From acting as the "vanguard of the working class," which required, or so they thought, that the party had to give precise orders to the labour movement, the Communists now publicly asked the labour leaders how the party could "best help" them in "maintaining and extending the unity of the trade union movement."[38] In line with this new style, the party at its Eighth Dominion Convention in 1937 adopted a resolution that called upon the All-Canadian Congress of Labour (ACCL) "to put an end to the futile and narrow National Unionism and to unite in action with their brothers and sisters of the International Union movement (AFL)...which can best serve the interests...of all working people."[39]

The party had not abandoned its cherished goal of leading the working class to socialism, but it now moderated the means by which this would be achieved. When Tom Ewen pronounced his eulogy at the demise of the WUL, he put forward a proposal that the labour movement build a "broad federated political party of the common people."[40] This had been attempted in the 1920s through the Canadian Labour Party but failed miserably. The Communists, through letters to J.S. Woodsworth and other prominent CCFers, urged the CCF to build such a party jointly in 1935, but that was turned down by the leaders and by various conventions of the CCF. It appeared in 1937 as a proposal for a trade union party with an anti-CCF flavour.

The CCF had been slow in taking part in the great organizing drive of the CIO and it was in response to the tremendous activity of the Communists in this movement that the leadership of the CCF entered the field. It sent a number of experienced trade union organizers, particularly into the CIO. It made deals with like-minded labour leaders such as Philip Murray, Sidney Hillman, David Dubinsky, and even John L. Lewis. It amended the CCF constitution in Ontario to permit the affiliation to the CCF of entire unions. Thus the stage was set for a major confrontation between the Communists and the CCF leaders over influence and control of the new unions, and over the political direction the trade union movement would take. There were relatively minor skirmishes at the outset. The fiercest battles took place after 1940, when the ACCL merged with the CIO to form a new and powerful federation called the Canadian Congress of Labour.

But even if the preliminary battles were minor, in a comparative sense, they were not considered so by the main contestants at the time. The

Communists knew, of course, that there would be no possibility at all for trade unions or federations to affiliate with or endorse the Communist party in federal, provincial, or municipal elections. Ironically, this applied to the Liberal party as well, even though the main leaders of the TLC were Liberals. But the CCF could and did win some affiliations or endorsations from unions or labour councils, and the Communists put forward as an alternative the idea of "independent labour political action." This appealed to many left-wing trade unionists and also to Liberal labour leaders as a way of opposing the CCF and having a voice in the politics of their union movement.

The Communists made a more explicit proposal to implement the general idea of independent labour political action by having the unions create labour representation associations. This proposal was adopted by several councils, including the most important one in the country, the Toronto and District Trades and Labour Council. It not only set up such a body but also endorsed J.B. Salsberg, the CP's trade union director, as the Labour Representation Association candidate in the 1937 provincial elections in St. Andrew riding, where a large bloc of garment workers resided.

This move presented the CCF with a dilemma, but David Lewis, then national secretary of the CCF, proposed that the St. Andrew CCF Constituency Association withdraw its candidate and support Salsberg, because he had the endorsation of the Trades and Labour Council. J.S. Woodsworth sharply rebuked Lewis for making this suggestion, and for not consulting him before he presented the idea to the constituency committee.[41]

Whatever steps the Communists made to improve their relations with the CCF, let alone bring about some kind of united front during this period, were in effect abandoned because of the hostility between the CCF and CPC in the trade union movement. It was hostility that grew incessantly, so that socialist-Communist unity, the main declared goal of the world Communist movement since the Seventh Congress, became a disaster in Canada.

COMMUNIST-CCF UNITY: AN IDEA THAT NEVER GOT OFF THE GROUND

At least from May 1934, the Communist party of Canada was aware of the discussions going on in the top circles of the Comintern concerning a major change in the tactics of world communism, especially with respect to relations with social democratic parties in the fight against fascism. It was in May that instructions had been received to establish a Canadian affiliate of the World Congress Against War and Fascism. A provisional committee to organize a founding convention was established in July and, in his capacity as a member of this committee, Leslie Morris, editor of The Worker and second-in-command in the executive of the CPC, addressed a letter to the CCF national convention, then in session, inviting the CCF to attend the forthcoming founding convention of the Canadian League Against War and Fascism.[42]

As was expected, the CCF convention rejected Leslie Morris's invitation, but the fact that Leslie Morris made such an appeal was surprising, coming as it did two weeks before the Seventh Convention of the Communist party, the first Communist convention since the foundation of the CCF. Morris knew that the convention was going to perpetuate the attack on the CCF contained in G. Pierce's (Stewart Smith's) book *Socialism and the CCF.*

If anything, the convention went farther. It addressed a manifesto which, among other things, called on the rank and file of the CCF, the AFL, and the ACCL to revolt against their leaders and join a united front with the Communist Party.[43] On the one hand, the CPC was busy organizing a congress against war and fascism, which was to be the beginning of a new approach to the CCF leaders, members, and supporters, yet simultaneously continue or escalate its onslaught against "social fascism" and "labour fakirs."

This apparent paradox was in part a reflection of the fact that the debate inside the Comintern was just beginning. To Maurice Thorez, the leader of the French Communist party, for example, the idea of a League Against War and Fascism was as far as he was willing to go in a united front with the French Socialists, and he believed that this would not necessitate any change in the long-standing hostility between Communists and Socialists in the forthcoming elections. It was the French Socialists who objected to that limited conception and insisted on a united front in the elections, which would include an agreement by the Communists to cease their name calling.[44]

J.S. Woodsworth, who had been a prime target of Communist name calling since 1928, made a similar point in a letter dated 23 April 1931, to his one-time friend and colleague Rev. A.E. Smith:

> It has seemed to me impossible to work closely with those who persistently denounce us as enemies of the working class.... It was the Communist party that disassociated itself from me, and denounced me.[45]

A.E. Smith's reply was typical. We will stop calling you an enemy of the working class, he said, as soon as you cease to be an enemy. Until his death in 1942, Woodsworth was labelled an enemy of the working class by the Communist party.

The name calling persisted during the whole of the popular front period, although it moderated slightly. On 9 January 1935, less than two months after his release from Kingston Penitentiary, Tim Buck issued a lengthy statement which was supposed to signal a change in the hitherto unwavering attitude of the Communist party towards the CCF and the main trade union organizations. The only concession that Buck made was that he did not explicitly call the CCF a capitalist party; he did, however, lambaste the leaders as "social-reformist charlatans...who are committing a terrible crime against the working people of Canada.... [S]uch CCF leaders...help the development of the fascist methods of deception."[46]

On 2 September 1935, *The Worker* published the revised election platform of the CP under the banner headline,

ELECT A MAJORITY OF COMMUNISTS, CCF CANDIDATES!

For the first time, the Communists admitted that the CCF was *not* a capitalist party, but was in fact a "part of the progressive forces in Canada today." The platform, however, went on to declare that this classification did not apply to many, perhaps most, of the CCF leaders, who, according to the CP, were "reactionary."

What was the criterion, according to the platform, by which most CCF leaders were judged "reactionary" and some "progressive"?

> The CCF candidates who oppose Communist candidates offer no program to the masses. They are acting as pawns of reactionary groups, splitting the united front and defeating the common interests of all progressive forces of the Canadian people.

By this standard A.A. Heaps, Labour MP for North Winnipeg since 1925, was labelled "reactionary" because he would not step aside in favour of Tim Buck of Toronto, who was brought in by the party to contest that riding.

In spite of the fact that this platform was drawn up well after the Seventh Congress of the Comintern, it did not advance a new analysis of the CCF by the Communist party of Canada, nor did the election campaign that followed, in which the party's attention was focused on the bitter battle waged between Tim Buck and A.A. Heaps.

A further, but not much different, analysis was made in the latter half of 1936 with the publication by the party of a 119-page book entitled *What the Communist Party Stands For*. According to this book the CCF was divided into three factions: right, centre, and left. It is dominated by "the old guard, Woodsworth and his group...who are rock-ribbed reactionaries, who refuse to admit that only a united front with the Communists can hurl back the attacks of the capitalists on the workers."

The centre "agrees in words with, and pays lip service to, the analysis of the Communist party on the need of unity within the ranks of the working-class, but in action carries out all the policies of the right wing and thus prevents unity."

The left faction "realizes the importance of united working-class action and, as in Toronto on May Day 1936, assists in the organization of real mass demonstrations of working-class strength."[47]

According to this analysis, the criterion that distinguished the three factions in the CCF was their attitude to a united front with the Communists, an attitude gauged by whether or not they were willing to take part in May Day and other street demonstrations.

The last official word by the Communist party of Canada during the united front period was contained in a 1939 pamphlet by Leslie Morris, "The Story of Tim Buck's Party 1922-1939." The main theme of this analysis was that the criticism by the party made in G. Pierce's book *Socialism and the CCF* failed to differentiate between the "hundreds of thousands of supporters" who sincerely believed in socialism via the CCF and "Mr. Woodsworth and a group of intellectuals with little experience in or knowledge of the throbbing labor movement."[48]

The denunciation of the CCF as "social fascist" or "labour fascist" was not mentioned in Leslie Morris's pamphlet. Even though this was the main ingredient that had poisoned the relations between Communists and social democrats, it was ignored in Canada. In fact, it was not until the Soviet Union admitted in 1971 that this had been a grievous mistake[49] that most Communist parties, including the Canadian, confessed that it had been an error.[50]

After the fiasco in CCF-Communist relations in the federal elections of 1935, the party adopted a novel proposition for carrying out the popular front in the political arena. In his speech to the Eighth Convention of the CPC in October 1937, entitled "The People vs. Monopoly," Tim Buck proposed "a democratic coalition." The coalition was to be made up of Communists, CCFers, Social Crediters, reform Liberals, Young Conservatives, and followers of H. H. Stevens, a former member of the Bennett Cabinet, all working to defend Canadian democracy from a forthcoming onslaught by the reactionary alliance of R. B. Bennett, Ontario Tory leader George Drew, Ontario Liberal Premier Mitchell Hepburn, and Quebec Premier Maurice Duplessis, which had all the potential for evolving into a fascist coup.[51] This proposal had already been rejected by the CCF on the grounds that it would divert the CCF from its struggle to establish itself as a strong Social Democratic political party from coast to coast.[52]

Buck's entire speech stood in sharp contrast to the speeches and resolutions of the previous party convention in July 1934, which was held under the slogan "For a Soviet Canada." At that convention, the language and the concepts were revolutionary in the extreme, although this was a continuation, even if in sharper words, of the tone of the party's previous six national gatherings. The Eighth Convention was, however, a point of departure. Here the language was soft and moderate, hardly distinguishable from that heard at gatherings of other political parties. Not only had the language changed, so had the ideas. The program was now stressing social reforms, democratic liberties, patriotism, and labour rights, including the incorporation of trade unions into the legal framework of the federal and provincial governments, a demand which had been repugnant to the Workers' Unity League. The achievement of socialism was still the ultimate goal, but it had to be put aside because of the urgency of the struggle for peace and democracy against fascism. Repeating the slogan that Dimitrov issued at the Seventh Congress, Buck declared:

> The decisive issue being fought out in the capitalist countries today is not fascism versus communism but fascism versus democracy.[53]

When Dimitrov first issued that slogan, it was accompanied by the directive that the Communist parties must shift from emphasizing the struggle for socialism to "the defence of the immediate economic and political interests of the working class.[54]

This represented a major tactical change, because previously the CPC had scorned any attempt to put immediate demands ahead of socialist goals. This had caused some tension between the few spokespersons that the

Canadian party had succeeded in getting elected to municipal bodies, and the local and national leaderships. Now these aldermen and school trustees could pursue the immediate issues with a clear conscience that they were not betraying Marxism-Leninism in so doing. In fact, at the Eighth Convention Tim Buck issued this appeal:

> A hundred Communist aldermen throughout Canada will be one of the best guarantees that civil liberties will be defended, that adequate relief will be provided for the unemployed, that children will be cared for and the burden of municipal taxation distributed more democratically than at present.[55]

Although they did not achieve that ambitious target, Canadian Communists were beginning to elect municipal representatives, including such well-known party officials as J.B. Salsberg and Stewart Smith to the Toronto City Council, John Weir to the Toronto School Board, and the Communists in Winnipeg, who were the first to elect two aldermen succeeded in 1938 in electing a third. Jim Litterick, the party's Manitoba leader, was elected to the Legislature in 1936, coming second out of ten in the multi-member riding of Winnipeg. In the 1935 federal elections, most of the Communist candidates for the House of Commons increased the Communist vote in their constituencies, Tim Buck leading this increase with 7,276 votes in North Winnipeg, and J.B. McLachlan with 6,450 votes in Cape Breton South. (Tim Buck came third, while A.A. Heaps was re-elected with 12,093 votes. McLachlan was second to the Liberal incumbent and resigned from the CP soon after because of its alliance with John L. Lewis.) There is no doubt that the improved standing in the Communist votes throughout the country was in some measure the result of the party's taking elections more seriously and paying more attention to the issues involved at each of the three levels of government.

The extent of the party's change in attitude can be seen in its submission to the Royal Commission on Dominion-Provincial Relations (Rowell-Sirois). The brief, which the party titled "Toward Democratic Unity for Canada," contained 123 pages of closely argued analyses of the strengths and weaknesses of Confederation. The argument supported the party's main demand—namely, that the federal government be given more powers at the expense of the provinces, to legislate social programs such as unemployment insurance, national minimum wage levels and living conditions, national health insurance, national standards of education, and guaranteed "minority rights" for the French Canadians in Quebec.[56]

This document was obviously prepared with great care and precision. The research was the work of several professionals in this field, including Alex Skelton, secretary of the Commission.[57] It presented an argument for the policies of the Mackenzie King government, although it went beyond them on several issues. It was very similar to the brief of the League for Social Reconstruction, the unofficial "brain trust" of the CCF, especially in its emphasis on strong central government.[58] Both submissions stressed the need for more federal power to enable the federal government to achieve progressive reforms for the whole country, but they also revealed an unmistakable bias toward central government with or without the social measures proposed.

The new tactics of the Communist party, the rising prestige of the Soviet Union because of its stand in the League of Nations to stop the advance of fascism, and the support for the popular front government of Spain increased the pressure within the CCF and within the labour movement for a united front in Canada. The provincial conventions of the CCF, together with the annual national convention, were witnesses to this conflict. Resolutions from many branches became the subject of heated debate as to whether or not to accept some or all of the appeals from the Communist party.[59] One of the most bitter fights took place in the Saskatchewan CCF over the decision made in 1938 by the CCF North Battleford federal constituency association to run Dorise Nielsen as a Unity candidate in the next federal elections, over the objection of the provincial executive.[60]

The arguments that the leadership advanced against a united front with the Communists had little or nothing to do with the policies involved. J.S. Woodsworth kept insisting that the CCF had fought and continued to fight in Parliament, in the legislatures, in the municipal governments, and in the trade union movement for all the issues which the Communists advocated as the basis of an alliance. His central objection to a united front was the unpopularity of the Communist party among average Canadians. Any association between the two parties, he said, would tar the CCF with the wrong brush. The CPC was, in Woodsworth's view, bound by the rules of the Comintern but would not be bound by the decision of a federated party. The Soviet Union, he asserted, was engaged at that very moment in history in purging most of the leaders who emerged under Lenin at open show trials in Moscow; this affected not only the people put to death after rigged trials but also thousands who were disappearing, never to return. The CCF could never be silent about its condemnation of these bloody purges, and the Communists could never do anything but support Stalin. How could these two parties, he asked, belong to the same political federation?

Yet the appeals by the Communist party were supported by a number of prominent intellectuals. One of the outstanding figures in Winnipeg who joined the united front was ex-Judge Lewis St. George Stubbs, who had been removed from the bench by R.B. Bennett for siding with people who were brought before him for stealing food or for participating in strikes or demonstrations. At the time he was ousted, *The Worker* warned its readers in Winnipeg not to enter into any united front relationship with this man, because having been a judge meant that he was a member of the capitalist class. Several readers wrote to protest such a narrow view, but it was not until a few years later, when the party was making the united front its prime task, that Stubbs became a valued ally, especially after he was elected to the Manitoba Legislature.[61]

Prior to the Seventh Congress of the Comintern, intellectuals had never been made welcome in party ranks. This was especially so under Stalin's regime. R. Palme Dutt, himself an intellectual and a close associate of Stalin, warned his colleagues as late as 1932 that they were in the party only on sufferance:

> [T]here is no special work and role for Communists from the bourgeois intellectual strata.... The intellectual who has joined the Communist party...should forget that he is an intellectual (except in moments of self-criticism) and remember only that he is a Communist.[62]

After Dimitrov's speech, however, everything changed. Intellectuals were accepted inside the party or on its fringes with respect, given special assignments, and especially were encouraged to take part in united front activities as "fellow travellers." In Canada, several cultural institutions were sponsored by the party, including the Progressive Arts Club, the Theatre of Action, and two magazines, *New Frontiers* and *Always Ready*, the latter being a lively magazine for children, edited by Dorothy Livesay.

Another lesson from the Seventh Congress that the Communists had to learn was the difference between "bourgeois nationalism" and "national nihilism." Dimitrov said Communists must shun the former without becoming practitioners of the latter. Readers of *The Worker* who might have missed that phrase from Dimitrov's speech must have been astonished by a heading in the 19 October 1935 issue:

COMMUNISM IS CANADIAN

Communist Party—a product of the Soil of the Canadian Labour Movement—A Canadian Party.

The American party was a bit more imaginative when it came out with this slogan:

COMMUNISM IS TWENTIETH-CENTURY AMERICANISM!

It could be argued, as it was at the time, that there was nothing wrong with either slogan. It had merely taken a long time for them to appear in Marxist-Leninist journals. It was only four years previously that an article by a party leader had appeared in *The Worker* denouncing the Ukrainian members for allowing the mandolin orchestra to sing and play "O Canada" at their national convention.[63] Now party members could do such things with a clear conscience, and they started doing them in an organized and more substantial way. One of the first results of a study of the Canadian heritage by Marxists was the publication by Stanley B. Ryerson of *1837—The Birth of Canadian Democracy*, and the naming of the Canadian contingent to the International Brigade in Spain the Mackenzie-Papineau Battalion.[64] The party's brief to the Royal Commission, cited above, was a major study of the political economy of Canada, the first of many.

The party began losing interest in further pursuing the united front with the CCF. Instead it became more anxious to follow its connections with the Liberal party. On 1 March 1939, the Vancouver *News Herald* carried an item headed "Vote Liberal, says Communist." Norman Freed, executive secretary of the Communist party, in a public address in Nanaimo stated that in the next elections, the Communists would give support to the Liberal government of Mackenzie King because it supported progressive policies, and was susceptible to mass pressure. Though he would like to see J.S. Woodsworth or Tim Buck as prime minister of Canada, he said, such a course was not possible now. The sane alternative was to re-elect the King government to prevent fascism in Canada.

The Communist party had made some tangible gains after the inauguration of the popular front tactic. It had ended its isolation, particularly in the labour movement. It had no success, however, in improving its relations with most of the leaders, members, and supporters of the CCF. It never really tried. Instead, from the beginning, it resorted to issuing ultimatums to the CCF leadership and imagined that, by so doing, it would separate the members, and perhaps even the second-line leaders, from the Woodsworth, Coldwell, Lewis, Heaps, and Frank Scott group. On the other hand, it had made important connections in the Liberal party through some of the main AFL-TLC leaders with whom it began to work out a labour political strategy to isolate the CCF, or at least to provide a counterweight to the CCF. The Communists were making remarkable progress in the CIO, which at that time was still in the TLC in Canada, and began working on a similar political strategy with some of the CIO leaders.

They also believed, however, that with the new connections in the AFL, TLC, and CIO, and with the support of some Liberal MPs in strong labour constituencies, such as Paul Martin in Windsor, they could become the Labour wing of what later did in fact emerge: a Liberal-Labour alliance. This had nothing to do with the main theme of the Seventh Congress—namely, a Communist-Social Democratic unity of the working class. Much of the new orientation ordered by the Comintern to end the so-called "third period" was beneficial to the Canadian party, but in its overall relations or lack of them with social democracy, the party's practice was still firmly rooted in the old tactic.

The black cloud of war loomed over Europe almost from the beginning of 1939. The Eighteenth Congress of the CPSU opened in March; in his speech to the opening session, Stalin dropped a hint of what might happen. He declared that the Soviet Union was "not going to pull the chestnuts out of the fire" for Britain and France. That ominous remark was translated into action in August, when the Soviet Union and Germany signed a non-aggression pact which permitted Hitler to move against Britain and France, knowing that the Soviet Union would not be at war with Germany.

Thus ended the era of the popular front. The Soviet Union had tried to utilize the Western Communist parties, particularly in France, to change the policies of their own governments to one of resistance to Hitler's drive to the East. It did not work and the Soviet Union, now isolated, deflected for a time an inevitable German attack.

The recasting of the Communist parties along the Seventh Congress blueprint brought about a complete change in the outlook of these parties, their tactics, and their alliances. Most of them, including the Canadian party, benefited greatly from these changes. In a few months, however, all of these benefits disappeared as the Communist parties, following the lead of the Soviet Union, opposed the war and were completely isolated as a result.

NOTES

1. R. Palme Dutt, *Fascism and Social Revolution* (New York: International Publishers, 1934), ix, x, xi.

2. Ibid., 286.

3. Ibid. After such a brilliant prognosis, Dutt was modest enough to explain to the Seventh Congress, a year later, how he was able to make such analyses: "We are able scientifically to predict the inevitable outcome because we are able to analyze the social conditions governing the consciousness, and the line of development of these social conditions." Quoted by Raphael Samuel in an article in *New Left Review* (London, March/April, 1986), 105.

4. G. Pierce, *Socialism and the CCF* (Montreal: Contemporary Publishing, February 1934), 143.

5. Georgi Dimitrov, *United Front Against Fascism*, 6th ed. (New York: New Century Publishers, September 1947), 112-13

6. Quoted in Hugo Dewar, *Communist Politics in Britain* (London: Pluto Press, 1976), 103.

7. J. Stalin, Report to the Seventeenth Congress of the CPSU (B), 26 January 1934, in J. Stalin, *Works*, Vol. 13 (Moscow: Foreign Languages Publishing House, 1953), 308-9.

8. Supra note 5, 31-2.

9. Jane Dégras, ed., *The Communist International Documents*, Vol. 3 (London: Frank Cass & Co. Ltd., 1971), 239.

10. Report of Congress, American Committee for Struggle Against War (New York, 1932), 4.

11. Supra note 9, Vol. 3, 239.

12. Philippe Robrieux, *Histoire intérieure du parti communiste 1920-1945* (Paris: Fayard, 1980), 419.

13. Report of the First Canadian Congress Against War and Fascism (Toronto, 1934), 20-2. See R. S. Kenny Papers at the Robarts Library, University of Toronto.

14. A. M. Stephen, *Hitlerism in Canada* (Vancouver: Canadian League Against War and Fascism, 1936). The author was a well-known poet of the day.

15. E. H. Carr, *The Comintern and the Spanish Civil War 1936-1939* (New York: Pantheon Books, 1984), 3-4.

16. *International Solidarity With the Spanish Republic 1936-1939* (Moscow: Progress Books, 1974). Also see Carr, supra note 15, 23: "No Russian joined the international brigades."

17. See Ted Allan and Sydney Gordon, *The Scalpel, the Sword* (Boston: Little, Brown and Company, 1952), 157-67; Roderick Stewart, *Bethune* (Toronto: New Press, 1973); David E. Shephard and Andrée Lévesque, (eds.), *Norman Bethune* (Ottawa: Canadian Public Health Association, 1982); *Bethune: Speech on Socialized Medicine* (Guelph: Alive Press).

18. See Victor Hoar, *The Mackenzie-Papineau Battalion* (Toronto: Copp Clark, 1969); *Steve Nelson, American Radical* (Pittsburgh: University of Pittsburgh, 1981), 183-239; John Gerassi, *The Premature Antifascists* (Westport, Connecticut: Praeger, 1986).

19. House of Commons Debates, 19 March 1937, 1939-62.

20. Ross Dowson, "A Tribute to Henry Scott Beattie," in *Forward* (5 January 1972); W. Krehm, *Spain: Revolution and Counter-Revolution* (Toronto, 1939).

21. Hoar, supra note 18, 41.

22. Supra note 9, Vol. 1, 307.

23. Harvey Klehr, *The Heyday of American Communism* (New York: Basic Books, 1984), 319-23. See also Donald H. Avery, *Canadian Communism and Popular Front Organizations*, paper presented at the Annual Conference of the Learned Societies, University of British Columbia, June 1983, 7.

24. Preamble to the Catalogue of the Canadian Youth Congress Papers (Hamilton: McMaster University).

25. Ben Lepkin, "The Youth Army Matches," in *Winnipeg Free Press Magazine* (10 September 1938), 3. See also Thompson and Seager, *Canada 1922-1939* (Toronto: McClelland & Stewart, 1985), 317, for the stand of French-Canadian Catholics on the Spanish Civil War.

26. Resolution at the Enlarged Plenum, Central Committee of the CPC, February 1931, 26.

27. Tom Ewen, "Unity Is the Workers' Lifeline," Report to the Third Dominion Convention of the WUL, 9 November 1935, 28.

28. Supra note 9, 365-6.

29. Supra note 27, 18.

30. Ibid., 19.

31. Ibid., 30.

32. Harvey Klehr, supra note 23, 228-30.

33. Harvey Levenstein, *Communism, Anticommunism and the CIO* (Westport, Connecticut: Greenwood Press, 1981), 49.

34. "The WUL Fights for Unity," Report by the "Fraction Secretary" to the Ninth Plenum of the Central Committee of the CPC, November 1935, and published under the title *Towards A Canadian People's Front*, 126, by the Central Committee, Communist party of Canada.

35. Harold A. Logan, *Trade Unions in Canada* (Toronto: Macmillan, 1948), 84 (Table 8).

36. Earl Browder, *The People's Front* (New York: International Publishers, 1938), 39.

37. Tim Buck, *The People vs Monopoly* (Toronto: New Era Publishers, 1937), 45. Report delivered to the Eighth Dominion Convention of the CPC, 8-13 October 1937.

38. J. B. Salsberg, "Maintain and Extend Trade Union Unity," in *A Democratic Front for Canada*, Reports, Speeches, and Resolutions at the Thirteenth Session of the Dominion Executive of the CPC, June 1938, 76.

39. "We Propose," Resolutions of the Eighth Dominion Convention of the CPC, 8-12 October, 1937, 11.

40. Supra note 27, 26.

41. CCF-NDP National Office Correspondence, PAC, MG28 IV-I: Items 160 (30 August 1937); 161 (30 August 1937); 162 (21 September 1937); 163 (27 September 1937).

42. Ibid., Item No. 143.

43. *The Worker*, 15 September 1934.

44. Daniel R. Brower, *The New Jacobins* (Ithaca, NY: Cornell University Press, 1968), 50-2.

45. Woodsworth Papers, PAC.

46. Tim Buck, "Statement to the Working People of Canada," in *The Worker*, 9 January 1935.

47. CPC, *What the Communist Party Stands For* (Montreal: Contemporary Publishers, 1936), 47.

48. Leslie Morris, *The Story of Tim Buck's Party* (Toronto: New Era Publishers, 1939), 25-6.

49. Central Committee of the CPSU, *Outline History of the Communist International* (Moscow: Progress Publishers, 1971), 312.

50. CPC, *The Canadian Party of Socialism* (Toronto: Progress Books, 1982), 109.

51. Supra note 37, 10-19, 31-41.

52. David Lewis, in *The Canadian Forum*, September 1936, 6-8.

53. Supra note 37, 39.

54. Supra note 9, 362.

55. Supra note 37, 44.

56. "Toward Democratic Unity For Canada," Stewart Smith, ed., CPC's Submission to the Royal Commission on Dominion-Provincial Relations, 1939.

57. Interview with one of the three top leaders of the CPC of that period by Norman Penner in 1986.

58. "Canada—One or Nine," Submission to the Royal Commission on Dominion-Provincial Relations by the League For Social Reconstruction, 1938.

59. Papers of The Cooperative Commonwealth Federation of the New Democratic Party 1918-1976, PAC, MG28 IV-I.

60. Ibid., Letter No. 58.

61. *The Worker,* 21 January 1933; 28 January 1933; 5 August 1933; also see Lewis St. George Stubbs, *A Majority of One* (Winnipeg: Queenston House, 1983).

62. R. Palme Dutt, *Communist Review,* September 1932, quoted in Jim Fyrth, ed., *Britain, Fascism, and the Popular Front* (London: Lawrence & Wishart, 1985), 160-1.

63. John Wevursky (Weir), "Federalism, Opportunism, and the Ukrainian Question," in *The Worker,* 10 January 1931.

64. Stanley Ryerson, *1837—The Birth of Canadian Democracy* (Toronto: Francis White Publisher, 1937).

THE FORMATION AND RISE TO POWER OF THE UNION NATIONALE

BY HERBERT QUINN

o

The Union Nationale had its origin in a revolt which took place within the ranks of the Liberal party in the early 1930s. This revolt began when a group of young left-wing Liberals, who called themselves L'Action Libérale Nationale (A.L.N.), became dissatisfied with the party's conservative economic policies and the tight control exercised over the party organization by Taschereau [Liberal Premier of Quebec] and a few close colleagues. The leader of the A.L.N. was Paul Gouin, the son of a former Liberal Prime Minister of Quebec and grandson of Honoré Mercier. Gouin and his associates, like most of the younger generation, had been influenced greatly by the nationalistic ideas of Bourassa, Groulx, and members of L'Action Nationale (formerly L'Action Française). As a consequence, they were alarmed at the threat which industrialism presented to the survival of the traditional French-Canadian culture and were critical of the close ties which existed between the Taschereau administration and the foreign capitalists.[1]

The original plan of the A.L.N. was to reform the Liberal party from within by forcing it to shift to the left in its economic and social policies and by persuading it to adopt a more nationalistic philosophy. However, within a short time the Gouin group became convinced of the futility of trying to reform the party or break the control of the ruling oligarchy. As a result, the A.L.N. severed all connections with the Liberals shortly before the provincial election of 1935 and set itself up as a separate political party. Aside from Gouin, other key figures in the A.L.N. at that time were Oscar Drouin, who was to become chief organizer of the new party, J.E. Grégoire, mayor of

Excerpt from Herbert Quinn, *The Union Nationale: Quebec Nationalism from Duplessis to Lévesque* (Toronto: University of Toronto Press Incorporated, Second Edition, 1979), pp. 48-72. Reprinted with permission of University of Toronto Press Incorporated.

Quebec City, and Dr. Philippe Hamel, a dentist by profession, also from Quebec City. Both Grégoire and Hamel were bitter enemies of what they termed "the electricity trust" and for some years had been campaigning for the nationalization of the power companies.

When the A.L.N. was launched it met with a favourable response from many sections of the population since its ideas conformed with the nationalist ideology then sweeping the province. It was endorsed by the influential L'Action Nationale,[2] and was looked upon favourably by the Union Catholique des Cultivateurs[3] and other Catholic Action groups. The new party had one handicap, however; most of its key figures had had little practical experience in politics. Very few of them had ever been candidates in either provincial or federal elections or played any kind of active political role before. In contrast, their Liberal opponents were skilled politicians, strongly entrenched in office, and with a powerful and well-financed political machine. Moreover, in a province where traditional habits of voting were an important factor in politics, the Liberals had been looked upon as the party of the French Canadian ever since 1897. In many families, particularly in the rural areas, political affiliation was inherited with the family farm, and a large number of people were Liberal for no better reason than the fact that their fathers had always voted that way. It was only too apparent that Taschereau's administration was not going to be easily dislodged by a new and untried party, led by a group of young men who, however idealistic and enthusiastic, had little knowledge of the "know how" of the political game. For all these reasons there were obvious advantages for the A.L.N. in making an alliance with some other group equally opposed to the Liberal administration but with more political experience and with a better electoral organization. The only group which could meet these requirements was the provincial Conservative party. A brief look at the political history of this party will indicate why it might be receptive to such an alliance.

The Conservative party had been the official opposition in the Quebec Legislature ever since its defeat at the polls in the election of 1897. From that time onward it was only on a few occasions that the party had been able to capture sufficient seats to present the Liberals with any kind of challenge. It suffered from its close association with the federal Conservative party which was, of course, looked upon by the average voter as the party of "British Imperialism," and, above all, as the party which had imposed conscription in 1917.

The leader of the Quebec Conservative party during the greater part of the 1920s was Arthur Sauvé, member of the Legislative Assembly for the electoral district of Deux Montagnes, who had become party leader in 1916. Acutely aware of the disadvantageous position in which his party was placed by its close connections with the federal Conservatives, Sauvé was determined to make every effort to dissociate the Quebec Conservative party from its federal counterpart. When the nationalist movement of Abbé Groulx and L'Action Française began to gain ground following the brief postwar depression of 1921 Sauvé adopted most of its ideas and slogans. He also gave his party a new orientation in matters of economic and social policy.

Although the Conservatives, like the Liberals, had been staunch supporters of laissez-faire capitalism during most of their history, the party now took a turn to the left. Sauvé began to criticize the role of foreign capital in the industrial development of the province and to attack the Liberals for their generous concessions to the business interests. In one election speech he made this statement: "Our natural resources must serve not only the ends of speculators, but the welfare of contemporary classes and of the generations to come.... The government...has sold our wealth to foreigners who shared with ministers and politicians, while our own people emigrated from the province." Sauvé proposed "that we develop, as far as possible, our natural resources by our own people and for our own people."[4]

Sauvé's attempt to dissociate his party from the federal Conservatives was only partly successful. It is true that the new orientation which he gave the Quebec Conservative party won it the editorial support of *Le Devoir* and *L'Action Catholique*,[5] and that it was soon on friendly terms with such groups as the U.C.C. whose agitation for a government-sponsored scheme of low-cost rural credit had been turned down by the Liberals. Sauvé was not able, however, to convince the vast majority of voters that the Quebec Conservatives were completely independent of the federal organization.[6] The reason for this failure is not hard to find. Sauvé's party still contained a strong right wing which was closely associated with the business interests and had strong ties with the federal Conservatives. This right wing had always been critical of his policies. In giving up the leadership shortly after the defeat suffered by his party in the 1927 election, Sauvé attacked this group for its hostile attitude.

> Une fraction du parti conservateur fédéral a toujours été hostile à ma direction. On m'accuse de nationalisme. Le nationalisme que j'ai prêché et pratiqué est celui de Cartier, c'est le conservatisme intégral et foncièrement national.... Mes efforts n'ont pas été couronnés de succès. Il convient donc que je laisse le commandement du parti.... [7]

In 1929 Camillien Houde, mayor of Montreal and member of the provincial legislature for Montreal-Ste Marie, succeeded Sauvé as party leader. Houde was a colourful politician who was to play an important role in municipal and provincial politics for the next twenty years. In the eastern and working class section of Montreal where he had been brought up Houde was affectionately known as "le petit gars de Ste Marie." Like Sauvé, Houde was a nationalist with radical ideas, but he showed a greater readiness to compromise on policy if the situation demanded it. Moreover, he was a much more dynamic and hard-hitting politician than his predecessor.

In the election campaign of 1931 Houde followed the same line of attack as Sauvé. His main accusation against the Liberals was that they had turned over the natural resources and wealth of the province to foreign capitalists, and he referred to them as "a nest of traitors to their race and their province."[8] His platform consisted of a number of social reforms which the trade unions, the farmers' organizations, and other groups had been demanding for a long time: government pensions for widows and the aged, a reduction in electricity rates, an intensified program of colonization [of northern Quebec], the establishment of a Ministry of Labour, and a government-sponsored scheme of low-cost rural credit.[9] Houde waged a vigorous campaign in all parts of the province and hopes were high in the ranks of the party that it would be able to defeat the Liberals. However, the latter emerged victorious once more and Houde himself lost his seat in the Assembly. When he resigned from the leadership a year later the party decided to call a convention made up of delegates from all parts of the province for the purpose of selecting a successor.

The Quebec Conservative party's convention was one of the most famous in the history of the province. Before the convention met, the name most prominently mentioned for the leadership was Maurice Duplessis. The son of a judge and a lawyer by profession, Duplessis had started his career in politics when he was elected as a Conservative member to the Legislative Assembly from the electoral district of Three Rivers in 1927. (He was to be returned to the legislature by that constituency in every election from that time until his sudden death in 1959.) Duplessis soon built up a reputation in the Assembly as a clever debater and able parliamentarian. He was also adept at those skillful manoeuvres which are an asset in rising to the top in the field of politics. A short while after Houde lost his seat in the Legislative Assembly in the election of 1931, Duplessis was chosen as temporary leader of the party in that House.

When the Conservative convention started its proceedings in the city of Sherbrooke on 3 October 1933, the delegates were divided into two factions.[10] One of them supported Duplessis as leader, and the other supported Onésime Gagnon, a Conservative member of the federal Parliament. The Gagnon faction has been organized by Camillien Houde, who was determined to block Duplessis' bid for the leadership. Houde's antagonism towards Duplessis arose out of a disagreement which had developed between these two forceful personalities shortly after the 1931 election over matters of party strategy. But Houde was not successful in his attempt to prevent Duplessis from capturing the leadership. While the latter had been temporary leader of the party in the Assembly he had built up a considerable following within the party ranks, and, as a result, he had control of the party machine by the time the convention was called. The chairman of that convention was one of his supporters. Moreover, he had the influential backing of most of the Conservative members of the federal Parliament from Quebec, and these federal Conservatives participated in the convention as voting delegates. When the time came for the balloting Duplessis was elected leader by 334 votes to 214 for his opponent.

Although it was not apparent at the time, the political ideas of the new Conservative leader differed from those of Sauvé and Houde in one very important respect. Duplessis was certainly a nationalist, but he was by no means a radical. As subsequent events were to show, he was a "practical politician" whose main objective was to defeat the Taschereau government and put the Conservative party in its place rather than to bring about sweeping economic and social reforms. However, it was only after the Union

Nationale's victory over the Liberals in 1936 that the economic conservatism of Duplessis was to be fully revealed.[11]

When Duplessis took over the Conservative leadership he inherited a party which had won only fourteen out of ninety seats in the previous election, a party whose chances of defeating the Liberals did not appear to be any brighter than they had been at any other time during the preceding thirty-five years. There were obvious advantages, with little to lose, in making an alliance with another group, such as L'Action Libérale Nationale, which was equally opposed to the Liberals. If the Conservative party could supply the practical knowledge of the techniques of politics and some of the financial backing, the A.L.N. could provide new men, new ideas, and considerable popular support.

Thus, a short while before the provincial election of 25 November 1935, Duplessis and Gouin entered into negotiations with a view to forming a united front against the Taschereau administration. These negotiations were successful and on 8 November the two leaders issued a joint statement announcing that their respective parties had joined forces against the Liberals. This statement read in part, "Répondant au désir de l'électorat du Québec, le parti conservateur provincial et L'Action Libérale Nationale déclarent par leurs représentants attirés qu'aux élections du 25 novembre, ils présenteront un front uni contre l'ennemi commun du peuple de la province de Québec: le régime Taschereau."[12] The new coalition was to be known as the Union Nationale Duplessis-Gouin.

The Duplessis-Gouin combination was soon joined by a number of independent nationalists who had hitherto taken little or no active part in politics, although many of them were leaders of various Catholic Action and patriotic organizations. The outstanding figures among these independents were Albert Rioux, a former president of the U.C.C., and René Chaloult, a Quebec City lawyer who was one of the directors of L'Action Nationale.

Undoubtedly one of the most important aspects of the Union Nationale was the nature of the program which it presented to the electorate. This program was significant in two respects: for the first time in the history of the province a political movement presented to the electorate a clear-cut and comprehensive set of proposals for economic, social and political reform; secondly, this program was to lay down the basic principles which were to be followed by all reform movements in the province for the next decade or so. It is essential, therefore, to understand just how this program originated, and the particular proposals for reform it put forward.

...the nationalist intellectuals of the twenties, in spite of their campaign against the industrial system, had never formulated any concrete and coherent program of social reform and had not been in agreement as to how the industrialists were to be curbed. In other words, their critique of the economic system was stronger than their positive suggestions for its transformation. With the spread of nationalistic sentiments to the masses of the people in the early thirties it soon became apparent that such a constructive program was urgently needed. It was the Roman Catholic hierarchy which provided the nationalists with the positive proposals for which they had been looking, proposals which were the result of a new orientation taking place in the social thinking of the Church after 1930.

Any discussion of the social philosophy of the Roman Catholic Church, whether in Quebec or elsewhere, must start with the encyclical letter, *Rerum Novarum*, of Pope Leo XIII, which appeared in 1891. This encyclical set forth the basic principles which were to underlie the Church's approach to labour and social problems.... In his encyclical Leo XIII rejected both socialism and economic liberalism as solutions to the problems of an industrial society. The rejection of socialism, it should be emphasized, was not merely because it involved the abolition of all right to private property and proposed the establishment of a completely collectivized economy, but also because the continental socialism of Leo's day, under the influence of Marxist doctrines, was strongly anti-religious and sometimes militantly atheistic. The consistent opposition of the Church to socialism since that time cannot be fully understood unless this vital point is kept in mind.

In opposition to the philosophy of economic liberalism, the Pope insisted that the state had a special obligation to intervene in the economy and protect the standard of living of the wage earner and other depressed classes. He criticized the treatment of labour as a mere commodity which is bought and sold in the market, and condemned the exploitation of workers by employers. He also defended the right of workers to organize into associations to promote their interests.

Although *Rerum Novarum* was, of course, not unknown to the Church in Quebec, Leo's critique of industrial capitalism and his call for reform had comparatively little impact on Catholic thought in that province until the depression decade. Even in the 1920s, when the Church had become aware of the challenge which the industrial system presented to the religious and cultural values of French Canada, it still showed comparatively little grasp of the serious social problems resulting from that system, and particularly of those which affected the urban worker. It is true, of course, that the Catholic trade union movement and other Catholic Action organizations founded in the 1920s were to a certain extent inspired by *Rerum Novarum*. It has been pointed out..., however, that the primary concern of the hierarchy in setting up these organizations was to promote the religious and moral advancement of their members rather than their economic well-being, although the latter objective was not altogether overlooked.[13]

There were a number of reasons for this neglect of the social problems of a capitalist civilization on the part of the Church in Quebec, but the most important one was the predominantly "ruralistic" character of the clergy's thinking—their preoccupation with the problems of a rural society and their strong belief that the trend towards industrialization could be reversed. In so far as the clergy did become aware of some of the problems faced by the urban worker, such as unemployment, the remedy suggested was more likely to be a return to the land than the introduction of unemployment insurance.

In the early thirties a change took place in the social thinking of the Quebec hierarchy and it was prompted to put forward a program of reform which would come to grips with the problems of an urban and industrial society. An immediate reason was that the breakdown of the capitalist system in the depression focused attention on certain social problems arising out of that system which could no longer be ignored. Even more persuasive was the appearance in 1931 of the encyclical, *Quadragesimo Anno*, of Pope Pius XI. This encyclical was the most important papal pronouncement on social questions since *Rerum Novarum*, and had a tremendous influence on Catholic thought in all parts of the world, including Quebec. Its purpose was to reaffirm the basic principles laid down in the earlier encyclical and to clarify and reinterpret those principles in the light of the changes which had taken place in industrial capitalism since the 1890s. Like his predecessor, Pius rejected both laissez-faire capitalism and socialism, although recognizing that one wing of the latter movement, democratic socialism, had moved away from the more extreme position of the Marxists. The Pope's critique of capitalism was expressed in statements such as this: "...the immense number of propertyless wage earners on the one hand, and the superabundant riches of the fortunate few on the other, is an unanswerable argument that the earthly goods so abundantly produced in this age of industrialism are far from rightly distributed and equitably shared among the various classes of men."[14] As a remedy for this situation, he called for a redistribution of private property.

A related consideration, nearer to home, also prompted the Quebec hierarchy to take a particular stand on the problems arising from the industrialization of that province. The depression had resulted in widespread dissatisfaction with the capitalist system, and unless the Church put forward a program of reform within the framework of Catholic social philosophy it was quite conceivable that it would be faced by the growth of a socialist or communist movement which might very well be not only secularistic but even militantly atheistic. The need to take some positive action seemed all the more imperative to the hierarchy, when the Cooperative Commonwealth Federation (CCF), an avowedly socialist party, was formed in western Canada in 1932 and announced its intention of spreading its doctrines to all provinces. An eminent theologian who had been assigned the task of making a careful study of the social philosophy of the new party came to the conclusion that the CCF "did not merit the support of Catholics" because of its promotion of the class war, its extensive program of socialization, and "its materialistic conception of the social order."[15] A different solution to the problems of the day was imperative.

The responsibility for the formulation of the Church's program of reform was entrusted by the hierarchy to an organization sponsored by the Jesuit Order in Montreal called the Ecole Sociale Populaire. This was not actually a school in the ordinary sense but an organization which had been set up before the First World War for the purpose of studying and propagating the teachings of the Church on a wide range of moral, educational, and social problems.

The Montreal Jesuits did not themselves draw up the proposed program. Instead, they called together a group of prominent Catholic laymen and gave them the assignment of outlining a set of proposals which would be a concrete application of the principles put forward in *Quadragesimo Anno* to the specific conditions and problems peculiar to Quebec. This group of laymen was composed of individuals playing a leading role in all phases of French-Canadian life: the Catholic trade unions, the farmers' organizations, the cooperatives and credit unions, the patriotic and professional societies, the universities. The most prominent members of the group were Albert Rioux, president of the Union Catholique des Cultivateurs; Alfred Charpentier, one of the leaders of the Catholic unions; Wilfrid Guérin, secretary of the Caisses Populaires, or credit unions, in the Montreal area; Esdras Minville, a professor at the Ecole des Hautes Etudes Commerciales in Montreal; and Dr. Philippe Hamel and René Chaloult of Quebec City. Most of these people were also directors of L'Action Nationale.

The Ecole Sociale Populaire published the conclusions arrived at by this study group in a pamphlet entitled *Le Programme de restauration sociale* which appeared in the fall of 1933.[16] This pamphlet contained proposals for reform in four different areas. "Rural Reconstruction" suggested the steps which should be taken to strengthen and even extend the agrarian sector of this economy; "The Labour Question" put forward an extensive scheme of labour and social legislation which would raise the incomes and provide greater economic security for the working class; "Trusts and Finance" dealt with measures which should be taken to curb the power of the public utilities and other large business enterprises; and "Political Reforms" called for legislation which would eliminate patronage politics and electoral and administrative corruption.

We come now to the immediate background of the program of the Union Nationale. The relationship of this program to the proposals of the Ecole Sociale Populaire can be traced back to the formation of L'Action Libérale Nationale. Paul Gouin, its leader, had not been a member of the group of Catholic laymen who had drawn up and formally affixed their signatures to *Le Programme de restauration sociale*, but he was in general sympathy with the ideas put forward for he had participated in some of the discussions leading up to the final proposals. It was not too surprising, therefore, that when he launched the A.L.N. a short while later he adopted the Ecole Sociale Populaire document as the basis for his own program.[17] He did, however, make some minor changes and included a few additional proposals of his own. When the alliance with Duplessis was arranged the following year one of the basic conditions which Gouin insisted upon was that the Conservative leader accept the complete A.L.N. program. In the light of later developments it is important to make it quite clear that Duplessis agreed to this condition at the time.[18] One of the clauses in the joint statement issued by the two leaders announcing the formation of the Union Nationale states this firmly:

> Après la défaite du régime anti-national et trustard de M. Taschereau, le parti conservateur provincial et L'Action Libérale Nationale formeront un gouvernement national dont le program sera celui de l'Action Libérale Nationale, program qui s'inspire des mêmes principes que celui du parti conservateur provincial.[19]

One other significant aspect of the Duplessis-Gouin program should be mentioned here. The fact that the reforms proposed by the two leaders were based on *Le Programme de restauration sociale* was a decisive factor in winning the support of such influential figures as Rioux, Hamel, and Chaloult, all of whom had participated in the drawing-up of the Jesuit-inspired program.

A brief summary of the more important proposals put forward in the program of the Union Nationale Dupesssis-Gouin of 1935 is now in order.[20]

AGRARIAN REFORMS

Reforms in the field of agriculture were given top priority in the Union Nationale's plan of action. They included a government-sponsored scheme of agricultural credit at low rates of interest, the extension of rural electrification, subsidies for certain types of farm products, government assistance in marketing, development of small and medium-size industries in rural regions which would be complementary to the farm economy. The monopolistic control exercised by "the milk trust" over the processing and marketing of dairy products was to be destroyed through the organization of farmers' cooperatives. Emphasis was placed on an extensive back-to-the-land and colonization program under which the government would spend large sums of money in building roads, schools, and churches and in draining the land. A special commission made up of independent experts and government officials would be set up to organize this program.

LABOUR AND SOCIAL REFORMS

In this area it was proposed that the laws governing minimum wages, hours of work, and industrial hygiene be strengthened and extended. A Labour code was to be drawn up which would bring together and clarify all existing labour legislation. The Workmen's Compensation Act was to be revised so as to give the workingman greater security and indemnity in case of injury. Industry would be compelled to give priority to wages over dividends and to provide the worker with an income which would not only give him a fair standard of living, but also enable him to acquire property. The social legislation proposed included health insurance, pensions for needy mothers (that is, married women with children whose husbands had died or deserted them), old-age pensions, and a slum clearance program.

INDUSTRIAL AND FINANCIAL REFORMS

The program called for "the destruction, by every possible means, of the stranglehold which the large financial institutions, the electricity trust and the paper industry trust have over the Province and the municipalities." Aside from the pulp and paper and power companies, the "trusts" which were singled out for particular attention were the coal, gasoline, and bread companies. It was proposed that a publicly owned hydroelectric system be established as a solution to the problem of high electricity rates. Its first task would be to develop all the unexploited water power resources of the Province. At the same time a special commission would be appointed to investigate the feasibility of the government gradually taking over all privately owned companies engaged in the production and distribution of electric power. The commission would be asked to determine whether the cost to the government of such a takeover would still permit a reduction of rates. The coal, gasoline and bread companies would be subjected to competition from state-owned enterprises in these fields if such a step was felt to be necessary in order to reduce prices. A thorough investigation would be made of the structure and methods of financing of all public utility companies in order to determine the extent of such abuses as watered stock and doctored financial statements. There would be a reduction in the rate of interest charged by banks on loans. The Companies Act would be more rigidly enforced.

GOVERNMENTAL AND ELECTORAL REFORMS

Under this heading it was suggested that cabinet ministers be prohibited from becoming shareholders or having any other form of financial interest in any company receiving contracts from the government. In addition, ministers would be barred from serving on the directorates of banks, insurance companies, financial houses, railways, or any company exploiting the province's water power or forest resources. Compulsory voting would be introduced, and a limitation would be placed on the amount of money which individuals or business concerns could contribute to the electoral funds of any political party. All voters in cities with a population over 10,000 would be required to have identification cards.

One of the most important features in this section of the program was the suggestion that Quebec's upper house, the Legislative Council, be abolished and replaced by an economic council which would act as an advisory body to the Legislative Assembly on all economic matters. This proposal was a step in the direction of the corporative system advocated by Pope Pius XI in his encyclical *Quadragesimo Anno*. Under this system employers and employees in each industry would be organized into a professional association or corporation, which would have considerable authority to make decisions regarding prices, wages, and general policy for that industry. All corporations would be joined together in an economic council at the top which would formulate policy for the economy as a whole.[21]

The comprehensive program summarized above indicates the wide extent of the economic, social, and political changes which the Union Nationale proposed to introduce. It also provides us with some valuable insights into the nature of the assumptions and basic principles underlying the whole approach of both the nationalists and the Church in the 1930s to the question of social reform.

In the first place, it is evident that the nationalists, like the Church, still idealized the rural way of life and were not yet fully reconciled to the new industrial society. They still hoped to maintain, or even to expand somewhat, the relative importance of the agrarian sector of the province's economy.

Secondly, their avowed aim of breaking the domination of foreign capital over the economy and bringing about French-Canadian participation in the wealth and natural resources of the province was to be accomplished by five different methods: (a) A policy of social legislation and higher wage scales which would enable the wage earner to acquire property; (b) The formation of cooperatives which would compete with the large monopolies in some fields and thus curb their power; (c) Encouragement and assistance to small- and medium-scale French-Canadian business establishments; (d) Government regulation and control of public utilities and other large-scale business enterprises; (e) Government ownership of certain industries, but only as a last resort, and provided that such a step was deemed absolutely necessary for the well-being of the community as a whole.

Finally, it can be said that the program taken as a whole, and following the inspiration of *Quadragesimo Anno* and other papal encyclicals, attempts to pursue a middle road between laissez-faire capitalism and socialism. Its objective is the redistribution of private property rather than its elimination. It is also interesting to note that in many respects Union Nationale's proposals were similar to those being incorporated about the same time in Roosevelt's New Deal in the United States.[22]

The formation of the Union Nationale meant that for the first time since the days of Honoré Mercier in the 1880s, a powerful nationalist movement had arisen to play an important role in provincial politics. Like Mercier's party, the Union Nationale was determined to maintain all those traditional values and rights which had always been considered essential for cultural survival. It differed, however, in that it was also concerned with a problem which, in the nature of things, Mercier did not have to contend with. This was the Union Nationales's determination to raise the economic status of the French Canadian by bringing about extensive reforms in the system of industrial capitalism. For this reason the Duplessis-Gouin coalition must be described, not merely as a nationalist movement, but as a radical nationalist movement.[23]

Perhaps the greatest source of strength of the Union Nationale was the fact that it had the unofficial, but nevertheless effective support of all the various Catholic Action and patriotic organizations across the province: the Catholic trade unions, the farmers' organizations, the cooperatives and the credit unions, the youth organizations, the associations of French-Canadian businessmen and merchants. All of these organizations were supposed to be neutral in politics, but...they were all strongly nationalistic and therefore opposed to the Liberal party's policy towards the industrialists.[24] Moreover, many of the leaders of these organizations had participated in drawing up the program of the Ecole Sociale Populaire which the Union Nationale had adopted. Needless to say, the new movement also had the enthusiastic backing of such nationalist publications as *L'Action Nationale* and the Montreal daily, *Le Devoir*. There was little doubt too that, although the hierarchy was careful that the Church as such should not become directly involved on one side or the other in the political struggle, most of the clergy were sympathetic towards the political movement which had adopted its program of social reform.

As a result of the wide support behind the Union Nationale the Liberals, for the first time in nearly forty years, were presented with a real challenge to their continued control over the provincial administration. The seriousness of this threat was to become apparent in the election of 1935, the first test of strength of the Duplessis-Gouin combination.

THE UNION NATIONALE COMES TO POWER

When Paul Gouin and a few other young Liberals formed L'Action Libérale Nationale in 1934 and began to attack the policies of the Liberal "old guard," neither Taschereau nor any of his colleagues took the new movement very seriously. It was only when the Gouin group began to win wider support, and then joined forces with the Liberals' traditional enemy, the Conservative party, that Taschereau slowly began to recognize the serious nature of the challenge with which he was faced. He was still confident, however, that his party would be able to weather the storm and retain control over the provincial administration as it had done so often in the past.

There were several good reasons for Taschereau's confidence. Although many Quebec voters might be dissatisfied with Taschereau's economic policies, the Liberal party was still looked upon as a staunch defender of the Quebec point of view on such vital issues as provincial autonomy and relations with Britain. Another factor was that the party's control over the provincial administration placed it in the advantageous position of being able to spend government money and give out government jobs in a purely partisan fashion. When the budget was drawn up each year the administration made sure that a good portion of the allocations to each department could be spent at the discretion of the minister, that is, in those ways which would be of most benefit to the party. Since the province lacked a nonpartisan competitive system for the selection of governmental personnel, the way was left open for all sorts of patronage. The Liberals held a further advantage in that their huge majority in the legislature enabled them to manipulate the electoral machinery along lines which would provide the greatest handicap to the opposition forces. This can be illustrated by a bill which the party put through the legislature in 1931. Shortly after the election of that year a large number of defeated Conservatives contested the election of their Liberal opponents before the courts. The Conservatives sought to nullify the election of these Liberals on the grounds that they had been guilty of fraudulent practices on polling day. While litigation was still under way the Liberal majority in the legislature pushed through a law, popularly known as the Dillon Act (after the name of its sponsor) and applying retroactively to the 1931 election which removed all such cases from the jurisdiction of the courts.[25]

When the election of 1935 was called, Taschereau toured the province denouncing the Union Nationale coalition as "un mariage qui va se terminer par un désastreux divorce."[26] He accused Duplessis of abandoning the principles for which the Conservative party stood and attacked Gouin for betraying the ideals of his father, Sir Lomer Gouin, who had preceded Taschereau as leader of the Liberal party. Taschereau also defended the policies which his administration had pursued in the past and contended that these policies had been of immeasurable benefit to the farmer, the worker, and other sections of the population. Although the Liberals had never shown much enthusiasm for the Ecole Sociale Populaire program,[27] Taschereau promised to introduce some of the reforms which it put forward, such as old-age pensions and a government-sponsored scheme of low-cost farm credit.

However, the Liberals did not rely solely on the introduction of a few reforms to win the support of the electorate. They had even more tangible benefits to offer. As in the past the government embarked on an extensive program of public works several months before the election. New roads, public buildings, and bridges were built, or at least started, in all parts of the province. Some of these projects were discontinued the day after the election. The public works program provided additional, if temporary employment, and meant sizable government orders for local hardware merchants and shopkeepers in various towns and villages. Whenever the government provided a community with some badly needed public facility it was able to present itself as a "benefactor" which had "done something" for that particular town or district. This was an important consideration for the average Quebec voter when he was trying to decide which party to vote for. Government candidates in most electoral districts also spent fairly large sums of money on the distribution of drinks of "whisky blanc" and handed out other gifts and favours which might help to convince the voters that the Liberals were "des bons garçons."

The willingness of the Liberal party to use any and all methods to win an election is exemplified in the operation of its well-oiled electoral machine in the Montreal area on polling day. When the polls opened it soon became apparent that the names of many voters who were known to be opponents of the régime had been left off the voting lists. At the same time hundreds or even thousands of fictitious names might have been added to these lists in a particular electoral district. Impersonation of voters, or "telegraphing," was carried out on a large scale, and in certain polls where the party might be expected to do poorly some of the ballot boxes disappeared altogether. In several constituencies "strong arm" squads went from poll to poll intimidating voters, and then proceeded to smash up the committee rooms of the opposition. These activities were often carried out under the eye and sometimes with the tacit approval, of election officials and the provincial police.[28]

The well-entrenched position of the Liberals, and their readiness to use all kinds of questionable tactics, obviously placed the Union Nationale in a disadvantageous position in the election campaign of 1935. However, shortly after the date of the election had been announced, the new coalition entered candidates in every electoral district and proceeded to wage a vigorous campaign in all parts of the province. Its appeal to the electorate was for the most part based on the comprehensive program of economic and social reform summarized above. The Union Nationale leaders also made strong attacks on the administrative and electoral abuses of the Taschereau government. In spite of the many handicaps under which it fought the election, the Duplessis-Gouin combination succeeded in capturing a total of forty-two seats, almost four times the number of seats held by the Conservative opposition in the previous legislature. Although the Liberals, with forty-eight members elected, still maintained control over the administration, they had only a narrow margin of six seats—five after the Speaker had been selected.

The results of the election were a serious setback for the Taschereau régime. The gains made by the Union Nationale coalition completely changed the situation in the legislature where the Liberals had always had an overwhelming majority and had thus been able to put their legislative program through with a minimum of obstruction. After the 1935 election the government was not only faced by a large and vigorous opposition, but one of the leaders of that opposition, Maurice Duplessis, was an astute politician who knew all the tricks of the parliamentary game.

When the 1936 session of the legislature was called, Duplessis used the many delaying tactics of the experienced parliamentarian to hold up the passing of the budget until such time as the government agreed to enact some of the proposals outlined in the Union Nationale program. The result was that as time went on the government found itself in increasing financial difficulties. The most telling blow struck by Duplessis, however, and the one which was to sound the death knell of the Taschereau régime, was the information he was able to bring to light concerning the administration's handling of public funds.

Ever since the early 1920s, the Conservative party had been accusing the Liberals of graft, corruption, and inefficiency in the administration of government departments. Owing to the weakness of the party in the legislature, however, it had never been able to coerce the government into setting up a parliamentary inquiry to investigate these alleged irregularities. The Public Accounts Committee, which was supposed to maintain a close check on how public money was being spent, had not met for a long time. Even if it had been called into session at any time before the election of 1935, the huge Liberal majority would have been able to dominate proceedings and prevent any serious investigation from taking place. In the legislature of 1936, however, the Liberals no longer enjoyed this strategic advantage. The opposition was not only successful in bringing the Public Accounts Committee back to life, but the strength of its forces in the Committee made it difficult for the Liberals to control the inquiry.

The Public Accounts Committee was in session from 5 May to 11 June, and under the skilful probing of Duplessis it quickly brought to light a picture of patronage, nepotism, and the squandering of public funds which involved most government departments.[29] It was discovered that members of the administration, from cabinet ministers down to the lowest level of the civil service, were using the contacts and influence which they had as government officials to increase their private incomes and those of their friends and relatives. Certain officials made a substantial income by selling materials of all kinds to various government departments at very high prices. One such case involved the director of the government-run School of Fine Arts who made sizable profits from the sale of automobile licence plates to the government.[30] The Treasury lost many thousands of dollars every year through the inflated travelling expenses of ministers and other individuals; this was especially true of the expenditures of the Department of Colonization.[31] One of the most startling discoveries was that a brother of the Prime Minister, who was the accountant of the Legislative Assembly had been putting the interest on bank deposits of government money into his own personal account. His only defence was that all his predecessors in the position of Assembly accountant had done the same thing.[32]

Another case investigated by the Committee concerned certain activities of the Assistant Attorney General. When the latter was questioned by Duplessis as to whether he had from time to time received fees for legal counsel from companies exploiting the province's natural resources he refused to answer.[33] A few days later he resigned from his government position. It should be mentioned here that for many years it had been common practice for the Prime Minister himself, as well as a good number of his ministers, to accept appointments to the board of directors of many of these companies. Although there was nothing illegal in this practice, it is obvious that it could result in a serious conflict of interests and loyalties when these companies came to the government for some new concession. Taschereau had always justified his acceptance of these directorships by arguing that, "the head of a government should meet business men around a directors' table, learn about business, and give the province the benefit of it."[34]

The Public Accounts Committee also found a good number of instances where unsuccessful Liberal candidates and other friends of the party had been put on government payrolls at unusually high salaries or had been paid some kind of commission or fee without having to do much work.[35] In some cases special positions or assignments were created for these individuals. The Prime Minister himself had no less than forty-five of his relatives employed in various government departments.[36]

One other interesting aspect of the committee's investigations was that they showed how the Liberals used their control over the provincial administration to build up a powerful political machine. In colonization regions, for instance, government subsidies and other forms of financial assistance to new colonists were not sent to the latter directly, but were turned over to the Liberal member or local organizer in that district, who saw to it that the money was distributed in ways which would be of greatest benefit to the party.[37] The government indirectly bought the support of a number of newspapers in the province by handing out sizable printing contracts at generous prices and by spending large sums of money on publicity and advertising for the various government departments.[38]

The revelations of the Public Accounts Committee created a sensation throughout the province and completely discredited the Taschereau administration. Around the beginning of June, when the committee was still in the midst of its deliberations, Taschereau suddenly announced his resignation as Prime Minister and recommended to the Lieutenant Governor that Adelard Godbout, Minister of Agriculture, be appointed in his place. At the same time the Legislative Assembly was dissolved and a new election was called for the following August.

Godbout was a logical choice for Prime Minister, for he was one of the few members of Taschereau's cabinet who had not been involved, either directly or indirectly, in the scandals of the administration. In selecting his cabinet the new Liberal leader reduced the number of ministers from fourteen to ten, and appointed only four members from the previous government.[39] Like Godbout himself, these men had not been involved in the investigations of the Public Accounts Committee. The strategy of the Liberals was to go before the electorate with "a government of new men," as they termed it. In an attempt to dissociate himself from the Taschereau regime, Godbout did not try to defend the policies of his predecessor, but instead promised that a Royal Commission of Inquiry would be set up to investigate every aspect of the provincial administration.

Godbout appeared determined to set up a government, not only of new men, but also of new policies, for he recognized the extent of the dissatisfaction throughout the province with the economic system and the widespread desire for social reform. When the election campaign of 1936 got under way he put forward a program which was similar in many respects to that of the Union Nationale. The main proposals in that program were: an extension of rural credit facilities, a program of rural electrification, and the provision of subsidies on certain farm products; an intensified colonization program; a sweeping reduction of electricity rates throughout the province; a public works program to solve the problem of unemployment; a minimum wage scale for industrial workers not covered by collective labour agreements, and the introduction of certain amendments to the Workmen's Compensation Act requested by the trade unions; the establishment of a system of needy mothers' allowances; and the elimination of the practice of cabinet ministers accepting directorships from companies doing business with the government.[40]

The most important difference between Godbout's appeal to the electorate and that of the Union Nationale was that the Liberal leader refrained from making a direct attack on the large corporations and business interests, and there was no attempt to stir up the nationalistic sentiments of the Quebec voter. Moreover, the Prime Minister, himself a farmer, tended to concentrate his efforts on winning the support of the rural rather than the urban voter. When announcing his progam he stressed the vital role of agriculture in the economy: "Restaurer l'agriculture pour restaurer toute notre vie économique; c'est le fond même de notre politique."[41] There was a very practical aspect to this strategy of emphasizing the concern of the Liberals for the interests of the farmer. Although the farm population of the province had been declining for many years, the rural vote was still the decisive factor in elections. This was because of the distorted nature of the electoral system, which gave the rural areas approximately 63 per cent of the seats in the legislature in spite of the fact that by 1931 only 37 per cent of the people of Quebec lived in rural districts.[42]

The Union Nationale entered the election campaign under the leadership of Maurice Duplessis. Paul Gouin had had a disagreement with the former Conservative leader and had quit the coalition shortly after the dissolution of the legislature.... Gouin's defection had little immediate effect on the strength of the Union Nationale as most of his Action Libérale Nationale followers, including such prominent figures as Oscar Drouin, Dr. Philippe Hamel, and J.E. Grégoire, remained in the coalition with Duplessis.

The election of 1936 was to demonstrate that the deathbed conversion of the Liberal party to social reform and honest administration had come too late. All through the election the opposition forces attacked the Liberals for the administrative and political corruption of the Taschereau regime and refused to absolve the Godbout government from the sins of the previous administration. They strongly denied that it was "a government of new men." As stated by Duplessis, "M. Godbout est l'héritier de M. Taschereau.... En politique comme ailleurs, l'héritier d'un régime assume la responsabilité des dettes et des méfaits de son auteur.... "[43] In another speech later in the campaign he repeated the charge that there had been no real change of direction: "Le gouvernement Godbout est une nouvelle pousse des branches décrépites du gouvernement Taschereau.... Pouvez-vous avoir confiance en un régime qui refuse de punir les voleurs d'élections en favorisant des lois électorales malhonnêtes? Lorsqu'un régime refuse de protéger la source même de la démocratie, on ne peut avoir confiance en lui."[44] Duplessis promised that if the Union Nationale was elected to office it would continue the investigations begun by the Public Accounts Committee into the administrative practices of the Taschereau regime, and all those found guilty of misusing public funds would be punished. A clean sweep would be made of the whole administration, graft and corruption would be eliminated, and an end would be put to the squandering of government money.

The Union Nationale also attacked the Liberals for promoting the interests of the large business corporations while ignoring the serious predicament of the unemployed and neglecting the needs of the common people. The administration was referred to as "ce régime de véritable trahison nationale" because of the extensive concessions it had granted to the companies exploiting the province's natural resources.[45] In a radio address one prominent Union Nationale candidate stated, "Ce mot 'Union' signifie la solidarité entre tous les gens de bonne volonté, afin de mettre à la raison les trusts et les monopoles qui ont été protégés jusqu'ici par le régime

Taschereau-Godbout-Bouchard et qui ont travaillé dans l'intérêt des financiers et des capitalistes, au détriment du peuple et de la masse des électeurs."[46] The trusts which were usually singled out for attack were the pulp and paper, timber, mining, coal, gasoline, and power companies. The opposition to the power companies was particularly strong as this industry was considered to be the most important single factor in "la dictature économique" which controlled the province.

Perhaps one of the most telling aspects of the Union Nationale's campaign was its appeal to the nationalistic and anti-English sentiments of the French-Canadian population. Antagonism towards the English reached a peak as Union Nationale orators, in meeting after meeting, warned the people of Quebec that their cultural values and their traditional way of life were threatened by the dominant role played by the British, American, and English-Canadian industrialists in the economic life of the province. The strong feelings of the nationalists towards "les étrangers" were forcibly expressed in a speech delivered at a mass meeting in Montreal by Dr. Philippe Hamel, the outstanding opponent of the large corporations, and particularly of "le trust de l'électricité":

> Or notre patrie, notre foi, nos traditions, nos libertés, tout cela est menacé. Nos ressources naturelles, elles ont été vendues par le régime pour un plat de lentilles aux étrangers. Vos foyers, ouvriers, on est en train de vous les arracher et déjà la lutte s'organise contre votre clocher par de sourdes menées anticléricales qui se font plus audacieuses et violentes.[47]

At another meeting Hamel's close associate, J.E. Grégoire of Quebec City, spoke in similar vein of the usurpations of "les étrangers":

> ...une calamité nous étreint de toutes parts. Chacun est exploité, l'épicier canadien-français, le bûcheron, le petit propriétaire. Les meilleures places sont prises par des étrangers.... Les usines sont fermées, parce que notre province a été vendue aux étrangers. Les produits agricoles ne se vendent pas, parce que l'on a fermé nos débouchés.[48]

On every possible occasion Duplessis and other prominent figures in the Union Nationale expressed their determination to take whatever steps were necessary to protect the interests of the small-scale French-Canadian business enterprise engaged in a life and death struggle with the larger and more firmly entrenched English-owned corporations. This meant the small independent grocer in competition with the large chain stores, the small insurance broker against the large companies, and the small manufacturing concern against the larger establishments. It was also promised that legislation would be enacted compelling the large corporations controlled by foreign capital to hire more French Canadians in the higher supervisory and managerial positions.

The Union Nationale's appeal to the nationalistic sentiments of the French Canadian, and its promises of economic, social, and administrative reform, met with an unequivocal response from the electorate. When the time came for the balloting the people of Quebec turned the Liberal party out of office and elected the nationalist movement led by Maurice Duplessis. The Union Nationale won seventy-six out of the ninety seats in the legislature, while the Liberals with only fourteen seats were now in the novel position of being the official opposition.

The chain of events leading to the Union Nationale victory of 1936 shows two things. First of all, the Quebec voter seemed to be convinced that the time had come for a government housecleaning, the elimination of graft and corruption and the introduction of extensive reforms in administrative and electoral practices. Even more important, the success of this new nationalist movement was a clear indication of the strong opposition which had developed to the Liberal party's policy of promoting the industrialization of the province through the intervention of foreign capital. The defeat of the Liberals was a protest, not only against an economic system which had changed the traditional way of life and brought economic insecurity in its wake, but also against the dominant role played by English-speaking industrialists in that system. This protest was accompanied by a demand that the new capitalist economy be reformed and modified and that positive steps be taken to enable the French Canadian to regain control over the wealth and natural resources of his province. The direction these reforms were to take was to be determined by the principles of social Catholicism as laid down in the encyclicals of Pope Leo XIII and Pope Pius XI.

NOTES

1. Many of Gouin's ideas are to be found in a number of speeches which he delivered to various groups in the 1930s and which are collected in his *Servir*, I, *La Cause nationale* (Montreal, 1938).

2. Maison Wade, *The French Canadians, 1760-1945* (Toronto, 1955), 906.

3. See statement of A. Rioux, president of U.C.C., *Le Devoir*, 7 août 1934.

4. *Montreal Star*, 10 May 1927.

5. Robert Rumilly, *Histoire de la Province de Québec*, XXVI, *Rayonnement de Québec* (Montréal, 1953), 157.

6 This was an important factor in the Liberal victory over the Conservatives in the provincial election of 1927. See Jean Hamelin, Jacques Letarte, and Marcel Hamelin, "Les Elections provinciales dans le Québec," *Cahiers de Géographie de Québec*, 7 (oct. 1959-mars 1960), 39. See also, "L'Election provinciale de 1927: les conservateurs de Québec battus par les conservateurs d'Ottawa," *Le Devoir*, 11 fév. 1950.

7. Robert Rumilly, *Histoire de la Province de Québec*, XXIX, *Vers l'âge d'or* (Montréal, 1956), 98.

8. *Montreal Star*, 6 July 1931.

9. *Canadian Annual Review*, 1932, 165.

10. A detailed description of the organization and proceedings of the convention is to be found in *La Presse*, 30 sept.-5 oct. 1933. See also Pierre Laporte, "Il y a 25 ans, la convention de Sherbrooke," *Le Devoir*, 1-3 oct 1958.

11. See *infra*, 73-5.

12. *Le Devoir*, 8 nov. 1935.

13. See *supra*, 40-1.

14. Pope Pius XI, *Quadragesimo Anno* (London, 1931), 29.

15. R.P. Georges Levesque, O.P., "La Cooperative Commonwealth Federation," *Pour la restauration sociale au Canada* (Montréal, 1933). An even stronger condemnation of the C.C.F. was made a year later by Archbishop Georges Gauthier of Montreal. See *Montreal Gazette*, 26 Feb. 1934. This ban on the party was not to be lifted until the bishops of Canada, both English and French, issued a joint statement in 1943 declaring that Catholics were free to support any Canadian party except the Communists. See *Canadian Register* (Kingston), 23 Oct. 1943.

16. A. Rioux et al., *Le Program de restauration sociale* (Montréal, 1933).

17. Gouin acknowledged his debt to the Ecole Sociale Populaire in a speech which he delivered in August, 1934: "Nous avons pris comme base d'étude et de discussion, pour préparer notre manifest, le program de Restauration sociale publié sous les auspices de l'Ecole sociale populaire...ce document reflétait de façon assez juste non seulement l'opinion de nos esprits les plus avertis mais aussi les sentiments, les aspirations et les besoins populaires." *Le Devoir*, 13 août 1934.

18. See *infra*, chap.v.

19. *Le Devoir*, 8 nov. 1935.

20. This program first appeared in *Le Devoir*, 28 juillet 1934, when it was the program of L'Action Libérale Nationale. A few weeks later Gouin delivered a speech in the town of St. Georges de Beauce in which he provided further amplification and explanation of his proposals. See *Le Devoir*, 13 août 1934....

21. Pius XI, *Quadragesimo Anno*, 36-44. The "professional corporatism" advocated in the encyclical is not the same as the "state corporatism" of Mussolini's Fascism. The latter system involves the total elimination of parliamentary democracy; the former merely suggests that some of the functions of government concerned with regulation and control over the economy should be entrusted to associations of employers and employees in each industry. The Church's corporatism finds its inspiration in the craft guilds of the Middle Ages and proposes to establish a system of self-government in industry similar in some respects to Roosevelt's N.R.A. [National Recovery Administration] codes of the early thirties. For a very brief but accurate description of the differences between Catholic and Fascist corporatism, see Ernest Barker, *Principles of Social and Political Theory* (London, 1961), 39-40.

22. When Paul Gouin formed his Action Libérale Nationale in 1934 he pointed out the similarity between his ideas and those of Roosevelt. See *Le Devoir*, 28 juillet 1934. There were, however, important differences between the two programs as well, such as the emphasis placed by Gouin on the agrarian sector of the economy.

23. In applying the term "radical" to the Union Nationale I mean only, of course, that its approach to economic policy was considered to be radical at the time. Many of its proposals for reform would not be considered very radical today.

24. The leaders of the U.C.C. had always been close to the old provincial Conservative party. Albert Rioux, president of the association until 1936, resigned his post to run as Union Nationale candidate in the election of that year. Several leaders of the Catholic unions supported Union Nationale candidates on the platform in the same election.

25. See *Canadian Annual Review*, 1932, 171.

26. *Le Devoir*, 11 nov. 1935.

27. When the program appeared Olivar Asselin, a prominent Liberal, stated, "It bears a greater resemblance

to a 'bleu' [Conservative party] pamphlet than to a work of social apostolacy." *Montreal Gazette*, 21 Nov. 1933.

28. The activities of the Liberal electoral machine in some of the Montreal constituencies in the election of 1935 are described in a series of articles in *Le Devoir*, 25 nov.-10 dec. 1935.

29. Although a stenographic report was made of the proceedings of the Public Accounts Committee, this report was never published. Consequently the discussion here of the evidence presented before the committee has had to be based on newspaper reports. For each case at least two sources have been referred to in order to make sure of the accuracy of the reporting. One of the main sources has been Montreal's *La Presse*, a newspaper which has usually been a strong supporter of the Liberal party. Another important source has been a series of articles published in *Le Devoir* shortly after the sessions of the committee had ended and entitled, "M. Godbout était ministre au temps des scandales révélés au comité des comptes publics." *Le Devoir* ws anything but friendly towards the Liberals at the time, but these articles are well documented and contain verbatim reports of many of the sessions.

30. See reports in *La Presse*, 13 mai 1936; *Le Devoir*, 23 juillet 1936; *Canadian Annual Review*, 1935-6, 283.

31. See *La Presse*, 9, 14, 29 mai and 2, 3, 4 juin 1936; *Canadian Annual Review*, 1935-6, 282-3.

32. See *La Presse*, 5, 6, 9, 10 juin 1936; *Le Devoir*, 6 août 1936; *Sherbrooke Daily Record*, 12 June 1936.

33. See *La Presse*, 15, 26 mai 1936; *Le Devoir*, 30 juillet 1936; *Sherbrooke Daily Record*, 12 June 1936.

34. *Canadian Annual Review*, 1928-9, 381.

35. For reports of some of these cases, see *La Presse*, 29, 30 mai 1936; *Le Devoir*, 13 août 1936.

36. Although this information is not directly based on evidence presented before the committee, it is nevertheless reliable. The Union Nationale organization made its own investigation into the Public Accounts and came up with a list of the names, occupations and salaries or fees of these forty-five relatives. See the party's booklet, *Le Catéchisme des électeurs*, (Montréal, 1936), 74-80. This publication is obviously partisan, but it is well documented.

37. See *La Presse*, 7 14 mai 1936; *Le Devoir*, 4, 13 août 1936.

38. See the case of the Quebec City newspaper, *Le Soleil*, as reported in *La Presse*, 29 mai 1936. *Le Catéchisme des électeurs*, 119-27, makes an analysis based on the Public Accounts for 1935 of the money paid out by the government to various newspapers in the province.

39. See *Sherbrooke Daily Record*, 28 June 1936.

40. These proposals were put forward by Godbout in a radio address. See *La Tribune* (Sherbrooke), 6 juillet 1936.

41. Ibid.

42. In 1936 there were 90 seats in the legislature. They are listed in Quebec, Legislative Assembly, *Report on the General Election of 1936* (Quebec, 1936), Appendix 1, 3-4. According to the 1931 census figures, 57 of these electoral districts were predominantly rural, and 33 were predominantly urban. Of the latter, 5 were in Quebec City, and 16 were in the Montreal metropolitan area. See *Census of Canada*, 1931 (Ottawa), II, Table 16.

43. *Le Devoir*, 24 juin 1936.

44. *La Tribune*, 6 août 1936.

45. See Union Nationale advertisement, *Le Devoir*, 15 août 1936.

46. *Le Devoir*, 15 août 1936.

47. Ibid., 13 août 1936.

48. *La Tribune*, 5 août 1936.

"I SWING TO THE LEFT": MITCH HEPBURN AND THE ONTARIO LIBERAL PARTY

BY JOHN SAYWELL

o

Mitch was not a poor man, but he had a much deeper personal experience of the Depression than either King or Bennett closeted in Ottawa. Mitch was a working farmer, who spent much of his time among Elgin farmers and St Thomas railwaymen. When not at home or in the Commons, he was on the road organizing the party, speaking in mining and mill towns, talking and drinking with local Liberals until the early hours of the morning. And as he lamented in the spring of 1932, the "suffering and privation one witnesses now in travelling throughout this land of ours would bring tears to the eyes of a Pharo [sic]."[1]

In that spring of 1932 it was difficult to imagine that the worst was yet to come. The captains of industry and finance no longer spoke of interruptions and dislocations. Sir Herbert Holt's assurance that "it is darkest just before dawn" may have comforted his Royal Bank shareholders, who received their customary dividend without the customary bonus, but it was of little consolation to the thousands without power because of unpaid hydro bills. The promised recovery in the summer of 1931, when 18 per cent of all wage earners in Ontario were unemployed, had not materialized. The ranks of the unemployed increased sharply over the winter, and by April trade unions reported that one-quarter of their members were unemployed, while many with jobs worked short shifts. Wages had held up reasonably well, but they too began to fall early in 1932.[2]

Some parts of the province suffered more than others. In April only one Torontonian in ten was on relief, but in the suburbs that had mushroomed during the 1920s the figure was one in five. In Oshawa and the Border Cities the automobile industry ran at one-sixth capacity. Three thousand people had fled Oshawa since 1929, and in East Windsor almost 40 per cent of the people were on relief. Much of northern Ontario was a wasteland. Failing commodity prices had closed many mines. Export markets and domestic consumption declined drastically and work in the logging camps came to a halt. Abitibi, typical of the troubled pulp and paper industry, closed half its mills. Single-industry towns were devastated. In the summer of 1931 two-thirds of the men in Sudbury had registered with the unemployment office and in the winter almost no one had a job in Sturgeon Falls. Transients moved restlessly from city to city, living in shack towns or squatter colonies like those in Toronto's Don Valley, where the men moved out of the ravines to panhandle in Rosedale or along the Danforth when the racoons returned from their night-time marauding.

Sporadic strikes produced few gains. Unionized or not, workers had little choice but to accept wage cuts or face unemployment. Organizing the unemployed became the special mission of the Workers' Unity League, an instrument of the Communist party, under the direction of Tom McEwen. Street demonstrations by the WUL led inevitably to confrontations with the police. Brigadier General Draper, chief of the Toronto city police and Major General Williams of the Ontario Provincial Police were not alone in their crusade to sweep the demonstrators from the streets. In August 1931 Attorney-General Price, encouraged by the federal minister of justice, ordered the arrest of McEwen, Tim Buck, and seven other communists. A compliant jury found them guilty under section 98 of the Criminal Code of being members of an unlawful association and of engaging in a seditious conspiracy. All received jail terms.

The players on Bay Street did not escape the ravages of the depression. Corporate profits slipped and the stock market continued its precipitous decline after the great crash of October 1929. By May 1932 it had fallen to 16 per cent of its 1929 peak and the paper value of fifty leading stocks had dropped from $6.2 billion to $880 million. There were fortunes to be made as Distillers Seagrams went begging at $3.50 and Imperial Oil at under $5.00. There were some with money to buy. Real wages of those who kept their job—civil servants, university professors, railway workers—improved as the cost of living fell 20 per cent between 1930 and 1932. The most fortunate were those with fixed-interest investments, the real value of which leaped 20 per cent. Life for many was not difficult, and life for the rich at the Hunt Club and the Royal Winter Fair, in Muskoka and Bermuda, went on much as before. Table talk about the newest colt or the pregnant maid, the troublesome headmistress at Bishop Strachan or the manliness of a Ridley master, tended to ignore the social misery on the other side of town.[3]

While the urban unemployed were the most visible and vocal casualties, Ontario farmers were also bleeding. Even with record farm incomes in 1928 and 1929—in part because of them—many farmers were overextended as the cost of new land, mechanization, and electrification was piled on old mortgages, and taxes rose faster than prices. Bountiful harvests in 1930 and 1931 were more than offset by falling prices. In Elgin wheat fell from $1.29 a bushel in 1929 to 50 cents in 1931; in 1932 Mitch got 48 cents for a bushel of beans that had brought $3.04 three years earlier. County agricultural agents monotonously reported prices below the cost of production, idle farms with food rotting in the ground, tractors left in barns as horses ploughed the fields, and many farmers unable to pay either their taxes or mortgage interest. By the end of 1931 the Henry government was forced to announce there would be no foreclosures on the $35 million farm mortgages held by the government.[4]

Mitch may have been in a quandary about how to solve the depression or relieve its acute distress, but he had no difficulty identifying those who suffered and those who did not. Those who did not certainly included the bankers, brokers, and bondholders who financed Henry's deficits at usurious interest rates; the oil companies who, behind Bennett's tariff, inflated the cost of crude to their Canadian subsidiaries, fixed prices, and exported their excessive profits to their American head offices; the tariff-protected manufacturers who cut wages to maintain profits; the middlemen who, as always, preserved an unconscionable price spread between producer and consumer; and the Tories, allies of all the exploiters, who showed little sympathy for the disinherited and used section 98 to sweep dissent from the street.

The Tories were an inviting target. During the 1930 campaign Bennett had attacked King for refusing to accept responsibility for the unemployed. Promising to end the dole, Bennett provided $20 million for provincial and municipal relief works and $4 million for direct relief, with the provinces and municipalities paying two-thirds of the cost. By the spring of 1932 the works program was an admitted failure as the costs far outweighed the benefits. Direct relief, however degrading, was financially ten times as efficient, and in 1932 grants to the provinces to pay for the dole became Bennett's answer to unemployment. In May 35,000 heads of families, their 110,000 dependants, and 5,000 single men and women in Ontario were dependent on direct relief. One year later they would number more than half a million.[5]

Mitch's criticism of reckless expenditures and irresponsible budgeting under Ferguson and Henry hit home when both local and provincial governments insisted they could not shoulder more of the financial burden of direct relief or public works projects. Ferguson had deliberately delegated more responsibilities to the local governments, and equally deliberately had denied them access to a broader tax base. Free of provincial control, municipal expenditures had soared beyond increases in the taxable assessment. Even before the Depression struck, many cities and towns had found the debt charges unbearable and were borrowing to meet current expenditures. As tax collections fell off leaving many municipalities on the verge of defaulting, in December 1931 Henry gave the Ontario Municipal Board power to declare a moratorium on debt repayment and in effect to act as trustees for insolvent municipalities. While the Border Cities were the first to go under, all the Toronto suburban governments, most of the northern resource towns, and even some of the older cities of central Ontario soon followed.[6]

As Mitch charged, the province also had borrowed heavily against the future. By 1930 Ontario's debt was the highest in the country as a percentage of revenue. Since Ferguson and Henry had charged public works and relief expenditures to the capital account, the debt soared. By 1931 the debt charges absorbed 21 per cent of total revenue and the bankers were insisting that the government control expenditure, make some provision for debt retirement, and increase taxes. Although the province had the lowest revenue as a percentage of income in the country, Henry was reluctant to do little more than levy modest increases on gasoline, liquor, and the minuscule corporation tax. Mitch promised that with the Liberals in office the rich would not get off so lightly.[7]

As the Depression deepened there was less humour and more anger in Mitch's attacks on the managers and defenders of the status quo. His friends noticed a new truculence when the session began in February 1932. Within a few days he had demanded the repeal of section 98 and asked whether the troops, stationed on Parliament Hill to defend it against a march of the unemployed, had orders to shoot. He attacked Bennett for giving the oil companies a tariff behind which they raked in excess profits of S20 million and pressed successfully to have the Banking and Commerce Committee, on which he sat, investigate the price of gasoline. Nor was he in any mood to put King's constitutional niceties above the interests of Canadian farmers when Bennett proposed to provide emergency seed grain under the lapsed 1931 Unemployment and Relief Act before it was passed again. King was determined to oppose the measure, and was angered by the opposition in caucus. "It is surprising how shortsighted some of the best men are, they want the 'immediate' thing, they see the need for seed grain, for relief in their constituencies & wd. jettison all Liberalism has fought & stood for to meet an immediate situation. I was surprised a little at Brown and Vallance— disgusted with Elliott and felt Hepburn was not big enough for a leader when all favoured not opposing the Govt. making grants under a 'dead statute'."[8]

When the bill came up for renewal, however, Mitch was one of the most effective opposition speakers. While King attacked form, he attacked substance: Bennett had used the act to give the banks a $29 million guarantee against losses on loans to the western wheat pool; to permit insurance companies to make a retroactive evaluation of their common stock assets; and to enable the cabinet to increase appropriations for the RCMP, buy riot bombs, and hire a secret service. In fact, Bennett had used the act "to give the glad hand to the big interests and the mailed fist to the unemployed." The backbenchers loved it; King admitted it was "a fighting speech" but described it as "claptrap."[9]

Mitch had already upset the establishment with another attack on Sun Life. Unlike most of its competitors, Sun had invested aggressively in common stocks and by 1930, despite repeated warnings from the superintendent of insurance that such a heavy investment "might at some time cause embarrassment to the company if not loss to the insuring public," had half its assets in stocks. As the market continued its steep decline in 1931 the company became increasingly vulnerable and, following another sudden plunge in September, G.D. Finlayson, the superintendent of insurance, informed Bennett that Sun's assets had fallen at least $15 million below its liabilities. Sun rejected Finlayson's request not to issue its usual dividend, and instead successfully appealed to Bennett to use an order-in-council under the Unemployment and Relief Act to permit insurance companies to value their stock retroactively as of 1 June 1931. Citing the real value of Sun's assets, J.J. Harpell charged in his *Journal of Commerce* that Sun was close to insolvency but had added $3 million to the shareholders' account at the expense of the policy holders. He enlisted Mitch's support to bring it before the Commons.[10]

Bennett was convinced the attack on Sun would shake the precarious foundations of Canadian finance and undermine the financial stability of the country. Britain had gone off the gold standard in September; the Canadian dollar had fallen as hundreds of millions of Canadian obligations were due to mature in New York; many securities firms were teetering on the edge; and several banks were severely overextended in the West Indies and South America. In October 1931 Bennett had called in the press on several occasions to discuss the perilous financial situation and plead for moderation. When Harpell's article was published in December, Bennett wired Howard Ferguson to see Harpell, then in London, and urge him "in the national interest" to stop the attack on Sun Life, "which may result in a run upon all companies for cash surrender of policies, with consequent liquidation at forced sale of Canadian bonds and complete demoralization of financial structure of the Dominion." Harpell replied bluntly that a return to a "sound industrial system" demanded the denunciation of "robbers" such as Wood, Gundy and T.B. Macaulay. When Bennett later warned him of the danger of a libel suit, Harpell said, "I prefer to go to jail."[11]

Michael Luchovitch, the UFA member for Vegreville, first raised the matter in the Commons, and Bennett solemnly asked the House to dispose of the resolution quickly and quietly so that no damage would be done to the company, "the men, women and children in every part of the world" who had Sun policies, or to the credit of the country. But Mitch was unwilling to let the resolution die quietly. In a long and angry speech, frequently interrupted by Bennett and the Sun Life lobbyist, Charles Cahan, he denounced Macaulay for Sun's "wild orgy of speculation" and attacked Bennett for saving the company from insolvency. Asked if he held a Sun Life policy, Mitch replied that he did, but "I am cashing in my policy in Sun Life because I sincerely believe that the assets of the company are seriously impaired, and I do not like the management."[12]

The response was immediate and inflamed, even among his Liberal colleagues. Percy Parker warned Mitch that "there has been a lot of unfavourable criticism of your attack, but of course chiefly among financial people," and from Windsor his friend Ellison Young of the *Border Cities Star* complained that the speech would "further impair the general public confidence that unfortunately is none too strong at this time." Even Elmore Philpott, now back at the *Globe*, termed his threat to cash in his policy a "colossal blunder" which "might have easily started a run on the Company equally as disastrous as a run on a bank," a concern perhaps influenced by the fact that most of Philpott's savings were in a Sun policy. "Your attack may appeal to the 'back concessions' and to the irresponsible in the cities," wrote one-time radical Patrick Donnelly, "but these two classes are of' little assistance at election time."

Win him support on the back concessions it did, perhaps more for its daring than its substance. "It's congratulations on your scrap about Sun Life," wrote Malcolm Macdonald, the sage of Springfield, who boasted that his political education had begun with "Sir John Aigh" and ended with "Laurie Aigh." "Still and all, if you were my boy, I'd spank you for gipping yourself. No votes in it, I mean.... They're going to hang you for disturbing our sleeping Finance-thing. Wrecker they say. Better to let the burglars burgle than to alarm the neighbourhood." Of course, Mitch was right, he concluded, but "being right is how folks get hung."[13] But Mitch would not back down. "Some of our right-wing Liberals feel that I have gone quite a way in criticizing the capitalistic system and the great financial people known as Sun Life," he replied to Macdonald. "However, I told them that if at any time they feel like kicking me out for not telling the truth that is their privilege."

As the Liberals feared, the Tories hoped to hang Mitch over Sun Life and sent William Finlayson, the tough minister of lands and forests, to St Thomas with the rope. It was clear that Hepburn was too young and irresponsible to be trusted with the leadership of a party, he warned a politely bipartisan crowd, perhaps even with a seat in the Commons. "These are serious times and you don't want a joker and a wisecracker who is attacking financial institutions. You want a man of sobriety, of business experience and a man of steadiness." Liberals prayed that Mitch would be steady and sober enough to ignore Finlayson's personal attack, and Senator Hardy begged him to follow King's commendable example of maintaining "absolute silence under the bitterest of attacks."[14]

Before an expectant crowd of over a thousand in St Thomas, Mitch struck back. Sun Life was a scandal, a scandal that exposed the unethical behaviour of big business and high finance, aided and abetted by Tory governments. And little could be expected of liberally inspired investigations, such as the one he had secured on the multinationals' control of gasoline prices, for the reformers were "up against a subsidized press. If the situation became unpleasant for the protected interests, $200,000 or $300,000 was released and distributed among newspapers for advertising." Right in St Thomas was it not fear of losing Sun advertising that led the *Times-Journal* to ignore his speech in the Commons? Commanding the reporters to report his statement accurately, Mitch stated that "If elected I would apply a capital levy to take the ill-gotten gains from the multi-millionaires of this country." The crowd loved it, and Gordon Reid, a prominent Tory who had driven from London to hear Mitch, reported to Bennett that "This bird is a bad actor but is making ground."

Albert Rogers, the left-wing Elgin Liberal, told King that "Mitch was at his best in a bold and daring broadside, the discretion of which is not for me to say," and "evidently shares the opinion of a growing multitude, namely, that the hour has struck for action—that capitalism is on its deathbed, and is lingering by virtue of 'hypos' and 'blood transfusions.'..." In politics, matters even up in the long run, King replied, forgetting Rogers's radicalism. "Mitch may be and is extreme in many things he says and this brings on his head much in the way of criticism and attack which he would otherwise escape. It is out of the pummelling of this kind that profounder judgements are evolved." Over time Mitch would become more moderate and, meanwhile, in "dealing with the forces that control at Queen's Park, he will perhaps gain more than he will lose by inclining, as he does, more to the left, than some, even of his close friends, may feel he should."[15]

Mitch's inclination was to move even further left during the West York by-election in May 1932. The riding ran north from Lake Ontario on both sides of the Humber River, and with the exception of that part of Etobicoke north of Dundas Street, was almost completely urban. It was also very heavily working class. Only Lambton Mills, now the fashionable Kingsway and Swansea area, was the preserve of the well-to-do. The other communities were populated by railwaymen and the lunch-bucket workers in the dozens of small industries in Weston and along the lakeshore. Over half the voters in West York were blue collar, and one in ten a farmer.

West York had voted Conservative since the turn of the century, and since 1907 had been owned by Dr Forbes Godfrey. With Godfrey gone, Liberal strategists believed they could win West York. It was an angry community. Along the lakeshore a quarter of the families were on direct relief, unemployment ran as high as 40 per cent, and most workers had experienced wage cuts and layoffs. Relief administrators asked to be allowed to keep guns. Some of the local governments made no effort to collect taxes, most could not pay their share of relief costs, and all were on the verge of defaulting.

The Liberal convention gave William Gardhouse, a popular reeve and cattle-breeder from Thistletown, a narrow victory over W.A. Edwards, a one-time mayor of Mimico who had strong labour support. And the Liberal chances of electing Gardhouse were immediately threatened by the decision of James Buckley, since 1929 the secretary of the Toronto and District Trades and Labour Council, to run as a Labour candidate. Buckley refused [Liberal party organizer] Harry Johnson's appeal to withdraw, and rejected Mitch's offer of a joint convention to nominate a Lib-Lab. Harry Price, the young Lambton businessman who ran for the Tories, faced a divided opposition.[16]

Mitch opened the campaign on Saturday night, 14 May, in Long Branch. Just two weeks earlier an epidemic of "Bolshephobia" led police across Ontario to move in force against May Day demonstrators. The Saturday morning newspapers reported a crisis, with relief vouchers and charges against a meat-packers' combine in the Commons. That night, outside Sir Adam Beck School, communist handouts urged the working class to take up arms against the capitalists. Inside, Mitch, with Arthur Roebuck, his constant companion during the campaign, and Bill Gardhouse, faced the largest crowd ever seen in West York, and probably the most unruly. Roebuck could hardly be heard above the heckling and when Gardhouse spoke one-third of the crowd followed two pugilists outside.[17]

But when Mitch took the platform, the battlers and their entourages returned. He ran over the well-worn arguments about the tariff, over-production and under-consumption, inequitable taxes and corrupt extravagance. Mitch insisted that his position on the political spectrum was unequivocal, but "there is one question which I fear will split even the Liberal party. There are men in Liberal ranks who are Tory at heart: there are men in Tory ranks who are reform at heart. I have met disapproval from Liberals when I said I wanted to see a definite decision in the matter of placing taxation on the shoulders where it belongs and not on the backs of the masses. I am not a Communist, but I go the whole way as a reformer." When the cheers died down, Mitch fielded questions from the floor. Asked if he supported J.S. Woodsworth, Mitch replied that he supported him fully in the attack on section 98. Asked if he favoured an alliance of Liberal and Labour forces, he replied:

> I favour and have advocated calling together the leaders of the Liberal and Progressive and Labour groups to pool our interests and see wherein we may follow a common road. Let me repeat that I swing well to the left where some Grits do not tread. If it is necessary to travel alone there, I will. One of the first things I will do if I form a government in this province will be to call together the best men of Labour, Progressives and Liberals and seek their advice. I hope to see a realignment of political thought in this country.

The "swing to the left" became the focus of the campaign. Everywhere Mitch's message was the same: "The increasing concentration of wealth in the hands of the few is our biggest problem today, and no man in public life seems to have the courage to come out and say so. If someone dares to boldly put his finger on the evil he draws upon his head the wrath of the capitalist class." At the Veterans' Hall in Earlscourt on the edge of the riding, he was praised as a radical and a socialist, and he promised to lead the fight against the moneylenders who, "like Alexander the Great have acquired so much that they have no more worlds to conquer—if you fellows support me."

Mitch also injected a new note into the campaign. By the spring of 1932 talk of inflation was in the air. In April, King found it difficult to persuade the western members of his caucus not to support a Progressive amendment calling for government control of the financial system and an expansion of the money supply. Roebuck had urged Mitch to jump on the bandwagon, for "it is on such popular measures that parties are swept into office and early reading of the public pulse is what constitutes political genius." During a 24 May speech Mitch accused the government and the moneylenders of collusion to keep interest rates high. He suggested that "inflation of currency might work here, though I do not advocate it at present, but something can be done to force down interest rates that increase the toll we pay to the moneylenders who exploit us. The masses cannot struggle any longer under this burden of debt that has been laid on them."[18]

After their unexpected loss in South Wellington, the Tories were determined to win West York. Rumours that they indirectly helped to finance the Buckley campaign were probably well founded. Premier Henry promised to take over the cost of relief from the insolvent municipalities and improve the food relief system. Half the cabinet entered the riding to warn that Hepburn's restraint program would mean cuts in relief payments, old-age pensions, and mother's allowances. Above all, Tory strategy centred on Mitch personally and his swing to the left. Health Minister Robb demanded to know exactly where Mitch stood: "Does Mitchell Hepburn mean he has communistic leanings when he talks of swinging to the left? Does he mean that he is condemning Canadian institutions that have stood the test of time? Does he mean that he does not believe in British institutions?"

The prize for invective went, as usual, to Leo Macaulay, who ministered to the needs of adjoining York South from his fashionable home on Humewood Drive. Hepburn was wild and reckless, his campaign "mass production in political bribery on the grandest scale yet attempted in Canada by anybody. It is trafficking in the suffering of the afflicted, the poor and unemployed." Macaulay mocked Mitch's promise to "disgorge" the millionaires when among his closest friends and supporters were millionaires Hardy, Parker, and George Fulford. Mitch was "their creature and he must be winking and nodding to them in the wings as the Liberal party goes on the Ontario stage: either that or there is an unscrupulous conspiracy...that they will hoodwink the people, the credulous working man with his wife and family—in the demagogic appeal—and doublecross them if, and when, they get into power."

George Henry ventured into West York on the last day of the campaign and could seldom be heard above the bedlam in New Toronto's Capitol Theatre. But finally he subdued the hecklers with a savage attack on Hepburn: his cowardly refusal to enter the legislature; his sell-out to American power interests whose propaganda he peddled; his promise to cut spending in times of social distress; and his dangerous swing to the left. The people of Ontario and Canada were measuring the calibre of West York voters. Would they tolerate a leader who swung well to the left? Would they desert their traditions and threaten their institutions?

Although Price defeated Gardhouse by 844 votes in a record turnout, the answer was ambiguous. The Liberals won easily in the rural areas, where Harry Nixon [former United Farmers of Ontario cabinet minister, turned Liberal] had campaigned. But Buckley ran second in most of the urban polls and won 23 per cent of the vote with a committee, he said, "largely composed of the unemployed, on Relief, with not a postage stamp between them." Seven out of ten working-class voters had cast their ballots against the Henry government. As *Saturday Night* commented and Mitch knew only too well, labour had become "a political entity that must be reckoned with by all political leaders."[19]

Exhausted by the campaign and even more by the winding down that went on into the early morning hours, Mitch returned home. The farm needed his attention, and there was much to think about. The alliance with Nixon seemed secure, but West York clearly revealed the danger of opposition on the left that might again deliver Ontario to the Tories. Some Liberals, such as Tom McQuesten, supported his proposed working arrangement with labour, and even Senator Hardy agreed that the Liberals had to have "a program radical enough to catch the radical third party...and take it into camp." But he warned that even the moderate statements in West York had caused "a good deal of talk about your 'Swinging to the Left' and you talked a good deal about making the rich man pay." That tactic might work in some ridings, "but I don't think it will get you anywhere. The rich man is paying as much as he is going to pay and still remain rich and that means remain with the party that takes from him more than he thinks it should." To drive the point home Hardy reminded Mitch that he had already experienced "the difficulty of getting away money from people who have it and also getting the support of those people." Generous as always, Hardy enclosed a cheque and begged Mitch not to burn the candle at both ends.[20]

But Mitch believed that the swing to the left had to be consummated by some alliance with labour. Speaking at Colin Campbell's nomination as the federal Liberal candidate in Frontenac-Addington, he expressed the hope that the November OLA convention in Ottawa would establish a committee to work out the details of an alliance. "There will be no submergence of the identity of the Liberal Party," he assured the rural Grits, "but I believe labour should be given a definite allocation of seats to contest in the next election and I am of the opinion that a labour section in the opposition ranks would be of benefit." Personally he was willing "to forget factional differences and go into camp with the Progressives or the Labour people," he told the Peterborough Liberals and, if they preferred, he would be prepared to step down for another leader.[21]

Mitch had already scheduled a meeting in Toronto to discuss an alliance with labour. Labour was represented by his friend Irwin Proctor, who believed the swing to the left "started in West York will quickly sweep this country from coast to coast," James Connors, secretary of the Toronto Labour party, and James Henderson. Mitch was accompanied by Roebuck, Nixon, Harry Johnson, and Colonel Hunter, the radical Toronto Liberal who had warned the London convention that the party must move to the left or die. The meeting was long, the rhetoric inspired. Discussion focused on the principles to be followed in allocating ridings and on the need for Mitch not only to define the swing to the left in policy terms but also to make it, in Hunter's words, "definite, drastic and irrevocable."

Proctor pressed Mitch to seize the initiative and earn his place in history. "Napoleon alone carved up the whole of Europe," he wrote him later. "*All history* demonstrates that in time of crisis, strong, even arbitrary, individual leadership is imperative." The time had come for Mitch to act, for if not, "some demagogue will assuredly arise and get the ear of an exasperated people.... An absolute and immediate break with the reactionary elements of your party, not only in fact, but avowed and apparent, is the only thing under Heaven that can now forestall a Fascist or Communist dictatorship in this Country."[22]

Arthur Roebuck, the self-styled "mummy at the feast," was far less enthusiastic. He questioned whether the riding associations would bow to the dictates of the leader and doubted the wisdom of formal manifestos that went beyond generalities. The Nixon alliance posed few problems because the Progressives were essentially agrarian Liberals, he argued, but labour was split among trade unionists and unorganized workers, moderate Lib-Labs and fire-breathing Marxists. "No one will hold it against you for hitching organized labour to the hub of your chariot," Roebuck cautioned, "but they will not march with you if you let the labour leaders become your charioteer."[23]

Mitch discovered that Roebuck was right when he canvassed the possibilities of allocating ridings or selecting joint candidates. He found it difficult, and sometimes impossible, to carry the local associations with him. Even in Windsor, where David Croll, the popular left-wing mayor, was willing to run as a Lib-Lab, there were rumblings among the Liberals. Yet Mitch remained convinced that some formal statement was essential to cement the association and, as Harry Johnson informed Norman Lambert, hoped that the Ottawa convention would pass a resolution to "cover extent to which Hepburn may deal with Farmers and/or Labour."[24]

Although the Progressive alliance was more manageable, it often took months of patient negotiations to persuade local Liberals or Progressives either to withdraw or to accept a joint nominating convention. Sometimes it was impossible. The advantages were demonstrated in the October federal by-election in South Huron necessitated by the death of Thomas McMillan, who had been elected as a Progressive in 1925 and as a Liberal the next year. The Progressives were particularly determined to reclaim the riding, because the provincial Liberals seemed certain to oppose William Medd, the Progressive MLA. Asking Mitch to enter the fray, King agreed to any course he wished to adopt for "there is nothing which matters quite as much as winning that particular contest." Hepburn and Nixon finally persuaded the Progressive candidate to withdraw with the promise that Medd would not be opposed in the next provincial election. To King, the subsequent capture of the seat by the Liberals was a personal triumph. To Mitch, it was a convincing demonstration of the need for a united opposition, and he hastened to thank Medd for his cooperation. But he also shared in the general Liberal enthusiasm and wrote his congenial drinking companion Larry McGuinness that the "Grits have their heads up and their tails over the dashboards since the wonderful victory in South Huron."[25]

Mitch had continued to hammer away at the hydro contracts in every public address, and by the fall of 1931 had Henry on the defensive. The cabinet had decided to hold a public inquiry after the South Wellington by-election but, following the totally unexpected defeat, Henry changed his mind. After Ferguson promised him there was nothing to hide, and the government-appointed accountants assured him the deals would bear public scrutiny, Henry reluctantly decided on a short inquiry. Mitch charged that the one-man commission under Mr. Justice Middleton was an "affront to the province." The inquiry was restricted to the Dominion Transmission and the Madawaska deals and the sole counsel was W.N. Tilley, who had never pretended to be politically independent. After two days of hearings Middleton fell ill and the inquiry was adjourned, but not before Aird [John Aird, Jr., son of the president of the Bank of Commerce] admitted that some of the Madawaska documents were missing and the press confirmed reports that they had been offered for sale.[26]

Before the Ontario inquiry resumed, Senator Haydon had told a Senate committee looking into Beauharnois that [R.O.] Sweezey [engineer, promoter, and investment dealer] had told him that Ferguson would not sign the Beauharnois contract "until he gets $200,000." Even the Tories agreed that after Haydon's statement Henry's inquiry was not "worth a hoot" and when it resumed under Mr. Justice Orde, the terms of reference had been extended to include Beauharnois. Sweezey testified again. He denied Haydon's story as well as the statement of George Kurdydyk and George Hyde of Winnipeg, passed on to Mitch by John Dafoe, that Sweezey had told them with some elation in November 1929 that he had got his contract but that "——— ——— Ferguson had just stuck him for $325.000." Sweezey stuck to his story that he "assumed" Aird was the Tory collector "properly constituted with authority" and while he did not think the payment was necessary to secure the contract, he believed it "would keep friendly relations between ourselves and the powers that be in Ontario." Sweezey knew that political parties did look for contributions and that "sooner or later we would get a request in some form from Ontario, and this had the appearance of it." Ferguson had raced back from England to testify at both inquiries. Under intense and disbelieving interrogation by Arthur Slaght, the brilliant counsel for the Liberals, he denied any knowledge of the $125,000—or indeed of campaign funds at all—and even implied it might have gone to the Liberals since the Airds were regarded as a Liberal family.

In the end Slaght could produce no hard evidence to tie the $125,000 to the Tories. Indeed, an independent investigation proved that Aird had the bonds in his possession in May, and while his devious method of cashing the coupons and paying the milkman and the children's nurse with $50 bills was unusual, there was little about John Aird Jr. that was not. Released in October, the report completely exonerated the government: the price paid for Dominion was reasonable; the "propriety" of the $50,000 Madawaska payment was unquestioned; and the $125,000 had "no relation" to the Beauharnois contract. But Henry's inept handling of the inquiry and the implausibility of so much of the testimony had more impact on a suspicious public than the earnest testimony of Hydro engineers or government-appointed accountants.[27]

Even before the final report appeared, the collapse of Abitibi sowed the seeds of another scandal that rocked the Henry government. The Abitibi deal was another of Ferguson's legacies, and the facts were as obscure as they seemed shady. In 1926, without consultation with Hydro, Ferguson had leased the Abitibi Canyon, the largest waterpower source in northern Ontario, to an Abitibi subsidiary. But the new Hydro chairman, Charles McGrath, advocated a policy of the rational development of northern power under Hydro and on the eve of the 1929 election persuaded a reluctant Ferguson to announce a policy of public development. Soon after the election, when INCO inquired about the possibility of securing 16,000 horsepower at Sudbury, Hydro engineers recommended harnessing the Mississagi River. However, there was persistent pressure from Alexander Smith, the president of Abitibi, to develop the canyon, and the Hydro commissioners finally turned the question over to the premier.[28]

A few months later Hydro engineers were forced to put their name to a report that they had neither written nor approved, and Hydro signed a contract with Abitibi for a 240,000 horsepower development on the canyon. Although there was little demand for power in the north, the government forced Hydro to buy back 100,000 horsepower from Abitibi. The agreement was so distasteful that the Hydro Commission demanded an order-in-council to protect it against any losses. Abitibi created the Ontario Power Service Corporation to carry out the contract, and as the company's prospectus made clear, the Hydro purchase was enough to cover the cost, including the interest of a $20 million bond issue, and leave the company with 100,000 horsepower as profit.

Strachan Johnson, one of Ferguson's close friends, negotiated the contract for the government. Ferguson's friend J. Homer Black became vice-president of Abitibi in charge of Ontario Power. Later he became head of Dominion Construction when it secured the construction contract. Coincidentally, Black's son-in-law was Hugh Aird of the Aird, McLeod brokerage firm and John Aird Jr.'s brother. As Ferguson admitted to Henry, it was a deal the "ordinary man" would find difficult to understand.[29]

The government was reluctant to divulge the details of the contract, either to Mitch and the Liberals or to inquiring *Financial Post* reporters. But late in February 1932 the agreement began to unravel. Alexander Smith told Henry that the OPSC did not have enough money to finish the project and that Abitibi itself could not borrow without government backing. Henry agreed to support Abitibi, but it soon became apparent it was going under as well. Sick in bed for much of March and April, Henry set a trusted team of Tory lawyers, accountants, and brokers to work out a solution. The negotiations dragged into June, when Arthur Meighen, who had become a Hydro commissioner in 1931, with broker J.H. Gundy and E.G. Long, visited Queen's Park. The premier was in the north, and Meighen, meeting alone with William Price, appealed to him to reach an early decision in the interests of the widows and orphans who were suffering as the bonds dropped to fire-sale prices. Another visitor was A.J. Nesbitt of the Power Corporation, which owned Northern Ontario Power, whose offer to finish the project on undisclosed terms was not accepted. Late in June the cabinet approved an agreement with the bondholders and instructed Hydro to exchange $18 million in government guaranteed bonds for the $20 million in OPSC bonds.

Mitch and the Liberals denounced the agreement as outrageous, another even more convincing demonstration of the corrupt relationship between the Tories and the financiers. What else could explain offering $90 for bonds that had been selling as low as $30 in June? Although the government replied that the real value of the bonds was much higher, the *Financial Post* concluded that the agreement was excessively generous and "based on considerations for bondholders and not on value...and every new fact brought to light indicates that the rights of taxpayers have been grossly overlooked." Mitch joined the *Post* in demanding an investigation. It was not long before the Liberals were hinting at corruption, not collusion.[30]

The Hydro revelations had done nothing to convince Mitch that his attack on the corrupt relationship between government and big business was unwarranted. When he returned to Ottawa for the fall session in October, Sun Life was again on his agenda, with the evidence more damning than before. In 1929 and 1930 Sun Life had become deeply involved in the financial affairs of the Insull financial and utility empire in the United States and Ivar Kreuger's Swedish match conglomerate. By the fall of 1932 the Insull empire was in receivership. Martin Insull had fled to Canada and his brother Samuel to Greece, and both were fighting extradition as the drama in a Chicago courtroom disclosed the involvement of T.B. Macaulay and other Sun executives with the Insulls. Kreuger had also gone bankrupt, and in March 1932 committed suicide in Paris. J.J. Harpell had continued his attack on "The World's Greatest Crook" and attempted to have Macaulay arrested for defrauding Sun policy-holders. Macaulay countered by charging Harpell with libel.[32]

When Mitch reached Ottawa, Harpell gave him a copy of the indictment he intended to use in court which, supported by a stinging rebuke of Sun from the superintendent of insurance, Mitch planned to use in the Commons. Aware of the seriousness of the charges, however, Mitch first consulted King, Hardy and other leading Liberals. All agreed that the crash of Sun could be imminent. King said he "tried to keep Hepburn from going too far, in precipitating a crisis thro' exposure in prlt.—until Govt. has had a chance to deal with Sun Life matters."[32]

The opportunity to implicate Bennett soon overcame King's concern for the financial stability of the country:

Hepburn tells me Bennett sold his common stock in the Eddy Match Co. to the Swedish Match Trust for $3,000,000 when he became leader of his party. That Macaulay of Sun Life too[k] Swedish Match Trust stock in that amt. to give the Trust money to pay Bennett for his stock. This has all been lost by Kreuger collapse. Bennett & Macaulay had preference stock between them. Bennett is said to have sold a lot of his poor stock to Macaulay, unloaded on him.— It is now gone. The Sun Co. shareholders' money is in Bennett's possession. Bennett and Macaulay are mixed up in the Insul [sic] Co. transactions, the Sun having acquired much of that stock—What collapse in important Co's may come once all this is public, I hesitate to predict.—It should be the end of R.B. & a very fitting end, if it be true.

Senator Hardy was convinced that a renewed attack on Sun Life would mean defeat in the next provincial election, for a run on the company would "mean bankruptcy for thousands of people including possibly one or two of our banks" and urged Mitch to proceed with "the utmost caution." Percy Parker phoned from Toronto to beg him to let others take the initiative. Arthur Roebuck wrote that "if Sun Life is ruined as these figures indicate, it will fall over or be absorbed, but if you push it over the anger of those who lose will be divided between yourself and those who actually wrecked it." The losers could be not just the "high financiers," he warned, but thousands of ordinary people. Moreover, "I am satisfied that there are dangers lurking all through this resolution, dangers which a courageous man should not, perhaps, fear to face, but which it may be are quite unnecessary to face. Libel actions are extremely costly. Personally I would feel greatly relieved if you handed over this job to someone else who is perhaps not carrying as you are conflicting responsibilities and whose personal fortunes in a dogfight of this kind are less important."[33]

Although King was prepared to let Hepburn bring a resolution before the House, the criticism in caucus infuriated Mitch. "Hepburn was much annoyed at the way Malcolm spoke," King noted, "re Liberals in Toronto seeking to prevent him from speaking out and said he would resign the leadership—his real problem is the financial one—no help from the political bosses, Parker et al." Mitch's attempt to raise the matter as a question of urgent public importance was ruled out of order by the Speaker, and Mitch was outraged when a number of Liberals, Fraser and Moore among them, voted to sustain the chair. But as King confessed, the arbitrary ruling, on which he did not vote, "really helped us all to meet Hepburn's situation and our own attitude. Only the very serious condition of Canada's financial institutions would justify the failure to clear up the Sun Life situation regardless of all else."

Deserted but undaunted, Mitch then secured the Speaker's assurance that he could bring the matter before the House as a notice of motion, but two days later when it was still not on the order paper he belligerently asked, "Is some official of this house exceeding his authority or is there some powerful influence at work to conceal from the people of Canada the true situation in connection with Sun Life?" The question was too important to be left to the Speaker, and Bennett was immediately on his feet to denounce Hepburn as Harpell's accomplice and state that since Harpell was being sued for libel in a Montreal court, Sun Life could not be discussed in Parliament.

Balked at every turn, Mitch angrily said he was "through," a decision happily relayed to A.B. Wood, the vice-president of Sun, by Jim Malcolm. But Mitch was incensed by the pressure from his own party. "Needless to say I was very much surprised to get your letter," he wrote to Arthur Roebuck:

> In my humble opinion the financial racketeers of this country have so disregarded the laws covering bribery and the manipulation of watered stocks and promotion schemes that there is an actual danger of our whole monitory [sic] system being destroyed.

In this particular case there is no doubt that the life savings of people have been dissipated by trustees who benefitted personally in the transaction. The Liberal Party is either for or against that kind of business and cannot occupy a neutral position, and for my part I do not wish to be a puppet of' St. James Street.

If the "hush, hush" advice I have been getting represents the majority opinion of the Liberal Party then I feel completely out of tune, and I believe that the matter should be discussed frankly at the coming annual meeting in Ottawa. When I made the statement in West York that I was swinging to the left I meant every word of it, and am more determined than ever to fight class legislation and special privileges.

In Montreal, Chief Justice Greenshields refused to let Mitch testify on Harpell's behalf and a well-instructed jury took only an hour-and-a-half to find Harpell guilty of libel. Despite the recommendation for clemency, Greenshields sentenced Harpell to three months in jail.[34]

For the year following his recovery [from kidney removal surgery], in the fall of 1931, Mitch maintained a feverish pace that would have taxed a man in good health. With the House in session he spent his weekends in eastern and central ridings wooing the Franco-Ontarians back into the fold, encouraging local organizations, resolving personal squabbles, and seeking potential candidates. There had been time for a trip to Sudbury with Ian Mackenzie, his good friend and fellow MP from Vancouver, and regular visits to Toronto to help oversee the assault on Queen's Park. Even in St. Thomas, where he spent part of the summer, there were countless visitors, political meetings in southern and western ridings, and endless correspondence. Yet, despite all his accomplishments, he still faced the implacable hostility of Sinclair and his friends, continual sniping from the *Globe* and the *Star*, and underground threats to his leadership.

In the spring of 1932 Mitch promised Bill Fraser, the MP for Northumberland, that he would hold a joint meeting of the federal and provincial members to discuss party organization and attempt a Hepburn-Sinclair reconciliation. But Mitch changed his mind, and earned a stinging four-page rebuke from Fraser, who warned that "noisy demonstrations of a certain class of people" would never bring the Liberals to power. Mitch's role was to unite the Liberal party, to realize that "suspicion breeds suspicion," and that a politician's "greatest assets are diplomacy and tolerance, and the ability to stoop to conquer. These abstracts, commodities or virtues, you refuse to recognize." The rank and file were concerned not with the Hepburn-Sinclair feud, he maintained, but with victory, and unless Mitch was prepared to find some accommodation with Sinclair and his followers in the caucus "for your own good, you should resign as Leader of the Ontario Party."[35]

Mitch may have respected the bluntness, but certainly not the content. As far as he was concerned, it was Sinclair who refused to put the party ahead of his own personal antagonisms. Although he disliked and distrusted Sinclair, he had repeatedly held out the olive branch, only to have it sullenly rejected. Sinclair, he believed, was perverse if not malicious, small-minded and stubborn, convinced that the party would some day realize its mistake and cast aside a man he detested. Billy Sinclair imagined himself to be a man of principle. But loyalty to the elected leader was not one of them. As far as Mitch was concerned, why should he "stoop to conquer"? Why should he resign because Sinclair and his small group of ardently dry followers refused to accept the will of the convention and endorse its leader and its platform?

Mitch also wondered whether Fraser could be trusted. Bill Fraser was a decade older than Mitch, a wealthy Trenton fruit-grower and businessman with real estate investments in Toronto and memberships in the Granite Club and the Royal Canadian Yacht Club. Mitch had campaigned for him in 1930, and Fraser had supported him for the leadership. But there were those who knew that he had been working behind the scenes against him at London. Moreover, late in 1931 Fraser had been closely associated with Moore and Sinclair in the organization of the Central Ontario Liberal Association, and despite Fraser's reassurances that the new body would strengthen both the federal and provincial parties, no attempt had been made to bring it under the Ontario Liberal Association umbrella. Fraser had made it clear that he had no use for the OLA office, for Harry Johnson and "your other henchmen in Toronto" who "purely and simply for their own selfish ends, feel they should run the Liberal Party in Ontario and are endeavouring to do this through the Liberal leader." And it was this "self appointed and selected advisory group," he believed, who were responsible for Mitch's refusal to stoop to conquer. At best, Billy Fraser was a question mark.[36]

Fraser was not alone in his hostility towards Johnson and the OLA office. Some of the old guard complained that control of the party seemed to be in the hands of their former Progressive enemies like Nixon and Roebuck, while others resented the new prominence of Frank O'Connor, Senator McGuire, and Percy Parker. Joe Atkinson [owner of the *Toronto Star*] refused to associate with Hepburn or the office, and even refused to serve on King's new National Liberal Federation because of its link with the OLA. And Hardy had been astute enough not to recommend any active members of the OLA executive or Management Committee to King, to "eliminate any possibility of a charge that we are looking after ourselves." The Management Committee had added a number of prominent Toronto financiers and businessmen—Albert Matthews, J.F. McKay and P.J. Mulqueen—in January 1932, but the criticism that the office was in the hands of a small clique persisted. Even Hardy warned Mitch on one occasion to consult some friends, "*but not those from Toronto.*" So disliked was Johnson that many of the MLAs refused to answer his letters. and the Central Ontario Association executive pointedly refused to invite him to the inaugural banquet. Johnson took the slight philosophically, and joked to Mitch that "If anything happens to you, this Office and I part company, *quick.*"[37]

By the fall of 1932 there were rumours that Mitch's leadership would be challenged at the November OLA convention. Ambrose O'Connor of

Oshawa warned Mitch of a conspiracy, with Fraser supplying the money and Moore the brains, to support Moore for the leadership. The arguments used, he wrote, were that "you are not proper leader, you are federal MP, elected by Beauharnois crowd." They plan to go to Ottawa "solidly against you and further I know that they have a bunch of really good fellows convinced that while you are an awfully nice chap you are not managing as you should."

But it was Sinclair who most visibly symbolized the threat to Mitch, and there were many Liberals who agreed with Patrick Donnelly that the party should "face the inevitable" and force Sinclair to resign as House leader. As always, Mitch was reluctant to make any move that might irreparably split the party, but Tom McQuesten argued that the issue had to be faced. While the OLA convention could not deal with the leadership, he suggested that a strong vote of confidence "might strengthen you in dealing with the Members. I feel that your position is even now strong enough to lay down the law to the members and read out of the party those who will not obey.... I believe you have one-half the members and it would be better to lose the rest than to trifle with the situation." Whatever the outcome, the issue had to be faced for the "average voter, particularly the one who has not strong party affiliations simply will not believe that Sinclair as House Leader does not represent and speak for the Liberal Party in Ontario."[38]

For a while in the fall of 1932 it looked as if the Ottawa convention would have to deal with the leadership, for Mitch spoke often and openly of resigning. The blistering pace he had maintained for a year had taken its toll. He had never fully recovered from his operation and its aftermath, and during the summer his health got worse. He was exhausted, perspiring heavily and unable to sleep at night, and unwilling to relax during the day. He lost seven pounds and by October his weight had fallen to 165 pounds. As usual when he was worn out, he got bronchitis, and was afraid that he had tuberculosis. And all the party did, it seemed, was to carp and criticize, while making more and more demands on his time and energy.[39]

To make matters worse, the promised financial support had not materialized. Of the five who promised to contribute, two had reneged by the fall of 1931, Hardy told Pat Donnelly, and "two of us have paid in a couple of thousand dollars each. I can't go any further and it would not be fair to ask young Mr. Fulford to do so either." By the summer of 1931 the office rent and Johnson's salary were overdue, and Parker complained that "Most people are so hard up that we have been at our wits end and have had to go into our own pockets." The rent had apparently been guaranteed by Senator Spence, but some bad business deals had pushed him close to bankruptcy and he was "worrying everybody sick" by the end of the year. "He's determined someone shall take it off his hands," Hardy told King, "so I gave him a good sharp letter today asking him why anybody should especially Percy Parker whom he's been urging to do so. I told him he had received a Senatorship and that he'd better pay for it like the rest of us. The old rascal has never put up a dollar for anything."[40]

In the Beauharnois fallout, an apologetic Percy Parker had suggested at the 1931 convention that each riding contribute $100 a year to the provincial office and that a dime a year from three hundred thousand Liberals would handily cover the costs. Later, the Management Committee accepted Arthur Roebuck's proposal that two thousand Liberals contribute five dollars each to a maintenance fund. Although this "begging scheme" was mocked by more cynical Liberals, Roebuck had raised $7,000 by November 1932 and the OLA debt had been cut in half. But it was far from enough. Rents and salaries were behind, Mitch had no staff except Eleanor Parker, his House of Commons secretary, and was covering most of his own expenses. In October he simply threw up his hands, and said the OLA executive would have to decide "whether they consider it advisable to try and carry the load much further" or close the Toronto office. At the same time Mitch wrote angrily to William Mulock that "I am not prepared to lose any more of my time and sessional indemnity running around the province like a greyhound.... As you are fully aware, the party has not lived up to any of its obligations. So far as I am concerned, I have done everything humanly possible to carry out my responsibilities. There is a limit to everything, and I have just about reached mine."

Soon after he reached Ottawa in October, Mitch told King he was sufficiently fed up to consider resigning as leader. "Between 6 & 7 I had a good talk with Mitch Hepburn and cleared up his mind on many things," King wrote. "He sees he has made a mistake in taking the Ontario leadership, he would like to get out, I advised him to stay. I would give him no assurance of a cabinet post—nor did be ask it though he mentioned the subject & told him events wd. decide whether or not it was best for him to remain in the federal or provincial fields—we wd. see which election came on first."[41]

However, there was no suggestion of frustration in Mitch's speech to the Twentieth Century Club banquet on 12 November. Mitch spoke with a gusto that belied his fatigue, and he brought the crowd to its feet time and time again as he leavened his anger with humour and sarcasm. Mitch did not back away from his swing to the left, but the tone was muted, the language restrained. He had been called a socialist and a communist because he dared to discuss conditions as they were. But his solutions were not revolutionary, for the evils of special privilege and industrial oppression could be removed by democratic means if there were "a fusion of all the forces that oppose Toryism." As far as he was concerned, he declared, a little more cautiously than before, "We are willing to extend a reasonable measure of support to other groups. We wish to remain close to our good friend, Harry Nixon.... We extend the hand of fellowship to Labour. (Cheers) We are not far apart in matters political." The Liberal party was a "virile fighting force ready for the fray. I want to say to Premier Henry, let him take his appeal to the people. We will be ready. We are ready now." The standing ovation should have removed any doubts about his future.[42]

Not even the Tory press could report an imminent revolt as the six hundred delegates gathered in Ottawa a week later. There was no discussion of' an alliance with labour, but the unanimous approval of Paul Martin's resolution that "the curtailment of socialistic and communistic thought by methods of direct coercion is ill-advised, and with a view of arriving at political and social truth, a free and unrestricted discussion of these and other questions is desirable" placed the party well to the left of the Tories. Mackenzie King praised Mitch and lectured the dissident. The time was approaching when Mitch would be assessing cabinet potential and aspiring candidates would have to "reveal their talents to the people." It was already time, King added, for "older men, who are somewhat critical because Mr. Hepburn is more radical than they," to still their criticism and get into the fight.

Mitch rose to thunderous applause and boisterous singing, and his speech was constantly punctuated with applause and laughter. King thought Mitch was "light & discursive—a little too much 'my friends'—& jumped about—but the sort of thing the crowd likes." The crowd certainly liked it, and was on its feet when Mitch promised that in the election expected in 1933 "we shall neither give nor take quarter." The new slate of officers confirmed Mitch's position. Tom McQuesten. the progressive Hamilton bachelor lawyer, was a loyal if distant colleague. Bay Street and the old guard may have been appeased when Albert Matthews accepted the vice-presidency. Percy Parker chaired the influential Management Committee and Frank O'Connor. who was becoming one of Mitch's close friends, became treasurer. Arthur Slaght joined the executive officially as the head of the Toronto and York regional association. The victory seemed complete.[43]

After the convention Mitch went on a twice-postponed northern jaunt from North Bay to Kenora with Peter Heenan. The trip was an unqualified success, and Mitch returned triumphantly to Toronto for a giant Liberal rally in Massey Hall on 15 December, the largest it was said since the days of Laurier. At the white tie banquet, Mackenzie King pictured Mitch as a "political knight errant" and the next premier of Ontario. In an unusually serious speech. Mitch promised cuts in expenditure, a review of taxation, a study of overlapping federal and provincial services, and the honest and efficient development of northern resources. Like King, he discussed the growing threat from the newly formed left-wing political party, the Cooperative Commonwealth Federation, and stressed not his radicalism but his moderation. Swinging to the left did not mean that he was out "to destroy capitalism," he assured the well-dressed audience. "If I thought for a moment the founding of a new order were necessary, I would not hesitate to join it for my first consideration is the welfare of the people. I believe in the capitalist system but I condemn in no uncertain terms the abuse of the capitalist system under the Tory administrations. I have long since learned that there is no Santa Claus, no pot of gold at the foot of the rainbow. I do not believe in sending people up a blind alley when we have the machinery for a sane democracy."[44]

Mitch went home for a much-deserved rest amid praise from all sides. Both McQuesten and Hardy saw a great improvement in the recent speeches, and Hardy added that he was "very glad to see certain people at the Toronto meeting and hope you can begin to chip away at the edges of that place before too long." Harry Johnson was euphoric. The speeches "have revealed you to the City man as a person of brains and common sense ideas on how to better conditions in the province. Old friends like J.F. McKay and Albert

Matthews are delighted at the address you delivered and the effect they have had on businessmen generally." From "where I sit, I see you a natural born poker player, with four aces and a king from the dealer." "An expert with a hand like that needs no advice from anyone," he added. "All you need is a Doctor to tell you to keep your feet warm and your head cool." Senator Hardy agreed, and warned Mitch to cut down on the after-dinner meetings: "You have your feet in the saddle now and we can't afford even a slight or temporary breakdown."

But to the *Farmers' Sun* it seemed that Mitch had abandoned his swing to the left and the attempt to rally farmers and labour under a progressive banner. His policy would be dictated by the interests of the federal Liberals and the *Globe*, "that senile old lady whose mind is so failed that she has forgotten her noble past." And at the Toronto Club, Leo Macaulay asked sardonically where was the man who would disgorge the millionaires of their "ill-gotten gains? The muffler on the exhaust has now become a silencer."[45]

NOTES

1. HP, Hepburn to T. McQuesten, 19 May 1932.

2. *Canadian Annual Review*, 1932, 690.

3. Henry Papers, W.J. Stewart, mayor of Toronto, to Henry, 21 Sept. 1931.

4. Ontario, Dept. of Agriculture, *Annual Report*, 1930-2; AO, Dept. of Agriculture, Agricultural Representatives Annual Reports, 1930-1; Canada, Dept. of Agriculture, *The Economic Analyst*, 1929-32, *passim.*

5. See James Struthers, *No Fault of Their Own: Unemployment and the Canadian Welfare State 1914-1941* (Toronto, 1983), 44.

6. Stewart Bates, *Financial History of Canadian Governments* (Ottawa, 1939)

7. AO, Treasury Dept., Series 11-3. H.A. Cotnam and W. Campbell, Report to the Provincial Treasurer on Sinking Funds and Debt Retirement.... 2 March 1936; Henry Papers, Henry to W. Finlayson, 31 Dec. 1931. The correspondence with the banks may be found in AO, Treasury Dept., files 1612-10 and 603/1.

8. *HCD*, 22 Feb. 1932, 384; 3 March 1932, 748; KD, 2 March 1932; House of Commons, Select Committee on Banking and Commerce, Minutes, Reference: Price of Gasoline, 1932.

9. *HCD*, 17 March 1932, 1222; KD, 17 March 1932.

10. Bennett Papers, Memorandum for the Hon. R.B. Bennett: re Policy Holders Association & Sun Life, 16 Apr. 1931; *Report of the Superintendent of Insurance for Canada...1928* (Ottawa, 1929), Vol. 2, xxxi; Bennett Papers, Finlayson to Bennett, 19, 26 Sept., 9 Oct. 1931; *Journal of Commerce*, Dec. 1931, Jan. 1932.

11. Spry Papers, Diary, 6 Oct. 1931; Ferguson Papers, Bennett, wire in code, to Ferguson, 18 Jan. 1932; Ferguson to Bennett, 25 Jan. 1932; interview, Sherwood Walters.

12. *HCD*, 14 March 1932, 1102, 1106.

13. HP, Parker to Hepburn, 19 March 1932; Young to Hepburn, 24 March 1932: Philpott to Hepburn, 6 April 1932; Donnelly to Hepburn, 6 April 1932; Macdonald to Hepburn, 4 April 1932; Hepburn to Macdonald, 19 April 1932.

14. *ME*, 1 April 1932; HP, Hardy to Hepburn, 7 April 1932.

15. *ME,* 13 April 1932; Bennett Papers, G. Reid to A.W. Merriam, 13 April 1932; *Hush,* 14 April 1932; KP, Rogers to King, 13 April 1932; King to Rogers, 16 April 1932.

16. HP, Johnson to Hepburn, 19 April 1932; KP, Johnson to King, 14 June 1932.

17. The account of the election is based on the four city papers, 11-30 May 1932.

18. H. Blair Neatby, *William Lyon Mackenzie King: The Prism of Unity 1932-1939* (Toronto, 1976), 30; HP, Roebuck to Hepburn, 22 May 1932.

19. *Globe, TDS, ME, TET,* 16-30 May 1932; Buckley Papers, MSS Reminiscences. n.d.; *Saturday Night,* 4 June 1932.

20. HP, McQuesten to Hepburn, 17 May 1932; Hardy to Hepburn, 31 May 1932.

21. *TDS,* 14, 30 June 1932.

22. HP, Proctor to Hepburn, 5 July 1932.

23. PC, Roebuck Papers, Roebuck to Hepburn, 13 July 1932.

24. HP, Hepburn to Hardy, 24 Aug. 1932; LD, 12 Oct. 1932.

25. Minutes of the East Lambton Liberal Association, 1932-1933; KP, Hepburn to King, 24 Aug.; King to Hepburn, 29 Aug. 1932; Neatby, *Prism of Unity,* 24; HP, Hepburn to Medd, 13 Oct. 1932; Hepburn to L. McGuinness, 12 Oct. 1932.

26. Henry Papers, Henry to Ferguson, 23 Nov. 1931; Ferguson to Henry, 10 Dec. 1931; *TDS, ME,* 3, 4 Feb. 1932.

27. Canada, Senate, *Report and Proceedings of the Special Committee...on the Beauharnois Power Project 1932,* 19; Bennett Papers, Arthur Ford to Bennett, 18 March 1932; HP, Dafoe to Hepburn, 16 March 1932; OHA, Royal Commission to enquire into certain matters appertaining to the Hydro Power Commission of Ontario 1932, *Hearings,* 5 vols., 920 (Sweezey), 769

(Ferguson); OHA, Royal Commission...1932, Special Report for W.N. Tilley re John Aird Jr. by Thorne, Mulholland, 9 May 1932.

28. OH, Minutes, Ontario Hydro, 4 Oct. 1929-11 April 1930.

29. OH Minutes, 11 April 1930; Henry Papers, Ferguson to Henry, 10 Dec. 1931.

30. *FP,* 26 Sept. 1931; OHA, Inquiry into the Hydro-Electric Power Commission, *Hearings,* 1011; *FP,* 30 July 1932.

31. See Forest Macdonald, *Insull* (Chicago, 1962).

32. *Farmers' Sun,* 13 Oct. 1932; HP, Harpell to Hepburn, 17 Oct. 1932; KD, 21 Oct. 1932; KP, Hardy to King, 22 Oct. 1932.

33. KD, 26, 27 Oct. 1932; KP, Hardy to King, 22 Oct. 1932; HP, Hardy to Hepburn, 22 Oct. 1932; Roebuck to Hepburn, 1 Nov. 1932.

34. KD, 2 Nov. 1932; *HCD,* 2 Nov. 1932, 744; 4 Nov. 1932, 845; Malcolm Papers, Malcolm to Wood, 15 Nov. 1932; HP, Hepburn to Roebuck, 3 Nov. 1932; Montreal *Gazette,* 28 Dec. 1932.

35. HP, Fraser to Hepburn, 21 June 1932.

36. HP, Hepburn to John Godfrey, 18 Feb. 1932; Fraser to Hepburn, 21 June 1932; Dunning Papers, Fraser to Dunning, 21 Dec. 1931.

37. KP, McCreath to King, 10, 20 Nov. 1931; Parliament to King, 5 Aug. 1932; Hardy to King, 20 Nov. 1932; HP, Hardy to Hepburn, 28 Nov. 1931; Johnson to Hepburn, 12 Jan. 1932.

38. HP, O'Connor to Hepburn, n.d.; AO, Roebuck Papers, Memorandum by Patrick Donnelly, n.d.; HP, McQuesten to Hepburn, 14 Oct. 1932.

39. HP, Medical Report, Nov. 1932.

40. Donnelly Papers, Hardy to Donnelly, 17 Sept. 1931; KP, Parker to King, 28 July, 4 Dec. 1931; Murphy Papers, Murphy to Sinclair, 11 May

1932; Murphy to M.J. Quinn, 23 Feb. 1932. Five years later Hardy told King that since 1919 he had put up $200,000 for the Liberal party, "25,000 of which went to help Mitch Hepburn chiefly because I knew if he could win Ontario we could make a better showing in the federal house." He added that he had loaned Spence money to save his seat in the Senate and had never got it back and was suing for recovery (KP, Hardy to King, 20 Aug. 1937).

41. KP, Charles Collins to Hardy, 22 Feb. 1932; Roebuck to King, 7 Dec. 1933, enc. Report of the Ontario Liberal Association Maintenance Fund 1933; HP, Hepburn to McQuesten, 15 Oct. 1931; Hepburn to Mulock, 21 Oct. 1932; KD, 19 Oct. 1932.

42. *ME*, 14 Nov. 1932.

43. Ibid., 19 Nov. 1932; KD, 17 Nov. 1932; Dewan Papers, Diary, 18 Nov. 1932.

44. *ME*, 16 Dec. 1932; *Farmers' Sun*, 22 Dec. 1932.

45. HP, McQuesten to Hepburn, 17 Dec. 1932; Hardy to Hepburn, 15 Dec. 1932; Johnson to Hepburn, 29 Nov. 1932; *Farmers' Sun*, 19 Jan. 1933; *TET*, 17 Dec. 1932.

CONTINUITY AND CHANGE, 1946-1998

○

INTRODUCTION

While the period 1918 to 1945 saw the demise of the two-party system and the "progressive" reform of the programs and structures of the old parties, much of the period since 1945 saw the reassertion of earlier, pre-1918 trends, at least at the federal level. One such trend was the return of two-party competition as the Liberals and Conservatives alternated in power in Ottawa, largely unopposed, until the 1990s, by other parties. Another trend was the domination of national politics by one of the two major parties, in this instance the Liberals. Nevertheless, there were changes. In contrast to the prewar years, victorious Liberal and Conservative parties had a much tougher time winning a majority of the seats, a reflection of the electorate's growing disillusionment with the major parties, or at least with their leaders. The re-emergence in force of regionally based protest parties in Ottawa in the 1990s presented additional challenges to the leading parties. The growing strength of these protest parties and the virtual disappearance of the Conservative party as a strong federal force in the elections of 1993 and 1997 further undermined the stability of federal politics. In provincial politics, the two-party system did not re-emerge after 1945. Provincially, third parties remained highly competitive. Add to all these trends the significant changes in electioneering methods that the federal and provincial parties themselves have undergone since 1945 and what emerges for this period is a rather blurry picture of continuity and change, an amalgam in many ways of the patterns of party politics since Confederation.

Perhaps the leading theme of the postwar period has been the domination of federal politics by the Liberal party. Of the sixteen general elections held since 1945, the Liberals have won ten. Assuming no change in government until the year 2001, they will have ruled for the equivalent of more than four decades since the last war. A remarkable record, indeed, and one that has earned the Liberal party the label "the government party." The reasons for this success are, as always, varied, although a combination of favourable economic conditions, attractive leaders, timely policies, rising Quebec nationalism, and opposition weakness account for much of it.

The immediate postwar years were not marked by nearly the same political turbulence as that which followed the First World War. Quite the opposite in fact. The transition to peace occurred smoothly and the country quickly entered into a period of unprecedented prosperity. Rapid economic growth fostered a widespread feeling of complacency that, combined with the uncertainties created by the Cold War and the nuclear age, made voters reluctant to switch their political loyalties. This reluctance, of course, benefitted the ruling Liberals, as did the party's decision in 1948 to replace the ailing Mackenzie King with then Minister of Justice Louis St. Laurent, a highly appealing figure whose liberal nationalism, unassailable integrity, and benevolent manner suited perfectly the laid back, cautiously progressive mood of the day. On the strength on their new leader's formidable campaigning skills and their government's expansion of the nation's infrastructure and social programs, the Liberals went on to resounding victories in the elections of 1949 and 1953.

Continuing prosperity, budgetary surpluses, further advances in social services, and the rapid growth of Canada's international stature foretold only more success. But this continued success was not to be. By 1957, Canadians were bored with the Liberals, figuring that because the party had appeared to govern so effortlessly and without much imagination, it was dispensable. Canadians were offended, too, by what they perceived to be the growing arrogance of a party too long in power. This trait was particularly visible during the 1956 pipeline debate over whether Parliament should approve funding to an American company's construction of the trans-Canada pipeline, when the government invoked closure four times to limit debate and the usually composed and benign St. Laurent lashed out against the united opposition for delaying passage of the bill in question. Nor did the insufficiently partisan prime minister help his party's cause by allowing key provincial Liberal organizations to whither during his tenure. Even so, the election of a Conservative minority government in 1957 led by John Diefenbaker came as a surprise to most commentators, who were certain that for all their grumbling the voters would never "shoot Santa Claus."[1]

What followed can only be described as a bumpy seven-year roller-coaster ride, during which the fortunes of the national Conservative party and the emotions of the voters who elected it went from euphoric highs to dismal lows. The high began with the massive victory of the Conservatives in 1958, when the party captured 208 of 265 seats, the largest majority to that point, much of it attributable to Diefenbaker's incredible energy on the campaign trail, his image as a champion of the underprivileged, his riveting oratorical flourishes, and his ability to evoke images of national greatness, in the manner of a Macdonald or a Laurier. All of this was in marked contrast to the platitudinous St. Laurent and to Diefenbaker's predecessor, George Drew, who, while feisty in his own way—perhaps too feisty at times—had expounded a brand of conservatism that the emerging welfare state was quickly rendering anachronistic and who had appeared to speak only for Ontario's urban, Protestant elite. As an outsider or anti-establishment figure, Diefenbaker placed an entirely new stamp on the party, giving it the broad appeal it had not had for many years.

Within four years, however, the Conservative party's popularity had plummeted. Garnering seventeen per cent less support than in 1958, it won only a minority of seats in the 1962 election. From within the Conservative party calls for Diefenbaker's resignation became louder. Certainly some of the party's demise was due to bad luck. Coming to power at the onset of the first serious recession since the Great Depression, the Tories were bound to take the brunt of the blame as economic conditions worsened. Scholars generally agree, however, that much of the misfortune that eventually befell the party was a direct result of its own—and especially its leader's— bungling. After winning an incredible fifty seats in Quebec in 1958, for example, the Tories did little to consolidate their gains, organizationally speaking, in that all-important province, or for that matter in any other province, for Diefenbaker was generally uninterested in party organization. More serious was the vacillation the Diefenbaker government displayed in a number of policy areas, foremost among them the question of whether or not to accept nuclear arms on Canadian soil. Its clumsy handling of the Coyne affair—in which Bank of Canada Governor James Coyne was forced to resign, ostensibly on a matter of personal integrity, but in reality as a scapegoat for the policy of high interest rates he was allowed to pursue at a time of rising unemployment (he did not go quietly)—and of other fiscal matters further enhanced the image of incompetence. As a result, the party was forced out of office by Lester Pearson's Liberals less than a year after its minority victory. What support the Conservatives retained after 1963 was concentrated among the over-thirty voters and in the rural areas of Ontario and the West, the new base of the party's support under the "prairie radical" Diefenbaker.

Back in office following the "Diefenbaker interlude," albeit with only a minority government, the Liberals struggled to improve their standing with the voters. New social programs were created, such as medicare and contributory old-age pensions, a distinctly Canadian flag was introduced, and efforts were made to reduce American cultural influences, although the latter two measures produced more division than consensus. The Liberals were somewhat more successful in their efforts to bolster their sagging popularity in Quebec. The departure of native son St. Laurent, combined with poor economic conditions, the government's decision to accept nuclear arms, the resignation of several Quebec ministers under a cloud of scandal, and the growth of Québécois nationalism had done much to undermine the Liberal party's popularity in that province since 1957. To reverse this trend, Pearson's government made concessions to Quebec's demands for greater provincial autonomy. The party also recruited several high-profile francophone candidates for the next election. These measures, aided immeasurably by the turmoil in the Conservative party, which was completely engrossed in a bitter debate over Diefenbaker's leadership, led to gains in the Liberals' seat totals in 1965, although still not enough to form a majority government. Outside the big cities of central Canada, the rather bland, intellectual Pearson was not able to arouse much enthusiasm for himself or his party, especially on the campaign trail, where he was no match for the rabble-rousing Diefenbaker. As a result, the Liberals won no seats in three provinces and a mere nine seats west of the Ontario-Manitoba border.

What restored the Liberals to a position of parliamentary pre-eminence was the sudden and unexpected accession to the leadership of the party of a young and relatively unknown liberal intellectual from Quebec, Pierre Elliott Trudeau. At a time when an increasingly younger populace was seeking from its political leaders youthful vigour and new, more progressive ideas, Trudeau—a "swinging bachelor" by all accounts—seemed to fit the bill in a way that the new, but stodgy leader of the Conservatives, Robert Stanfield, and the folksy, time-worn leader of the NDP, Tommy Douglas, did not. Trudeau also possessed abundant charm and candor as well as the ability to evoke unlimited possibilities, qualities rare among traditional politicians and well suited, indeed, to the confident, adventurous spirit of the Expo '67 generation. Just as important to many voters was Trudeau's determination to affirm the powers of the federal government against Quebec's insistent demands for more power while at the same time promising to make his French-speaking compatriots feel welcome in all of Canada. The Trudeau factor, more than any other, swept the Liberals back into office in June of 1968 with their first majority in fifteen years. And with representation in all provinces save PEI, the Liberals also became a genuinely national party once again. Both were no small accomplishments in a period of mounting social polarization and student protests, phenomena that had many experts predicting the demise of the middle-of-the-road Liberal party.

Under Trudeau the Liberals dominated federal politics in the 1970s and early 1980s, winning elections in 1972, 1974, and 1980. It would be wrong to say, however, that the party's electoral accomplishments came easily or were largely the result of its own doing. These were, in fact, very difficult years for the Liberals and their success can be attributed as much to luck as to concerted effort. It wasn't too long before Trudeau became a liability for the party outside Quebec, quickly gaining a reputation for arrogance and aloofness. At a time of rising unemployment, taxes and prices, Trudeau was further perceived as uncaring and overly preoccupied with constitutional matters. Voters punished the Liberals for this perception in 1972, forcing them to seek the support of the NDP in Parliament to keep their minority government afloat. His political future in jeopardy, a chastened Trudeau quickly took steps to restore his party's popularity. To rebuild local party organizations and to revamp his poor image, he turned to the party's "backroom boys," whose assistance—and that of grassroots Liberals generally—the notoriously apolitical Prime Minister had to that point spurned. In part to satisfy the NDP, but mostly to satisfy voters, his government also implemented a number of costly left-nationalist measures, including higher spending on social programs, with benefits indexed to the inflation rate, and the Foreign Investment Review Agency, to limit American investment in Canada. Trudeau's conversion to traditional politician was complete when on the advice of his new political handlers he took to the campaign trail in 1974 (having refused to do so two years prior) and managed to endear himself to the legions of voters he met along the way. The end result of this rehabilitation program was a comfortable Liberal majority.

The Liberals' next brush with political death occurred in 1979. After a brief honeymoon following the 1974 victory, the party's popularity once again began to fall. By 1976 it was at its lowest in over three decades. Economic factors were largely to blame, as unemployment and inflation continued to rise, but Trudeau, whom voters loved to hate, also contributed greatly to the decline. Marital problems and the coming to power of the separatists in Quebec in 1976 had made the Prime Minister particularly irritable, and he often vented his frustrations on his opponents in Parliament and in the media. Forced finally to call an election in the spring of 1979, the Liberals were unceremoniously removed from office. What's more, it looked as though this situation would endure, for although the Conservatives had only a minority government and were now led by the much-maligned Joe

Clark, they felt certain that with a referendum on sovereignty-association looming in Quebec and with Trudeau planning to resign shortly as Liberal leader, another election would not come for some time, giving them ample opportunity to prove themselves in office.

What transpired, instead, is truly the stuff of political thrillers. Seven months into its mandate and not long after Trudeau had effectively surrendered the Liberal leadership, the Clark government introduced its first budget, the central feature of which was a major hike in gas taxes, a measure sure to alienate gas-guzzling Ontario. The unexpected defeat of the budget on a vote in the House by the combined NDP-Liberal opposition led to the calling of another election. In an equally surprising move, Trudeau was asked to once again lead the Liberal party in the upcoming campaign. Feeling more relaxed and content than he had for some time, and believing it was important to have a French-speaking federalist as Prime Minister during the Quebec referendum called for May 1980 by the Quebec government, he agreed. In the campaign that followed, however, his aids kept him out of the spotlight, aware that anti-Trudeau sentiment still ran high in English Canada. They counted, instead, on the unpopularity of Joe Clark and of his government's budget to win them the election. It was a shrewd strategy and it worked. In what must be counted as the most dramatic political comeback since Mackenzie King in 1926, the Liberals were returned to office in 1980 with an eleven-seat majority, pushing the Trudeau era into its third decade.

What the elections between 1968 and 1980 demonstrate above all is that while the Liberal party enjoyed much success, it was often in spite of its leader, its policies, or its organization. The best organization in the world would not have likely saved the Liberals in 1979, so unpopular was their leader and their record. Rather, the Liberals were fortunate to have been faced in this period with a Tory party whose leaders, for all their decency and intelligence, were distinctly lacking in public appeal, and whose policies were very much out of tune with the public mood for much of the period. Both Stanfield and Clark were decent, capable individuals but in the television age neither could hold a candle to the charismatic and telegenic Trudeau. Similar shortcomings hurt the party on the policy front. Many English Canadians considered the Conservatives' "two nations" approach to the Quebec "problem"—whereby Canada was said to consist of two nations, not one—a sop to Quebec separatists, disliked the idea of giving more power to the provinces, feared the imposition of wage and price controls promised by Stanfield in 1974, and, at least in central Canada, still valued such nationalist programs as the Foreign Investment Review Agency and Petro-Canada, both of which the Tories promised to dismantle. Add to these voter concerns the party's continued neglect of Quebec, organizationally and otherwise (which cost the Conservatives a majority government in 1979), and it seems fair to say that except for 1968, the Liberals did not win the elections of these years as much as the Tories lost them. The quick reversal in Liberal popularity following each election, 1980 included, further suggests as much.

Two developments in the early 1980s spelled a more prolonged interruption to the Liberal party's hold on national power. The first development was the growing conservatism of the period. In the context of high unemployment, double-digit interest and inflation rates, rising taxes, and growing deficits, problems that Liberal governments were unable to resolve and for which they were often blamed, voters began turning away from the liberal-interventionist philosophy of the postwar years to embrace a neo-conservative, "get the government off the people's back" agenda espoused by such popular leaders as US President Ronald Reagan and British Prime Minister Margaret Thatcher. Alongside this development emerged a similar antipathy toward centralized federalism, an antipathy that Quebec governments had held for some time, but that was now being echoed by most western provinces as well. The Progressive Conservative party, with its more right-of-centre, decentralist philosophy was the prime beneficiary of this shift in the public mood, particularly in western Canada, where the Trudeau governments' oil pricing and foreign investment review policies had been wildly unpopular.

The other development was the Conservative party's selection of Brian Mulroney as Joe Clark's replacement in 1983. The party, whose base of support had shifted markedly westward and toward the rural areas during and since the Diefenbaker years, now had at its helm an urbane, fluently bilingual Quebecker who promised to do whatever was necessary to secure for the Conservatives the support of his home province, while at the same time maintaining the party's rural western stronghold. Under Mulroney, who unlike his predecessors could communicate effectively through the media— a crucial difference—the Conservatives spoke, therefore, of constitutional decentralization, fiscal responsibility, better relations with the US, privatizing key public assets, and deregulating industry, all the while preserving the essential elements of the welfare state. These two developments, assisted by a poorly run Liberal campaign and the active support of many Quebec separatists, whom Mulroney had courted with promises of favours, brought the Tories to the seat of national power once again. In 1984 they carried a surprising 211 seats, three more than in the Diefenbaker landslide of 1958. Sixty of the seats were in Quebec, a sign that perhaps the Conservatives were on the verge of displacing the almighty Liberals in that province.

The 1984 election inaugurated what might be called the Conservative party's first mini-dynasty at the federal level this century, as it gained re-election four years later with a reduced, but still sizable majority. Aside from the key factors just outlined, the Conservatives' back-to-back majorities can be attributed to the vastly improved economic conditions of the late eighties and the fulfillment of some of its main promises, including the dismantling of the Liberals' economic-nationalist programs, the signing of a free trade agreement with the US (lavishly promoted by the business community in the 1988 campaign), and the devolution of constitutional powers, exemplified by the Meech Lake constitutional accord of 1987, all of which met with reasonably high approval ratings at the time. The Liberals, meanwhile, were unable to persuade voters that despite the more right-wing orientation of their new leader, John Turner, they were really very different from the Trudeau Liberals or that they were capable, in view of Turner's rather stiff and awkward public presence, of running the country efficiently. In an age of rapidly falling trade and communication barriers, moreover, the liberal-nationalist appeal that had stood the party in good stead for many years did not quite evoke the same response it once had, although in the "free trade" election of 1988 the Liberals certainly tried. The fact that the party was also quite divided between its left and right wings over social policy and consti-tutional questions—even more so than it had been in the Pearson-Trudeau years—only made matters worse, especially when it came time to rebuild the party's tattered electoral machinery. Therefore, even though Turner had helped restore his party's parliamentary representation to a respectable eighty-three seats in 1988, the Liberals replaced him two years later with Jean Chrétien, another veteran from the Trudeau era.

What eventually brought the Conservatives down was a combination of unpopular leadership, stagnant economic growth, and failed constitutional initiatives. In 1984 Mulroney had given the impression that he was going to do politics differently, that backroom deals, pork-barrelling, and petty patronage were to be significantly reduced, if not eliminated. When the exact opposite occurred, and a slough of ministers were forced to resign for various improprieties, Canadians felt betrayed. The cynicism and lack of trust voters came to feel toward Mulroney and his administrations were amplified by the failure of free trade to produce the promised gains, the creation of a Goods and Services Tax, which offset any gains to consumers from lower import duties, and the government's inability to reduce its sizable and still growing budgetary deficit. The severe downturn in the economy—the most serious since the Great Depression—was an additional liability. Perhaps the most damaging factor, however, was the government's failed attempts at constitu-tional reform. The defeat of the Meech Lake and Charlottetown Accords in the early 1990s, both of which sought to meet the often irreconcilable demands of various social groups and provincial governments for constitu-tional recognition and greater powers, produced widespread disillusionment and constitutional weariness, in turn sparking the rise of new and fundamentally opposed regional protest parties in Quebec and the West. These parties (discussed below) cut deeply into Tory support in the 1993 federal election. Even under its newly chosen, and first female leader, former Defence Minister Kim Campbell, the party was unable to stave off the inevitable thrashing it received from the voters in that election. It won a mere two seats, and for the first time since 1867 was not recognized as an official parliamentary party.

The Liberals, on the other hand, were restored to their traditional position as the ruling party with a strong majority. Once again, however, it had triumphed less on its own strengths and more on the weaknesses of its opponents. Apart from having to bear the crushing legacy of the Mulroney years, Campbell's Conservatives had run a poor campaign, one that included a tasteless attack on the physical infirmities of the Liberal leader. Furthermore, the Tories had had to share for the first time a large portion of the right-wing vote with another party, the western-based Reform party, allowing the Liberals to win plurality victories in many ridings.

Nevertheless, the Liberal government managed to consolidate its support during its first term. It made substantial progress in reducing the deficit, paid little attention to constitutional matters (in deference to the constitutional fatigue across Canada), avoided the sorts of scandals that had plagued its predecessors, and, in true Mackenzie King fashion, did little to alienate voters. Granted, this approach to governing was unexciting and entailed little in the way of bold initiatives, but in the cynical atmosphere of the nineties, with voter regard for politicians at an all time low, this lack of excitement, too, probably worked to the party's advantage, as did Prime Minister Chrétien's more laid back, down-to-earth public persona and a more favourable economic climate. As a result, the Liberals were re-elected with a second consecutive (albeit slim) majority in June 1997 and both the party and its leader continue to enjoy high public approval ratings. Whether we have a new Liberal dynasty in the making is, of course, anyone's guess, but continued economic growth, a divided opposition (now consisting of four official parties) that shows few signs of coalescing, and continued progress toward balancing the budget all bode well for Canada's government party into the millennium.

While the domination of federal politics by the Liberals is perhaps the most salient feature of Canadian party politics since 1945, the general picture of continuity and stability should not be exaggerated, for this was also a period in which old-party loyalties were far more tenuous than before. The move away from old-party loyalties was most evident in the relatively high number of minority governments elected after the war—six out of sixteen governments, compared to only two between 1867 and 1945. In part the greater number of minority governments is attributable to the Diefenbaker phenomenon. The Conservative leader's charismatic personality and more populist approach to issues jarred traditional Liberal attachments, particularly at a time when voters were bored with that party and its uninspiring leader. The growing convergence of the two parties in terms of their platforms—with differences centred largely on the details of the welfare state that each was promising to expand—merely reinforced this trend. Underlying the looseness of party affiliation, moreover, was the changing nature of the electorate itself, particularly by the 1960s. Under the influence of the baby boom generation and the more liberal, experimental atmosphere it helped inaugurate, voters became less attached to traditional politicians and parties. Hence the tremendous popularity, initially, of Diefenbaker and Trudeau. In the absence of, or after greater acquaintance with such leaders, however, voters seemed more willing than ever to transfer their allegiance between the main parties, or to third parties, or, in the era of "participatory democracy," to bypass parties altogether in favour of more direct forms of political protest, such as public demonstrations and private lobbying. The volatility of public opinion polls between elections and the regularly high undecided vote just before them are further testimony to the chameleon-like behaviour of Canadian voters in this period.

A more visible limitation on the portrait of one-party rule outlined above is the vitality of third parties at both the federal and provincial level in this period. Initially, the federal CCF and the Social Credit parties remained the leading third parties in terms of seats and popular vote. Postwar prosperity reduced somewhat the support of each. The CCF was burdened additionally by the public's Cold War-induced fear of socialism, a program that during a time of tremendous growth predicted recession, the CCF's growing ties to organized labour, and the piecemeal adoption of its program by the old parties. Both the CCF and Social Credit benefited somewhat in the mid-fifties from the growing disaffection with the Liberals and increasing unemployment, but they did not benefit nearly as much as the Conservatives. The Diefenbaker landslide of 1958 left the CCF with a paltry eight seats (only one more than it held in 1935) and the Social Credit party with none. What's more, both parties remained predominantly regional, with the bulk of their support in the West.

The failure to advance after the war led the CCF to undertake a process of ideological and organizational renewal in the late fifties. While the party continued to stress the need for state economic planning, it placed less emphasis on government ownership and more on social policies, such as national health insurance, low-cost housing, and aid to universities. More significant, it took the lead in the formation of a "New Party," one with closer ties and greater appeal to organized labour and the rapidly expanding urban middle class. This process culminated in the formation of the New Democratic Party (NDP) in Ottawa in 1961, led by former CCF premier of Saskatchewan Tommy Douglas. The NDP's popularity rose only slowly, however, and in 1968 it still had fewer seats than at the height of its previous incarnation. There were several reasons for this lack of success, including the widespread belief that the NDP was dominated by powerful unions, the implementation of several key NDP policies by the ruling Liberals, and serious intraparty divisions over policy, which did little to inspire public confidence. The appearance at the helm of the old parties of charismatic, populist-type leaders, who cut deeply into areas of NDP strength, and the electorate's desire in these years to restore stable, majority government by voting for the opposition party most likely to replace the ruling party, were important factors as well.

NDP fortunes improved considerably in the 1970s. Led by the popular CCF veteran David Lewis, and having expelled its troublesome radical faction, the so-called Waffle, the party benefitted from the left-wing nationalist shift in public opinion at this time, mostly at the expense of the centrist Liberals. As such, the NDP held the balance of power in Parliament between 1972 and 1974 and controlled an average of twenty-six seats for the decade as a whole. After a sharp decline in support in the early 1980s, when doubts were expressed about its very survival, the NDP surged to new levels in popular support later in the decade. With only minor changes to its moderate social democratic program and now led by another highly popular figure, Ed Broadbent, the NDP added to its traditional base of working-class support that of former Liberal voters disillusioned with John Turner and his party's pro-business drift. By the summer of 1987 the NDP was actually the most popular party in Canada, and many believed it would form the next

Official Opposition. Indeed it would likely have done so had the resurrected Liberals not monopolized so effectively the anti-free trade issue in the 1988 election campaign and had the NDP achieved the expected breakthrough in Quebec. As it was, the NDP finished an impressive, but disappointing third with forty-three seats, all of them west of Quebec. This election was followed by another period of decline. Broadbent retired in 1990 in favour of the less appealing (or effective) Audrey McLaughlin. The NDP's traditional "tax and spend" program became even less attractive at a time when voters complained of high taxes and government debt. In addition, the unpopularity of several provincial NDP governments rebounded negatively on the federal party. The result was a loss of thirty-four seats in 1993 and, along with this, the loss of official party status. Only when federal cuts to transfer payments began to be felt and after several key Liberal promises went unfulfilled did support for the NDP once again rise. The replacement of McLaughlin with the feisty former leader of the Nova Scotia NDP, Alexa McDonough, helped too. In 1997 the NDP regained official party status with twenty-one seats, including an historic eight seats in the long-barren Atlantic provinces, a region hit hard by federal cuts to transfer payments and unemployment insurance.

While less successful than the CCF/NDP, the federal Social Credit party was also a political force for much of the postwar period. Led initially by Solon Low, who replaced John Blackmore as federal leader in 1945, and boasting a stridently anti-socialist, pro-private-enterprise platform, one that nevertheless continued to favour monthly social dividends as a way of maintaining purchasing power, Social Credit held an average of fifteen seats from 1946 to 1962, all of them from Alberta and British Columbia. In the early sixties, however, the locus of the movement's support shifted almost entirely to Quebec, where a weaker economy, deep disillusionment with the two old parties, and a highly charismatic leader in the person of Réal Caouette resulted in a surprising surge in support for *Le Railliement des Créditistes de Québec* (RC), the newly formed, soon-to-be allied Quebec wing of the Social Credit movement. Caouette was to rural and small-town French Canada what Diefenbaker was to rural English Canada at the time, an evangelical populist leader whose emotional attacks against economic exploitation by unseen corporate villains held strong appeal among those who felt most anxious about their livelihood, especially poor farmers, the unemployed, and the unskilled. When those villains were painted in ethnic terms, the RC also captured some of the growing nationalist vote in the province. Just as important was Caouette's skilled use of television and the impressive street- and factory-floor level organization his followers put in place to deliver the Social Credit message. As a result, the party won thirty seats in 1962, twenty-six of them in Quebec, enough to hold the balance of power in Parliament. Thereafter, basic differences over policy between the then head of the federal party, Robert Thompson, and his Quebec lieutenant, Caouette, caused an irreparable split, with each section going its separate way. No longer a national party speaking with one voice, and faced with improved economic conditions by the mid-1960s, Social Credit went into gradual decline. The RC maintained a corporals' guard of MPs throughout the 1970s, but by 1980 no Social Crediters sat in the federal Parliament or have appeared since.

In some ways the Alberta- and Quebec-based Social Credit parties were replaced in the late 1980s by two new and much more successful regional movements: the Reform party, formed in Alberta in 1987 under the leadership of Preston Manning, son of Alberta's long-time Social Credit premier Ernest Manning, and the Bloc Québécois, a strictly Quebec-based party established in 1990 and led by former federal Tory cabinet minister Lucien Bouchard. While the roots of each can be traced back to at least the 1970s, their immediate origins lie in the Meech Lake Accord. To the West, Meech was symbolic of a number of simmering grievances, in particular a perceived excessive attention to Quebec's demands by federal politicians and the failure of governments to consult broadly with the public in the process leading up to the Accord. To many in Quebec, the failure of all the provinces to ratify Meech constituted an explicit rejection, yet again, of Quebec's constitutional demands and thus of Quebec itself. Reform and the Bloc were the political expressions of these regional discontents.

But whereas the Bloc's agenda is quite narrow, namely, to effect Quebec's separation from the rest of Canada, Reform's is much broader. As an expression, first and foremost, of western alienation, Reform is simply the latest in a line of regional protest parties stretching back to the Progressives and Social Credit. With the former it shares an aversion to the existing political system, which it considers too expensive and too remote from the people, as well as to state-bestowed privileges for individual provinces or groups. Hence it calls for a balanced federal budget, lower, non-progressive taxes, a more powerful, elective, and egalitarian Senate, and an end to constitutional or legislative "special status" arrangements. With Social Credit it shares a conservative social and economic philosophy, one that holds traditional family values, individual self-reliance, and private enterprise in high regard, but that has also shown signs—in its rejection of official biculturalism and multiculturalism for example—of ethnic intolerance.

What distinguishes the Reform party from its regional predecessors, however, is its political strength and durability. In 1993, with a popular vote of nineteen percent, it won fifty-two seats, only two fewer than the Bloc, and in 1997 it gained an additional eight seats, replacing the Bloc as Official Opposition. While its representation remains entirely western-based, the Reform party continues to attract strong support from Ontario, where it captured 19 per cent of the vote in the last election, a sign that Reform's regional grievances—particularly its calls for deficit reduction and no special constitutional status for Quebec—are to a significant degree shared by English-speaking Canadians elsewhere. The Bloc's fall to third place, with forty-four seats, reflects the departure of the popular Bouchard as party leader as well, perhaps, as the waning support for separatism in a province more concerned about its staggering debt and stagnant economy than the constitution. Nevertheless, both parties have had, and will continue to have, a powerful impact on Canadian politics. Reform, for instance, has cut deeply into Conservative support, particularly in the West and Ontario; indeed, recent efforts by Reform to moderate its image on the national unity issue, by appearing less "anti-Quebec," and to "unite the right" by essentially absorbing right-wing Conservatives and their supporters in Ontario under some form of broader, reconstituted Reform party, may not only spell the end for the Tories, but may also present a formidable challenge to the Liberals at the next election. The Bloc, meanwhile, has left the federal Liberal and Conservative parties distant runners-up in Quebec. In short, the most recent surge of political protest has weakened considerably the "national" complexion of the old parties—with Liberal seats concentrated primarily in Ontario and Conservative seats mostly in Atlantic Canada—and created the most regionalized Parliament in Canadian history, developments that do not augur well for national unity.

Third-party vitality in the postwar era has been even more in evidence at the provincial level, especially in the West. In Alberta, which elected its first third-party government in 1921, Social Credit enjoyed a remarkable tenure, stretching uninterrupted from 1935 to 1971. Its success in neighbouring British Columbia was only slightly less impressive. There it ruled from 1952 to 1972, and again from 1975 to 1991, alternating power with the CCF/NDP. In all, British Columbia has been under the administration of a non-Liberal, non-Conservative party since the Second World War. Saskatchewan and Manitoba have also seen their share of third-party rule. In the former, the CCF/NDP has held sway for much of the postwar period, ruling under a number of leaders for thirty-nine of the past fifty-four years. In Manitoba, where a United Farmer government predominated for much of the interwar period, the NDP has been in office for fifteen of the past twenty-nine years. What all of this suggests is that in western Canada, at least, it is the Liberals and Conservatives who have been the real "third" parties, provincially, since 1945.

But even in central Canada, where the old parties have deeper roots, third parties have done well. In Quebec, either the Union Nationale or the Parti Québécois has been in office for thirty-three of the past fifty-four years, while in Ontario, the NDP has been truly competitive since 1967, holding an average of twenty-nine seats, forming the Official Opposition on two occasions, and winning power in 1990 for the first time in its history.

None of the above statistics is meant to imply any radically new directions in governing at the provincial level. What they do suggest, however, is that the undisputed hegemony of the Liberal and Conservative parties at the national level, until very recently, must be considered alongside the impressive performance of third parties provincially, parties that have been more successful in articulating the growing regional, ethnic, and class discontents of an increasingly diverse, politically aware, urban-industrial society.

The final development worth noting for this period is the change that has taken place in the structures and electioneering methods of Canada's political parties. Structurally, the old parties continued along the path of democratization, a process begun in the interwar period and accelerated by the wave of youth-led "participatory democracy" that swept over much of the western world in the 1960s. While most power over program and party affairs still rested with the parliamentary caucuses of these parties, particularly the party leaders, regular Liberal and Conservative members nevertheless gained a larger voice in determining policy and selecting leaders and candidates. Beginning in the late fifties, for example, both the Liberals and Conservatives began holding larger, more inclusive conventions and policy rallies, and by the 1970s party leaders and MPs no longer anointed their successors before stepping down. This democratization process has also included a broadening of the old parties' financial base. Whereas in the past the Liberals and Conservatives relied almost exclusively on contributions from the corporate sector, they now rely almost as much on funding from individuals, through such techniques as computerized direct-mail solicitation and social fundraisers. Changes in the early 1970s to the laws governing election expenses, whereby individual financial contributions now qualified as tax credits, were largely responsible for the new approach.

More noticeable were the changes in the approach of all parties to the voters at election time, changes arising from the spread of television and the development of more sophisticated polling techniques after the war. Television not only meant less face-to-face contact with voters by party leaders and workers, but also less emphasis by parties on conveying their range of policy positions to the public. Parties tried to focus the public's attention, instead, on their leader, whose public persona or image was crafted in the most favourable light possible. The result is that elections became essentially personality contests between cleverly "packaged" party leaders instead of partisan contests per se. Polling facilitated this process by telling parties which policies and which leadership qualities were especially appealing to voters. In short, electioneering became more professional, involving as it did the services of paid professionals, such as pollsters, advertisers, and communications experts, in addition to—and, increasingly, in place of—grassroots volunteers. Of course trying to increase support for one's party by tailoring its image and program to suit the tastes of the day is hardly new to Canadian politics. What the new electronic media of the past half-century have done is simply to make this kind of manipulation easier (and also more expensive) for parties to do. Consequently, slick ads, catchy slogans, and staged photo opportunities, all focused more or less on the party leader, have increasingly become staples of election campaigns since the war.

The changing electioneering methods of Canadian parties raises, as well, the issue of whether parties have declined in importance of late, as some political scientists claim. Certainly less is required of the partisan grassroots supporters and local candidates at election time, given the heavy reliance on paid professionals and their technology to gauge and shape public opinion. The expansion of state bureaucracies has to some extent undermined the role of parties in formulating policies. The concurrent emergence of a more aggressive, autonomous journalism has also reduced somewhat the opposi-tional role held by parties out of office. Moreover, the traditional brokerage function of the leading parties—as mediators and spokespersons for a variety of groups—has been weakened by the growth of single-issue interest groups and, with the arrival of the Charter of Rights and Freedoms in 1982, the greater resort of such groups to the courts to achieve their legislative goals. On the other hand, the unchanging levels of voter turnout, the intense rivalry among party members to secure candidate and leadership nominations, the high numbers of delegates attending party conventions, the greater financial security parties generally enjoy, and the parties' on-going role in raising money, defining issues, building voter coalitions, and getting out the vote all seem to confirm Zev Paltiel's observation that there is "little evidence...Canadian parliamentary parties are either moribund or in decline."[2] The impressive strength of regional parties in recent years reinforces this view.

The central themes of continuity and change that have defined Canadian party politics since 1945 are well illustrated by the readings in this section. In the first, Reg Whitaker demonstrates how in the postwar years the federal Liberals became the "government party," whereby the organizational and policy-making functions of the party were increasingly concentrated in government structures, particularly the bureaucracy, leaving the party's extra-parliamentary wing in a much-weakened condition. In so doing he provides an intriguing explanation for both the success and the eventual decline of the Liberals in the immediate postwar years. The tribulations of the party that replaced the Liberals in 1957 form the subject of the next piece, by George Perlin. Professor Perlin examines the 1960s' manifestation of what he calls "the Tory syndrome," the Conservative party's historic tendency toward internal divisions over leadership, in this case John Diefenbaker's, divisions that arose from and contributed to the party's repeated electoral failure. The author makes clear, nevertheless, that Diefenbaker was to a large extent the architect of his party's demise.

The next three articles highlight the themes of provincial third-party persistence, decline, and buoyancy. My own study of the Ontario CCF/NDP seeks to explain the reasons for both the stagnation and survival of that party—and, by extension, much of Canada's democratic socialist movement—during a difficult period, while at the same time challenging the common view that the CCF/NDP forsook its identity for the sake of electoral gain. Historian Alvin Finkel looks at the virtual disappearance of the once-mighty Social Credit party in Alberta in the 1970s, which the author attributes primarily to the departure of the pragmatic and scrupulous Ernest Manning as leader, the electorate's desire for a change after thirty-five years of Social Credit rule, and the success of the Lougheed Conservatives in assuming the role of regional defenders against federal intrusions. Finkel's comparisons of the party's post-Manning leaders and programs with those of earlier Social Credit administrations provide, as well, an indirect explanation for the tremendous popularity of the party prior to the 1970s. Finkel's piece is followed by Graham Fraser's colourful description of the Parti Québécois' rise to power in Quebec, a development based largely on the unpopularity of then-Premier Robert Bourassa and the nationalist passions unleashed by the air traffic controllers strike of 1976. From this piece we also learn much about the PQ's serious internal divisions over such things as language policy, relations with organized labour, and internal party democracy, divisions that, much to the relief of most federalists, continue to plague the separatist movement.

The remaining selections in this chapter are taken from the works of prominent political journalists and combine a number of the themes discussed above. The recent surge of third-party protest at the federal level, for example, is the subject of studies by Sydney Sharpe and Don Braid, and Judy Steed. Sharpe and Braid provide a succinct account of the birth and explosive growth of the Reform party in the late 1980s, an account that captures skillfully the unique mix of circumstance, ideology, and personality so often the cause of such dramatic political phenomena. Steed, too, focuses on a third party whose popularity rose quickly in the 1980s, in this case the NDP. By detailing the many weaknesses in the party's 1988 campaign strategy and organization, as well as the deep intraparty divisions following its disappointing third-place finish, she conveys clearly the sense of opportunity lost for Canada's perennial third party. Her piece also highlights the importance of modern campaign techniques to the fate of contemporary political parties. This theme also dominates the excerpt from Christina McCall-Newman's *Grits*, an "intimate" look at the workings of the Liberal party since 1957. McCall-Newman recounts the successful efforts of several key political managers to rescue the Trudeau Liberals after the 1972 election debacle using modern campaign techniques, especially image manipulation. Essentially a story about "the making of the Prime Minister," this lively piece also provides valuable insight into the limitations of the "new politics" under the auspices of a stubborn party leader and an increasingly cynical electorate. The last article is a chapter from Jeffrey Simpson's *The Spoils of Power*. Simpson reminds the reader that despite the new methods of political marketing detailed by McCall-Newman, older methods also remained important tools of governing parties—in this case patronage distribution by the Mulroney Conservatives. In the process, Simpson shows how changing forms of political participation and the public's growing intolerance of old-style patronage politics forced the Conservatives to adopt more modern methods of mobilizing support, in turn extending their tenure by another term.

N O T E S

1. Cited in J.M. Beck, *Pendulum of Power: Canada's Federal Elections* (Scarborough: Prentice-Hall, Ltd., 1968), 300.

2. Khayyam Zev Paltiel, "Political Marketing, Party Finance, and the Decline of Canadian Parties," in A. Gagnon and B. Tanguay, eds., *Parties in Transition: Discourse, Organization, Representation* (Scarborough: Nelson, 1989), 343.

PARTY AND STATE IN THE LIBERAL ERA

BY REGINALD WHITAKER

o

It is now possible to summarize the main conclusions of this study. There are two limitations immediately apparent on theoretical generalizations. First, the major thrust of this study has been descriptive rather than analytical, based on the sufficient grounds that so little has been known about Liberal party organization and financing in this period that the mere marshalling of the historical evidence from primary sources is of legitimate interest. Second, the limitation of this study to the period from 1930 to 1958 forbids facile generalizations linking the party structures of that era to those of today. It would be a tempting, but inevitably superficial exercise to draw out lines of historical development from this earlier period to the present. It is to be hoped that studies like the present one will in fact make such broader analyzes possible, but such a task lies outside the scope of this work. The conclusions are thus confined to what can be inferred directly from the evidence here presented.

ENVIRONMENTAL CONSTRAINTS

The environmental constraints on the Liberal party would appear to have been dominated by three factors. The Canadian political system is liberal-democratic, which, as C.B. Macpherson has ably argued,[1] is a system characterized by a fundamental, or structural ambiguity: the coexistence of the democratic and egalitarian values of the political institutions based on universal adult suffrage and the inegalitarian nature of the liberal capitalist

Excerpt from Reginald Whitaker, *The Government Party: Organizing and Financing the Liberal Party of Canada, 1930-58* (Toronto: University of Toronto Press Incorporated, 1977), pp. 401-22. Reprinted with permission of Reginald Whitaker and University of Toronto Press Incorporated.

economic structures upon which the political structures arose historically. The Liberal party was operating in an environment in which two sometimes contradictory forces were at work in shaping the party's role. On the one hand, the party had to finance its operations as a party as well as to manage capitalist economy as a government, both of which left it vulnerable to the demands of the corporate capitalist world. On the other hand, the party had to get votes, which left it vulnerable to the demands of public opinion. Contradictions were not always in evidence between these two forces, but when they were the party was in a state of crisis. Crisis can mean not only danger but opportunity. The Liberal party demonstrated superior skill at calling in one of these forces to redress the balance when the other became too dominating. In the King period this often meant calling in the force of the voters to compensate for the opposition of the private economic interests, but in the St. Laurent period it more often meant calling in the force of corporate capitalism to restrain and manage public opinion. In either event, both the political power of the voters and the economic power of corporate capitalism were in effect resources with which the party, as an intermediary force, could bargain. The ambiguity of this role was heightened, and even cultivated, by the ambiguous ideological role of the party fashioned by Mackenzie King. That the party never rejected the support of the vested capitalist interests, while at the same time never entirely losing its credibility with the voters as a party of democratic reform, left it precisely the flexibility and freedom of action to "wheel and deal" in the centre of the political spectrum and to make the kind of practical accommodations necessary to maintain its hold on power.

The third environmental factor, this somewhat more specific to Canada, was the regional diversity and political fragmentation inherent in a federal society as decentralized as Canada. This factor is at the same time so obvious as to be almost taken for granted, and yet so important that it can scarcely be overestimated. The relatively weak impact of the dominant *class* cleavages of modern industrial society on Canadian party politics in the face of economic regionalization and cultural divisions not only simplified the role of the Liberals as the centre party exploiting the ambiguities and contradictions of liberal-democracy—rather than becoming a victim of them, as in the case of the British Liberal party—but also gave a very particular cast to the structure of the party. It is no exaggeration to say that the structure of the Liberal party in this era can *only* be understood in the light of the impact of federalism on the inherited political structures of the British parliamentary system.

PARTY FINANCE

The relationship between the party and its financial supporters was a complex one, to a degree which rather forbids easy generalizations. The celebrated Beauharnois affair of 1930 [involving improper donations from the Beauharnois Power Company to the Liberal party] was a highly misleading guide to the financial state of the party. The penury into which the party fell following the defeat of that year illustrates two points: first, whatever the motives of corporate donors to political parties, a party which sustained a major defeat was quickly abandoned. This was particularly crucial for the Liberal party whose traditional links had been more to government contractors than to significant sections of big business whose interests closely related to party policy or ideology. A party which depends heavily on government contractors is in obvious difficulties when faced with a period out of office. The second point to emerge from this period is that the party was clearly unwilling to compromise its policies in return for financial support. In the case of the banks and the mining companies, as well as the railway unification issue and the wheat marketing board, there is evidence that the party—and here the role of the party leader must be emphasized— would not alter policy at the behest of businessmen armed with financial inducements. On the other hand, the party's own ideological bent, while it might distance itself from some capitalists interests, drew it close to certain sectors of the corporate world. Capitalism is not a monolithic set of interests, except in those comparatively rare moments when it is challenged by other classes from below or external enemies from without. There were always some sectors of the corporate world, even if not the greater part, which were willing to work with the Liberals, particularly where their interests coincided closely with Liberal policy. Even while still in opposition there were those who found such an identity of outlook—particularly the retail chain stores and the meat packing industry. Later, the Liberal party in office was able to greatly widen the scope of its friendly relations with the corporate world, as the identity of interests broadened and deepened with the years of power.

With the victory of 1935 a major structural problem in financing the party—its separation from office—was ended. Another problem soon manifested itself, however, in the form of Mitch Hepburn's financial blockade of the federal party. The capacity of a strategically well-situated provincial party to dominate certain crucial sectors of private financial support for the party, in this case the resource industries, and to use this financial power to attempt to force its own policy goals on the federal party, was a salutary lesson to the national party both as to the growing decentralization of the structure of Canadian federalism as a result of the growing peripheralization, or Balkanization, of the economy, as well as to the continuing vulnerability of the party, even in office, to the withdrawal of financial support for the campaign fund. Any government in a liberal-democracy is aware of the crucial significance of "business confidence." This general dependence of governments on the private sector was matched by the dependence of the Government party on the continued support of the same interests for the party treasury. In both cases, on the other hand, the party was not without resources of its own with which to bargain—although in neither case was it in a position to ignore these interests altogether. The party's principal resource was its continued hold on office. Hepburn's blockade could only work in the long run if he were able to dislodge the Liberals from power at Ottawa. Failing that, the Liberals would have to be dealt with as the Government party, and business could not afford to ignore the implications of this for its continued relations with government.

The contract levy system which Norman Lambert enforced in the late 1930s was predicated upon the desire of business to maintain good public relations with government as a major purchaser of goods and services from the private sector. This system not only was maintained after Lambert's departure from active party work, but was extended and deepened. Two developments made this consolidation possible. The enormous growth of government intervention in the private sector, arising out of the demands of the wartime economy and the commitment to interventionist Keynesian fiscal policies following the war, along with the maintenance of relatively high levels of defence expenditure in the Cold War period, had a specific meaning for the financing of the Government party. A greatly expanded state sector which involved government in continuous interaction with private corporations as sellers of goods and services to this sector, enhanced the scope for party finance—on a contract levy system where tenders were in force, or on a straight patronage basis where public bidding was not the practice. That this growth of state activity was expressed initially through the federal government, and that this centralization was closely associated with the policies of the Liberal party, also meant that the position of the federal party was reinforced in relation to its provincial counterparts. Of course, business generally wishes to retain good relations with government parties, especially when government intervention in the private sector becomes less predictable than in the past. There is also the motive of wishing to purchase access to decision-makers in case of difficulty. Thus, with or without the specific connection of government contracts, the federal Liberal party was able to increase its capacity for financing its activities as a partisan organization through the 1940s and into the 1950s. Another sign of this improved financial position was the growing regularization of funding over the inter-election period, reflected in the growing ability of the party in the 1950s to finance its day-to-day operations on a normal business basis—a condition which had certainly not existed in the 1930s.

Party finance was not an isolated factor; party organization was intimately, even inextricably, bound up with the problem of party finance. Adequate financing was the necessary, although not the sufficient, condition for the vitality of the party as an organization. The genesis of the National Liberal Federation in the early 1930s was as much, if not more, a matter of fundraising as it was a matter of creating an extra-parliamentary organization for electoral purposes. Vincent Massey was selected by the party leader most of all because of his presumed access to sources of party funds, and his desire for post-election assignment to the London High Commission was used by Mackenzie King as a club to force Massey unwillingly to abandon a policy-making role to concentrate on fundraising. Norman Lambert, as Massey's successor, was above all a finance chairman and "fixer" for linking financial supporters with government business. Following the war the close connection between NFL officials and fundraising continued, from Gordon Fogo through Duncan MacTavish through Alan Woodrow to Bruce Matthews.

This concentration of the extra-parliamentary party on fundraising may indicate an endemic condition of cadre parties, with their aversion to mass membership participation in policy-making or leadership selection, and their extreme vulnerability to a small number of corporate donors, but it also illustrates two specific factors of the Canadian political experience in this era. First, the Liberal party, especially under King's leadership, was haunted by the spectre of the Beauharnois affair, and found considerable political utility in a formal separation of the fundraising apparatus from the parliamentary leadership of the party. Duverger's notion of "contagion from the left" impelling cadre parties into extra-parliamentary organization proves to be of limited significance here. There is very little evidence of demands for participation by the rank-and-file membership in policy-making or even leadership selection in this era of the Liberal party's history. Nor is there much, if any, evidence of a perception of electoral threat from mass party techniques of campaigning. The move of the Liberal party toward extra-parliamentary organization had much more to do with the demands of party finance.

The second major factor forcing the national party's attention on party finance was the divergence between the concentration of economic power in the private sector—both in the corporate and in the regional sense—in a small handful of influential corporations in Toronto and Montreal and the decentralized nature of the formal political system. As a political organization, the Liberal party was based on the constitutional distribution of elective offices into more than two hundred local constituencies and nine provinces (ten after Newfoundland's entry into Confederation). However much the central regions might dominate the party as a whole, such centralization could in no way match the centralization of private economic power. Indeed, the autonomy of the local units of the party in a political and electoral sense was one of the characteristics of the Liberal party as an organization, and the very structure of the formal institutional arrangements of election under the parliamentary system of single-member constituency voting ensured that this would be so. Consequently, the scope of such political activities as electoral organization and policy-making on the part of an extra-parliamentary national office was necessarily limited; on the other hand, the importance of the small number of party donors in two concentrated geographical locations meant that local units of the party at the provincial and constituency level were generally incapable of generating the necessary contacts for fundraising purposes—but for the crucial exception of the provincial units in these areas. With this exception and its consequent problems aside, it is clear that party finance would necessarily be one area of party activity best left to an extra-parliamentary wing of the national party. Hence the high degree of concentration on this one activity most relevant to the extra-parliamentary national party.

PARTY ORGANIZATION

There is no doubt that the Liberal party was a cadre party in many of the senses that Duverger uses the term: parliamentary in origin, small in membership, deriving support from local notables, etc. Yet I have already suggested that there is little evidence of Duverger's "contagion from the left" as a factor shaping the party's structure. The growth of an extra-parliamentary party alongside the parliamentary party did not come about as the emulation of a successful mass socialist party organization on the left—since such never did develop fully at the national level in Canada—but rather as the consequence of electoral defeat, in 1930, or the fear of defeat during the Second World War. Even when, as in the latter case, it was fear of a leftward trend in public opinion and the possible capitalization of the CCF on this trend which moved the party to change its approach, the specific *organizational* changes introduced in the party were not very significant; changes rather took place on the level of policy and party program. There was no democratization of the party organization or any shift of influence from the parliamentary to the extra-parliamentary party; rather the parliamentary leadership skilfully manipulated the extra-parliamentary structure to help initiate desired policy changes. Once the next election was won, the organization reverted to its former state.

The point is that a cadre party operating in a federal system is particularly vulnerable in an organizational sense to the loss of office, not only because the fruits of power are useful resources for party organization but also because the party lacks a firm and loyal *class* basis of support in the electorate. Moreover, the fact that the party's provincial bases are not really bases at all, but rather problematic elements in the overall structure of the national party, with different electorates, different concerns, and even different sources of party funding, means that a national cadre party out of office cannot rely on the provincial parties as a second, fallback position for the national party in its hour of organizational need. Conversely, if it does (as in the case of Ontario in the 1930s), it may be creating organizational and political problems for itself in the long run.

The alternative in this situation is for the defeated cadre party to create an extra-parliamentary structure to undertake some of the functions normally carried out by the cabinet ministers while in office. This in turn reflects the particular cast which federalism gives to cadre parties in office, which can be called a *ministerialist* system of party organization. This system places a premium on the regional representativeness of the executive, and encourages the emergence of regional power brokers as key cabinet ministers, who thus play a double role as administrators and as political leaders of regions. When the administrative powers of patronage are severed from the political role of regional power-broking, ministerialist organization becomes a liability rather than an asset to the party. Hence the attempt to create an extra-parliamentary wing of the party as an electoral alternative, particularly when the party leader, as in the case of King from 1930 to 1935, is unwilling to personally assume the organizational burden.

On the other hand, when the party returns to power the extra-parliamentary party diminishes drastically in importance in the face of the return to ministerialism. In the case of the Liberal party after 1935, however, one can see a new factor entering into the parliamentary versus extra-parliamentary equation. In the absence of strong class bases to national politics, cadre-ministerialist party organization rests most comfortably on what can be loosely called a patron-client model. The regional discontinuities of the country lend themselves to a clientist type of politics in which one sees vertical integration of subcultures and horizontal accommodation among the elites generated by these subcultures. So long as politics revolves mainly around questions of patronage and regional bargaining, ministerialism fits in well with the needs of the party as an organization. Even out of office, as with the creation of the NFL in the early 1930s, the promise of future patronage considerations is a powerful weapon to line up political support. Yet to the extent that the forces of industrialism and urbanism and events such as depressions and world wars intrude on this somewhat petty little political stage (the provincialism and sordidness of which was noted by earlier outside observers such as Lord Bryce and André Siegfried),[2] the attention of governments is drawn inevitably toward wider problems, which demand universalist, bureaucratic solutions rather than the old-fashioned particu-larist solutions of patronage political cultures. Under the pressure of these external forces, ministerialist government becomes administrative government, politics turns into bureaucracy, and the Liberal party becomes the Government party. Paradoxically, ministerialist organization thus becomes an impediment to the political health of the party as a patronage organization, as well as the source of the necessary instruments of that type of politics. In these conditions there is a continued need for some sort of extra-parliamentary wing of the party to maintain the necessary contacts between the party's external supporters and the largesse of the government, to coordinate the patronage side of the party's operations, and to remind it constantly of its role as an electoral as well as an administrative organization. Thus the NFL did not disappear entirely after the return to office in 1935, as had happened in 1921. The partisan ceasefire in the war years coupled with the intense and accelerated bureaucratization and centralization of the wartime government led to such a political crisis for the Liberal party that it found it necessary to call the extra-parliamentary party back into existence to help get the electoral machine functioning once again. Ministerialism thus generated its own limitations.

The electoral victory of 1945, in which the party's ability to respond to *class* politics as well as regional politics was tested, and the return of prosperity in the aftermath of war, laid the foundations for an apparent reversal of the relationships just indicated. After the war the extra-parlia-mentary party was relegated to the status of a mere paper "democratic" legitimatization of ministerialist organization. Even party publicity was in effect "farmed out" to a private advertising agency in return for government business, thus directly linking party publicity with state publicity. The Liberal party's transformation into the Government party had reached its logical culmination, with the virtual fusion of party and state. The Liberals won two general elections under this arrangement, and convinced most observers that they could continue indefinitely. But they lost the third election, and then suffered a devastating collapse when faced with the necessity of running while out of office, suddenly bereft of ministerialist organization, yet lacking any real extra-parliamentary party organization.

Ministerialist organization thus appears as a curiously ambiguous factor in party organization. Partly as a result of this ambiguity, the role of the national leader in the Liberal party was of paramount importance. When the party was out of office in the early 1930s the leader was in a very real sense the sole representative of the national party. In the aftermath of defeat, it is no exaggeration to assert that Mackenzie King had become the sole personal embodiment of the party in any significant way. The parliamentary party remained, but without clear responsibilities, and often without either the inclination or the ability to function as a continuing party organization. Hence King's frantic efforts to set up an extra-parliamentary organization for purposes of election planning and especially fundraising, since the responsibility for these activities was forcing an intolerable burden on his own shoulders. It should also be noted that when out of office the potential patronage powers of the leader of the opposition in a future government are almost the only inducements available to the party for organizational purposes. This places the leader squarely at the centre of the political stage, to a degree which would appear to almost match the domination of the party by an incumbent prime minister. There is no doubt that Mackenzie King returned to office in 1935 in a stronger and more commanding position over his parliamentary party and his ministers than that which he had enjoyed before defeat. The circumstances of that period of opposition may have been exceptional, and no attempt should be made to generalize on the role of the leader of a party on the strength of this example. What is clear, however, is that the crucial role of the leader in the party organization was enhanced by this experience, and that the creation of an extra-parliamentary party was not a detraction from the role of the leader but rather an instrument of the leader's continued influence over all aspects of the party's operations.

The well-known patronage powers of an incumbent prime minister, his direct relationship with the voters, his prerogative of dissolution, and his financial control over the fortunes of individual candidates, all demonstrate that the role of the party leader while in power is of enormous importance. Yet ministerialist organization, as well as the concentration of the prime minister on policy and administrative matters, tended to push the Liberal party in power toward a somewhat more diffuse distribution of responsibilities for party organization than had been the case while out of office. This tendency became quite striking when a new leader, Louis St. Laurent, who showed not the slightest interest in matters of party organization, allowed a still greater degree of devolution of responsibility in these matters to his ministers. Paradoxically perhaps, the greater strength of ministerialism in the St. Laurent years is itself an indication of the discretionary role of the leader in shaping the party organization; Liberal leaders had the capacity to leave their personal stamp on the party structure, even if, as in St. Laurent's case, this stamp was delegation of authority to his cabinet colleagues. Under King's direction the party organization, as well as the cabinet, was under tighter control. Yet it must also be pointed out that this greater control was only a matter of degree. It is clear from the historical record that King's ability to dominate his colleagues was limited, the limit being well recognized by King himself. Ministerialism was more than a tactic of a certain kind of prime minister; it was a structural feature of cabinet government in a regionally divided society. The historical circumstances and the accident of personality might allow greater or lesser scope for ministerialism, but the *fact* of ministerialism was not subject to these vicissitudes. National party organization when the Liberal party was in office derived its basic structure from the interplay of the leadership of the prime minister and the ministerialist distribution of responsibilities.

The domination of the extra-parliamentary by the parliamentary leadership was an inevitable feature of a cadre-ministerialist party in a federal political system. This did not make the administrative task of the extra-parliamentary officials an easy one, in the sense of a division of responsibilities and recognition for their work. In the case of both Vincent Massey and Norman Lambert, the problems of status and position were acute. Massey was obviously over-qualified in the sense of social prestige and self-evaluation for the instrumental task which King had set him. The severe personal problems which beset the relationship between the NLF president and the party leader during Massey's short tenure indicated that in future less "weighty" persons would have to be selected for the NLF. Norman Lambert was much less prestigious a figure than Massey—as well as being more appropriate for the position in terms of skills and interests—but Lambert's difficulties in dealing with the party leader arose from another, although related source. In order to do the job of national organizer, fundraiser, party "fixer," and director of the party publicity office, Lambert believed that as NLF president he must be given official recognition by the party leadership, in order that the requisite authority be vested in the position. The reluctance of the party leader to grant this recognition, and the consequent inability of Lambert to deal on a level of equal footing with the cabinet ministers, meant that his capacity to carry out his duties was constantly hemmed in by frustration and sometimes by direct opposition of elements of the parliamentary party.

In this situation there would appear to be more than the structural constraints of ministerialism and federalism at work: to King, party organization work was "dirty work," slightly tainted, not quite respectable, and above all to be kept at arm's length to avoid any possibility of his own office being infected with scandal. To St. Laurent, party politics was rather boring and unworthy of much attention, best left to those with a taste for that sort of thing. In either event, the result was the same: the extra-parliamentary party lacked prestige and authority. Lambert, as well as some of his financial collectors, found this invidious position intolerable, and eventually parted ways with the Liberal parliamentary leadership. While direct historical evidence of dissatisfaction on the part of later incumbents in the NLF presidency is lacking, it is clear that none of Lambert's successors held positions of any greater prestige than Lambert. If they were satisfied with their role it could only be because their expectations were lower than

Lambert's had been. Finally, when one reaches the level of the secretariat of the national office, there is no question of the strictly instrumental role expected of these officers. People like H.E. Kidd and Paul Lafond displayed the utmost modesty and self-effacement in their dealings with the parliamentary leadership, as well as in their relationship to the NFL president and executive. They were the closest thing in the Canadian context to party bureaucrats. It is a mark of the domination of the parliamentary leadership as well as the weak level of extra-parliamentary organization in this country that these party bureaucrats never became, as sometimes happened in the European context, "apparatchiks," men of indirect but powerful influence on the party. Since they were not holding the levels of power they could not manipulate them. More to the point, there is no evidence that they harboured such ambitions; if they had, they would not have assumed such positions.

The weakest aspects of the extra-parliamentary party in this era were the policy-making function and the question of leadership selection. Mackenzie King derived his ultimate legitimacy as party leader from the 1919 convention, but it was a legitimacy which he never allowed to be put to the test of renewal by the assembled party membership. Since there was no provision in the party constitution and no overwhelming party demand for national conventions during King's tenure, a generation passed without a single assembly embodying the membership base of the party in any significant sense. The advisory council meetings held infrequently over the years were the closest approximation to conventions but in terms of numbers and of authority they were far from substitutes. Advisory councils were effectively dominated by the parliamentary party and rarely fulfilled other than honorific and formal duties. The one apparent exception was the 1943 meeting which adopted the welfarist program which the party carried into the 1945 election campaign. This was not the result of autonomous action, however, but of superbly executed manipulation by a parliamentary leadership which wished to legitimize new directions in policy which had been planned by the civil service and advisers to the prime minister.

Massey's attempts at policy-making in the early 1930s met the active hostility of the party leader and the indifference of the parliamentary caucus as a whole. That the party leadership expended considerable anxiety and energy at the various advisory council meetings over the question of preventing anything remotely critical of the parliamentary party's policies from being aired is a striking indication of how far parliamentary control over policy went: the extra-parliamentary membership was not only to be powerless in deciding policy, but it had to be *seen* to be powerless as well. The smallest hint of disagreement over policy among Liberals—which is to say, the hint of any dissension from the policies adopted by the parliamentary leadership—was to be avoided at all costs. Democratic legitimization of the internal processes of decision-making in the party was accepted, but only at the most rarefied and abstract level, that of the mandate of the party leader derived from the majority vote of a party convention at one point in time. The autonomy of the parliamentary party in policy-making was justified in rhetorical terms by the invocation of the constitutional supremacy of

Parliament. Whatever the merits of that argument, it was rendered somewhat problematic by the increasing bureaucratic influence on the policies of the parliamentary leadership, to the extent that by the last years of the St. Laurent period virtually all Liberal policy was formulated by the permanent civil service. Policy-making was delegated to an institution which was, in the formal sense at least, non-political as well as non-partisan. The exclusion of the extra-parliamentary party membership from policy-making may thus be viewed as a mater of practical expediency rather than as one of constitutional principle. The party membership was not judged competent to formulate policy.

The 1948 national convention which chose Louis St. Laurent as King's successor best illustrates these relationships within the Liberal party. The extraordinary lengths to which the party leadership went, in this unique example of a national party meeting throughout the period of this study, to prevent any public manifestation of criticism or disagreement within the membership extended not only to policy questions but to the matter of leadership itself. The evidence clearly indicates that the convention format was manipulated throughout to ensure that King's chosen successor should receive as little opposition as possible. On the other hand, the necessary democratic legitimization seemed to demand that St. Laurent receive some token opposition. Both imperatives were carried out in a remarkable example of stage-managed conflict, in which the two genuine opponents of St. Laurent were effectively utilized for maximum public effect and minimum internal impact. Even in the case of the selection of the party leader then, the "democratic" mandate becomes highly questionable, and the domination of the party by the parliamentary leadership is seen to be decisive.

Conventions at the constituency level during this era would appear to have served equivalent legitimization purposes for the parliamentary élite. Nomination votes by the constituency association membership were often, although not always, called before elections. Rarely were these exercises more than empty formalities. Sitting members were virtually assured of renomination; defeated candidates from the previous election had the inside track; and if neither of these conditions obtained, the local cabinet minister and his organizers would normally anoint the man they wanted for the nomination. The association would then ratify the choice. It did not happen like this in every instance, but it was the general rule. Observers of contemporary Canadian political culture who have noted the "quasi-participative" nature of Canadian democracy[3] might examine the role of the Liberal party, the dominant party in Canadian politics for well over a generation, in the political socialization of its members and supporters. The Liberal party was certainly no training ground for participatory democracy, however loosely that phrase might be defined. If anything, the dominant values which it propagated as a mediating institution between the state and the mass of the citizens were those of deference and unreflective loyalty.

Deference and loyalty are political values appropriate to the clientist web of relationships which formed the basic structure of the party. Clientist relationships, moreover, flourished in the era of one-party dominance, when the Liberals as the Government party monopolized the basic medium of exchange in patron-client politics: patronage. But the general condition referred to earlier, the transformation of politics into bureaucracy in the period of one-party dominance, had a double effect on the party as an organization. The use of the state as a reward system for party loyalty effectively drained away the human resources of the party as a partisan organization into levels of the bureaucracy and judiciary where they could no longer be of political use to the party. Second, as an inevitable consequence of the first problem, the party had to rely heavily on direct cooperation from the bureaucracy or the private sector to replenish its parliamentary leadership. Thus it merged more and more intimately with the senior civil service, both in terms of policies and personnel, and with the corporate élite outside the state system itself but in regular contact with government. For these organizational reasons, as well as for the more general ones mentioned earlier, the party became less and less distinct as an entity, its separation from the state system and the private sector more and more blurred. The Government party was becoming in a curious sense a non-partisan party, so long as its hold on office was not challenged. Some might prefer to argue that it was a case of the bureaucrats being made into Liberals. Yet however one approaches the question, it seems reasonable to conclude that the Liberal party, as a political party, was growing less distinct, that the party was more a vehicle for élite accommodation, involving not only the élites of the two linguistic and cultural groups in Canada but the bureaucratic and corporate élites as well, than a partisan organization. When partisanship got in the way of élite accommodation it was partisanship which was usually discarded. No better example of this can be found than in the examination of federal-provincial relations within the Liberal party in this era.

FEDERAL-PROVINCIAL PARTY RELATIONS

The relations between the federal and provincial wings of the Liberal party were examined in some depth. The conclusions of this examination may be most usefully divided into two parts: the central provinces of Ontario and Quebec and the hinterland or peripheral area of the West and the East.

Quebec, as the homeland of French Canada, held a special status within the national Liberal party, based on tradition and a mild form of consociational tolerance. Yet it was Ontario, with its strong and semi-autonomous economic base, which mounted the toughest challenge to the dominance of the national party in this era. In both cases the federal party ran into difficulties with its provincial counterpart, to a moderate degree in Quebec and to an extreme degree in Ontario. In Quebec, electoral defeat for the provincial party in the mid-1930s gave the federal party, which remained ascendant in its own electoral sphere, the opportunity to control the provincial party, even to the extent of guiding it back into office briefly. Eventually, the federal party settled into a pattern of constituency collaboration with its provincial party's enemy, and more or less accommodative intergovernmental relationships with the Union Nationale in terms of federal-provincial affairs, including accommodations which sometimes drastically undercut the political position of its provincial counterpart. In Ontario, a politically (and even financially) stronger provincial party in the mid-1930s waged open war on the federal party, even extending its campaign to Quebec, both on the intergovernmental and political fronts. This vigorous challenge was finally defeated by intelligent mobilization of the federal party's resources, and the intervention of an external event, the coming of the Second World War. Following the provincial defeat, the federal Liberals managed very well in Ontario by allowing a much weakened and discredited provincial party to flounder unaided in the further reaches of opposition, while dealing with the Conservative provincial government in federal-provincial relations with little regard to partisan considerations. Thus, in both cases, the long-run result was the same: the federal party prospered in the two largest provinces without a strong provincial wing. Little was done to aid the provincial parties, and, in the Quebec case, much was done to damage the provincials. This distant relationship was matched by an emphasis on intergovernmental relations with the provincial administrations of the opposite political colour. In other words, executive federalism overrode federal-provincial party solidarity. The Government party at Ottawa preferred to deal with other governments.

Intra-party relationships with the hinterland regions of Canada were not normally troubled by financial competition between the federal and provincial wings. The financial superiority of the federal party was almost always evident. In the Atlantic provinces this financial strength in conjunction with competitive two-party systems and patronage political cultures resulted in highly integrated party organizations and low levels of intra-party strains. Newfoundland was a somewhat exceptional case, representing one-man provincial rule in close cooperation with the federal Liberal party and the federal state, but even here there was a close meshing of the two parties, albeit with rather more provincial direction than in the Maritime provinces. Basically the Atlantic provinces represent a case study of the Liberal party as an integrative device within Confederation drawing the provincial units into the federal sphere of influence and control, a political reflection of economic and administrative domination of poor and underdeveloped provinces by the federal government.

The West presents a striking contrast with the Atlantic region. Although very much in a state of economic inferiority to central Canada, the western provinces resisted a status of political inferiority to the Government party at Ottawa, first by giving relatively weak electoral support to the party in federal elections and second by tending to strike out on experimental routes with the party system in provincial politics. Thus the Liberal parties in Manitoba and British Columbia entered coalitions at the provincial level while maintaining their full partisan identities in federal politics. Even in Alberta unsuccessful moves were attempted in this direction. In all cases severe intra-party strains became apparent. Only in Saskatchewan was a consistently high level of federal-provincial party integration maintained, due to tradition, strong partisan leadership, and relative provincial political strength. Yet even in Saskatchewan prolonged relegation to provincial opposition bred growing internal party disunity. The Liberal party at Ottawa during its long period of domination grew further apart from its provincial counterparts in the West which were either cooperating with its federal party competitors or floundering in opposition. Eventually, a pattern of intergovernmental relations with provincial administrations ranging in partisan colouration from quasi-Liberal to social democratic to Social Credit began to predominate over the kind of intra-party integrations which the Saskatchewan Liberal machine had once represented. The Liberal party's experiences in the West were very different from those in central Canada. Yet the same basic result was reached from different routes: executive federalism proved stronger than federal-provincial party solidarity.

The underlying reasons for the prevalence of executive federalism over political federalism in Canada have been explored at length by other writers. Attention has also been given to the general question of federal-provincial intra-party relations.[4] This study in effect constitutes a documentation of the growing "confederalization" of the Liberal party over a period of almost thirty years. It should be emphasized that this process does not necessarily imply the attenuation of federal dominance over provincial wings of the party. Indeed, in most cases examined, the federal party emerged as the more successful. That this took place in the two central provinces, those best situated in economic, political, and even cultural (in the case of Quebec) terms to mount effective challenges to federal domination of the Liberal party, is a striking indication of the ability of the senior level of the party to maintain its superior position. But confederalization did mean the separation of the two wings in terms of senior personnel, career patterns, party finance, and even ideology. This means that by the 1950s the Government party in Ottawa was loosely linked with unsuccessful opposition parties in Quebec City, Toronto, and three western provinces—parties whose weakness was more or less enforced by the very success of the federal party. Nor was this distinctly asymmetrical relationship simply an accident; rather it reflected a crucial problem in federal-provincial relations.

The problem revolves around the inevitable conflict in which two wings of the same party in the same province must engage for the available human resources. An increasing separation and insulation of the two wings at the level of parliamentary leadership was never matched by an equivalent separation of the membership at the constituency level. The critical problem faced by all parties of the mobilization of the party rank and file at election time to perform the multiple organizational tasks necessary for successful electioneering, could become itself a cause of contention and competition between two wings of the party in the same area. Only in the extreme—and in the Canadian context, unlikely—eventuality of complete jurisdictional accord between the province and the national government might political conflict at the governmental level not cause conflict at the party level. Another factor capable of overriding intra-party divisions might be a cross-provincial ideological cohesiveness within the party; in the case of a brokerage party like the Liberals, this was never true in practice, and doubtful in theory. Nor could pure patronage politics serve to override divisions.... A preoccupation with patronage politics was itself a disturbing factor in federal-provincial intra-party relations.

E.R. Black has suggested that "just as the virtual independence of a provincial government's policy-making depends to a considerable extent on its provincial resources, so the effective control of provincial organization by the local officers depends upon the local unit's political resources in comparison with those of the central party: such resources are considered to be size and commitment of membership, financial capabilities, quality and appeal of leadership, and, of course, electoral success." Black then goes on to note that while the policy objectives and organizational requirements in the federal and provincial arenas are often quite different, nevertheless "both sets of leaders must rely in large measure on the relatively small group of people and on the same resources in their field work."[5]

In the case of Hepburn's challenge to federal domination, it was precisely this lack of organizational differentiation at the local level which proved to be his undoing. To blockade successfully the federal party Hepburn had to mobilize the local Liberal activists to withdraw their allegiance and support from the federal Liberals. This he attempted to do by discrediting the federal party in the eyes of Ontario voters and by forming alliances with federal Conservatives. Yet so long as the Liberals remained in office in Ottawa, this campaign achieved little success. Thus Hepburn was driven by the logic of his position to more and more extreme opposition to his own national party. Since he was ultimately unable to extend his efforts beyond his own province, the much wider base of the national party was not sufficiently undercut to give tangible evidence of success. Hence his struggle developed in a manner which seemed irrational and self-defeating to the local Liberal activists. The financial resources of the provincial party were not enough to counteract the political resources of the federal party, especially after the outbreak of the Second World War. In the end it was the provincial party which was driven into opposition; the provincial Liberals have never, since Hepburn's failure, attracted the kind of local organizational strength characteristic of the federal Liberals in that province.

In Quebec a superficially different, but essentially similar, pattern developed. Provincial disputes spilled over into federal constituency politics; the federal party reasserted stability by the subordination of the provincial wing, first by directly placing it in office, later by abandoning it to successive terms of opposition while collaborating with its opponent. The capacity of the federal wing to enforce a permanent opposition status on its provincial counterpart derived from its superior political and financial resources accruing from the national office, and its evident unwillingness—except in the very special circumstances of 1939 [to defeat the Union Nationale government for its criticism of the federal government's war effort]—to utilize these resources on behalf of the provincial party. Superior political and financial resources combined to ensure superiority in the attraction of human resources. Yet, in the long run, the provincial Liberals were able to rebuild their strength, not through prior solution of their financial problem but by generating new and separate organizational structures which could serve as alternative sources for the mobilization of human resources. In other words, political resources were developed independently of the federal party.

To a degree in Manitoba and much more so in British Columbia, coalition arrangements in provincial politics put severe strains on constituency organization and the loyalties of local party activists. There is definite evidence for British Columbia that the federal Liberals were in a much stronger position when the provincial party went into opposition in the 1950s than when it had been the dominant provincial coalition partner earlier. Saskatchewan, in the period of joint Liberal rule in both capitals from 1935 to 1944, appears to offer a contrast, inasmuch as party integration was smoother than it was later when the provincial party was out of office. In this case, Saskatchewan is closer to the example of the Atlantic provinces where intra-party unity was bought at the price of clear federal domination—exercised in the Saskatchewan case, however, with some autonomy at the level of the federal cabinet by Jimmy Gardiner as the regional prairie power-broker at Ottawa. In other words, federal Liberal domination within Saskatchewan did not preclude regional representation of some significance within the cabinet, a regional power which was backed precisely by the high level of intra-party integration and the bargaining leverage this placed in Gardiner's hands. Saskatchewan thus represented a model of party politics as a vehicle of regional representation quite different from those adopted elsewhere in the West. The Liberal parties of the Atlantic provinces, on the other hand, did not appear to utilize party integration as a bargaining lever within the federal cabinet to the same extent. Here party loyalty overrode regional discontent and the same local activists could be mobilized equally for either level of electoral politics with the same well-integrated set of rewards backed by the political financing of Montreal and the coordinated patronage inducements of the federal and provincial states. Only in Newfoundland is there real evidence of this Liberal loyalty being translated into any real provincial influence on the federal party, but here the small size of the province and its state of underdevelopment and poverty severely limited its power. The Maritimes aside, it is clear that in the case of Saskatchewan federal-provincial integration as a vehicle of provincial political representation is not without strain when one party loses office. In the late 1940s and 1950s it became apparent that a certain tension between the two wings at the leadership level was being reflected in problems at the local level.

There is a sense, then, in which federal and provincial wings of a party are often locked into a rather self-destructive relationship. If, as many observers have argued, political parties act mainly as recruitment agencies for the staffing of elective office—and the weakness of the Liberal party as a channel of demands on the political system through extra-parliamentary policy formation appears to give added weight to this emphasis—then federal and provincial wings of the same party are necessarily locked into competition for the same pool of human resources. Provincial weakness matched by federal strength guarantees the latter wing against too much competition. Dealing with governments of another political colour at the provincial level, on the other hand, avoids this problem. The claims of other governments can be treated as a matter of intergovernmental negotiation. The claims of party become a complicating factor, adding new levels of conflict which can be avoided when the problem is simply intergovernmental. The intra-party dimension of federal-provincial relations is thus a matter of *additional* complexity. It is difficult to generalize beyond this from the limited time period which has been examined, but it does seem safe to conclude that a Government party will prudently seek to avoid such complications. They may opt, as the federal Liberals did in Ontario and Quebec, for underwriting the position of their provincial wings as permanent opposition parties, thus keeping the party name before the provincial voters while at the same time minimizing their impact on the federal level. Thus the dominant strategy of the federal Liberals in confronting this organizational problem in Ontario and Quebec was to downplay partisanship between levels of government.

In a country as diverse and as decentralized as Canada, and especially in the case of provinces as crucially influential in relationship to the federal government as Ontario and Quebec, a party in power in Ottawa could not afford the intra-party strains involved in attempting to use the party as an integrative device in federal-provincial relations. Instead, the Liberal party reverted to intergovernmental, even interbureaucratic, relations as the major channels of accommodation. This not only helped account for the weak and underdeveloped nature of extra-parliamentary national party organization in this era, but also strongly reinforced the tendency already present in the Government party to transform politics into bureaucracy and party into state.

Perhaps this may be the final, paradoxical, conclusion to be drawn from this study. The curious lack of definition of Canadian parties, which has troubled so many observers of our politics, is only reinforced as the evidence concerning their structures is marshalled. The Liberal party was an organization seeking not so much to consolidate its distinct partisan identity as to embed itself within the institutional structures of government. Its fulfillment was not so much organizational survival as it was institutionalization as an aspect of government: control over recruitment channels to senior levels of office. The deadening of political controversy, the silence, the greyness which clothed political life at the national level in the 1950s, were reflections of a Liberal ideal of an apolitical public life. In place of politics there was bureaucracy and technology. This in no sense meant that Canada stood still. Profound changes were taking place in the nation's political economy. But these changes tended to take place outside the realm of traditional political debate. Instead, it was between the great bureaucracies, whether public (federal and provincial) or private (Canadian and American), that debate and policy refinement took place. The Liberal party had truly become the Government party—an instrument for the depoliticization and bureaucratization of Canadian public life. The vision of Mackenzie King in his almost forgotten *Industry and Humanity* had begun to take shape: "whether political and industrial government will merge into one, or tend to remain separate and distinct" was King's question for the future in 1918. He concluded that "the probabilities are that for years to come they will exist side by side, mostly distinguishable, but, in much, so merged that separateness will be possible in theory only."[6]

The pipeline fiasco of 1956 and the Liberal defeat the following year were episodes in an apparent crisis of the Government party and its vision of the world. Whether this crisis was merely an ephemeral case of instability, or something more serious, is a question which cannot be answered here. It is enough to point out that many of the structural preconditions of Government party organization, as described in this study, remain in place today. On the other hand, the extent of political fragmentation, conflict, and instability in Canada since the Diefenbaker interlude of 1957-63 makes the continuation of the Liberal party as the permanent Government party much more doubtful than in the King-St. Laurent era. To Liberals, at least, the world was simpler then.

NOTES

1. C.B. Macpherson, *The Real World of Democracy* (Toronto, 1965), and *Democratic Theory: Essays in Retrieval* (London, 1973).

2. André Siegfried, *The Race Question in Canada* (1906; new ed., Toronto, 1966); James Bryce, *Canada: An Actual Democracy* (Toronto, 1921).

3. R.J. Van Loon, "Political Participation in Canada: The 1965 Election," *Canadian Journal of Political Science,* III, 3 (Sept. 1970), 376-99; Robert Presthus, *Elite Accommodation in Canadian Politics* (Toronto, 1973).

4. D.V. Smiley, *Canada in Question: Federalism in the Seventies,* 2nd ed. (Toronto, 1976).

5. E.R. Black, "Federal Strains within a Canadian Party," in H.G. Thorburn, ed., *Party Politics in Canada,* 3rd ed. (Scarborough, 1972), 129-30.

6. William Lyon Mackenzie King, *Industry and Humanity* (1918; new ed., Toronto, 1973), 246.

THE TORY SYNDROME: CONFLICTS
OVER DIEFENBAKER'S LEADERSHIP

BY GEORGE PERLIN

o

In the general election of 1962 John Diefenbaker's government lost its majority in Parliament. Eight months later, in February 1963, with the government in difficulty in Parliament, a group of ministers tried to depose Diefenbaker. The coup failed but the divisions it exposed left the Conservative party severely weakened. Forced into a new election, the Diefenbaker government was defeated.

Diefenbaker's leadership was soon the focus for renewed conflict within the party. This conflict grew progressively wider and more intense. It reached its climax at the annual meeting of the National Association in 1966 when, by a small majority, the delegates voted to call a leadership convention.

This chapter will discuss the factors which contributed to these conflicts over Diefenbaker's leadership. Each episode will be described and analyzed separately.

THE CABINET REVOLT OF 1963

The most important factor in the background to the cabinet revolt of 1963 was the precipitous decline in popular support for the Conservative government which began in 1959. Between January 1959 and September 1960 support for the Conservatives in the Canadian Institution of Public Opinion poll fell from 59 per cent to 38 per cent[1] and it did not again rise above 40 per cent. In the federal election of 1962 the Conservative share of the popular vote fell to 37 per cent

Excerpt from George C. Perlin, *The Tory Syndrome: Leadership Politics in the Progressive Conservative Party* (Montreal, McGill-Queen's University Press, 1980), pp. 61-83. Reprinted by permission of George C. Perlin and McGill-Queen's University Press.

(from 54 per cent in 1958) and the party lost so many seats that it was reduced to the status of a minority government. Among the factors which contributed to this dramatic change, three appear to have been particularly important.

First, the Conservatives had assumed office just as the country was entering a recession. Over the next five years the annual rate of economic growth declined, unemployment reached its highest levels since the Depression, and there was persistent pressure on the Canadian dollar. The government was slow in its attempts to deal with these problems. In part this was because it was frustrated by a conflict with the governor of the Bank of Canada, James Coyne, over the control and appropriate course of monetary policy.[2] Another cause of delay was the cautious advice it received from the officials of the Department of Finance.[3] But what was most important was the cabinet's own approach to policy-making which tended to protract the period in which every decision was taken.[4] This general proclivity to delay meant not only that policies were not approved in time to deal effectively with problems, but also that decisions had the appearance of being taken and often were taken in an atmosphere of crisis.

A good illustration was the devaluation of the Canadian dollar which was forced on the government in the middle of the 1962 election campaign. This decision became the central issue in the campaign—with damaging consequences for the government.[5]

The contrast between the promise of Diefenbaker's messianic appeal in 1958 and the performance of the government was a second factor in the government's political decline. Diefenbaker's own behaviour added to this credibility gap. In response to criticism of government economic policy the prime minister was evasive, attacking his critics or accusing privileged interests of conspiring to frustrate the government's purpose. He also resorted to the same kind of arbitrary acts for which he had so effectively criticized the Liberals in 1956 and 1957. A notable example was his personal comportment in and the government's collective handling of the dismissal of James Coyne from his position at the Bank of Canada. There was a good case to be made against Coyne's attempt to pursue a course independent of the cabinet, but the government chose instead to emphasize the charge that Coyne had acted improperly in approving an increase in his pension which had been voted by the Bank's board of directors.[6] Coyne was provoked by this tactic to resist the efforts to have him resign and the government was drawn into an extended public confrontation in which it appeared to be bullying Coyne. The government's image was further damaged by its refusal to permit Coyne to be heard before a committee of the House of Commons.[7]

Another illustration of the discrepancy between the standard Diefenbaker applied in his criticism of the former Liberal administration and his own behaviour was his response to critical evaluations of the government by journalists. Both publicly and privately he accused members of the parliamentary press gallery of partisan bias and he tried to restrict the reporting opportunities of journalists whose stories and commentaries he found particularly offensive.[8] Quite apart from its effect on his image as an advocate of popular rights, this response was a serious mistake in press relations.

Whatever the original disposition of the journalists, Diefenbaker's accusations and harassments could only serve to colour their judgements and analyses. By 1962 the prime minister's relationships with members of the press gallery had "reached the breaking point" and his government had been widely stigmatized in editorial comment as evasive and high-handed.

A third factor in the government's decline was its handling of Quebec. It was unfortunate for the Conservatives that they had come to office just when important social, economic, and cultural changes were taking shape in Quebec.[10] Diefenbaker was prepared to make some symbolic gestures toward the recognition of French-Canadian concerns[11] but they were not sufficient to satisfy the aspirations of a new, more liberal, and assertive French-Canadian nationalism.

Substantively and symbolically, one of Diefenbaker's biggest mistakes was his failure to give French Canada strong representation in his cabinet. French Canadians were never accorded a proportionate share of senior cabinet portfolios; in fact they held no senior portfolio at all until 1960. In addition, there was no French-Canadian minister with enough support or stature among his colleagues to assume the natural leadership of the Quebec wing of the party and Diefenbaker refused to designate a French-Canadian lieutenant. The French-Canadian presence was further weakened by Diefenbaker's refusal to permit the Quebec members to meet together as a provincial caucus to discuss their distinctive concerns.[12]

The party's dependence on the Union Nationale created another set of difficulties. For one thing the dominant faction in the Union Nationale was out of touch with the changes which were taking place in Quebec.[13] This was reflected in its defeat in the provincial election of 1960. Equally important, when the Union Nationale fell from power Conservative organization in Quebec was severely weakened. But no effort was made either to respond to appeals from the Union Nationale for help in shoring up provincial party organization[14] or to establish an independent Conservative organization. As a result, the party fought the 1962 election in Quebec with an organization hardly more effective than the one it had had in 1957.

In the general election in June 1962, the Progressive Conservative party lost ninety-two seats. The government was able to retain office only because Conservative losses in Quebec had not been matched by Liberal gains, large numbers of Quebec voters having abandoned both established parties to vote for Social Credit candidates. In the new House the Conservatives held 116 seats, the Liberals ninety-eight, Social Credit thirty, and the New Democratic Party (NDP)—formed in 1961 from an alliance of trade unions and the CCF—nineteen.

The election struck a damaging blow at Diefenbaker's leadership. For one thing, it was apparent that, as public opinion polls had suggested, he no longer enjoyed the popular appeal which had made such a substantial contribution to the party's victory in 1958.[15] He was thus deprived of one of his most valuable political resources. In addition, most ministers believed the party's losses were the result of mistakes which the government could have avoided and some ascribed the blame for these mistakes to the prime minister.

The main complaint against Diefenbaker's leadership was that he was indecisive. Even ministers who were to remain loyal to him shared this view.[16] The prime minister insisted that every cabinet decision be unanimous. If there was only a small dissenting group he would still defer decisions and permit discussions to continue repetitiously. This meant not only that important problems remained unsolved but also that ministers wasted time in unnecessary meetings of the cabinet.

There had been tension in the relationship between Diefenbaker and some members of the cabinet long before 1962. Alvin Hamilton, a minister sympathetic to Diefenbaker, claimed the basis of this tension was "conservative" resistance to Diefenbaker's "progressive" policies.[17] On the face of the evidence about policy conflicts within the cabinet, it is difficult to sustain this explanation. The cabinet did not divide into consistent voting blocs which persisted from issue to issue. Moreover, even in the early conflicts over economic policy, the alignments which occurred did not conform to a simple distinction between "progressives" and "conservatives."[18] Yet there is a sense in which this explanation identifies a source of discontent within the cabinet. In seeking to make himself the advocate of "the average Canadian," Diefenbaker had cast himself as the adversary of "big interests." Some ministers were disturbed by this aspect of his political style not because of any policy in which it had resulted but because of the effect of its tone on the party's relations with big business.[19]

On balance, however, this seems to have been far less important as a source of tension than the nature of the prime minister's personal interactions with many of his ministers. Diefenbaker treated most members of the cabinet who had not supported him in 1956 with continuing mistrust;[20] he frequently expressed his disapproval of ministerial actions in outbursts of temper which humiliated the ministers concerned;[21] he sought personal credit for all of the government's achievements while blaming other members of the cabinet for its mistakes;[22] and he sometimes gossiped about the private lives of his ministers, or made unflattering personal remarks to colleagues about ministers whom he disliked.[23]

The extent of cabinet alienation immediately following the 1962 election is not wholly clear. Most of the ministers who ultimately opposed Diefenbaker have said that despite whatever misgivings they may have had at that time it was several months before they reached the conclusion that Diefenbaker should go. In any event, by February 1963 close to half the cabinet was ready to seek a change.

Four factors helped transform the discontent within the cabinet into the challenge to Diefenbaker's leadership.

First, the prime minister would not commit himself to a clear position in the discussion of a long-delayed decision about the acquisition of nuclear weapons for Canadian forces in NATO and the North American Air Defence Command. Since the Cuban missile crisis in October there had been increasing public pressure, reinforced by pressure from the American government, for some action in this matter. The government had appeared to agree to the acquisition of nuclear weapons in 1959 when it undertook to equip Canadian forces with delivery vehicles designed to carry nuclear explosives. However, it began to hedge its position in 1961 as a result of its foreign policy commitment to act as a mediator in the negotiation of nuclear disarmament. A decision had been required for some time because Canada had begun to equip its forces with the new delivery vehicles. Most members of the cabinet wanted to proceed with the acquisition of nuclear weapons, at least for the Bomarc missiles installed in Canada as part of the continental air defence agreement.[24]

Second, no progress had been made toward the formulation of a new budget. This was a cause of particular concern in relation to the government's position in Parliament because the 1962 budget had never been formally adopted. Although a cabinet committee on economic policy had completed its work in November, the prime minister had made no effort to have its proposals presented to cabinet for discussion.

Third, the prime minister had refused to cooperate in efforts to negotiate terms with the thirty Social Credit members of Parliament for stabilizing the government's position in Parliament. Social Credit votes had kept the government in office throughout the autumn, but the Social Credit leader, Robert Thompson, had warned government representatives that his party's support would not continue without some clear indication of government attention to outstanding problems.[25]

Fourth, criticism of the government outside Parliament had spread to include its own nominal supporters, among them several Conservative newspapers and some officers of the National Association. One source of party criticism was the fact that during the Cuban missile crisis the government had delayed for forty-two hours before acceding to the American request that Canada place its armed forces on full alert. Another was the government's failure to execute an agreement with the United States for the acquisition of nuclear weapons.[26]

Rumours of cabinet dissatisfaction with the prime minister had reached the press as early as November and had prompted a number of speculative newspaper articles about a change in the party leadership. But there had been no serious discussion of attempting to force Diefenbaker to resign. In fact, the challenge to Diefenbaker occurred by accident rather than as the result of any prior plan.

The series of events which led to it began when the House of Commons met on 21 January and the opposition pressed the government for an explanation of its nuclear weapons policy. In response, on 25 January, Diefenbaker made a long and ambiguous speech. On 28 January, Douglas Harkness, the minister of defence, issued a statement claiming that, contrary to press interpretations of the prime minister's speech, it had been clear that Diefenbaker had confirmed the government's intention to accept nuclear weapons. In the House, Diefenbaker refused to make any further comment, either in elaboration of his speech or in confirmation of the statement of the defence minister. Two days later, the American State Department published a statement in which it offered its own clarification of and correction to the prime minister's speech. This so angered Diefenbaker that he recalled the Canadian ambassador to Washington and began to canvass the opinion of some of his closest advisers about the possibility of calling an election on the issue of American interference in Canadian affairs.

This suggestion, along with the determination of Harkness to secure acceptance of nuclear weapons, created a crisis in the cabinet. On the morning of 3 February, Diefenbaker met members of the cabinet at his home.[27] The prime minister proposed that Parliament be dissolved and an election fought on the issue of relations with the United States. George Hees, the minister of trade and commerce, opposed him and raised the nuclear weapons issue. Then Harkness attacked the prime minister, asserting that he had lost the confidence of the country. Diefenbaker interrupted him to demand that those who were with him stand up. When eleven of the twenty-one ministers present remained seated, Diefenbaker announced that he would resign and left the room. After the prime minister left, several ministers said they had not stood up because they did not know whether they were being asked to vote on the question of the dissolution or on the question of Diefenbaker's leadership. A memorandum was therefore drafted, urging Diefenbaker not to resign and not to seek a dissolution. Harkness refused to sign this memorandum and declared that in any event he would have to resign.

In the Commons on the following day, Social Credit leader Robert Thompson introduced a motion of non-confidence which seemed likely to have the support of the Liberal and New Democratic parties. When the House adjourned, five ministers—George Hees, George Nowlan, Wallace McCutcheon, Pierre Sévigny, and Léon Balcer—met with Thompson to see if it might be possible to save the government. Thompson made it clear that he would only be willing to support the Conservatives if Diefenbaker were replaced. As a result, the five ministers agreed to ask Diefenbaker to resign. On the morning of 5 February, Hees presented this request to the prime minister, but Diefenbaker refused.

It was now impossible to escape defeat in the House that evening. However, the ministers who had met with Thompson believed that if they could force Diefenbaker to resign they could form a government under a new leader and avoid an election. They believed there might be as many as eleven of the remaining ministers willing to depose Diefenbaker, while he could count on only nine. They therefore decided to confront Diefenbaker at a cabinet meeting scheduled for the next morning. While the rebels knew they lacked the support of the caucus, which was to meet immediately following the cabinet meeting, they hoped to present caucus with a *fait accompli*. But Diefenbaker, having learned of their plans, advanced the time of the caucus meeting so that it took place before the cabinet meeting. He therefore ensured that the confrontation took place in a forum in which he had a substantial majority. The result was the capitulation of the rebels. Hees, who had led the attack in caucus, was chosen to announce to the press that the party was united behind its leader and ready to fight a new election.

Three days later Hees and Pierre Sévigny, the associate minister of defence, resigned—ostensibly because of the prime minister's failure to satisfy their concerns about defence policy. Hees claimed that the prime minister had repudiated a privately made promise, given during the caucus on 6 February, to satisfy his objections to defence policy. Behind this public explanation there was another. After the caucus on 6 February, two close friends—E. A. Goodman, a member of the national executive, and John Bassett, the publisher of the Toronto *Telegram*—pressured him to resign, arguing that by continuing in the cabinet he was humiliating himself and breaking faith with them. (Both Goodman and Bassett had given public and private support to the efforts to force Diefenbaker out and both were pledged to help Hees succeed to the leadership.) Goodman said in an interview that when he learned Hees had not resigned he went to see him and "told him he had been conned. When he found out that he had been had, he quit."[28] Sévigny has made it clear that it was not defence policy, but a personal slight he had received from Diefenbaker that led him to resign. Since the resignation of Harkness he had been acting minister of defence. On 7 February a press release issued by the Defence Department described Sévigny as the minister. When asked whether the omission of the word "acting" indicated that Sévigny had been permanently assigned to the new portfolio, Diefenbaker replied "Certainly not!" As a result, Sévigny writes: "I felt as if my face had been slapped. Something snapped in my mind. Why should I take this abuse? It was bad enough being utterly concerned with defence principles and policies that could no longer be explained. Why should I furthermore be insulted and accept such treatment? There was only one answer and that was to resign."[29]

Together, Hees and Sévigny tried to persuade other anti-Diefenbaker ministers to join them. Their principal target was Balcer. Balcer said in an interview that Hees and Sévigny had told him that Diefenbaker was going to make a speech repudiating what they felt was an undertaking to acquire nuclear weapons. He explained his response and reaction as follows: "I said 'What are you going to tell the press?' I thought they would look foolish. I said 'Let us wait and see what [Diefenbaker] says.' I had no personal reason to resign. I was in a good position to get reelected. I knew the government would be defeated, but I thought Diefenbaker would go after the election and that we would carry on."[30] Thus Balcer refused to participate in this further act of rebellion. Although three other anti-Diefenbaker ministers, Davie Fulton, Ernest Halpenny, and Donald Fleming, decided not to run in the election, they continued in the cabinet for the duration of the campaign. Fulton had announced in November that he planned to return to British Columbia to accept the leadership of the provincial party which was attempting to rebuild itself, while Fleming and Halpenny both announced that they wished to retire for personal reasons of a non-political nature. All three of these ministers had strained relations with Diefenbaker and both Fulton and Halpenny had been active in the efforts to force him to resign. Although Fleming had not been active, he was regarded as a potential supporter of the rebels.

It was the prime minister's refusal to make an unequivocal commitment to nuclear weapons that had led to the conflict. At a substantive level this had evoked concern about the effectiveness of the country's defences against nuclear attack, the strength of its commitment to its allies, and the state of its relations with the United States. Yet only Harkness had thought defence policy sufficiently important to stake his career on it. Other ministers, including Hees and Sévigny, had been prepared to defer a decision even longer if delay could be explained in politically credible terms. (Both of them had been among a group who tried to persuade Harkness on 1 February that he should agree to give his support to the prime minister until after the NATO foreign ministers' meeting in May, when Diefenbaker had promised to take a definitive position.)[31]

In fact, for most of the anti-Diefenbaker ministers, the substance of defence policy was less important than the political implications of the conflict it had produced. The prime minister seemed to be unable or unwilling to lead the cabinet to a decision on any question about which there existed or was likely to be disagreement. Moreover, his reaction to the pressure of the American government convinced them that he had lost his political judgement. They believed Diefenbaker's continued leadership would destroy the government. What was at stake was their political survival. If the cabinet could not be mobilized to action the government would fall. Beyond defeat in Parliament they saw defeat in a general election.

Their political analysis reflected an assessment of the situation in the metropolitan heartland of the country. It was in the densely populated industrial corridor running along Lake Ontario and the St. Lawrence River that the party had suffered its most substantial losses in 1962. It was from the press and party in this area that the most severe criticism of the government had been coming. Quite apart from its implications for the party's plurality in Parliament, a further loss in Conservative votes here threatened many of them personally. Thus, out of eleven ministers who had seats in this area, only three were clearly committed to Diefenbaker.

Undoubtedly, their own interest in the leadership influenced the behaviour of some of the rebel ministers. Fulton, Hees, Nowlan, and Fleming had all been mentioned as possible successors. As early as November, Hees had been engaged in discussions with friends outside the caucus to plan a leadership campaign, although he claims that these discussions were held in anticipation of Diefenbaker's resignation and not with the intention of forcing it. Some of the ministers sympathetic to Diefenbaker claim that Fulton participated only because he had what one of them called "an unholy ambition to be Prime Minister."[32]

The strain in their personal relations with the prime minister was a contributing factor in the estrangement of some of the anti-Diefenbaker ministers. None of them felt any bond of affection for him and some of them disliked him intensely. By his behaviour toward them he had deprived himself of a reserve of personal support which might have served to restrain their discontent when the sanctioning effect of his popular appeal had lost its potency.

On the other side of the conflict, the substance of defence policy had even less importance. Most of the ministers who supported Diefenbaker agreed with anti-Diefenbaker ministers that the country should accept nuclear weapons.[33] Their loyalty was based on a strong bond of affection, empathy with Diefenbaker's populism, and gratitude for their political success.

The emotional commitment was of over-riding importance.[34] In part, this was a personal commitment, but it was also a group commitment. Diefenbaker had created a circle of "insiders" within the cabinet. They were not all his social intimates, but they were all accorded his trust. Their affective ties to Diefenbaker as a personality were reinforced by affective ties to the Diefenbaker group.

Paradoxically, the solidarity of this group appears to have been reinforced by the feeling of some of its members that socially and politically they were outsiders. An interesting piece of evidence in this regard is found by using the social characteristics of members of the cabinet to rank them on a scale measuring their social distance from the centres of national power. As Table 1 shows, the fewer "establishment" social characteristics a minister possessed, the more likely the minister was to be a Diefenbaker loyalist. (The characteristics used in creating the scale are explained in the table.) It seems reasonable to suppose that these ministers were attracted to Diefenbaker because his symbolic attacks on negative stereotypes of the dominant elite in the country (and the party) gave expression to their feelings of exclusion from the establishment. In any event, some of them clearly felt a special debt of gratitude to him for their political success, believing they might not have been appointed to the cabinet by another prime minister. Michael Starr, for example, was deeply conscious of the fact that, as the son of Ukrainian immigrants, he was the first person of a non-charter ethnic group to be appointed to a federal cabinet.[35] It was not just a matter of gratitude for their elevation to the cabinet which instilled loyalty; there were still sections of the electorate among whom Diefenbaker remained very popular. In fact, despite the decline in his rating in the polls, there was reason to believe that Diefenbaker was still more appealing to voters than the Liberal leader, Lester Pearson.[36] Thus, some ministers saw his continued leadership not as a threat to their political survival but as a condition for its achievement.

TABLE 1. *PERCENTAGE OF "DIEFENBAKER LOYALISTS" AMONG MINISTERS BY THEIR SCORES ON A SCALE OF ESTABLISHED SOCIAL CHARACTERISTICS*

		SCALE OF ESTABLISHMENT CHARACTERISTICS[a]				
		4	3	2	1	0
Percentage Loyal to Diefenbaker[b]		13	67	75	100	100
	N[c]	(8)	(6)	(4)	(2)	(1)

a) Each minister was accorded one "point" for each of the following characteristics: representative of an Ontario or Quebec riding; representative of a wholly urban riding; in a major professional (e.g., lawyer, doctor, engineer) or corporate occupation; university-educated.
b) A "Diefenbaker loyalist" is defined as a minister who took an unequivocal stance in support of Diefenbaker at every stage in the conflict. These ministers were Gordon Churchill, Howard Green, Alvin Hamilton, Raymond O'Hurley, Hugh John Flemming, J. Angus MacLean, Michael Starr, Walter Dinsdale, and J. Waldo Monteith. (It has been suggested that H.J. Flemming was part of the coup attempt; in an interview Flemming said he "never at any time opposed Mr. Diefenbaker's continued leadership.")
c) Number of people questioned.

THE REVOLT IN THE PARTY: 1964-66

In the 1963 election the Diefenbaker government lost an additional twenty-one seats and with them its plurality in Parliament. As a result, the Liberal party took office under the leadership of Lester Pearson.

Since there was no longer a cabinet, the institutional centre of dissatisfaction with Diefenbaker's leadership had been eliminated. The only other institution with a continuing life where the issue might be raised was the caucus and there Diefenbaker faced no immediate threat. Even before the election, as we have seen, he had the support of a substantial majority in the caucus. The election had strengthened his position because it had removed some of the members who might have been disposed to challenge him. The elected wing of the caucus now consisted predominantly of members from the prairies, the Maritimes, and rural and small town sections of the central provinces (mainly Ontario)—members who had reason to have a strong sense of identification with and dependency on Diefenbaker. The shifting balance of power in the caucus is reflected in the fact that, after the 1957 election, prairie members comprised 13 per cent and Ontario members 54 per cent of the elected membership, and after the 1963 election, prairie members comprised 43 per cent and Ontario members 28 per cent.

Opinion of Diefenbaker's leadership outside the caucus was more critical, but dissidents had no national forum in which to express their views. Thus, it was not until the annual meeting of the National Association in February 1964 that any new evidence of discontent appeared. The issue was raised by a motion to conduct the normally routine vote of confidence in the leader by secret ballot. Since the vote of confidence always before had been a standing vote, Diefenbaker chose to fight the secret ballot. Although he won a substantial majority, because the decision to reject the secret ballot was itself taken by a standing vote, the true strength of opposition to him remained in doubt. The overwhelming vote of confidence he ultimately received therefore did not settle the issue.

Douglas Harkness had been the only member of Parliament to vote against Diefenbaker at the annual meeting, but by the middle of 1964 there was a small group in the caucus which had begun informally to discuss the need for a change in leadership. They were particularly concerned by the state of personal relations within the caucus. The conflict of 1963 had left a residue of bitterness which infected these relations. Diefenbaker made a direct personal contribution to the perpetuation of ill-feeling by subjecting known or suspected dissidents to personal slights and petty harassments. The intensity of his hostility and the lengths to which he was prepared to go in expressing it are reflected in his attempt during a defence policy debate in October 1963 to prevent Harkness from speaking to the House. It actually required a formal vote of the whole House to override Diefenbaker's objection to a speech on defence policy from a man who only ten months before had been the minister of defence. Such acts created serious strains among Conservatives in Parliament. Several of the new members elected in

1962 and 1963 "were shocked by the internal condition of the party...[and] by Diefenbaker's behaviour."[37]

The strains within the caucus were seriously aggravated in the autumn of 1964 when Diefenbaker decided to stage a parliamentary filibuster to try to block the adoption of a new national flag. Most of the eight remaining francophone members of the caucus saw Diefenbaker's opposition to a distinctive national flag—establishing more clearly Canada's independence of Britain—as one further indication that he was insensitive to the feelings of French Canadians. They already had a good deal of evidence to support this view: the conflict over his choice of nominators at the 1956 leadership convention; the win-without-Quebec strategy he adopted in the 1957 election campaign; his failure to give a senior portfolio to a French-Canadian minister before 1960; his refusal to designate a Quebec lieutenant while he was prime minister; and his constant affirmation of his conception of the country as "one Canada," a view which seemed to deny the French-Canadian claim to distinctive cultural recognition.

In 1964, in an attempt to overcome the charge that he was unsympathetic to French Canada, Diefenbaker had at last appointed a Quebec lieutenant— Léon Balcer. This act proved to be an empty gesture. Balcer was given a place of prominence seated next to the leader in the House, but Diefenbaker did not accord him any commensurate role in party decision-making. (In fact, even though they were seatmates, Diefenbaker rarely spoke to Balcer, even to exchange a formal greeting.)[38]

The filibuster decision also struck a further blow at external support for his leadership. He was criticized in the press both because of the anti-French implication of his position and because of the effect of the filibuster in delaying other parts of the government's legislative program. It was argued that Diefenbaker was obstructing the government and undermining public confidence in the parliamentary system by abusing the right of the opposition to debate government proposals.

The criticism in the press provoked concern among leading members of the extra-parliamentary party as well as among members of the caucus. Equally important, members of the extra-parliamentary leadership were aware that party fundraisers were finding it difficult to meet the party's financial needs and it was being made clear that this financial problem was directly related to Diefenbaker's continued leadership. When Senator Wallace McCutcheon, a key figure in the business community, tried to establish a sustaining fund for national headquarters he received more than sixty letters which said contributions would only be made if Diefenbaker were replaced.[39]

There was open criticism of Diefenbaker's leadership at a meeting of the national executive in December. A few days later Balcer called upon the government to use closure to end the flag debate. Following this open break with his leader, Balcer mobilized Quebec members of caucus behind an appeal to the national executive for the convening of a leadership convention. When the national executive met in February 1965, Diefenbaker confronted it with a challenge to its right to deal with the issue. On 5 February, the day before the executive meeting, Diefenbaker had secured a vote of confidence in his Commons leadership from his loyal majority in the caucus. He had thus presented the extra-parliamentary party with the possibility of a conflict over its authority. "Decide on your convention," he reportedly told the executive, "but I'm not going to accept it. I'll have to go back to caucus. They've just given me a vote of confidence."[40]

Members of the executive were to be asked to answer two questions which had been formulated by the principal officers.[41] The first asked whether a leadership convention should be called; the second sought an assessment of Diefenbaker's leadership.

After Diefenbaker had delivered his challenge, Erik Nielsen, an MP loyal to the leader, argued that the executive should not deal with the question of confidence and moved that it not be presented to the meeting. Nielsen's amendment was passed by a majority of only two votes and the five principal officers, most of whom were anti-Diefenbaker, had abstained. Subsequently, by a larger majority, the call for a leadership convention was defeated. While the constitutional issue had been avoided, Diefenbaker had unambiguous evidence that he had lost the confidence of a large part of the national executive. Yet he chose to treat the executive's decision as a reaffirmation of support for his continued leadership, forgetting his statement to the national president that if more than 30 percent of the national executive voted against him, he would feel compelled to resign.[42]

On 19 February 1965, one of the francophone members of the caucus, Remi Paul, left the Conservative party to become an Independent. For two months Balcer resisted pressures to follow a similar course. His resignation was ultimately provoked by a debate in caucus over Diefenbaker's opposition to government proposals which would have had the effect of permitting some provinces to develop distinctive areas of legislative and administrative jurisdiction. Diefenbaker was prepared to commit the party to another extended parliamentary battle on this issue on the ground that to permit some provinces powers which other provinces did not possess was to endanger national unity. Balcer saw in this position another attack on French-Canadian interests both because there was strong feeling in Quebec that that province would require distinctive constitutional arrangements if it were to be able to give adequate protection to its French-Canadian culture and because one of the proposed pieces of legislation touched directly upon an agreement between the federal government and the government of Quebec. For reasons that are not clear Diefenbaker agreed to moderate his position,[43] but for Balcer the acrimony and invective of the struggle had been too much. His motives and character had been impugned by crude gossip which was repeated directly and by innuendo in the virtually continuous heckling to which he was subjected whenever he spoke in caucus. Despite the pleas of several colleagues, Balcer decided to resign from the caucus because life there had become unbearable.[44]

In the fall of 1965, Prime Minister Pearson called a new election. Despite the intensity of feeling within the Progressive Conservative party, a facade of unity was created for the campaign. Two of the ministers who had resigned in 1963, Hees and Fulton, sought re-election; E. A. Goodman, a leading member of the extra-parliamentary party who had refused to take an active role in the 1963 campaign, became campaign chairman; and the four Conservative provincial premiers provided a public display of support. One reason for the return of these rebels, according to Goodman, was that there was a risk the party would fall completely into the hands of a Diefenbaker rump.[45] For Fulton and Hees there was the additional motive of personal ambition. Fulton's efforts to rebuild the electoral base of the provincial party in British Columbia had failed disastrously, while Hees had found private life "less exciting" than politics. Both aspired to succeed Diefenbaker and wished to re-establish their standing in the national party in preparation for a leadership convention which they believed would not be long in coming.[46]

For all its outward appearance of unity the party was not entirely free of inner conflict during the 1965 campaign. In some ridings, Diefenbaker partisans attempted to replace candidates whose loyalty to the leader was doubtful, among them Gordon Fairweather, a member of caucus who had supported the resolution calling for a leadership convention at the national executive meeting in February. These efforts, while not systematically organized or supported, reflected the extent to which the party was in danger of complete factional polarization. Activity of this kind at the constituency level was unprecedented in the modern history of the party.

The outcome of the 1965 election failed to alter the basic distribution of power in the Commons, each of the two major parties achieving a net gain of two seats. The complexion of the Conservative caucus was also basically unchanged which meant that Diefenbaker could still command a substantial majority there.

It was not until the following spring that the conflict over Diefenbaker's leadership was resumed.[47] The principal figure this time was Dalton Camp, the president of the National Association.

Camp's career in the party had been built upon his skills as a publicist and political strategist. Until 1963 his main interest and sphere of activity had been provincial politics. He had had an important role in provincial campaigns in Nova Scotia, New Brunswick, Newfoundland, Prince Edward Island, and Manitoba and retained a close relationship with Premier Robert Stanfield of Nova Scotia and Premier Duff Roblin of Manitoba. Camp had been chosen by Diefenbaker to manage the national campaign in 1963, and in 1964 he was elected president of the association.

Camp and Diefenbaker had had a good working relationship in the 1963 campaign but some strain began to develop when Camp, in an appraisal of the campaign, told a party meeting that the party could not afford "to make a god of its leader." In 1964 this strain was deepened by Diefenbaker's criticism of Camp's plan for a conference of intellectuals to discuss Conservative policies for the future. The leader treated the conference with public disdain and made only a token appearance. Later in the year, Camp found the relationship growing even more difficult after he advised Diefenbaker that the Conservative filibuster in the flag debate was hurting the party. In January 1965 newspaper stories implied that Camp was involved with the Balcer challenge to Diefenbaker's leadership. Apparently, in consequence, Camp was approached by a member of caucus who, to test his loyalty, tried to trap him into making critical statements about the leader. Camp was disturbed by the paranoiac atmosphere this suggested and was subsequently shocked by Diefenbaker's behaviour during a six-hour meeting in which the leader was by turns "recriminating, abusive and flattering. [He seemed to be] prepared to wreck the party...to avoid becoming the fall guy."[48]

But the national president was not yet prepared (in 1965) to join the fight against Diefenbaker. He believed Diefenbaker had the right to lead the party in another election and that if the party were to lose, Diefenbaker would resign—if he were given time to do so with dignity. Camp's reluctance to become a rebel in 1965 was probably also related to his own interest in becoming a candidate for the succession. He had worked hard to maintain "open lines" with all sections of the party and believed that if he could acquire some parliamentary experience he might be able to establish credibility as a leadership candidate.

In the spring of 1966 two factors convinced Camp that it would no longer do to wait for Diefenbaker to resign. One was the decision by James Johnston, the new national director, to dismiss Flora MacDonald, the senior permanent member of the staff of national headquarters, who was an experienced and well-liked figure in the party organization. This decision seemed to suggest that anyone whose loyalty to Diefenbaker was even remotely suspected might be purged, no matter what the cost to the party. The second factor was that Diefenbaker, by persistent efforts in Parliament to force another election, had made it clear that he did not intend to resign. Although "it occurred to [him] that by opposing Diefenbaker [he] would dismiss [his] own leadership chances for ten years,"[49] Camp decided to launch a campaign to get a proposal before the annual meeting of the association in the fall to hold a leadership convention before the summer of 1968. In a speech to a private meeting of Conservatives in May and in informal conversations through the spring and summer he argued that since the Liberals were also in consid-erable difficulty, electoral advantage would lie with the Conservatives if they were to effect an early "renewal." In September he publicly called for a reassessment of the leadership.

Camp's strategy was to cast the struggle in terms of a principle. He did not attack Diefenbaker personally nor did he even mention the leader by name. The issue, he argued, was party democracy, the right of the membership to submit its leader to some evaluation that was more than a *pro forma* or ritual exercise.

Diefenbaker's supporters responded by making an issue of the propriety of Camp's behaviour. They attacked him personally, arguing that he was abusing the prerogatives of his office as national president in using it to launch his reassessment campaign. A second element of their strategy was to evoke Conservative fears about the party's reputation for disloyalty to its leaders. They argued that, intrinsically and in the interest of party cohesion, loyalty to the leader was a principle which ought to be respected.

Inevitably, Camp's re-election as president became a critical issue. Camp decided to make this issue a test of confidence in his call for leadership review. The Diefenbaker forces chose Arthur Maloney, a popular former member of Parliament who had been an active supporter of Fleming in 1956, to run against Camp.

There was little Camp could do to secure the election of committed constituency delegates. This would have required months of intensive organization. His strategy, therefore, was to try to elect as many supporters as possible among the new provincial association executives which were to be chosen before the annual meeting. The realization of this objective had four potential benefits. First, under the rules then in force, the provincial executives controlled the appointment of a large number of delegates-at-large; second, representatives of the provincial executives were more likely than constituency delegates to attend the meeting;[50] third, their opinion-leadership might have some effect on the decisions of constituency delegates; and fourth, the representatives of the provincial executives would be members of the national executive where critical procedural questions would have to be resolved.

With the help of Flora MacDonald, who knew most of the leading activists across the country, Camp was able to develop a loose network of contacts among all the groups within the party who believed there was a need for leadership review. A national speaking tour of Young Progressive Conservative (YPC) associations and Progressive Conservative Student federations (PCSF), where there was known to be considerable anti-Diefenbaker feeling,[51] provided him a relatively uncritical forum in which to publicize his campaign. It also helped to mobilize younger party members who might otherwise have remained inactive.

Diefenbaker, through Johnston, the national director, controlled the party's national headquarters, but his advantage was of limited value. For one thing, as was pointed out earlier, the locus of power in party organization in most parts of the country is at the provincial level.[52] In addition, in the fall of 1966, communications between national headquarters and local party associations were not very effective because Johnston had had virtually no experience in national party affairs and neither knew nor was well known among provincial and local activists.

The success of Camp's strategy became apparent when the national executive assembled to give final approval to procedural arrangements for the association meeting. Johnston had prepared an agenda deferring the election of officers until the last day of the meeting. Camp challenged the agenda, believing that his advantage lay in avoiding an early debate of the reassessment resolution. If the executive election were held first, his personal victory could be symbolically influential in the vote on the resolution and he would have the authority of a renewed mandate from which to deal with procedural issues raised in the presentation of the resolution. The national executive redrew the agenda, placing the election of officers first. Among Camp's supporters on this crucial vote were most of the officers of the National Association, the YPC and PCSF representatives, the representatives of the provincial associations from Quebec, Ontario, and British Columbia, and significant proportions of the representatives of the four Atlantic provincial associations, the Manitoba association, and the Alberta association.

This defeat placed Diefenbaker on the defensive. When he addressed the formal opening of the meeting he tried to deal with the question of leadership review by attacking Camp. The result was disastrous. Camp supporters had been directed to the auditorium early and had occupied most of the seats. Thus Diefenbaker faced a hostile audience: "Diefenbaker called on the unlistening crowd to work together to build the party. He quoted at length an earlier statement by Camp that praised his leadership. He was building towards the question: why did the change take place? But he never had a chance. He was greeted by hoots and catcalls. The Old Chief lost his stride; he poked and prodded and searched for a civilized response, but could not get one."[53]

It is impossible to assess the direct influence of Diefenbaker's speech on delegate opinion, but the reception he received had a disruptive effect on his organization, as Robert Coates observes:

> The humiliating treatment by the Camp forces on the Monday evening probably cost Arthur Maloney the election as President. Members of Parliament had to immediately leave the Chateau and meet on the Hill in an effort to salvage from the ruins a foundation on which Diefenbaker could stand. The necessity for the elective wing to move immediately cost Maloney support, for the Members could not be in two places at the same time. If the Party were to be saved, it had to continue as an effective opposition in the House of Commons. It could only operate effectively if John Diefenbaker continued as leader. The time required to consolidate the leader's position was at the moment when Maloney needed active supporters the most, on the eve of the voting.[54]

The result of the presidential election revealed the seriousness of the division within the party. Camp had 564 votes and Maloney 502.

Maloney's defeat further demoralized Diefenbaker's organization with the result that it was not prepared for a procedural manoeuvre which brought the question of the leadership to an early vote during debate on resolutions on the following day. Many of Diefenbaker's supporters had left the hall to join a procession escorting the leader to the meeting when— under the guidance of E. A. Goodman, who was chairman of the resolutions committee—a motion was quickly introduced and adopted to conduct the vote on the question of confidence in the leader by secret ballot. A resolution was then presented which affirmed confidence in Diefenbaker but proposed that "in view of the present situation in the party" a leadership convention be held before 1 January 1968. Goodman succeeded in limiting debate on the resolution and bringing it to a vote before the Diefenbaker forces could respond. As a result, the resolution was adopted 563 votes to 209.

In a general sense, the motives of participants in the conflict of 1966 were very much like those of the participants in the conflict in 1963. One factor which was different was the absence of any immediate disagreement about the substance of specific policies. There was no one question of policy that brought the conflict to a head. This was not to suggest that policy motives were unimportant in the conflict. To the contrary, they were important in four ways.

First, there had been growing concern within the party about Diefenbaker's attitude toward French Canada. There were French-Canadian Conservatives who supported Diefenbaker, but they were few in number and they did not represent the prevailing attitude in the party's Quebec wing. Léon Balcer was a better representative of that attitude.[55] By his own account he was "not an ardent nationalist" but believed—intrinsically and in the interest of combating separatism—in expanding protection for French-Canadian culture and in getting more French Canadians involved in federal matters. "The main stumbling block was that Diefenbaker never trusted French-Canadians.... He was hostile to French Canadians. His attitude was that the constitution gave the French Canadian everything he needed.... Essentially he was prejudiced.[56] Not everyone shared the view that Diefenbaker was prejudiced, but it was apparent that his conception of the role of French Canadians in Confederation did not recognize the changes which most Quebec opinion leaders now felt essential to the survival of French-Canadian culture. This influenced not only French-speaking Conservatives but also English-speaking Conservatives who were concerned about national unity.[57]

Diefenbaker's attacks on the big economic interests of Toronto and Montreal could be seen to be a second policy-based cause of opposition to his leadership. These attacks did not embrace any specific proposals which might be seen to threaten corporate power. Indeed, if anything, Diefenbaker's policy positions were less interventionist than those of the Pearson government. But members of the corporate elite were suspicious of his rhetoric and, rightly or wrongly, they blamed him for the economic problems the country had experienced between 1960 and 1963. The fact that members of the corporate establishment were solidly arrayed against Diefenbaker was brought forcibly to the attention of members of the party's extra-parliamentary elite by the response to their appeals for financial support. Whatever their own relationships with and views of big business, they could see that Diefenbaker's continued leadership had seriously weakened the party financially.

Third, there is a sense in which criticism of Diefenbaker's personality can be said to have been policy-motivated. One of the most common complaints about his personality related to its effect on the process of making policy. There was a widely held view that his indecisiveness, obsessively suspicious nature, insensitivity to the feelings of colleagues, and unpredictable temperament were qualities which would immobilize any cabinet under his leadership. In addition, several members of Parliament were upset about the way in which policy was made in the caucus. One of them, a committee chairman, said that between 1963 and 1966 the discussion and formulation of policy grew progressively more disorganized: "I found...that certain stands were being taken independently, without any consultation, by people with access to Mr. Diefenbaker's ear.... There were some embarrassing situations. Decisions were made [in some matters] by people without any comprehension [of the issues involved]. The chairmen were consulted less and less. There was no communication at all. The people who were asked to consult were those who would reflect what Mr. Diefenbaker wanted to hear."[58]

Finally, policy disagreements had been significant in the behaviour of some of Diefenbaker's opponents in the sense that an initial disagreement about some issue had led to a strain in personal relations which continued after the original controversy passed. The mutual animus between Diefenbaker and Harkness is the best example. The ill-feeling which developed in this relationship illustrates the general point made by several members of both the caucus and the extra-parliamentary party that once they had expressed some disagreement with Diefenbaker they were never again fully trusted.

Quite apart from any feelings that they may have had about policy or policy-making, as such, members of the anti-Diefenbaker coalition shared the belief that the style of Diefenbaker's leadership and some of his opinions about issues had made him an electoral liability to the party. The view was spreading, especially among members of the extra-parliamentary party, that the Conservatives could never return to power under Diefenbaker's leadership because he could not appeal successfully to urban, middle-class, and young voters. Anti-Diefenbaker sentiment among these groups was such that in some constituencies it had become a threat to the preservation of the party's corps of activists. One member of caucus had been told by members of his constituency executive, for example, "that a number of them were going to resign or at least stand aside" if he did not support the calling of a leadership convention.[59]

The dilemma at the heart of the conflict lay here. Most members of the caucus majority which supported Diefenbaker, quite apart from any other consideration, perceived him as an electoral asset and many of them feared the consequences for the security of their own seats if he were forced to resign. These members came from the rural areas and small towns and/or the hinterland provinces in which Diefenbaker's political style and policies had had greatest appeal. Most of the anti-Diefenbaker group, which was drawn predominantly from the extra-parliamentary party, saw his continued leadership as an obstacle to their own or to the party's achievement of office precisely because he was unable to appeal beyond these areas. There was no way to resolve this dilemma if Diefenbaker did not choose to resolve it by resigning because both sides were probably right.

There were bigger career stakes for some of the participants on both sides of the conflict. Some of the more prominent figures in the anti-Diefenbaker coalition had a direct personal interest in the leadership. Fulton had actually formed a committee to organize his leadership campaign even before he was re-elected to Parliament in 1965 and members of his committee had an active role in the anti-Diefenbaker coalition. Others could expect the benefit of positions of greater influence under a new leader. Conversely, many supporters of Diefenbaker had reason to be grateful to him for their positions of prominence and to fear the loss of these positions if he were removed. In this regard, however, Diefenbaker had contributed to the weakening of his power by becoming too generous in his promises of future cabinet appointments. One member of Parliament said that virtually every person in caucus had at one time or another been promised some portfolio. The result was that such promises had less and less credibility. Yet he still possessed institutional prerogatives which gave some buttress to his position in the caucus, particularly for those members who had little expectation or desire for ministerial careers.

Affective dispositions appear to have contributed more to the conflict in 1966 than they had in 1963. The leader evoked very strong negative feelings among some of his colleagues, if not for any intrinsic characteristic of his personality, at least for his manner in dealing with them.

One member of Parliament, a former minister, observed that "[Diefenbaker] approached MPs on a bullying basis...rather than trying to convince them. It was a matter of leadership style.... He was always looking over his shoulder. He seemed to create opposition [by suspecting it]. I don't see how anybody who professed himself to be stable can possibly have had anything but an unsatisfactory relationship with someone who is as emotionally unstable as Mr. Diefenbaker has been through all the years."[60] Another pointed out that there were some members to whom Diefenbaker never spoke and several with whom he had "very awkward personal relationships. At the same time he never seemed to appreciate those who were loyal. He couldn't manage people."[61]

David MacDonald, one of the MPs who opposed Diefenbaker, emphasized the importance of the positive affective ties Diefenbaker had created in preserving the loyalty of the caucus majority. "They didn't relate to the issue in intellectual terms; even now [1970] they relate to it in emotional terms. [They were bound to Diefenbaker] by deep-seated emotional ties, ties that were totally beyond the rational."[62] In support of this analysis, MacDonald cites the case of a former minister who told MacDonald of his concern with the chaotic process of decision-making within the Diefenbaker cabinet and caucus but explained that he could not bring himself to oppose Diefenbaker because of his strong personal attachment to the leader.[63]

One way to explain such attachments is to see them simply in terms of the emotional attraction that certain personalities appear to generate by their very nature—that is, in terms of the appeal of what is popularly called charisma. Diefenbaker was a rare public personality, a man who was widely seen to possess this charismatic quality. But there is a second less idiosyncratic way to explain the strength of personal attachments to him. As we have seen, in the cabinet revolt of 1963 the ministers who were most loyal to him were for the most part those whose social characteristics placed them outside the Canadian establishment. An analysis of the social backgrounds of members of caucus reveals a similar pattern in his support after 1963. As

Table 2 shows, the less similar the social characteristics of members to those of the dominant elite in the country, the more likely they were to support him. Diefenbaker's appeal to these social "outsiders" was essentially emotional. He sought to mobilize their support by attacking the "powerful interests," the sinister and anonymous "they" who were the hidden rulers of the country. The use of vague negative symbols of this kind provides an outlet for feelings of status insecurity. It provides an object on which to displace the frustration of being an "outsider."

TABLE 2. *PERCENTAGE OF MEMBERS OF PARLIAMENT SUPPORTING DIEFENBAKER BY SCORES ON A SCALE OF ESTABLISHED SOCIAL CHARACTERISTICS*

| | | SCALE OF ESTABLISHMENT CHARACTERISTICS[a] | | | |
	4	3	2	1	0
Percentage Loyal to Diefenbaker[b]	50	43	65	88	100
N[c]	(2)	(21)	(23)	(25)	(23)

a) Each member was accorded one "point" for each of the following characteristics: representative of an Ontario or Quebec riding; representative of a wholly urban riding; in a major professional (e.g., lawyer, doctor, engineer) or corporate occupation; university-educated.

b) The members supporting Diefenbaker were identified from a caucus petition in support of Diefenbaker which was circulated immediately following the 1966 annual meeting.

c) Number of people questioned.

Regardless of the role of such emotional dispositions in creating the conflict, an emotional content of its own appeared as it continued. In the caucus in particular, members found themselves increasingly isolated in relationships of suspicion and ill-feeling. As A.D. Hales observed: "It got so bad around here that you were labelled depending on who you were seen talking to. You had to be careful about whose office you were seen going into. It was a terrible situation."[64]

Robert Coates writes that at the annual meeting of the association in 1966 "emotion overcame reason and bitterness replaced composure."[65] Feeling ran so high at the annual meeting that there were occasions when physical blows were exchanged.[66] Even the most dispassionate of the leading participants admitted to succumbing in some measure to the emotional intensity of the situation. The development of these affective interactions helped divide the party elite into two factions which found their internal cohesion in common attitudes toward Diefenbaker and toward the rival faction...this factional split became the dominant cleavage in the internal politics of the party.

NOTES

1. Canadian Institute of Public Opinion, "Liberals edge ahead in party standings," *Release*, 28 September 1960.

2. The problem with Coyne originated in the position of the previous government accepted by the Conservative minister of finance, Donald Fleming, soon after he assumed office, that the Bank of Canada had complete autonomy in the determination of national monetary policy. In early 1960 when the government began to consider a policy of economic expansion to deal with unemployment, Coyne was one of the senior public servants who advocated a restrictive policy. Unlike the other opponents of expansion, Coyne was in a position because of the autonomy doctrine, to act on his own and resist any movement toward expansion by maintaining tight credit.

3. Cf. Roy Faibish, cited in Peter Stursberg, *Diefenbaker, Leadership Gained, 1956-62* (Toronto: University of Toronto Press, 1975), 211.

4. Cf. Douglas Harkness, Roy Faibish, Davie Fulton and Donald Fleming, ibid., 177-8.

5. There had been discussion of pegging the dollar (which had been allowed to float since 1950) for eighteen months. The immediate crisis was created by a run on the dollar but the government had had ample warning of this danger since there had been an intensive drain on reserves, reducing them by nearly 25 per cent, in the four previous months.

6. The minister of finance, Donald Fleming, claimed he had not been informed of the decision to increase the pension, and it ought not to have been taken without his approval. Coyne responded that Fleming should have known about it since his deputy minister was aware of it. Fleming has since said that the deputy minister came to him after the controversy developed and apologized to him for not reporting the decision. Cited in Stursberg, *Diefenbaker, Leadership Gained*, 240. While it was Fleming who recommended to cabinet that Coyne be removed, it is not clear that he was responsible for emphasizing the pension issue. Some members of the cabinet said in interviews that they thought Diefenbaker had been responsible. Certainly, Diefenbaker emphasized this aspect of the controversy when he spoke to caucus about it. Cf. R.A. Bell, cited in Stursberg, *Diefenbaker, Leadership Gained*, 241-2.

7. It was Fleming who refused the opposition request that the matter be submitted to committee. He subsequently claimed he had consulted with Diefenbaker and had had cabinet approval for his decision (cited in Stursberg, *Diefenbaker, Leadership Gained*, 245), although at least three ministers—Alvin Hamilton, Davie Fulton, and David Walker—say they had wanted to let Coyne be heard. (Interviews.) Fleming does not appear to have foreseen that Coyne would be able to get a hearing in the Senate where the Liberals held a large majority. Thus Coyne did get his opportunity to testify—in a situation controlled by the government's political enemies.

8. Diefenbaker was allegedly involved in an attempt to suppress a CBC program, *Preview Commentary*, on which there had been criticism of the government. There is no direct evidence to support this allegation. When it was investigated by a parliamentary committee, the CBC official who had been responsible for the decision to suspend the program testified that "never at any time has an offer or directive been given to me, or to my president, by [the minister responsible for the CBC] or by any member of parliament, or by anyone else who could

be said to wield political influence." Cited in Peter C. Newman, *Renegade in Power: The Diefenbaker Years* (Toronto: McClelland and Stewart, 1963), 235.

9. Ibid., 244,

10. On aspects of the Conservative party's problems in Quebec, see Marc La Terreur, *Les tribulations des Conservateurs au Québec* (Quebec: Les Presses de l'Université Laval, 1973).

11. These included the appointment of the first French-Canadian governor general, Georges Vanier, the decision to have all government cheques printed in both official languages, and the provision of simultaneous translation facilities in the House of Commons.

12. Léon Balcer, interview.

13. Ibid., Paul Sauvé who succeeded to the leadership of the Union Nationale and the premiership of Quebec upon the death of Maurice Duplessis in 1959 appeared to be more sensitive than Duplessis to the changes occurring in the province. He introduced a series of social and political reforms intended to respond to these changes. However, less than four months after his succession, Sauvé died.

14. Senator Jacques Flynn, interview. Senator Flynn said Union Nationale officials had wanted patronage support from the federal Conservatives and were "furious" when they did not receive it.

15. Between 1958 and 1962 the proportion of voters in Canadian Institute of Public Opinion surveys who said Diefenbaker "would make the best leader for Canada at present" fell from 50 per cent to 35 per cent. Cited in Peter Regenstreif, *The Diefenbaker Interlude* (Don Mills, Ontario: Longmans, 1965), 71.

16. Cf. the comments by Howard Green and Angus MacLean in Stursberg, *Diefenbaker, Leadership Gained,* 179.

17. Alvin Hamilton, interview.

18. Cf. the comment by Merrill Menzies in Stursberg, *Diefenbaker, Leadership Gained,* 125. Of eight ministers whom Menzies identified as supporters of the "progressive" policy of economic expansion, there were only three whom he described as unqualified "progressives" and there were three to whom he said the term definitely did not apply. None of the other ministers interviewed for the study accepted the thesis that such policy blocs existed.

19. Diefenbaker was himself sufficiently concerned about the perception of the government in big business circles to look for a representative of big business to sit in the cabinet. In August 1962, he appointed Wallace McCutcheon, an executive and director of several large corporations, to the Senate and made him minister without portfolio.

20. Cf. Newman, *Renegade in Power,* 94-5, and Pierre Sévigny, *This Game of Politics* (Toronto: McClelland and Stewart, 1965), 177-8, et passim. In an interview, Davie Fulton, the minister of justice, who had been a rival candidate for the leadership in 1956, gave an example of the extent of Diefenbaker's mistrust. He said that twice in 1958 he was called into the prime minister's office and accused of being disloyal, although Diefenbaker did not cite any evidence or any specific ground for his accusation. Fulton later came to the conclusion that the accusation arose from a newspaper article which described him as, next to the prime minister, the most powerful man in the cabinet.

21. Cf. Sévigny, *This Game of Politics,* 179-80, and Patrick Nicholson, *Vision and Indecision* (Don Mills, Ontario: Longmans Canada, 1968), 140. In an interview, Ellen Fairclough described him as a person who was "mercurial and given to temperamental outbursts." Another minister, see 81, described him as "unstable."

22. Cf. the comments by George Hees in Stursberg, *Diefenbaker, Leadership Gained*, 180.

23. One of Diefenbaker's closest and most loyal associates who asked not to be identified made the following comment in an interview: "John Diefenbaker was a highly principled man...but there was one way in which you could say he was unprincipled. He would talk to some ministers about other members of the cabinet behind their backs and this would get back to them."

24. For a full discussion of the background to this issue see Newman, *Renegade in Power*, 333-54, and Nicholson, *Vision and Indecision*, 145-78, 196-226.

25. Cf. Nicholson, ibid., 243-6. Nicholson had helped arrange the meetings between Thompson and representatives of the government.

26. An indication of the strength of party feeling is the fact that despite an appeal from Diefenbaker not to tie his hands in the matter, one-third of the delegates to the annual meeting of the National Association in January supported a resolution calling on the government to accept nuclear weapons if no progress had been made toward nuclear disarmament by the end of the year.

27. Newman, *Renegade in Power*, 363-78 and Nicholson, *Vision and Indecision*, 230-63, have both provided fairly full descriptions of the events between 3-6 February. While they both agree on the main points, there are differences between the two accounts on some of the details.

28. E. A. Goodman, interview.

29. Sévigny, *This Game of Politics*, 284.

30. Léon Balcer, interview.

31. Cf. Newman, *Renegade in Power*, 363. Hees and Sévigny had both indicated to other ministers before they resigned that they accepted this proposal.

32. J. W. Monteith, interview. Diefenbaker claimed that Fulton asked him at a private meeting on 4 February to designate him as his successor.

33. Howard Green, the minister of external affairs, was the only minister strongly opposed to the acquisition of nuclear weapons.

34. All of the ministers who were interviewed stressed this point.

35. Michael Starr, interview.

36. Diefenbaker ran ahead of Pearson in every published survey prior to the 1963 election, even though his support had declined substantially from 1958.

37. Gordon Fairweather, interview.

38. Léon Balcer, interview.

39. Typical of the replies were these:

    (a) My sympathies have been with the Conservative party for many years, however, I would be less than frank in saying that I cannot subscribe to the philosophies being expounded by the present leader of the party. Mine is a very small voice of complaint and no doubt I am very much in the minority in suggesting that the time is long overdue when the party should look for a new leadership....

    In the meantime because I feel so strongly about the present situation, I think it would be hypocritical to send a contribution to you, at this time. However, if and when this situation is rectified, I hope you will feel disposed to ask me again. In the meantime I should say that I have not abandoned the Conservative cause and my allegiance and financial support is directed to the Provincial Party.

        - President, large Toronto real estate company

    (b) On the other hand I would be less than frank if I did not tell you that my support of the two-party system does not go so far as to support any party headed by Mr. Diefenbaker. I think his leadership in itself is a great deterrent to the success of the party he heads, and it would be inconsistent with my views and my principles were I to support anything with which he is identified.

- Partner, Toronto law firm

(c) I support Conservative principles where I can find them, but the Conservative party at present is seemingly without any adherence to such principles—and the last Conservative Prime Minister was a travesty while in office. Why then, is he retained as Leader? Surely not on the thoroughly disproven basis that he is a vote-getter. I think you must act in this matter before soliciting funds for support. If I am wrong, please let me know.

- General Manager, I national life insurance company

(d) On a corporate basis, we have taken the position that we believe in the two-party system, and it is right and proper that the national funds of the party in power and the opposition should be given an annual contribution. We make no secret of it and seek no quid pro quo. However, after giving it a good deal of thought, I can't bring myself to quite such an objective position. I no longer have confidence in Mr. Diefenbaker's ability to govern and, therefore, I do not feel that I wish to give tacit approval by contributing to the party funds now. Should the situation change and you still want help from me, I will be glad to reconsider.

- President, national communications and publishing company

These quotations are derived from a file provided the author by a confidential source.

40. Peter C. Newman, *Distemper of Our Times* (Toronto: McClelland and Stewart, 1968), 117.

41. This group had no formal constitutional status but acted on its own authority in dealing with questions of agenda and procedure.

42. Dalton Camp, interview.

43. Marcel Lambert, chairman of a caucus subcommittee directed to consider one of the controversial pieces of legislation, said in an interview he knew nothing of Diefenbaker's decision until he was told by the party's house leader on the afternoon the bill was to be introduced for second reading that he would lead off the debate. Lambert was surprised since he had opposed Diefenbaker's apparent intention to make an issue of the bill on the grounds that "there was nothing in it. It was a 'Mickey Mouse' bill." When he asked what the party's position was to be, he was told to do as he saw fit. Lambert says he believes Diefenbaker had lost interest in the bill because he could no longer see any political advantage to it. Marcel Lambert, interview. Another explanation is that Diefenbaker's plan to fight on this issue had brought protests from three of the four Conservative provincial premiers, including John Robarts of Ontario.

44. Léon Balcer and others, interviews.

45. E. A. Goodman, interview.

46. George Hees and Davie Fulton, interviews.

47. One reason was an inquiry ordered by the Liberals into the relationship between Pierre Sévigny, when he had been associate minister of defence, and Gerda Munsinger, an immigrant from Germany who was once alleged to have been an espionage agent. The inquiry touched upon both the extent to which the relationship had constituted a security risk and the role of Diefenbaker, as prime minister, and Fulton, as minister of justice, in handling the case. Although the inquiry was being conducted by Wishart Spence, a justice of the Supreme Court, it was widely seen by Conservatives as an act of partisan vengeance, having been provoked

in the heat of a difficult debate in the House. Its immediate effect, therefore, was to unite the party.

48. Dalton Camp, interview.

49. Ibid.

50. Perhaps the most important reason was money. Constituency delegates were expected to meet most of these costs from personal resources, while there was some party support, from their provincial association, for the ex-officio delegates.

51. The Progressive Conservative Student Federation had challenged Diefenbaker as early as 1964 when it voted to ask the National Association to conduct its vote of confidence in the leader by secret ballot. Both the PCSF and YPC representatives had supported the motion for a leadership convention at the National Executive meeting in February 1965, and a few weeks later a delegation of officers from the PCSF (led by its president, Joe Clark) had called on Diefenbaker to urge him to resign.

52. See George Perlin, *The Tory Syndrome*, Ch. 2.

53. James Johnston, *The Party's Over* (Don Mills, Ontario: Longmans Canada, 1971).

54. Robert Coates, *The Night of the Knives* (Fredericton, New Brunswick: Brunswick Press, 1969), 60.

55. Data from the survey of delegates to the 1967 leadership convention support this view.

56. Léon Balcer, interview.

57. Robert Stanfield and Gordon Fairweather, interviews.

58. Marcel Lambert, interview.

59. Ibid.

60. Confidential interview.

61. Tom Bell, interview.

62. David MacDonald, interview.

63. Ibid.

64. A. D. Hales, interview.

65. Coates, *The Night of the Knives*, 53.

66. Ibid., 55-7.

"A DESPERATE HOLDING ACTION": THE SURVIVAL OF THE ONTARIO CCF/NDP, 1948-1964

BY DAN AZOULAY

o

For some time now, the dominant interpretation in the historiography of the Cooperative Commonwealth Federation/New Democratic Party (CCF/NDP) has been the alluring "movement to party" or "protest movement becalmed" thesis, which holds that the CCF/NDP's development was shaped by the essentially antagonistic interaction of its "movement" and "party" elements, with the latter prevailing as the CCF/NDP sought to increase its level of support. This interpretation has been most clearly and extensively articulated by the late Walter Young in his classic study of the national CCF. As the party aged, states Young, "the increasing attention that was paid to electoral activity, the increasing emphasis on organization, and the lessened emphasis on education marked the decline of the movement aspect of the CCF and the predominance of the party aspect." To this list most academics, including Young, have added several related themes, such as the centralization of power in the hands of the party establishment, the expansion of the party bureaucracy, and the moderation or dilution of the CCF's principles, particularly the decreased emphasis on public ownership.[1]

But the movement/party thesis has come under attack in recent years. In his memoirs, veteran party activist David Lewis called it "historical nonsense" and proceeded to make the case that "the CCF was never a movement which degenerated into a party [but]...was always both at the same time.[2] Yet Lewis remained a sort of lone wolf, prompting an appeal

Dan Azoulay, "'A Desperate Holding Action': The Survival of the Ontario CCF/NDP, 1948-1964," Ontario History, Vol. LXXXV, Number 1 (March 1993). Reprinted with the permission of The Ontario Historical Society.

several years later from Professor Alan Whitehorn, one of Lewis's research assistants, for distinctly new approaches. "While there have been numerous writings on the CCF and, to a lesser degree, the NDP," wrote Whitehorn in 1985, "there has not been sufficient diversity in the themes presented." The "protest movement becalmed framework," he insisted, "should not...be belaboured."[3] His appeal, however, has gone largely unanswered. Since then the literature relating to the party has been mostly biographical, with little questioning of the standard interpretation.[4] The lure of the movement/party thesis thus remains strong....

Not surprisingly, the Ontario CCF/NDP has been viewed from primarily the same perspective, in both the national studies as well as the less numerous provincial studies.[5] Leo Zakuta's examination of the party up to 1961, suggestively entitled *A Protest Movement Becalmed*, typifies the standard approach. What began as a "movement"—democratic in structure, socialist in ideology, administered by selfless volunteers, and committed above all to educating voters in the principles of democratic socialism— ended up as a "party" not unlike the others—authoritarian in structure, " liberal-reformist" in ideology, run by paid bureaucrats, and geared primarily to winning elections. Zakuta concludes, in short, that the CCF underwent "that sequence of changes in which a new crusading group loses its original character as it becomes enmeshed in the surrounding society and develops an increasing resemblance to the established bodies against whose very nature it initially arose to protest."[6] A more novel approach is presented by J.T. Morley in the only other full-length study of the Ontario party. Morley argues that the CCF/NDP has developed in a manner analogous to the human individual—from a phase of immaturity, in which it isolated itself from the world around it, to one of maturity, in which it successfully adapted to its sociocultural milieu, all the while retaining its fundamental identity, or "personality" as Morley calls it; he appropriately entities this process "secularization." So, while the party made some changes in its program and rhetoric to suit the changing concerns and mood of Ontario voters, and some minor changes in its structure, such as giving affiliated members a greater voice in the party, the CCF/NDP's essential features—its structure and ideology—remained basically unchanged.[7] While one can easily take issue with the sociological dynamic underlying Morley's secular- ization thesis, his analysis is, nevertheless, a refreshing change from the standard fare.

Unfortunately, neither interpretation is particularly useful in explaining the evolution of the Ontario CCF/NDP during what was unquestionably its most difficult period, from 1948 to 1964. The CCF/NDP experienced few highs and many lows in these years. Despite the rapid growth in the province's population after the war, party membership levels fell sharply and did not recover until late in the period; party morale, especially at the grassroots, experienced a similar downward trend; money was increasingly hard to come by; and election after election yielded little in the way of popular support or legislative representation.[8] The highly publicized formation of the NDP in 1961 was a grandiose attempt to reverse the decline, but by 1964 the rechristened CCF still held only seven seats, in an expanded legislature, and garnered three percentage points less in popular support than its predecessor had in the disastrous election of 1951.[8] These were indeed, as one party leader recalls, "desperate" years.[9]

The Cold War atmosphere and the overall prosperity of the period were key factors in this decline. The former tended to mute notions of class conflict, government intervention, or socio-economic equality upon which much of the CCF/NDP's philosophy and program was based. Most Ontarians, in fact, called for an "end to ideology" and for a united front in the face of the so-called international communist threat. Dissent was viewed as dangerous, even subversive, especially if it took the form of left-wing agitation. "Throughout the whole of the Western world," CCF leader Ted Jolliffe told delegates at the party's 1952 convention, "constructive popular interest in social welfare, in social ownership, in all forms of social progress, is increasingly overshadowed by the clouds of international uncertainty. Domestic issues...do not receive the attention they deserve because the world is living in fear—not so much fear of poverty at this time as fear of war."[10] The CCF/NDP suffered greatly as a result of this widespread phobia, even more so when enemies of the party openly linked it with the communists at home, as they did before and during the 1955 election and at various times in 1962 and 1963. This, coupled with the breakdown of East-West cooperation after the Second World War, left many CCFers demoralized, and the result was a rapid spiral of declining support and membership.[11]

The second factor, economic prosperity, is virtually self-explanatory. After having endured six long years of wartime sacrifice, self-restraint, and government regulation in the name of a noble cause, most Ontarians were in no mood come peacetime to create a socialist heaven on earth, especially one directed by bureaucrats. They wished only to drive their new cars down one of Ontario's many new expressways, or mow their suburban lawns, or watch their new television sets. And as jobs were plentiful, wages high, and inflation low, many more could afford to do these "frivolous" things. "We seemed to wither on the vine [in the 1950s]," recalls former CCF/NDP leader, Donald MacDonald, "partly by reason of the whole atmosphere of the time and the apathy of the Eisenhower period.... Everybody just wanted to relax. The normal apathy of the electorate vis-à-vis politics became even more pronounced with relatively good times."[12] In this context, the CCF/NDP was an anachronism.

Cold War and economic prosperity aside, the party also had to contend with the immense popularity and cunning of Leslie Frost, the province's premier for most of this period. By carefully cultivating the down-to-earth, folksy public image that was his trademark, and diffusing his opponents' assaults with an ample stock of charm and anodynes, Frost carried the Conservative party to massive victories. His successor, John Robarts, was also a very capable and appealing figure. Although less the politician than Frost, Robarts's low-key, pragmatic management style was appropriate to the growing role government was being asked to play by the early sixties. Both Tory leaders were well served, moreover, by capable provincial organizers:

Alex McKenzie and Eddie Goodman under Frost, and Ernie Jackson under Robarts.[13] To some extent, therefore, the decline and stagnation of the CCF/NDP was also due to the exceptional political and organizational leadership which they faced in these years.

Surely, then, if there was ever a period in which one might expect to see the CCF/ NDP shedding its movement elements and becoming more like the other parties, simply for the sake of survival, this was it, especially if, as Young argues, "the [electoral] failure of the party was largely through the crippling effects of the movement."[14] But such was not the case. It will be argued, first, that in almost every respect cited by the movement/party proponents to support their thesis—structure, ideology, and motives—the Ontario CCF/NDP retained its basic character in this period. The much-heralded movement/party model, in other words, does not shed much light on the particular events of this period.

But neither does the secularization thesis. Although its central conclusion is correct—that the party's character did not undergo any fundamental changes—it goes no further, leaving us to wonder what, in fact, *did* happen to the CCF/NDP in these years. Where Morley's study is particularly weak is in its tendency to substitute theory for rigorous, empirical analysis. He labels this particular stage in the party's evolution, for example, "The Quest for Respectability," one of the stages through which individual personalities (and therefore left-wing parties) supposedly pass on their way to maturity. By itself the designation is ambiguous enough to be meaningless, as this quest could apply to any stage depending on how it is defined. But to Morley, respectability specifically means creating "a genuine organizational capacity," experiencing "ideological divisions," and exposing government "scandals."[15] Yet even these themes, with the exception of the last, are not unique to this period, in kind or degree. There is, as well, no explanation of how these themes or the numerous other developments of the period, such as the selection of a new leader or the decision to form a "new" party, relate to one another. And apart from the rather dubious secularization model, Morley's analysis fails to explain *why* these developments arise, *why* certain decisions are taken. In short, the secularization thesis fails to tie the central facts of the party's experience together in a coherent, logical fashion, something which at least the movement/party model has accomplished. It is, at best, an extended critique of that model, with no alternative paradigm.

The other purpose of this paper, therefore, is to provide an alternative explanation for the Ontario CCF/NDP's evolution in this period. It will be argued that the period 1948 to 1964 is best understood in terms of one central theme: basic organizational survival, inspired and directed by a dedicated, idealistic core of party leaders. Basic organization—namely rebuilding and maintaining the party's membership, finances, and morale—was without question the main activity of the CCF/NDP in this period, particularly at its highest levels.[16] Almost every action the party took, from revising its program, to electing a new leader, to devising new organizing techniques, even to transforming itself into the NDP, can be linked to this fundamental imperative. Nor could it have been otherwise, for the party's survival was, as the facts clearly demonstrate, very much in doubt. Other themes were present, to be sure, such as the party's ongoing effort to broaden its organizational base among farmers, unionists, and the middle class. But the overriding theme of the period 1948 to 1964, simply because it consumed so much of the time and energy of the party, particularly its leaders, was this business of basic organizational survival.

But before elaborating on this central theme, it is necessary to deal with the prevailing notion that this period was marked primarily by the ongoing transformation of the CCF/NDP from a movement to a party.[17] One of the key elements of this model holds that, typical of a cadre-like party, power and overall responsibility within the CCF/NDP devolved over time to party leaders and bureaucrats in the provincial office, and that this process was inevitable according to Robert Michels's "iron law of oligarchy."[18] As the years passed, writes Zakuta, "the CCF's top governing bodies acquired greater powers, both actual and constitutional."[19] Such, however, was not the case for the period 1948 to 1964. There were, to begin with, no formal constitutional changes that had the effect of centralizing power within the party; the essentially democratic structure of the CCF/NDP remained intact, with sovereignty residing in the membership, whose collective will regarding party policy and other matters was expressed through the annual convention. If anything, the structure became *more* democratic in this period. Until 1961, for example, most members of the party's executive committee were elected by the Provincial Council; with the formation of the NDP in 1961, however, the party decided that all members of the executive would thereafter be elected by the convention.[20] Nor was this structure at all threatened by a self-perpetuating clique of party leaders, as some have alleged,[21] for the turnover rate on the council and executive from one year to the next was quite substantial.[22] There is no denying that, as Morley states, "a few individuals were particularly influential" in each phase of the party's history—that successive "oligarchies" did exist—but there is no evidence that the oligarchies of this period had *more* power than those which preceded them. The important point is that these and other leaders continued to operate within a democratic structure, and were annually accountable to the membership gathered in convention.

It is true, however, that party leaders assumed greater responsibilities in this period, and that the size of the provincial office staff expanded. But two important qualifications are necessary. First, there was nothing inevitable or Machiavellian about this, notwithstanding the views of Michels and others who see the drive for personal power as endemic to mass parties. Administrative centralization was, instead, a necessity borne of the disintegration of the party's basic organization and the concomitant desire of party leaders to preserve the party as a viable political entity. The provincial office was forced to assume more of the burden of fundraising, recruiting members, membership education, and so on, because fewer people at the grassroots were willing to do this. Rank-and-file apathy, and not the inexorable laws of party evolution, led to the centralization of responsibility in the 1950s.

Moreover, rather than covet power, CCF/NDP leaders were forever trying to return the burden of organizing to the local level, by restoring the strength and augmenting the power of the constituency associations so that *less* organizational responsibility would rest with the leadership. They succeeded, to some extent, with the "regional organizer" plan of the early 1960s and the accretion of electioneering responsibilities at the constituency association and area council levels.[23]

The second point worth noting is that the "bureaucracy"—that is, the number of paid party officials in the provincial office—did not grow linearly in this period in response to any inherent centralizing tendencies. Rather, the number of full-time provincial organizers tended to fluctuate according to the party's financial resources. In 1952 there were two. For a while in 1954 there were four, but for the remainder of the decade the staff was again reduced to two. It remained at that level until 1962, when the number of organizers was expanded to six, thanks in small part to the influx of funds for the regional organizer plan. In short, the impetus to hire more organizers, to expand the "bureaucracy," was not something which grew stronger in this period. The will was present from the start—the money was not. As a result, much of the organizational work continued to be done on a part-time volunteer basis, often by members of the Provincial Council. Even the party's 1953 decision to pay a salary to its provincial leader was purely pragmatic and did not reflect a fundamentally new orientation in the party. Because there was no guarantee that the provincial leader would be elected and thus receive a legislative stipend, as Ted Jolliffe did between 1945 and 1948, and again between 1951 and 1953, the party decided that it would only be fair, particularly in cases where the leader lacked independent financial means, to ensure his or her livelihood.[24]

Related to the notion that power within the CCF/NDP shifted from the rank and file to the leadership as the party aged is the belief that party leaders also placed less emphasis on membership education and instead concentrated more on "organization" and winning elections. By the 1950s, asserts Young, "more time and attention were devoted to organization and winning votes than to discussion of the many aspects of socialism and the development of more telling social criticism."[25] But again, evidence of such a change is lacking, at least for the period 1948 to 1964. If the term "organization" is defined broadly to mean the direct and indirect methods adopted by political parties to gain support, including membership education, then the question is not whether the CCF/NDP increased its commitment to organization, but rather, where the organizational emphasis lay in this period. And in this case, for reasons already cited, the emphasis was on basic organization.

Nevertheless, even if organization is taken to mean "basic organization," it cannot be said that the latter loomed larger in the CCF/NDP's calculations as the period unfolded. It is true that after the 1951 election disaster the party began emphasizing basic organization over other activities. This was done to reverse the precipitous decline in members and finances, which, in any case, deprived the CCF of the funds necessary for other activities, such as producing new literature, obtaining interesting guest speakers, or holding political education conferences. The result was that membership interest in socialism was not stimulated and literature sales to the ridings remained low. But once membership and finances stabilized in the mid-fifties, education assumed its former position. Judging from the amount of literature ordered by riding associations and the attendance at regional education conferences, the level of membership education was substantially higher in the mid-to-late fifties than earlier in the decade.[26] In fact, depending on the circumstances, education was sometimes emphasized over other activities. The rank and file spent a good deal of time, for example, discussing drafts of the party's 1955, 1959, and 1962 programs, as well as the 1956 Winnipeg Declaration and drafts of the "New Party" (as the NDP was originally called) program and constitution. This served the party's organizational purposes well, insofar as it stimulated interest in the party, increased understanding of democratic socialism and motivated members to do more to rebuild the party's basic organization. But at other times, particularly when membership figures and revenues fell suddenly, fundraising and membership recruitment received priority. There was, in other words, no continuous shift towards basic organization at the expense of membership education in this period; rather, the balance between basic organization and education fluctuated according to the circumstances of the day.

Nor is it clear that the CCF paid more attention to electoral activity in these years. The party simply did what it could with the resources, always insufficient, at its disposal. As a result, much more money and effort went into the 1951 campaign than into the subsequent election because of the party's weaker financial condition by 1955.[27] The same could be said for by-elections. Whether the party chose to contest these depended on a number of factors, primarily its resources and the prospect of victory, and there was no steady increase in the proportion of by-elections contested by the CCF/NDP in this period.[28] In fact, except for the 1963 campaign, the number of ridings contested by the party over each general election actually declined, as the party chose to concentrate its meagre resources in the more winnable ridings.[29] It might even be argued that with the CCF/NDP's electoral chances more remote and its basic organization weaker, *less* effort and enthusiasm was expended on the election campaigns of this period than those of the mid-forties, when prospects were far brighter.[30] The party was mainly concerned with simply surviving each election, politically, and using the excitement generated by an impending election to rebuild its basic organization.

Implicit in the charge that by the 1950s the CCF/NDP was paying more attention to electoral contests is the suggestion that the motives of party members were not what one would expect to find in a genuine "movement," and that the leaders, in particular, were driven largely by the desire to secure their power within the party hierarchy; David Lewis is the most frequently cited example of this.[31] It is a line of argument which is virtually indistinguishable from that expounded by some of the leading political theorists of this century, who argue that as left-wing parties age, their leaders are increasingly driven by a ruthless desire for electoral success and self-aggrandizement.[32] In reality, what kept CCF/NDP leaders and the small core of dedicated, grassroots activists going through these incredibly trying times was, first and foremost, their unshaken belief in democratic socialism. "The Kingdom of God...was still a beacon there that you were working towards," recalls former provincial organizer, Fred Young. Dudley Bristow, a two-time CCF candidate in Toronto and chair of the party's organization committee in the early fifties, echoes the sentiment. "The question of whether we would win [elections] wasn't important," he asserts. "I was elated when we did well and disappointed when we did poorly, but it didn't affect my level of activity because I believed strongly in what we were doing." No doubt it was people such as Young and Bristow whom the party's prescient national secretary had in mind when he wrote, shortly after the 1951 election, that CCF activists "have a conviction in the justice of their cause and the leadership and spirit necessary to tackle anew the task of building the organizational foundation which can one day win power in Ontario."[33]

The theorists argue, as well, that feelings of solidarity and devotion are not enough to keep a left-wing party alive in the long run—that there must be material incentives.[34] In fact, the other main motive of CCF/NDP activists was *precisely* the feeling of camaraderie and devotion, of not wanting to let one's colleagues down by doing any less than they for the cause. Fred Young recalls with warm affection the "people who were willing to spend time, energy, and money to hold on to what we had," and that this inspired him to make similar sacrifices. Doc Ames, the party's northern provincial organizer, was one such individual. "Everybody loved Doc," states a former leader:

> He was always up. I never knew him to be down. He was marvellous. It was a joy to go up there [to northern Ontario]...because you could just feel all the love and warmth. It was the kind of feeling you felt that this party was about and which was very much there all through the '40s and '50s.... He exemplified the fellowship, the human love between people working for a cause. And that's what you felt with people like Doc, and Fred, and Donald, and Ken [Bryden]. That's what nurtured us.

It is out of this same sense of fellowship that Donald MacDonald dedicates his memoirs, in part, to "the thousands of working people who shared the vision of the Cooperative Commonwealth Federation and the New Democratic Party," and whose "labours and sacrifice were an inspiration for those to whom they entrusted the responsibilities of leadership." Surely Tommy Douglas's biographer is well off the mark, then, when she states flatly that while "the old concepts of political brotherhood were alive" in Saskatchewan in the 1950s, "in Ontario they were sour, irrelevant, and empty, a poor joke."[35]

The qualities of self-sacrifice and perseverance in the name of high principle and fellowship, which many leaders and certain followers in the party displayed in these difficult years, clearly distinguished the CCF/NDP as something more than just another political party driven by the potential spoils of office. "Movements have a vitality and a tenacity which parties lack," writes Walter Young, "because they are organizations of like-minded people dedicated to a cause that is predicated on what are seen as high moral values."[36] By his own criteria, then, Young and his followers would be forced to admit that in at least one important respect—ideologically-based vitality and tenacity—the "movement" aspect of the CCF was stronger in this period than before.

The final, and perhaps most important, element on which the standard interpretation of the Ontario CCF/NDP is based is ideology. It is argued that for the sake of electoral gain the party diluted its ideology (and program), to the point where it became less socialist than it had been in its early days. "As it neared the 1960s," writes Zakuta, "the CCF seemed to be turning into a liberal, reform party," and "the socialism that emerged," states Young, "was more and more, a kind of remedial liberalism."[37] An analysis of each of the party's programs between 1948 and 1964, however, yields a very different conclusion. To begin with, the party's democratic socialist philosophy of placing human need before profit and cooperation before competition, and of redistributing wealth more equitably, remained unchanged. In its 1948 program, entitled *First Term Program*, this was stated clearly and succinctly at the outset: "The Cooperative Commonwealth Federation is a democratic movement which believes that people are more important than profits. It stands for economic planning and social ownership to develop our natural resources for the good of *all* the people." Although not always spelled out in a separate section, these basic principles were clearly embedded in subsequent programs, in 1955,1958, and 1963.[38] Nor did the means for achieving these ultimate goals change very much. The primary method was always extensive government intervention in the economy, either through regulation or outright ownership, as well as other areas of everyday life.

In fact, the only indication that the CCF/NDP became more opportunistic in its quest for greater support—in the sense of subverting something essential about itself for the sake of votes—was its adoption of modern electioneering techniques in the early sixties. These included polls, slick advertising, and the increased use of radio and television, where the main objective was not to "sell" the party's program or philosophy, as it had been in the past, but to sell a particular policy or leader according to what the polls said would win votes and to do so using the emotional-visual appeal of manipulative advertising. The Provincial Council expressed this new direction in no uncertain terms when it stated, shortly before the 1963 provincial election, that "our policy and program won't get us elected" and that "we must look for and devise other tactics to win."[39]

But for the most part, the much-acclaimed movement/party thesis does not explain the CCF/NDP's evolution between 1948 and 1964. The presumed shift to a more centralized, bureaucratic, electoral-minded, power-seeking, liberal-reformist "party" is not very discernible. This is not to suggest that the movement/party thesis is invalid, only that such a model does not shed much light on the evolution of the CCF/NDP at a time of increasing prosperity and Cold War anti-communism, when one might have expected a more party-oriented transformation. Perhaps a broader time frame would yield such a shift, although adherents would likely be hard-pressed to find examples of how the CCF subverted its basic beliefs for the sake of gaining power—this being perhaps the essential difference between a movement and a party, the rest being simply a question of tactics. In the end they may well conclude, as did David Lewis, that "the CCF was never a movement which degenerated into a party [but]...was always both at the same time.[40]

Rather, the dominant theme in this period was the party's sustained effort to rebuild and expand its basic organization, with virtually every major party initiative geared to achieving this goal. This phase in the party's history began in earnest after the devastating provincial election defeat of November 1951, which stunned the party and left both leaders and rank and file searching frantically for answers. Although there was serious disagreement as to who or what was to blame for the sudden change of fortunes, most agreed that the immediate problem was one of weak basic organization—not enough members or money. Indeed, both had fallen dramatically in a number of ridings since 1949, and without a strong organization in those ridings the party was unable to get its message across or its supporters to the polls on election day.[41] This organizational decline was itself a symptom of the severe disillusionment and apathy from which so many party members suffered in the early 1950s and which, in turn, stemmed from the CCF's declining popularity following the heady years of the party's "golden era."

In any case, the CCF/NDP's evolution in the dozen or so years following the 1951 election can best be understood as a series of increasingly innovative and sophisticated plans, emanating from the provincial office, to rebuild the party's basic organization. One of the earliest was the "CCF Brigade." Devised by the chair of the party's organization committee, Marjorie Pinney, in the summer of 1954, its object was to persuade an army of two hundred party members, particularly some of the "dead wood" on the Provincial Council, to openly pledge themselves to sign up fifty new members over a two-year period. It emerged at a time when membership levels had taken a sudden and unexpected plunge, after an impressive recovery in 1952 and 1953, and leaders were desperate to avoid another blood-letting of members, such as that which occurred in the twenty-four months prior to the 1951 election. The Brigade's goal was to expand the membership lists, and its crudity was a reflection of the anxiety the provincial office felt at the time.[42]

But with the stabilization of membership and finance levels came more sophisticated schemes, such as poll organization. Initially proposed by the national office in 1952, and adopted in earnest by the provincial office late the following year, poll organization involved the creation of a poll committee for each poll within a riding, either in place of or in addition to the regular CCF club.[43] The committee would act as the local contact point of the party and would consist of active CCF supporters within the poll, such as former campaign workers, who would be trained in organizing techniques through a regional conference, and whose main responsibility would be to attract new members, renew old memberships, and raise money; existing CCF clubs and riding associations were to continue as educational and recreational centres, but would "henceforth assume a major responsibility building poll committees within the area from which their membership is drawn." The primary goal of poll organization was not simply to obtain a larger membership, which is what the CCF chose to emphasize whenever membership figures and finances declined sharply, but to create a more *active* membership, working through a new instrument, the poll committee.[44]

By late 1953, with membership levels once again at their 1949 level and with a significant improvement in its finances, the CCF could approach the question of organization more calmly and rationally, with less of the anxiety engendered by the earlier haemorrhaging of members. This more relaxed disposition, plus the apparent success of poll organizing techniques in York South during the 1953 federal election, resulted in a more refined organizational strategy, and the provincial office spent most of its time in the mid-fifties promoting poll committees.[45]

There were numerous other techniques used to rebuild the party's basic organization, some of which became permanent features in this period, such as the annual membership and finance drives, the regional educational conferences, and the policy of concentration. Even things like issuing new literature and revising the official program were intended primarily to attract members and funds to the party, indirectly, by wresting members from their apathetic state so that they would take responsibility for constituency-level organization. But for the most part these methods failed, for they could not overcome the pervasive apathy and demoralization which had beset the CCF/NDP in these years. And with fewer members willing to find new recruits, publicize the CCF message, contribute money, or serve as candidates, the party did that much more poorly on election day, which only bred further disillusionment and apathy. Any signs of renewed spirit and vitality at the local level between elections were based largely on the innovative schemes and tireless efforts of the provincial office staff, but rarely translated into overall organizational expansion, as growth in some areas was inevitably matched by decline in areas which the provincial organizers were forced to neglect. Hopes and spirit would revive somewhat as an election approached, resulting in a flurry of last-minute preparation, and therefore an improvement in membership levels and finances; expectations would be further inflated by promises of assistance from the labour movement or by a juicy election theme. But this eleventh-hour activity was never enough to stave off defeat, after which the cycle would resume.[46]

The boldest plan devised to restore the party's organizational vitality was the 1958 decision to create a "new" party. This was a federal party initiative, which actually began in 1956 with the issuance of the Winnipeg Declaration, a new statement of principles aimed at giving the CCF a more moderate, up-to-date image and attracting support from those progressive farmers, blue-collar workers, and middle-class professionals who had been alienated by the socialist rhetoric of the CCF's first statement, the Regina Manifesto. At the same time, party leaders decided that this new coalition of the left should be accommodated in a new political instrument, with the old

CCF as its core. The Ontario CCF, although initially lukewarm towards the New Party idea, came to realize its great potential as another tool with which to restore its basic organization and adapted it to serve this end. Consequently, CCF leaders in Ontario permitted "liberal-minded" non-CCFers to participate in the movement to build the New Party only to the extent that they *filled gaps in the CCF's existing organization* or upheld the image of a broadly based party of the left. The New Party clubs which were set up as a temporary vehicle for the participation of the liberal-minded, for example, were only promoted in those areas where the CCF did not have a strong organizational presence and explicitly excluded unionists, for fear that organized labour would be accused of dominating the New Party. Moreover, non-CCFers were given only token representation on the important decision-making bodies during the New Party's gestation period, in order to convey the image of a new, genuinely broadly-based party.[47] Unfortunately, this overriding concern with restoring the CCF's basic organization and only admitting new blood in a selective, symbolic fashion meant that much of the rapid rise in potential support among workers and the "liberal-minded" middle class was never mobilized, and as a result, the New Party experiment was no more successful than previous methods had been in reviving the CCF organizationally. The NDP's membership, popular support, and proportion of legislative representation was not much higher than that of its predecessor twelve years earlier.[48]

Closely related to the "organization" theme is the dominant role played by party leaders in attempting to restore the CCF/NDP's organizational vitality. There can be no question that the party owes its very survival to a small group of top leaders who were willing to take hold of the party at a most difficult phase in its history and guide it through to better times. These could have been forgiven for joining the grassroots in their apathy and demoralization, or for abandoning the party altogether. At a time when to be a democratic socialist was more difficult, socially, than it had ever been before, it would have been much easier to opt for political inactivity. But many did not. Instead, driven by a burning belief in the righteousness of what the movement stood for and by the loyalty and affection they felt for one another, they redoubled their efforts and continued to make the sacrifices required to save the CCF/NDP from extinction. Fred Young recalls, without regret, the endless hours he spent criss-crossing the province as a provincial organizer:

> You were always travelling, living in hotels, or sleeping in cots in spare rooms, and on the floor sometimes and in the back seat of the car...trying to keep your expenses as low as you could.... It was just a case of digging in your heels, all the time. You were just struggling to keep the membership, struggling to keep leadership, and I just had the feeling all those years, up until the early '60s, of just standing there, pushing.... It was a desperate holding action.

On top of all of this, Young had to endure the loneliness of constant travelling, the disappointment of successive electoral defeats, and a wife who, while supportive, was not altogether pleased that he had left the ministry to do CCF work. Another prominent organizer, Marjorie Pinney, also recalls the tribulations of the period:

> The '50s, especially, were tough years. Nobody knows how close the party came to going under in Ontario in the '50s it was so bad. But it was mainly because most of us were there working our heads off...so you admire all the people you remember from then.... I have thought that this party, if it means anything today, is here because of that group of people in that period, because we could easily have packed it in.[49]

And then there was Donald MacDonald, the party's chieftain for much of this period, whose Herculean feats and unflagging dedication played a key role in the party's survival. Although his precise impact is, of course, difficult to measure, it can be argued that at the very least he attracted new members to the CCF and inspired existing ones to greater efforts. From the minute he assumed the position of leader in late 1953, MacDonald was determined to make himself seen and heard in Ontario politics. Before and after his election to the legislature in June 1955, for instance, he undertook extensive tours of the province at least once each year, speaking at various party, labour, and farmer gatherings and making numerous appearances on radio and television, particularly in northern Ontario, where MacDonald spent much of his time when he wasn't in the legislature. In a widely circulated newspaper article in December 1955, columnist Don O'Hearn documented the leader's high visibility across the province:

> The CCF...is a very lively party.... This stems primarily from the activities of one man: leader Donald MacDonald.... The fact is that for a one-man show, Mr. MacDonald is carrying out a mammoth task. He is organizer, leader and publicity man rolled into one. And he is doing such a good job that in each category he is doing better than the whole Liberal organization. The buildings see a lot of Mr. MacDonald. The province sees a lot of him. And the press hears a lot from him. He is always on the go, and he usually has a statement ready on any issue of importance. The impression inevitably is left that the CCF is an active party, and this is going to win it votes.[50]

The CCF/NDP leader was equally vigilant inside the legislature, both in airing the party's policy priorities and exposing government immorality, and this, too, inspired party members to greater efforts.[51]

Perhaps the most telling indication of just how hard MacDonald worked to revive the party's fortunes was his performance during the 1963 provincial election campaign. Ably assisted by the federal secretary, Terry Grier, who wrote many of his speeches and planned his itinerary, MacDonald covered every square inch of the province. He drove ten thousand miles [16 090 km], addressed forty-one public meetings, issued at least forty press releases, and spent over thirty hours on the phone with his advisers. And because most of the party's election funds were being put into organizers and expensive radio and television advertising, MacDonald was also forced to raise money along the way to finance his campaign. But as usual, he was the quintessential political warrior, loving almost every minute of his frenetic, dawn-to-dusk schedule. He never seemed to tire, and on the last day of the campaign told reporters that he had never felt more invigorated. "The thing about these elections," he remarked casually, "is that you feel fine up to a day after the election, then you fall apart." Somehow one doubts this was true in MacDonald's case. Morley's observation, that MacDonald "almost single-handedly...kept the party alive in the darkest days, is therefore only a slight exaggeration.[52]

There is one other salient characteristic of the CCF/NDP in this period, related to the question of organizational revival, which deserves mention, if for no other reason than to dispel some myths: namely, the CCF/NDP's attempt to broaden its organizational base among farmers, organized labour, and the middle class. Actually, the efforts to attract the middle class, or the "liberal-minded" as they were called, were halfhearted at best. Although most of the party's top leaders came from middle-class families of ministers, social workers, teachers, and lawyers, as did a substantial percentage of the rank and file, the party did not target the middle class, either in its election propaganda or its recruitment efforts. There was, for example, no middle-class equivalent of the CCF's trade union committee or farm committee within the party's organizational apparatus. There was, it is true, the Woodsworth Foundation, a socialist education and research centre which had at first hoped to attract middle-class members to the CCF. But this body was not formally part of the CCF and after 1952 shifted its educational emphasis toward the working class.[53] Not until the late fifties did the liberal-minded officially become a target group, and even then the effort to mobilize their support was mostly symbolic. Any possibility that large numbers of liberal-minded would joint the NDP after its birth, moreover, was likely dashed by continuing organizational neglect and widespread rumours that the NDP was "dominated" by labour.[54]

Instead, the CCF/NDP reached out to other occupational groups, such as farmers and blue-collar workers, groups with mass organizations in place that could more easily be tapped for support and who were more likely to sympathize with the party's philosophy and program. The attempt to attract farmers, however, was largely unsuccessful. The farmers' suspicion that the CCF had a hidden, communist agenda, their long-standing antagonism towards organized labour, the non-partisanship of the leading farm organizations in the province, and the CCF/NDP's shortage of rural organizers, all contributed to the party's perpetually low membership and support in rural ridings.[55]

The party enjoyed much more success among organized labour, but even here its record was unenviable. The CCF's relationship with labour, always rather tenuous, began to deteriorate by the early 1950s and had not improved very much by the time the CLC and CCF joined hands under the NDP banner in 1961. Fears in some quarters of the party that labour was trying to "dominate" the CCF by securing an unduly large voice in party affairs—one which many felt would render the CCF less democratic and less socialist—without first committing itself more formally and permanently to the party, were met with resentment from the many non-affiliated unions. They felt that the CCF was willing to take their money and assistance during elections, but was not willing to give them a say in matters of policy, candidate selection, and party matters generally; there was truth in each perspective.[56] This mutual antagonism became less overt as the decade progressed, but it did not disappear. It resurfaced briefly in northern Ontario during the New Party development, at a time when unions were increasingly viewed as corrupt and violent, and grew to a fever pitch in the twenty-four months following the NDP's founding convention, as old fears of labour domination once again took hold.[57]

This mutual antagonism naturally soured relations between the two organizations at all levels. Even during the New Party development, the essence of which was to finally make labour an integral part of a "new" left-wing realignment, the two sides had a hard time cooperating and pooling resources. A serious conflict between the OFL and CCF over the allocation of part-time New Party organizers came very close to destroying the whole New Party project and was ample testimony to the mutual suspicion and organizational rivalry between labour and the party, as each side scrambled to ensure itself sufficient representation at the founding conventions.[58] In the months following the birth of the NDP, relations worsened. Unfounded charges that labour was controlling the New Party, combined with the reluctance of labour to get involved with the party for fear of lending credibility to these charges, led many party members to question once again the wisdom of the NDP-labour connection.

In organizational terms, the strained relations between labour and the CCF/NDP meant that for the period 1948 to 1964 joint political action was restricted to elections, in the form of "parallel" CCF and OFL campaigns. Between elections there was some informal consultation at the highest level, and even some formal organizational cooperation through the party's trade union committee for a short while, but this rarely extended to the local level. Where unionists did get involved with the CCF at the riding level, they more often than not formed a majority in the riding association, so that, in fact, there was little mixing of unionists and non-unionists. So Zakuta's assertion that "the dominant trend throughout the whole period was the growing role of the trade unions in party affairs and the steady meshing of the two organizations in conducting the operations of the CCF" is not very persuasive.[59]

Several additional points are worth noting to complete the picture of CCF-labour relations. First, although mutual suspicion and resentment were key reasons for the sporadic cooperation, they were not the only reasons. Union leaders, particularly in the immediate postwar years, were very busy with their own union affairs, and this usually left little time for political action. As a result, the party was regularly deprived of capable local leaders, candidates, and organizational assistance.[60] Furthermore, union leaders sympathetic to the CCF were often reluctant to disrupt newly established unions by introducing the always divisive issue of political action. And where political action was encouraged, by local political action committees (PACs) for example, rank-and-file unionists frequently complained of having the CCF shoved down their throats.[61] All of these factors militated against sustained and substantial political action by the labour movement and, in turn, gave rise to the sometimes bitter feeling among CCFers that when it came to helping the party, labour was all talk and no action.

The second point is that despite its arms-length relationship with the CCF/NDP, labour's contribution to the party must not be understated. Many of the party's members and local leaders, for example, were unionists, who often used what influence they had in their own organizations to win adherents to the party. As well, in election after election the PAC raised large sums of money for the CCF/NDP (most of which paid for its advertising), distributed leaflets, provided candidates and organizers, and brought out the union vote on election day.[62] Ken Bryden, the one-time provincial secretary and former MPP points to the generosity of the Steelworkers, in particular, who in 1952 agreed to pay the salaries of the party's only full-time organizers, Ames and Young; without this, he doubts the CCF would have survived. Labour also played a leading role in the formation of the NDP, as seen in the large number of union delegates at the founding convention, and in placing the new party on a stronger financial footing through the sudden rise in affiliations which followed.[63]

Finally, it must be noted that the argument that feelings of tension were a significant feature of the labour-CCF/NDP relationship between 1948 and 1964 does not appear in the existing studies of the Ontario party, or the national party. Neither Morley nor Zakuta deals with the issue directly, but both strongly imply that compatibility and cooperation were touchstones of the relationship. Gad Horowitz, in his full-length study of labour's political activities prior to 1960, concedes that relations between labour and the party were poor in the early fifties, but suggests nevertheless that, at least at the highest levels, the two sides enjoyed an increasingly warm and close relationship thereafter, culminating in the formation of the NDP in 1961.[64] What is clear, however, is that the tensions which emerged forcefully in the early 1950s persisted, and were manifested just as forcefully during the New Party development and during the honeymoon which followed.

Having said this, however, it is clear that most party leaders did not harbour strong feelings against labour and, in fact, saw the alliance as a prerequisite to the CCF/NDP becoming a major force in provincial politics. Much of the anti-labour sentiment seems to have been concentrated at the local level, particularly among the sizable minority of old-time CCFers, particularly in northern Ontario, who felt they had a vested interest in preserving, unchanged, the party they had done so much to build.[65] The majority of (non-union) party members viewed labour with indifference or, at worst, grudging acceptance. This would account for why the New Party idea was accepted almost unanimously by the membership, but without much enthusiasm and why, in 1961, a large number of CCFers, leaders included, opposed the granting of full voting rights at constituency meetings to affiliated (i.e., union) members.[66]

It has been argued that the prevailing movement-to-party interpretation of the Ontario CCF/NDP, between 1948 and 1964 at least, is not very persuasive, for there are few indications that the party became more centralized, bureaucratic, and election-minded, or less socialist in ideology and motivation. Instead, to understand what this period was really all about, one must appreciate the CCF/NDP's primary concern with rebuilding its basic organization. Almost all of the major initiatives and developments of this period can be linked to this imperative. That the emphasis on basic organization was so strong should not, however, come as a surprise. If the CCF was to avoid extinction, the only option was to intensify basic organizational efforts. Sometimes the methods were desperate and crude, like the CCF Brigade, and sometimes sophisticated, like the poll committee structure. And sometimes they were grand and deceptive, like the formation of the NDP. But they were always essential.

Consequently, the years 1948 to 1964 represent a distinct phase in the party's history. Unlike the mid-forties, when policy research and legislative performance were important elements of the party's organizational strategy, and unlike the late 1960s and beyond, when modern campaigning methods were combined with the maturation of the poll committee structure, and greater attention was given to producing party literature, the years from 1948 to 1964 were heavily coloured by techniques, gimmicks, and plans aimed at reinforcing the very foundations of the party. In the future, therefore, it might be more useful for academics to view the CCF/NDP's history from the point of view of "organization," of how the party has gone about trying to mobilize enough support to get itself elected, or to just survive. But this will require that the term "organization" not only be broadly defined, but that it also be divested of its sinister connotations. Marjorie Pinney, among others, was forever trying to convey this to party members, many of whom, like the movement/party theorists themselves, interpreted organization to mean a sell-out of the CCF/NDP's basic beliefs and character. "For too long," Pinney told party members in 1955,

> ...we have...refused to face up to the hard facts of political life—that we are a political party and must organize as one.... We've been suspicious of the very word organization; thinking it is some soulless monster that will rob us of that which sets us apart from other political parties...[believing that] our goal is to educate, to influence, to create programs, etc. All that must be done in achieving our goal, but should not be substituted for it.... An organization is nothing more than a sane, sensible mobilization of our human resources to work towards a common goal.[67]

Pinney's message, that movement and party were not necessarily incompatible, would eventually be understood. Until then, however, she and a tiny band of stalwarts continued their "desperate holding action," hopeful that perhaps one day the means by which their common goal—the establishment of a cooperative commonwealth—would be within their grasp.

NOTES

1. Walter Young, *The Anatomy of a Party: The National CCF 1932-61* (Toronto: University of Toronto Press, 1969), 60. See also Leo Zakuta, *A Protest Movement Becalmed: A Study of Change in the CCF* (Toronto: University of Toronto Press, 1964); Michael Cross, *The Decline and Fall of a Good Idea: CCF/NDP Manifestos 1932-1969* (Toronto: Hogtown Press, 1974); Kenneth McNaught, *A Prophet in Politics: A Biography of J.S. Woodsworth* (Toronto: University of Toronto Press, 1959); Peter Sinclair, "The Saskatchewan CCF: Ascent to Power and the Decline of Socialism," *Canadian Historical Review* 54 (December 1973), 419-33; and Christina Nichol, "In Pursuit of the Voter: The British Columbia CCF, 1945-1950," in J. William Brennan, ed., *Building the Cooperative Commonwealth: Essays on the Democratic Socialist Tradition in Canada* (Regina: Canadian Plains Research Centre, 1984), 123-40.

2. David Lewis, *The Good Fight: Political Memoirs, 1909-1958* (Toronto: Macmillan of Canada, 1981), 446-7.

3. Alan Whitehorn, "An Analysis of the Historiography of the CCF-NDP: The Protest Movement Becalmed Tradition," in Brennan, ed., *Building the Co-operative Commonwealth*, 1, 14. Whitehorn's article is the most comprehensive review of CCF/NDP literature and the shortcomings of the movement-party thesis.

4. See, for example, Donald C. MacDonald, *The Happy Warrior: Political Memoirs* (Markham, Ontario: Fitzhenry and Whiteside, 1988); Judy Steed, *Ed Broadbent: The Pursuit of Power* (Toronto: Penguin Books, 1989); Betty Dyck, *Running to Beat Hell, A Biography of A.M. (Sandy) Nicholson* (Regina: Canadian Plains Research Centre, University of Regina, 1988);

Thomas McLeod and Ian McLeod, *Tommy Douglas: The Road to Jerusalem* (Edmonton: Hurtig Publishers, 1987); Gerry Harrop, *Clairie Gillis, M.P.* (Hantsport, Nova Scotia: Lancelot Press, 1987); Allen Mills, *Fool for Christ: The Intellectual Politics of J.S. Woodsworth* (Toronto: University of Toronto Press, 1991); Cameron Smith, *Unfinished Journey: The Lewis Family* (Toronto: Summerhill Press, 1989); Olenka Melnyk, *Remembering the CCF: No Bankers in Heaven* (Toronto: McGraw-Hill Ryerson, 1989); and Lynn McDonald, *The Party that Changed Canada: The New Democratic Party, Then and Now* (Toronto: Macmillan of Canada, 1987).

5. The only published studies of the Ontario CCF/NDP are Gerald Caplan, *The Dilemma of Canadian Socialism: The CCF in Ontario* (Toronto: McClelland and Stewart, 1973); Leo Zakuta, *Protest Movement*; and J.T. Morley, *Secular Socialists: The CCF/NDP in Ontario, A Biography* (Kingston: McGill-Queen's University Press, 1984). There are, as well, several dissertations on the Ontario party. The most comprehensive are Dan Azoulay's, "Keeping the Dream Alive: the CCF/NDP of Ontario, 1951-1963" (Ph.D. diss., York University, 1991), and Peter Campbell's, "'Truly Grass Roots People,' The Cooperative Commonwealth Federation in Northern Ontario" (MA thesis, Laurentian University, 1986).

6. Zakuta, *Protest Movement*, 4-5.

7. On the question of internal power, Morley does note a shift in power from the extra-parliamentary party leadership to the caucus by the late sixties. He also details the existence of an influential party "oligarchy," but does not argue, as do the movement/party theorists, that its power vis-à-vis the rank and file increased over time.

8. The number of regular members, for example, declined from approximately 11,000 in 1948 to just under 6,000 in 1950, and did not recover to the 1948 level until 1961; provincial office revenues fell from over $30,000 in 1948 to just over $20,000 in 1952, and didn't surpass the 1948 level until 1959; and in terms of legislative representation and popular support, the CCF went from twenty-one seats and 27 per cent of the popular vote in the election of 1948 to two seats and 19 per cent two years later. After the 1963 election it still held only seven seats and 16 per cent of the popular vote. Ontario, *Reports of the Chief Electoral Officer*, 1948-1963; Azoulay, "Keeping the Dream Alive," 549-51.

9. Marjorie Pinney, taped interview by author, 1 June 1990, Toronto, Ontario.

10. National Archives of Canada (NAC), Ottawa, Ontario, CCF/NDP Papers, CCF, Ontario, "Report of the Eighteenth Annual Convention."

11. Lewis, *The Good Fight*, 412-13; Zakuta, *Protest Movement*, 113-25; Reginald Whitaker, *Double Standard: The Secret History of Canadian Immigration* (Toronto: Lester and Orpens Dennys, 1987), 16-18; Canadian Broadcasting Corporation, *Cold War in Canada*, transcript of "Ideas" broadcast, 6-27 March 1984; CCF/NDP Papers, CCF, Ontario, Minutes of Provincial Council, 10, 11 February; 29 September 1951; 12, 13 January 1952; Donald MacDonald, taped interview by author, 16 May 1990, Toronto, Ontario; Fred Young, taped interview by author, 29 April 1990, Toronto, Ontario.

12. MacDonald, interview by Ontario Historical Studies Series, 6 June 1972, transcript, OHSS; see also quote by Lewis in Morley, *Secular Socialists*, 58. For more on Ontario's tremendous economic growth after 1945, and the social changes this wrought, see K.J. Rea, *The Prosperous Years: The Economic*

13. For more on the Tory administration and organization in this period, see MacDonald, *The Happy Warrior;* Roger Graham, *Old Man Ontario: Leslie M. Frost* (Toronto: University of Toronto Press, 1990); Jonathan Manthorpe, *The Power and the Tories: Ontario Politics—1943 to the Present* (Toronto: Macmillan of Canada, 1974); and Eddie Goodman, *Life of the Party: The Memoirs of Eddie Goodman* (Toronto: Key Porter Books, 1988).

14. Young, *Anatomy of a Party*, 11.

15. Morley, *Secular Socialists*, 57-89.

16. The CCF itself defined the term "organization" as the method whereby the information produced by research and conveyed to party members through education was communicated to the public at large, to attract new members, funds, and electoral support. Party organization differs from party "structure" in that the latter usually refers to the *general* distribution of constitutional powers and obligations within the party, while the former refers to the *specific* methods and policies adopted to increase party support.

17. While this seems to be the *raison d'être* of Morley's study, even here the latter is only partially convincing, for the central components of the movement/party model are not challenged directly or with ample cogency. Morley does not discuss the motivation of party members, for example, or the specific question of bureaucratic centralization, and his conclusions on the ideological evolution of the party are arrived at without having looked at any of the party's official programs in this period.

18. In his classic study of political parties, Robert Michels contends that all organizations are subject to centralizing tendencies that result sooner or later in the establishment

History of Ontario, 1939-1975 (Toronto: University of Toronto Press, 1985).

of oligarchy. "Organization implies the tendency to oligarchy," he wrote. "In every organization, whether it be a political party, a professional union, or any other association of the kind, the aristocratic tendency manifests itself very clearly. The mechanism of the organization, while conferring a solidity of structure, induces serious changes in the organized mass, completely inverting the respective position of the leaders and the led." Michels calls this a "sociological law" and those who deny it, dangerous liars. Robert Michels, *Political Parties: A Sociological Study of the Oligarchical Tendencies of Modern Democracy*, trans. Eden & Cedar Paul (n.p.: Hearst's International Library, 1915; New York: Dover Publications, 1959), 32-5.

19. Zakuta, *Protest Movement*, 65.

20. The democratic structure of the CCF/NDP is outlined in detail by Frederick Engelmann in "Membership Participation in Policy-making in the CCF," *Canadian Journal of Economics and Political Science* 22 (May 1956), 161-73. For more on the constitutional modifications during this period, see Morley, *Secular Socialists*, 101-14.

21. See, for example, Zakuta, *Protest Movement*, 26-30; Frank Underhill, "Power Politics in the Ontario CCF," *Canadian Forum* 32 (April 1952), 7-8; and Lloyd Harrington, "What's Left," *Canadian Forum* 31 (March 1952), 269-70.

22. From 1948 to 1956, for example, the composition of the nineteen-member provincial executive changed considerably. Close to sixty different individuals sat on the executive in this period and with the exception of the provincial leaders, who sat on the executive automatically, no one served for longer than five years, twelve people served from four to five years, and the remaining forty to forty-five individuals served for three years or less. The turnover rate on the much larger and less exclusive Provincial

Council was, of course, even greater. Queen's University Archives, Kingston, Ontario CCF/NDP Papers, CCF, Ontario, "Reports of the Annual Convention, 1948-1956."

23. Ontario CCF/NDP Papers, NDP, Ontario, Minutes of Table Officers, 23 July 1962; Minutes of Provincial Executive, 2 August 1962; Azoulay, "Keeping the Dream Alive," 498. The regional organizer plan was an effort to get area councils to finance their own organizers, through contributions from local labour bodies, who would work in their areas exclusively except for Toronto and Hamilton. It was largely unsuccessful.

24. CCF/NDP Papers, CCF, Ontario, Minutes of Provincial Council, 5 September 1953.

25. Young, *Anatomy of a Party*, 122; see also Zakuta, *Protest Movement*, 73, 112, 133, 142; and Morley, *Secular Socialists*, 57-8.

26. McMaster University Archives, Hamilton, Ontario, Ontario CCF/NDP Collection, CCF, Ontario, Minutes of Membership Education Committee, 4 October 1952, and Report of same to Provincial Council, 4, 5 October 1952; Ontario CCF/NDP Papers, Minutes of Membership Education Committee, 17 October, 3 November 1953, and Report of Literature Committee to 1952 convention; CCF/NDP Papers, Minutes of Provincial Council, 8 September, 8 December 1956; "Report of the Twenty-second Annual Convention," Minutes of Provincial Executive, 21 November 1956, Provincial Council, 24, 25 August 1956.

27. For the 1951 election, the provincial office set aside a budget of over $50,000 for election expenses. In 1955, the figure was $10,000, or 20 per cent of the preceding election. In 1951 the CCF ran candidates in seventy-seven of ninety ridings (i.e., 86 per cent), whereas in 1955 it contested seventy-nine of ninety-

eight ridings (81 per cent). CCF/NDP Papers, CCF, Ontario, Minutes of Provincial Council, October 1951, and Minutes of Provincial Executive, 19 April 1955.

28. In the period 1948 to 1953, the CCF contested every by-election, federal and provincial, but from 1954 to 1960, it contested only 58 per cent of them. *Canadian Parliamentary Guide, 1938-1962;* Ontario, Returns of By-Elections, 1948-1962.

29. Ontario, *Returns of the Chief Electoral Officer, 1948-1963.* The policy of "concentration" was adopted in 1955, and it meant that provincial organizers paid more attention to ridings in urban-industrial areas of southern Ontario, and the North, where the CCF had traditionally done well. CCF/NDP Papers, CCF, Ontario, Minutes of Organization Committee, 4 October 1952, Provincial Council, 25 June 1955, Provincial Executive, 16 June 1955.

30. In terms of money spent to hire organizers, publish election material, and find candidates, the CCF was clearly far more concerned with "electoral activity" in the period 1943 to 1948 than it would be for many years after. "In many ways," concludes Gerald Caplan, "the Ontario CCF was better prepared for these campaigns [the June 1945 federal and provincial elections] than any in its history." *The Dilemma of Canadian Socialism,* 110-13, 118, 163-5.

31. Young, *Anatomy of a Party,* 95, 163; see also Zakuta, *Protest Movement,* 59-60, 68, 142.

32. Michels, *Political Parties;* M. Ostrogorski, *Democracy and the Organization of Political Parties,* vol. 1, *England,* 2d. ed. (New York: Anchor Books, 1964), Ch. 8, and "Introduction" by S.M. Lipset; and Maurice Duverger, *Political Parties: Their Organization and Activity in the Modern State,* 3d. ed. (New York: John Wiley and Sons, 1966), "Introduction."

33. Fred Young, interview by author; Dudley Bristow, interview by author, 8 May 1990, Mississauga, Ontario, notes; NAC, Canadian Labour Congress (CLC) Papers, Canadian Congress of Labour, Political Action Committee, *Newsletter,* December 1951. Perhaps the best account of the sorts of sacrifices which CCF activists across Canada chose to make is Melnyk's *Remembering the CCF.*

34. Leon Epstein, *Political Parties in Western Democracies* (New York: Frederick Praeger, 1967; reprint, New Brunswick, NJ: Transaction, 1980), 102.

35. Marjorie Pinney, taped interview by author, 1 June 1990, Toronto, Ontario; MacDonald, *Happy Warrior;* Doris Shackleton, *Tommy Douglas* (Toronto: McClelland and Stewart, 1975), 248.

36. Young, *Anatomy of a Party,* 4.

37. Zakuta, *Protest Movement,* 103; Young, *Anatomy of a Party,* 65. See also Cross, ed., *Decline and Fall of a Good Idea,* 11-13; Desmond Morton, *The New Democrats 1961-1986: The Politics of Change* (Toronto: Copp Clark Pitman, 1986), 20; Gad Horowitz, *Canadian Labour in Politics* (Toronto: University of Toronto Press, 1968), 173-4; and Ivan Avakumovic, *Socialism in Canada: A Study of the CCF/NDP in Federal and Provincial Politics* (Toronto: McClelland and Stewart, 1978), 164-5.

38. CCF/NDP Papers, CCF, Ontario, *First Term Program* (1948). The 1959 program, *For a Better Ontario,* is illustrative. It promises that a CCF government "will plan the use of our resources for the benefit of our people.... Its aims will be to stimulate a steady increase in provincial wealth, to ensure fair distribution of that wealth, and to use a reasonable part of it for necessary public services." The 1963 program promises likewise: "to produce the greatest wealth of which our province is capable...to distribute it fairly

among all the people, to make health and other essential services available to all who need them, to develop educational and cultural opportunities, and to protect and extend the rights and liberties of the individual." CCF/NDP Papers, CCF, Ontario, "Looking to the Future: The CCF Program for Ontario" (1955); *Challenge for Ontario* (1958); NDP, Ontario, *A New and Democratic Program for Ontario* (1963).

39. Ontario CCF/NDP Papers, NDP, Ontario, Minutes of Provincial Council, 20, 21 April 1963.

40. Lewis, *The Good Fight*, 447.

41. CCF/NDP Papers, MacDonald to Lazarus, 10 March 1952; CCF, Ontario, Minutes of Provincial Executive, 31 July 1951; Donald MacDonald, Organization Report to National Council, 1, 2 March 1952; Ontario CCF/NDP Papers, CCF, Ontario, Minutes of Provincial Council, 12 January 1952; Report of Organizing Committee to Provincial Council, 29, 30 September 1951; Riding Report to Provincial Council, 14 April 1951.

42. CCF/NDP Papers, CCF, Ontario, Minutes of Provincial Council, 26, 27 June 1954; *CCF News*, August 1954; Pinney, interview by author; Queen's University Archives, George Grube Papers, CCF, Ontario, Minutes of Organization Committee, 31 August 1954.

43. It should be noted that riding "clubs" were distinct from riding "associations." The CCF constitution stated that "CCF members in any locality with the approval of the constituency association or the provincial council may form themselves into a CCF club for social, educational and political purposes, hold meetings, elect officers and raise from among themselves the necessary monies to carry on local activities, provided that, for the purposes of electing candidates and fighting election campaigns, members of all clubs in the constituency shall act through the constituency

association." CCF, Ontario, "Constitution of the CCF (Ontario Section), April 1955," in Zakuta, *Protest Movement*, Appendix B.

44. CCF/NDP Papers, Donald MacDonald, Memorandum on Proposals for Ontario Organization, January 1952. "By itself," explained the Organization Committee, "a membership drive is of limited value, even if it is completely successful in terms of increased membership. We certainly need an increased membership, but even more, we need a more active membership." Ontario CCF/NDP Papers, CCF, Ontario, Minutes of Organization Committee, 4 September 1953.

45. CCF/NDP Papers, CCF, Ontario, Minutes of Provincial Council, 4, 5 October 1952, and Financial Statement, appended to Provincial Council Minutes, 16,17 January 1954; CCF, federal, Provincial Reports to National Council, 1953; Ontario CCF/NDP Papers, CCF, Ontario, Minutes of Finance Committee, 13 August 1953.

46. Based on reports from its provincial organizers, the Organization Committee concluded in 1952 that in "more than half of the ridings outside Toronto and District," membership levels were either stagnant or falling because of "the reluctance of our local people...to tackle the job of building an effective organization." Ontario CCF/NDP Papers, CCF, Ontario, Report of Organization Committee to Provincial Council, 4, 5 October 1952, and 17, 18 January 1953; CCF/NDP Papers, CCF, federal, "Organizer's Report—Fred Young," 20 October 1952.

47. For more on the Ontario CCF's pragmatic and deceptive approach to forming the NDP, see Azoulay, "'This March Forward to a Genuine People's Party'?: Rivalry and Deception in the Founding of the Ontario NDP, 1948-1961," *Canadian Historical Review* 74 (March 1993), 1-27.

48. There were numerous signs that the liberal-minded were interested in the New Party, including the large number who joined New Party Clubs (almost as many as belonged to the CCF, in fact), the well-attended and enthusiastic liberal-minded conferences arranged to discuss the New Party's program and constitution, the larger number of "undecided" voters in opinion polls, the strong showing of New Party candidates in two by-elections in 1960, and the spirit shown by New Party Club delegates at the national and provincial founding conventions the following year. Azoulay, "'This March Forward.'"

49. Young and Pinney, interviews by author.

50. CCF/NDP Papers, CCF, Ontario, "Report of the Twentieth Annual Convention"; Minutes of Provincial Council, 27, 28 March 1954; *CCF News*, February 1954, December 1955.

51. Queen's University Archives, Donald MacDonald Papers, Doc Ames, Organization Report, 29 February 1956; *CCF News*, April, June 1956; for more on MacDonald's activities in these years, see his *Happy Warrior*, Chs. 4-7.

52. "MacDonald's Day Spent on Foot Greeting Electors in York South," *Globe and Mail*, 25 September 1963; Morley, *Secular Socialists*, xvii.

53. Morley, *Secular Socialists*, 178-82. For more on the Woodsworth Foundation, see R. Douglas Francis, "The Ontario Woodsworth House Controversy: 1944-1954," *Ontario History* 71 (March 1979), 27-37, and Azoulay, "The Cold War Within: The CCF, the Ginger Group, and the Woodsworth Foundation, 1944-1953," *Ontario History* 84 (June 1992), 78-104.

54. See Morton, *The Politics of Change*, 29; and Azoulay, "Keeping the Dream Alive," 445-6, 458-62.

55. CCF/NDP Papers, CCF, Ontario, Minutes of Farm Committee, 20 May 1950; Minutes of Provincial Council, 22 October 1950; 14 April 1951; 12, 13 January 1952; 16, 17 January 1954; 11 December 1954; 5 November 1955; Ontario CCF/NDP Collection, Farm Committee Report to Provincial Council, 4, 5 October 1952; Von Pilis to Bell, 8 May 1954, and Bell to Von Pilis, 10 May 1954; CCF *News*, June 1953; York University Archives, North York, Ontario, Paul Fox Collection, David Lewis, interview by Paul Fox, 1961, transcript; MacDonald, *Happy Warrior*, 265-88.

56. CCF/NDP Papers, CCF, federal, Minutes of Provincial Executive, 10 May 1952; MacDonald to Lazarus, 12 September 1952; CLC Papers, Ingle to Weisbach, 2 May 1952; Canadian Labour Congress, "Memorandum Re CLC Convention Resolution on New Political Party," [1958]; Weisbach to MacDonald (CLC), 1 May 1952; MacDonald to Carlin, 13 September 1952; Matt Quinn to MacDonald, 3 November 1951; MacDonald to Fred Young, 6 February 1952; Murray Cotterill, taped interview by author, 4 June 1990, Toronto, Ontario; McMaster University Archives, United Steelworkers of America Papers, Bill Sefton to Larry Sefton, 18 June 1959.

57. Azoulay, "Keeping the Dream Alive," 415-21, 458-66, 475-81.

58. Azoulay, "'This March Forward'."

59. Cotterill, Pinney, Young, and Bryden, interviews by author; Lewis, *The Good Fight*, 301; CLC Papers, Weisbach, "Memorandum to Cleve Kidd for the OFL Executive," 27 October 1952; CCL, "Report of the Political Action Department," 15 June 1954; "Report of the PAC to the Executive Council of the CCL," [1955]; CCF/NDP Papers, CCF, Ontario, Minutes of Provincial Council, 12, 13 January 1952, and Provincial Executive, 8 March 1952; NAC, OFL Papers, OFL-PAC, Report to OFL Executive, December 1951; Report of Annual Convention, 1, 2 February 1952; Zakuta, *Protest Movement*, 109.

60. In relation to the 1951 election, for example, see CCF/NDP Papers, MacDonald to Leo Lalonde, Timmins, Ontario, 8 May 1951, to Arnold Peters, Timmins, Ontario, 10 May 1951, and to Lazarus, 12 September 1952; Quinn to MacDonald, 3 November 1951; Thomas Fisher Rare Books Library, University of Toronto, Woodsworth Memorial Collection, CCF, Ontario, "Report of the Eighteenth Annual Convention, 10-12 April 1952."

61. Cotterill, interview by author; Ontario CCF/NDP Papers, CCF, Ontario, Report of NED Planning Conference, 4 February 1951; OFL Papers, OFL, Report of PAC Director to OFL Executive, December 1951.

62. Labour's contribution to the 1955 campaign was typical. The PAC mobilized its own campaign workers, enumerators, and canvassers, to assist the party, and provided the CCF with four full-time organizers. It also spent $16,000 on newspaper and radio advertising and prepared several leaflets on the CCF for distribution among workers; these efforts were combined with repeated pleas by OFL leaders to its members to get out and vote, and more important, to vote for the CCF. As well, more than half of the CCF's eighty-one candidates were union members. OFL Papers, OFL, "Election Guide for Labour council and local Union PACs," 1955, and "Report of the Annual Convention"; CCF/NDP Papers, CCF, Ontario, Minutes of Provincial Council, 22, 23 January, 25 June 1955, and Executive Committee, 31 March, 16 June, 25 June 1955; Ontario CCF/NDP Papers, Eady to CCF Riding Associations in Toronto and District, 13 May 1955.

63. Fifty-five per cent of the delegates were union members. Bryden, interview by author; Woodsworth Memorial Collection, NDP, Ontario, "Capsule Report on Founding Convention, 7-9 October 1961."

64. Horowitz, *Canadian Labour,* especially Chs. 4-6.

65. Young and Cotterill, interviews by author; Caplan, *Dilemma,* Ch. 2; Ian MacPherson, "The 1945 Collapse of the CCF in Windsor," *Ontario History* 61 (1969), 203-5; MacDonald Papers, MacDonald to Irene Ames, 10 September 1958; Ontario CCF/NDP Papers, CCF, Ontario, "Confidential By-Election Analysis," 3 October 1960; CCF/NDP Papers, Macdonald to Hamilton, 1 December 1959; Murdo Martin, "Report to CCF National Executive," 20 June 1959.

66. OFL Papers, OFL, "Confidential Memo for OFL-PAC Special Meeting, 26 May 1958"; CCF/NDP Papers, CCF, Ontario, "Report of the 24th Annual Convention, 11-13 October 1958"; Ontario CCF/NDP Papers, Peg Stewart, Confidential Memo to CCF members of Ontario Committee for the New Party (OCNP), [July 1961]; "MacDonald to Archer, 16 July 1961; OCNP, Minutes, 16 August, 13 September, 6 October 1961; Stewart to Archer, 25 July and Archer to Stewart, 26 July 1961.

67. *CCF News,* November 1955, November 1956.

SOCIAL CREDIT IN ALBERTA:
THE ROAD TO DISINTEGRATION

BY ALVIN FINKEL

o

In September 1968 Ernest C. Manning announced that he was retiring from the premiership of Alberta after more than a quarter-century in the post. A leadership convention two months later, the first in the Social Credit League's [Social Credit party] history, chose Municipal Affairs Minister Harry Strom as Manning's replacement. Strom ran the province for only two and a half years before facing his first election as premier. In that election, the resurgent Progressive Conservatives carried two-thirds of the seats and ended thirty-six years of Social Credit rule. Used to the spoils of power, Social Credit proved an inept opposition party. Its attempts to find ideological ground not covered by the Conservatives gave the party a sharply reactionary image and, for those leery of the aura of wealth and slickness about the new governing party, reduced its ability to provide a reasonable alternative. Ultimately the party's ranks thinned to the point where other right-wing parties, particularly a western separatist party, moved in on Social Credit's much-reduced stock of voters. Finally, deprived of both members and voters, it was taken over by right-wing extremists of the type Manning had purged in the late forties. By the mid-eighties, no one of importance connected with the Social Credit government and party of the Manning and Strom periods remained in Alberta's Social Credit League; it had become the exclusive property of bigots and kooks. In this chapter, I trace the party's fall in the post-Manning period and question whether the slide that seemed to begin once the venerable premier left could not have been reversed at various points.

Excerpt from Alvin Finkel, *The Social Credit Phenomenon in Alberta* (Toronto: University of Toronto Press Incorporated, 1989), pp. 177-201. Reprinted by permission of University of Toronto Press Incorporated.

Shortly after the resignation of Manning came the report of the Kirby Commission into alleged influence-peddling by [E.W.] Hinman [a former provincial treasurer] and [Alfred] Hooke [a cabinet minister]. Like the 1956 commission on ministers' activities, this commission found no evidence that a government minister had clearly abused his high office. But, like the 1956 [report Mahaffy], the 1968 commission raised questions about the internal operations of the Social Credit government. The Mahaffy report had suggested a pattern of informality in government contract-granting and purchasing that would have been unacceptable in any large, private corporation. Such informality, coupled with the fact that the government was riddled with poor appointments based on patronage and nepotism, suggests that the public image of Social Credit as providing a "businesslike" if unimaginative administration of the province's affairs was somewhat mythological.

The Kirby report raised doubts about the public-mindedness of the two cabinet ministers it investigated, even if it concluded that neither had used his position to pressure government agencies or private individuals to make certain decisions that resulted in a personal benefit. But the John J. Barr interpretation, which accorded with the Social Credit interpretation of the time, that Kirby merely "chided" their "lack of discretion in some of their business dealings"[1] is an understatement indeed. Kirby outlined a variety of their dealings, which on the surface could appear as conflicts of interest with their ministerial duties. Lord Asquith, the British prime minister from 1908 to 1916, he noted, had said that ministers must not enter transactions "whereby their private pecuniary interest might, even conceivably, come into conflict with their public duty."[2] By these standards, Hooke and Hinman came off badly.

Hooke was involved in a variety of land deals while he was minister of municipal affairs. There was no evidence, for example, that he used his office to press for the development of Sherwood Park, a bedroom community near Edmonton where he owned land and made a profit of $64,000 from its sale once the government approved suburban development.[3] "However, Mr. Hooke's involvement in this development could, and indeed did, give rise to the suspicion that he was using his office for the personal gain of himself and his associate Campbell. In so exposing himself to such suspicion his conduct in my view was imprudent in the sense of the observation made by Prime Minister Asquith quoted earlier in this Report."[4] Similarly, Hooke was judged harshly by Kirby for getting personally involved, as co-owner of a house-building firm, in a damage claim against the City of Edmonton for failing to renew a certain lease at the same time that Edmonton was appearing before the Local Authorities Board trying to annex industrial areas adjacent to the city. Wrote Kirby: "In my view, it was imprudent for Mr. Hooke, in view of his position as Minister of Municipal Affairs to have become personally involved to the extent that he did in a dispute between a company in which he had a substantial financial interest and a municipal corporation, and thereby create apprehension on the part of the City Commissioners, particularly Hamilton, even though it was unfounded."[5]

Edgar Hinman's amassing of a private fortune during ten years in the cabinet also drew barbs from Kirby. Regarding Hinman's association with wealthy Edmonton businessman Jacob Superstein, Kirby wrote:

> Superstein assumed he was deriving substantial benefits from his association with the Provincial Treasurer. This assumption demonstrates how imprudent it was of Mr. Hinman to have placed himself under obligation to Superstein by accepting the loan to B and R Service, and the personal loan to himself, and to have become involved to the extent that he did in Superstein's business affairs.... By this imprudence he rendered himself open to the same assumption by anyone aware of this relationship, notwithstanding, as pointed out by Davey, Superintendent of Treasury Branches, that the granting of credit by Treasury Branch is not subject to any control either by the Provincial Treasurer or by the Treasury Board, of which Hinman was Chairman, and that he did not in fact in any way intervene with respect to this interim financing.[6]

It might be unkind to question whether a minister need "intervene" to get what he wished from a civil service rife with patronage and nepotism in which the interests and desires of the minister would be likely commonly known. In any case, however, Kirby was clear that neither Hinman nor Hooke could, by the laws of evidence—one is innocent until proven guilty—be labelled guilty of [Garth] Turcott's [NDP MLA] explicit charge that the ministers had set out to use their offices to gain benefits.

But just as the wealth of Norman Tanner [former Social Credit cabinet minister] had surprised many Albertans who regarded their government as being composed of plain folk like themselves, the report on Hinman and Hooke illustrated again that Social Credit ministers, during or after their stay in government, appeared miraculously to prosper. The point was particularly emphasized when, within months of leaving government, Manning had become a director of the Canadian Imperial Bank of Commerce, Stelco, Pacific Western Airlines, Manufacturers Life, Melton's Real Estate, Alberta Gas Trunk, McIntyre Porcupine, and Underwood and McLellan.[7] The bank directorship particularly shocked old Social Crediters like Hooke,[8] just as Tanner's appointment to the board of the Dominion Bank of Canada shortly after leaving the cabinet in the fifties had raised questions about the sincerity of Social Credit ministers' thunderbolts against financial orthodoxy. Such events weakened remaining pretensions that Social Credit was qualitatively different from other conservative administrations: more high-minded, and governed by God rather than by Mammon. Increasingly its halo tarnished, and Social Credit and its leaders had to bear comparison with the Progressive Conservatives and their image-conscious leader, Peter Lougheed. Harry Strom, Manning's successor, and his handlers understood the challenge before them, but the ideological restraints of "social conservatism" set by Manning made their task difficult.

For twenty-five years Alberta Social Credit and Ernest C. Manning had been synonymous. He had established early in his premiership that his ideas must prevail in cabinet and caucus, and his purge of extremist rightists and of Arthur Wray, who clung to the fuzzy radicalism of the Aberhart period, showed his resoluteness. Despite his serious manner and his social reserve, Manning, thanks to Aberhart and the Bible Institute, had developed a sense of theatricality that became an important asset in establishing his presence among Albertans. In Manning, it was felt, one could trust implicitly that the province was in clean hands. The business community in particular came to admire his philosophical individualism, particularly since it caused him to accept their opposition to government programs whose specific aim was to redistribute wealth.

Although many of Manning's ministers through the years were competent in their portfolios, none other perhaps than the colourful Alfred J. Hooke developed much of a public profile. Day-to-day administration night be in their hands but policy development, such as it was, always seemed to be Manning's province. In any case, the Social Credit-sponsored radio and television programs to propagandize government achievements made little use of ministers other than Manning when new policies were introduced.

In the last years of Manning's regime, he appeared to consult not with his cabinet colleagues but with his friends from big business, who were hoping to woo him to the national scene, with his son, Preston, and with Preston's young, educated, technocratic right-wing friends.[9] But Manning groomed no heir apparent either from the cabinet or from his latter-day consultants and there were no ministers in his government who appeared obvious contenders for his job and adequate opponents to the upstart Conservative leader.

Ultimately, Preston Manning and his friends proved to be kingmakers. Having won the senior Manning to their view that modern business and scientific ideas could be applied to find conservative solutions to social problems, they sought a successor for the premier who was similarly receptive. There was no obvious candidate among the fuddy-duddy old men of the Manning cabinet. Robert Clark, the minister of youth, might be a possibility but he was still in his twenties and unlikely to be acceptable to older party members. In the end, they settled on Harry Strom, who had become municipal affairs minister earlier that year and previously had served as agriculture minister. A wealthy farmer from southern Alberta, Strom was the type of successful, religious, rural family man likely to appeal to older party members. His appeal to the young Turks of the party was that he was open to new ideas.

The year before, for example, Strom had demonstrated his receptivity to the idea of "preventive welfare," a notion that the "systems approach" group favoured. As chairman of the new Human Resources Development Authority, a major product of the Manning White Paper on Human Resources, Strom locked horns with crusty Alfred Hooke, who regarded the new technocrats, with some justification, as half-baked flakes. Hooke had only recently become minister of public welfare and he raised serious objections to the fuzziness of the Preventive Social Service Act of 1966. This act, which had been encouraged for several years by department officials,[10] set aside funds to be granted to municipal programs designed to get—and to keep—people off the welfare rolls.[11] Its parameters were so poorly defined that, in Hooke's view, municipalities were rushing to create vague programs so that they could receive government funds and reduce their own welfare costs. While Hooke attempted to convince Manning that no further grants be approved, so as to allow a balanced budget for 1968,[12] the Human Resources Development Authority moved to reduce Hooke's authority to delay approval of preventive social service programs.[13] Although Strom's officials may have played a greater role here than Strom himself, within government circles Strom became clearly associated with the side of the experimenters, not the traditionalists.

Strom promised little during his leadership campaign except to initiate a "Head Start" program for the children of the poor, modelled after the largely futile "Great Society" program the United States designed to equalize educational opportunities for ghetto children in that country, and to launch a major study of educational programs necessary to carry Alberta into the twenty-first century.[14] The stress on education and training fit in well with the ideas of the "social conservative" systems-approach group who believed that conservatives must raise such issues as poverty, which theretofore had become the property of liberals and socialists by default. But while leftists might call for collectivist solutions such as government job creation and wealth redistribution, the social conservatives called for better educational opportunities and other community opportunities directed at individuals who might then be expected to pull themselves out of poverty.[15]

Preston Manning's involvement in the Strom campaign made it appear, probably correctly, that Premier Manning, nominally neutral, favoured Strom as his successor over Raymond Reierson and Gordon Taylor, the other strong contenders and men who might be regarded as old-fashioned conservatives, little interested in the mumbo-jumbo of the white paper.[16] Strom indeed won, but a fifty-five-year-old farmer from southern Alberta would have a difficult row to hoe to convince the increasingly alienated urbanites of the province that he represented the political change that Albertans increasingly seemed to want.

The young Turks, as they had hoped, came to play a significant role in the evolution of policy during the brief Strom period. Among their number were talented individuals such as Owen Anderson, executive assistant to Strom for a period and later coordinator of federal-provincial research and policy development; John Barr, executive assistant to the minister of education; and Don Hamilton, Strom's executive assistant at the time of the 1971 election. Anderson was only twenty-three when Strom became premier but had already played a role in the determination of the contents of Manning's White Paper on Human Resources. He was also...responsible for producing a thesis that provided the first detailed profile of the Social Credit League membership and its views. Barr was twenty-five and had a background in journalism, while Hamilton, who entered the lists as a Social Credit candidate against Don Getty in Whitemud in 1971, was a United Church minister "who made a modest success of business before turning to politics."[17]

These three, according to David G. Wood, "were responsible for the Task Force on Urbanization and the Future; for the creation of the Intergovernmental Affairs office; for early childhood programs; for a province-wide magazine, 'Land for Living.'"[18]

None of these young men nor Strom himself had anything to say about monetary policy. They were social conservatives rather than social crediters and they supported an activist government whose aim was to promote individual opportunity and, in so doing, minimize the socialist threat. They did not always speak respectfully of the Social Credit party as it had operated in the preceding decades or of the party faithful from that period who remained active and demonstrated hostility to proponents of change. Just months before the 1971 election, for example, Hamilton provided this irreverent overview of party history in *Insight*, the glossy party organ which in the Strom period replaced the black-and-white little magazine, *The Busy Bee*, that served as party house organ from 1956 to 1968.

My analysis is that Social Credit started as a movement of the people—almost a revolutionary movement which began really on the left in many ways, but had the characteristics of the Western Canadian—independence, individual responsibility and that sort of thing.

Beginning about the end of the 1940s, it went progressively to the right, and in the 1950s was very much a right-wing kind of party. I think partly due to the influence of Preston Manning on his father's thinking, the party veered back to the left in such things as the White Paper on Human Resources and the concepts contained in it.

Now I see it in the centre with some good social legislation and a feeling they want to stay on the right instead of the left. But there is a tension in the party created by some of the younger, newer thinkers who have come in and are pressing the social legislation and the old-line thinkers who came into the party in the late 1940s and see it as it was then.[19]

Someone who could find leftism, however vague, in Manning's white paper would be confusing technique with ideology since Manning expressed no important change of view in this document, except to claim that a "systems approach" would help to rationalize programs and better serve the "social conservative" ends he had espoused throughout his premiership. His comments on the Carter Commission [federal Royal Commission on Taxation] later that year and his government's rebate of 100 per cent of estate taxes to everyone including the very rich demonstrated his continued opposition to wealth redistribution and "regimentation" of industry. But to the young Social Crediters, mesmerized by technique, the battle with the Social Credit old-timers to achieve a "scientific" right-wing approach to problems rather than rely on seat-of the-pants solutions was a crucial one. It was also coincidentally a battle to change the Social Credit image in the public mind and to convince voters that the old Social Credit government was renewing itself and that there was no need to turn to Peter Lougheed's untried Conservatives.

The new approach produced a major governmental reorganization in 1971, with health and social development combined, a hospital services commission established, and a department of the environment with its own minister launched. Alberta was indeed the first province to establish a ministry of the environment. Earlier...intergovernmental affairs was established as a ministry. All in all, the government had been rearranged so that questions susceptible to the systems approach had been separated out and placed under a single authority.[20]

Reorganization of government departments, however, while it may lay the basis for better planning of programs, has little immediate impact on voters. Responding to the public's desire for ever-increasing educational opportunities and to increasingly fashionable "human capital" views, whose currency among conservatives was obvious in the evidence before the Royal Commission on Education in the fifties as well as in Manning's white paper, the government vastly expanded education spending at every level. From 15.1 per cent of provincial expenditures as a percentage of receipts in 1956, education had climbed to 20.4 per cent in 1966, and then over the next five years soared to 33.4 per cent of the total budget.[21] Interestingly, while a 13 per cent surplus of receipts over expenditures had been recorded in 1966, huge increases in educational spending over the next five years wiped it out. The government posted small deficits in 1970 and 1971 and drew on surpluses of earlier years to the hypocritical shock of the Tories, for whom government expenditures on education were never high enough.[22]

Despite their willingness to fund ambitious building programs by the universities, colleges, and technical schools as well as to provide more money for the schools, the Strom government would not accept the long-standing position of all opposition parties that the government should place an upper limit on property taxes resulting from education costs. Nor would it take over the municipal portion of welfare costs. In these areas, the "social conservative" (that is, Manning) view, that local governments and/or individuals must bear a share of costs for services delivered on their behalf as a deterrent to unwise spending, remained intact.[23]

Similarly intact was the Alberta government's opposition to federal programs which Manning had attacked. Bilingualism and biculturalism, tax reform, medicare, and regional developmental programs were subjects of hostile attack. Interestingly, however, while Manning had attempted to present his opposition to federal programs mainly in ideological terms, the Strom team preferred to emphasize regional concerns. Obviously, Manning's positions were formed in part by his perceptions of provincial interests, but unlike Harry Strom he seemed to feel little need to invoke provincial pride. He rarely spoke of regional interests because he was well aware that on most issues of federal-provincial relations the four western provinces and/or the three Prairie provinces were not in agreement. But the young men behind

Strom, aware of the power of Quebec's appeal as a separate culture and region requiring special treatment from the federal government, wished to cast western Canada in the same light.

A book of essays edited by Barr and Anderson in 1971 exemplified the new approach. Its title *The Unfinished Revolt: Some Views on Western Independence* shamefully exploited the emergence of separatism as a major issue in Canada after the Parti Québécois took 24 per cent of the votes in a provincial election in 1970. There was no western independence movement in 1971, but Barr and Anderson nonetheless correctly noted that such old western grievances as freight rates and tariffs still caused disgruntlement among westerners. They threw the new federal programs of the fifties and sixties into the same bag as the traditional western grievances, labelling them as eastern-inspired and a burden on western Canada.

For example, Barr in his article "Beyond Bitterness" attacked proposed federal tax reforms in regional terms. Finance Minister Edgar Benson had offered a watered-down version of the Carter [Commission] reforms in a white paper presented to parliament in November 1969, and business pressure from all regions of the country eventually forced a further weakening of the reforms before an emasculated set of tax reforms reached parliament in 1971. Nonetheless, Barr, ignoring the national character of conservative resistance to tax reform, including measures designed to favour domestic investors over foreign investors, commented: "The thought that Mr. Benson was prepared to sabotage United States investment in Western Canada as a part of a federal tax-reform scenario outraged Westerners, not because they love Americans but because they know what the alternative to American investment is for *them:* a return to economic stagnation."[24]

What had been for Manning a national imperative—the need for American investment—became for the new Social Credit team merely a regional question. Similarly, while Manning had argued against official encouragement of bilingualism and biculturalism by proclaiming that the whole nation should be left alone to produce a single culture (the standard "melting pot" argument), the Strom group were more inclined to view the language issue from a regional perspective. Wrote Barr: "...the creation of a French-language television station in Edmonton—where fewer than six per cent of the viewers list French as their mother tongue but almost eight per cent of the viewers list German and eight per cent Ukrainian as their mother tongue—says some interesting things about the determination of the federal government to push a bilingual policy on all parts of the country, regardless of local needs or circumstances."[25]

The rejection of bilingualism did not prevent these champions of western Canada from invoking Louis Riel, whose efforts had brought official bilingualism to the west, as a spiritual forbear. Although the Social Credit government had done little more for the descendants of Riel's Métis than to place some of their number in bleak colonies that received little provincial funding, Owen Anderson chose to regard the French-speaking Métis leader as an integral part of a tradition of western dissent to which Social Credit was also heir. That the federal government suppression of the 1885 rebellion had largely cleared the way for European settlers to inhabit Indian and Métis lands did not appear to becloud the argument that the West, like Quebec, had a history of resistance to Ottawa's rule.[26]

Anderson, the major figure in Alberta's new federal-provincial relations bureaucracy, seemed, like Barr, to slip invariably into Quebec-bashing in his comments on federal policy towards Alberta. In this respect he probably fairly reflected the feelings of many westerners, who, however, unfairly, regarded the federal government as overly solicitous of the views of Quebec voters. For example, Anderson claimed that Ottawa had erected barriers to the entry of western oil into eastern markets which, at the time, were mainly served by oil imported from Venezuela. He charged that the federal government refused to discourage imports at a time when only half of the country's oil needs were provided internally because Quebec voters would react bitterly to having to pay one or two cents more per gallon of gasoline.[27]

In general, Anderson and Barr argued for a less interventionist federal government as the solution to most problems and in this sense were not far off the Manning position. Interestingly, however, these new-wave Alberta conservatives seemed not to share Manning's concern over salacious and subversive movies. While Manning had asked the federal government to keep such offerings off the airwaves in God's province, Anderson denounced the "cultural censorship" implied in the policy of the new Canadian Radio-television and Telecommunications Commission's limiting of American offerings on the Canadian networks.[28]

Premier Strom, influenced by his young advisers, proposed that much of Ottawa's alleged interference in areas of provincial jurisdiction and its resultant need for more tax dollars could be jettisoned in favour of a federally financed guaranteed national income plan.[29] Talk of such a plan was widespread at the time, although not all of its proponents by any means saw it as an actual replacement of but rather as a supplement to existing federal programs whose total impact on the distribution of wealth in Canada had, incidentally, been marginal. Barr expressed the conservative vision of a guaranteed income plan. It would: "replace the present ineffective patchwork-quilt of regional incentives and regional development programs. The plan would create a modest level of guaranteed income, sufficient to enable one to live at a spartan but healthy level. Beyond that the problem of 'regional inequality' would be left to the working of the free market and stepped-up programs of manpower retraining and mobility grants by the federal government."[30]

The guaranteed income plan along with a call for an elected Senate with equal representation from all regions provided Barr's main prescriptions for dealing with alleged regional inequalities. The elected Senate idea would be a recurring one among Albertans claiming that central Canada exerted overwhelming pressure within the existing federal system.[31]

The "social conservative" philosophy joining traditional conservatism to scientific management with a bit of old-fashioned regional dissension tossed in for good measure failed to provide the Strom government with the image of dynamism that its younger civil servants tried to create. An ecology corps was created "to give unemployed students an income and a role to play in environmental protection," and at the last minute a Department of the Environment with regulatory power was established.[32] Employees of Alberta Government Telephones were given access to the Alberta Labour Act, removing the Manning tradition of treating Crown corporation employees as civil servants to be denied full bargaining powers (such as they were under the Alberta Labour Act).[33] Royal commissions on the future of the cities and on post-secondary education were established.[34] But none of this seemed to remove the impression that the new Social Credit team was merely borrowing ideas from the Lougheed legislative group. Strom himself, as John Barr notes, appeared remote and dour on television despite being warmhearted in person.[35] Lougheed and some of his deskmates, meanwhile, seemed to be masters of the medium.

The Conservatives began to gather momentum before Strom had an opportunity to present a legislative program. In February 1969, just two months after Strom became leader, Bill Yurko, an Edmonton engineer, carried Manning's Edmonton seat in a by-election. Later that year when Liberal Bill Switzer died, the Conservatives carried his Calgary seat. When the remaining Liberal in the legislature subsequently defected to the Tories, followed in a few months by the Independent member for Banff-Cochrane, the crystallization of the Conservatives as *the* non-socialist opposition to Social Credit was complete.[36] The provincial Liberal party, damaged by the renewed unpopularity of its federal wing, lapsed into a two-decade coma.

The Conservatives presented themselves as a party of openness and of fresh ideas. In the 1969 session, for example, their calls for open government included pleas for greater independence of constituency MLAs from party discipline, the opening of legislative committees to the public, and the opening of the legislature to radio and television coverage.[37] The largely urban Tories also demonstrated their sympathy with urbanites' frustrations over Social Credit priorities by calling for provincial financing for urban transportation. The newly elected Bill Yurko noted that urban residents were increasingly dependent on "automobile and high speed transportation systems" for work and recreational purposes and that the attraction of industry was dependent as well upon good transportation facilities. He called for the establishment of a commission with representation from the province's nine urban areas to: "(1) Study in detail the future of existing new satellite cities and towns and traffic patterns in and around said areas of Alberta and evolve blueprint for the year 2000. (2) Study and make specific recommendations respecting long-range financing of urban transportation systems."[38]

The establishment a year and a half later of the even more wide-ranging Task Force on Urbanization and the Future indicated the government's understanding that it was increasingly perceived as out of sympathy with the needs of non-rural residents. But while an opposition calling for a commission of investigation may receive public support for being innovative, a government which follows such advice and does no more—

particularly a government perceived as old and creaking in the seams—simply appears vacillating. And the task force was established too close to the 1971 election to report, never mind have its recommendations implemented.

In the 1970 legislative session, the Conservatives stole the spotlight with twenty-one bills designed to present themselves as an alternative to the cautious Social Credit regime. More important, the Conservatives were busily engaged in organizing strong constituency organizations and developing a campaign for the next provincial election which revolved around Lougheed as a leader. Lougheed had himself determined such an approach even before Manning's retirement, stressing in a July 1968 document that a leader "along the Trudeau style" and using "the Kennedy approach of a set speech with some improvisation" would provide the most effective campaign. The replacement of the respected Manning with a lesser-known figure made this approach even more promising.[39]

Lougheed did not wait for the election to make himself known personally to Albertans. He travelled the province, in each area meeting local officials and leaders of business, farm, and labour organizations. His burgeoning party held policy conferences and, in general, did all that was possible to establish itself as a competent alternative to the old Socred administration.[40] Short on policy specifics, the Conservatives nonetheless appeared open to what the people had to say—a convenient position open only to opposition parties, from whom endless willingness to listen cannot be read as an excuse for inaction.

Strom and his associates attempted to respond in kind to the Conservative image-building thrust. Edmonton lawyer Bill Johnson became league president in 1969, replacing the redoubtable Orvis Kennedy. The next year, Johnson and his executive announced a "new look" for the league's annual convention. The party would have a new logo, featuring a stylized "S" above with a "C" below, all in fluorescent green. Cabinet ministers would face newscasters from "hot benches" to account for the government's performance. Up to six additional delegateships per constituency were reserved for the minuscule group of party members between the ages of eighteen and twenty-five to disguise the fact that...party members on average were over fifty years old.[41] Attempts were made, meanwhile, to revive dormant constituency organizations, and the party claimed more than 30,000 members at the time of the 1971 election.[42] This figure, if accurate, was an increase of about a third since 1967 and indicated that in rural constituencies at least candidates for a Social Credit nomination still thought it worthwhile to beat the bush to sign up their supporters as party members.

The major cities, however, according to the "rates and information" pamphlet for *Insight*, the party publication, remained barren terrain for Social Credit recruitment. Only 19.3 per cent of copies of *Insight*, sent to all members, were mailed to addresses in Edmonton and Calgary, where more than half the population lived. While 10.8 per cent of copies went to "intermediate urban centres" (an undefined category), 35.7 per cent went to rural areas and 34.2 per cent to small towns and villages.[43] The Social Credit geographical profile of membership reflected the Alberta of 1935 rather than of 1971.

Nonetheless, the electoral map still gave over-representation to the rural population, although the under-representation of the cities had been alleviated somewhat by the Strom administration. Ten seats were added in an electoral redistribution before the 1971 election, seven of them in the two large centres. It was in the cities, it was generally conceded, that further Tory gains were inevitable. But the countryside, many felt before the election would remain loyal to Social Credit, which had bequeathed upon them endless miles of highways and large grants to schools whose trustees appeared far more grateful for the bounty than did their still-complaining urban counterparts.

Differences between the two major parties were not easy to discern. The Tories, as indicated previously, called for greater provincial spending to alleviate municipal spending on education and transportation, at the same time denouncing the tiny deficits of the last two years of Social Credit rule. While the Conservatives generally appeared more interventionist in their orientation than Social Credit, one of their bills in 1971 called upon the government to consider handing over unspecified Crown corporations and operations to private enterprise. And while Highways Minister Gordon Taylor, speaking for the government against the motion, said "the interests of the people of Alberta have to come first," four government MLAs joined in supporting the Tory motion. Two of the dissidents, Alfred Hooke, representing Rocky Mountain House, and John Landeryou, from Lethbridge, had been among the first crop of Aberhart members in 1935.[44] Hooke indeed, excluded from cabinet after Strom's accession to power, often seemed to be a member of the opposition rather than the government, and Strom's inability either to convince him to tone down his public criticisms or to sit as an independent created dissension within the party and caucus. Ironically, Hooke's independent stance and his ability to carry with him a small group of government backbenchers on some issues refuted the Lougheed charge that Social Credit, at least in the Strom years, stifled its backbenchers. But the bitterness of the Hooke attack and the premier's bafflement before it did not likely aid the government's cause.[45]

During the election, the two major parties made similar promises. Social Credit promised one thousand dollar cash grants for home purchasers, while the Tories promised to double the provincial housing budget. Both parties promised urban transportation funds and various subsidies for pensioners. The Tories, however, went somewhat further than the government in some of their spending and tax-concession promises. They would eliminate, they said, the portion of property tax then used to pay for basic education programs and would provide property tax credits to homeowners and renters.[46]

In the end, however, specific promises doubtless played less of a role than the issue of whether, after thirty-six years of government by the same party, Alberta did not need a change. "Alberta deserves a fresh start and the Lougheed Team can provide it" was the Conservative theme for 1971.[47] Lougheed had been briefly, in the 1950s, a quarterback for the Edmonton Eskimos; the emphasis on him as a vigorous man in the prime of life and a successful team player in sports, business, and law appealed to many voters to whom Social Credit, with Manning gone, appeared a tired old machine with its engine removed. As Allan Hustak writes in his favourable biography of Peter Lougheed: "Thirty-six years of 'God's government' had come to an end. It was an awesome victory for Lougheed but in terms of Alberta's history it was a triumph of style rather than of substance—the secular equivalent of a revival meeting—a new minister had been selected to do a better job than the old one but the faith remained the same. There was no substantive change in political philosophy."[48]

The "awesome victory for Lougheed" bore no resemblance to the election of 1935 that had brought Social Credit to power. Although Albertans have been painted exaggeratedly as followers of Pied Pipers who leap together from one party to another, leaving their former political home in shambles, Social Credit suffered no resounding defeat in 1971. The Progressive Conservatives carried forty-nine seats to twenty-five for Social Credit and one for the NDP. With a third of the legislative seats, an opposition party could hardly be said to be on the way to extinction.

The popular vote indeed demonstrated once again how easily the first-past-the-post system of voting distorted the intentions of Alberta voters. With 46.4 per cent of the total vote the Conservatives had won almost two-thirds of the legislative seats. Social Credit, with 41 per cent of the vote, had lost only 3.5 per cent of its vote it 1967; indeed, with a larger electoral turn-out in 1971, the absolute number voting Social Credit in 1971 was marginally higher than in 1967.[49]

The major difference between 1971 and 1967, indeed between 1971 and every election since 1940, was that Social Credit faced a fairly united opposition. Lougheed, by turning the provincial Conservative party into a personal vehicle, de-emphasized the connection of this party with the federal Conservatives who had dumped John Diefenbaker in 1967, making it a comfortable political home both for traditional western Conservatives as well as for federal Liberals whose provincial party had collapsed before their eyes. The New Democratic Party, led since 1968 by young schoolteacher and party organizer Grant Notley, had sunk all its capital in the ultimately failed attempt to pursue Hooke and Hinman before Justice Kirby. Its political purse empty, the party concentrated on a small number of seats and managed barely to elect Notley in the Spirit River-Fairview seat in the Peace River district. But its overall vote had fallen from 16 to 11 per cent between 1967 and 1971.[50]

Social Credit, thus, need not have felt in 1971 that Albertans had massively rejected the party. There were, however, ominous portents. The party had managed to carry fourteen of twenty seats in the two big cities in 1967 with only 39 per cent of the vote, thanks to large numbers of three- and four-way contests in which the split of opposition party votes allowed Social Crediters to win with modest pluralities. In 1971, its vote shaved by another five per cent in the metropolitan ridings, Social Credit carried only three of twenty-seven seats in the big cities, all three in Calgary. Indeed, outside

Edmonton and Calgary, the Conservatives overtook Social Credit in only twenty-five of forty-seven seats (excluding the NDP-won seat) and were slightly behind the Strom forces in popular vote. So any rebuilding of Social Credit either would have to seek to restore party popularity in the cities or would have to reject the urban voters altogether and attempt to build upon rural resentments against the metropolis to firm up a still-mighty sentiment in favour of "God's government."

First, however, Social Credit had to come to terms with being in opposition. Never before had this party been in opposition. It had nary a provincial member before the electoral sweep of 1935 and then for thirty-six years—going through several guises—never lost its position as the party of government. Its initial radical and monetary-panacea phases having passed before the death of Aberhart, the party had gradually become the lapdog of Premier Manning, whose combination of evangelical religion, anti-socialist rhetoric, courting of the oil companies, and lavish spending on schools and education eventually bore the label of "social conservatism." Under Strom the ideological content of the "*social* conservatism" had not been made clear, and it now became necessary for the Social Credit opposition caucus and the Social Credit League as a whole to determine whether they had any fundamental differences with the Conservatives. Lougheed's caginess between 1967 and 1971, sometimes attacking the government from the right, sometimes from the left, made it difficult for the league to plan strategy before the new government showed its hand.

In their controversial account of the economic strategies undertaken by Saskatchewan and Alberta in the 1970s to free themselves from over-reliance on resource extraction for economic survival, Larry Pratt and John Richards attempt a social portrait of the Lougheed Conservatives. For these authors, Lougheed's "interventionist provincial government" served as an instrument to "nurture the development and defend the interests of an ascendant regional bourgeoisie."[51] During the seventies, they argue, this bourgeoisie, via the Conservative government, attempted to increase revenue from the province's energy resources in order to finance policies that would encourage economic diversification in Alberta, with an emphasis on secondary manufacturing. Among the members of this arriviste bourgeoisie these authors count Alberta-based energy and construction giants such as Mannix-Loram, Nova, ATCO, and the Alberta Energy Company. More generally, within the ranks of those tired of the "passive rentier" approach of Social Credit were the professional groups who benefited from the growth of the Alberta economy—including corporate lawyers, engineers, geologists, and financial consultants—and feared that failure to diversify would result in stagnation of that economy as resources were depleted.[52]

Richards and Pratt were guardedly optimistic in 1979, when world oil prices were at record highs, that the strategy of the Alberta Tories might work. Many commentators at the time were sceptical, but, with the drop in oil prices and oil demand that began in 1982, hopes of diversification dimmed and questions were raised over whether the Tories had not frittered away monies that might have aided in diversification.[53] Pratt himself had noted in an earlier book that the Alberta government, in its eagerness to support development of the Athabasca tar sands, poured in millions of dollars in infrastructural, training, and financing costs without ensuring that the multinational companies involved provide opportunities for Alberta-based firms to develop and profit from technologies required to service the giant projects.[54]

It would seem, in fact, that the oil boom, which Conservative rhetoric treated as the opportunity to fund diversification of the Alberta economy, proved to be its opposite. Private investment in the province was largely attracted to the energy sector and to a booming real estate market, while government funds, as Pratt's earlier book indicated, were also largely directed towards the needs of the energy sector.

Nonetheless, the success or failure of the rhetorical Lougheed strategy for the Alberta economy, as it emerged gradually after the election of the Conservatives in 1971, does not disprove the Richards-Pratt analysis of who the new political rulers of Alberta were. Indeed, as is often the case with regional bourgeoisies hoping to gain greater influence within their colonial-dominated economies, the ideological commitment to the existing economic system—which in Canadian terms means state subsidies for major business ventures as much as it means any supposed free operation of the marketplace—limits the degree to which new policies designed to strengthen local capitalists are pursued. In Alberta's case, although the Tories did skirmish with the multinational oil companies over royalties, the main target of attack was the federal government, which, especially after the spectacular rise of oil prices in late 1973 after the Yom Kippur Middle East war, was seen as trying to muscle in on Alberta's resources by attempting to increase its own revenues and to control prices charged Canadian consumers of Alberta energy.

The Conservatives' ability to rally rich and middle-class Albertans behind their banner and to drape their party in the provincial flag as champions of western interest against the hated "East" (central Canada) left Social Credit in a precarious position. The Manning Socreds, as we have seen, were largely a party of farmers, small-business people, and lower-middle-class rural residents. Although the big oil companies were happy to finance the party's electoral needs, their executives played no conspicuous role in either the government or the party. The unlikely marriage between the major benefactors of the Alberta boom and the more modest party membership was performed by Manning with his religiously based opposition to all forms of socialism and advanced liberalism. Many members of the upper-middle-class of professionals and executives had supported Manning with their votes, grateful for the low taxes his regime levied upon them, but few joined his party, which, because of its origins, appeared too plebeian. Many, as the Social Credit poll in 1956 revealed, supported free-enterprise opposition parties, which they regarded presumably as less ideology-bound than the Manning party. The latter-day Manning attempt to renovate his party's dogmatic laissez-faire image with a new technocratic language and an emphasis on social engineering had won only a coterie of middle-class converts to the aging government party, especially since the Lougheed conservatives provided an alternative political home for the "arriviste bourgeoisie" with a chance of unseating Aberhart's successors. Even in 1971, despite nominating thirty-seven new candidates for the seventy-five Alberta seats, "a breakdown of candidates' occupations shows the continued domination of small businessmen, teachers and agriculturists in the Socred election team."[55] While some of the "small businessmen" were indeed big fish within the areas in which they lived, they were generally men who had made their money in the service sector and were indirectly dependent upon the health of the resources sector for their prosperity.[56] Lougheed's candidates included eleven lawyers, but Social Credit had only two lawyers on its slate. Nonetheless, the relatively modest circumstances of the 1971 Social Credit candidates should not be overstated. The party had gone out of its way to attract a broader base of candidates, and it did nominate several professionals and substantial businessmen, none of whom, however, won their seats.

Once the election was over, Social Credit's ability to keep even its small group of well-educated and/or rich members declined. It no longer offered the spoils of power, and its remaining activists were not the younger opportunists recruited by Strom's young men but the older, dogmatic members of the Manning period who embodied the classic "petite bourgeois" values of thrift and self-reliance and appeared unconcerned that the "social conservative" philosophy of their long-time leader had allowed the Alberta economy to become overly dependent upon resource extraction, foreign-controlled, and riddled with glaring inequalities. The interventionist state, after all, like the banks and the labour movement, was part of the insidious conspiracy aimed at enslaving ordinary people like themselves.

Harry Strom was not particularly representative of their thinking. Although he was a religious, well-to-do rancher of conservative bent, he was not the ideologue that Manning was and he seemed to lack any clear vision for his party. As leader of the opposition, he found little in the new government's actions to which he could take strong objection.[57] He did not protest when the Lougheed government, shortly after it assumed office, announced its intention to increase petroleum royalties. Although he warned that such action could limit new investment in the energy sector,[58] neither he nor his colleagues could find much enthusiasm for a defence of companies whose large profits would be touched rather slightly by the new government's gesture. In December 1972 Strom resigned as leader so that the party might attempt to find a younger leader who might develop a profile over the next few years as a dynamic alternative to Lougheed.

Strom's mantle was supposed to fall on Robert Clark, a successful farmer in his early thirties who represented Olds-Didsbury and had served as minister of youth under Manning and minister of education under Strom. Clark had chaired Strom's leadership campaign in 1968, and like Strom he was a flexible right-winger who would have preserved Social Credit more as an alternative administration than as an alternative vision to the Progressive

Conservatives. Enjoying caucus support and the support of the younger Social Crediters, Clark was expected to win the well-attended convention in February 1973, which chose the party's new leader.

The dictates of political realism almost allowed predictions of Clark's win to come true. A youngish, non-dogmatic, articulate, experienced former cabinet minister who held a fairly safe legislative seat could present Social Credit as a voice of the future rather than of days of past glory. But a party majority, unhappy with the timid attack of Strom and company on the new government, wanted a leader who would represent more forcefully a traditional Manning vision for Alberta as an alternative to the interventionism of the slick lawyers and businessmen who then held the levers of political power. For some, Gordon Taylor, the veteran highways minister of the Manning period and member for Drumheller since 1940, served the purpose. But most, despite being aged themselves, recognized that a leader in his sixties would be a liability.

And so it was that the convention in February 1973 turned to a political unknown: Werner Schmidt, a forty-one-year-old educational administrator whose religiosity and reactionary views endeared him to the Manning generation of Social Crediters. Schmidt had been raised on his family's farm near Coledale in the far south of the province, where Social Credit support was particularly high in the party's years in office, and had been employed in the sugar-beet fields and as a trucker while working towards his two university degrees. From 1966 to 1969 he had served as executive director of the Alberta School Trustees Association. In 1971 he ran unsuccessfully as a Social Credit candidate in the provincial seat of Edmonton-Belmont and was soundly defeated by a Conservative in that party's sweep of the capital city.[59]

Schmidt won a second-ballot victory over Clark of 814 to 775 votes[60] and proceeded over the next two years to provide Albertans with an alternative vision for the province's economic development to that represented by Lougheed. For example, the new government created the Alberta Energy Company as a vehicle for increasing participation by Alberta investors in all facets of petroleum development. The corporation was to be partly under public ownership and partly controlled by private shareholders. It followed, in fact, a model set by Manning when Alberta Gas Trunk Line Company was established in 1954 with a monopoly over gas-gathering within Alberta. Although common stock shares in AGTL were issued, voting shares and membership on the company board were divided equally among four groups: gas producers, gas exporters, Alberta's gas utilities, and the Alberta government.

For Werner Schmidt, however, the Alberta Energy Company, rather than being a logical extension of past Social Credit policy, was a massive government entry into areas where "private enterprise has managed heretofore." He claimed to see no government role in "the pipeline business, the electrical power business, the gas exploration and development business, and the tar sands oil extraction business," all areas in which the Alberta Energy Company would have some involvement.[61] In contradistinction to Conservative interventionism to favour Alberta-based capitalists, Schmidt counselled "a minimum of government."[62] But his zealous opposition to all involvement of government in the economy outside of the social services and education areas proved no asset to his party. Instead of concentrating on who was mainly benefiting from Conservative expenditures in the economic development area, as Clark might have done, Schmidt limited himself to a blanket ideological attack on the government with little comment about the specifics of its programs.

The Social Credit platform in 1975 reflected Schmidt's lack of political realism, if also his courage of political convictions. Not only should resources be developed solely by private enterprise but, he believed, even farmers must stop relying on government for subsidies: "Our agricultural economy will operate most efficiently when it 'stands on its own.' Government should assist only in research, technical advice, marketing assistance to farmers and farmer organizations, and meeting emergencies and catastrophies."[63] Even Ernest Manning, for all his devotion to the justice inherent in the operations of the marketplace, had not been willing to attack assistance to farmers, especially since most of it came from the federal government. Schmidt was indeed rather more consistent than Manning, who...was happy to implement government regulations when the oil industry required them and to protect the Calgary Power hydroelectric monopoly. Schmidt simply wanted the government to absent itself from the operation of the economy altogether.

Schmidt's a priorism neither held his party together nor attracted much support from Albertans. In June 1973, four months after becoming party leader, Schmidt ran in a by-election in the riding of Calgary Foothills and was badly trounced by the Conservative candidate. In September, Social Credit house leader James Henderson left the party to sit as an Independent and caucus chose Bob Clark, Schmidt's rival for the leadership, as his replacement.[64] Party membership, which had stood at 30,000 for the election year of 1971, reached only 6000 before the 1975 election, reflecting the disinterest in Social Credit nominations outside of ridings already held by the party.[65]

Lougheed called the election for March 1975, promising an all-out defence of Alberta interests in dealing with the federal government regarding the energy sector and announcing the establishment of a trust fund, to be called the Alberta Heritage Investments and Savings Fund, in which a portion of oil royalties annually would be banked to make room for investments by the province in economic development and diversification.[66] Against the image of a forward-looking, province-protecting white knight projected by Lougheed, the earnest-looking Schmidt appeared a dinosaur clinging to a political viewpoint that, while having some support in generalities among rural residents, had little support in the details.

Social Credit incumbents tended to run local-oriented campaigns in which little was said directly either of Loughheed or of Schmidt. They appealed to their constituents to remember the services they had performed for them as local representatives and played upon feelings among many rural people that Lougheed and company were city slickers who did not concern themselves as much with rural issues as did the incumbent Social Crediters.

This strategy worked for only five of the seventeen incumbents who chose to run, of whom one, the veteran Gordon Taylor, ran as an Independent Social Crediter. No previously unelected Social Crediter came even close to taking a seat,[67] and Schmidt lost in Taber by almost two to one to a Conservative. The once-might party of Aberhart and Manning suffered a humiliating defeat, dropping from 41 per cent of the vote in 1971 to only 18 per cent in 1975. The party that had lost urban Alberta in 1971 after becoming too identified as a rural party had now also lost most of its rural strongholds, having failed to develop a politics that could express rural reservations with Lougheed without having to promise to leave farmers almost totally without government aid.

The Progressive Conservatives carried sixty-nine of Alberta's seventy-five ridings with 63 per cent of the vote in 1975, a better performance in the popular vote than even Social Credit had ever achieved. Social Credit had four seats, while Grant Notley of the NDP and Gordon Taylor held the remaining two seats. A new political dynasty had been established, and the future for Social Credit looked bleak. The province was wealthier than ever, and while Tory policies, much as Social Credit policies, favoured the better-off, there was enough money to go around to keep most voters happy.

The hapless Schmidt resigned as party leader shortly after the election. He had been a disaster looking for a place to happen and he left behind a practically non-existent provincial organization: short of members, finances, and self-confidence. The party now turned to Bob Clark, who had been re-elected handily in Olds-Didsbury and had not entirely given up on the party's chances to outlive the Schmidt fiasco and to offer a viable, right-wing alternative to the Lougheed forces. Clark did not reject Schmidt's position against government involvement in productive enterprises, and he promised that a Social Credit government would sell government shares in the Alberta Energy Company, in the Syncrude tar sands plant near Fort McMurray, and in Pacific Western Airlines, all of which had been acquired in the Lougheed years.[68]

But Clark did not limit himself to listing things government should not do. While he attacked "big government, big business and big labour" as being in cahoots in Alberta, it was not his view that small business people and farmers, the backbone of what was left of his party, needed no government help.

Indeed, the party now "promised a comprehensive program of support of small business," including start-up capital grants and low-interest loans. It also proposed "renewed emphasis on people programs, especially on innovative programs in the health and education fields,"[69] echoing complaints from the NDP and myriad pressure groups that the purse-strings of the provincial treasury were held rather close where social spending was concerned. The Manning and Strom governments, because they had spent little on economic development, had poured large chunks of their revenues into "people programs," and the declining portion of provincial expenditures going to education and social services was cited as a turning away from humane priorities. Social Credit in 1979 promised to extend Alberta Health

Care Insurance Plan coverage to include dental care for children under twelve and to expand dramatically educational services to the handicapped and home-care services to the old and the ill.[70]

But Social Credit's most attractive vote-getting promise in 1979 was the elimination of provincial income tax on the first $16,000 of taxable income. Such a move would have exempted three-quarters of Alberta taxpayers from provincial income tax and cut everyone else's taxes as well. Revenue for this measure, it was claimed, was easily available from the then-large provincial budget surplus.[71] Ironically, except in its last few years of office, Social Credit had regarded budgets without current-account surpluses as anathema, leading the province back to the humiliating dependence on bankers that had plagued Alberta governments before 1945.

Social Credit faced mighty difficulties in selling the Clark package as an alternative to Lougheed's triumphalism. The party's losing image had lost it financial support from business and electoral worker support from former members. Above all, the party had to contend with Peter Lougheed, who had convinced large numbers of Albertans of all social classes that his alleged program to develop and diversify the economy was for the benefit of all. More to the point, perhaps, his continual battles with the federal government provided him with a well-cultivated image as champion of the exploited Alberta people against the hated "East." Ignoring the fact that no provincial party had opposed his government's positions in federal-provincial relations, Lougheed in 1979, as in 1975, tried to turn the election into a plebiscite in which Albertans were asked to elect only Conservative MLAs so that the government could claim that it spoke for all Albertans when it negotiated with the federal government.

Whether or not the plebiscitary logic of the government captured the public imagination, discontent with the Conservatives was still too meagre for Social Credit to stage a comeback. The four sitting MLAs were re-elected, but they were not joined by new deskmates. The party's popular vote had increased marginally from 18 to 20 per cent,[72] but there was no indication that any revival was in sight. Indeed, 1979 would prove to be the last year in which Social Credit contested an Alberta election as a serious political outfit. The rise of separatist sentiment in the province over the next several years, provoked in part by Lougheed's demagoguery, provided a new outlet for right-wing sentiment and left Social Credit without a constituency.

Western separatist movements, fuelled by redneck hatred of Pierre Trudeau, bilingualism and biculturalism, the metric system, and high taxes, came and went in the seventies in western Canada, usually finding their greatest strength in central Alberta. But it took the October 1980 budget of the Trudeau government to bring respectable elements into the movement and to give it a serious audience in the province. The federal government, fulfilling promises made in the February 1980 election that had overturned the short-lived Joe Clark Conservative minority government, introduced a so-called National Energy Policy. This policy, which envisaged a transfer of a large share of petroleum assets from American multinationals to Canadian investors, also increased the federal government's share of revenues from oil production. All aspects of the policy were denounced by Peter Lougheed, who promptly announced a cutback in the flow of oil and gas to central Canada until the budget policies were withdrawn.

Some sections of the petroleum industry went further and called for outright separation of the West from Canada in order to protect industry profits and American investors. Carl Nickle, millionaire oilman and former Conservative MP, led this group. He allied himself with West-Fed, a separatist group led by wealthy and cranky implements-dealer Elmer Knutson. Knutson was rabidly anti-Quebec and patented a curious constitutional theory that the 1931 Statute of Westminster had given sovereignty to the Canadian provinces, thus removing the federal government's right, without specific authorization by provinces, to make rules within their territories. "Oil-well-servicing businessmen, consultants and drilling contractors" were attracted to the new separatist groups, which also included a party called Western Canada Concept, the creature of British Columbian Doug Christie, a right-wing Victoria lawyer. But the hard-core supporters "were rural residents, small businessmen, and farmers throughout the West."[73]

The attraction of separatism for right-wing elements of their natural constituency bode ill for Social Credit, which had been heir to a regional protest with which it had consciously identified in the Strom years, though rather less so in the Manning years. The party leaders, however, remained federalist and seemed generally to take a "me too" stance on issues of federal-provincial relations raised by Lougheed.

February 1982 marked a watershed both for Social Credit and for the separatists. Bob Clark had resigned as party leader in 1981 and a convention in late 1981 had chosen Rod Sykes, former mayor of Calgary and lifelong Liberal, as his successor. When Clark subsequently resigned his Olds-Didsbury seat to become a private consultant, a by-election was called by Lougheed for February 1982. It was during this by-election that Gordon Kesler, oil company scout and rodeo rider, created a political upset by carrying a seat for the Western Canada Concept. Kesler, taking advantage of his constituents' paranoia about Trudeau's intentions regarding constitutional revision (failure to include a property-rights guarantee was regarded as proof of imminent Communist takeover), appealed for voters to send both Edmonton and Ottawa a message of anger. A vote for the status quo, which in Olds-Didsbury was Social Credit, would not be noticed; a vote for a separatist would not be missed.[74]

Social Credit's failure to hold one of its remaining strongholds precipitated a coming apart at what were, by then, rather loose seams. Sykes found a pretext to resign; Fred Mandeville, one of the remaining three MLAs, announced that he would not be a candidate in the next provincial election; and Ray Speaker and Walter Buck, the other Socred MLAs, announced that they would run as Independents. The Social Credit party's career, even as a minor political force, was over.[75]

Social Credit ran only a handful of candidates in the provincial election of 1982 and received less than 1 per cent of the total vote.[76] The party might have been allowed a decent burial except that its corpse proved a convenient vehicle for a small core of Douglasite [C.H. Douglas, father of social credit theories] monetary fundamentalists and a vicious group of Nazi apologists and hatemongers who felt comfortable with Douglas's racial views.

In December 1982, Jim Keegstra, mayor of Eckville, was fired from his teaching job by the Lacombe County schoolboard for his rabid anti-Semitic teachings in his high school social studies classes. His firing was widely publicized and he was subsequently prosecuted and convicted for violations of federal hate laws. Shortly after his firing, Keegstra was elected second vice-president for Alberta of the national Social Credit party. The national party leader, J. Martin Hattersley, an Edmonton lawyer who was committed to Douglasite monetary views but rejected Douglas's racism, attempted to fire Keegstra from his new position. He cancelled the party memberships of Keegstra and two party officials who were openly supporting Keegstra and his teachings that Jews were taking over the world by stealth in a bid to eradicate Christianity and capitalism and that, along the way, they had invented the Holocaust out of whole cloth to win sympathy for themselves. But in the end, Hattersley lost. "At a special executive meeting the dismissals and cancellations were overturned and Hattersley himself was forced to leave the party. Keegstra once again became vice-president. There is not much left of the federal Social Credit party in Canada or in Alberta today, but what there is seems to be as anti-Semitic as Douglas Social Credit ever was."[77]

Thus, the post-Manning period began with Social Credit charting a moderate right-wing route having little to do with the monetary radicalism of its founders, the social radicalism of its thirties urban activists, or the bigotry of some of its activists and elected representatives of the forties. It ended fifteen years later with the party moribund and its corpse invaded by racist body-snatchers. Their racist venom, reminiscent of Douglas's bigoted views, should not, however, obscure the fact that Social Credit, in office, whatever the conspiratorial views of its leaders, had been authoritarian and right-wing but never fascist and genocidal. It was only the departure of the respected party leaders and most of the members that left the party shell available to kooks and fascists. It is indeed unfortunate for democracy in Alberta that Bob Clark narrowly failed to gain his party's leadership in 1973 and to keep the party alive as a moderate right-wing alternative for those who felt excluded from Lougheed's Conservative clique of better-educated business and professional people but disdained the left-wing alternative offered by the NDP. But the fear and distrust of government involvement in the economy and of the welfare state engendered by Ernest Manning attracted members who, in many cases, were even more consistent in holding these views than the practical Manning deemed feasible in political life. The result was that Social Credit, for a period, failed to articulate the real wishes of its constituency—to kick welfare recipients in the rear but also to provide extensive subsidies for virtuous farmers and small businessmen. Unhappily, by the time it again expressed its more traditional views, the party had fallen too far into disrepair to be taken seriously by many people.

NOTES

1. John J. Barr, *The Dynasty: The Rise and Fall of Social Credit in Alberta* (Toronto: McClelland & Stewart, 1974), 163.

2. Provincial Archives of Alberta, Premier Manning Papers, Box 58, File 630, *The Report of the Honourable Mr. Justice W.J.C. Kirby, In the Matter of an Inquiry by a Royal Commission into the Matters Set Out by Order-in-Council 861/67 respecting the Use or Attempted Use by the Honourable Alfred J. Hooke of his Office as a Member of the Executive Council of Alberta, and the Use or Attempted Use by Edgar W. Hinman of his Office as a Member of the Executive Council of Alberta*, October 1968, 7.

3. Ibid., 84.

4. Ibid., 85.

5. Ibid., 89.

6. Ibid., 302.

7. Alfred J. Hooke, *30 + 5: I Know, I Was There* (Edmonton: Institute of Applied Art, 1971), 259.

8. Ibid.

9. Ibid., 252-5.

10. Premier Manning Papers, Box 31, File 346(a), D.W. Rogers, deputy minister, Department of Public Welfare, to R.D. Jorgenson, minister of public welfare, 30 July 1962. Rogers proposed the establishment of a preventive social services program in welfare in this memo, four years before the legislation establishing such a program came into effect.

11. Premier Manning Papers, Box 70, File 764, Government of the Province of Alberta, Department of Public Welfare Social Planning and Development Branch, "Administration and Policy Guide to the Preventive Social Service Program—Preventive Social Service Act, April 1966." This document noted: "In essence, a preventive social service is one designed to develop community awareness and resources, to strengthen and preserve human initiative and to preclude individual and family breakdown. It is any activity which is available to all members of the community on a voluntary basis for the enrichment of their physical, mental and social well-being."

12. Premier Manning Papers, Box 70, File 764, Alfred J. Hooke, minister of public welfare, to Manning, 20 December 1967.

13. Premier Manning Papers, Box 70, File 764, J.E. Oberholtzer, director, Human Resources Development Authority, to Harry Strom, minister of agriculture and chairman of the Human Resources Development Authority, 29 December 1967. This memo observed that at a meeting of the HRDA, chaired by Strom on 28 December 1967, it had been observed that several recommendations of the Advisory Committee on Preventive Social Services were not being followed up by the minister of welfare. It was therefore decided to set up a committee, composed of representatives of Welfare, Health, Youth, and Education, to make recommendations relative to preventive social services. This decision was a transparent attempt to remove Hooke's authority in the area.

14. Barr, *The Dynasty*, 179-80.

15. See the discussion of Premier Manning's book, *Political Realignment*, in Alvin Finkel, *The Social Credit Phenomenon in Alberta*, Ch. 6.

16. Barr, *The Dynasty*, 179-80; Hooke, *30 + 5*, 256-8.

17. *Insight* (Alberta Social Credit League organ), 1:4 (June-July 1971), 4.

18. David G. Wood, *The Lougheed Legacy* (Toronto: Key Porter Books, 1985), 71.

19. *Insight*, 1:4 (June-July 1971), 4-5.

20. *Edmonton Journal,* 19 November 1970.

21. Ed Shaffer, "The Political Economy of Oil in Alberta," in David Leadbeater, ed., *Essays on the Political Economy of Alberta* (Toronto: New Hogtown Press, 1984), 184.

22. *Edmonton Journal,* 19 February 1970.

23. Lougheed had raised the property tax issue in his motion of non-confidence on 4 March 1968; he raised it again in his reaction to the first Throne Speech from Strom (*Journals of the Legislative Assembly of Alberta,* 27 February 1968 and 17 February 1969). Though minor changes were made to the Public Welfare Act in 1970, the municipalities continued to pay 20 per cent of welfare costs (*Revised Statutes of the Province of Alberta,* 1970, Ch. 104).

24. John J. Barr, "Beyond Bitterness," in John J. Barr and Owen Anderson, *The Unfinished Revolt: Some Views on Western Independence* (Toronto: McClelland & Stewart, 1971), 15.

25. Ibid., 16

26. Owen Anderson, "The Unfinished Revolt," in John J. Barr and Owen Anderson, *The Unfinished Revolt: Some Views on Western Independence* (Toronto: McClelland & Stewart, 1971), 42.

27. Ibid., 43.

28. Ibid., 46.

29. *Edmonton Journal,* 13 March 1970.

30. Barr, "Beyond Bitterness," 29.

31. Ibid.

32. Barr, *The Dynasty,* 187; *Edmonton Journal,* 19 November 1970.

33. Provincial Archives of Alberta, Research Division, Alberta Department of Labour, "A History of Labour and Social Welfare Legislation in Alberta," 1973.

34. *Insight* 1:1 (September 1970), 2; 1:2 (November 1970), 9.

35. Barr, *The Dynasty,* 188.

36. Meir Serfaty, "The Conservative Party of Alberta under Lougheed, 1965-71: Building an Image and an Organization," *Prairie Forum* 6:1 (Spring 1981), 67.

37. Ibid., 67.

38. *Journals of the Legislative Assembly of Alberta,* 6 May 1969.

39. Serfaty, "The Conservative Party of Alberta under Lougheed, 69-70.

40. Ibid., 63-5.

41. *Insight* 1:2 (November 1970), 8-10.

42. *Insight* 1:4 (June-July 1971), 3.

43. Provincial Archives of Alberta, Alberta Social Credit League Papers, Box 2, "Rates and Information" for *Insight,* "Official Bulletin of Alberta Social Credit League," n.d. (journal began publication in September 1970).

44. Alberta Social Credit League Papers, Box 3, "Newsclippings, pre-election 1971."

45. Barr, *The Dynasty,* 189-90.

46. *Calgary Herald,* 3 August 1971.

47. Wood, *The Lougheed Legacy,* 73.

48. Allan Hustak, *Peter Lougheed: A Biography* (Toronto: McClelland & Stewart, 1979), 138.

49. *Canadian Parliamentary Guide,* 1972; Kenneth Wark, *A Report on Alberta Elections 1905-1982* (Edmonton: Government of Alberta, 1983), 17.

50. Larry Pratt, "Grant Notley: Politics as a Calling," in Larry Pratt, ed., *Socialism and Democracy in Alberta: Essays in Honour of Grant Notley* (Edmonton: NeWest Press, 1986), 28-9, 33-7.

51. John Richards and Larry Pratt, *Prairie Capitalism: Power and Influence in the New West* (Toronto: McClelland & Stewart, 1979), 215.

52. Ibid., 167-8.

53. Ed Shaffer, "Oil, Class and Development in Alberta," in Larry Pratt, ed., *Socialism and Democracy in Alberta* (Edmonton: NeWest Press, 1986), 119-25.

54. Larry Pratt, *The Tar Sands: Syncrude and the Politics of Oil* (Edmonton: Hurtig, 1976).

55. Alberta Social Credit League Papers, Box 3, "Newsclippings, pre-election 1971."

56. *Insight* 2:1 (March 1971), 12-14, provided biographies of most of the new Socred candidates.

57. His few speeches in *Alberta Hansard* in 1971 and 1972 indicate a lack of focus or even conviction in his criticisms of government policy.

58. *Edmonton Journal*, 10 November 1971.

59. *Insight* 2:1 (March 1971), 12.

60. Ernest Watkins, *The Golden Province: A Political History of Alberta* (Calgary: Sandstone Publishing, 1980), 213.

61. Alberta Social Credit League Papers, Box 2, *Alberta Challenge* (Alberta Social Credit League newspaper), October 1973, 7.

62. Ibid., 1.

63. Alberta Social Credit League Papers, Box 2, *Social Credit...on the Move* (Alberta Social Credit League Newspaper, 1975, 3.

64. *Alberta Challenge*, October 1973, 1.

65. *Social Credit...on the Move*, 1975, 2.

66. Watkins, *The Golden Province*, 213.

67. *Canadian Parliamentary Guide*, 1976; Wark, *A Report on Alberta Elections*, 17.

68. Alberta Social Credit League Papers, Box 2, *New SCene* (Alberta Social Credit League newspaper), 2:1, 1979.

69. Alberta Social Credit League Papers, Box 2, Election leaflets, 1979.

70. *New SCene* 2:1, 1979.

71. Ibid.

72. *Canadian Parliamentary Guide*, 1980; Wark, *A Report on Alberta Elections*, 18.

73. On the rise of western separatism, see Denise Harrington, "Who Are the Separatists?" in Larry Pratt and Garth Stevenson, eds., *Western Separatism: The Myths, Realities and Dangers* (Edmonton: Hurtig, 1981), 23-44.

74. While there are academic writings on the rise of Alberta separatism in general, particularly the articles in the Pratt and Stevenson book cited above, little interest in the flash-in-the-pan Kesler win has been shown, probably because his party's weak showing in the general election later that year—11 percent of the provincial vote and no seats—dampened earlier interest.

75. *Edmonton Journal*, various issues, February-May 1982.

76. *Canadian Parliamentary Guide*, 1983; Wark, *A Report on Alberta Elections*, 18.

77. David Bercuson and Douglas Wertheimer, *A Trust Betrayed: The Keegstra Affair* (Toronto: Seal, 1987), 39.

RENÉ LÉVESQUE AND THE RISE
OF THE PARTI QUÉBÉCOIS

BY GRAHAM FRASER

○

René Lévesque was now simply the Liberal member for Laurier, in opposition. He was not comfortable in opposition; he never liked the legislature much, and he was not comfortable in the Liberal party. Much of parliamentary life struck him is an archaic waste of time, and he spent more time preparing his weekly column for *Dimanche Matin* than participating in debates in what the new government had renamed the National Assembly.

However, the fact of being in opposition forced Lévesque—and the rest of the party—to think about issues that had been put aside during the intensity of day-to-day government. In defeat, the Quebec Liberals were tearing each other apart. At their convention in November 1966, [Quebec Liberal leader Jean] Lesage blamed the election defeat on the "idealistic illusions" and "perfectionism" of some people. As Dominique Clift [political commentator/journalist] observed, everyone understood this to be directed at Lévesque, Kierans, and Gérin-Lajoie. Even more explicitly, the outgoing party president, Dr. Irenée Lapierre, said in a CBC interview that Lévesque should quit the party.

However, the party was in no mood for this. The reform elements had gathered around Lévesque and Kierans and their slate for the party executive. Despite Lesage's speech, Kierans was elected to the presidency of the party, and an apology was exacted from Lapierre by the delegates. Lesage, who had come close to throwing Lévesque out of the cabinet after the "lâchez-pas" incident, clearly did not have the power to throw him out of the

Excerpt from Graham Fraser, *René Lévesque and the Parti Québécois in Power* (Toronto: Macmillan, 1984), pp. 39-70. Reprinted by permission of Graham Fraser and Macmillan Canada.

party. Still, even the relationship of Kierans and Lévesque as reformers in the cabinet and their personal friendship could not maintain their alliance. Lévesque was to evolve in a direction that Kierans would not follow.

There was a new intensity to the nationalist debate; with the election of Daniel Johnson [Union Nationale party leader], tensions between Quebec and the federal government moved to a new stage. Instead of dismissing Claude Morin, who had done Lesage's strategic planning on the federal-provincial front, Johnson kept him on; Morin became even more influential than before. At his first federal-provincial conference, Johnson stunned English Canada by calling for one hundred per cent control of personal income taxes, succession duties, and corporation taxes on natural-resource firms by 1972. The implied threat was clear.

In this new stage of the debate between Ottawa and Quebec, Pierre Trudeau, Jean Marchand, and Gérard Pelletier were no longer meeting Lévesque to argue, they were in Ottawa as MPs—Marchand was minister of manpower and Trudeau parliamentary secretary to the prime minister, Lester Pearson—and advising the finance minister, Mitchell Sharp, on how to repel these attacks.

On the weekend of 1-2 April 1967, there was a weekend meeting of some twenty reform Liberals at Mont Tremblant to discuss new policy directions for the party. It was here that Lévesque presented the first germ of what was to become sovereignty-association: a call for dramatically more powers for Quebec—although the word "sovereignty" was not mentioned.

After Mont Tremblant, Lévesque began meeting with a smaller group that included Jean-Roch Boivin, his law partner Rosaire Beaulé, labour lawyer Marc Brière, André Brassard, and a young MNA, Robert Bourassa. Although the issue of Quebec sovereignty had not yet entered their discussions, there was already an indication of the direction Lévesque's thinking was going in. Readers of his column in *Dimanche Matin* could see his views becoming firmer. He began to write about the demographic threat that immigration represented to Quebec—since immigrants were being overwhelmingly assimilated into the English-speaking minority—and about the failure of Confederation to protect the interests of Quebec, and the interests of French Canadians. But he had tossed off bitter remarks about federalism and the federal government for years; he only dropped hints of where he was evolving. He concluded one column: "Where does that lead us? In any case, certainly not to a second centennial."

When Lévesque went off on holidays to Maine, he told Jean-Roch Boivin and the others that he would write a statement of the position he was still groping for. He didn't get around to it, but when he got back, things suddenly began to move very quickly. For on 24 July, Charles de Gaulle shouted "Vive le Québec libre!" from the balcony of the Montreal City Hall. Lévesque was, if anything, annoyed. He didn't want his statement to seem inspired by this incident. At Lesage's insistence, the Liberal caucus passed a motion criticizing de Gaulle, and François Aquin resigned from the party as a result. Lévesque tried to persuade him not to quit; he wasn't ready—yet— to leave. His ideas were still coming together.

In August and September, the group he had been discussing things with had been meeting at Robert Bourassa's house. At the last meeting they were to hold before Lévesque's riding association meeting, he read a thirty-five-page statement that he had finished in Bourassa's basement. It called for "the essential components of independence," and "the complete mastery of every last area of collective decision-making" along with economic association with the rest of Canada. "This means that Quebec must become sovereign as soon as possible."

Despite the months of discussion, Lévesque's blunt statement took the group by surprise. André Brassard and Jean-Roch Boivin were hesitant. Lévesque had hoped that Bourassa would support him—he had a great deal of respect for Bourassa's economic expertise—but Bourassa took him aside and said, "René, I can't join you. You don't seem to realize that political independence goes with monetary independence. Quebec cannot be sovereign and pay its bills with Canadian dollars."

Lévesque shrugged. "Monetary system, economic system, all this is plumbing. One doesn't worry about plumbing when one fights for the destiny of a people."

But even then the rupture was not complete. The statement remained a policy which he was going to present to the Laurier riding association to be endorsed as a proposal for the Liberal party policy convention.

On 18 September, Lévesque's statement was ready for the riding-association meeting, which had already been postponed once so that he could finish it. The constitutional debate had picked up in intensity: the Progressive Conservatives had held their leadership convention ten days earlier, choosing Robert Stanfield but rejecting the concept of "two nations" which had emerged at a Conservative policy conference that summer and which Stanfield supported. The Ontario premier, John Robarts, had asked the other provincial premiers to a "Confederation of Tomorrow" conference in November. The Friday before, the newspapers had reported Jean Lesage as accusing Pierre Trudeau—by now minister of justice—of intransigence; over the weekend, Senator Maurice Lamontagne had urged the federal Liberals to accept the idea of special status for Quebec.

So the debate ranged from the functional pragmatism of the Progressive Conservatives and federal Liberals to the explicitly anti-colonial "liberation" arguments of the Rassemblement pour l'indépendance nationale (RIN).

When Lévesque rose to make his presentation of a resolution that his riding association would endorse for the party convention in October, he made a wide-ranging three-hour speech.

Often expanding on his text, he talked about how he felt more at home in the United States than in English Canada; about how diminished people felt when they were told "I can't speak French" in stores in Montreal; about how the French explorers gave "lessons of audacity and heroism" and how, as a boy of thirteen, he had spent weeks drawing up an outline for a novel about the soldier and sailor Pierre Le Moyne d'Iberville, who defeated the English in Hudson Bay.

While managing to cover every possible justification for breaking the federal link, Lévesque still emerged with a formula for independence that remained ambiguous. For if there was an appeal to pride and history in his speech, there was also a kind of frustrated pragmatism. Stronger than his nationalist message was the suggestion that he could accomplish a great deal for Quebec if it weren't for the waste of energy caused by the bickering and squabbling of federal-provincial relations.

"Either we have to modify [the system] profoundly, or else build another, because it's paralyzing," he said. "There is a vital minimum, a prudent minimum, a vital minimum of change [needed] to assure our collective security. And this is a minimum which, for the rest of the country, is a completely unacceptable maximum."

The next day, the *Toronto Star* ran a major front-page story on the speech, along with a background piece which began, "Partisans of Quebec independence waited seven years for René Lévesque. He arrived last night."

On Friday night, 13 October, the Liberal convention opened at the Château Frontenac in Quebec. Kierans was chairing the meeting as president, but had arranged to withdraw for the procedural wrangles. Lévesque's supporters were pushing to get a secret ballot on the constitutional question, but this was defeated overwhelmingly. On Saturday, there were some last-minute abortive attempts to mediate. On Saturday afternoon, as he came into the ballroom, Lévesque was greeted by delegates chanting "Lévesque dehors! Lévesque dehors!" (Lévesque out.) Walking beside him, Jean-Roch Boivin said, "I'm nervous; this is the first time I have physically felt hatred."

"You should have been nervous before the decision," Lévesque replied. "Once it's taken, it's all right."

Bourassa came up to him and, in a last attempt to keep him in the party, reminded him that Aneurin Bevan had stayed in the Labour party when his position on nuclear arms was rejected.

After making his presentation and seeing that it was going to be defeated overwhelmingly, René Lévesque made a short statement and walked out of the ballroom of the Château Frontenac, and out of the Quebec Liberal party.

Doris Lussier, an old friend, followed, sadly removing his delegate badge and dropping it in a hotel ashtray, looking, in the words of a reporter, "like an American student burning his draft card." In the press section, a twenty-one-year-old student named Claude Charron, accredited with the Université de Montréal student paper, said, "That's enough." He whipped off his press badge, and headed after Lévesque.

Followed by a cluster of supporters and a crowd of reporters, Lévesque walked across Place d'Armes to the Clarendon Hotel, and held a press conference. A reporter asked him if he would be founding a political party. "I don't know," Lévesque replied "We're going to meet. But if we do, we'll get twenty per cent of the vote." There was a burst of laughter.

After the press conference, Lévesque's group went for dinner at the Old Homestead Restaurant on Place d'Armes. At the end of the meal, Jean-Roch Boivin grabbed a placemat and said, "I'm going to make you all sign, in case it becomes historic."

Lévesque signed at the top left corner; thirty-eight others signed with him. An era had ended; a new one had begun.

The period between 1967 and 1970 was transitional; a substantial change in political leadership occurred both in Canada and in Quebec.

Lévesque had ambiguous feelings on leadership. On the one hand, he carefully adopted a non-leadership style: an apologetic shrug, a modest "sorry-to-bother-you" manner. When a journalist described him as a "national leader" in 1969, Lévesque wrote him a letter, saying, "if you *do* have to make me any kind of leader (ugh)—I'd much prefer you made me 'party l[eader].' But, please, not 'national leader'!" But on the other hand, he could be harsh and resentful towards those who did not give him total loyalty.

During these years, three men in particular were to act in counterpoint with Lévesque: sometimes enraging him, sometimes provoking him, and sometimes defining him. The three were Pierre Bourgault, Pierre Trudeau, and Robert Bourassa. All three were graduates of the best-known élite character-shaping Jesuit classical college in Quebec: Collège Jean-de-Brébeuf.

Bourgault had been an actor and a journalist when, in 1960, almost by accident, he found himself at an RIN meeting. But suddenly, he found his vocation: he was an orator. There was an icy brilliance to his style: a theatrical, precise rhetoric that had none of the slang or joual that marked the speech of many Quebec politicians.

He had an intensity that was almost frightening, and a style that shone with its simplicity. He often began his speeches with the Conquest: Quebeckers were a conquered people, a colonized people. Confederation was imposed upon them. It worked to their constant economic disadvantage, having been designed for Ontario. From there, he would look at other countries. Independence was not something outrageous. but something normal. Why was it something appropriate for the Swedes and the Dutch, the Mexicans and the Brazilians—but not Quebeckers?

It was a provocative question that stirred the imagination and the indignation of thousands. But Bourgault was not simply a powerful orator, he was a fiery, impulsive personality, living on adrenaline, fighting to keep the often divided party together, and often with no fixed address. He was a homosexual—a fact he would not discuss publicly until fifteen years later, but which gave Lévesque the creeps.

The indépendantistes dreamed of Lévesque and Bourgault working together; the prospect unnerved Lévesque. Whatever happened, he was determined to keep his new political organization as far away as possible from the RIN.

Similarly, Lévesque had never liked Pierre Trudeau. He found him arrogant, condescending, élitist, and exasperating. Trudeau's cold Jesuitical logic infuriated him. But while Lévesque was leaving the Quebec Liberal party and setting out to build a political organization that he could control, Trudeau was engaged in a process that would result in his taking over the Liberal party of Canada, and controlling it. The arguments the two men had always had would become a central part of the dynamic of politics in Canada and Quebec over the next fifteen years.

Of the three, Lévesque was closest to Bourassa, and had most hoped that he would join him. When Bourassa didn't, Lévesque was hurt, feeling that Bourassa had made his decision for careerist reasons. But others who were at the meetings at Bourassa's house in the summer and fall of 1967 suggest that the idea that Bourassa was on the point of joining Lévesque has been exaggerated; that Bourassa always made his disagreement clear. He tried to keep Lévesque in the party, and when Lévesque left, Bourassa said sadly, "The party will no longer be insured against lapses into bourgeois complacency."

On 20 April 1968, Pierre Elliott Trudeau was sworn in as prime minister of Canada. Gérard Pelletier was sworn in the same day as a minister without portfolio, joining Jean Marchand in the cabinet.

That same day, in Montreal, there was a convention of the Mouvement Souveraineté-Association at the Maurice Richard Arena, and already splits in the movement were beginning to show. It had started very spontaneously and idealistically. The night of its conception over dinner at the Old Homestead, Jean-Roch Boivin had later dropped in to a Liberal suite at the Château Frontenac, where Pierre Laporte [former Liberal cabinet minister] told him that he could not take the idea seriously because of Lévesque's insistence that there be no secret election fund, financed by corporate donations. But at Lévesque's riding office on Saint-Denis Street, the mail began to pour in: between five and six hundred letters, many containing dollar bills and two-dollar bills. Nervously, Lévesque and his friends decided that the movement could hire a student as a secretary, at fifty dollars a week.

After inviting everyone who had written or got in touch, Lévesque held a public meeting at the Dominican monastery on Côte Sainte-Catherine, on the weekend of 18-19 November, and the Mouvement Souveraineté-Association [MSA] was founded. He began gathering together academics and civil servants, while developing a platform and consulting [economist] Jacques Parizeau in some detail on the economic proposals. In January 1968, the 18 September speech, fleshed out, was published as a book: Option-Québec. This provided the basis for speeches, debates, interviews, all aimed at laying the groundwork for the April convention.

By the time of the convention, the MSA had a provisional executive, and a set of policy proposals, ranging from the essentials of sovereignty-association to the creation of new ministries of planning, compulsory civic service for young people, a modest army, and the suggestion that all lawyers should be employed by the state.

The delegates debated various parts of the proposed program—but the big fight was on language. The proposal from the policy committee said that the state of French in Quebec "reflects sadly enough the very state of a threatened nation"—and made its restoration "a question of dignity, certainly, but also a question of life itself. Quebec will be the country of a people speaking French."

The specific recommendations called for French as the only official language of a sovereign Quebec, but gave the right to add English to French in municipalities that held a referendum on this, and also gave the right to anglophones to communicate with the public administration in English. Non-French-speaking immigrants were to be required to pass a French test before becoming citizens.

But the mood of the convention was not conciliatory. A paragraph in the preamble saying that Quebeckers "should make it a point of honour to show great respect for the rights of its important linguistic minority" was deleted by a vote of 418 to 240.

This led to a dramatic floor fight between Lévesque and his fellow-independent in the National Assembly, François Aquin, who made a motion calling for stricter measures: a special tax on any company seeking to use English in a sign, or operate an English TV or radio station; the cutting off of social-security payments to any immigrant who did not enroll his or her child in a French school. Another motion called for the phasing out of state support for English-language schools.

Lévesque urged generosity, saying that to adopt the motions would be to imitate the most repugnant aspects of Anglo-Canadian repression of the French minorities outside Quebec. Aquin replied, saying that the English minority was different. "It has economic control. It is the best-off minority in the world," he said. "I don't want vengeance, I simply want to create a French society." He was cheered.

The debate raged on: some arguing that there would be no minorities in an independent Quebec, and that they might as well stay in Confederation if they were going to "pamper the English" and encourage "the cancer of bilingualism"; others argued that such a policy was unacceptable, and proof of an inferiority complex. Those opposing the amendment were booed, those endorsing it were cheered.

Then, at 11.10 p.m., Lévesque came to the microphone and made it clear how crucial he felt the movement's language policy to be. "The result [of the vote] will require a period of reflection on my part," he said. "For my name is attached to the movement."

Aquin came to the microphone to repeat that state funding for English-language education was not a right but a privilege, but Lévesque's implied threat had turned the tide. Aquin's amendment was defeated, 481-243.

Once the convention was over, the next job to be done was to resolve the question of negotiations with the RIN. Lévesque's chief negotiator was Jean-Roch Boivin, and neither he nor Lévesque wanted to fuse their movement with Bourgault's party. They didn't like his style: he had made too many inflammatory remarks, led too many demonstrations. So Boivin's main tactic was to stall. In June, two events gave Lévesque and Boivin the pretext to break off negotiations.

The first, was the involvement of the RIN in the language dispute in Saint-Léonard, a largely Italian suburb in northeastern Montreal. The schoolboard had refused to permit an English high school to be built, which had provoked the fury of the Italian community. This, in turn, had drawn the attention of the nationalist groups to Saint-Léonard as an example of their fears of immigrants assimilating into the English-speaking minority. The Mouvement pour l'Intégration Scolaire was formed, which demanded that all courses in Saint-Léonard be taught in French. In June, the MIS occupied a school, and RIN members participated, arousing Lévesque to accuse them of over-dramatizing the situation.

Then, on 24 June, the day before the federal election, violence erupted during the St. Jean Baptiste parade in Montreal. Pierre Trudeau stayed on the reviewing stand, grimly refusing to retreat from the hurled bottles and stones—a gesture of personal courage widely thought to have sealed his parliamentary majority next day. The riot lasted five hours; 292 people were arrested, and 96 policemen injured. One of those arrested was Pierre Bourgault.

Lévesque was outraged, and broke off discussions with the RIN, whose members became convinced he had never wanted a fusion. "They were right," he told an interviewer years later. "We weren't exactly eager to merge with them because of their image. Political realism was what we needed to fashion something new.... We were already getting members [from the RIN], except for the off-fringe."

In fact he had always hoped that the RIN—or some other formation— would develop to the left of his movement, to draw off the idealists and ideologues who harassed and undermined him. Increasingly, he wanted the PQ to have a solid, middle-class base of support from what he was later to call "normal people." After the breakdown of negotiations with the RIN, he pursued discussions with Gilles Grégoire, the former Social Credit MP who had become the leader of the right-wing indépendantiste Ralliement National in the fall of 1966.

At the same time, work was continuing for the fall convention that would found a new party: preparation of party statutes and party policies. Lévesque and the group of people around him who had left the Liberal party, like Boivin, Beaulé, and Marc Brière, were worried that the disruptive elements of the RIN might take control of the party. On the other hand, younger intellectuals who had been in the Liberal party but had become very disenchanted with its authoritarian structure were determined that the new party should be controlled by its members, and not by a small élite working on a "political commission" named by the leader. This conflict was to mark the new party throughout its first years of existence.

In the months that led up to the October convention that founded the Parti Québécois, a group of young researchers had been drawing up possible constitutions for the party. André Larocque was a political scientist working on his doctorate at the Université de Montréal who, thanks to a sympathetic department head, was able to work virtually full-time on politics. He had assembled a range of examples, stretching from what he considered the authoritarian model of the Quebec Liberals to much more decentralized, member-controlled parties. He argued that in the Quebec Liberal party policy was usually dictated by the political commission, while in more democratic parties policy was worked out at the grassroots.

The MSA executive consisted largely of former Liberals, and Jean-Roch Boivin was in charge of party statutes. Boivin was a tall, earthy, tough-talking lawyer. Born in Bagotville, he had graduated from the Université d'Ottawa and studied law at the Université de Montréal. He had worked with Lévesque since 1962; he remained totally loyal to his interests. Boivin was dead set against the kind of grassroots control of the party that Larocque was pushing for, but he was even more worried about the nationalist left taking over the first executive.

Boivin and Rosaire Beaulé invited Larocque and a colleague to lunch, and proposed a deal. They were prepared to accept Larocque's constitution, with its idealistic commitment to grassroots control of the party, if Larocque would agree that there should be no left-wing challenge to the proposed executive. Larocque agreed. The deal gave Boivin and Lévesque the executive they wanted at the foundation of the party, but it laid the basis for a continuing debate between the leadership and the membership.

On the weekend of 11-14 October 1968, in Quebec City, the Parti Québécois was founded, and delegates spent the weekend debating hundreds of resolutions that had been submitted by riding associations to modify the draft program drawn up at the April MSA convention.

Formally, the party was a fusion between the MSA and Gilles Grégoire's Ralliement National. However, this was an illusion; Grégoire had lied in claiming that there were fifteen thousand members in his right-wing nationalist-Créditiste party, and many RIN members had already left the floundering left-wing party to join Lévesque

Lévesque had hoped that the new party would be called the Parti Souveraineté-Association, or the Parti Souverainiste—and those were the only names on the ballot. But, by lobbying furiously, Grégoire managed to get enough people to write in the name Parti Québécois to give it a majority.

The creation of the PQ meant the end of the line for the RIN. At a special convention ten days later, there was a vote to dissolve the party, and Bourgault urged the members to join the PQ, concluding "For the last time in my life I say 'Vive le RIN'—and for the first time in my life I say 'Vive le Parti Québécois!'"

The RIN members were to bring a strong commitment to a social-democratic program to the PQ. But they were also to bring an intensity and a partisan rigour which unnerved and irritated Lévesque. When Bourgault and the RINistes joined the party—and by 1972 it was estimated that seventy-two percent of the RIN members had—they strengthened the uncompromisingly indépendantiste wing against Lévesque and the moderates. This remained a fundamental conflict in the new party.

In the months that followed the formation of the Parti Québécois, Lévesque worked to give it a reassuring image of stability and competence. At the 1969 convention, he asked the delegates to vote for unity and moderation in electing the executive—a hint that he did not want Pierre Bourgault elected. The convention responded, electing Claude Charron, then twenty-three and a student leader, to the executive instead of Bourgault. The party's goal of respectability was immeasurably bolstered in September 1969, when the economist Jacques Parizeau announced that he would be a candidate for it in the next election.

The departure of René Lévesque did not solve the problems of the Quebec Liberal party. On 28 August 1969, after some public criticisms of his leadership, Jean Lesage resigned. On 17 October 1969, Robert Bourassa announced that he was a leadership candidate. The other candidates were Claude Wagner, forty-four, the former minister of justice and a tough law-and-order man, and Pierre Laporte, forty-eight, the former minister of municipal affairs.

Bourassa was then thirty-six. The only son of Aubert Bourassa, a modest civil servant in the federal ministry of transport who had died suddenly when his son was sixteen, he had been a scholarship student at Brébeuf. After studying law at the Université de Montréal, where he graduated in 1966 with the Governor General's Medal, and being admitted to the Bar, Bourassa won a fellowship to Oxford, where he read Philosophy, Politics, and Economics. He also became interested in British politics, and worked for the Labour party while he was at Oxford. This was followed by a year at Harvard studying taxation and fiscal law in the International Tax Program.

From 1960 until 1963, Bourassa worked in Ottawa for the Department of National Revenue as a fiscal adviser, and taught economics and public finance at the University of Ottawa. Then, from 1963 until 1965, he was secretary and director of research for the Bélanger Commission on Taxation, which was studying the Quebec fiscal system. In 1966, he returned to Ottawa with a team of specialists studying the Carter report on tax reform, but he did not stay long.

For in June 1966, encouraged by Jean Lesage, Bourassa won the Montreal riding of Mercier, and was appointed opposition finance critic. It was then that he became friendly with Lévesque and tried to mediate between him and the less nationalist Liberals.

When he declared his candidacy for the leadership, he had one major asset. Paul Desrochers, the secretary-general of the Quebec Liberal party, had commissioned an American polling firm, Social Research Inc. of Chicago, to do a massive study of the opinions of Quebec voters. The party officials were surprised to learn the importance the voters placed on the economy; the poll showed they were looking for a leader who could stimulate an economic recovery. Moreover, they saw such a recovery as the solution of another major preoccupation: the generation gap. In summary, according to Social Research, the ideal leader was seen as "helping bridge the gap between the generations...a good representative of the Quebec people, the kind of man who could be strong enough to deal with Ottawa, the titans of finance, and most aspects of a highly sophisticated world."

"We were stupefied," a senior party official said later. "The identikit sketch resembled neither Laporte nor Wagner. The leader people were looking for was a young businessman, with a very detailed knowledge of the economy. The man who best corresponded to the picture was Bourassa. I barely knew him at the time, but, without knowing him, I agreed he should become leader."

Armed with the poll and the power that his position in the party gave him, Paul Desrochers went to work to set the stage for Bourassa to succeed Lesage. Bourassa seemed like a fresh alternative to old, tired, familiar faces. Claude Ryan wrote approvingly in Le Devoir that. "The rational functionalism of this man who studies before speaking, who knows not only how to count but how to read, who maintains a responsible tone in every circumstance, makes for a man who is superior to his two rivals." On 17 January 1970, Bourassa won the Liberal leadership on the first ballot, with 53.2 percent of the vote.

Two months later, Premier Jean-Jacques Bertrand [the late Daniel Johnson's successor] called an election....

The Union Nationale government was clearly in trouble. Jean-Jacques Bertrand, a decent, colourless man, had been unable to avoid the language crisis that exploded over the conflict in Saint-Léonard in 1968, and his 1969 law, Bill 63, which gave freedom of choice in the language of education. The economy was in bad shape, with unemployment over nine percent, and the finance minister, Mario Beaulieu, had not presented a budget, before the National Assembly was dissolved.

The Union Nationale ran an erratic campaign, trying to be more nationalist than the Liberals (whom they portrayed as federal puppets) but to appear more responsible than the Parti Québécois (whom they described as revolutionaries). When the polls showed the UN running third, Bertrand lashed out in a tantrum against the corporate élite accusing them of using the Montreal newspapers to defeat the UN and elect Bourassa, In a paragraph he did not actually read but which was distributed to reporters, he charged that the public-opinion polls had been faked. But the only obvious fake was an elaborate gesture which became known as the "coup de la Brinks." On 27 April, at dawn, eight Brink's trucks loaded with millions of dollars' worth of securities drove off to Toronto. A Gazette photographer was tipped off, and the pictures made an enormous impact.

That night, the justice minister, Rémi Paul, told an audience in Terrebonne that when they got home they would learn of the millions being moved out of Quebec. "That's the result of political instability in the province, the threat of independence, separatism," he said. "René Lévesque is the Fidel Castro of Quebec."

Bourassa campaigned on a slogan of "Non au séparatisme," promising a hundred thousand jobs. The PQ ran a positive, almost therapeutically affirmative campaign, with a slogan of "Oui!" Lévesque told an ecstatic crowd in Paul Sauvé Arena on 27 April that victory was possible. "But in any case—the object was not necessarily to take power right away," he added, "it was not necessarily to jump right into soft jobs in a powerless province; it was to smash, once and for all, the ice of our fears, our complexes, our impotence!"

But sometimes the positive mood cracked. A Montreal Star editorial compared Lévesque to Kerensky, the Russian democrat who was deposed by Lenin and the Bolsheviks, and alluded to "the propensity of Quebec leaders, throughout history, toward authoritarianism and dictatorship."

The next night, speaking in English at a public meeting in his own riding, Lévesque let his outrage pour out. He described the editorial as the "first lovely confirmation" of the English community's view that "we, basically, are not civilized enough as a society for self-government."

"That's an insult, a collective insult to a civilized people which in fact has no goddam lesson to get from the *Montreal Star*, or from any of the exploiters of both the English and the French groups in Quebec—and they're among the worst!" he raged. "And I'd like to say that we've got no lesson on that score to take...from anyone that has been dominating Quebec like a bunch of Rhodesians—the white group. If we had colours here, you'd feel it."

The Liberals won a sweeping victory, taking 71 out of 108 seats: the biggest victory they had won since 1931, the strongest majority since Duplessis won 77 out of 86 seats in 1956. The UN became the official opposition with 16 seats, the Créditistes won 13 seats and the PQ only 7. Six of these were in Montreal: Dr. Camille Laurin was elected in Bourget; Robert Burns in Maisonneuve, Claude Charron in Saint-Jacques, Charles Tremblay in Sainte-Marie, Guy Joron in Gouin, and Marcel Léger in Lafontaine. The only seat off the Island of Montreal was Saguenay, won by Lucien Lessard.

English Canada reacted with euphoria: The Toronto *Telegram* ran a banner headline saying "Quebec: A vote for Canada." But the reaction in the PQ was bitter resentment, and a feeling that they had been cheated by the electoral system. For with 24 percent of the popular vote the PQ had won less than 6 percent of the seats; the Liberals had won 65 percent of the seats with 44 percent of the votes.

With his shy grin and boyish cowlick, Robert Bourassa seemed to be a portent of a new generation of technocrat politicians—unpretentious, contemporary, and accessible: a politician-expert more at ease with job-creation statistics than with the deceptive reassurances of campaign rhetoric. As newly elected premier, he continued to stay in a $9-a-day room in Old Quebec, drifting unrecognized among the youngsters on the rue Saint-Jean.

The October Crisis changed all that.

With the kidnapping of the British Trade Commissioner, James Cross, on 5 October 1970, and of Pierre Laporte, Bourassa's labour minister on 10 October, the imposition of the War Measures Act and the arrest of over 450 people, and the subsequent discovery that Laporte had been murdered, Quebec's political life was thrown into chaos.

René Lévesque was appalled. When he heard the news that Laporte had been killed, he sat in his office at the PQ headquarters and wept. Laporte had been a friend. When he had run as an independent in 1956, Lévesque had covered his campaign; Laporte had covered Lévesque's for *Le Devoir* in 1960. They had played tennis together regularly as cabinet colleagues.

Lévesque and Claude Ryan both opposed the proclamation of the War Measures Act, and were part of a group that called on the federal government to negotiate with the FLQ. This became the basis for the suggestion, made to Peter C. and Christina McCall-Newman, that there was a plan to replace the Bourassa government with a "provisional government."

The October Crisis did harden lines in Quebec, but the identification of independence with terrorism, which Lévesque had feared so much, did not happen—or, if it did, it did not last. Some people, like Pierre Marc Johnson, the late premier's son, decided that Pierre Trudeau was defining all nationalists as terrorists and, in their anger, decided to join the PQ. And only a few months after the crisis, in the by-election to fill Pierre Laporte's seat, Pierre Marois ran and held his vote from six months earlier. But the short-term effect of the October Crisis on reform politics was devastating. The War Measures Act virtually eradicated FRAP, the municipal reform party in Montreal, giving Mayor Jean Drapeau a complete victory at the polls. And it transformed Robert Bourassa.

The $9-a-night room vanished overnight in favour of the premier's suite; security became a constant fact of life, with Bourassa moving into the recently completed, impregnable premier's office that was quickly dubbed "le bunker," and functioning in a swirl of bodyguards, walkie-talkies, limousines, and helicopters.

Bourassa's first mandate, from 1970 to 1973, was a stormy mixture of explosive conflicts, ambitious plans, sweeping reforms—and breathtaking sellouts to foreign investors. The growth of the state had continued unabated for a decade. For ten years, Quebeckers had increasingly looked to the state to provide equipment, institutions, infrastructure. Under Lesage, Hydro-Québec was expanded, and the Ministry of Education, the Caisse de Dépôt, SIDBEC, Quebec's steel corporation, and SOQUEM, Quebec's mining corporation, were all created. Under the Union Nationale, the trend had continued, with the province taking control of the church-run hospitals, and the creation of Radio-Québec and the government-owned oil and gas company SOQUIP.

Now began a decade of conflict over social issues: language, immigration, power. Under Bourassa, with Claude Castonguay as his minister of social affairs, the great social reform was a full medical-insurance plan, with a whole centralized system of delivering social services, and the creation of a network of social-service centres: Centres Locaux de Services Communautaires (CLSC).

But the conflicts came quickly. The Union Nationale had lost its credibility on the issue of language; Bourassa tried, and failed, to end a General Motors strike in which the right of workers to use French at work was a key issue. He postponed introducing a language law of his own, saying that he was waiting for the report of the Gendron Commission that had been set up to examine the question.

In 1971, Bourassa at first agreed in principle, along with the other nine provincial premiers, to the "Victoria Charter," the federal government's proposal for patriating and amending the constitution. Under the Charter Ottawa would have had to consult the provinces on a range of decisions, and a province could opt out of federal social programs. Opinion in Quebec, led by Claude Ryan in *Le Devoir* and encouraged by the Parti Québécois, demanded that the province should receive from Ottawa the financial equivalent of programs from which it opted out. After a week of hesitation, Bourassa announced that he would not sign the Charter; thus acquiring a reputation for weakness both in Ottawa, for having vacillated, and in Quebec for not having won.

Meanwhile the PQ was having its own problems. Camille Laurin, an imperturbable psychiatrist highly respected in the party, became parliamentary leader. Robert Burns, a tall, cheerful labour lawyer became House leader. Laurin had to spend a great deal of energy easing the tensions between the caucus and Lévesque who, having been defeated at the polls, was back in Montreal, writing a daily column and leading the party.

But soon the party gained a major asset. Louis Bernard, the assistant deputy minister for intergovernmental affairs, resigned in June to become Laurin's chief of staff, and his presence was to provide technocratic expertise at the heart of the party.

The tensions between Lévesque and the caucus were not the only ones. The bitterness of the 1970 election defeat and the October Crisis surged onto the convention floor in February 1971. Again, Lévesque vowed to resign if a language resolution calling for an end to subsidized English schools were passed, and urged the delegates to elect a "harmonious" executive. The language resolution was defeated—but this time Lévesque could not keep Pierre Bourgault off the executive.

In an electrifying five-minute speech, Bourgault won over the convention. He summed up in a nutshell the party's unease about what the members saw as the increasingly cautious pragmatism of the leadership, and attacked that pragmatism openly and directly, accusing the party of seeking security instead of liberty, respectability instead of solidarity. He concluded with a series of metaphors that appalled Lévesque, confirming every prejudice he had against Bourgault; he listened with his face in his hands.

"Ho Chi Minh was not respectable; he became so. Castro was not respectable; he became so. De Gaulle was not respectable; he became so. Because they remained faithful to the dreams of their youth!" he shouted. "And that is what I want the Parti Québécois to do—to remain faithful to the dream that it has given birth to!"

There was a storm of applause. The speech had drawn lines very clearly inside the party; Ho Chi Minh and Castro were certainly not part of Lévesque's dream. Lévesque was also challenged for the presidency—for the first and last time—by André Larocque, who used the campaign to argue the "participationist" position, as it was called—that more power should be given to the membership of the party.

Lévesque won handily, but the convention established a pattern of giving him most of what he wanted, but not everything. The divisions became even clearer, as labour unrest grew in Quebec. There was tension between Lévesque and the caucus, where men like Burns and Charron were urging the party to become more involved with the labour movement.

The unions had become increasingly radicalized, developing a neo-Marxist ideology and a sweeping critique of the government. Labour unrest exploded in the fall of 1971, first with a strike at *La Presse*, and then with a general strike in the public sector after the leaders of the three union federations, Louis Laberge, Marcel Pepin, and Yvon Charbonneau, were jailed for urging strikers to defy an injunction ordering them back to work.

Robert Burns argued vigorously that the PQ should join a march on *La Presse* on 29 October. Lévesque, who had been warned by a union official that the march might become violent, was strongly opposed. The PQ executive backed Lévesque—by one vote. Burns marched anyway. By the end of the march, several buses were burned, eight policemen were injured, seven demonstrators were in hospital and thirty under arrest. One demonstrator died of an asthma attack.

A month later, the party held a closed-door national council meeting to clear the air, and issued a lengthy statement by Lévesque, clearly dissociating the party from violence and the excesses of the labour movement. And, although the debates continued inside the party over the next few years, as the 1973 election drew near the party pulled together, bolstered by the presence of "respectable" candidates like Claude Morin.

In September Bourassa called an election for 29 October. For the first, time, the PQ campaigned on the assumption that it could win. The major party figures travelled together across the province, and were greeted by huge rallies of wildly cheering supporters. But it was a deceptive enthusiasm, and journalists sympathetic to it failed to see the electorate's fear of a Parti Québécois victory.

The PQ provided the Liberals with one heaven-sent opportunity. To reassure people of the financial safety of independence, the PQ executive decided (over his objections) that Jacques Parizeau should produce a model budget for an independent Quebec. The result, was the notorious Budget de l'An 1. The document assumed that economic growth would continue after a PQ victory, that there would be a 9.5 percent increase in GNP. The Liberals pounced on it, found miscalculations, mocked the optimistic assumptions, and succeeded in putting the PQ on the defensive.

Lévesque had often repeated since the 1970 defeat that the only way for the PQ to win power would be for the Union Nationale to disappear. This was one of his major arguments for a moderate campaign: that it was essential to win over UN supporters. He was wrong. In 1973, the Union Nationale and Créditiste support collapsed—and the result was a Liberal landslide of 102 out of 108 seats. The PQ increased its share of the popular vote to thirty-three percent—and won one seat less than in 1970, losing three members (Camille Laurin, Guy Joron, and Charles Tremblay) and gaining two, Jacques-Yvan Morin and Marc-André Bédard. Lévesque again failed to win a seat. At the election-night rally in Paul Sauvé Arena, Laurin put his head on Lévesque's shoulder and wept uncontrollably.

The defeat was traumatic—even more so than in 1970, because it was more unexpected. Lévesque was particularly disheartened; Pierre Marois had again failed to get elected, and when Lévesque thought about quitting he wished that Marois had been elected so that he could succeed him as leader.

The defeat further widened the gap between the PQ national office and the parliamentary wing. Camille Laurin could no longer play the role of father-confessor and go-between. The caucus had split three-three between Jacques-Yvan Morin and Burns for the parliamentary leadership, and Lévesque broke the tie in Morin's favor. Unfortunately Morin did not have Laurin's skills, or his respect from all sides of the party. This split only contributed to the festering of the bitterness on the left of the party about Lévesque's leadership. The tension between his faction and Burns's became more intense.

The 1974 convention was marked by an uneasy compromise agreement on a referendum on sovereignty-association which left the indépendantistes unhappy. Also at that convention, Lévesque asked Burns to go on the party executive, which Burns thought would be a waste of time. Finally they struck a deal: Burns would go on the executive if Lévesque would come to Quebec City for caucus meetings. But Lévesque would not keep his part of the bargain. He had his own grievance: by then he was working full-time for the party for only $18,000 a year. The pension he was entitled to as a former MNA was going entirely to his estranged wife.

Tempers flared after he refused to run in a by-election, and the organization of the by-election was a shambles The party's fundamental problem was a small parliamentary group in Quebec City with an unelected leader in Montreal. While the overworked caucus was forced to make its decisions on the fly in the assembly and in committees, the party's prestigious spokesmen, Lévesque, Parizeau on the economy, and Claude Morin on intergovernmental relations, were free to speak out at their leisure. The results were often contradictory, with Lévesque casually reversing positions that had been fought for strongly in the National Assembly.

But the Liberals suffered even more than the PQ from the problems created by the 1973 landslide. First, there was an accumulation of accusations of patronage and favouritism. A Liberal MNA was forced to resign because of a conflict of interest; Bourassa's wife and his brother-in-law, Tourism Minister Claude Simard, were part owners of the holding company that owned Paragon Business Forms, which did a million dollars' worth of government business. More substantially, the government failed to negotiate from strength with the construction unions building the massive James Bay hydroelectric project, or those building the Olympic Stadium. The Cliche Report found that the union goons who had sabotaged the James Bay LG2 site had benefited from a private deal with Paul Desrochers, Bourassa's chief adviser.

Bourassa began to appear manipulative and image-obsessed, hiring a hairdresser as his bodyguard. The American ambassador Thomas Enders privately compared him to Richard Nixon, saying they were "both creeps." While the comparison was tempting, it was fundamentally unfair; Bourassa was not paranoid, but blandly confident he could reach an agreement with everyone.

He did not hate his adversaries. He called them "tu," offered them jobs or cabinet posts, and assumed he could undercut their support, absorb their passion, contain and redirect their energies. Were his opponents and critics social democrats? So was he. Were they conservatives? He could slow the pace of change. His was the arrogance of consensus, the ultimate Liberal belief that all differences could be ironed out, all problems could be solved, all setbacks and failures rationalized and explained.

By 1976 the constituent parts of the Liberal consensus were falling away, and Robert Bourassa appeared a weak, cynical, Machiavellian figure; the people in his office, whizkids in 1970, now seemed to be cynics, sycophants, or liars.

Bourassa's language legislation, Bill 22, became the ultimate disaster in consensus politics: it outraged every constituency of the language issue, and satisfied virtually no-one. The English were horrified at the prospect of any restrictions in access to the English school system, and angry at the regulations making knowledge of French compulsory in various professions. Quebec nationalists were appalled that any immigrant or francophone child who could be coached to pass a test could enter the English, rather than the French, school system.

The most devastating critique of Bill 22—and of Bourassa— came from Pierre Trudeau. On 5 March, leaving lunch with Bourassa in Quebec City, Trudeau quipped "He only eats hot dogs, that guy"—a mocking reference to a recent magazine cover showing Bourassa with a hot dog on a silver platter. That night, for an hour, Trudeau was scathing in his treatment of Bourassa in a speech, saying how hard Bill 22 made it for Liberals to sell bilingualism to the rest of Canada. He also attacked Bourassa's handling of the Olympics and the constitution.

In the spring of 1976, Quebec nationalist anger focused on the rule that French-speaking pilots must talk to French-speaking air-traffic controllers in English. It was a question that struck at the heart of the French fact in Canada, and cut across all party lines.

The conflict had been brewing since 1975, when a Bilingual Communications Project (BILCOM) recommended to the federal ministry of transport that bilingual air-traffic control services be extended in Quebec. The Canadian Airline Pilots Association (CALPA) and the Canadian Air Traffic Control Association (CATCA) objected. After a year of increasingly heated argument, and the formation of a new association, Les Gens de l'Air to represent Quebeckers in aviation, CATCA voted to go on strike on 20 June, arguing that the extension of bilingual service threatened air safety. The pilots decided to support the air controllers.

The result was chaos in Canadian airports before a peak holiday period and just before the Olympics. Worse, it revealed a profound sense in English Canada, where there was heavy support for the strike, that French was a cultural luxury with no place in a technological environment. The fact that English-speaking pilots might hear French between another pilot and the control tower was seen as a threat to safety; the fact that a French-speaking pilot in a private plane had to use a second language to speak to the tower was not.

As Trudeau put it, "We can't force Quebeckers to learn English, and if they don't want to within their own province, they will say 'Well, this is basically the separatist issue. If we can't operate even within our own language, then what the hell are we doing in this country?' Do you know the answer to that? I can't answer the separatists."

When the federal transport minister, Otto Lang, signed an agreement with air controllers and pilots on 27 June to end the strike, and conceded the controllers a virtual veto over the introduction of bilingual air-traffic control, there was outrage in Quebec. Jean Marchand resigned, saying he could "not stay in a government that is prepared to negotiate bilingualism."

The reaction in Quebec was spontaneous and massive. As [historian] John Saywell observed, "It is possible that there has never been such unanimity among Quebec francophones in the history of Canada." A massive public campaign in support of the Gens de l'Air gathered steam during the summer, and two Liberal MPs, Serge Joyal and Pierre de Bané, joined the Quebec labour lawyer Clément Richard as counsel for the association. The two committees of support were chaired by active PQ members: Claude Morin in Quebec City, and Guy Bisaillon in Montreal: Pierre Péladeau donated full-page advertisements in his tabloids for endorsations by figures as various as Dominique Michel, a TV star, and the hockey idol Maurice Richard. The unanimity of the outrage added to the sense that the Liberals had failed to protect the French language, either in Quebec or in Ottawa.

Ironically, the Gens de l'Air fight added to the growing tensions inside the PQ leadership. During the summer, Lévesque began to view the non-partisan common front with suspicion. He distrusted Joyal and de Bané and disliked Bisaillon, a union activist working on the campaign full-time. As a result, a special executive meeting at the Auberge Handfield in Saint-Marc-sur-le-Richelieu at the end of August ended in a major explosion. Lévesque came to the meeting with a paper calling on the executive to urge PQ members not to get involved with the Gens de l'Air, arguing that, they would end up being manipulated by the federal Liberals working in the campaign. When tempers began to flicker, Lévesque banged his fist on the table and said, "We're going to settle this."

Burns, who has as much of a hair-trigger temper as Lévesque, flared up and uttered the caucus's complaints: they weren't being consulted, they were being embarrassed by Lévesque's shoot-from-the-hip policy-making; Lévesque had broken his agreement to come to caucus, and it had all gone too far. "I don't recognize you as my leader any more, it's as simple as that," Burns said. "You have no idea how to work as part of a team."

"You're right, I don't believe in it," Lévesque said bluntly. "That's the way it is."

Burns was appalled. He felt he had offered to go halfway to work with Lévesque, but on the condition that there be some commitment to the idea of teamwork. Now Lévesque had confirmed his worst suspicions. Lévesque's paper on participation in the Gens de l'Air was shelved, and there was a motion of confidence in his leadership, which he won—by one vote.

Michel Carpentier, Lévesque's executive assistant, left the meeting devastated. He was convinced that if there were no election that fall, the tensions would blow the party apart at the convention scheduled for the spring, and Bourassa would win again. If that happened, Lévesque would clearly be unable to survive as leader.

The idea of calling an election in the fall of 1976, two years before his mandate expired, had been maturing in Bourassa's mind over the summer. The federal-provincial discussions of constitutional reform which had ended with the failure of the Victoria Charter had resumed in 1975. Through the winter and spring of 1976, Trudeau began talking about the need to patriate the BNA Act. Traditionally, Quebec had always opposed this until a new division of powers was agreed on. Through the summer and early fall, Bourassa became convinced that Trudeau was determined to proceed with unilateral patriation, and came to the conclusion that the only way to stop him was to hold an election on the issue.

In mid-September, he made a list of factors in favour of a fall 1976 election, and those favouring waiting until fall 1977. In support of September 1977, he came up with three reasons: it would be a normal four-year mandate; it would mean waiting until the memory of the strikes of 1976 had faded; and he knew that there were severe tensions inside the PQ which might boil over at the 1977 convention. He listed eleven reasons in favour of an earlier election, including the fact that the Union Nationale had climbed from eight to fourteen percent in the polls over the summer; the government's borrowing was up and would go higher; the Olympic finances had left a mess and an arrangement for payment would have to be imposed on Montreal; there was a police contract coming up in the spring of 1977 which looked as if it would produce a strike; the economy was facing a downturn because of an expected slackening of investment after the American presidential elections; unemployment was expected to climb higher through the winter with the post-Olympic construction slump in Montreal; his leadership was increasingly contested. The overriding reason, though, was the threat of unilateral patriation of the constitution by Trudeau.

His cabinet expressed strong opposition at a meeting in Sherbrooke on 29 September, but Bourassa did not change his mind. His decision was confirmed when, in the Speech from the Throne, Trudeau made it clear that he was determined to proceed with unilateral patriation. On 18 October, the election was announced.

For the Liberals, the campaign was a disaster. Quebeckers began to see TV clips on the news of Bourassa being jostled by Hydro-Québec strikers in Saint-Jérôme, and mobbed by angry Alcan strikers in Jonquière. Meetings began to be disrupted by loud, persistent hecklers. There was an unnerving sense of passions barely under control, of currents of rage and contempt towards Bourassa swirling around smaller currents in the English and ethnic communities of resentment, feelings of betrayal, and fear of the Parti Québécois. Instead of dying down, anger over Bill 22 began to intensify, and wide divergences in the party became public.

The election campaign proved to be exactly what the Parti Québécois needed to submerge the anger and internal conflict of the previous three years. Lévesque campaigned vigorously, attacking the government for having won "the Triple Crown: the championships of unemployment, taxes, and debt," but did so with the calm conviction that he could not win more than forty seats.

Lévesque himself coined the phrase "On a besoin d'un vrai gouvernement" (We need a real government)—the main slogan of the campaign. The other slogans were "On mérite mieux que ça" (We deserve better than that) and "René Lévesque: un vrai chef'."

A key element in the PQ's platform was the commitment to hold a referendum on Quebec's future. In the dying days of the 1973 campaign, the PQ had promised a referendum taking out full-page advertisements on the last day of the campaign. But it was not until after that election that the question of a referendum was actually debated by the party. At the convention of 1974, the party committed itself to hold a referendum to ratify the constitution of an independent Quebec—indicating that this would be after independence was declared. Now, just as he had watered down the party policy in 1973, Lévesque changed this to mean that a PQ government would not proceed towards achieving independence until it had got the authorization of a referendum.

Lévesque focused the campaign on the announcement of a series of commitments: policies that had been developed by Louis Bernard, Jacques-Yvan Morin's chief of staff, and a party official, Claude Malette. They were nitty-gritty, bread-and-butter promises: free drugs for people over sixty-five, new industrial health and safety legislation, agricultural zoning, stringent election-financing legislation, the reform of municipal financing, and a promise to change the language law, Bill 22.

Like Bourassa, Lévesque and Carpentier had underestimated the revival of the Union Nationale. Its new leader, the tall, bearded political neophyte, Rodrigue Biron, succeeded in capitalizing on public disenchantment with the Bourassa government and unease with the PQ, making the election of the first Lévesque government possible. But the phenomenon of the revival of the moribund Union Nationale with its sewer-pipe-maker leader is explicable only by the rage and sense of betrayal in the non-French-speaking community.

Bourassa began to worry that English-speaking anger would create a split vote; in the middle of the campaign, he introduced changes to Bill 22, and, after a speech at the Canadian Club on 8 November, made a personal appeal to the *Gazette* publisher, Ross Munro. With Bryce Mackasey, he talked with Munro for a couple of hours, impressing upon him the danger of a split vote, and warning him that, having just moved to Montreal from Edmonton, he should know that there were reporters on his staff sympathetic to the PQ. In addition, Arnie Masters, Mackasey's campaign manager, prepared an analysis of thirty-one ridings that the Liberals could lose because of the erosion of English and immigrant support.

Munro was impressed: more, so when, on Wednesday, 10 November, the Hamilton-Pinard poll was published showing that a PQ victory was probable unless there was a massive shift of undecided voters to the Liberals. Upset by the prospect, Munro sat down and, in a white heat, wrote an editorial which began, "The central issue in Monday's provincial election is separation." It was an awkward, passionate, sometimes ungrammatical diatribe, which argued that the election of the PQ would be a disaster for Quebec.

Faced with the prospect of an argument with his editorial-page editor, Tim Creery, Munro signed it and took it to the news desk. No-one dared edit it, and it ran as a front-page editorial on Saturday, 13 November. On page 3, there was an advertisement, taken out by thirty-six reporters publicly dissociating themselves from Munro's position.

Excess became the order of the day in that last week. In the north-end Montreal riding of Crémazie, Education Minister Jean Bienvenue distributed voting cards which said in Italian that Quebec was in peril because "they want to separate from Canada" and that only a Liberal vote was a guarantee against losing old-age pensions, family allowances, and health insurance.

Ross Munro was not the only prominent member of the English-speaking community to succumb to the Liberal pressure. Charles Bronfman, of the distilling family, had also talked with Bourassa and heard him at the Canadian Club, and he became more and more upset. At a special election meeting in the Allied Jewish Community Services Hall on Côte Sainte-Catherine, his rage and frustration exploded. "Don't vote with your heads—your heads tell you that Bourassa's a bum. But he hasn't done such a bad job," he said.

He told his audience that, unbelievable as it might seem, Bourassa was not aware of the "injury, pain, and distress" Bill 22 had caused. "I swear to God this is true! It's incredible to believe, but the premier just didn't know. *He knows now!*

"If we turn our backs on the Liberals," he continued, "we are committing suicide. It would be worse than a disaster, it would be criminal—putting spears and daggers into our own backs. The election *is* the referendum...the referendum on whether we live or die...because they are a bunch of bastards who are trying to kill us!"

No-one was to express so dramatically the mood of near panic that gripped parts of the English-speaking community in Montreal at the prospect that the Parti Québécois might take power.

On election day, 15 November, Lévesque was tired but quietly hopeful; he thought he would probably win his own seat, and he felt that the PQ might, at last, make the breakthrough, and win as many as forty seats. Robert Bourassa had a more realistic sense of how things were going; the night before, his chief of staff, Jean Prieur, had told him that he would lose his own seat. Bourassa prided himself on being a cerebral, rational man; he believed it, and he was not particularly upset. It had happened before, he told himself, to Mackenzie King. Nevertheless, it had made it harder to get to sleep.

Both men spent the day touring their ridings, visiting the polls, shaking hands with the election workers. At four o'clock, the campaign committee had its final meeting at party headquarters as campaign director Michel Carpentier briefed Lévesque for the last time on how the voting had gone during the day, and what the latest projections were.

Throughout the campaign, the organizers had kept themselves from being too optimistic, refusing to believe Michel Lepage and Pierre Drouilly, their own poll-takers, who had projected victory. At the meeting, Carpentier presented three possibilities. The PQ might, as a minimum, get between 20 and 25 seats if only the most successful candidates pulled through. If things went better, they might get between 40 and 45 seats. Or, if the most optimistic scenario worked out, the party might get over 60 seats and form the government. Lévesque listened to the breakdown and then said, "We can forget, about that last one."

At seven o'clock, the polls closed. Until three minutes earlier, Bourassa was still touring the polls. Finally, two minutes before they closed, having greeted the voters standing in line at a poll on Saint-Urbain Street, he climbed back into the limousine. As he had done in 1970 and 1973, he went first to the Centre Notre Dame, an athletic centre opposite St. Joseph's Oratory, for a swim. His mind swirling, speculating on the range of possibilities, Bourassa decided to swim a little more than his usual third of a mile. He wanted to be as relaxed as possible, and he wanted to have some news when he got, out.

When he climbed out of the pool and walked dripping into the locker room, shortly after 7.30, he was struck by the fact that none of his entourage was there waiting. The news must be bad, he thought, there was only his son François, white-faced with shock.

"Papa, I think you're beaten," he said.

"Why?" replied his father, still breathing hard from the exertion and towelling himself off.

"It's six to one for the Parti Québécois," the boy replied.

"That's it," Bourassa thought. He dressed and headed off to visit his eighty-year-old mother, who was staying with his sister in Saint-Bruno, on the south shore. She was almost relieved at the news.

In Longueuil, René Lévesque arrived at the campaign office in a small shopping centre about 6.45. He listened intently to the early returns on the radio, and when the first results came in for Taillon showing that he had a substantial lead, he gave a sudden little jerk of joy with his fist, his face breaking into a glow of triumph. It was one of his few smiles of the night.

About 7.15, Lévesque turned to his campaign aides and said abruptly, "We're going upstairs." With Jean-Roch Boivin, Robert Mackay, and Pierre Bellemare, he headed up to a small apartment above the storefront office and turned on the television set. Someone offered him a Scotch; he took a glass of water instead, and sat down at a small round table opposite the television set. Boivin, Mackay, and Bellemare sat on a sofa, and found they were watching Lévesque as much as the television.

The results began to come in quickly. At 7.33, the PQ was leading in 21 seats, the Liberals in 18. Five minutes later, the PQ was leading in 27, the Liberals in 19. Getting tenser and tenser, Lévesque was almost twitching as he smoked one cigarette after another. "C'est pas possible, c'est pas possible," he muttered.

At eight o'clock, Bernard Dérôme announced that Pierre de Bellefeuille, a journalist and former director of Expo 67, had defeated the most nationalist member of the Bourassa cabinet. Denise Filiatrault, a popular actress who was the co-host at Paul Sauvé Arena, began to jump up and down with delight before running to the microphone to make the announcement.

The reaction was delirious. No-one had expected the PQ to win Deux-Montagnes; the announcement was a quick, sudden cue to everyone inside the party organization that this was a victory. In Longueuil, Lévesque violently stubbed the cigarette he was smoking and reached for another. Robert Mackay said quietly. "Those polls that Drouilly and Lepage did—perhaps they are not as stupid as all that." There was a ten-second silence, and Lévesque snapped, "Stop exaggerating."

But a minute or so later, Bertrand Bélanger, a senior party organizer working in the riding, came up to the apartment and said to Lévesque, "You'd better get to work on the 'miracle' speech, because that's what it looks like."

Similarly, Deux-Montagnes was all the news that Michel Carpentier needed; as soon as he heard, he decided he didn't need to wait any longer, and left Paul Sauvé Arena to drive to the party headquarters and start the wheels in motion for the transition: getting in touch with the Quebec police force so that the security could take over immediately, getting on the phone to Lévesque, and waiting for the key people to arrive back at headquarters and get to work.

At 8.40, Bernard Dérôme made the announcement: the Parti Québécois would form a majority government. That night, the PQ won 69 seats—and two more were added later on recounts for 71. The Liberals were reduced to 26 seats, the Union Nationale won 11, the Créditistes 1, and the Parti National Populaire 1. It was a sweeping victory; when Lévesque finished speaking to the ecstatic crowd at Paul Sauvé Arena, throngs poured onto the streets.

The newly elected members and party organizers made their way to PQ headquarters, where euphoria was total. But more than one person was struck by Lévesque's silence. He congratulated a few people, but said little, staying for about an hour, subdued and serious in the sea of elated faces. Then he headed home to brood on his too-sudden victory. Already, the new job had begun: Roland Giroux, the president of Hydro-Québec, had phoned and asked Lévesque to show up at the Hydro-Québec office the next morning to be briefed on a major international bond issue.

In the streets of Montreal, there were the sounds of triumph: honking horns and whoops of joy. Along the rue Saint-Denis and in Old Montreal, exuberant celebrants rode on the hoods of cars, waving Quebec flags.

About four in the morning, the last revellers left the Lasalle Hotel, where the Montreal Centre ridings had been having a victory party, and climbed into their cars. Then, without any previous discussion, they headed west.

It is an old custom in rural Quebec that after elections, the victors parade past the homes of the losers. Spontaneously, a line of cars formed and headed north, into Westmount, up past the brick townhouses, up the tree-lined streets where the houses grew larger, up to the symbolic peak of Upper Westmount, Summit Circle. And there, at the top, the cars drove around and around, honking their horns in taunting, nose-thumbing delight.

STORMING BABYLON: PRESTON MANNING AND THE REFORM PARTY OF CANADA

BY SYDNEY SHARPE AND DON BRAID

o

"I have to laugh when I hear people say he's new to politics. After all, this is Senator Manning's son!"

- Historian Desmond Morton

"I'm building a kite and I need wind for it to fly."

- Preston Manning

In a remarkably short time, the Reform party has come charging out of the West to assault all the towers of "Old Canada"—the three traditional parties, a federal system that costs too much and delivers too little, politicians who try to placate Quebec, the discredited champions of bilingualism and multiculturalism. Reformers see all these forces as agents of a corrupt, bankrupt system that no longer represents their traditional faith in family, frugality, the rights of the individual, and one united but decentralized nation. They hear a Babel of Canadian voices, too many new voices, all contradictory, many incomprehensible, none saying what they want to hear. They yearn for a simple, clean-cut Canada with home-spun verities at its heart. To achieve their "New Canada," they are ready to storm the federal Babylon and throw out the unbelievers. Their increasingly powerful siege engine, an organization with more than 100,000 members by the beginning of 1992, is not so much a political party as a populist movement unlike anything Canada has seen since the 1920s and 1930s.

Excerpt from Sydney Sharpe and Don Braid, *Storming Babylon: Preston Manning and the Rise of the Reform Party* (Toronto: Key Porter Books, 1992), pp. 1-14. Used by permission of Key Porter Books.

The leader of these political shock troops is Ernest Preston Manning, age 49, the son of Ernest Charles Manning, who was Social Credit Premier of Alberta from 1943 to 1969. Preston Manning seems fresh to many Canadians because he is new on the national scene, but he has been active in politics for 25 years, and he has been preparing himself for leadership all that time. "I have to laugh when I hear people say he's new to politics," says University of Toronto historian Desmond Morton. "After all, this is Senator Manning's son!" (Ernest Manning, the enemy of almost everything the federal Liberals stand for, accepted a Senate appointment from Pierre Trudeau in 1970 and served until 1983.)

Preston Manning seems to be the very opposite of a slick and seasoned politician. He could easily be mistaken for the shy, modest proprietor of a religious supply store in rural Alberta. When he appears on a podium or a TV screen, he has the darting, big-eyed look of a nervous owl ready to pounce on some misplaced fact. His nickname among friends—"Press"—is as plain as his appearance, and his family life appears so uneventful that one relative calls Preston and Sandra Manning "Mr. and Mrs. Perfect." But this meek demeanour masks a political will cast in iron, skills as polished as a tap dancer's shoes, and beliefs so radical they would entirely change the nature of Canada.

The deep religious convictions of the Manning family, rooted in evangelical Christianity, are central to Preston Manning's political beliefs. For many years he appeared on his father's evangelical radio show, "Canada's National Bible Hour." He believes that every word of the Bible is true and knows that he has a calling to translate those words into political action. Every one of his policies, from his views on capitalism to privatization, can be traced in a straight line back to his vision of the proper Christian society. He is convinced that Canada is hell-bent for damnation but can be saved by turning sharply toward the heavenly beacon of the Reform party's New Canada. Ernest Manning once said, referring to Social Credit, "No other philosophy in the world today offers anything but ultimate slavery." Today the Reform party espouses much the same philosophy and Preston Manning believes the stakes are just as high.

Anyone who gets close to Manning senses at once his intensity and his burning devotion to the Reform cause. In conversation he can be restless and fidgety, often squirming impatiently when he hears something with which he does not agree. His manner is pleasant and his responses are always polite, but behind them lies a strong mind that settled on most of the answers long ago. There are very few political issues Preston Manning has not studied and pondered deeply. His attention to detail is almost obsessive, his concentration legendary among friends. He once spent an entire day honing a single sentence of a policy definition. His brother-in-law, Phillip Stuffco, remembers stopping his car a few feet from where Manning was sitting behind a picture window. "I blew the horn and the guy didn't even hear me," Stuffco recalls. "He was writing a paper or something."

Manning's personal sense of duty and obligation, implanted by religion and family example, is both his strength and his burden. His father served in the Alberta legislature and the Senate for an astounding total of 47 years. Now 83, Ernest Manning still preaches damnation and salvation on the radio twice a month, his powerful voice reminiscent of the charismatic Social Credit founder William "Bible Bill" Aberhart. Many sons would run from a model so daunting, and Preston Manning may once have tried in his quiet way to escape. For his first two years at the University of Alberta he studied physics and considered a career in pure science, far from the world of politics. Then he switched to economics and embraced political life, propelled by duty, aptitude, and perhaps by a trace of guilt, for there was a quiet tragedy in the Manning family. Preston Manning's older brother and only sibling, William Keith Manning, was afflicted by cerebral palsy and institutionalized for much of his short life. From his youngest days, Preston Manning felt responsible for his brother, and his sense of loss was immense when Keith Manning died in 1986. Fundamentalist religion and his father's impressive service created in Preston Manning, the lucky healthy son, a profound sense of obligation and mission. As his father would say, Preston Manning felt a call from the Lord. The call from his family circumstances was just as loud and compelling.

Manning is the polar opposite of Prime Minister Brian Mulroney, the leader whose regime he challenges so fiercely. Mulroney has always been far more interested in people than policy. He knows nearly every important decision-maker in Canada and counts his friends and acquaintances in the hundreds. As John Sawatsky shows in *Mulroney: The Politics of Ambition*, the prime minister is an extroverted charmer who measures success by his influence over people. Manning, on the other hand, is a true crusader whose main interest is the mission. Despite his deep faith in the individual, he does not have the born politician's burning desire to win over every person he meets. He tends to be shy and even awkward with strangers. Ron Nicholls, a Calgary Tory and friend of Mulroney's, once encountered Manning in a store in Arizona while both were on holiday. "I'd never met him," Nicholls recalls, "so I introduced myself and said, 'I used to be president of the provincial Tory party in Alberta.' I might have been a convert just ripe for convincing, but he didn't seem very interested. He just sort of said 'hello' and drifted off." Mulroney has always made a point of cultivating key people in other parties, but Manning hardly seems interested. (In Nicholls' case he should have been; the Calgary architect wrote a report for Mulroney on the Reform party's prospects in Alberta.) Very few people know Manning well, and the vast majority of decision-makers in Canadian politics and business have never met him. While Mulroney was climbing the ladder in the Montreal business establishment, making contacts all over the country, Manning worked in Slave Lake, Alberta, trying to pull a small town up by its bootstraps. His relatively limited circle of friends and acquaintances tend to work at the policy-making levels of business, government, and consulting.

His zeal for the cause has never diminished. Over the years, Manning was quietly involved in many political causes and ventures, always waiting for just the right moment to found a new federal party. His timing was excellent; he moved in the spring of 1987, just before English Canada's discontent began to explode into a true fury over Meech Lake, the national debt, the Goods and Services Tax, Quebec's law against English signs, the rise of the Bloc Québécois, and criminal charges against Tory politicians.

From the start Manning hoped that his new populist movement, once firmly rooted in the West, would become truly national. He did not want just another western-based party that would shout briefly at Ottawa and fade away: no Western Canada Concept or West-Fed for him. "I'm building a kite and I need wind for it to fly," he told Quebec journalist Michel Vastel in 1987. In this sense, too his timing was impeccable. Pollsters began to notice in the late 1980s that "western" issues were becoming "national" issues. The same things that bothered westerners for so many years—high taxes, the seemingly unending focus on Quebec, the feeling that the federal system is a foe rather than a friend—were now common perceptions in Ontario and Atlantic Canada as well. At the same time there were lingering memories of outrages such as the Liberals' 1980 National Energy Program and the Mulroney government's decision in 1986 to award the CF-18 fighter maintenance contract to Montreal rather than Winnipeg. For all these reasons, Manning's ideal of taking a regional party to the national stage was suddenly possible.

Roger Gibbins, one of Canada's leading experts on regional alienation, does not see the Reformers as a regional movement at all. "Two things have happened," says the University of Calgary professor. "The western Canadian electorate has been nationalized in the sense that their concerns are not parochial any more. And second, the primary issues the Reform party is addressing are not really regional. It's a much more broadly based movement."

The party also taps into powerful international currents that are eroding old systems far from Canada. The death of the Soviet Communist party, the defeat of socialism in Sweden, the redrawing of borders along ethnic lines in Eastern Europe, all fit the Reformers' belief in the bankruptcy of "collectivist" government. So does the growth of populist, anti-establishment parties in nearly every country of western Europe. Like many of those groups, the Reformers want decentralized government, state functions in private hands, social needs met by free enterprise, and more citizen control over politicians. They are even ready to contemplate Canada's ultimate ethnic split, the cleavage of Quebec from the rest of Canada, if Quebec will not accept their vision of the country. They believe that local control is better than central control in everything from politics to economics. Now they are convinced that the world is moving their way.

Manning sees his movement as part of these international trends, and he identifies with the leaders in eastern Europe. He was powerfully impressed by a meeting he had with the Polish, Hungarian, and Czechoslovakian ambassadors to Canada. "These guys are trying to change the system on every front," Manning said in an interview. "They're trying to convert from a Marxist economy to a market economy. They're trying to go from a totali-tarian system to a democratic system, and they're trying to get beyond this left-right stuff. These are populist type things, they're bottom-up, democratic, and market-oriented. The difference, of course, is that in Canada we have all this freedom. These guys can't understand why if Canada wants to make systemic changes it shouldn't be about the easiest thing in the world."

As an avid amateur historian, Manning is also attracted to the populist tradition in Canada. The Reform party echoes the great western populist movements of the 1930s: The Progressives, the Cooperative Commonwealth Federation (CCF) and Social Credit. Some of Reform's rhetoric, especially about Quebec, is powerfully reminiscent of the One Canada speeches of the late Tory Prime Minister John Diefenbaker, the last leader whose western voice found wide national appeal.

But the main parallel lies deeper in the past. The left-liberal Progressives, lead by farmers and workers, who won 65 seats in the 1921 federal election, are the tactical model for the Reformers as they march onto the national stage. The rightist Social Credit movement, which ruled Alberta from 1935 to 1971 and elected many federal MPs, provides the strategic goals, the grand design for Canada. Most of the ideas espoused by the Reform party today, in fact, were developed by Manning and his father in the late 1960s as they tried to keep the populist spirit alive in a form appealing to modern Canada.

Populism can have its dark side, as Manning knows very well. Alberta Social Credit was often blatantly anti-Semitic, and today there are racists among the Reformers. Manning admits this is a problem but argues that his party can purge extremists merely by growing beyond them. Meanwhile, though, some people in the party come very close to the perceptive definition of American observer Kevin Phillips: "Populism likes flags, criticizes welfare as well as Wall Street, and keeps a gun in the pick-up truck."

All Manning's careful planning, mixed with good timing and even better luck, propelled the Reformers to national attention with shocking speed. In May of 1987, 300 disgruntled westerners went to Vancouver for the Western Assembly on Canada's Political and Economic Future. By November of that year in Winnipeg, the same group created the Reform party of Canada with Manning as leader. The new party had fewer than 1,000 members, a vaguely crackpot image, and money in the bank only because rich donors believed enough to give. Soon the Reformers gained just the kind of national attention they needed in the 1988 federal election, especially from Manning's unsuccessful run at Joe Clark in Alberta's Yellowhead riding. In 1989, Reform candidates in Alberta won both a by-election and that province's peculiar provincial election to choose a Senate candidate.

The real surge in Reform support came after the collapse of the Meech Lake Accord in the summer of 1990, and the passage of the GST at the end of that year. The party began 1990 with 27,000 members and finished the year with 54,000. By the end of 1991, the membership had nearly doubled again, to about 100,000. Similarly, the party collected $200,000 in donations in 1988, $1.1 million in 1989, and more than $2 million in 1990. For 1991 the figure was expected to top $4 million. Canada has not seen a new federal party grow so explosively since the Progressives burst out of the West and Ontario to finish second to Mackenzie King's Liberals in the 1921 election.

Nevertheless, the Reformers are not the Progressives or anything like them. Above the genuine populism at the grassroots sits a modern political apparatus that operates out of the party headquarters on 4th Avenue Southwest in Calgary. Nearly every day, computer operators open sacks of mail and pour out new membership applications, each with $10 enclosed. By fall of 1991 the party had launched a major drive for corporate donations, headed by Reform chairman Cliff Fryers; hired Frank Luntz, a Republican pollster and campaign planner who used to work in Ronald Reagan's White House; engaged national pollsters; and signed Hayhurst Communications, a sharp Calgary-based advertising firm, to sell its image. (The contract was sensitive for Hayhurst: the company first asked all its other clients if they had any objections to the Reform account.)

The party's original slogan, "The West Wants In," disappeared with expansion into Ontario. So did the red-white-and-blue logo, to be replaced with green, the hot colour of the 90s. "For us [green] denotes growth and vibrancy and freshness," said Manning's new executive assistant, Diane Ablonczy. The old logo was also too close to Tory colours for comfort. Yet many of the party's structures, including Reform Fund Canada, draw heavily on Progressive Conservative models. This is only natural, Manning says, when 70 percent of Reformers in Alberta are former Tories. "What they know about constituency organization is mainly from the Conservatives. Reform Fund Canada is exactly the same as the PC Canada Fund." When the party assaults the towers of Old Canada in the next election, it will fire the same weapons as the occupants.

Not surprisingly, some westerners see these changes as compromises with the very system that the party is trying to change. Elmer Knutson, founder of the Confederation of Regions party, accused Manning of selling out to Ontario power brokers. On 24 September 1991, the day after his party had won eight provincial seats in New Brunswick, Knutson told *The Edmonton Journal*: "He said at first he was a western-based party.... Then he wasn't going to go beyond the Manitoba-Ontario border. [Westerners] are now seeing that Manning is taking his orders from Bay Street." Later Knutson added: "He's a wimp if I ever met one."

The accusations did not seem to slow Manning in the West or anywhere else. The major reason for the growth of Reform, beyond doubt, is deep discontent with all traditional politicians, and especially with the governing Tories. "Very little of the Reform party would have come about if it had not been for the blundering of this awful Conservative government," says NDP icon Stephen Lewis, with only slight exaggeration. This bitterness against the Tories is so powerful, as Roger Gibbins points out, that the content of Reform policies is almost irrelevant. "There is a lot of anger and discontent searching for a home," he says. "The Reform party provides the vehicle. That opportunity for people to express themselves is going to be more important than any of the policies the Reform party has.... With the almost total collapse of the Conservatives, literally hundreds of thousands of people are looking for something else, and that doesn't involve a very careful search among the alternatives." Yet the Reform party does have a full set of proposals for Canada: radical ones. If they were all implemented, this would be a vastly different country, and very likely a country without Quebec.

The Reformers want a nation at once united and decentralized, a country without public debt where all people are declared equal but no individual receives special help. They believe that women should make their way without affirmative action or any federal programs to lift them up. "They have a very traditional view of women, if they think of women at all," says long-time women's advocate Doris Anderson.

The Reformers apply the same thinking to special groups within society such as recent immigrants, people of colour, other "visible minorities," and, of course, Quebec. There would be no official multiculturalism, sharply limited bilingualism, and no funding for any private group to preserve its identity. The provinces could develop their own policies in these areas but without federal money. Provincial governments would also have full control over medicare and most social programs. Ottawa would become a federal referee, an impartial arbiter of constitutional rules with a negligible role in social issues. All this brings fierce charges that the party is racist and right-wing because it would ignore minorities and the underprivileged.

The point of all these policies, the broad Reform party goal, is to create a Canada where citizens shed their hyphenated identities and everyone has equal opportunity but no state guarantees of equal outcomes. Collective values, such as the principle that the state has the major responsibility for helping the poor, would be virtually wiped off the slate and replaced by the Reformers' brand of frontier individualism. Indeed, this belief in the individual is the Reformers' core value, and for their leader it has a religious root. All people must be as free as possible, Preston Manning believes, in order to find God in their own way.

On this point alone the Reform party and modern Quebec are fundamentally incompatible. While Quebec politicians increasingly try to foster *la collectivité* (the francophone majority), the Reformers always stress the rights of the individual. The Reform party has no intention of reconciling these disparate visions. If Quebec cannot accept the Reform view of Canada, the party says, it should seriously consider leaving. The Reform party invites Quebec to consider these ideas, then come back and talk after "New Quebec" has defined itself. Yet there is no indication that Quebec is ready to accept either the invitation or any of the Reform party's prescriptions for Canada. Reform is the only national party that makes no effort to accommodate Quebec within Canada. Its policy boils down to: "Here's our view of the country, take it or leave it." The unilingual Manning's view of himself as a skilled conciliator, based mainly on his business record, does not extend to his attitude toward Quebec.

"He says he wants to show Reform is not a redneck party," notes Vastel, who followed Manning through western Canada for 10 days in 1987. "Yet he uses anti-Quebec feelings to make points in his speeches.... He doesn't look like he's full of himself but you get the strange feeling that he might be a demagogue. He scares me a bit. At the same time, I kind of like him."

Political institutions would also be very different in Preston Manning's

New Canada. Every province would have the same number of senators, those senators would be elected, members of Parliament would no longer be under the thumb of their party leaders, and federal election dates would be fixed rather than decided by the prime minister. The voters could start petitions to kick out their MPs, launch new legislation through citizen initiatives, and generally have much more direct influence over the system. These policies respond to the deep conviction that politicians no longer represent the people. Yet, when taken together, they would radically change Canada's system of representative democracy to an unfamiliar hybrid of representation and direct democracy.

Combine all these policies, and the result is a truly radical blueprint for Canada. Many Reformers do not seem to be aware of this, however. A good number who join the party are not familiar with the full range of policies, but seize one or two that appeal to them. As a result, many newer Reform party members are more moderate than the leader or party officials. Those who joined Reform at its inception, on the other hand, are often more radical than the leadership. Manning's cautious statements as he tries to walk a line between these groups show how tricky life can be for the leader of a populist movement.

The Reform party's appeal is also uneven in the regions of Canada: it is very strong in British Columbia and Alberta, less so in Saskatchewan and Manitoba, powerful in pockets of rural southern Ontario, but limited in Toronto and other big cities. For obvious reasons the party will try to field candidates in every riding in Canada, except in Quebec.

By late 1991 support in Atlantic Canada was weak at best, so Manning set off on a tour of all four provinces to win converts. Ever the optimist, he told people in Nova Scotia that his party is not a western interloper, but a natural heir to the great Nova Scotia reformer Joseph Howe. On an earlier trip Manning held a news conference under Howe's statue, and did the same in Ottawa under the monuments to Robert Baldwin and Louis-Hippolyte LaFontaine, early reformers of central Canada. Preston Manning knows his history and uses it to advantage.

There is a powerful reform tradition in all of Canada, not just in the West, Manning insists. But he allows that Atlantic Canada will be hard to crack because under his policies the region would have to accept less help from Ottawa. The Reform party's appeal, he concedes, "is offset by this psychological depression that accompanies the economic depression in Atlantic Canada. People believe you can't change the system. They read our *Blue Book* [on policy] and say, 'That's right, we've got exactly the same views.' But when it comes to political actions or doing something about it, it's a harder sell."

Yet some Maritime observers, including Nova Scotia author and playwright Silver Donald Cameron, feel the sell could be easier than many believe. "Until now, Maritimes have been content to take care of themselves from within the power structure," he says. "But the Tories seem to be saying, 'you're on your own.' That will release a tremendous rage and the Reform party could do quite well." Only two days after Cameron made the remark, the 23 September provincial election in New Brunswick seemed to bear him out. The Confederation of Regions party [CoR] won eight seats with 20 percent of the popular vote, showing clearly that some Maritimers are just as discontented as westerners and Ontarians. Many CoR attitudes, especially annoyance at official bilingualism, echo precisely the feelings of Reformers.

Few experts now doubt that the Reform party of Canada will have a major impact on the next federal election. Its powerful momentum, born of anger, enthusiasm, and fierce dedication to a cause, shows no sign of abating. "They'll be spoilers at least," says Patrick Gossage, a Toronto media consultant and former press secretary to Pierre Trudeau, reflecting a common view.

Preston Manning is a veteran leading a party of newcomers. Many of his followers, including party executives and organizers, had never attended a rally or joined a party before they found his Reform movement. But they are speaking out now, most for the first time in their lives, through a swelling party with its cerebral and pious leader. They have become the surging, bitter voice of a growing group of tradition-minded Canadians who feel excluded and ignored.

Great numbers of Canadians obviously welcome this assault on the bastions of the old Canada. Others echo the dark thought of a newspaper editor in St. Catharines, Ontario, who wrote after Social Credit swept into Alberta in 1935: "The whole thing is a chimera, a nightmare that passeth all understanding." Supporters see Manning and his followers as popular heroes led by a new prince of democracy, while enemies paint them as maddened, irrational rednecks storming the ramparts with pitchforks. There is truth in both images, for little about this movement is as simple as it seems. One thing is clear: Preston Manning and his party will continue to provoke deep and bitter controversy as they storm the old federal order, Canada's Babylon.

SHATTERED DREAMS: THE NDP'S
1988 ELECTION CAMPAIGN

BY JUDY STEED

o

On Sunday, 2 October 1988, after months of speculation, billions of dollars' worth of promises and intense media attention, Prime Minister Brian Mulroney finally called the election. Fifty-one days later, on 21 November I was driving east on the 401, from Toronto to Oshawa, to witness election night at Ed Broadbent's headquarters. There was a full moon beaming coldly on the dark highway; apprehension hung as thick as smog in the air. Everybody knew it; the NDP campaign had not gone well.

In the opinion of Lawrence Wolf, the savvy advertising man who orchestrated the NDP's ads in 1979 and 1980, "The New Democrats had a wonderful product, a wonderful leader in Broadbent, but they shot themselves in the foot. Their commercials had no teeth. They didn't sell themselves well." At the Canadian Auto Workers' Local 222 building on Bond Street in Oshawa, where Broadbent first won the New Democratic Party nomination in 1968, booze tickets cost $2 and an old woman at the front door tried to rouse spirits with her boisterous harmonica playing. But there wasn't much revelry.

Up on the stage, an attractive colour poster of the party leader—"This time, Ed"—had been taped to a plain wooden podium. Along one wall, the media people were packed like pigeons on a window ledge. Rows of tables, pushed up against each other, were buried in technological hardware: laptop computers, banks of TV sets and thick ropes of wires and cables snaking everywhere. It was hot and bright under the lights that turned the

Excerpt from Judy Steed, *Ed Broadbent: The Pursuit of Power*. (Toronto: Penguin Books, copyright Judy Steed, 1988), pp. 9-44. Used by permission of Livingston Cooke, Inc.

auditorium into a makeshift TV studio. Most people—journalists, technicians, citizens of Oshawa—were dressed in casual clothes, jeans and T-shirts, lounging around, sipping coffee, sweating, waiting. The female TV interviewers stuck out in the crowd; they were wearing suits, pancake make-up, shadowed cheekbones and red lips.

Bent over a soundman's sound-board was Anne Carroll, Broadbent's executive assistant who had been wagonmaster on the campaign plane (named Air Apparent and J'esp-air, a poignant reminder of great expectations gone awry). Responsible for the myriad of complex details that kept the tour moving, with buses, hotels and planes ready when they were supposed to be, Carroll had, by all reports, done a magnificent job. Tonight, she was tightlipped, looking exhausted and thin. When she's tense, she can't eat. Smoking Du Maurier cigarettes, with black headphones mussing her coiffed strawberry blonde hair, she was making notes on a pad. "Jack Harris has been defeated in St. John's East," she muttered. "We've lost St. John's East." It was 7.30 p.m. The returns were just beginning to come in from the Maritimes, and it looked like it was going to be a long night of personally painful losses for Broadbent.

At 8.40 p.m. the CBC predicted a majority Conservative government, with no seats for the NDP east of Oshawa. The New Democrats were shut out, again, in Quebec. Rémy Trudel and Phil Edmonston, for whom Broadbent had the highest hopes in Quebec, had come close, but they had lost.

Broadbent was absorbing the bad news in his suite at Oshawa's Holiday Inn. He was devastated. His wife Lucille was in tears, as were, at various times, the close friends who spend the evening with them: Mary Ellen McQuay, a former federal secretary who is now a professional photographer; Terry Grier, former chairman of the Election Planning committee, now president of Ryerson Polytechnic Institute in Toronto and one of the men who would share the blame for the campaign's failures; Bill Knight, federal secretary, the shrewd Saskatchewan party professional who pretended to be a prairie hayseed; Knight's fiancée, Tessa Hebb, a member of the NDP's international affairs committee who'd run for and lost a federal nomination in Halifax; George Nakitsas, Chief of staff, an intense Montrealer of Greek ancestry who had endured his father's death and an attempted coup mid-campaign, with his wife Cathy; Rob Mingay, a Vancouver film producer-director-writer who was events coordinator for the campaign; and Christine, the Broadbent's somewhat rebellious teenage daughter who of all of them seemed the least disturbed—but then, she had never particularly enjoyed having her father in politics.

"It was a very emotional night," said Rob Mingay. "I guess we felt it was Ed's last campaign. I mean, how much of this can a guy take? It was his fourth election as leader in ten years, he'd been an MP twenty years, and it hurt to think he was going to leave like this." Mingay knew more than most people about the failures of the campaign, about the anguish many staff members felt, convinced they had let down their leader in what should have been his finest hour.

Broadbent was most distraught about being shut out in Quebec. He didn't know it then, but a month prior to election day, the Montreal *Gazette*, followed by *The Globe and Mail*, had received detailed information about an RCMP criminal investigation into the alleged wrongdoings, involving illegal kickbacks, of Richard Grise, the Tory MP in Chambly, Edmonston's Montreal-area riding. The information obtained by both papers showed a remarkable scandal was brewing, but neither paper would touch the story—before the election. According to journalists close to the situation, Edmonston would have won if the news about the Tory candidate had leaked out—and the NDP would have gained its crucial toehold in Quebec. However, the Liberals were just as eager as the Tories that the story not appear: the Liberal candidate was running third and the revelation of allegations against Grise would likely have put Edmonston over the top.

He agonized about losing Dr. Rémy Trudel, former president of the University of Quebec at Rouyn-Noranda. The NDP had spent almost $7 million on the election, with $2 million going to Quebec, which made for a very expensive regional campaign that delivered no seats. The energy of the Quebec NDP had been dissipated by internal battles—normal enough in any organization that was growing as fast as it was—and by struggles to get itself heard in Ottawa, where Nakitsas was the only key figure in Broadbent's inner circle who was fluent in French. Another factor that worked against electoral success was Broadbent's anti-free-trade stance, which had gone against the grain of the Quebec mood. Days before the election, Parti Québécois leader Jacques Parizeau, who promotes separatism and free trade, said that the Conservative agenda, free trade and the Meech Lake Accord, would weaken Canada and that was why he thought most Québécois supported it.

Broadbent did not venture out of the Holiday Inn until late in the evening. Back at Local 222, the drone of election returns continued. The mood was less than festive. At intervals throughout the evening, the sound of the CBC's Peter Mansbridge broadcasting results was interrupted when Broadbent's constituency representative, Nestor Pidwerbecki, got up on stage to promote the sale of raffle tickets for a colour TV. That night Nestor wasn't his usual ebullient self. In the municipal elections a week earlier, he had lost a bid for a seat on regional council by thirty-three votes.

Brian Harling, chief organizer for the Ontario NDP, was being interviewed by everyone all evening. He was the only party official available to explain why the Ontario breakthrough wasn't happening as NDP MPs went down to defeat: Michael Cassidy lost by 762 votes to a Liberal in Ottawa, Lynn McDonald by 1,192 votes to a Liberal in Toronto, Marion Dewar by 64 votes to a Liberal in Hamilton. Something else Broadbent didn't know was that Bob White, president of the Canadian Auto Workers and a vice-president of the NDP, was viewing the election results with increasing distress; later, he termed it "watching the disintegration of what should have been the New Democratic Party's finest hour." But that night, the critics were still mute. Patiently, Harling repeated himself to reporters: "Yes, it's tough to be the third party in an election that's polarized over one issue." In an aside, he acknowledged, "If we get forty seats, I'll heave a sigh of relief." Alexa McDonough, leader of the Nova Scotia NDP, appeared on TV to state that "strategic voting" had hurt the party's chances. The Liberals' anti-free-trade campaign, she said, had drawn votes away from the New Democrats.

Ed Broadbent finally arrived late in the evening. He was shielded by security Mounties and surrounded by a media pack that clung to him like a plague of locusts, bristling with microphones and TV cameras. Accompanied by his wife Lucille, followed by a solemn George Nakitsas and an expressionless Bill Knight, Broadbent did not mingle with the crowd. Standing on the stage, with Lucille smiling bravely by his side, he spoke very briefly, thanking the people of Oshawa for his personal success, the seventh time they'd elected him since 1968; this time, his margin of victory was a modest 4,000 votes. He was still optimistic, he said, about the results coming in from western Canada, and he was right. The New Democrats took 10 out of 14 seats in Saskatchewan and 19 out of 32 in British Columbia, winning more seats than ever before, but in Vancouver centre NDP federal president Johanna den Hertog lost by 269 votes to Tory Kim Campbell, a former Social Credit MLA. Broadbent had not hidden his desire to see the multilingual den Hertog replace him as party leader.

Broadbent spoke about his disappointment in Quebec, where the results were now final: Rémy Trudel, the New Democrats' great Québécois hope, won 15,621 votes but came second to Tory Gabriel Desjardins' 19,100. In any other election, 15,000 votes for a New Democrat would have been considered a breakthrough; most times, New Democrats did better than expected. Not this time. It was hard to believe, at this point, that they had once dreamed of winning 100 seats, that Eric Gourdeau, defeated in Quebec City, had once predicted the party would take 40 Quebec ridings "if the campaign is properly organized." One thing was clear: no political leader in Canada seriously seeking power could afford to be less than fluently bilingual. Broadbent's earnest efforts to speak French, as sincere as they were, were not good enough.

But one had to appreciate his bulldogged pursuit of power to realize how much he was hurting. Gone was gregarious Ed; his smile was tight and he looked like a wax figure. The strain of having to appear jaunty was so great that he seemed to be having a hard time speaking. Followed by the media pack and the police, he was hustled out of the hall into a waiting limousine. The car roared off into the night carrying a bitterly disappointed man who had allowed his hopes to soar.

The final standing were: 168 Conservatives, 83 Liberals, 43 New Democrats and one vacant, a Tory candidate having died just after being elected. (Redistribution increased the number of seats from 282 in 1984 to 295 in 1988. Standings after the '84 election were Tories 211, Liberals 40, NDP 30; after dissolution of the House in '88, Tories 205, Liberals 38, NDP 32, 3 independent, 4 vacant.)

Within days of the election, Richard Grise, the Tory MP elected in Chambly, was forced to withdraw from caucus. *Globe* reporter Stevie Cameron then noted in her column what she ironically termed "a coincidence" that occurred 22 November, the day after the election, when the RCMP started the raids on Mr. Grise and his associates that finally broke the scandal, so long delayed. The *Globe* revealed that early in November, Peter White, Mulroney's principal secretary, was aware that "Grise was 'worried' because he believed he was involved in 'improprieties.'" These activities allegedly included "the use of federal job creation funds for political purposes," and various other forms of under-the-table dealings and alleged kickbacks and payoffs.

"While the comments contained in this letter are my own, I can tell you that I've never seen such a level of disappointment and anger among our activists, leaders of the labour movement and candidates, at how the party strategists conducted the campaign," wrote Bob White, on a letter dated 28 November and made public 7 December. "We went into this election with the Liberals in disarray, with the respect for Ed Broadbent and the NDP at an all time pre-election high. What happened?"

Bad luck, rigid planning, inflexibility, personnel problems, bad timing, too few people for too much work, misreading the signals—it all added up to trouble. It was the free-trade election. It was the continued-dominance-of-Quebec election. And it was the first time in recent memory that an NDP campaign had gone belly-up. In the past, the NDP was expected to lose. Not this time. The New Democrats, poised to replace the Liberals as the number two party, were after big game. They needed significant gains in Ontario and a breakthrough in Quebec to live up to their promise that this campaign, their first all-out national effort, was going to be a tight three-way race. It didn't happen. The party's election planning committee made a serious strategic error. It didn't anticipate the passions that the fight over free trade would arouse, even though it was the NDP that initially mounted the sharpest attack on the Mulroney-Reagan trade deal. And when the election polarized, despite Broadbent's efforts to broaden the range of issues under discussion, the NDP had no effective strategy to disrupt the return to the rut of traditional Tory-Liberal, Liberal-Tory Ping-Pong, a game which was facilitated by media coverage.

Adman Lawrence Wolfe figures the New Democrats entered the race at a disadvantage of their own making. "The problem," he says, "was a lack of professionalism in advertising and media management. They hired party hacks out of misplaced loyalty. They were preaching to the converted." Now, the Wolf, Richards, Taylor agency would have dearly loved to have had the NDP account, so in a sense Larry Wolf has an axe to grind. Yet Michael Morgan and Associates, the Vancouver communications firm that designed the campaign, argued that it had responded to the wishes of its client; nevertheless, regardless of who is to blame, says Wolf, the NDP displayed the same ineptness selling its message and leader that crippled Michael Dukakis and the Democrats in the 1988 US presidential election.

"In Ed, the New Democrats had a very attractive guy, but he looked like hell in the commercials," says Wolf. "He came across as far more strident than he is in fact. They needed to make him more intimate and statesmanlike, but he seemed to be shouting." As for the famous environmental commercial showing a grandfather walking beside a lake with his grandchild, Wolf says, "it was pretty to look at, but so what? Everybody is against pollution. It didn't tell you anything about the New Democrats vis-à-vis the other players. Compare that to the Liberal one where two businessmen erased the border line between Canada and the US, a vivid image that positioned the Liberals strongly against the Conservatives."

In Wolf's opinion, "the NDP and Broadbent seemed almost irrelevant this election in eastern Canada. And in the west, it's not so much that they did better but that the Tories did worse because of that right-wing fringe group (the western Reform party)." Conventional wisdom had it that free trade was an economic issue and that the NDP had little credibility on economic issues. The party intended to lead with its strengths, talking about the environment, tax reform, daycare, social programs, women's issues, showing how free trade would hurt these areas. Broadbent was part of the team that made the decision about the NDP's overall approach, and later he would defend it. But the campaign ended up looking soft, unable to focus the fierce emotions raised over fears about Canadian sovereignty. As co-campaign director Robin Sears later said, "We should have approached the issues differently, in reverse order. We said, 'We need to protect the environment; here's how the trade deal hurts our ability to do that.' That didn't work because the trade deal had become the number one concern. People thought we weren't tackling it. We should have said, 'The trade deal hurts the environment; here's how.'" Sear's point is a classic example of how the order of expression of ideas affects the message received. It's not so much what you say, but how say it. Hard lessons.

The anti-free-traders won their battle but lost the war. Most Canadians voted against free trade and the Tories' share of the popular vote dropped from nearly 50 percent in 1984 to 43 percent in '88, but it wasn't enough to unseat Mulroney.

The Conservative victory demonstrated that Montreal is the political capital of Canada, and that the party that taps both the Toronto financial community and Quebec's "native son" commitment is unbeatable. This was the formula that guaranteed power to Pierre Trudeau for almost two decades. But with a difference: Mulroney's Conservatives took over Liberal turf by uniting the old Union Nationale right-wingers with the new Quebec business class which was, ironically, liberated by the social democratic policies of René Lévesque's Parti Québécois. At the same time, Mulroney passionately embraced Toronto's Bay Street power brokers who had always been suspicious of Trudeau's socialist sentiments. (Interestingly, the '88 vote showed clear class divisions: lower- to middle-income Canadians voted almost exclusively for the Liberals or New Democrats, while middle- to upper-income Canadians voted Conservative.)

Never before in Canadian history had the business community so visibly intruded in an election. Through the Business Council on National Issues and the Canadian Alliance for Trade and Job Opportunities, business leaders threatened disaster for the Canadian economy if the free trade deal didn't go through. They sent mass mailings of letters to employees, suggesting that it would be best for them if they voted Conservative. They held "information sessions," at which employees were instructed in the benefits of the deal. "In a grey-walled meeting room in a downtown Toronto office building, about 400 employees of a major Canadian insurance company are having what is called an open discussion on the Canadian-US free-trade agreement," wrote Mary Gooderham in the *Globe* on 15 November 1988. "The only speaker at the front of the room is a company vice-president, economist and self-proclaimed 'staunch free-trade advocate,' despite the fact that the meeting has been billed as an information session on the trade deal." The speaker was Leo de Bever, a vice-president of Crown Life Insurance, who said later, somewhat defensively, that "the reason for the meeting is not to round up the troops and deliver the vote."

This extraordinary rounding-up of the troops was repeated hundreds of times in office buildings and corporations across the country, leading to charges that some companies were intimidating their workers to vote Conservative. Executives defended their actions saying that they were merely countering the aggressive anti-free trade campaign funded by Canadian unions. Yet the so-called might of the union movement was much exaggerated: only 36 percent of Canada's non-agricultural workers belong to a union, and almost half that group belong to unions which are not part of the Canadian Labour Congress and stayed out of the trade wars.

Various business groups, not restricted by the same spending limits as political parties, invested millions of dollars advertising the benefits of free trade. One Liberal insider figured the business ads cost almost as much as each party was allowed to spend on the entire campaign, which was nearly $7 million. This was the most expensive election in Canadian history. In the weeks preceding the call, the Mulroney government outdid itself in what was widely perceived as a wild spending spree to buy votes. The estimated tab exceeded $16 billion.

The outcome was, after all, predictable. The Gallup poll of 1 October, at the beginning of the election, showed the Tories at 43 percent, the Liberals at 33, the NDP at 22—which was the way it turned out. Mulroney appeared to have the whole thing wrapped up, as the nation was glued to its TV screens, watching the public death of a badly wounded Liberal leader. John Turner's torment was, in fact, the main story at the early stages of the campaign. The Liberal leader continued to stumble, tripped up at every step by his party's own in-fighting. Reporter Greg Weston's book, *Reign of Error,* hit the bestseller lists, portraying Turner as a vacillating, bad-tempered, ideologically bankrupt leader with a nasty wife, a bad marriage and no political prospects.

At the end of the first week of campaigning, the pundits delivered their interim verdicts, which everybody already knew from watching TV: Turner was in serious trouble. Mulroney was incommunicado, protected behind the much-photographed portable plastic chains that kept the press at bay, heading a seamless campaign so polished that the Tory leader seemed to be sealed inside a transparent cocoon. And Broadbent was looking good, though his early campaign successes have long since been buried in criticism. "After a week travelling with the fast-paced, superbly organized Broadbent tour—it was not only the first off the ground but also went from sea to sea—it is clear the NDP has finally come of age as a modern political party with all the trappings of professionalism, financing, research and programming," wrote Hugh Winsor, the *Globe's* national political columnist, on 10 October. "This time, Ed" was the NDP's slogan. Observed Winsor: "And if it isn't the time for J. Edward Broadbent, he'll never have a better chance."

Yet the NDP had already made a serious error: Broadbent's opening speech did not focus on free trade, an omission that would come to haunt him, though George Nakitsas insisted later that in the campaign opener, "Ed talked about the future of Canada, about how we needed to be able to control our own destiny." But it was not specific enough.

Even with Broadbent soft-pedalling the trade issue, at the beginning it looked as if the trends were shifting in his direction. On 11 October, the *Globe's* main headline blared that, according to the latest Environics poll, the New Democrats had moved into second place, bumping the Liberals to third. The Tories had a wide lead, with 42 percent of decided voters, while the NDP was at 29 and the Liberals at 25. Broadbent couldn't contain his exuberance and made what his wife thought was his major mistake in predicting the demise of the Liberal party.

Television clips showed John Turner limping from a pinched nerve in his back, trying stoically to put a good face on a bad situation. Then the CBC's national news anchor Peter Mansbridge revealed that key Liberal strategists were plotting to dump Turner mid-campaign, a sensational story that was denied on all sides but that insiders later swore was true. Regardless of the truth, the harm was done. Turner looked more and more like a wounded animal who'd become prey for the encircling wolves.

Then came the great debate. Unfortunately for Broadbent, the French debate was first, on Monday, 24 October. Exhausted by his efforts to communicate in French, he moved directly into the English debate the next night, where the unexpected happened: John Turner did well. Turner's voice settled into his chest, his speech was cleared of the nervous chokes and coughs that had plagued him, and he looked good, Mulroney, as usual, seemed too glib—the usual "negative," in pollsters' jargon, that has dogged his public image. Broadbent, according to adman Larry Wolf, who is keenly attuned to image, "wasn't as well lit as the other guys. Ed looked to be in the shadows; it was as if the lighting accentuated the shadows around him. It was subtle but it hurt the way he came across." Broadbent did indeed look murky. In contrast to Turner's crisp white shirt and red tie, Broadbent wore a blue shirt, a dull tie. Then there was his performance, for which he received varied reviews. Lucille Broadbent, watching TV at home—she decided not to sit in the Ottawa studio where the debate was held because "I wanted to see that the public was seeing"—thought her husband did well. "Ed got his points across effectively," she said, "and I was surprised, afterwards, by the reaction of the media."

Broadbent confronted Mulroney on energy provisions and subsidy definitions in the trade deal, he pushed on daycare and the environment, and he personally felt he had done all right. "Any review of the debate footage makes it clear that Ed took every opportunity to blast the trade deal," wrote NDP pollster Vic Fingerhut in a confidential memo to the election review caucus, after it was all over. Fingerhut was trying to analyze why "the shift in our fortunes vis-à-vis both the Tories and the Liberals came as a result of the debate, and even more importantly the coverage of the debate." Fingerhut noted in "a cursory content analysis of the first hour's Turner/Ed confrontation" that "Turner spoke for 56 percent of the time versus Ed's 44 percent of the time, and the moderator (Rosie Abella) interrupted Ed/Turner exchanges on five separate occasions—and in every single one of them directed Ed (three in semi-scolding terms) to 'let Mr. Turner have his chance...'"

At times, Broadbent seemed to lose his cool and sounded too strident, trying to get his points across, while Turner stole the show, attacking Mulroney for selling out Canada in what was to become the most dramatic, most frequently re-played clip of the election. Turner had frequently said his fight against free trade was "the fight of my life," and the night of the debate he looked like he meant it.

"I knew it right away," says Bill Knight, of "that moment" when Turner confronted Mulroney and wouldn't let up, charging that Mulroney had sold Canada to the United States. Watching from backstage, Knight realized "the New Dems" were in trouble. Their worst-case scenario, an election polarized on free trade, was being born. Robin Sears also recognized the weight of what he, too, terms "that moment." When he saw it, he says, he looked over at Knight, their eyes locked, and they exchanged a wordless acknowledgement of the damage that had been done.

"There's no doubt that Turner did superbly in that moment," says Joe Levitt, Broadbent's close friend who watched the entire campaign very carefully. "Turner hit a raw nerve, the country woke up to its fears about free trade and all bets were off. Ed was put in a catch-up position." Unfortunately, Broadbent couldn't catch up. The post-debate fallout lathered praise on Turner and buried Broadbent by dismissing him from the fight. George Nakitsas remains convinced that the media shaped the post-debate atmosphere. The almost drooling coverage of Turner's performance seems excessive now when one looks again at the tapes; but there is no doubt that coverage had a massive influence in the week after the debate. One could argue that the media, having driven Turner to the brink of destruction, had decided to resurrect him, partly out of its own insatiable need for drama. A Liberal-Tory clash, which is the traditional rivalry in Canadian politics, was deemed essential to keep electoral conflict interesting. To find the central drama in an NDP-Tory clash would be to accept the NDP as a main stage player, and the media, says Nakitsas, was not prepared to do that. Its own vested interests were at stake.

This is a touchy subject among journalists, but there is no doubt that reporters and editors are conditioned into a sensitivity toward the leanings of their corporate owners. The result is a subtle form of censorship which pervades the media. In the United States, Noam Chomsky, linguistics professor at the Massachusetts Institute of Technology, has long argued that media owners actually function as propagandists for the ruling elite. The so-called free press, he says, is largely a fantasy, the role of the media being "to inculcate and defend the economic, social and political agenda of privileged groups," he writes in his book, *Manufacturing Consent.* "As Chomsky sees it," observed Martin Mittelstaedt in the *Globe,* "the media also have structural biases that preclude a full explanation of dissenting views through devices such as the short clips that typify television news or the short op-ed pieces in newspapers. Media conventions, he said, 'ensure that you cannot say anything unusual without sounding outlandish.'"

Anyone questioning why the NDP cannot break through negative perceptions in eastern Canada has to consider one crucial element: media ownership, particularly in print. Toronto's three major newspapers make no secret of their bias, which affects more than their editorials: the biggest and richest, the *Toronto Star,* is relentlessly Liberal; the smallest and most upscale, *The Globe and Mail,* is relentlessly Conservative; the fastest-growing upstart, *The Toronto Sun,* is also flagrantly Conservative. Similar allegiances tie Montreal's papers to either Liberal or Tory fortunes.

A study of the major newspapers' reportage of the opening day of the free-trade debate in the House of Commons demonstrates this bias at work. The *Globe* ran a big front-page picture of Mulroney accompanying a headline about why free trade was so good for Canada. The *Toronto Star* ran a big front-page picture of Turner and a headline about why free trade would damage Canadian sovereignty. The *Toronto Sun* ran the same of Mulroney and the wonders of free trade. Ed Broadbent and the New Democratic Party, which had initiated the opposition to free trade, were nowhere to be seen; a casual reader would have concluded that Broadbent had nothing to say about the deal, though in fact he had delivered a speech as long and as impassioned as those of his political rivals. But he didn't get the prime, front-page coverage.

It is not surprising that Broadbent's broad-focus approach to the election soon lost favour with the media. What got headlines was Mulroney's "managing change" refrain, which came from pollster Allan Gregg's divinations about the deeper worries of Canadians; and Turner's transformation. Even if Turner was "talking nonsense as a born-again nationalist," in the words of one of his corporate buddies, he was first and foremost, like Mulroney, a member of the elite served by the media. Thus the drama of John Turner's resurrection, his brave "Last Stand" against free trade, as the media played it, overshadowed Ed Broadbent's brief rise as potential leader of the Opposition. Not that Broadbent made all the right moves, but looking back at the coverage of the parties it is astounding how the media's shift, from pre-debate approval to post-debate rejection of the NDP campaign, killed Broadbent's chances. Turner, the media told us, had captured the public affection and mounting opposition to free trade—which the polls then supported, for a while. But support for Turner would prove soft and the post-debate euphoria for the Liberals would appear as a small blip. The irony was that Turner was unable to broaden his message; basically, he had not much to say and was criticized for running a single-issue, anti-free trade campaign. Mulroney, meanwhile, had the media on his side, the vast majority of newspapers, with the notable exception of the *Toronto Star*, being ardent supporters of free trade. The only real criticism Mulroney was subjected to was that his campaign was too tightly structured, that he was inaccessible. Accordingly his organizers responded by loosening things up; they packed away the white plastic chains and staged events showing Mulroney talking to real people about "managing change."

And there was Broadbent, being criticized for trying to talk about too many issues. The polls showed that people cared about the environment, tax reform, child care, and Broadbent addressed these issues. But the media didn't give him approving coverage. Instead, he was ridiculed for not attacking the trade deal enough, a charge that puzzled Lucille Broadbent. "Everywhere I travelled with him." she says, "he was always attacking free trade."

Later, *Globe* columnist Jeffrey Simpson would reflect a similar opinion. "From the first press conference," he wrote, "Mr. Broadbent never stopped hammering away at free trade. Almost every other issue he mentioned—the environment, child care, regional development, social programs—was tied to free trade. If Mr. Broadbent said it once he said it two hundred times that the reforms in those fields would be made difficult, if not impossible, by the free trade agreement."

Bob White and his friends, however, would not let the New Democrats off the hook. "We should never have let John Turner and the Liberals steal this issue," he wrote, "but somehow the strategists thought we could skate through this election announcing programs on other issues, when we knew free trade would and should be the issue." White hammered home his point: "Immediately after the leaders' debate, the largest NDP rally up to that time [in the campaign] was held in London, with over 1,200 people attending. I personally called NDP headquarters to ensure that Ed had the Fleck story." James Fleck, an ardent free-trader, owner of Fleck Manufacturing, member of the Business Council on National Issues, had recently closed down an auto parts plant and moved it to Mexico's so-called free trade zone, where cheap labour ensures bigger profits—and deprives North Americans of jobs.

As Bob White pointed out, "this was a major story in the London area.... *The London Free Press*, not a favourable newspaper, carried major stories on Fleck, including sending a reporter to Mexico." White's staff gave Broadbent's staff all the information about the Fleck case, "presented the documentation to the leader's tour, upon arrival in London. Ed spoke, and never mentioned Fleck." Astonished, White started to get really mad. Broadbent, in White's opinion, was blowing it. Afterwards, Broadbent admitted that the omission was a mistake. He hadn't been informed about the Fleck situation; if he'd known, he would have talked about it. But at that point, in the frenzy of a national campaign, he was captive to his staff. If they didn't tell him, he didn't know; and his staff was already having problems.

In the week after the debate, Broadbent slumped. "He responds badly when he thinks he's done badly," said an insider. "He won't sleep. He worries. It affects his performance." Normally an aggressive, upbeat campaigner, he had a hard time shaking the post-debate fallout. "Ed knew he'd been grandslammed," says Knight, who in the darkest hours that week feared the party could drop as low as twenty-three seats. "There was no question: we'd been hammered, hit off course. It got pretty hairy." Nor could they recover. One week after the debate, the news was out. On 1 November, a *Globe*-Environics poll showed the Liberals soaring to 37, the Tories dropping to 31, and the NDP down to 26. The next Gallup Poll, on 7 November, was even more startling. In what the *Toronto Star* termed "an unprecedented mid-campaign turnaround," the Liberals hit 43, the PCs 31, and the NDP was back down to a dismal 22.

The party was heading into its own internal crisis. On Monday, 31 October, George Nakitsas's father died. At 2 a.m., an exhausted Bill Knight, who was having trouble sleeping and wasn't feeling well, had just fallen asleep in his Ottawa apartment when the phone rang. It was Nakitsas, who announced grimly that he had to go to Montreal for his father's funeral. Knight was summoned onto the plane.

Nakitsas was torn apart. He hated to leave the tour during a rough period when the leader was in particular need of support. Broadbent was also in conflict, experiencing "cross-pressures of guilt and responsibility in relation to George's father's death," said an insider. "Ed had been away when his own mother died, he had been estranged from his father, so he felt guilty; at the same time, he needed George and he was deeply affected by what George was going through."

Broadbent says simply that "for George to lose his father at a time like that was obviously extremely difficult. In Greek culture, there's so much ritual around death and George was the only son. He had chosen not to play the traditional role. God only knows how that affected his psyche."

Broadbent had become dependent on Nakitsas and felt closest to him, perhaps, of anyone in his inner circle, partly through their shared commitment to a breakthrough in Quebec. And Nakitsas, according to observers, had submerged his life into his profession, a common political hazard. Some of his colleagues thought he had lost the professional detachment that is crucial on the field of battle. "George bonded psychologically with Ed in a way that Bill Knight didn't do," said one. "As chief of staff, Knight always kept his distance; you have to stand aloof in some respects, in that job. Sometimes you have to give very tough advice to the leader and you need a degree of separation to be able to stand back and be critical. George crossed over that line. His life was interwoven with Ed in a way that's not always helpful."

Nakitsas flew to Montreal. Knight flew to Toronto to join the tour, taking Nakitsas's place. Robin Sears was left in Ottawa to take charge of headquarters. Everyone was in rough shape, suffering from the post-debate blues. At that point, the NDP's tiny band of strategists, all red-eyed from working eighteen-hour days, seven days a week, felt overwhelmed in their fight against the fat cat Tories, whose financial resources afforded them such a lavish display of strategical expertise that there could be no question about who was the underdog.

Broadbent was aware of the stress that was wearing down the ranks. Before his departure, Nakitsas had found it difficult at key moments to step back and detach himself. "George really suffered at every up and down," said one campaign worker, who attributed Nakitsas's rocky ride to his high expectations; but then, all New Democrats were hurt by the gap between pre-electoral hopes and post-debate reality. The staff who'd been cocooned on Parliament Hill were, perhaps, suffering the most, the danger in that insulated environment being a willingness to believe their own best press releases.

"The hothouse atmosphere of the Hill is seductive," said one insider. "It's too easy to be captured by the mythologies of that world." And it was hard to follow the advice of veteran NDP strategist Cliff Scotton: "Never get so low you can't climb back in your chair," he liked to say, "and never get so high you can't sustain the fall."

Knight was not prepared for what he found when he joined the NDP plane less than a month before the election. Some of the key staff members closest to Broadbent were on the brink of mutiny. The press had not spelled out the personnel problems in detail, though "the Dobermans on the plane were hitting the bone with their bite," according to an insider.

Knight was able, through sheer force of personality—he specializes in laid-back, low-key, prairie-hayseed charm—to soothe ruffled tempers. "Bill gets an enormous amount of credit for handling that period," says Sears. "He took Ed for a vanilla milkshake and cooled everybody down. He pretended he was so relaxed that he was bored; in reality he was churning away inside. He got so sick from the stress that he coughed up blood." Asked about coughing up blood, Knight later acknowledged that it was true, "but it didn't happen until I got back to Ottawa at the end of that week." He chortled. "The strain got to me," he said, with some amazement at how bad it must have been if it got to *him*.

It was a dismal Friday in British Columbia when Bill Knight left the tour, having calmed things down, and returned to headquarters in Ottawa. Little did he know that a revolt would soon be triggered. Nakitsas had rejoined the tour the previous evening—some organizers thought he wasn't ready but he insisted—just hours before "the shit hit the fan in Quebec," according to Sears. Nakitsas, a Montrealer, fluent in French, in charge of Quebec, had been incommunicado, all week. Sears, who knew nothing about who was doing what to whom in the on-going battle within the Quebec NDP, had stumbled into a messy situation. Quebec NDP leaders Michel Agnaieff and Jean-Paul Harney represented a "gang of seven" candidates who, that Friday, "decided to articulate a new policy for the NDP on certain constitutional matters," in the ironic words of the *Globe's* Jeffrey Simpson. Broadbent, needless to say, was furious; NDP candidates do not hold press conferences to announce their bright ideas as official party positions. As reported in the *Globe*, the Agnaieff-

Harney policy "would allow Quebec to override the Canadian Charter of Rights and Freedoms in order to protect French language and culture. It would also allow the Quebec government to invoke the notwithstanding clause in the event that the Supreme Court of Canada rules that parts of Bill 101, outlawing bilingual signs, are unconstitutional." Which was what Premier Robert Bourassa did—invoke the notwithstanding clause to outlaw outdoor bilingual signs—when the Supreme Court subsequently declared that parts of Bill 101 were unconstitutional. But the position taken by Agnaieff's group sounded, in some English reports, as if the NDP was abandoning its long-held principles of support for minority rights. Party stalwarts were enraged by such a possibility, Broadbent was flabbergasted and "I didn't have a clue what was going on," says Sears. "George had been in mourning for his father at the precise moment they [Agnaieff and Harney] had cooked up this little masterpiece." That fiasco reached its peak on 11 November, when he was on a ship in the middle of the icy St. Lawrence river between Quebec City and Lévis. He was there to hold a news conference announcing a multi-million dollar plan to clean up the St. Lawrence River and the Great Lakes. But instead of being queried on the NDP's proposal for new water-treatment and sewage facilities, he was pummelled over alleged inconsistencies in the party's position on Quebec's controversial Bill 101, designed to protect the French language, and the use of the notwithstanding clause.

But on Friday, 4 November, trouble was brewing on the leader's tour, then in Nanaimo, BC. In Mingay's opinion, "when George was on the plane, the tour didn't work. When Bill came on, it worked. Those of us on tour lost confidence in George. He should have taken himself out of it, but he wouldn't."

Yet another senior New Democratic organizer rejects the attack on Nakitsas. "It would be a miscarriage of justice to lay the problems of the campaign at George's feet. There were misunderstandings, yes, directed at George, but I could never get to the bottom of the problems. George carried an enormous load and handled it well. The truth is, the campaign went off the rails after the debate. What can I say? Our reach exceeded our grasp. You make your best judgement, plan your strategy, organize your resources in that direction, commit yourself and you go. You hope the wind blows in your direction, because if it doesn't, and you have to change course, you can't turn it around in three weeks. That's the reality we were faced with. We had a wonderful campaign in the first three weeks, things were going well, then the debate hit and it started going badly for us. The media got fixated on Turner. Ed writing the Liberals off into oblivion didn't help. But there we were. You don't have any more resources left, you don't have a back-up strategy. I don't care what anybody says; you throw everything you have into it. We tried so hard we were bleeding."

Back on the NDP plane, Broadbent seemed sometimes to be carrying his tattered gang on his own back. He kept going, doing what he was supposed to do, but the strain showed. The campaign was in a nosedive and nobody was able to grasp the steering wheel and correct the flight. Later, he would refuse to criticize the performance of any of his staff. "The ability to shift course is in part a function of the people you've got at headquarters, monitoring what's going on. Our human resources were stretched to the limit, even beyond the limit. We had ten people where the Tories and Liberals had thirty to forty each. The more people you've got, the more ideas you get."

There were few new ideas emerging from the NDP campaign. The only detectable addition was a repeated attack on John Turner. From the New Democrats' point of view, they couldn't believe voters would accept Turner's hastily created image as a left-leaning Canadian nationalist, when his tract record as finance minister and corporate lawyer gave him a decidedly right-wing, pro-multinational tilt. But at this stage of the campaign, Turner's aggressive stance opposing the Mulroney sellout was popular with the public. Broadbent ended up looking as if a) he was bashing a defender of Canadian sovereignty, which didn't help his cause or b) he was sending undecided voters scurrying back to the Tories. Frustrated New Democratic voters wanted to hear Broadbent's impassioned attacks on the trade deal, not on Turner.

And so the NDP campaign entered its grimmest, final weeks. Not surprisingly, Nakitsas became terse and uncommunicative. He was unhappy with the performance of Arlene Wortsman, director of research; she was unhappy with his interference. Hilarie McMurray, Broadbent's chief speech-writer, found Nakitsas difficult to work with as did, on occasion, Anne Carroll. At one point, there were resignation threats. "Hilarie said she was going to quit," says Mingay, "and I said I'd quit if she did, but we realized we couldn't do that to Ed so we agreed to stay on. We hung in for Ed and Ed only."

"It's like military combat," says Robin Sears, describing the experience of going through an election campaign. "You're like soldiers in the trenches, getting bombed day after day. You smoke too much, eat shitty food, get no sleep, no exercise, get tense, and one day someone freaks out and can't stand it any more." There were explosions, confrontations, tears, hand-wringing, guilt. They all worried about the impact their dissension was having on Broadbent, the man who had to carry the flag and look optimistic at every public moment. He carried on "like a trouper," said Mingay. "Ed was incredible." But as leader, Ed was also responsible, and would later be held responsible, for the decisions that had led to this impasse.

By Saturday night, 5 November, the tour was back in Ottawa, conflicts still bubbling. At the Sunday strategy meeting, the usual discussion continued, on the surface; beneath the group politeness, individual differences crackled, with Nakitsas trying to keep the lid on and dissenters trying to push it off, buttonholing senior organizers in the washroom. But further eruptions were unavoidable; finally the key players had to pay a special call on Broadbent at his home that evening. One side wanted Nakitsas off the tour but he insisted he could manage. Eventually Broadbent was forced to accept a compromise "solution," which was that Nakitsas would stay on the plane and would be joined by Knight. That plan never really worked and Knight characterized his role, by that point, as "playing the part of the village idiot, with nobody ever really knowing what I was doing or where I'd show up next."

"We had decided," said Mingay, "that this was a tour through hell, we'd checked in for the duration and couldn't jump ship. So we stuck it out. But it wasn't a lot of fun." The NDP's major problem, said Mingay, was "the refusal to acknowledge that there was a problem. Whenever a difficult subject came up, discussion was cut off. No one was willing, or able, to say what was wrong."

During that period, Broadbent did something unusual: normal practice for Sunday strategy meetings was to exclude the leader so that people could be entirely frank. Two weeks before election day, Broadbent insisted that he attend a session. Much to the staff's surprise, he delivered a spontaneous and very moving talk in which he told them he was aware of the difficulties they were enduring and that he was very proud of their effort. "It was his way of saying that he knew more than we thought he knew, that he appreciated us—and it meant a lot," says Sears. Then he did the same thing for the clerical staff "and gave everybody a significant lift," says a staffer. Still, the pressures didn't let up.

In the *Toronto Star* on Sunday, 13 November, Martin Cohn, with the Broadbent campaign, wrote a devastating critique of the New Democrats' tour: "The New Democratic Party has come a long way in four years. Now, in the campaign homestretch, it's going nowhere." Cohn described Broadbent moving "in slow motion. Weighed down by a curious inertia, he behaves like a frontrunner protecting a handsome lead—anxious to avoid mistakes, loath to take risks...clinging to an outdated game plan that aims for power in a close three-way race." Toronto journalists were highly critical of Broadbent staging photo ops on a Sunday afternoon at deserted downtown bank towers.

The lesson Rob Mingay took from all this was "don't plan your strategy too far in advance; ours was etched in stone six months before the election." When the ground started to shift during the campaign, "we were stuck. The landscape changed and we didn't change with it." In the last weeks of the campaign, Broadbent's major "sound bite" was a tired refrain of street names, linking Mulroney to Wall Street, Turner to Bay Street, and the New Democrats to Main Street. It was a wornout cliché that revived the ghost of an old-fashioned party with a knee-jerk, anti-business attitude. The same old Liberal-Tory, Tory-Liberal tussle was continuing, with the New Democrats struggling as usual to alter the traditional alignments of Canadian politics. The difference this time out was that they had been in the game, but partly through their own errors had fouled out.

Still, there were some good moments: on Monday, 14 November, the biggest rally in Quebec in NDP history had 2,000 people cheering Broadbent in a standing ovation that gave him a jolt of adrenaline he desperately needed. "I've been waiting all my political life for this," he said at the time. Mingay, watching his boss's reaction, said, "*That* was a *moment*." Even the *Toronto Sun,* notable for dishing out a steady diet of socialist bashing, observed that "Broadbent delivered one of his finest performances yet." A couple of days later in Edmonton, on a radio phone-in show with Ron

Collister in Edmonton, Broadbent was again his charming, witty self. To one caller, who projected a Tory majority, Broadbent said: "I don't know what you've been smoking, but..."

Each day brought similar contrasts for each leader, days when it was clear no one knew which buttons to press to achieve the desired result; this election wasn't over until it was over. "People who say they know what's going to happen don't know what they're talking about," said a weary *Globe* columnist, Jeff Simpson, on Friday, 18 November, having spent fifty days on the road. But Allan Gregg had told him, he said, that a Tory majority was in the bag. Gregg was right.

At the end of November, Leo Gerard, Ontario director of the United Steelworkers of America, told 1,400 delegates to a Toronto conference that unnamed party strategists were to blame for setting bad campaign directions without consultation, joining a chorus of critics dumping on the party's failure to tackle the trade deal.

At the beginning of December, labour's top gun, Bob White, released his seven-page letter headlined "Lost Opportunity," addressed to "NDP Officers and Executive Members." To Broadbent's deep dismay—since he utterly opposes washing dirty linen in public—White's letter made front-page headlines across the country. White's conclusion: "We didn't fail by accident—but rather, we failed by design." The reason? Again, in White's view, because the party tried to avoid free trade.

"Unnamed party strategists" were quick to come forward and confess to certain errors. "We were amiss on our strategy to manage the trade deal," Bill Knight admits. "We didn't have a sufficient grip on it and I don't know if we could have. This is the problem: Canadians don't yet trust the New Democratic Party to handle economic issues. On social policy, we can't be beat. On trade related to social policy, we had a lot of running room. But on managing trade, we were in the cellar."

But if the NDP ever hopes to form a government, it has to confront this last, major stumbling block to power—and it must become credible on economic issues; a party aiming at power has got to persuade people to trust its ability to manage the economy. Indeed one of Broadbent's major contributions to the party, through the late '70s and early '80s, was his focus on economic development and industrial strategy, while advisers like Gerry Caplan kept pushing him to retreat to the NDP's traditional area of strength, social policy. It was Ed Broadbent who brought in political economist Jim Laxer as research director for a few troubled years before the 1984 election; their ill-fated partnership was based on a shared vision of developing the Swedish or West German model of industrial development for Canada.

Related to the problem of trust, in Knight's view, was the matter of candidates. "We needed every known, experienced New Democrat on the ticket. We had to look like we were playing for keeps. We had to be able to point: that's who'll be minister of finance." But the ideal minister of finance, for instance—Allan Blakeney, the former premier of Saskatchewan who had been responsible for balancing the Saskatchewan budget for many years—decided not to run.

An allied problem was the party's apparent, and traditional hostility to the business community, which seems outdated to young entrepreneurs and other baby boomers born in the computer age. Broadbent wanted to reach these people, as candidates and voters, but had to deal with their apparent discomfort with the spectre of "big labour," which also haunts the party's traditional power base in Saskatchewan, where farmers are suspicious of "unions dictating NDP policy." Union leaders are suspicious of the party's tendency to ignore them. Urban intellectuals don't like being referred to as "ordinary Canadians." Academics think the party is too populist. Purists think it's too middle-of-the-road. The Québécois see the NDP as a centralist anglo plot out to deprive Quebec of its freedom. The business community is suspicious of Broadbent's overtures, and labour wonders what kind of sweetheart deal he's pursuing. Broadbent, aware of the perils on all sides, tried to find a balance and failed to find a compromise that pleased any of his potential partners.

But how he tried. Personally he gave everything he had to a gruelling schedule that had him on the road, living out of a suitcase, throughout 1987 and 1988. By reaching out to all regions of Canada, he set the party an enormous task in terms of its ability to manage its own growth. Perhaps he pushed too far too fast. In Quebec, there were inevitable growing pains and shakedowns as the surge in party membership brought with it new personalities and rivalries as yet unresolved. Some of Broadbent's personnel decisions did not work out. In the year before the election, the handful of senior posts in the party hierarchy changed faces: Bill Knight went from chief of staff where many insiders say he should have stayed, to federal secretary. He was replaced by George Nakitsas, who many think did a better job as research director than as chief of staff. Nakitsas's old job in research was filled by Arlene Wortsman, a talented women who didn't have time to find her feet before being immersed in the frenzy of an election campaign.

Bill Knight figures that "after the Dennis Young blowout"—Young was fired as federal secretary, amid much acrimony, in 1987—"we'd been through a big family fight, so we wanted to patch things together. Maybe we accommodated each other too much. Maybe we should have had more arguments, before the election. But we didn't."

The campaign itself became a maze of sheer logistical problems, which overwhelmed the New Democrats. "In terms of dealing with the size of the campaign," says Knight, "we were still going through growing pains. We needed more experienced hands in Quebec. George Nakitsas should have stayed in Montreal to run Quebec, where things were very bumpy. But I remain convinced that one of our major problems was our lack of capacity to persuade Canadians that we had the team, that we could manage power politics." In the end, the phrase that Tory pollster Allan Gregg had picked up, "managing change," became what the election was all about. The Tories convinced enough people in individual ridings that they could manage the trade question better than the others.

Another major problem for the New Democrats concerned issues. "On foreign policy, because we were so worried about NATO, the international affairs committee was forced to hammer out a really credible foreign policy," says Knight. "We did the same thing with agriculture. We conferred with the provincial NDP in Saskatchewan, Manitoba and Alberta, and out of it came a very good farm policy that went down well in Saskatchewan. We should have had the same consultations on the trade issue. Sure, we went through all the party committees, but we didn't sit down together. We ought to have brought all parts of the party together in a big room and said, "This is what the campaign looks like, here's how we're going to do it.'"

One of the two most difficult moments of the campaign, says Sears, was "that moment—watching the clip from the debate, Turner against Mulroney, and thinking goddamn it." The second came two weeks after that, when the Quebec Gang of Seven held a press conference about language policy and Broadbent was forced to respond to it with no briefing beforehand. "I had the feeling, as someone once said, of a bucket of shit to the heart. A feeling of being absolutely done in. Oh well. As my grandmother said, 'Count your blessings, young man.'"

Stephen Lewis, son of [former NDP leader] David [Lewis], stepped forward and said the party should return to its traditional, honourable role of "conscience of the nation." The NDP exists, he said, "primarily to shape public policy, not to govern." His good friend Gerry Caplan, who personally dislikes Broadbent and was excluded from the party's inner circle for the last four years, agreed. Bob White took a different tack: "Defeat is not the issue here. Strategy, timing, direction and input are." White argued that the party must escape the clutches of a group of strategists who isolate the leader, and that it must change its tack if it wants to talk seriously about forming a government. Instead of trying "to finesse our way through," New Democrats, he suggested, must stand for principles while still aiming for power.

The party leader continued to believe that the pursuit of power was compatible with his social democratic principles; he would never agree to relegating the New Democrats to eternal fringe status. But Ed Broadbent was elusive after the election. He wanted to lick his wounds in private; he will never be a man who bares his soul in public. There was a lot for him to think about, apart from his own future. Bill Knight was gone, having accepted a senior position with the Canadian Cooperative Credit Society, a national umbrella group for the nation's credit unions. George Nakitsas, enjoying what he termed "the sanity" of family life, was leaning towards leaving too, especially given the criticism heaped on him privately. Robin Sears was back in Toronto as chief of staff to the Ontario NDP leader, Bob Rae. Sears was having difficulty settling in again with his son and wife, both of whom had disliked the long separation necessitated by an election campaign.

Criticism of Broadbent's direction of the national campaign continued, from inside and outside caucus, while speculation mounted about the possibility of the leader stepping down. At a weekend caucus retreat in January, MP John Rodriguez said Broadbent would have to go, then apologized for his untimely remarks. Windsor MP Howard McCurdy got into a shouting match with Broadbent, in front of the other MPs, over the party's failure to tackle the trade issue. McCurdy commented later that, "I actually heard a pin drop." It was an unusual eruption in NDP caucus, yet another signal that the second honeymoon Broadbent had enjoyed with the party from 1984 to 1988 was over.

Anne Carroll, who had performed so brilliantly throughout, had nothing to say about any of it: "No comment in any way, shape or kind." Such was her loyalty to her boss that her friends felt if Broadbent quit, she'd be gone too....

...What went wrong? For Broadbent, the furor about the "perceived setback" boils down to a judgement call on the overall approach to the election. The strategy was developed by the forty-member Election Planning Committee over a period of more than two years; every sector of the party had input into the process, including labour. And to repeat an old cliché, it seemed like a great idea at the time.

In every campaign, Broadbent says, "you can go back over what went wrong, the things we didn't do that we should have done. Because we didn't get the results we wanted, certain particulars were cited with varying degrees of intensity." On the basic thrust, "when the campaign is seen in a historical perspective, I think I would still defend what we were trying to do. [Allan] Blakeney phoned me two weeks after the election, at home, 'to celebrate and commiserate,' as he put it, and he said, 'I don't know, I wasn't at the strategy meetings, but I assumed you wanted to avoid a single-issue campaign, which would clearly have favoured Mulroney with the two opposition parties going at each other. So I figured you tried to put trade into the mix of a social democratic agenda to give people more reasons to vote NDP.'" Recounting the conversation, Broadbent leaned back in his chair and took a puff on his cigar. "I told Blakeney he was absolutely right. He said, 'If I'd been there, I would have done the same thing.'"

The key question that had lingered for Broadbent, after strategy meetings during the campaign, was, "Does it make sense to stay on [a pre-arranged] course even though the election has become polarized over a single issue?" He was told, he said, that "the basic argument of the EPC [Election Planning Committee] was to hang tough. I accepted that. Was that a mistake? If we were to change direction, what should we have changed it to?" For him, at the time, the all-consuming demands of the election, performing, travelling, spreading the message, following the plan, made him dependent on decisions made by his staff. Essentially, a party leader does what he's told to do during an election and has no time for second-guessing.

On the details of the campaign, he remained most disturbed about the misunderstanding that arose over the language issue in Quebec.

"A lot of negative stories came out about me being unwilling to defend minority rights," he said later, still fuming a little. "Bad decisions," he added, were made internally; his staff had not handled the issue well and it continued to bother him because of "my own deep commitment to individual and minority rights as well as to the right to the Québécois to protect their language. He was annoyed that some people tried "to equate the position of the English minority in Quebec with the French minority in Canada. You can't do it. It's not the same thing. We saw the nature of the problem on our campaign plane. There were fights between the English and French media. The French were sympathetic to our position but the English criticized me for abandoning our commitment to minority rights."

If in the past he had had a more convivial relationship with the press, because nobody took his party seriously, this time out Broadbent had to deal with a hard-edged scrutiny that subjected his every misstep to amplification. As his friend Joe Levitt said, politics is like a war and no one comes out of it unscathed.

The other part of the campaign that he will admit to not exactly relishing was the last two weeks, when his major message was a recitation of the Wall Street-Bay Street-Main Street theme. At one point, his handlers thought it would be a bright idea to take Broadbent to Wall Street in New York City and have him photographed against the backdrop of America's investment district. That plan was scotched, perhaps because a similar trip to Toronto's Bay Street had not played well. "I was as uncomfortable as anyone repeating the Bay Street-Wall Street variant; I'm uncomfortable with clichés," he said. But he was told it was working; it was the script he was given. The trouble was, in the heat of the campaign, "if it's not clicking, you don't know," at least not until the polls come out a week later.

The final irony was that the NDP finally played personality politics in one of the few elections in Canadian history that was not about leadership. They had an obvious asset, the most popular political leader in Canada, up against a prime minister nobody trusted, according to the polls, and a Liberal leader who was going nowhere. "Never had an NDP campaign been bound so tightly to the popularity of its leader," wrote Jeffrey Simpson. "In 1988, New Democratic candidates embraced the persona of Mr. Broadbent as never before, to the point of placing his picture on lawn signs instead of their own, and introducing themselves on the doorstep as 'your member of the Ed Broadbent team.'" Then, as Larry Wolf put it, the party failed to sell their leader effectively while the media endorsed the status quo.

Broadbent could comfort himself with the words of the man who inspired his Ph.D. thesis, John Stuart Mill, who wrote: "It is better to be Socrates dissatisfied than a pig satisfied." Broadbent is dissatisfied; he has, at one level, failed in his pursuit of power. He believed, as Bob White put it, that this election was a historic opportunity which has now passed....

...After it was all over, Lucille, asked if she was tired, responded, "I'm disillusioned. I'm very disappointed about Quebec, very apprehensive about what's going to happen from here on, with Bill 101 in Quebec, with Meech Lake, free trade.... We have very difficult decisions to make as a nation. There are no magic solutions. It's upsetting: the majority opposed free trade but we got it. I find it bizarre that Canadians went for three years thinking they knew what they wanted and then things turned overnight. Did they really want a fairer tax system or better daycare? Did they mean it when they said they believed there was a greater need for environmental protection? They seemed not to want to hear discussion of these matters during the election.

We have one million children living in poverty. Nobody discussed it. Maybe in the end all we need is a better jingle." Uncharacteristically cynical, she too was pondering a future outside politics, with the possibility of more freedom and more time to spend with her husband.

As for Broadbent, the 1988 election demonstrated, in negative terms, the truth of a Bill Knight axiom. "Politics is a tornado," Knight had said earlier. "The eye of the storm is the leadership. It drives the mass of energy forward but it's got to be calm at the centre.... If you ever start consuming the leader's energy, it's not working." During the latter part of the 1988 campaign, the disorder on the tour was so corrosive it consumed the leader's energy—at least, part of it. One long-time party worker remembers seeing the NDP plane coming in and out of western Canada through October and November, and "the leader was not being supported or complemented by his staff. In terms of leader management, it was god-awful." There it was: a campaign focused on the leader, in which the leader was drained.

Broadbent has spent twenty-one years in the trenches of political life. First elected in 1968, he became interim leader in 1974, was elected party leader at the 1975 convention, and has spent fifteen years as head of North American's only national social democratic political organization. It all seemed to lead up to this election, and the results were shattering.

But the principles that have made him still remain firm. "If you believe what you're fighting for—and I deeply believe in the need to build a social democratic society—then without egoism I can say that being the leader of the New Democratic Party is the most important job in Canada. Those who say we have to return to this idea of being the conscience of the nation, that's defeatism to me. We have a moral obligation to be passionately committed to what social democracy is all about in the world, and we have a moral obligation to pursue power. Because we're still the third party, we always have to establish a relevant reason for voting NDP. If voters are mad at the government, they vote for the largest opposition party, and that's what we're up against. We want to create a fairer world with more equal opportunity, and the people of Canada came closer to choosing us, I'm convinced, than they ever have."

JAMES COUTTS AND THE POLITICS OF MANIPULATION: THE LIBERAL PARTY, 1972-1977

BY CHRISTINA MCCALL-NEWMAN

o

I

The twenty-sixth of March, 1979, that miserable Monday when Pierre Trudeau finally called the federal election he had been postponing for more than a year, was not the kind of day James Coutts, his principal secretary, enjoyed.[1] Coutts had been working for weeks activating the battle plan for the campaign to come, and the last-minute details he had to attend to on Monday were dispatched with his usual efficiency but not his usual zest. Coutts loved to conduct every aspect of his life with what he thought of as style. He didn't like sandwiches at his desk, whiners on the telephone, pessimistic forecasts, or criticisms of Liberalism; and he had been forced to put up with all of these annoyances on the twenty-sixth of March.

What he really liked was having his secretary summon important Liberals to eat lunch with him on Sundays in the mock splendour of the Park Plaza dining room not far from his clever little house in downtown Toronto where he usually spent his weekends. Or ordering up mineral water with a twist of lime from room service at the Inn of the Provinces where he stayed in Ottawa during the week, before settling down in his suite to gossip the late-night hours away with a Liberal crony from out of town. Or sauntering over to enjoy a long lunch at the Chateau Laurier across the road from his office in the Langevin Block after a morning spent in agreeable tasks, such as

Excerpt from Christina McCall-Newman, *Grits: An Intimate Portrait of the Liberal Party* (Toronto: Macmillan of Canada, 1982,) pp. 137-60. Used by permission of Christina McCall and Macmillan of Canada.

advising the PM on an important appointment or consulting with the Clerk of the Privy Council on the cabinet agenda.

Ever since he had become Trudeau's right-hand man in August 1975, Coutts had made the Chateau Grill his personal lunching club. Such was his importance in the city in the late 1970s that his presence there had turned the restaurant into a more fashionable place to eat at noon than the Rideau Club or Le Cercle Universitaire. He was seen in the Grill as often as three or four times a week, always in the fourth alcove on the east side of the room, his fair head clearly visible in the gloom beneath the green flocked hangings that gave the place the aura of a bordello in a story by de Maupassant. He would sit on the velvet banquette like an Irish landowner on rent day, bestowing his benign interest on the waiters ("How's your wife, Pasquale?"), ordering the same food and drink (martini straight up, minced steak medium rare, sliced tomatoes, black coffee, and then, oh sin, oh sweet sublimity, a fat chocolate cream from the silver bonbon dish that was brought only to the tables of the favoured), dropping his pearly perceptions for the benefit of his guests, waving in acknowledgement as privy councillors and deputy ministers respectfully passed by, his clear eyes surveying, small presence commanding, the room that lay before him. It had taken Coutts a quarter of a century to propel himself to that table and he was shrewd enough to savour its significance.

He knew that within a few months of his second coming to the capital—he had been Lester Pearson's appointments secretary from 1963 to 1966—people had begun to say he was a political wizard, capable of concocting strategies that would have taxed the ingenuity of Jack Pickersgill [former Liberal cabinet minister] in his prime. In a way, Coutts's devotion to Liberalism was very much like Pickersgill's. He was a party man, first, last, and always. He served Liberal prime ministers because he believed in Liberalism. It was almost as if he had encompassed the party's past, sponged up its primordial lessons, and turned them into personal truths.

Outside the concentric circles of the Canadian elites, he was very little known before he came to Trudeau's office, though during the second year he was in town, journalists filing background reports from Ottawa who were accustomed previously to attributing rumours of intra-party deals to "the Prime Minister's chief honcho, Senator Keith Davey" took to writing sentences that began, "The Prime Minister's closest political advisers, Keith Davey *and* Jim Coutts, are known to have urged him...". Inside the party itself Coutts's name began to be mentioned more often than Davey's as the arch "fixer," the man operating in the vortex of power and operating surpassingly well. A dozen scenes were telegraphed along the Liberal information exchange: Coutts conducting the search for Margaret Trudeau the weekend she ran away from home with the Rolling Stones and gave her Mountie escort the slip; Coutts meeting secretly with Jack Horner, the Alberta MP, when he was skittish as a brood mare about leaving the Conservative party for a seat on the Liberal front bench, promising a Senate seat if all went wrong at the next election and a cabinet portfolio in the meantime; Coutts having lunch with Dr. John Evans, the president of the University of Toronto, helping him screw up his courage to run for the Liberals in Rosedale; Coutts gravely discussing with the Prime Minister what to do about the "j'accuse" letter that betrayed the indiscretions of Francis Fox, the Solicitor General and MP for Argenteuil-Deux Montagnes, who had signed another man's name on an Ottawa hospital form in order to obtain an abortion for a woman who was not his wife; Coutts ringing up Al Johnson, president of the CBC, during a federal-provincial conference on the constitution to complain that the proceedings were not being broadcast on the English network, a failure he described as a blow to national unity, which in his eyes meant a blow to Liberalism as well; Coutts dropping in on deputy ministers' meetings, Anti-inflation Board meetings, cabinet committee meetings, with messages from the Prime Minister, messages from the hinterland, messages from the party regulars, to be stuffed in the ears of his elders and his equals. All for the party's good.

Coutts, Coutts, Coutts. How did he get to that banquette in the Chateau? What did his success mean?

I I

Coutts was in his late thirties when he came to work for Trudeau, but his looks remained remarkably boyish, so that it was possible to imagine him easily as an undersized, rosy-cheeked fourteen-year-old, riding his bicycle down a side street in his home town of Nanton, Alberta (population 1100), on that idle summer Sunday in 1952, when the direction of his life was set. He had stopped to gaze over a hedge at the guests enjoying a backyard breakfast in honour of the Alberta provincial Liberal leader, Harper Prowse. The hostess told him to "Get off that bike and come on in, you hear, Jimmy! Harper's going to speak." Harper did speak, eloquently, about the miracles of eternal progress, the importance of "little people," and similar sacred touchstones of Liberalism, and young Coutts was hooked for life by the romance of the moment and the force of the Liberal myth.

Coutts's father, Ewart, sold insurance and real estate in Nanton, a CPR town fifty miles [80 km] south of Calgary, and his mother, Alberta, worked in drygoods and variety stores and at playing the piano in a movie house. Jim was a lively boy, imbued with Western hustle and fascinated by the goings-on of the townspeople, both proclivities that he could indulge while he made money after school running the projector at the Broxy Theatre or sweeping floors and setting type at the *Nanton News*. ("I've always had hunches about people," he said when he was an adult. "Somehow I just know what they are going to do in certain situations, and that comes out of being a kid in a town where you knew everybody and could watch their behaviour for years.")

Politics for him was a ticket to the world outside Nanton, where the goings-on were even more fascinating, where he could stretch his mind and perfect his talents, where a face like a kid in a toothpaste commercial and a mind like Niccolò Machiavelli's were both formidable assets—especially when you knew instinctively the advantages to be wrung from one and the importance of concealing the other.

When he was in his teens and twenties, Coutts loved politicians and politicians loved him. He was adorable in those days, with his red-blond hair and his china-blue peepers, getting up at riding association meetings to cut short the ramblings of his elders with his surefire jim-dandy ideas; volunteering to work for Joe McIntyre, a mine manager and local riding boss, when he ran for the Liberals in the 1953 federal campaign and reaping publicity out of the fact that there he was, a campaign manager, at the tender age of fifteen; fetching up at the University of Alberta a few years later as Liberal prime minister in the model parliament along with another boy from southern Alberta, named Joe Clark, who was a member of the Tory opposition. A few years after that, when Coutts was just out of law school and articling in a Calgary firm, he was elected national president of the National Young Liberal Federation and began to form the cross-country network of friends who were to prove so important later in his life.

By the time the federal campaign rolled around in 1962, when the Liberals were all set to save the country from John Diefenbaker, Keith Davey talked Coutts into running as the candidate in his home riding of Macleod. He lost resoundingly but cheerfully. (In fair times and foul, good Liberals are supposed to be cheerful, and Coutts learned early on how to be a good Liberal above all else.) The next year Davey, who liked Coutts's sunny style and reputed left-Liberal leanings, named him campaign chairman for Alberta, a job no one else wanted, mainly because the province had been hostile to Liberalism since 1921 when the United Farmers of Alberta had swept the Liberal party out of power provincially apparently forever. Again Coutts performed optimistically and well, helping elect Harry Hays, the former mayor of Calgary who had been cajoled into running by Keith Davey, almost against his will and certainly against his better judgment.

That was the campaign when Keith Davey's natural ebullience ran away with him and he thought up a series of gimmicky ideas, including the anti-Diefenbaker Election Colouring Book, which might have wowed them on the U. of T. campus in 1948 but left the editorialists dripping sarcasm and the politicians plainly hostile in 1963. When Coutts was sent copies of the colouring book—which featured a series of wiseacre cartoons of John Diefenbaker with captions like "This is the Prime Minister and his Cabinet. They have just disagreed with him. He doesn't like people to disagree with him. Colour the P.M. purple."—he promptly telephoned party headquarters in Ottawa from Calgary, deep in the heart of Diefenbaker's West, and said without preamble, "Listen, Davey, colour me *pissed off*."[2] It was entirely in character for Keith Davey to love the line and to go around Ottawa repeating it to everybody he met, with proud glee at Coutts's acuity.

Later that spring when Coutts was invited by Lester Pearson to work in Ottawa, on the recommendation of Davey and Gordon, he already had a reputation in Liberal circles as a wit, "a natural," "a great little guy." Few people realized how circumspect he had been at checking out what he was getting into and how determined he was to learn from every experience that came his way. He was twenty-five years old and he already knew the basic lessons about how to climb the ladder of success—the "greasy pole" as he was given to describing it—who you needed to know, how you ought to dress, the ways in which to ally yourself with other men on the move. He had asked his friend Tony Abbott, an easterner who had been working in Calgary when Coutts was articling in a law firm there, to introduce him to his father, Mr. Justice Douglas Abbott, finance minister in Louis St. Laurent's cabinet, long since gone to his reward on the Supreme Court bench.

Before beginning his job in Pearson's office, Coutts had trotted along to consult the senior Abbott in his august red-carpeted chambers about what to expect from political Ottawa. Abbott told him that a political assistant's job could be an invaluable training but to keep his mouth shut, and his eyes open, and on no account to stay at that level in Ottawa too long. Two years preferably and certainly no more than three. After that, Abbott warned him, you're liable to turn into an Old Faithful, to get hooked on the trappings of power and to be of diminishing use to the party and of no use at all to yourself. Best to get out and make a stake in the business world and run for office when you have an established reputation of your own.

Coutts stayed three years in Pearson's office and afterwards he remembered them as the most valuable learning experience of his life. From the beginning he was entranced with Pearson and his wonderful anecdotes about international affairs and cataclysmic events, his self-disparaging wit, his seemingly casual attitude to the power of his office, his liberalism. Pearson made Coutts feel like an instant insider and Coutts was able to watch the government system from the centre and to figure out how it worked. Weekdays he sat in Pearson's outer office on the second floor of the East Block, keeping the Leader's appointments calendar, making friends with the powerful, and the has-beens, and the would-bes, who waited there before passing through the ancient green baize doors on their way to talk to "good old Mike." Evenings he went to big cocktail parties and to little dinners and to have drinks in hotel bars, soaking up news of what was happening from middle-echelon civil servants, minor diplomats, Press Gallery reporters, Liberals from the outlands. He was friendly to everybody, from the political assistants in ministers' offices to the wives of his associates in the PMO, who found Coutts cosy, funny, and altogether—well, adorable was the word. He watched monetary crises and cabinet scandals and the rise and fall of the reputations of many men. He came to understand who did well at politics and who did badly and why. And he accomplished all this without making his elders uneasy or his contemporaries jealous. He was so popular, in fact, that when a television documentary called *Mr. Pearson* was made by Richard Ballentine at the urging of Pearson's press secretary, Richard O'Hagan, in 1964, nobody minded that Coutts seemed to figure prominently in frame after frame, though Pearson joked that it "looks as if my grandson is running the country."

By the spring of 1966, when the Gordon-Davey group had fallen apart after the disappointment of the previous fall's election, Coutts had served his apprenticeship. He announced to his friends that he was not going to go back to Calgary to practise law since he had met the tough admission standards of the Harvard Business School and meant to amble down to Cambridge, Mass., to get his MBA.

During the next two years at Harvard, Coutts made friends with other young and ambitious managerial men from all over the United States and Canada, went to seminars on corporate management and political power given by famous American academics—Henry Kissinger and Richard Neustadt among them—and finished his degree with creditable standing.

He then went to work briefly in New York City with the management consultancy firm of McKinsey and Company and, among other duties, took part in a study of the organization of John Lindsay's mayoralty office. In 1969 McKinsey sent him to Toronto. But functioning within a local partnership of a US firm was not to Coutts's taste and he soon struck out on his own with half a dozen other young men, some of whom had also been to Harvard. They formed the Canada Consulting Group, which was described in its handsome brochure as a firm of "management consultants to the Private and Public Sectors."

The Canada Consulting Group had a "business philosophy" which was formed on Harvard principles. It set out to meet the needs of "top managers," to provide them with "strategies...to keep [their] organizations effective in a changing environment."[3] In brief, they were hiring themselves out as troubleshooters to the men in the executive suites, advising a vice-president here and a deputy minister there, instigating analytical studies, proposing "concepts" that would help Canadian businessmen "turn the profit corner" and Canadian bureaucrats "actualize" their political masters' plans, using Harvard Business School jargon and Harvard Business School techniques to dazzle their clients a couple of decades after these notions had begun to wow them in New York and Washington.

It was the perfect setting for Coutts at that point in his career, and, coincidentally, the perfect finishing-school experience for a man who was to find himself chief fixer for the prime minister of Canada five years later. Canada Consulting allowed him to draw on his professional education and his practical understanding of Ottawa and to connect once more with the cross-country network he had made in his student Liberal and appointments-secretary days. It also taught him how the Canadian business world worked. John Aird, the Liberal senator and fundraiser; Tom Kent, the former policy adviser to Pearson who had become first a deputy minister and then the president of the Cape Breton Development Corporation; Paul Desmarais, the chairman of Power Corporation in Montreal; Tony Abbott, who was working for Jake Moore, the president of Brascan; Maurice Strong, executive director of the Environment Program of the United Nations Secretariat; Sylvia and Bernard Ostry, who were fast becoming the best-known civil servants in Ottawa, she as the chief statistician and he as assistant under-secretary of state; and Michael Pitfield, deputy secretary to the cabinet, who had all the right connections in English Montreal. All these people were old friends who were able to provide entrée for him. Coutts went to Africa to do studies at the behest of Strong. Coutts went to Cape Breton at the behest of Kent. Coutts stayed with Desmarais at his hunting lodge on Anticosti Island. Coutts met Aird's business friends and discussed with Aird, the prototypical old Toronto establishment man, all the little details of his career. Coutts went up to Ottawa to consult with government officials and conducted important studies of Central Mortgage and Housing and of the power of deputy ministers; and all his old friends in the bureaucracy, from Michael Pitfield on, were pleased that Jimmy was doing so well.

Coutts had a talent for other kinds of friendships, too. He loved the arts world and the media world and the glitter that went with both. His old friend Martin Goodman, who had been in the Ottawa Press Gallery in the 1960s, became the editor-in-chief of the *Toronto Star* in the 1970s, and Goodman's wife, Janice, an interior designer, helped Coutts decorate his Toronto house. His old friend John Roberts, who had been an executive assistant to Maurice Sauvé during the Pearson years, had become MP for York-Simcoe and married Beverley Rockett, a Toronto fashion photographer, and Coutts did his Paul Martin and Mitchell Sharp imitations at their parties. Coutts went to the ballet and to the commercial art galleries downtown and filled his house with Canadian paintings. Coutts was seen with beautiful women at beautiful parties and in beautiful bars. Coutts began to wear bright-red braces to hold up the trousers of his well-cut suits and to snap them at odd moments as a kind of deliberate put-on, lest anyone think he was taking himself too seriously or that he had forgotten his small-town roots. Coutts went on sailing holidays in the Grenadines, and to weddings of Harvard classmates in Virginia, and to hear Mabel Mercer singing at the St. Regis in New York.

And Coutts kept away from politics "like an addict keeping away from his drug,"[4] as he himself described it. Keith Davey was still his closest friend and he saw other Liberals, particularly John Aird, George Elliott, the party's advertising man, and John Nichol, John Roberts, and Tony Abbott, almost as often as he had of old. But, essentially, in the first Trudeau regime, Coutts's most important party connections—the self-described Pearsonian Liberals— "were out of the play," to use their euphemism. For four years the Prime Minister ignored them and they were lying low. They still talked politics constantly. They still kept track of whose career was on the up and whose was on the down, who had the leader's ear, who brought on his fury or his frowns. But no matter how knowledgeable they were about the party's affairs, none of them could have forecast in 1972 how radically the situation of Liberals would be altered after the election in October of that year when Trudeau was returned shakily to office as leader of a minority government with a margin of only two seats over the Tories.[5]

III

Within hours of absorbing the first shock of the Liberals' poor showing in the 1972 election, the Toronto lawyers Jerry Grafstein and Gordon Dryden were on the phone to each other urgently discussing what could be done "to save the party."[6] Though neither of them had ever run for office, both men were still almost as devoted to the Cause as they had been in the heady days of the new politics. Grafstein was now thirty-seven, a successful communications lawyer, the kinetically energetic, chronically enthusiastic son of an immigrant Polish Jew who had owned a catering business in London, Ontario; Dryden was now forty-eight, a dutiful tax expert working for the Unity Bank, still known for his loquacity, his loyalty, and his horse sense. What they shared was a kind of mystical approach to Liberalism. They were not just true Grits but true believers. For them the party was a vehicle for progress, a marvellously adaptable institution that was able to renew itself generation after generation for the greater good of Canadians. They were given to reminding their confrères, in bad electoral times like these, of Mackenzie King's rule of thumb that if you straddle the centre and lean to the left in Canada you will triumph. They believed implicitly that whenever the Liberal party turned right—as they thought it had in the first Trudeau regime—it lost its way and its natural constituency. Grafstein and Dryden decided during that post-election conversation that something had to be done to save the party from the forces of reaction, and they set about convening a meeting of Liberal friends in Grafstein's office on Richmond Street West to decide just what that "something" should be.

Many such meetings were held over the next few weeks with a dozen people in attendance at most of them—Keith Davey, Jim Coutts, Dorothy Petrie, Kathy Robinson, Chris Yankou, Martin O'Connell, John Roberts, Boyd Upper, Tony Abbott, Bob Kaplan, Gordon Floyd and, of course, Dryden and Grafstein.[7] None of them was quite as mystical in his attitude to the party as Grafstein and Dryden were—though Coutts once told Grafstein that it was his belief that there were two hundred good men in Canada, something like the Twelve Just Men of Judaism expanded into a great big Liberal team, who would come together instinctively when Liberalism was in trouble in order to put it right. But they all thought of themselves as progressive and ultra-loyal Liberals and they were all intensely pragmatic in their approach to politics.

They quickly came to a conclusion—worthy of Canada Consulting—that as a group they had three priorities: first, to re-establish their political presence in the party by devising a winning plan for the next campaign; second, to convince the Prime Minister that he needed the group; and, third, to get Keith Davey named co-chairman of the National Campaign Committee. They were tough goals because of Trudeau's known disdain for professional politicians and because of Davey's deflated reputation as an organizer.

The Senator was dragging with him, nearly a decade after the fact, the blame for Lester Pearson's failure to win a clear majority in the three elections of the early 1960s. It was an article of the modem Liberal faith that the leader was never blamed for disasters; the leader had to be beyond reproach. St. Laurent was not blamed for 1957; it was C. D. Howe's fault for being so arrogant. Pearson was never faulted for the failures of 1962, 1963, and 1965; it was Keith Davey's fault or Walter Gordon's fault for not getting him a majority; they gave him the wrong advice, they let him down. This same attitude was put to work for Trudeau after the near defeat of 1972. It was his advisers, Ivan Head, Jim Davey, and the rest of the technocrats in the PMO, who were blamed for having "isolated the PM from the political process," as if he were some passive object without free will.

Despite the drawbacks his reputation as a three-time near-loser represented, Davey was still the best-known and best-liked member of the Toronto group, both inside and outside the party. He possessed what the American senator Eugene McCarthy once described as "the perfect political mentality—that of a football coach, combining the will to win with the belief that the game is important." Even after seven years on the sidelines, Davey had maintained his network across the country among Liberals in the party's English-Canadian progressive wing.

That network was lobbied vigorously by the Toronto group on Davey's behalf in the early months of 1973; pressure was put on every MP, senator, and party organizer the group knew to "speak to the PM about Keith." Eventually Davey was granted an interview with Trudeau and went to his office, "briefed to the eyeballs" with a list of "seven reasons, Mr. Prime Minister, why you should *not* appoint me your campaign chairman." It was a gimmick that was "a real stopper—it caught his interest, definitely," Davey reported to Coutts on the phone.

As part of the same campaign to get Davey appointed, John Roberts, who had a temporary job in the PMO as a policy adviser, arranged a dinner for the Toronto group at 24 Sussex Drive. The Torontonians made their pitch, summing up what had gone wrong with the campaign just past ("no juice, no guts, no fight") and pledging that they would work their fingers to the bone and their brains to the nub in the campaign to come ("lotsa juice, lotsa guts, lotsa fight") if the leader saw fit to use their talents and heed their advice.

After a few minutes of this rhetoric, Pierre Trudeau cast upon the assembled company his cold, cold eye and said in quizzical tones, "Look, when my friends and I came into politics in 1965, we had a fire in our bellies—we wanted certain things for Quebec. But I don't understand what motivates you guys. What's in it for you anyway?"

The Torontonians were furious: they felt they were being insulted, treated as though they were nothing but ward pols on the make.[8] Abbott wanted to say, "Well, we had a fire in our bellies in the Second World War when you were riding around like a goddam fool on a motorcycle wearing a Nazi helmet," and Grafstein felt like hollering, "Listen, I was a Liberal—a *real* Liberal—when you were attacking Mr. Pearson in *Cité libre*." But they contained their anger, having promised themselves that they weren't there to score debating points, they were there to "save the party." Instead, they patiently explained to Trudeau what the party meant in their lives—the whole "vehicle for progress, circle of friends" number they did so well.

Trudeau was sceptical, but he was also desperate. Having first succumbed to a deep shock that lasted for several weeks after the election, he had roused himself to go over the 1972 results riding by riding. He and his French-Canadian colleagues, particularly Marc Lalonde, were convinced they were the victims of an English backlash against French power. At the same time, Trudeau knew he needed to take deliberate political action to win back the allegiance of English Canada.

He set about trying to mollify the various English-Canadian power groups in a way that caused Jean Marchand later to say sadly, "At first he was wonderful, like a philosopher's ideal leader. But after 1972, he had to become too political."[9] In his cabinet-making, Trudeau had appointed John Turner finance minister in the hope that the business community, which had been distraught over the actions of the previous minister, Edgar Benson, would be mollified. He had made approaches to the New Democratic Party with promises of Liberal legislation compatible with their goals in return for their agreement to maintain him in office despite the minority situation. And in response to the complaints of his English-Canadian MPs, he changed the makeup of his office, substituting for the technocrat intellectuals of his first regime a more politically experienced staff that included two defeated MPs, Martin O'Connell and John Roberts, as well as Eddie Rubin, his sometime assistant from the justice department. (Rubin had been practising law in Hong Kong for three years until his firm, Phillips & Vineberg, which had its head offices in Montreal, agreed to bring him back to Canada for the minority government's duration.) After many consultations and much thought, he finally decided in the spring of 1973 that the Toronto group was the best vehicle available to provide him with organizational and political advice, and he telephoned Keith Davey to ask him to be co-chairman with Jean Marchand of the campaign committee for the next election.

Davey was in the Senate lounge watching a Stanley Cup playoff game on television when he was summoned to answer Trudeau's call. After asking him to take on the job, Trudeau said politely he hoped he wasn't interrupting Davey's dinner. Davey told him he was watching hockey and added that the Buffalo Sabres were winning the game. There was an awkward pause at the other end of the line and then Trudeau said, "Oh, I see. What inning are they in?"

Davey loved that story. In fact, he loved any kind of story that showed up intellectuals as impractical, not to mention ignorant, about ordinary affairs. It reinforced his equanimity about losing the Senior Stick and dropping out of law school. "I'm no egghead," he would say emphatically; "that's what makes me valuable as a political adviser—I'm just an ordinary guy." That this was a fiction, that he was, in fact, shrewd, competent, and unusually empathetic, Davey would never admit. He figured his "ordinary guy" stance allowed him to josh Trudeau constantly, to tell him things that more pretentious advisers would have been too wary to suggest, to play the bad-news messenger no leader could afford to shoot.

In the year following Davey's appointment, Trudeau and the Toronto group were fused into an electoral team under the Senator's prodding, with Coutts figuratively hovering at his elbow providing expert managerial advice. In the end, Trudeau learned their tricks and they learned his.

Davey convened a series of dinner meetings with Liberal workers so that Trudeau could hear their complaints, their ideas, their inchoate yearnings. Trudeau learned to keep quiet when the yearnings got sufficiently inchoate to arouse his ire. What Davey was doing was trying to rehearse the Prime Minister for the stance he wanted him to take during the campaign to come:

he had to show an understanding of Davey's belief that "the public likes a politician to be a politician." Davey wanted Trudeau to project a double image of contrition (forgive me, for I have sinned in my arrogance) and pugnacity (but I'm the best man for the job).

For his part, Trudeau convinced Davey that secrecy was a virtue; under the pressure of constant reminders from Coutts, the Senator managed to restrain his normal impulse to talk openly to everyone he met, including members of the press. In the 1960s, Davey had been known in the Parliamentary Press Gallery as the "best leak in town," a much-repeated description that once prompted a sour reporter to reply, "Hell, that's no leak, that's a gusher." Now, in the 1970s, Davey went about his work in Ottawa and elsewhere with a lapel button stuck inside his wallet that read "Stifle Yourself," so that every time he reached for a credit card, his new behaviour pattern was reinforced.

During this whole period Trudeau was anxious that no "election psychosis" be created. He was busy handling a volatile minority situation in the House of Commons with the nimble aid of the House Leader, Allan MacEachen, and he didn't want an election triggered before both he and the party were ready. Behind the scenes, preparations went on and some of Liberalism's oldest precepts were brought into play. Patronage of one kind or another was used to dazzling effect, to repay the worn-out and to make way for the ambitious, just as it had been used for decades by Grits on the "Them that has gives and gits" principle. Dozens of Pearson Liberals were drawn back into active party work so that their skills and connections could be called on once the election writs were issued. Campaign jobs were roughly outlined and assigned in secret to the ablest people available. Finally, in early May the minority Liberal government engineered its own defeat and was released, at last, from the grip of the NDP, which as a condition for its continuing support in the Commons had forced the Trudeau cabinet into more progressive legislation in eighteen months than had been passed in the previous four years. The Liberals had indexed personal income taxes, announced a new energy policy, set up the Foreign Investment Review Agency, established the Food Prices Review Board, passed the Election Expenses Act, raised old-age pensions and family allowances, and initiated a precedent-setting inquiry into a proposed gas pipeline in the Mackenzie Valley, under the direction of Mr. Justice Thomas Berger, a former NDP MP from British Columbia.

Once the election was called, the Toronto group let it be known to the press that the Prime Minister had not wanted it at this time (which was partly true, since Trudeau disliked campaigns and never wanted an election) and pretended the party apparatus was in disarray. In fact, the party was so geared up for the election that in the next eight weeks the Toronto Liberals were able to conduct the campaign of their dreams, the campaign that rivalled in their fevered minds the Kennedy campaign of 1960 for sheer professional style. Davey operated from his Senate office in Ottawa, directing and coordinating the national and provincial campaigns by telephone, with particular attention paid to Ontario, the crucial province, where Dorothy

Petrie was in charge of the campaign committee, replacing Clem Neiman, who had the job in 1972. (Davey and Petrie functioned so well as a team that six months after the campaign was over, the Senator left Isobel Davey, his wife of more than twenty years, and Mrs. Petrie left her husband, an accountant named Bill Petrie, and both sought divorces. They were married in December of 1978.)

To fill what he regarded as the campaign's other key appointment, the party's liaison man travelling with the Prime Minister, Davey had told Trudeau that the best person would be Coutts. Coutts pleaded reluctance on the grounds that the job would take too much time away from his business, until Davey arranged to have Trudeau himself telephone to convince Coutts his presence was crucially important.

"When I heard about that phone call I practically choked," another member of the Toronto group said later. "It was so much a Davey-Coutts caper. Deals within deals. Everything Coutts had observed over the months we had been negotiating with Trudeau convinced him that to have purchase with this guy you had to be bringing him something, not just asking him for something, you had to have your own base. Coutts didn't want to look eager and he figured his return to a public role in politics could come later when he had built up his financial stake, unless the conditions were absolutely right. At the same time, Davey knew that Trudeau was worried about having Coutts in such a key advisory position in case his own staff was disturbed. Finally, everybody was finagled out of their fears. Davey got what he wanted. Coutts got what he wanted. Trudeau got the adviser he needed. And it was seen as an all-around triumph."

Coutts had known Trudeau when he was Lester Pearson's parliamentary secretary and Coutts was still in the PMO as appointments secretary. But they were a long way from cronies, and, like most of his Liberal friends, Coutts was wary of Trudeau. But, unlike most of them, Coutts knew how to make a personal connection with the Prime Minister. He spoke the language of technocrats, he had read the requisite American journals and the touchstone books, he had been to Harvard, he had travelled widely in Europe and Africa, he knew some French. He was tough, he was witty, he was smooth. He was able to bring twenty years of political experience in English Canada to the job. And if Trudeau wanted to be cold-eyed, well, what the hell, Coutts could be cold-eyed too.

What Trudeau wanted was to win, and Coutts knew how to help him do it. He accompanied Trudeau by train, plane, limousine, and cable-car for eight weeks and he talked all day long. He talked to Trudeau's staff, smoothing their feelings. He asked Ivan Head to write major policy statements and Jim Davey to give him advice on transportation policy, fitting their ideas into speeches written by an expert team that included Head himself as well as Alan Grossman, a former writer for Life and for Democratic politicians in the United States.

Weekends Coutts talked non-stop to Davey in the suite where they holed up in the Carleton Towers hotel in Ottawa. Weekdays Coutts talked to Davey back in Ottawa by telephone, as often as four times a day, describing what was going on, fitting in the "tactics" with the "strategy," i.e., what do we do today that will fit in with our overall game plan? Coutts talked to Liberals out in the country, that vast network of strivers and achievers who were giving their all lest the party lose and they lose with it. Most of all, Coutts talked to Trudeau, cajoling, persuading, informing, entertaining, reminding him at every stop who was important locally, what kind of one-line joke the crowd might respond to, which policy might attract notice from the press.

They made an odd pair, sitting at the front of the Liberals' chartered DC-9 campaign plane: Coutts with his fair hair over his coat collar, his face still rosy, his eyes as lively as a twenty-year-old's, Trudeau with his angular cheekbones, his expression opaque as a Chinese mandarin's, his mouth an austere line. Under Coutts's influence, Trudeau not only bounded onto platforms and made crassly political speeches every day, it got so that he actually enjoyed them. It seemed as if Coutts had made another friend, or at least an admirer of his considerable talents.

Looking back, Coutts decided that a crucial moment in their relationship came in the railroad station in Rimouski, Quebec. Very early in the campaign after the Trudeau entourage had just finished an old-fashioned campaign-train swing through the Maritimes, Jean Marchand and Gérard Pelletier, Trudeau's old friends, climbed aboard the train to report to the Prime Minister, like barons reporting to their prince on how things were going in this part of his fiefdom. Coutts immediately rose to move into the next train car but Trudeau called out that he should stay, and turning to his confrères remarked that Jim spoke French and they needed his advice. Coutts knew that the Liberal French never talked to the Liberal English about strategy: to be in on the inside talk about Rimouski as well as Red Deer was a sign of acceptance beyond his expectations. He also knew better than to give the slightest sign that he thought this was unusual. So he snapped his red galluses for good luck and casually sauntered back to sit down.

None of the other members of Davey's campaign team had roles quite as visible or as delicate as Coutts's but they all ran full out, their collective enthusiasm fuelled in equal parts by their lust for victory, their fear of failure, and the fun they were having together. Grafstein conducted a lively ad campaign from Toronto through a newly formed organization called Red Leaf Communications. Dryden, as party treasurer, managed the flow of money. Policies were made by an ad hoc committee that included Jack Austin, a lawyer from Vancouver who was now Trudeau's principal secretary, and Eddie Rubin, as well as Martin O'Connell, Davey, and Coutts. The policies concocted were highly political in content, coordinated closely with what Keith Davey was hearing from his professional pollster, Martin Goldfarb of Toronto, who had been talking to the electorate for months trying to gauge their concerns. During the course of the campaign, Trudeau promised easier home ownership for the aspiring middle class, more equality for women, fairer freight rates for the West, an industrial-development strategy, and a broadened social security system for the aged—all "progressive" legislation that was designed to attract the left-wing vote from the NDP. When he was attacked in Calgary over oil prices, in Metro Toronto over the planned Pickering Airport, and almost everywhere on inflation, Trudeau responded brilliantly, turning aside his hecklers with strength, charm, and some elegantly elliptical evasions of his past record. The party's most popular English-Canadian cabinet ministers, John Turner, Eugene Whelan, and Bryce Mackasey, were persuaded to stump the country tirelessly on the Liberals' behalf and the French-Canadian cabinet ministers were persuaded to stay home. (When a party worker mistakenly booked Jean Chrétien to give a speech at a riding meeting in Ontario, she was reprimanded; French power was being downplayed, though it was the raison d'être of the leader's political life.)

In brief, the Toronto group scripted a role for Trudeau and he, the consummate actor, was able to play it to perfection. They turned him into something they themselves could admire: a fighting leader, a gentle father, an adoring husband, and an all-around "beautiful guy" as his bride of three years, Margaret Sinclair Trudeau, described him in a speech in Vancouver. This was no arrogant intellectual, the Liberal strategists told the Liberal troops and the bug-eyed press. This was a misunderstood man, running as an underdog, a supporter of the little man, fighting against the heinous wage-and-price-control policies of Robert Stanfield, the Conservative leader, that awkward, not-so-beautiful guy, who was forecasting economic doom and who wanted to freeze wages to forestall it. Tory times are bad times, remember! Liberal times are boom times! Trudeau cares!

The whole campaign drove home this theme. The standard Trudeau speech, contrived to make him seem if not folksy at least accessible, ridiculed Stanfield mercilessly for his honestly considered solutions to the country's economic problems. The television free-time films, made under the aegis of Jerry Goodis, the Toronto advertising-agency president and a member of the Red Leaf conglomerate, idealized the new "loving" Trudeau. Goodis called them "straight propaganda, featuring ordinary Canadians in fedoras and glasses, ethnics, country people, kids—films full of uglies and one beautiful guy." By contrast, Stanfield was made to look old and David Lewis to look irrelevant. Neither was able to regain the kind of momentum they had achieved in the 1972 campaign, when Stanfield had been so effective attacking the Liberals from the right on their Unemployment Insurance Commission policies and Lewis had attacked them from the left, using his "corporate welfare bums" phrase as a basis for his critique of Liberal economic policy. Fresh photo and story "opportunities" were provided for the press and the television cameras: the three days of old-fashioned whistle-stop campaigning on the train in the Maritimes, ethnic group picnics outdoors in the wonderful June weather, shopping-plaza rallies packed with party supporters cheering themselves hoarse, hand-shaking and cheek-kissing with voters in outdoor markets, all with generous visual access to Margaret Trudeau, who was actually stumping the country with her husband for the first time.

Since Trudeau's marriage in 1971, he had been obsessively concerned that his wife, Margaret, not be exposed to press scrutiny. On a state visit to Russia in May 1971, shortly after their wedding, his press secretary, Peter

Roberts, had instructed the accompanying journalists on their first morning in Moscow that they were on no account to speak to the bride, and this directive had held, with a couple of exceptions, ever since. But now, Mrs. Trudeau, dressed as an artless young mother in simple blouses, skirts, and earth shoes, was seen on the television news almost nightly, speaking out on her husband's behalf, shaking voters' hands, or publicly hugging her nursing baby, her second son, Sacha, who was only six months old. Her presence inspired some of the most favourable prose ever printed about a Canadian public figure—prose that when read later, particularly in juxtaposition with Margaret Trudeau's own book about the period, *Beyond Reason,* sounded as much like Liberal propaganda as the party's own effusions. June Callwood, one of the country's best-known journalists, wrote in *Maclean's* that Margaret was "a perfectly preserved flower child" who listened at rallies "with an ethereal smile and rapt eyes full on her husband as he delivered his speeches," a woman "whose truthfulness and trust are like the artistry of a high wire act, all guts and beauty."[10] (This was written just six week before Mrs. Trudeau went to a celebrity tennis match in the United States and fell in love with the prominent politician she referred to as "my American," her attempted suicide with a kitchen knife at the prime minister's weekend retreat at Harrington Lake, and her subsequent admittance for severe depression to a hospital in Montreal.) "She was so flaky, even then, we were scared as hell every time she spoke during that campaign," one of the Liberals from Toronto said later, "but we were counting on her being mostly seen and not heard."

In Quebec, Mrs. Trudeau was seen very little and heard not at all, since her French was thought by the Quebec campaign committee to be inadequate and her manner a little outré. In fact, the Quebec campaign was left to Quebeckers, as English-speaking Liberals had left it since the time of Laurier. It was under the direction of Jean Marchand, as it had been in 1968 and 1972. All he took from the national campaign was the redesigned Liberal logo, a big "L" with a little maple leaf tucked in the corner, part of the Grafstein group's clever graphics for advertisements and campaign posters, a logo that said implicitly the flag is Liberal, the country is Liberal, we're the Government Party. All Marchand promised in return was that he would deliver the party between fifty and sixty of the seventy-four Quebec seats, a promise as sure as God makes the maple sap run in the Eastern Townships in March.

In sum the Liberals drew on nearly every political axiom in their considerable repertoire and their concerted effort worked. On 8 July the party won a majority, a victory far more telling than even the most optimistic among the original Toronto group had ever dared hope.[11] For the first time in twenty years and eight campaigns, the Liberals ended a campaign with a higher percentage of the electorate's support than the polls had given them at the start.

A few days later, a triumphant dinner was staged at 24 Sussex Drive in honour of the "key players" in the campaign, the kind of celebration Trudeau had never held in his life but that Coutts and Davey believed in as crucial for maintaining morale. A group photograph was taken on the lawn behind the house, to be mounted later on the office walls of several of the English-Canadian Liberals, their hour of glory frozen in an eight-by-ten glossy and framed in aluminum, with Pierre and Margaret standing in the middle of the group, hands clasped in front of them, smiling demurely into the camera like a Presbyterian minister and his sweet young wife at a church elders' picnic.

After dinner, toasts were proposed and speeches made, contrived of inside jokes and fulsome flattery for all concerned, and finally Trudeau got to his feet amid loud applause. He paid tribute with becoming if unaccustomed modesty to the party that had just rescued him from the ignominy of a defeat that had seemed almost certain since 1972 and then told a story that proved to the assembled company that he had indeed been "humanized" by the campaign.

Trudeau said that his first experience with politics had been through his father, Charlie Trudeau, an ardent Conservative. What he remembered best from the election nights of his childhood was his parents' friends damning the all-too-often-successful "Liberal machine" with righteous fury. These outbursts had so impressed him that until he was well into his teens he had visualized the machine as some huge Rube Goldbergian device that whirred, clicked, and threw off sparks which had a diabolical influence on the electorate.

Above the loud laughter this story inspired, Jean Marchand called out, "But Pierre, haven't they showed it to you yet'?" The Anglos in the room greeted that sally with even louder laughter. For them a "machine" was what had existed during the bad old days of C.D. Howe and Jimmy Gardiner, and that existed still in Quebec, though they would never have been so indiscreet as to say this in front of French Canadians. But *they* weren't a machine. *They* were a company of stouthearted friends with admirably liberal ideas, and they left Sussex Drive that night on a wave of euphoria.

They felt a new Liberal alliance between French and English had been forged. They thought they had taught Trudeau what Liberalism was all about and delivered him from the technocrats who held him captive in the PMO. They were certain he would henceforth run a government that would be consistently more "political" and therefore more "progressive," more reflective of his real nature and of their lifelong belief in liberalism.

What they did not realize was that Trudeau had never been the captive of anyone, that he had run his government from 1968 to 1972 in the way that he himself thought best, that his approach to people would remain elitist, and that, in fact, he did think of them as a machine. They did not know either that the next five years would turn into a bad dream for the Liberal party, that before those years were over they *would* behave like machine pols, and would argue desperately among themselves about whether their leader should be told that for God's sake and the party's he really must step down. But all that was far in the future. On that victorious July night in 1974, they all went happily home bathed in self-satisfaction, bilingual bonhomie, and the afterglow of the *vin mousseux*.

NOTES

1. Biographical material in this section is from several interviews with James Coutts, principally on 9 July 1974, 28 June 1977, 10 September 1977, and 22 November 1979, and from other interviews with many people over several years.

2. Keith Davey to the author, February 1963.

3. From a brochure printed and distributed by the Canada Consulting Group in 1970.

4. James Coutts to the author, 9 July 1974.

5. House of Commons party standings after the election of 1972 were: Liberals 109, Conservatives 107, NDP 31, Social Credit 15, Independent 2.

6. The material on the Toronto group and the election of 1974 in this section is from interviews with Grafstein (12 July 1974) and Dryden (13 Sept. 1977) and with Keith Davey (9 July 1974), Dorothy Petrie (18 July 1974), Eddie Rubin (28 June 1974), Jerry Goodis (5 July 1974), and James Coutts (9 July 1974).

7. Kaplan, Roberts, and O'Connell were defeated Toronto MPs; Upper, Yankou, and Petrie were experienced Liberal activists; Abbott, Coutt's old friend from Calgary who by now had left an executive job at Brascan to operate a furniture-stripping business in Oakville, Ontario, was thinking of running in the next election; Kathy Robinson was a law student; and Floyd was a young aide to Robert Nixon, the Ontario Liberal leader.

8. The encounter between the Toronto Liberals and Pierre Trudeau was described to the author by Jerry Grafstein (12 July 1974) and Keith Davey (9 July 1974) and expanded on later in a conversation with Anthony Abbott (1 October 1974).

9. Jean Marchand to the author, 6 June 1978.

10. From "Margaret's First Hurrah" by June Callwood in Maclean's magazine, August 1974.

11. Party standings after the federal election of July 1974 were Liberals 141, Progressive Conservatives 95, NDP 16, Social Credit 11, Independent 1.

MULRONEY 1988: POWER DESPOILED

BY JEFFREY SIMPSON

o

"I'm not trying to hang onto patronage. I think it's a pain in the neck. I mean to have to go and appoint an unemployment insurance commissioner in North Bay and then you find out that his sister happened to be married to the brother of someone who was a Conservative candidate in the provincial election, and all of a sudden it's Question Period time. We need that like a hole in the head."

- Prime Minister Brian Mulroney

Liberal senator Pierre De Bané attended Laval University law school with Brian Mulroney when new ideologies and fresh interpretations of old ones were swirling through the intellectual air of Quebec. The law school, De Bané recalled, featured students of every stripe: nationalist, federalist, separatist, Liberal, Conservative, Union Nationale, socialist, capitalist. Into this swirl of ideas and factions strode Brian Mulroney, friends with everyone in his first year and, upon graduation, still friends with everyone. All through law school Mulroney made every group believe that he supported its ideas. Almost every student fits into a pigeonhole; Mulroney fitted into them all, or so his classmates believed. It was, concluded De Bané, an astonishing performance.

This desire to be liked by everyone runs deep in Brian Mulroney's character. So does a willingness to act according to the demands of the moment, whether pleasing everyone at Laval, or stroking people as he moved upwards through Quebec society, or reassuring Conservatives in the 1983 leadership campaign that he would never support free trade with the

United States, or insisting privately that the Conservatives should drop the intellectual precursor of the Meech Lake constitutional accord—Joe Clark's "community of communities"—or promising Conservatives free drinks at the patronage bar. An almost morbid fascination with what others, especially the media, think of him represents the flip side of this intense desire to please. Mannerisms also reflect this desire to make a good impression: the darting eyes scanning a room; the smoothing or adjusting of his impeccable, conventional clothes; the ham performances; the blarney; the unctuous phrases. His Irish background is often advanced to explain these affectations. An abiding insecurity provides a better explanation.

While most of his politically minded classmates at Laval embraced the Liberal party or the *indépendantiste* movement, Mulroney, became a Conservative, a decision, whether through accident or design, that displayed courage. He admired Union Nationale Premier Daniel Johnson, the last of Quebec's old-style *patroneux*, but by the time Mulroney began immersing himself in politics, the Union Nationale was heading towards extinction, a fate with which federal Conservatives in Quebec had periodically flirted.

Nowhere in Canada did conspiratorial politics rage more virulently than among Quebec Conservatives. After the Union Nationale breathed its last, pathetic sighs, the *bleus* of Quebec held nothing but their memories and their resentments, which they often took out upon each other. The deaths of Premier Maurice Duplessis, his successor Paul Sauvé and then Daniel Johnson robbed them of their *chefs*; the defeat of Prime Minister John Diefenbaker deprived them of an erstwhile ally. By the late 1960s, the *bleus* of Quebec were leaderless and dispirited, a rabble army without a cause. Those dedicated to provincial politics chose other options; those interested in federal politics could join the Liberals, encourage the Social Credit, or suffer with the Conservatives.

A Conservative political rally in the 1970s or early 1980s combined low farce with pathos. On the seats, or at least those that were filled, sat the blue-rinse set bused from miles around, bribed with an offer of a free meal or a break in their daily routine. Around the periphery of the hall stood the organizers and hangers-on, men in shiny suits with bulging ambitions but few accomplishments, men invariably scratching for action in their own communities, peripheral players in the political game, quick-buck artists in the economy. A few preliminary speakers tried to whip up enthusiasm, usually with excessively histrionic performances, before the colossal letdown of a Robert Stanfield or Joe Clark speech delivered in earnest, mangled French. Having endured this agony, the crowd filed towards the buses for the long rides home and the organizers retired to a nearby watering hole to stiffen their pretensions with liquor. The media hustled to the phones to deal yet another blow to the Conservatives' already dismal prospects by reporting accurately just what a prefabricated fiasco the whole affair had really been.

Here and there, in the private clubs and hotel bars where Quebec's political players cut deals and swapped stories, the odd Conservative swam in the Liberal sea. A few lingered from the Duplessis-Johnson years; others had joined the apparently forlorn cause later on. The *bleus* of Quebec business and law had the cheques to keep the tattered Tory flag flying, pay the lost deposits, grease the proper palms, but they deliberately kept a low profile in the party and the province. They played politics in the shadows, their kinship apparently forged by the shared fate of being political "outs." A sense of Quebec nationalism seemed to provide an additional cement, for many of them rejected what they believed to be the astringent, centralizing federalism of Pierre Trudeau. Mulroney, however, insisted to his listeners at the Mount Royal Club and the downstairs bar at the Ritz Hotel that the Conservatives should stop playing footsie with Quebec nationalists, forget about "deux nations" or "community of communities," or any other sop to nationalist politics, and get on with replacing the Liberals as the defenders of a strong central government.

It is almost an iron law of politics that the more marginal the party, the greater the factionalism. The Conservatives of Quebec provided a splendid example of this iron law at work. Deprived through repeated defeat of the opportunity to run anything substantial, they squabbled furiously over the right to direct something inconsequential, namely themselves. In 1976, the intrigues and bitterness between the Claude Wagner and Brian Mulroney camps at the Conservative leadership campaign was the stuff, if not of legends, then of lingering and profound recriminations. Wagner's death left Mulroney as Quebec's only indigenous pretender to the Conservative leadership, although by dint of hard work and pluck Joe Clark gained a respectable toehold among Quebec Conservatives, a toehold he expanded into a bridgehead. In 1981, while professing undying fidelity to Clark's leadership, Mulroney agitated quietly for the stab in the back. At the convention to test Clark's leadership, the anti-Clark forces from Quebec whom Mulroney had helped to organize gathered in a Hull motel. They stayed clear of the convention until the hour of voting, when they slipped into the hall, cast their ballots for a leadership review, then retired furtively into the night, their mission almost accomplished.

Once Mulroney declared his candidacy—after Clark's second unsuccessful attempt to rally more than two-thirds of the party to his side— trench warfare erupted again in Quebec. Tales of instant delegates from the Old Brewery Mission in Montreal, payoffs, appeals against delegates' credentials punctuated the 1983 leadership campaign. As if all this did not adversely colour Mulroney's triumph, misty stories followed about offshore contributions to Mulroney from financier Walter Wolf.

Mulroney emerged from this conspiratorial, almost brutal, world of Quebec Conservative politics to lead the national party. Years of intrigue had taught him the value of loyalty, a loyalty that he required for his own political purposes and that his personality seemed to demand. Mulroney understood acutely from his Quebec Conservative background the pain of permanent exclusion from power; worse, the silent scorn of all the movers and shakers of the establishment. And he also appreciated, for he had witnessed this in Quebec, the factionalism of the Conservative party. Its failure to understand the discipline of power had stamped too many party supporters with the mentality of the "outs" whereby doubts ate at confidence, suspicions bred distrust, and convictions hardened into impractical, impossible positions the urgency of which bore an inverse relationship to their likelihood of ever being implemented.

Intrigue among Quebec Conservatives was never driven by ideology or intellectual conviction, but by personal rivalries and relationships sealed in telephone calls and secret meetings. In the politics of the shadows, networks of personal contacts counted for almost everything, and at this Mulroney excelled, for his capacity to reward friendship is matched by his intolerance of slights. More at home with a telephone than a book, more comfortable with conversation than briefing-papers, more attuned to the psyche of person-alities than to the stimulation of ideas, Mulroney became a superb network politician, reaching out to stroke his interlocutors with just the right words and the hint or promise of a desired reward.

When Mulroney stepped onto the national stage, he could not shake the habits of politics in the shadows. These habits, combined with the special needs of the Conservative party across Canada, perfectly suited the old-style politics of patronage, which depended upon a network of intense personal relationships, a commitment to personalities rather than ideas, and the need to expand political coalitions and mobilize participation by the expectation or receipt of rewards. Mulroney thus spoke from a mixture of conviction and expediency when in the 1983 leadership campaign he promised Conservatives an extended spell at the patronage trough. Genuine sympathy for a fellow political warrior, as well as the love of a good phrase, produced Mulroney's "there's no whore like an old whore" crack about Bryce Mackasey. It was entirely fitting, although supremely hypocritical for Mulroney to quietly select the chairmen of the Conservative patronage committees (PACs) across the country, during an election campaign in which he excoriated Liberals for patronage excesses and pummelled a hapless John Turner—"You had an option, sir"—in their television debate. It was therefore not in the least surprising that upon becoming prime minister Mulroney should have approached patronage in the traditional way. Nor was it surprising that the country, increasingly skeptical of patronage before Mulroney, then grossly misled during the campaign about his intentions, hoisted him on the petard of his own rhetoric and so forced the halting retreat from the traditional politics of patronage that marked the latter part of his mandate

In a broad historical sense, Mulroney and Trudeau, prime ministers during the transitional stage of the politics of patronage through which the country is still moving, were polar opposites. Trudeau arrived in office seeing the inadequacies of traditional patronage for mobilizing support and encouraging participation, and he tried through his early years as prime minister to temper or even eliminate some traditional manifestations of patronage. But Trudeau abandoned those efforts in his later years, then ended his career with an outlandish display that inflamed the country's reduced tolerance for patronage. Mulroney, conversely, entered 24 Sussex Drive without sensing how the country's tolerance had changed, let alone how he had accentuated that change, and so began practising the traditional politics of patronage, only to realize later, as Trudeau had at the beginning, that the old ways would no longer suffice. They were both stuck with a power their parties demanded be used, the use of which, without suitable and convincing explanations, simply irritated the country and widened the gap between the political elites and the rest of the population. Neither could summon the courage to explain forthrightly why patronage, properly and sensibly used, could assist the better functioning of parties and parliamentary democracy.

The Conservatives' provincial and national advisory committees on patronage took awhile to click into action. The PAC chairmen met in Ottawa the day before the swearing-in of the Mulroney cabinet. The PAC chairmen had to find suitable Conservatives to fill their committees, and ministers needed time to settle into their portfolios.... But by December, 1984, the PAC system was fully operational, and the first wave of appointments began. They were preceded, however, by a bit of political camouflage which pleased Mulroney greatly, since he proudly informed his staff that the appointment of former Ontario NDP leader Stephen Lewis as ambassador to the United Nations would blunt any criticism of the forthcoming Conservative wave. So would the appointment of former Commons Speaker Lloyd Francis, a Liberal, as ambassador to Portugal.

When the Conservative wave began breaking, followed by another and another and another, newspapers quickly reminded readers of the previous Mulroney hyperbole. "There's not a Grit left in town. They've all gone to Grit heaven" (9 July 1984). "They [Trudeau and Turner] have dishonoured the system...and it shall never happen again with a Conservative government" (12 July 1984). "Every morning that every citizen in the Sept-Iles region gets up and goes to work, remember that every tax dollar you pay to the end of your days will go to pay for the golden retirement of tired Liberals. It's a deceit and a sham. It has to be corrected by dramatic gestures and I propose to take them" (14 July 1984). "They [the Liberal appointments] confirm the old boys' network is back in town—that the boys are back and that the Liberal party doesn't want change" (25 July 1984). And, of course, there was Mulroney's justifiably famous line from the televised debate: "You had an option, sir. You could have said 'I am not going to do it. I'm not going to ask Canadians to pay the price.' You had an option to say no and you chose to say yes to the old stories of the Liberal party.... You could have done better" (25 July 1984).

Mulroney's "better" way consisted of replacing Liberals with Conservatives or filling vacancies with Conservatives. This began with twenty appointments on 4 December, most to Mulroney's personal friends or Conservative organizers. To the Citizenship Court, a favoured Liberal repository of patronage, went Helga Paide, for many years chief financial officer of the Conservative party of Ontario, and Huguette Pageau, the widow of Rodrique Pageau, one of Mulroney's *bleu* mentors in Quebec, who died of cancer shortly after the election. Two Conservatives from Sept-Iles, site of a Mulroney denunciation of Liberal patronage, received positions. On the last Friday before Christmas, the timing designed to minimize publicity, another long list of Conservatives appeared; it replaced eleven Liberals with Conservatives on the board of directors of Petro-Canada.

Three months later, Mulroney disbursed one of Ottawa's prized patronage plums: positions on the board of directors of Air Canada with their accompanying free passes. The appointments caused immediate political trouble, inside the Conservative party and beyond. Like all Opposition politicians, Mulroney had pledged to appoint only men and women of superior ability. And yet here was Gayle Christie, a perfectly competent municipal politician in Toronto and a Conservative, replying to a question about her qualifications by saying that she knew how to drive a car. And here were thirteen Conservatives, only two of whom had any demonstrable experience in areas related to travel. Worse still from the party's perspective, four of the new board members were PAC chairmen. Nine out of ten PAC chairmen had quickly received patronage posts—four on the Air Canada board, two on the Petro-Canada board, one on the Bank of Canada board, one on the bench, and one as commission counsel to a royal commission. The grumbling of the rank and file grew everywhere, because it justifiably appeared that the mini-patrons, the PAC chairmen, cared for themselves first, and only thought later of supporters or political clients.

Trouble, too, was brewing in the multicultural communities. A Carol Goar column in *The Toronto Star* praised the prime minister for appointing women and Francophones but noted the paucity of so-called ethnic appointments. The column caught Mulroney's eye—what didn't, in the media?—because he had given instructions that multicultural appointments should be a priority; he liked to recall that in the smashing triumph of 1984 only among Mediterranean Catholics had the Conservatives failed to win a majority of the votes. Historically, the Conservatives had done poorly among many ethnic groups, and Mulroney, like Trudeau, sought to employ the symbolism of patronage to appoint leading members of the ethnic communities. Yet the first spate of Conservative nominees reflected the traditional Anglo-Saxon and new-found French elements in the party. Peter White, in charge of the appointments system in the Prime Minister's Office, therefore created a multicultural advisory board in Ontario to assist that province's PAC.

That helped somewhat, but Conservative MPs in Toronto remained unhappy with the party's approach to the multicultural communities. In a draft report of a Metro caucus sub-committee, dated September, 1986, the members recommended a series of changes, including improved relations with the ethnic press. "High standards should be maintained for the news packages supplied to media outlets, a process the effectiveness of which can be maximized by 'spoonfeeding' the media. It is imperative that unfavourable news be displaced quickly from the headlines." The report reflected the traditional hostility of MPs towards any non-elected official dispensing or advising on patronage. "PAC and NAC should be replaced by regional caucus and MPs." Money, of course, provided the surest means to political exposure. "MPs may improve their visibility among ethnic groups by presenting grant cheques at events as often as possible." Money should be directed to politically favourable groups. "Liberal funding patterns among ethnic groups should not be retained, especially if they prove to be stumbling-blocks to the implementation of politically effectual PC funding." The lack of sufficient ethnic appointments rankled. "Increasing the number of ethno-cultural appointments should be recognized as an immediate priority, as appointments continue to be predominantly Anglo. Effective communication of multiculturalism policy and ethnic appointments must be seen to be as important as the policy and appointments themselves."

While Conservative appointments to boards, agencies and commissions—the new motherlodes of political patronage—continued apace, Mulroney wisely resisted the counsel of certain advisers to recast the civil service in a Conservative mould. Some Conservatives, searching for scapegoats other than themselves, fingered the civil service for having contributed to the Joe Clark debacle. They wanted heads to roll, just as Mulroney had promised in the Conservative leadership campaign. During planning for the transition of power, frontbencher Don Mazankowski (later the deputy prime minister) had recommended placing near the top of every civil service department a partisan assistant deputy minister to ensure that the civil servants followed the government's political priorities. This insidious scheme quickly evaporated when subjected to withering scrutiny by other members of Mulroney's transition team who correctly asserted that the civil service would follow proper ministerial direction. But pockets of deep hostility towards the civil service remained, even within the prime minister's entourage. Peter White, the appointments secretary who left after two years to work for business tycoon Conrad Black, was among the hard men of the Conservative party agitating for significant changes. White's imperious, dismissive attitude struck his more moderate successor Marjory LeBreton as so distasteful that she shredded some of White's memoranda.

Only two notable cases of political vengeance marred an otherwise commendable record. The Conservatives fired Edmund Clark from the Energy department because they considered him the author of the Liberals' detested National Energy Program. Robert Rabinovitch, who had served Clark with distinction in the Privy Council Office, was nevertheless viewed by Conservatives as a protégé of former Privy Council clerk Michael Pitfield. Rabinovitch, too, was fired in an act of senseless vengeance. But some Mulroney appointments—Montreal lawyer Stanley Hart as deputy minister of finance, Montreal economist Judith Maxwell as chairman of the Economic Council of Canada, Frank Iacobucci from the University of Toronto law school as deputy minister of justice—reflected a refreshing desire to leaven the civil service with top-quality, non-partisan talent, and not to use it as a playpen for Conservative worthies.

The same could not be said for Mulroney's approach to the diplomatic service. The temptation to use the diplomatic service for party purposes had been present from 1926 when Canada began sending its own diplomats overseas without prior approval of the British government. Indeed, even before that Canadian governments had sent as High Commissioners to London men with links to the party in power—Charles Tupper, one of John

A. Macdonald's closest political associates, was Canada's first High Commissioner to London. Prime Minister Mackenzie King made eighteen partisan appointments over twenty-two years in a service a fraction of the size of today's diplomatic corps. Prime Minister R.B. Bennett appointed two partisans in five years; Prime Minister Louis St. Laurent four in eight years; Prime Minister John Diefenbaker four in six years; Prime Minister Lester Pearson three in five years. Prime Minister Pierre Trudeau revived King's habit by appointing eighteen Liberal partisans over sixteen years, including four members of his personal staff and seven former cabinet ministers.

Three weeks after taking office, Mulroney wrote to the Professional Association of Foreign Service Officers (PAFSO), "The Canadian diplomatic corps is to be commended for the high esteem in which it is held by the international community. I can assure you the standard of professionalism so characteristic of our foreign service will be maintained by my government and reflected in the diplomatic appointments we will be making." This echoed his colleague John Crosbie's laments during the election campaign that "the diplomatic corps, once the pride of Canada and of the world...is being penetrated by a new kind of termite, the Liberal politician." The presumption, when combined with Mulroney's campaign promises, was therefore inescapable that the Conservatives would not use the diplomatic service for patronage. Instead, within the first fifteen months, nine Conservatives or friends of Mulroney received diplomatic posts. These appointments were all engineered by Mulroney himself, sometimes over the objections of Secretary of State for External Affairs Joe Clark. In one case, the department had decided to close the consul-general's office in Philadelphia as an economy measure. But Mulroney instructed the post be kept open for a friend, Pierrette Lucas. When the office eventually did close, Lucas became consul-general in Boston.

When Mulroney staffer Patrick MacAdam received a position in London already designated for a foreign service officer, PAFSO predictably cried foul. They sought to prove that Mulroney had more severely damaged morale within the service than had any previous prime minister. Although Mulroney had certainly used the diplomatic service for partisan purposes, PAFSO exaggerated the impact. Montreal mayor Jean Drapeau's appointment as ambassador to the United Nations Educational, Scientific and Cultural Organization in Paris was undoubtedly a poor one—Drapeau was too infirm to continue as mayor of Montreal—but not a patronage one, although elements of the media and Opposition parties so described it. Drapeau had never rendered service to the Conservative party, nor would he in recompense for the Paris post. The appointment of Mulroney's friend Lucien Bouchard, a lawyer from Chicoutimi and a former member of the Parti Québécois, proved to be inspired. Bouchard, although a diplomatic neophyte, adeptly negotiated the minefields of French politics, especially in organizing the first summits of La Francophonie. He became Secretary of State, then won a by-election in the early summer of 1988.

Bouchard's appointment reflected part of Mulroney's approach to building the Conservative party in Quebec. Mulroney delivered spectacularly on his solemn promise to the Conservative party. They won fifty-eight seats in that formerly hostile province, but everyone associated with that remarkable triumph understood that the party remained rootless in Quebec. A particular set of circumstances gave Mulroney the opportunity he brilliantly exploited—the departure of Trudeau, the factionalism of the Liberal party without his cementing presence, Mulroney's clear victory over Turner in the French-language television debate, a well-heeled and organized Conservative campaign, the recruitment of some excellent Conservative candidates, the willingness of Parti Québécois supporters to participate in federal politics after the defeat of the referendum on sovereignty-association, the knowledge seeping through Quebec that a Conservative bandwagon was rolling in the rest of Canada, and a desire for change. But his 1984 Quebec coalition, which included many provincial Liberals and *péquistes,* represented a dalliance rather than a political marriage. The Conservatives' overriding political priority therefore became to cement their standing in Quebec, for without a respectable number of Quebec seats, the Conservatives would continue to be Canada's minority party. For this cause, then, Mulroney deployed the instruments of patronage, sometimes in a heavy-handed and politically injurious manner, but with that overriding priority always in mind. There was, too, the prime minister's belief that the process of reconciling the former supporters of sovereignty-association with their Canadian future could be accelerated if a few of them received federal appointments. Within three years, former *péquistes* found themselves as the Canadian ambassador to France, a senior executive of Via Rail, an officer of Telefilm Canada, and a member of the board of governors of the Bank of Canada.

The Quebec PAC committee reviewed appointments from that province Thursday nights at the Ritz Hotel. Members would gather before the meeting in the main-floor bar, where various supplicants and would-be contractors hung about hoping for a word with Fernand Roberge and the other members of the committee. There was nothing terribly secretive about these meetings. It seemed as if *le tout Montréal* knew about them, and the notice board in the Ritz lobby indicated the where and when of the meeting upstairs.

The 1984 Conservative triumph in Quebec brought to Ottawa the widest possible range of MPs. The vast majority of newly elected Quebec MPs had never been actively involved in politics. They had often been recruited by Bernard Roy, Mulroney's close friend and Conservative organizer who all but dropped his solid legal practice for a year prior to the election to beat the bushes in Quebec for candidates. Some of these men and women were intellectually impressive and philosophically progressive. Person for person, the Quebec Conservative caucus could match in talent any provincial group within the national party caucus, a considerable testimonial for so green a group.

Yet at the margin of this inexperienced caucus, a handful of MPs and two ministers still thought politics could be played the old way, and their presumptions and activities got the Conservatives into serious trouble. To this group, the game of politics still revolved around spoils for supporters.

The Conservatives could count themselves fortunate that although rumours flew throughout Quebec about kickbacks, *ristournes,* and stern messages to contractors that without political contributions they could forget about further business, no newspaper could ever lay its hands upon a smoking gun.

Roch LaSalle, the last of the old-style *patroneux,* never hid his commitment to patronage for securing allegiance and rewarding friends. As a minister in Joe Clark's government, LaSalle said that Conservatives in Quebec "can look forward to being on the receiving end of government work and service contracts," because "patronage is a fact of life at all levels. Obviously, it was a tool that was used by the Liberals during their tenure in office, and I don't intend to pass up our opportunity. As you know, we haven't done very well in attracting Francophone votes, so this way we will at least be able to make some inroads with them."

Although the Conservatives won fifty-eight of seventy-five seats in Quebec, that left seventeen seats in Liberal hands, seventeen seats where local contractors and Conservatives might not know where to turn for advice. So LaSalle instituted a "Godfather" system in certain parts of Quebec, whereby Conservative MPs were assigned Liberal ridings in which to maintain political contacts. There was nothing startling about this development; parties had been covering seats held by Opposition parties for patronage and contract recommendations since John A. Macdonald's day. Michel Gravel, MP for the Montreal riding of Gamelin, took the responsibility for the Liberal riding of Hull where, among other projects, the federal government was funding the massive Museum of Civilization. On 15 May 1986, Gravel was charged with ten counts of bribery or attempted bribery, thirty-two of defrauding the government, and eight of breach of trust. The charges alleged that Mr. Gravel peddled influence "in Montreal, Hull and Ottawa and elsewhere in Canada between 1 December 1984 and 1 February 1986." Gravel's lawyer, however, had prevented the charges from going further than the arraignment stage, until Quebec's attorney-general, utilizing a seldom-invoked procedure, ordered Gravel to stand trial.

The Oerlikon affair, which broke in January, 1986, brought the immediate dismissal of a cabinet minister, André Bissonnette. It involved land flips of property near Saint-Jean-sur-Richelieu selected by the Oerlikon company after it received a $600 million contract to build Canada's low-level air-defence system. In eleven days the property changed hands and soared in value from $800,000 to nearly $3 million. An ashen-faced Mulroney told the press he had demanded Bissonnette's resignation and asked the RCMP to conduct a complete investigation. That investigation produced charges of conspiracy, fraud and breach of trust against Bissonnette and his top political organizer, Normand Ouellette. Bissonnette was found innocent, Ouellette guilty.

There were, too, pinprick stories which, when added together, furthered the impression of a party eager to use the spoils of power for dubious purposes. The assistant to MP Marcel Tremblay sent a "personal and confidential letter" to contractors in his Québec-Est riding informing them that the department of public works gave more than a billion dollars in contracts of which less than $30,000 went without competitive bidding. The letter said Québec-Est should gear up for a share of this money. The letter discussed preparation of a list of suitable companies, suitability being defined, among other criteria, by "subscribers to the 1984 campaign," and "members of the Club Brian Mulroney." Tremblay said the letter had been a mistake and apologized publicly for this "erroneous information."

Pierre Blouin, a Conservative advance-man in the 1984 campaign, pleaded guilty to accepting or demanding $70,000 to use his influence in the awarding of a contract for the renting of space at a Canada Employment and Immigration Commission centre in Drummondville. He was fined $3,000.

More serious by far was the resignation of Michel Coté, a minister from Quebec City whose political star fell further, faster than any other in the Conservative cabinet. The reason for his dismissal was failure to report, as the conflict-of-interest guidelines required, a loan secured from a personal friend. But the whole Coté affair was tinged with sadness, since the break-up of his marriage and failure to handle the pressure of Ottawa placed financial and psychological burdens on Coté. He had become the poodle of some prominent Quebec Conservatives of the old style, and his downfall cast the public eye, however briefly, on a part of the Conservative party in Quebec that knew nothing but the politics of the shadows.

The winning of contracts and the granting of permits had always brought businessmen, lawyers and middlemen to Ottawa eager by fair means or foul to win a slice of government work. In the nineteenth century, when Ottawa was a rough-hewn lumber town masquerading as a capital city, the contractors and lobbyists frequented the same hotels as the politicians, drank in the same bars, and wandered freely through the corridors of the Parliament Buildings searching for the right political shoulder to tap. Until well into the twentieth century, prominent politicians held directorships, collected legal fees or received personal campaign contributions from firms doing business with the government. A variety of embarrassing scandals, conflict-of-interest guidelines, more rigorous tendering procedures and new election-financing legislation had shredded many of the direct links between politicians and contractors, but the sheer volume of government work on offer made the pursuit of influence and information an abiding preoccupation of some corporate concerns.

In the Trudeau years a new breed of firms therefore took root in Ottawa, staffed by men with experience in government and the right political connections who then sold both to companies for handsome fees. The appellation "lobbyist" pained almost everyone to whom it was applied, for the word connoted a series of unsavoury practices they vehemently denied. By the waning Trudeau years, these firms had multiplied in number and expanded in size. The two largest—Executive Consultants Limited and Public Affairs International—took special umbrage with the appellation "lobbyist," since they insisted they supplied only information about government activities without ever seeking directly to influence a government decision on behalf of a client. They provided only advice so that clients could present a more effective case to the government. Or so ran the firms' credo. Staffed by former civil servants and political aides, the firms quickly amassed an impressive list of corporate clients.

The arrival of the Mulroney government sent these firms, heavily stocked with Liberals, hustling to recruit Conservatives. For example, William Neville, former chief of staff to Joe Clark, signed on as president of Public Affairs International, a position he left for personal reasons in 1987. But the most dramatic change occurred with the creation of Government Consultants Incorporated, a high-powered firm established by Mulroney's buddy Frank Moores, former premier of Newfoundland; Gerry Doucet, the brother of a senior Mulroney staffer; and Gary Ouellet, a long-time Mulroney friend from Quebec City. Despite occasional protestations of political innocence, GCI clearly capitalized handsomely on its Conservative connections. Moores, after all, had been among the leading schemers trying to engineer Clark's defeat by Mulroney. One day Moores would tell a columnist at lunch he had no special entrée to the Prime Minister's Office; the next day he would be seen dining with Ian Anderson, the prime minister's deputy principal secretary. He claimed he had no special contacts with the prime minister, but still spent New Year's Eve 1987 at Mulroney's home. He claimed he did not lobby—the word ostensibly pained him—but his firm did precisely that for a variety of corporate clients, even on one occasion charging money to set up a meeting with a minister. His firm threw a big party for Deputy Prime Minister Don Mazankowski upon his receipt of an honorary degree from the Technical University of Nova Scotia. Moores and his colleagues—and the smaller firms established by former Conservative aides such as Harry Near and William Fox—epitomized this new style of influence in Mulroney's Ottawa: pervasive, expensive and clearly based on the right political credentials. The test of that assertion was a simple one. Would these men have plied their trade with such success had a Liberal or NDP government been in office? The answer could only be a resounding no.

The ethics of these politico-corporate operators sparked periodic debates in Ottawa and the media, especially since some of them had jumped directly from government or political service into lobbying. And the ethical principles of Moores himself became the subject of debate when it was revealed that he had accepted a patronage position on the board of Air Canada, although his firm represented two of Air Canada's competitors: Wardair and Nordair. A row in Parliament and prominent newspaper stories forced Moores to resign his Air Canada directorship.

The swirl of Mulroney's friends trying to peddle their political connections around Ottawa gave rise to the charge of "cronyism" around the prime minister. This charge bore some weight, but not too much. Certainly, almost every friend and political associate of Mulroney got his reward within the first eighteen months of the government. But that sort of behaviour was hardly new in Canadian affairs, since those who had served Macdonald, Laurier, King and other prime ministers had invariably received their rewards. To have served Pierre Trudeau was a ticket to an appointment, if one were so desired. What gave the charge its heft was not that the prime minister surrounded himself with some friends and rewarded others, but that many of these people lacked the talents and judgment their positions demanded. Within a year, it became abundantly clear that many of those who had assisted Mulroney in winning the Conservative leadership were political liabilities, whereas those who had supported Joe Clark—the Establishment of the Conservative party—held the government together. Only when Mulroney rid himself of his friends and brought experienced and talented people to his side did the fortunes of his government improve.

The lobbyists thus joined the pollsters and admen, long since arrived in federal politics, to form the new triumvirate of clients at the top of the political patronage system, with the important twist that the pollsters and admen got their patronage directly while the lobbyists received theirs indirectly through retainers and percentages from clients. Predictably enough, the Conservatives moved quickly to give the government's advertising business to friendly firms, although not as quickly as they might have liked. The Liberals, who since the days of Mackenzie King had considered advertising a tidy reward for their own friends in the business, had left few hostages to fortune. Sensing the *fin du régime*, the Trudeau cabinet gave $26.4 million worth of advertising contracts to friendly firms during its last eight months in power. The Conservatives immediately fired the three Liberal admen in the Supply and Services department, put there by a special Treasury Board ruling that waived the normal practices for public-sector hiring, and installed two of their own. From there, the entire panoply of advertising patronage opened out to Conservative firms whenever contracts became available.

First to go, predictably enough, was the tourism account. It went to Camp Advertising, whose president happened to be Norman Atkins, Conservative campaign chairman. Another early winner turned out to be Lawson Murray Ltd. for placing advertisements for government bonds. The bonds program, of course, is the responsibility of the Finance department, and the Opposition immediately cried personal favouritisrn when they discovered that Lawson Murray's principal was none other than Finance Minister Michael Wilson's brother-in-law. But then, family ties did seem to carry weight with Conservative ministers. Joe Clark's brother-in-law was named legal counsel for all federal government work associated with the Calgary Olympics.

These sorts of patronage earned the prerequisite howls from the Opposition and headlines in the media. Although each incident was quickly forgotten, the cumulative impression of rampant favouritism stuck like a barnacle to the Mulroney government. Then the Sinclair Stevens affair attracted intermittent headlines from May, 1986 to February, 1987, and made another splash when a judicial inquiry under Judge William Parker found that Stevens had been in repeated conflicts of interest as a senior member of the Mulroney cabinet.

Sinclair Stevens was an odd duck in the Conservative party and, as such, considerably misunderstood. He acquired the nickname "Slasher" in the Clark government for his attempt to reduce the size of the civil service. The media depicted him as a right-winger in the party; in fact, he was nothing more than a pragmatist. Making deals, rather than propounding ideological nostrums, made Stevens happy. He often got angry with bureaucrats, red tape, even ministerial colleagues who questioned the deals he made as Minister of Regional Industrial Expansion. He professed to distrust big government, but he delighted in using government as a spur to economic growth or a partner with private concerns. An MP from an affluent riding north of Toronto, he developed a deep interest in Cape Breton, one of the country's most depressed economic areas.

Stevens, who smiled easily and had about him a certain bonhomie, nevertheless remained a loner in the Conservative party. Although a frontbencher in Clark's government, he was never close to the prime minister, and when the Conservatives lost power in 1980, he quietly joined the anti-Clark group within the party. In 1983, Stevens was the only prominent frontbencher from the Clark government who actively supported Brian Mulroney. He wished to be named finance minister, but his poor reputation on Bay Street—a holdover from his days with the ill-fated Western Bank—destroyed that possibility. He settled instead for what Mulroney offered, and quickly began making deals.

Unfortunately, as the Parker Inquiry report documented in numbing detail, while making deals for the government he also dealt with private interests on behalf of the York Centre group of companies he headed. On fourteen occasions, Judge Parker found, Stevens violated conflict-of interest guidelines.

In the long sweep of Canadian history, Sinclair Stevens' conflicts of interest might well be considered almost the norm. Until well on into this century, leading politicians routinely carried on their business dealings while cabinet ministers, and the question of conflict of interest came to be asked only when their ministerial decisions clearly produced private advantage. They had to earn their bread elsewhere because politics was a part-time, poorly paid occupation. Prime ministers accepted trust funds, premiers sat on boards of directors, cabinet ministers carried on legal practices, senators openly pressed business interests. But by the 1960s, especially in the wake of the mini-scandals that buffeted the Pearson government, a new attitude took hold: The law of Caesar's wife applied to politicians. Conflict-of-interest guidelines arrived under Pierre Trudeau, but they remained just that: guidelines instructing ministers how to arrange their personal affairs to avoid the reality or appearance of a conflict of interest. A major study under former Liberal cabinet minister Mitchell Sharp and former Conservative minister Michael Starr examined the issue again and recommended a commissioner of ethics to whom ministers could turn for advice. Then Mulroney introduced a conflict-of-interest code. All of these guidelines, studies and codes stopped short of mandatory full disclosure, on the theory that a balance should be struck between protecting the public interest and the private affairs of ministers.

Judge Parker, however, rejected the balance, recommending instead full disclosure and, if necessary, divestiture of assets. He also fully sanctioned an approach to conflict of interest whereby the potential of an appearance of a conflict of interest sufficed to place a minister in an unacceptable position. It was no longer enough, argued the judge, for conflicts to be real or even apparent; that a situation had the potential for creating real or apparent conflicts would condemn a minister to a conflict of interest. This exceptionally wide approach, which until recently would have been beyond the comprehension of most politicians, received almost universal acclaim in the media, reflecting inadequate analysis and the kind of rigid moralism adopted by those outside politics.

A Gallup poll in October, 1986, with the Stevens affair fresh in the public mind, showed that forty-nine percent of respondents believed "favouritism and corruption" were increasing in Ottawa, compared with thirteen percent who thought it was in decline. However, previous polls—in 1974 and 1966— had also found many more people who believed favouritism and corruption were rising rather than declining. If these numbers showed anything, it was not so much that the Mulroney government had soured people on the integrity of the political process, but that for several decades confidence in the integrity of politicians, and politics generally, had been on the wane. Although the disappointments of the Mulroney government undoubtedly contributed to this erosion, the sapping of public faith in politicians and their institutions—Parliament and the political parties—had been growing apace for decades. In response to this decline, and to the poor image of his government, Mulroney introduced conflict-of-interest legislation which fortunately stopped short of full disclosure. It envisaged a commission of ethics responsible to Parliament to which members would be forced to report their personal affairs. If necessary, the commission could then decide to make public such affairs as it deemed appropriate.

The decline of commitment to political parties holds profound consequences for all aspects of political life, including the practice of patronage. As government has grown, the influence of parties on the government they purport to run has shrunk. Quasi-judicial or largely independent agencies, over which the cabinet has limited review powers, hold sway in crucial areas of economic activity: communications, transportation, regional development, international trade. A minister in a sprawling department such as Transport must acknowledge, if honesty counts for anything, that with all his other ministerial responsibilities and the plethora of cabinet committee meetings requiring his attendance, he can only immerse himself in a handful of departmental dossiers. Further and further down the bureaucratic hierarchy are found the pressure points for the special interests and the trade associations or lobbyists who represent them. In the post-Charter of Rights era, even the courts beckon citizens or groups to press their claims in the legal rather than the political arena.

The atomization of politics breaks down the coalition-building functions of parties, because an increasing number of individuals participate through single-interest groups. Parties, by definition, force compromises upon their members; single-interest groups try to play for all or nothing. The proliferation of these groups may have increased democratic participation, but the participation lies outside political parties. They seek the achievement of their alms by influencing key bureaucrats, public opinion through the media, the courts through legal arguments, government tribunals through represen- tations—and political parties not by joining but by often relentless letter-writing, personal contacts, confrontational meetings, position papers, conferences and whatever other means they have the wit to devise.

Paradoxically, the parties have unwittingly assisted in their own decline by offering massive amounts of state funding to all manner of interest groups, a development that exploded in the early Trudeau years when "participatory democracy" was much in vogue. The consequence for natives, women's groups, linguistic minorities—to name just a few examples—was that members channelled their energies and offered their allegiance not to the government that funded them, and the parties vying for control of that government, but to the organizations themselves. Even large corporations, in the era after reforms to the *Elections Act*, often spent more money on trade associations, the Business Council on National Issues, or lobbying firms than they did on contributing to the non-socialist political parties. For them political contributions are a kind of civic duty, whereas the money spent on lobbyists and the like can directly reward self-interest.

In such circumstances, the old political patronage of material or honorific rewards seemed an increasingly feeble inducement to participation. Patronage worked best as a mobilizer when governing was largely about accommodating elites, brokering interests, winning the loyalty of key players who held sway over large numbers of followers. But as elite accommodation faltered in face of the pursuit of self-interest through single-issue groups, the massive, intermittent but utterly vicarious participation of television viewers, and the burgeoning bureaucratization of government, the mobilizing capabilities of patronage diminished. Even worse, patronage came to be viewed as a vestigial remnant of a political culture that only some of the political actors themselves seemed to think still existed.

The gap between demand for place and supply of positions, a gap that had tormented every Canadian political leader and driven a few of them to rage and despair, remained, and a new gap opened. The political elites insisted on using patronage for themselves. The rest of the population, finding they could no longer dream of receiving any material benefit or preferential treatment through the exercise of political discretion, were attracted by other inducements for political participation. This new gap so terrified politicians that none of them dared explain that political patronage, sensibly and moderately used, could still be justified. None of them dared argue that the very explosion of government made political control more problematic, and that therefore men and women who shared the broad philosophy and specific goals of the winning party might help further the democratically expressed desire for new approaches. Nor would they dare say that patronage often advanced the cause of minorities more rapidly than any other political tool, that an appointment could more quickly offer opportunities for participation in public life than the vagaries of electoral politics, and that an abiding purpose of national parties in such a diverse country lay in their integrative function, a function assisted by patronage.

Nor would they dare insist that the satisfaction of a reward held the feet of some men and women to the political fire, and by so doing sustained their commitment to the public life of their country.

In Opposition no politicians would dare do anything but feed the public outrage about patronage, an outrage which they would then confront themselves if given a chance to govern. Instead, modern-day politicians treated patronage as a matter of raw justice and even retribution. They refused in Opposition to explain honestly how they proposed to handle patronage; in government they therefore could not compellingly defend what they had previously lambasted. So patronage remained, like pornography, a subject closed to rational discourse, obscured by perfervid rhetoric, clouded by an enveloping hypocrisy, the peep show of politics.

The decline of patronage in the face of urbanization, modernization, better education, television, an aroused public opinion, among other factors, left parties in a terrible predicament. Many of their supporters continued to demand it, but the more politicians acceded to these demands, the more they risked alienating an unsympathetic public. If they curtailed patronage, then they would have to search for other means of securing participation and mobilizing commitment and these means proved elusive. It was easy to decry patronage and certainly possible to limit it. But what would take its place, and prove as effective as patronage had once been in cementing loyalties and encouraging participation? The answer seemed to be, as Mulroney belatedly discovered, participation driven by an intellectual or emotional commitment to a set of vigorously pursued, clearly articulated policies. Indeed, his experience and that of Trudeau in the current transitional stage of Canadian politics seemed to suggest that the "psychic patronage" of ideas had replaced material or honorific patronage as the great mobilizer of public participation.

Similarly, the time-honoured practices of political porkbarrelling seemed to be paying fewer political dividends. With the explosion in government activity, battles for private needs got carried into the political arena, and with the arrival of persistent deficit financing came a massive increase in the political temptation to spend vast sums of public money. This temptation had always been central to the Canadian political experience. The promise of a railway branch line, the construction of a new canal or bridge, the paving of a road, the opening of a post office—these were the stuff of local political debates in Canada, and few politicians ignored the political possibilities of such promises or projects. In the modern era all that changed was the scale and scope of government spending, but the change represented a quantum leap from what had gone on before. Although programs carried the prerequisite regulations and bureaucratic norms, by either adjusting these norms or simply overriding them with an act of political discretion, politicians could try to turn these programs to their political advantage. In this, the Mulroney government differed not a whit from its Liberal predecessors.

The tip-off that nothing had changed came early. Six months after the election, Domtar threatened to close its mill at Windsor, Quebec, unless it received money from Ottawa to finance a modernization. Domtar, whose biggest shareholders were agencies of the Quebec government, was turning a profit, yet it threatened seven hundred jobs. Sinclair Stevens, then minister for Regional Industrial Expansion, looked at Domtar's balance sheet, heard complaints from other pulp and paper producers, and correctly said no. But the political pressure from Quebec intensified, for a succession of Liberal governments had not accustomed the province to hearing no. So the prime minister got involved in the dossier, rejected Domtar's grab for a federal grant, and settled instead for an interest-free loan.

The Domtar decision signalled that political pressure—not economic reasoning—would sway this supposedly market-oriented government. Thereafter, the government littered the landscape with government assistance packages to industries and individual firms that had succeeded in generating the prerequisite political heat. An initial $1-billion payment to grain farmers was followed by another dollop the next year; there was assistance for Cominco's modernization of a smelter at Trail. Re-opening the old Cyprus Anvil Mine in the Yukon; keeping Sysco afloat in Sydney; handing the oil patch $350 million; helping Algoma Steel at Sault Ste. Marie; offering money to General Motors, the world's largest corporation, for its plant at Ste. Thérèse, Quebec—each of these decisions and many others like them served merely to tighten the political squeeze on the Mulroney government. Assistance to one region immediately set off a chain reaction from other regions for similar treatment, a reaction made more insistent by the uneven pattern of economic growth across the country.

The awarding of the CF-18 maintenance contract provided a classic illustration of the inflationary consequences of political bribery. A panel of seventy-five government experts analyzed bids from a Halifax consortium, Bristol Aerospace of Winnipeg, and Canadair of Montreal. They soon dismissed the Halifax bid as technically inadequate, but after an exhaustive analysis awarded Bristol 926 out of a possible 1,000 points for technical merit, compared with only 843 for Canadair. They also found that for the core element of the contract—"systems engineering"—Bristol's bid was thirteen percent lower, and three percent lower over all in the first three and a half years of the contract. Despite the experts' clear verdict, the prime minister and other Quebec ministers steered the contract to Canadair, devising a rationale about technology transfer to camouflage a purely political decision. Manitoba, having been defeated by Quebec's superior clout, then received the consolation prizes of the maintenance contract for the older CF-5 aircraft and a Health Sciences project proudly announced by Manitoba's senior minister, Jake Epp.

The policy of assisting first this company or region, then another, seldom brings a discernible political benefit and often lands the government in the unwinnable game of meeting exaggerated expectations everywhere. The game continues, however, because refusal to act may produce penalties even though the decision to act does not automatically bring advantages. A fear of what may happen if discretion is not exercised, rather than the certainty of benefit if discretion is applied, drags politicians into the vortex of exaggerated expectations. In the CF-18 case, no immediate political gratitude greeted the decision in Montreal; outrage, however, persisted in Winnipeg.

By the early months of 1987, the Mulroney government had been rocked by so many allegations, ministerial resignations, screaming headlines about political patronage and other damaging assaults that its popularity had sunk to depths that made recovery seem improbable, if not impossible. When Mulroney entered 24 Sussex Drive, he spoke enviously of what he called US President Ronald Reagan's "comfort zone" with the American people: the broad acceptance of the president's values and the widespread approval of his personality that encouraged Americans to forgive policy mistakes or presidential blunders. Americans liked their president, even though they did not always agree with him. Mulroney's search to establish his own "comfort zone" with the Canadian people produced completely the opposite result. Many Canadians felt uncomfortable with his values, distrusted his integrity, remained confused about where he wished to lead the country so that every error, allegation and damaging incident stuck to him. Instead of creating a "comfort zone" with the Canadian people, Mulroney became the flypaper Prime Minister.

And yet, very slowly and quite painfully, Mulroney was learning about the changed political culture with its reduced tolerance for political favouritism and its intense focus on the attitudes and values of the political leader. The classic network politician, the man who loved to spend hours on the telephone rapping with friends or simply touching base with those whom he thought might be helpful, increasingly understood that brokerage politics in the modern age was more difficult than he had imagined. He began a searching re-examination of what had gone wrong, and began listening to those who recommended remedial action. He completely overhauled the personnel in his office, and the new advisers were seasoned professionals: Dalton Camp and Marjory LeBreton from the Conservative party, Derek Burney from External Affairs. A weekly tactics meeting chaired by Deputy Prime Minister Don Mazankowski improved the government's performance in the Commons. Mulroney began distancing himself from secondary issues, concentrating instead on major dossiers brought to a successful conclusion: the Meech Lake constitutional accord and a trade agreement with the United States. He curbed his blarney, as best he could.

Still plagued by the allegations of favouritism and patronage, the government launched a multi-faceted series of reforms. It persevered with an earlier change allowing Commons committees the right to hear testimony from order-in-council appointments. It sent a white paper on lobbying to a parliamentary committee, which recommended the registration of lobbyists. It responded to the Parker Inquiry with an ethics-in-government package that tried yet again to define how ministers should avoid conflicts of interest. As part of the Meech Lake accord, Mulroney yielded up most of the prime minister's historic powers of appointing senators. And the party wound up the provincial advisory committees, and so bade farewell to another in a long series of efforts winding through the political history of Canada to balance the conflicting demands of political patrons and clients.

The PACs had been central to the Conservatives' attempts to involve the extra-parliamentary party in patronage. They had created a series of mini-patrons, the PAC chairmen, beholden to the prime minister, the ultimate political patron, but possessed of considerable powers themselves to act as mini-patrons. The PACs had never been popular with MPs who resented extra-parliamentary interference in what they considered the prerogatives of elected officials. Too many grassroots Conservatives disliked the closed appearance of the PACs which seemed to be recommending appointments largely for friends of the members. Ministers found the PACs cumbersome and sometimes inadequate in recruiting the most suitable candidates. The prime minister and his new senior staff, aware of the damage that the government use of patronage had done to the Conservative cause and the Mulroney image, believed the PACs persisted in recommending Conservatives for a partisanship unblemished by special qualifications. In December, 1987, Cabinet decided to abolish the PACs; on 1 February 1988, a majority of the PAC chairmen learned in a telephone call from LeBreton that the responsibilities they had been secretly given during the election campaign of 1984 were ended.

The wheel of politics brought the Conservatives full circle. They replaced the PACs with a system almost identical to the Trudeau system: A political minister, the caucus chairman, and the campaign director would recommend the patronage in each province. John A. Macdonald, who ran the patronage himself and through senior ministers, would have smiled.

The new system pleased the parliamentary party. Whether it would produce better-qualified candidates, and whether it could contribute to using patronage in a less politically injurious way remained open questions. Indeed, after four years of Mulroney, the future of political patronage in Canada remained uncertain. That patronage could never be abolished—indeed, should not be abolished—seemed clear, since the exercise of political discretion would always be central to democratic politics. The question remained, however, how governments would use the tool of patronage.

Provincial governments provided, roughly speaking, three models, at least for the patronage of appointments. In the western provinces, the political fight had evolved into a struggle between social democrats and free-enterprisers. Each change in government brought considerable shifts in personnel justified by the need to staff departments, boards, agencies and commissions with those philosophically, even ideologically, attuned to the government of the day. In Ontario and Quebec, a more managerial politics prevailed; new governments moved cautiously, albeit methodically, to reward supporters and left the civil service largely intact. In Atlantic Canada, the old-style politics of patronage was slowly dying, but with economic dependence still a regrettable fact of life, the scope and demand for patronage remained greater there than anywhere else in Canada.

As Mulroney himself admitted several times, his government would pay for having misled the public in the 1984 campaign and having misread the changed political tolerance towards patronage in Canada. How much the government had paid could only be sorted out by pollsters and academic specialists who picked over the voters' reasons for judgment. In a historical sense, it was perhaps fitting that political patronage, which drove nineteenth-century reformers into demanding responsible government and helped to glue Canada's nation-wide parties together after Confederation, should even in the latter part of the twentieth century still be enticing and tormenting the practitioners of Canadian politics. The centrality of patronage in Canadian political life had disappeared, but the practice of patronage remained, challenging all those charged with exercising political discretion and currying democratic support to practise craftily and judiciously this most demanding of the political arts.

FURTHER READING

○

What follows is a list of some of the more useful historical monographs, excluding memoirs and biographies (which alone could fill a book), specifically on Canadian political parties since 1867. The list is by no means inclusive, however. Those interested in exploring the subject further should refer to the following guides: G. Heggie, ed., *Canadian Political Parties, 1867-1968: A Historical Bibliography* (Toronto: Macmillan Canada, 1977); J. Gregor, *Bibliographical Guide to Canadian Government and Politics, 1968-1980* (Monticello, IL: Vance Bibliographies, 1986); and R. Jackson, *Canadian Government and Politics* (Ottawa: Department of the Secretary of State of Canada, 1988).

POLITICAL PARTIES: GENERAL

Bakvis, Herman, ed. *Canadian Political Parties: Leaders, Candidates and Organization.* Toronto: Dundurn Press, 1991.

Christian, William, and Colin Campbell. *Parties, Leaders and Ideologies in Canada.* Toronto: McGraw-Hill Ryerson Limited, 1996.

Elkins, D, and Richard Simeon, eds. *Small Worlds: Provinces and Parties in Canadian Political Life.* Toronto: Methuen Publications, 1980.

Engelmann, Frederick, and Mildred Schwartz. *Canadian Political Parties: Origins, Character, Impact.* Scarborough, ON: Prentice-Hall Canada, Inc., 1975.

Gagnon, A., and A. Brian Tanguay, eds. *Canadian Parties in Transition: Discourse, Organization, Representation.* Scarborough, ON: Nelson Canada, 1989.

Robin, Martin. *Canadian Provincial Politics: The Party Systems of the Ten Provinces.* Scarborough, ON: Prentice-Hall Canada, Inc. 1972.

Stewart, Gordon. *The Origins of Canadian Politics: A Comparative Approach.* Vancouver: University of British Columbia Press, 1986.

Thorburn, Hugh, ed. *Party Politics in Canada.* Scarborough, ON: Prentice-Hall Canada, Inc., 1996.

Underhill, Frank. *Canadian Political Parties.* Ottawa: Canadian Historical Association Booklets, no. 8, 1968.

Wearing, Joseph. *Strained Relations: Canadian Parties and Voters.* Toronto: McClelland & Stewart, 1988.

Winn, Conrad, and John McMenemy, eds. *Political Parties in Canada.* Toronto: McGraw-Hill Ryerson Limited, 1976.

LIBERALS

McCall-Newman, Christina. *Grits: An Intimate Portrait of the Liberal Party.* Toronto: Macmillan Canada, 1982.
Neatby, H. Blair. *Laurier and a Liberal Quebec.* Toronto: McClelland & Stewart, 1973.
Pickersgill, J.W. *The Liberal Party.* Toronto: McClelland & Stewart, 1962.
Smith, David. *The Regional Decline of a National Party: Liberals on the Prairies.* Toronto: University of Toronto Press, 1981.
_____. *Prairie Liberalism: The Liberal Party in Saskatchewan, 1905-71.* Toronto: University of Toronto Press, 1975.
Thomas, L.G. *The Liberal Party in Alberta: A History of Politics in the Province of Alberta: 1905-1921.* Toronto: University of Toronto Press, 1959.
Wearing, Joseph. *The L-Shaped Party: The Liberal Party of Canada 1958-1980.* Toronto: McGraw-Hill Ryerson Limited, 1981.
Whitaker, Reginald. *The Government Party: Organizing and Financing the Liberal Party of Canada 1930-1958.* Toronto: University of Toronto Press, 1977.
Wilson, Barry. *Politics of Defeat: The Decline of the Liberal Party in Saskatchewan.* Saskatoon, SK: Western Producer Prairie Books, 1980.

CONSERVATIVES

Camp, Dalton. *Gentlemen, Players and Politicians.* Toronto: McClelland & Stewart, 1970.
English, John. *The Decline of Politics: The Conservatives and the Party System 1901-20.* Toronto: University of Toronto Press, 1977.
Fraser, Graham. *Playing for Keeps: Making of the Prime Minister, 1988.* Toronto: McClelland & Stewart, 1989.
Glassford, Larry. *Reaction and Reform: The Politics of the Conservative Party under R.B. Bennett, 1927-1938.* Toronto: University of Toronto Press, 1992.
Granatstein, J.L. *The Politics of Survival: The Conservative Party of Canada, 1939-1945.* Toronto: University of Toronto Press, 1967.
Macquarrie, Heath. *The Conservative Party.* Toronto: McClelland & Stewart, 1965.
Manthorpe, Jonathan. *The Power and the Tories: Ontario Politics: 1943 to the Present.* Toronto: Macmillan Canada, 1974.
Martin, Patrick, et. al. *Contenders: the Tory Quest for Power.* Scarborough, ON: Prentice-Hall Canada, Inc., 1983.
Perlin, George. *The Tory Syndrome: Leadership Politics in the Progressive Conservative Party.* Montreal: McGill-Queen's University Press, 1980.
Regenstreif, Peter. *The Diefenbaker Interlude: Parties and Voting in Canada, an Interpretation.* Toronto: Longmans, 1965.
Williams, John Ryan. *The Conservative Party of Canada, 1920-1949.* Durham: Duke University Press, 1956.

COMMUNISTS

Angus, Ian. *Canadian Bolsheviks: The Early Years of the Communist Party of Canada.* Montreal: Vanguard Publications, 1981.

Avakumovic, Ivan. *The Communist Party in Canada: A History.* Toronto: McClelland & Stewart, 1975.

Comeau, Robert, and B. Dionne. *Communists in Quebec, 1936-1956: The Communist Party of Canada, Labor-Progressive Party.* Montreal: Presses de L'Unité, 1982

Penner, Norman. *Canadian Communism: The Stalin Years and Beyond.* Agincourt, ON: Methuen, 1988.

Rodney, William. *Soldiers of the International: A History of the Communist Party of Canada, 1919-1929.* Toronto: University of Toronto Press, 1968.

CCF/NDP

Avakumovic, Ivan. *Socialism in Canada: A Study of the CCF-NDP in Federal and Provincial Politics.* Toronto: McClelland & Stewart, 1978.

Azoulay, Dan. *Keeping the Dream Alive: The Survival of the Ontario CCF/NDP, 1950-1963.* Montreal: McGill-Queen's University Press, 1997.

Brennan, William, ed. *Building the Co-operative Commonwealth: Essays on the Democratic Socialist Tradition in Canada.* Regina, SK: Canadian Plains Research Center, 1985.

Caplan, Gerald. *The Dilemma of Canadian Socialism.* Toronto: McClelland & Stewart, 1973.

Lipset, Seymour Martin. *Agrarian Socialism: The Cooperative Commonwealth Federation in Saskatchewan.* Los Angeles: University of California Press, 1950.

McHenry, Dean. *The Third Force in Canada: The Cooperative Commonwealth Federation, 1932-48.* Berkeley: University of California Press, 1950.

Melnyk, Olenka. *No Bankers in Heaven: Remembering the CCF.* Toronto: McGraw-Hill Ryerson Limited, 1989.

Morley, J.T. *Secular Socialists: The CCF/NDP in Ontario, a Biography.* Montreal: McGill-Queen's University Press, 1984.

Penner, Norman. *From Protest to Power: Social Democracy in Canada 1900-Present.* Toronto: James Lorimer & Company, Publishers, 1992.

Pratt, L., ed. *Socialism and Democracy in Alberta: Essays in Honour of Grant Notley.* Edmonton: NeWest Publishers Ltd., 1986.

Whitehorn, Alan. *Canadian Socialism: Essays on the CCF-NDP.* Toronto: Oxford University Press, 1992.

Wiseman, Nelson. *Social Democracy in Manitoba: A History of the CCF-NDP.* Winnipeg: University of Manitoba Press, 1984.

Young, Walter D. *The Anatomy of a Party: The National CCF 1932-1961.* Toronto: University of Toronto Press, 1969.

Zakuta, Leo. *A Protest Movement Becalmed: A Study of Change in the CCF.* Toronto: University of Toronto Press, 1964.

SOCIAL CREDIT

Barr, John. *The Dynasty: The Rise and Fall of Social Credit in Alberta.* Toronto: McClelland & Stewart, 1974.

Finkel, Alvin. *The Social Credit Phenomenon in Alberta.* Toronto: University of Toronto Press, 1989.

Irving, John. *The Social Credit Movement in Alberta.* Toronto: University of Toronto Press, 1959.

Macpherson, C.B. *Democracy in Alberta: Social Credit and the Party System.* Toronto: University of Toronto Press, 1953.

Mallory, J.R. *Social Credit and the Federal Power in Canada.* Toronto: University of Toronto Press, 1954.

Pinard, Maurice. *The Rise of a Third Party: A Study in Crisis Politics.* Scarborough, ON: Prentice-Hall Canada, Inc., 1971.

Stein, Michael. *The Dynamics of Right-Wing Protest: A Political Analysis of Social Credit in Quebec.* Toronto: University of Toronto Press, 1973.

Thomas, L., ed. *William Aberhart and Social Credit in Alberta.* Vancouver: Copp Clark Pitman, 1977.

OTHER THIRD PARTIES

Comeau, Paul-André. *Le Bloc populaire, 1942, 1948.* Montréal: Québec/Amérique, 1982.

Cornellier, Manon. *The Bloc.* Toronto: James Lorimer & Company, Publishers, 1995.

Dobbin, Murray. *Preston Manning and the Reform Party.* Toronto: James Lorimer & Company, Publishers, 1991.

Flanagan, Thomas. *Waiting for the Wave: The Reform Party and Preston Manning.* Toronto: Stoddart Publishing Co. Limited, 1995.

Fraser, Graham. *P.Q.: René Lévesque and the Parti Québécois in Power.* Toronto: Gage Educational Publishing Company, 1984.

Harrison, Trevor. *Of Passionate Intensity: Right-Wing Populism and the Reform Party of Canada.* Toronto: University of Toronto Press, 1995.

Morton, William. *The Progressive Party in Canada.* Toronto: University of Toronto Press, 1950.

Quinn, Herbert. *The Union Nationale: A Study in Quebec Nationalism.* 2d ed. Toronto: University of Toronto Press, 1979.

Saywell, John. *The Rise of the Parti Québécois, 1967-1976.* Toronto: University of Toronto Press, 1977.

Sharpe, Sydney, and Don Braid. *Storming Babylon: Preston Manning and the Rise of the Reform Party.* Toronto: Key Porter Books Limited, 1992.